BUSINESS

TWELFTH EDITION

William M. Pride

Texas A&M University

Robert J. Hughes

Dallas County Community Colleges

Jack R. Kapoor

College of DuPage

SOUTH-WESTERN
CENGAGE Learning

Australia • Brazil • Japan • Korea • Mexico • Singapore • Spain • United Kingdom • United States

Business, Twelfth Edition

William M. Pride, Robert J. Hughes, Jack R. Kapoor

Senior Vice President, LRS/Acquisitions & Solutions Planning: Jack W. Calhoun

Editorial Director, Business & Economics: Erin Joyner

Acquisitions Editor: Jason Fremder

Managing Developmental Editor: Joanne Dauksewicz

Editorial Assistant: Megan Fischer

Brand Manager: Robin Lefevre

Market Development Manager: Jonathan Monahan

Sr. Content Project Manager: Emily Nesheim, Holly Henjum

Supervising Media Editor: Scott Fidler

Manufacturing Planner: Ron Montgomery

Production Service: Integra Software Services, LLC

Sr. Art Director: Stacy Jenkins Shirley

Cover and Internal Designer: Joe Devine/ Red Hangar Design

Cover Image: © Jorg Greuel/Getty Images

Rights Acquisitions Specialist: Deanna Ettinger

Exam*View*® is a registered trademark of eInstruction Corp. Windows is a registered trademark of the Microsoft Corporation used herein under license. Macintosh and Power Macintosh are registered trademarks of Apple Computer, Inc. used herein under license.

© 2008 Cengage Learning. All Rights Reserved.

Library of Congress Control Number: 2012947815

ISBN-13: 978-1-133-59585-4
ISBN-10: 1-133-59585-5

Looseleaf Version ISBN 13: 978-1-133-93667-1
Looseleaf Version ISBN 10: 1-133-93667-9

South-Western
5191 Natorp Boulevard
Mason, OH 45040
USA

Cengage Learning is a leading provider of customized learning solutions with office locations around the globe, including Singapore, the United Kingdom, Australia, Mexico, Brazil, and Japan. Locate your local office at: **www.cengage.com/global**

Cengage Learning products are represented in Canada by Nelson Education, Ltd.

For your course and learning solutions, visit **www.cengage.com**
Purchase any of our products at your local college store or at our preferred online store **www.cengagebrain.com**

Printed in the United States of America
1 2 3 4 5 6 7 16 15 14 13 12

To Nancy, Allen, Mike, Ashley, and Charlie Pride

To my wife Peggy and to my mother Barbara Hughes

To my wife Theresa; my children Karen, Kathryn, and Dave; and in memory of my parents Ram and Sheela Kapoor

BRIEF CONTENTS

The following appendixes appear on the companion site www.cengage.brain.com
Appendix A: Careers in Business
Appendix B: Risk Management and Insurance
Appendix C: Business Law, Regulation, and Taxation

v

CONTENTS

Chapter 3: Exploring Global Business 69

2 Business Ownership and Entrepreneurship 103

Chapter 4: Choosing a Form of Business Ownership 104

Chapter 5: Small Business, Entrepreneurship, and Franchises 133

3 Management and Organization 163

Chapter 8: Producing Quality Goods and Services 211

4   Human Resources 243

Chapter 9: Attracting and Retaining the Best Employees 244

5 Marketing 329

Contents

6   Social Media, e-Business, and Accounting 455

7 Finance and Investment 519

Chapter 20: Understanding Personal Finances and Investments 579

The following appendixes appear on the companion site
www.cengage.brain.com
Appendix A: Careers in Business
Appendix B: Risk Management and Insurance
Appendix C: Business Law, Regulation, and Taxation

WILLIAM M. PRIDE
TEXAS A&M UNIVERSITY

William M. Pride is professor of marketing, Mays Business School at Texas A&M University. He received his PhD from Louisiana State University. He is the author of Cengage Learning's *Marketing*, 15th edition, and a market leader. Dr. Pride's research interests are in advertising, promotion, and distribution channels. Dr. Pride's research articles have appeared in major journals in the fields of advertising and marketing, such as *Journal of Marketing, Journal of Marketing Research, Journal of the Academy of Marketing Science*, and the *Journal of Advertising*. Dr. Pride is a member of the American Marketing Association, Academy of Marketing Science, Association of Collegiate Marketing Educators, Society for Marketing Advances, and the Marketing Management Association. Dr. Pride has taught principles of marketing and other marketing courses for more than 30 years at both the undergraduate and graduate levels.

ROBERT J. HUGHES
RICHLAND COLLEGE, DALLAS COUNTY COMMUNITY COLLEGES

Robert J. Hughes (EdD, University of North Texas) specializes in business administration and college instruction. He has taught Introduction to Business for more than 35 years both on campus and online for Richland College—one of seven campuses that are part of the Dallas County Community College District. In addition to *Business* and *Foundations of Business*, published by Cengage Learning, he has authored college textbooks in personal finance and business mathematics; served as a content consultant for two popular national television series, *It's Strictly Business* and *Dollars & Sense: Personal Finance for the 21st Century*; and is the lead author for a business math project utilizing computer-assisted instruction funded by the ALEKS Corporation. He is also active in many academic and professional organizations and has served as a consultant and investment advisor to individuals, businesses, and charitable organizations. Dr. Hughes is the recipient of three different Teaching in Excellence Awards at Richland College. According to Dr. Hughes, after 35 years of teaching Introduction to Business, the course is still exciting: "There's nothing quite like the thrill of seeing students succeed, especially in a course like Introduction to Business, which provides the foundation for not only academic courses, but also life in the real world."

JACK R. KAPOOR
COLLEGE OF DUPAGE

Jack R. Kapoor (EdD, Northern Illinois University) is professor of business and economics in the Business and Technology Division at the College of DuPage, where he has taught Introduction to Business, Marketing, Management, Economics, and Personal Finance since 1969. He previously taught at Illinois Institute of Technology's Stuart School of Management, San Francisco State University's School of World Business, and other colleges. Professor Kapoor was awarded the Business and Services Division's Outstanding Professor Award for 1999–2000. He served as an Assistant National Bank Examiner for the U.S. Treasury Department and as an international trade consultant to Bolting Manufacturing Co., Ltd., Mumbai, India.

Dr. Kapoor is known internationally as a coauthor of several textbooks, including *Foundations of Business*, 3rd edition (Cengage Learning), has served as a content consultant for the popular national television series *The Business File: An Introduction to Business*, and developed two full-length audio courses in business and personal finance. He has been quoted in many national newspapers and magazines, including *USA Today, U.S. News & World Report,* the *Chicago Sun-Times, Crain's Small Business,* the *Chicago Tribune,* and other publications.

Dr. Kapoor has traveled around the world and has studied business practices in capitalist, socialist, and communist countries.

ACKNOWLEDGEMENTS

The quality of this book and its supplements program has been helped immensely by the insightful and rich comments of a special set of instructors. In particular, we wish to thank the Advisory Board who focused on our series:

Michael Bento
 Owens Community College
Patricia Bernson
 County College of Morris
Brennan Carr
 Long Beach City College
Paul Coakley
 The Community College of
 Baltimore County
Donna K. Fisher
 Georgia Southern University
Charles R. Foley
 Columbus State Community College
Connie Golden
 Lakeland Community College
John Guess
 Delgado Community College
Frank Harber
 Indian River State College

Anita Kelley
 Harold Washington College
Mary Beth Klinger
 College of Southern Maryland
Pamela G. McElligott
 St. Louis Community College
 Meramec
Mark Nagel
 Normandale Community College
Angela J. Rabatin
 Prince George's Community College
Anthony Racka
 Oakland Community College—
 Auburn Hills Campus
Carol Rowey
 Community College of Rhode
 Island
Christy Shell
 Houston Community College

Cindy Simerly
 Lakeland Community College
Yolanda I. Smith
 Northern Virginia Community
 College
Gail South
 Montgomery College
Rieann Spence-Gale
 Northern Virginia Comm. College—
 Alexandria Campus
Kurt Stanberry
 University of Houston, Downtown
John Striebich
 Monroe Community College
Keith Taylor
 Lansing Community College
Tricia Troyer
 Waubonsee Community College

We are also indebted to the following reviewers for this and previous editions. Their suggestions have helped us improve and refine the text as well as the whole instructional package.

John Adams
 San Diego Mesa College
David V. Aiken
 Hocking College
Phyllis C. Alderdice
 Jefferson Community College
Marilyn Amaker
 Orangeburg-Calhoun Technical
 College
Harold Amsbaugh
 North Central Technical College
Carole Anderson
 Clarion University
Lydia E. Anderson
 Fresno City College

Ken Anglin
 Minnesota State University,
 Mankato
Maria Aria
 Camden County College
James O. Armstrong, II
 John Tyler Community College
Ed Atzenhoefer
 Clark State Community College
Harold C. Babson
 Columbus State Community College
Xenia P. Balabkins
 Middlesex County College
Gloria Bemben
 Finger Lakes Community College

Charles Bennett
 Tyler Junior College
Ellen A. Benowitz
 Mercer County Community College
Patricia Bernson
 County College of Morris
Robert W. Bitter
 Southwest Missouri State University
Angela Blackwood
 Belmont Abbey College
Wayne Blue
 Allegany College of Maryland
Mary Jo Boehms
 Jackson State Community
 College

Stewart Bonem
Cincinnati Technical College

James Boyle
Glendale Community College

Steve Bradley
Austin Community College

Lyle V. Brenna
Pikes Peak Community College

Tom Brinkman
Cincinnati Technical College

Robert Brinkmeyer
University of Cincinnati

Harvey S. Bronstein
*Oakland Community College—
Orchard Ridge*

Edward Brown
Franklin University

Joseph Brum
Fayetteville Technical Institute

Janice Bryan
Jacksonville College

Howard R. Budner
Manhattan Community College

Clara Buitenbos
Pan American University

Laura Bulas
Central Community College, NE

C. Alan Burns
Lee College

Frank Busch
Louisiana Technical University

Paul Callahan
Cincinnati State University

Joseph E. Cantrell
DeAnza College

Brahm Canzer
John Abbot College

Don Cappa
Chabot College

Robert Carrel
Vincennes University

Richard M. Chamberlain
Lorain County Community College

Bruce H. Charnov
Hofstra University

Lawrence Chase
*Tompkins Cortland Community
College*

Felipe Chia
Harrisburg Area Community College

Michael Cicero
Highline Community College

William Clarey
Bradley University

Robert Coiro
LaGuardia Community College

Jean Condon
Mid-Plains Community College

Mary Cooke
Surry Community College

Don Coppa
Chabot College

Robert J. Cox
Salt Lake Community College

Susan Cremins
Westchester Community College

Bruce Cudney
Middlesex Community College

Andrew Curran
*Antonelli Institute of Art and
Photography*

Gary Cutler
Dyersburg State Community College

Rex R. Cutshall
Vincennes University

John Daily
St. Edward's University

Dean Danielson
San Joaquin Delta College

Brian Davis
Weber State University

Gregory Davis
*Georgia Southwestern State
University*

Helen M. Davis
Jefferson Community College

Peter Dawson
Collin County Community College

Harris D. Dean
Lansing Community College

Wayne H. Decker
Memphis State University

Sharon Dexter
Southeast Community College

William M. Dickson
Green River Community College

John Donnellan
Holyoke Community College

Gary Donnelly
Casper College

M. Dougherty
Madison Area Technical College

Michael Drafke
College of DuPage

Richard Dugger
Kilgore College

Sam Dunbar
Delgado Community College

Karen Edwards
Chemeketa Community College

Robert Elk
Seminole Community College

Pat Ellebracht
*Northeastern Missouri State
University*

Pat Ellsberg
Lower Columbia College

John H. Espey
Cecil Community College

Carleton S. Everett
*Des Moines Area Community
College*

Frank M. Falcetta
Middlesex County College

Thomas Falcone
Indiana University of Pennsylvania

Janice Feldbauer
Austin Community College

Coe Fields
Tarrant County Junior College

Carol Fischer
University of Wisconsin—Waukesha

Larry A. Flick
Three Rivers Community College

Gregory F. Fox
Erie Community College

Mark Fox
Indiana University—South Bend

Michael Fritz
*Portland Community College at
Rock Creek*

Fred Fry
Bradley University

Eduardo F. Garcia
Laredo Junior College

Arlen Gastineau
Valencia Community College

Richard Ghidella
Citrus College

Carmine Paul Gibaldi
St. John's University

Edwin Giermak
College of DuPage

Debbie Gilliard
Metropolitan State College

R. Gillingham
Vincennes University

Robert Googins
Shasta College

Karen Gore
*Ivy Tech Community College—
Evansville*

Carol Gottuso
Metropolitan Community College

W. Michael Gough
DeAnza College

Cheryl Davisson Gracie
Washtenaw Community College

Joseph Gray
  Nassau Community College
Michael Griffin
  University of Massachusetts—Dartmouth
Ricky W. Griffin
  Texas A & M University
Stephen W. Griffin
  Tarrant County Junior College
Roy Grundy
  College of DuPage
John Gubbay
  Moraine Valley Community College
Rick Guidicessi
  Des Moines Area Community College
Ronald Hadley
  St. Petersburg Junior College
Carnella Hardin
  Glendale Community College
Aristotle Haretos
  Flagler College
Keith Harman
  National-Louis University
Richard Hartley
  Solano Community College
Richard Haskey
  University of Wisconsin
Carolyn Hatton
  Cincinnati State University
Linda Hefferin
  Elgin Community College
Sanford Helman
  Middlesex County College
Victor B. Heltzer
  Middlesex County College
Tom Hendricks
  Oakland Community College
Ronald L. Hensell
  Mendocino College
Leonard Herzstein
  Skyline College
Donald Hiebert
  Northern Oklahoma College
Nathan Himelstein
  Essex County College
L. Duke Hobbs
  Texas A & M University
Charles Hobson
  Indiana University Northwest
Marie R. Hodge
  Bowling Green State University
Gerald Hollier
  University of Texas—Brownsville
Jay S. Hollowell
  Commonwealth College

Townsend Hopper
  Community College of Allegheny County—Allegheny
Joseph Hrebenak
  Community College of Allegheny County—Allegheny
John Humphreys
  Eastern New Mexico University
James L. Hyek
  Los Angeles Valley College
James V. Isherwood
  Community College of Rhode Island
Charleen S. Jaeb
  Cuyahoga Community College
Sally Jefferson
  Western Illinois University
Jenna Johannpeter
  Belleville Area College
Gene E. A. Johnson
  Clark College
Carol A. Jones
  Cuyahoga Community College
Pat Jones
  Eastern New Mexico University
Eileen Kearney
  Montgomery Community College
Robert Kegel
  Cypress College
Isaac W. J. Keim, III
  Delta College
George Kelley
  Erie Community College
Marshall Keyser
  Moorpark College
Betty Ann Kirk
  Tallahassee Community College
Edward Kirk
  Vincennes University
Judith Kizzie
  Clinton Community College
Karl Kleiner
  Ocean County College
Clyde Kobberdahl
  Cincinnati Technical College
Connie Koehler
  McHenry County College
Robert Kreitner
  Arizona State University
David Kroeker
  Tabor College
Patrick Kroll
  University of Minnesota, General College
Bruce Kusch
  Brigham Young University

Kenneth Lacho
  University of New Orleans
John Lathrop
  New Mexico Junior College
R. Michael Lebda
  DeVry Institute of Technology
Martin Lecker
  SUNY Rockland Community College
George Leonard
  St. Petersburg Junior College
Marvin Levine
  Orange County Community College
Chad Lewis
  Everett Community College
Jianwen Liao
  Robert Morris College
Ronnie Liggett
  University of Texas at Arlington
William M. Lindsay
  Northern Kentucky University
Natasha Linsey
  University of North Alabama
Carl H. Lippold
  Embry-Riddle Aeronautical University
Thomas Lloyd
  Westmoreland County Community College
J. B. Locke
  University of Mobile
Paul James Londrigan
  Mott Community College
Kathleen Lorencz
  Oakland Community College
Fritz Lotz
  Southwestern College
Robert C. Lowery
  Brookdale Community College
Anthony Lucas
  Community College of Allegheny County—Allegheny
Robert Lupton
  Central Washington University
Monty Lynn
  Abilene Christian University
Sheldon A. Mador
  Los Angeles Trade and Technical College
John Mago
  Anoka Ramsey Community College
Rebecca J. Mahr
  Western Illinois University
Joan Mansfield
  Central Missouri State University
Gayle J. Marco
  Robert Morris College

John Martin
  Mt. San Antonio Community College
Irving Mason
  Herkimer County Community College
Douglas McCabe
  Georgetown University
Barry McCarthy
  Irvine Valley College
John F. McDonough
  Menlo College
Catherine McElroy
  Bucks County Community College
L. J. McGlamory
  North Harris County College
Myke McMullen
  Long Beach City College
Charles Meiser
  Lake Superior State University
Ina Midkiff-Kennedy
  Austin Community College—Northridge
Tony Mifsud
  Rowan Cabarrus Community College
Carol Miller
  Community College of Denver
Edwin Miner
  Phoenix College
Nancy Ray-Mitchaell
  McLennan Community College
Jim Moes
  Johnson County Community College
Dominic Montileone
  Delaware Valley College
Linda Morable
  Dallas County Community Colleges
Charles Morrow
  Cuyahoga Community College
Jadeip Motwani
  Grand Valley State
T. Mouzopoulos
  American College of Greece
Gary Mrozinski
  Broome Community College
W. Gale Mueller
  Spokane Community College
C. Mullery
  Humboldt State University
Robert J. Mullin
  Orange County Community College
Patricia Murray
  Virginia Union University
Robert Nay
  Stark Technical College
James Nead
  Vincennes University

Jerry Novak
  Alaska Pacific University
Grantley Nurse
  Raritan Valley Community College
Gerald O'Bryan
  Danville Area Community College
Larry Olanrewaju
  Virginia Union University
David G. Oliver
  Edison Community College
John R. Pappalardo
  Keene State College
Dennis Pappas
  Columbus Technical Institute
Roberta F. Passenant
  Berkshire Community College
Clarissa M. H. Patterson
  Bryant College
Dyan Pease
  Sacramento City College
Kenneth Peissig
  College of Menominee Nation
Jeffrey D. Penley
  Catawba Valley Community College
Constantine Petrides
  Manhattan Community College
Donald Pettit
  Suffolk County Community College
Norman Petty
  Central Piedmont Community College
Joseph Platts
  Miami-Dade Community College
Gloria D. Poplawsky
  University of Toledo
Greg Powell
  Southern Utah University
Fred D. Pragasam
  SUNY at Cobleskill
Peter Quinn
  Commonwealth College
Kimberly Ray
  North Carolina A & T State University
Robert Reinke
  University of South Dakota
Dwight Riley
  Richland College
William Ritchie
  Florida Gulf Coast University
Kenneth Robinson
  Wesley College
Kim Rocha
  Barton College
John Roisch
  Clark County Community College

Rick Rowray
  Ball State University
Jill Russell
  Camden County College
Karl C. Rutkowski
  Pierce Junior College
Martin S. St. John
  Westmoreland County Community College
Ben Sackmary
  Buffalo State College
Eddie Sanders, Jr.
  Chicago State University
P. L. Sandlin
  East Los Angeles College
Nicholas Sarantakes
  Austin Community College
Wallace Satchell
  St. Philip's College
Warren Schlesinger
  Ithaca College
Marilyn Schwartz
  College of Marin
Jon E. Seely
  Tulsa Junior College
John E. Seitz
  Oakton Community College
J. Gregory Service
  Broward Community College—North Campus
Lynne M. Severance
  Eastern Washington University
Dennis Shannon
  Southwestern Illinois College
Richard Shapiro
  Cuyahoga Community College
Raymond Shea
  Monroe Community College
Lynette Shishido
  Santa Monica College
Cindy Simerly
  Lakeland Community College
Anthony Slone
  Elizabeth Community & Technical College
Anne Smevog
  Cleveland Technical College
James Smith
  Rocky Mountain College
David Sollars
  Auburn University Montgomery
Carl Sonntag
  Pikes Peak Community College
Gail South
  Montgomery College—Germantown
Russell W. Southhall
  Laney College

Raymond Sparks
Pima College
John Spence
University of Southwestern Louisiana
Rieann Spence-Gale
Northern Virginia Community College
Nancy Z. Spillman
President, Economic Education Enterprises
Richard J. Stanish
Tulsa Junior College
Jeffrey Stauffer
Ventura College
Jim Steele
Chattanooga State Technical Community College
William A. Steiden
Jefferson Community College
E. George Stook
Anne Arundel Community College
W. Sidney Sugg
Lakeland Community College
Lynn Suksdorf
Salt Lake Community College
Richard L. Sutton
University of Nevada—Las Vegas
Robert E. Swindle
Glendale Community College
William A. Syvertsen
Fresno City College
Lynette Teal
Ivy Technical State College
Raymond D. Tewell
American River College
George Thomas
Johnston Technical College
Karen Thomas
St. Cloud University

Judy Thompson
Briar Cliff College
Paula Thompson
Florida Institute of Technology
William C. Thompson
Foothill Community College
James B. Thurman
George Washington University
Patric S. Tillman
Grayson County College
Frank Titlow
St. Petersburg College
Leo Trudel
University of Main—Fort Kent
Charles E. Tychsen
Northern Virginia Community College—Annandale
Ted Valvoda
Lakeland Community College
Robert H. Vaughn
Lakeland Community College
Frederick A. Viohl
Troy State University
C. Thomas Vogt
Allan Hancock College
Loren K. Waldman
Franklin University
Stephen R. Walsh
Providence College
Elizabeth Wark
Springfield College
John Warner
The University of New Mexico—Albuquerque
Randy Waterman
Richland College
W. J. Waters, Jr.
Central Piedmont Community College
Philip A. Weatherford
Embry-Riddle Aeronautical University

Martin Welc
Saddleback College
Kenneth Wendeln
Indiana University
Jerry E. Wheat
Indiana University, Southeast Campus
Elizabeth White
Orange County Community College
Benjamin Wieder
Queensborough Community College
Ralph Wilcox
Kirkwood Community College
Leslie Wiletzky
Pierce College—Ft. Steilacoom
Anne Williams
Gateway Community College
Charlotte Williams
Jones County Junior College
Larry Williams
Palomar College
Paul Williams
Mott Community College
Steven Winter
Orange County Community College
Wallace Wirth
South Suburban College
Amy Wojciechowski
West Shore Community College
Nathaniel Woods
Columbus State Community College
Gregory J. Worosz
Schoolcraft College
Marilyn Young
Tulsa Junior College

We also wish to acknowledge Colette Wolfson and Linda Hoffman of Ivy Tech Community College for their contributions to the Instructor's Resource Manual, as well as Julie Boyles of Portland State University for her help in developing the Test Bank. For our CengageNOW and CourseMate content, we would again like to thank Julie Boyles as well as LuAnn Bean of the Florida Institute of Technology, Amit Shah of Frostburg State University, Ashli Lane of Texas State University, and our Digital Consultant, Martin Karamian. We thank the R. Jan LeCroy Center for Educational Telecommunications of the Dallas County Community College District for their Telecourse partnership and for providing the related student and instructor materials. Finally, we thank the following people for their professional and technical assistance: Stacy Landreth Grau, Marian Wood, Amy Ray, Elisa Adams, Courtney Bohannon, Jamie Jahns, Whitney Pearce, Laurie Marshall, Clarissa Means, Theresa Kapoor, David Pierce, Kathryn Thumme, Margaret Hill, Nathan Heller, Karen Tucker, and Dave Kapoor.

Many talented professionals at Cengage Learning have contributed to the development of Business, 12e. We are especially grateful to Mike Schenk, Jason Fremder, Kristen Hurd, Joanne Dauksewicz, Emily Nesheim, Holly Henjum, Stacy Shirley, Kristen Meere, and Megan Fischer. Their inspiration, patience, support, and friendship are invaluable.

The Environment of Business

PART 1

In Part 1 of *Business,* we begin by examining the world of business and how the economy affects your life. Next, we discuss ethical and social responsibility issues that affect business firms and our society. Then we explore the increasing importance of international business.

CHAPTER 1   Exploring the World of Business and Economics
CHAPTER 2   Being Ethical and Socially Responsible
CHAPTER 3   Exploring Global Business

1 Exploring the World of Business and Economics

LEARNING OBJECTIVES

What you will be able to do once you complete this chapter:

1. Discuss what you must do to be successful in the world of business.

2. Define *business* and identify potential risks and rewards.

3. Define *economics* and describe the two types of economic systems: capitalism and command economy.

4. Identify the ways to measure economic performance.

5. Examine the different phases in the typical business cycle.

6. Outline the four types of competition.

7. Summarize the factors that affect the business environment and the challenges that American businesses will encounter in the future.

Zynga Zooms into Business

Zynga, named for its founder's American bulldog, is the fast-growing business behind some of the social media world's fastest-growing games. If you've ever tended crops on FarmVille, you know how addictive a Zynga game can be. Even though FarmVille was developed and launched in only six weeks, it instantly captured the imagination of millions of players who eagerly logged onto their Facebook accounts to plant trees or exchange seeds with "neighbors." Other popular Zynga games include CityVille, CastleVille, and Words with Friends.

Founder and CEO Mark Pincus is a seasoned entrepreneur who earned an MBA from Harvard University. Before Zynga, he had started four other Internet businesses—and earned millions of dollars from their success. In 2007, he came up with the idea for a game business in which players could get ahead by connecting with friends (think "neighbors" in FarmVille) and buying special items (such as virtual tractors and cows) that would give them a competitive edge.

Now, when players worldwide buy digital tractors and cows in FarmVille, they can pay with real money, which is why Zynga's profits are real. So real, in fact, that on the basis of its track record, Zynga was able to go public and sell shares of its corporate stock in December, 2011.

As Zynga continues to grow, Pincus and his managers are keeping their workforce satisfied by offering benefits such as surprise vacations and by making the workplace as comfortable as possible. Like many other high-tech firms, Zynga offers free lunch and dinner. Dogs are welcome at the San Francisco headquarters (and they get free dog nibbles, too). Employees can grab a cup of fresh-brewed espresso at the office's gourmet coffee station, sip tea in the Zen-style tea garden, work out in the fitness center, or take a break to play arcade games in the company lounge.

In today's fast-paced business environment, the online games that get everyone talking and clicking right now can become has-beens as soon as the next new thing comes to market. That's why Pincus and his entire team are working hard to keep Zynga zooming ahead year after year.[1]

Did You Know?

Zynga's CityVille game is the fastest-growing online game in history, attracting more than 84 million players within its first month of release on Facebook.

Wow! What a challenging world we live in. Just for a moment, think about the economic problems listed here and how they affect not only you, but also businesses in the United States and the global economy.

- U.S. unemployment rates hovering around 8 percent
- Reduced spending by worried consumers
- Increased government spending to stimulate a troubled economy that created the largest national debt in the nation's history
- A volatile stock market and concerns about banks and financial institutions
- Reform movements including the "Occupy Wall Street" movement that protest differences in wealth and income

In fact, just about every person around the globe was affected in some way by the economic crisis that began in late 2007. Despite the efforts of the U.S. government and other world governments to provide the economic stimulus needed to stabilize the economy, it took nearly four years before the economy began to improve. Today, even with signs of modest improvement, people still worry about their economic future and the future of the nation. Hopefully, by the time you read this material, the nation's economy will be much stronger. Still, it is important to remember the old adage, "History is a great teacher." Both the nation and individuals should take a look at what went wrong to avoid making the same mistakes in the future.

In addition, it helps to keep one factor in mind: Our economy continues to adapt and change to meet the challenges of an ever-changing world and to provide opportunities for those who want to achieve success. Our economic system provides an amazing amount of freedom that allows businesses like Zynga—the Internet gaming company profiled in the Inside Business opening case for this chapter—to adapt to changing business environments. Despite troubling economic times and a weak economy, Zynga—and its 3,000 employees—is a success because it was able to introduce new games that players love, earn a profit, and sell stock to the general public.

Within certain limits, imposed mainly to ensure public safety, the owners of a business can produce any legal good or service they choose and attempt to sell it at the price they set. This system of business, in which individuals decide what to produce, how to produce it, and at what price to sell it, is called **free enterprise**. Our free-enterprise system ensures, for example, that Amazon.com can sell everything from televisions, toys, and tools to computers, cameras, and clothing. Our system gives Amazon's owners and stockholders the right to make a profit from the company's success. It gives Amazon's management the right to compete with bookstore rival Barnes & Noble and electronics giant Sony. It also gives you the right to choose.

In this chapter, we look briefly at what business is and how it became that way. First, we discuss what you must do to be successful in the world of business and explore some important reasons for studying business. Then we define *business*, noting how business organizations satisfy their customers' needs and earn profits. Next, we examine how capitalism and command economies answer four basic economic questions. Then our focus shifts to how the nations of the world measure economic performance, the phases in a typical business cycle, and the four types of competitive situations. Next, we look at the events that helped shape today's business system, the current business environment, and the challenges that businesses face.

YOUR FUTURE IN THE CHANGING WORLD OF BUSINESS

Discuss what you must do to be successful in the world of business.

The key word in this heading is *changing*. When faced with both economic problems and increasing competition not only from firms in the United States but also from international firms located in other parts of the world, employees and managers began to ask the question: What do we do now? Although this is a fair question, it is difficult to answer. Certainly, for a college student taking business courses or an employee just starting a career, the question is even more difficult to answer. Yet there are still opportunities out there for people who are willing to work hard, continue to learn, and possess the ability to adapt to change. Let's begin our discussion in this section with three basic concepts.

- What do you want?
- Why do you want it?
- Write it down!

During a segment on a national television talk show, Joe Dudley, one of the world's most respected black business owners, gave the preceding advice to anyone who wanted to succeed in business. His advice can help you achieve success. What is so amazing about Dudley's success is that he started a manufacturing business in his own kitchen, with his wife and children serving as the new firm's only employees. He went on to develop his own line of hair-care and cosmetic products sold directly to cosmetologists, barbers, beauty schools, and consumers in the United States and 18 foreign countries. Today, Mr. Dudley has a multimillion-dollar empire—one of the

free enterprise the system of business in which individuals are free to decide what to produce, how to produce it, and at what price to sell it

most successful minority-owned companies in the nation. He is not only a successful business owner but also a winner of the Horatio Alger Award—an award given to outstanding individuals who have succeeded in the face of adversity.[2]

Although many people would say that Joe Dudley was just lucky or happened to be in the right place at the right time, the truth is that he became a success because he had a dream and worked hard to turn his dream into a reality. Today, Dudley's vision is to see people succeed—to realize "The American Dream." He would be the first to tell you that you have the same opportunities that he had. According to Mr. Dudley, "Success is a journey, not just a destination."[3]

Whether you want to obtain part-time employment to pay college and living expenses, begin your career as a full-time employee, or start a business, you must *bring* something to the table that makes you different from the next person. Employers and our economic system are more demanding than ever before. Ask yourself: What can I do that will make employers want to pay me a salary? What skills do I have that employers need? With these two questions in mind, we begin the next section with another basic question: Why study business?

Why Study Business?

The potential benefits of higher education are enormous. To begin with, there are economic benefits. Over their lifetimes, college graduates on average earn much more than high school graduates. Although lifetime earnings are substantially higher for college graduates, so are annual income amounts (see Figure 1.1). In addition to higher income, you will find at least five compelling reasons for studying business.

For Help in Choosing a Career

What do you want to do with the rest of your life? At some time in your life, someone probably has asked you this same question. Like many people, you may find it a difficult question to answer. This business course will introduce you to a wide array of employment opportunities. In private enterprise, these range from small, local businesses owned by one individual to large companies such as American Express and Marriott International that are owned by thousands of stockholders. There are also employment opportunities with federal, state, county, and local governments and with charitable organizations such as the Red Cross and Save the Children. For help in deciding which career might be right for you, read Appendix A: Careers in Business, which appears on the text Web site. To view this information:

1. Go to www.cengagebrain.com.
2. At the CengageBrain.com home page, search for the ISBN for your book (located on the back cover of your book) using the search box at the top of the page. This will take you to the product page where free companion resources can be found.

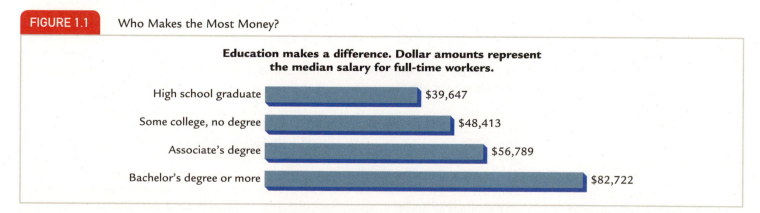

FIGURE 1.1   Who Makes the Most Money?

Education makes a difference. Dollar amounts represent the median salary for full-time workers.

High school graduate	$39,647
Some college, no degree	$48,413
Associate's degree	$56,789
Bachelor's degree or more	$82,722

Source: The 2012 Statistical Abstract of the U.S. Web site at www.census.gov (accessed January 10, 2012). Salary amounts were obtained from Table 692.

Career SUCCESS

Show Off Your Skills with Digital Merit Badges

Made of pixels instead of fabric, the next generation of merit badges is on its way, bringing new possibilities for showing off your skills via digital badges on your Web site, blog, or Facebook page. The point is to encourage students, career-changers, veterans, and learners of all ages to acquire or polish skills that can be helpful in career moves and in life. Whether you're just entering the workforce or you want to branch out into a new field, take a look at what digital merit badges have to offer.

The MacArthur Foundation is partnering with organizations such as the Smithsonian and the U.S. Department of Veterans Affairs to encourage and recognize skill attainment in a variety of areas through its "Badges for Lifelong Learning" program.

In the works are badges for financial literacy, engineering design, filmmaking, mathematics proficiency, natural history, and military experience. "The badges are another way to tell the story of who you are and what you know," explains a MacArthur executive.

TopCoder, a Connecticut company, awards digital badges (and cash) to those who earn top scores in its international programming competitions. NASA has teamed up with the Boy Scouts of America and the Girl Scouts of America to offer badges in robotics. Is a digital merit badge in your future?

Sources: Based on information in Anne Eisenberg, "For Job Hunters, Digital Merit Badges," *New York Times*, November 20, 2011, p. BU-3; Sam Kilb, "Credentials, the Next Generation," *New York Times Education Life*, November 6, 2011, p. 10; Leslie Katz, "Boy Scouts Can Now Earn Robotics Merit Badge," *Cnet News*, April 10, 2011, http://news.cnet.com.

In addition to career information in Appendix A, a number of additional Web sites provide information about career development. For more information, visit the following sites:

- Career Builder at www.careerbuilder.com
- Career One Stop at www.careeronestop.org
- Monster at www.monster.com

To click your career into high gear, you can also use online networking to advance your career. Web sites like Facebook, Twitter, LinkedIn, and other social media sites can help you locate job openings, help prospective employers to find you, and make a good impression on current and future bosses. To make the most of online networking, begin by identifying and joining sites where you can connect with potential employers, former classmates, and others who may have or may hear of job openings. Next, be sure your online profiles, photographs, and posts communicate your abilities and interest without being offensive or overly revealing. Finally, be ready to respond quickly when you spot a job opening.

One thing to remember as you think about what your ideal career might be is that a person's choice of a career ultimately is just a reflection of what he or she values and holds most important. What will give one individual personal satisfaction may not satisfy another. For example, one person may dream of a career as a corporate executive and becoming a millionaire before the age of 30. Another may choose a career that has more modest monetary rewards but that provides the opportunity to help others. What you choose to do with your life will be based on what you feel is most important. And *you* are a very important part of that decision.

To Be a Successful Employee Deciding on the type of career you want is only the first step. To get a job in your chosen field and to be successful at it, you will have to develop a plan, or a road map, that ensures that you have the skills and knowledge the job requires. You will also be expected to have the ability to work well with many types of people in a culturally diverse workforce. **Cultural (or workplace) diversity** refers to the differences among people in a workforce owing to race, ethnicity, and

cultural (or workplace) diversity differences among people in a workforce owing to race, ethnicity, and gender

gender. These skills, together with a working knowledge of the American business system and an appreciation for a culturally diverse workplace, can give you an inside edge when you are interviewing with a prospective employer.

This course, your instructor, and all of the resources available at your college or university can help you to acquire the skills and knowledge you will need for a successful career. But do not underestimate your part in making your dream a reality. In addition to the job-related skills and knowledge you'll need to be successful in a specific job, employers will also look for the following characteristics when hiring a new employee or promoting an existing employee:

- Honesty and integrity
- Willingness to work hard
- Dependability
- Time management skills
- Self-confidence
- Motivation
- Willingness to learn
- Communication skills
- Professionalism

Employers will also be interested in any work experience you may have had in cooperative work/school programs, during summer vacations, or in part-time jobs during the school year. These things can make a difference when it is time to apply for the job you really want.

Personal APPS

Sometimes you have to reach for success! There's an old saying that if you choose a career you like, you never have to work a day in your life. For most people, the first decision is choosing a career. Then the material in the sections "To Be a Successful Employee" and "To Improve Your Management Skills" can help you achieve success.

To Improve Your Management Skills Often, employees become managers or supervisors. In fact, many employees want to become managers because managers often receive higher salaries. Although management obviously can be a rewarding career, what is not so obvious is the amount of time and hard work needed to achieve the higher salaries. For starters, employers expect more from managers and supervisors than ever before. Typically, the heavy workload requires that managers work long hours, and most do not get paid overtime. They also face increased problems created by the economic crisis, increased competition, employee downsizing, the quest for improved quality, and the need for efficient use of the firm's resources.

To be an effective manager, managers must be able to perform four basic management functions: planning, organizing, leading and motivating, and controlling. All four topics are discussed in Chapter 6, Understanding the Management Process. To successfully perform these management functions, managers must possess four very important skills.

- *Interpersonal skills*—The ability to deal effectively with individual employees, other managers within the firm, and people outside the firm.
- *Analytic skills*—The ability to identify problems correctly, generate reasonable alternatives, and select the "best" alternatives to solve problems.
- *Technical skills*—The skill required to accomplish a specific kind of work being done in an organization. Although managers may not actually perform the technical tasks, they should be able to train employees and answer technical questions.
- *Conceptual skills*—The ability to think in abstract terms in order to see the "big picture." Conceptual skills help managers understand how the various parts of an organization or idea can fit together.

In addition to the four skills just described, a successful manager will need many of the same characteristics that an employee needs to be successful.

To Start Your Own Business Some people prefer to work for themselves, and they open their own businesses. To be successful, business owners must possess many of the same characteristics that successful employees have, and they must be willing to work hard and put in long hours.

It also helps if your small business can provide a product or service that customers want. For example, Steve Demeter, the CEO and founder of the software development firm Demiforce, began his career by creating the *Trism* application for the Apple iPhone. *Trism* was an immediate sensation and sold 50,000 copies at $4.99 in its first two months on Apple's AppStore. Now Demeter and the employees at Demiforce are working with a number of promising ideas in the works all with one goal in mind: to provide games and applications that people want.[4]

Unfortunately, many small-business firms fail: Approximately 70 percent of them fail within the first ten years. Typical reasons for business failures include undercapitalization (not enough money), poor business location, poor customer service, unqualified or untrained employees, fraud, lack of a proper business plan, and failure to seek outside professional help. The material in Chapter 5, Small Business, Entrepreneurship, and Franchises, and selected topics and examples throughout this text will help you to decide whether you want to open your own business. This material will also help you to overcome many of these problems.

To Become a Better Informed Consumer and Investor The world of business surrounds us. You cannot buy a home, a new Ford Fusion Hybrid from the local Ford dealer, a pair of jeans at Gap Inc., or a hot dog from a street vendor without entering a business transaction. Because you no doubt will engage in business transactions almost every day of your life, one very good reason for studying business is to become a more fully informed consumer.

Many people also rely on a basic understanding of business to help them to invest for the future. According to Julie Stav, Hispanic stockbroker-turned-author/radio personality, "Take $25, add to it drive plus determination and then watch it multiply into an empire."[5] The author of *Get Your Share* believes that it is important to learn the basics about the economy and business, stocks, mutual funds, and other alternatives before investing your money. She also believes that it is never too early to start investing. Although this is an obvious conclusion, just dreaming of being rich does not make it happen. In fact, like many facets of life, it takes planning and determination to establish the type of investment program that will help you to accomplish your financial goals.

Special Note to Business Students

It is important to begin reading this text with one thing in mind: *This business course does not have to be difficult.* We have done everything possible to eliminate the problems that you encounter in a typical class. All of the features in each chapter have been evaluated and recommended by instructors with years of teaching experience. In addition, business students were asked to critique each chapter component. Based on this feedback, the text includes the following features:

- *Learning objectives* appear at the beginning of each chapter.
- *Inside Business* is a chapter-opening case that highlights how successful companies do business on a day-to-day basis.
- *Margin notes* are used throughout the text to reinforce both learning objectives and key terms.
- *Two boxed features* in each chapter chosen from Career Success, Entrepreneurial Success, Ethical Success or Failure?, and Going for Success highlight how both employees and entrepreneurs can be successful.

- *Two Personal Apps* in each chapter provide special student-centered examples and explanations that help you immediately grasp and retain the material.
- *Sustaining the Planet* features provide information about companies working to protect the environment.
- *Social Media* features provide examples of how businesses and individuals are using social networking and social media sites.
- *End-of-chapter materials* provide questions about the opening case, a chapter summary, a list of key terms, review and discussion questions, and two cases.
- The last section of every chapter is entitled Building Skills for Career Success and includes exercises devoted to enhancing your social media skills, building communication skills with a journal exercise, developing critical-thinking skills, building team skills, and researching different careers.
- *End-of-part materials* provide a continuing video case about Graeter's Ice Cream, a company that operates a chain of retail outlets in the Cincinnati, Ohio, area and sells to Kroger Stores throughout the country. Also, at the end of each major part is an exercise designed to help you to develop the components that are included in a typical business plan.

In addition to the text, a number of student supplements will help you to explore the world of business. We are especially proud of the Web site that accompanies this edition. There, you will find online study aids, such as interactive quizzes, key terms and definitions, student PowerPoint slides, crossword puzzles, and links to the videos for each chapter. If you want to take a look at the Internet support materials available for this edition of *Business*,

1. Go to www.cengagebrain.com.
2. At the CengageBrain.com home page, search for the ISBN for your book (located on the back cover of your book) using the search box at the top of the page. This will take you to the textbook Web site where free companion resources can be found.

As authors, we want you to be successful. We know that your time is valuable and that your schedule is crowded with many different activities. We also appreciate the fact that textbooks are expensive. Therefore, we want you to use this text and get the most out of your investment. To help you get off to a good start, a number of suggestions for developing effective study skills and using this text are provided in Table 1.1.

TABLE 1.1 Seven Ways to Use this Text and Its Resources

1. Prepare before you go to class.	Early preparation is the key to success in many of life's activities. Certainly, early preparation can help you to participate in class, ask questions, and improve your performance on examinations.
2. Read the chapter.	Although it may seem like an obvious suggestion, many students never take the time to really read the material. Find a quiet space where there are no distractions, and invest enough time to become a "content expert."
3. Underline or highlight important concepts.	Make this text yours. Do not be afraid to write on the pages of your text or highlight important material. It is much easier to review material if you have identified important concepts.
4. Take notes.	While reading, take the time to jot down important points and summarize concepts in your own words. Also, take notes in class.
5. Apply the concepts.	Learning is always easier if you can apply the content to your real-life situation. Think about how you could use the material either now or in the future.
6. Practice critical thinking.	Test the material in the text. Do the concepts make sense? To build critical-thinking skills, answer the questions that accompany the cases at the end of each chapter. Also, many of the exercises in the Building Skills for Career Success require critical thinking.
7. Prepare for the examinations.	Allow enough time to review the material before the examinations. Check out the summary and review questions at the end of the chapter. Then use the resources on the text Web site.

Why not take a look at these suggestions and use them to help you succeed in this course and earn a higher grade. Remember what Joe Dudley said, "Success is a journey, not just a destination."

Because a text should always be evaluated by the students and instructors who use it, we would welcome and sincerely appreciate your comments and suggestions. Please feel free to contact us by using one of the following e-mail addresses:

Bill Pride: w-pride@tamu.edu
Bob Hughes: bhughes@dcccd.edu
Jack Kapoor: kapoorj@cod.edu

Define *business* and identify potential risks and rewards.

BUSINESS: A DEFINITION

Business is the organized effort of individuals to produce and sell, for a profit, the goods and services that satisfy society's needs. The general term *business* refers to all such efforts within a society (as in "American business"). However, *a business* is a particular organization, such as Kraft Foods, Inc., or Cracker Barrel Old Country Stores. To be successful, a business must perform three activities. It must be organized, it must satisfy needs, and it must earn a profit.

The Organized Effort of Individuals

For a business to be organized, it must combine four kinds of resources: material, human, financial, and informational. *Material* resources include the raw materials used in manufacturing processes as well as buildings and machinery. For example, Sara Lee (now part of Hillshire Brands) needs flour, sugar, butter, eggs, and other raw materials to produce the food products it sells worldwide. In addition, this Illinois-based company needs human, financial, and informational resources. *Human* resources are the people who furnish their labor to the business in return for wages. The *financial* resource is the money required to pay employees, purchase materials, and generally keep the business operating. *Information* is the resource that tells the managers of the business how effectively the other three resources are being combined and used (see Figure 1.2).

business the organized effort of individuals to produce and sell, for a profit, the goods and services that satisfy society's needs

Today, businesses are usually organized as one of three specific types. *Service businesses* produce services, such as haircuts, legal advice, or tax preparation. H&R Block provides tax preparation, retail banking, and various business advisory and consulting services in the United States, Canada, and Australia. *Manufacturing businesses* process various materials into tangible goods, such as delivery trucks, towels, or computers. Intel, for example, produces computer chips that, in turn, are sold to companies that manufacture computers. Finally, some firms called *marketing intermediaries* buy products from manufacturers and then resell them. Sony Corporation is a manufacturer that produces stereo equipment, televisions, and other electronic products. These products may be sold to a marketing intermediary such as Best Buy or Walmart, which then resells the manufactured goods to consumers in their retail stores.

© ANTON GVZDOKOV/SHUTTERSTOCK

Organization when it counts. Imagine what would happen if the medical professionals in a hospital operating room weren't organized—especially if you were the patient. Like a surgical operating room, a business must be organized in order to meet the needs of its customers and earn a profit.

Satisfying Needs

The ultimate objective of every firm must be to satisfy the needs of its customers. People generally do not buy goods and services simply to own them; they buy goods and services to satisfy

FIGURE 1.2   Combining Resources

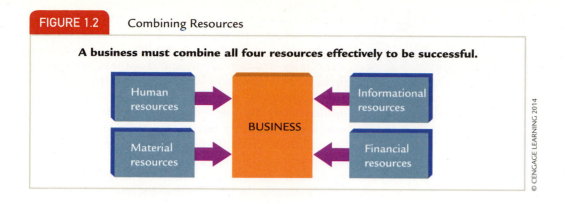

A business must combine all four resources effectively to be successful.

particular needs. Some of us may feel that the need for transportation is best satisfied by an air-conditioned BMW with navigation system, stereo system, heated and cooled seats, automatic transmission, power windows, and remote-control side mirrors. Others may believe that a Chevrolet Sonic with a stick shift will do just fine. Both products are available to those who want them, along with a wide variety of other products that satisfy the need for transportation.

When firms lose sight of their customers' needs, they are likely to find the going rough. However, when businesses understand their customers' needs and work to satisfy those needs, they are usually successful. Back in 1962, Sam Walton opened his first discount store in Rogers, Arkansas. Although the original store was quite different from the Walmart Superstores you see today, the basic ideas of providing customer service and offering goods that satisfied needs at low prices are part of the reason why this firm has grown to become the largest retailer in the world. Although Walmart has over 10,000 stores in the United States and 27 other countries, this highly successful discount-store organization continues to open new stores to meet the needs of its customers around the globe.[6]

Business Profit

A business receives money (sales revenue) from its customers in exchange for goods or services. It must also pay out money to cover the expenses involved in doing business. If the firm's sales revenues are greater than its expenses, it has earned a profit. More specifically, as shown in Figure 1.3, **profit** is what remains after all business expenses have been deducted from sales revenue.

A negative profit, which results when a firm's expenses are greater than its sales revenue, is called a *loss*. A business cannot continue to operate at a loss for an indefinite period of time. Management and employees must find some way to increase sales revenues and reduce expenses to return to profitability. If some

FIGURE 1.3   The Relationship Between Sales Revenue and Profit

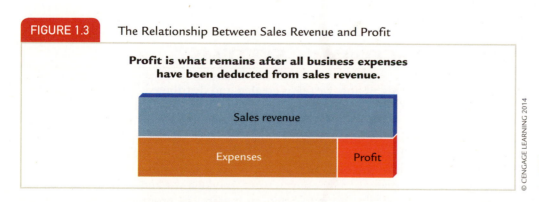

Profit is what remains after all business expenses have been deducted from sales revenue.

profit what remains after all business expenses have been deducted from sales revenue

Sustaining the PLANET

Honda: Not Just Another Automobile Manufacturer

When you hear the name Honda, you typically think about automobiles. But Honda is much more than that. Honda product lines include motorcycles, financial services, and even walk assist devices to help the disabled. The company continues to innovate and create products with a global perspective but they balance innovation with a commitment to the preservation of the environment both globally and in the local communities where they operate. Take a look at http://corporate.honda.com/innovation/ or http://corporate.honda.com/environment/.

specific actions are not taken to eliminate losses, a firm may be forced to close its doors or file for bankruptcy protection. Although many people—especially stockholders and business owners—believe that profit is literally the bottom line or most important goal for a business, many stakeholders may be just as concerned about a firm's social responsibility record. The term **stakeholders** is used to describe all the different people or groups of people who are affected by the policies, decisions, and activities made by an organization. Many corporations, for example, are careful to point out their efforts to sustain the planet, participate in the green ecological movement, and help people to live better lives in an annual social responsibility report. In its 86-page social responsibility report, General Mills describes how it contributed $100 million in 2010—a 10 percent increase when compared to 2009—to a wide variety of causes, including support for programs that feed the hungry and non-profit organizations in the United States and around the globe.[7] Although stockholders and business owners sometimes argue that the money that a business contributes to charitable causes could have been used to pay larger dividends to stockholders or increase the return on the owners' investment, the fact is that most socially responsible business firms feel social responsibility is the right thing to do and is good for business.

The profit earned by a business becomes the property of its owners. Thus, in one sense, profit is the reward business owners receive for producing goods and services that customers want. Profit is also the payment that business owners receive for assuming the considerable risks of business ownership. One of these is the risk of not being paid. Everyone else—employees, suppliers, and lenders—must be paid before the owners.

A second risk that owners undertake is the risk of losing whatever they have invested into the business. A business that cannot earn a profit is very likely to fail, in which case the owners lose whatever money, effort, and time they have invested.

To satisfy society's needs and make a profit, a business must operate within the parameters of a nation's economic system. In the next section, we define economics and describe two different types of economic systems.

Define *economics* and describe the two types of economic systems: capitalism and command economy.

stakeholders all the different people or groups of people who are affected by the policies and decisions made by an organization

TYPES OF ECONOMIC SYSTEMS

Economics is the study of how wealth is created and distributed. By *wealth*, we mean "anything of value," including the goods and services produced and sold by business. *How wealth is distributed* simply means "who gets what." Experts often use economics to explain the choices we make and how these choices change as we cope with the demands of everyday life. In simple terms, individuals, businesses, governments, and society must make decisions that reflect what is important to each group at a particular time. For example, suppose you want to take a weekend trip to some exotic vacation spot, and you also want to begin an investment program. Because of your

Entrepreneurial SUCCESS

Building a Million-Dollar App Business

Nick D'Aloisio, who lives in the south of London, England, created his first iPhone app when he was 12. Two apps later, teen entrepreneur D'Aloisio hit upon a new app idea that has brought him into the major leagues of the app business world.

D'Aloisio was searching the Internet for information for a term paper when he realized how much time it takes to determine the content of each web page. To speed things up, he developed an algorithm that summarizes the key points in a few words. He named this app Trimit, priced it at 99 cents per download, released it on Apple's App Store, and earned $1,600 within the first three days.

To accelerate Trimit's momentum, D'Aloisio decided to give it away instead of charging for it. The app's download numbers skyrocketed, bringing it to the attention of Horizon Ventures, a firm that invests in businesses when they're in the early stages of growth. Horizon invested $250,000 to commercialize the app, which was renamed Summly and relaunched a few months later. As Summly, the app was downloaded 30,000 times in the first week alone, putting D'Aloisio squarely on the path toward his goal of building a $1 million app business.

Sources: Based on information in Jane Wakefield, "British Teenage Designer of Summly App Hits Jackpot," *BBC News*, December 28, 2011, www.bbc.co.uk; Parmy Olson, "Teen Programmer Hopes to Make a Million from A.I. App," *Forbes*, September 1, 2011, www.forbes.com; Kit Eaton, "The 15-year-old Creator of the Trimit App Makes Regular Old Entrepreneurs Seem Like Slackers," *Fast Company*, August 11, 2011, www.fastcompany.com.

---

financial resources, though, you cannot do both, so you must decide what is most important. Business firms, governments, and to some extent society face the same types of decisions. Each group must deal with scarcity when making important decisions. In this case, *scarcity* means "lack of resources"—money, time, natural resources, and so on—that are needed to satisfy a want or need.

Today, experts often study economic problems from two different perspectives: microeconomics and macroeconomics. **Microeconomics** is the study of the decisions made by individuals and businesses. Microeconomics, for example, examines how the prices of homes affect the number of homes individuals will buy. On the other hand, **macroeconomics** is the study of the national economy and the global economy. Macroeconomics examines the economic effect of national income, unemployment, inflation, taxes, government spending, interest rates, and similar factors on a nation and society.

The decisions that individuals, business firms, government, and society make, and the way in which people deal with the creation and distribution of wealth determine the kind of economic system, or **economy**, that a nation has.

Over the years, the economic systems of the world have differed in essentially two ways: (1) the ownership of the factors of production and (2) how they answer four basic economic questions that direct a nation's economic activity.

Factors of production are the resources used to produce goods and services. There are four such factors:

- *Land and natural resources*—elements that can be used in the production process to make appliances, automobiles, and other products. Typical examples include crude oil, forests, minerals, land, water, and even air.
- *Labor*—the time and effort that we use to produce goods and services. It includes human resources such as managers and employees.
- *Capital*—the money, facilities, equipment, and machines used in the operation of organizations. Although most people think of capital as just money, it can also be the manufacturing equipment in a Pepperidge Farm production facility or a computer used in the corporate offices of McDonald's.

economics the study of how wealth is created and distributed

microeconomics the study of the decisions made by individuals and businesses

macroeconomics the study of the national economy and the global economy

economy the way in which people deal with the creation and distribution of wealth

factors of production resources used to produce goods and services

Saving natural resources one bus at a time. While "green" used to refer to a color in a box of crayons, now it has taken on a whole new meaning. For consumers, the government, *and* businesses, green means a new way to save natural resources, to protect the environment, and often to reduce our dependence on oil from foreign countries.

- *Entrepreneurship*—the activity that organizes land, labor, and capital. It is the willingness to take risks and the knowledge and ability to use the other factors of production efficiently. An **entrepreneur** is a person who risks his or her time, effort, and money to start and operate a business.

A nation's economic system significantly affects all the economic activities of its citizens and organizations. This far-reaching impact becomes more apparent when we consider that a country's economic system determines how the factors of production are used to meet the needs of society. Today, two different economic systems exist: capitalism and command economies. The way each system answers the four basic economic questions listed here determines a nation's economy.

1. *What* goods and services—and how much of each—will be produced?
2. *How* will these goods and services be produced?
3. *For whom* will these goods and services be produced?
4. *Who* owns and who controls the major factors of production?

Capitalism

Capitalism is an economic system in which individuals own and operate the majority of businesses that provide goods and services. Capitalism stems from the theories of the 18th-century Scottish economist Adam Smith. In his book *Wealth of Nations*, published in 1776, Smith argued that a society's interests are best served when the individuals within that society are allowed to pursue their own self-interest. According to Smith, when individuals act to improve their own fortunes, they indirectly promote the good of their community and the people in that community. Smith went on to call this concept the "invisible hand." The **invisible hand** is a term created by Adam Smith to describe how an individual's own personal gain benefits others and a nation's economy. For example, the only way a small-business owner who produces shoes can increase personal wealth is to sell shoes to customers. To become even more prosperous, the small-business owner must hire workers to produce even more shoes. According to the invisible hand, people in the small-business owner's community not only would have shoes but also would have jobs working for the shoemaker. Thus, the success of people in the community and, to some extent, the nation's economy is tied indirectly to the success of the small-business owner.

Adam Smith's capitalism is based on the following fundamental issues—also see Figure 1.4.

1. The creation of wealth is properly the concern of private individuals, not the government.
2. Private individuals must own private property and the resources used to create wealth.
3. Economic freedom ensures the existence of competitive markets that allow both sellers and buyers to enter and exit the market as they choose.
4. The role of government should be limited to providing defense against foreign enemies, ensuring internal order, and furnishing public works and education.

entrepreneur a person who risks time, effort, and money to start and operate a business

capitalism an economic system in which individuals own and operate the majority of businesses that provide goods and services

invisible hand a term created by Adam Smith to describe how an individual's personal gain benefits others and a nation's economy

| FIGURE 1.4 | Basic Assumptions for Adam Smith's Laissez-Faire Capitalism |

Laissez-Faire capitalism

Right to create wealth

Right to own private property and resources

Right to economic freedom and freedom to compete

Right to limited government intervention

© CENGAGE LEARNING 2014

One factor that Smith felt was extremely important was the role of government. He believed that government should act only as rule maker and umpire. The French term *laissez faire* describes Smith's capitalistic system and implies that there should be no government interference in the economy. Loosely translated, this term means "let them do" (as they see fit).

Adam Smith's laissez-faire capitalism is also based on the concept of a market economy. A **market economy** (sometimes referred to as a *free-market economy*) is an economic system in which businesses and individuals decide what to produce and buy, and the market determines prices and quantities sold. The owners of resources should be free to determine how these resources are used and also to enjoy the income, profits, and other benefits derived from ownership of these resources.

Capitalism in the United States

Our economic system is rooted in the laissez-faire capitalism of Adam Smith. However, our real-world economy is not as laissez-faire as Smith would have liked because government participates as more than umpire and rule maker. Our economy is, in fact, a **mixed economy**, one that exhibits elements of both capitalism and socialism.

In a mixed economy, the four basic economic questions discussed at the beginning of this section (*what, how, for whom,* and *who*) are answered through the interaction of households, businesses, and governments. The interactions among these three groups are shown in Figure 1.5.

An apple a day . . . Regarded as one of the most successful and profitable businesses in the very competitive technology industry, Apple has a history of introducing state-of-the-art consumer products like the iPhone and iPad. Although there are many ways to obtain Apple products, one way to "try out" the latest products is to visit one of their retail stores.

| FIGURE 1.5 | The Circular Flow in Our Mixed Economy |

Our economic system is guided by the interaction of buyers and sellers, with the role of government being taken into account.

Resource markets

Natural resources · Labor · Capital · Income
Natural resources · Labor · Capital · Wages · Rent · Interest
Govt. spending · Resources

Households — Taxes → Governments — Taxes → Businesses
Service ← Governments → Service

Consumer spending · Goods · Services
Govt. spending · Products
Sales revenue · Goods · Services

Product markets

© CENGAGE LEARNING 2014

market economy an economic system in which businesses and individuals decide what to produce and buy, and the market determines quantities sold and prices

mixed economy an economy that exhibits elements of both capitalism and socialism

Households Households, made up of individuals, are the consumers of goods and services as well as owners of some of the factors of production. As *resource owners*, the members of households provide businesses with labor, capital, and other resources. In return, businesses pay wages, rent, and dividends and interest, which households receive as income.

As *consumers*, household members use their income to purchase the goods and services produced by business. Today, approximately 70 percent of our nation's total production consists of **consumer products**—goods and services purchased by individuals for personal consumption.[8] This means that consumers, as a group, are the biggest customers of American business.

Businesses Like households, businesses are engaged in two different exchanges. They exchange money for natural resources, labor, and capital and use these resources to produce goods and services. Then they exchange their goods and services for sales revenue. This sales revenue, in turn, is exchanged for additional resources, which are used to produce and sell more goods and services.

Along the way, of course, business owners would like to remove something from the circular flow in the form of profits. When business profits are distributed to business owners, these profits become household income. (Business owners are, after all, members of households.) Households try to retain some income as savings. But are profits and savings really removed from the flow? Usually not! When the economy is running smoothly, households are willing to invest their savings in businesses. They can do so directly by buying stocks issued by businesses, by purchasing shares in mutual funds that purchase stocks in businesses, or by lending money to businesses. They can also invest indirectly by placing their savings in bank accounts. Banks and other financial institutions then invest these savings as part of their normal business operations. Thus, business profits, too, are retained in the business system, and the circular flow in Figure 1.5 is complete. How, then, does government fit in?

Governments The Preamble to the Constitution sets forth the responsibility of the government to protect and promote public welfare. The numerous government services are important but they (1) would either not be produced by private business firms or (2) would be produced only for those who could afford them. Typical services include national defense, police, fire protection, education, and construction of roads and highways. To pay for all these services, governments collect a variety of taxes from households (such as personal income taxes and sales taxes) and from businesses (corporate income taxes).

Figure 1.5 shows this exchange of taxes for government services. It also shows government spending of tax dollars for resources and products required to provide these services.

Actually, with government included, our circular flow looks more like a combination of several flows. In reality, it is. The important point is that together the various flows make up a single unit—a complete economic system that effectively provides answers to the basic economic questions. Simply put, the system works.

Command Economies

Before we discuss how to measure a nation's economic performance, we look quickly at another economic system called a command economy. A **command economy** is an economic system in which the government decides *what* goods and services will be produced, *how* they will be produced, *for whom* available goods and services will be produced, and *who* owns and controls the major factors of production. The answers to all four basic economic questions are determined, at least to some degree, through centralized government planning. Today, two types of economic systems—*socialism* and *communism*—serve as examples of command economies.

consumer products goods and services purchased by individuals for personal consumption

command economy an economic system in which the government decides what goods and services will be produced, how they will be produced, for whom available goods and services will be produced, and who owns and controls the major factors of production

Socialism In a socialist economy, the key industries are owned and controlled by the government. Such industries usually include transportation, utilities, communications, banking, and industries producing important materials such as steel. Land, buildings, and raw materials may also be the property of the state in a socialist economy. Depending on the country, private ownership of smaller businesses is permitted to varying degrees. Usually, people may choose their own occupations, although many work in state-owned industries.

What to produce and how to produce it are determined in accordance with national goals, which are based on projected needs and the availability of resources. The distribution of goods and services—who gets what—is also controlled by the state to the extent that it controls taxes, rents, and wages. Among the professed aims of socialist countries are the equitable distribution of income, the elimination of poverty, and the distribution of social services (such as medical care) to all who need them. The disadvantages of socialism include increased taxation and loss of incentive and motivation for both individuals and business owners.

Today, many of the nations that have been labeled as socialist nations traditionally, including France, Sweden, and India, are transitioning to a free-market economy. Currently, many countries that were once thought of as communist countries are now often referred to as socialist countries. Examples of former communist countries often referred to as socialists (or even capitalists) include most of the nations that were formerly part of the Union of Soviet Socialist Republics, China, and Vietnam.

Communism If Adam Smith was the father of capitalism, Karl Marx was the father of communism. In his writings during the mid-19th century, Marx advocated a classless society whose citizens together owned all economic resources. All workers would then contribute to this *communist* society according to their ability and would receive benefits according to their need.

Since the breakup of the Soviet Union and economic reforms in China and most of the Eastern European countries, the best remaining examples of communism are North Korea and Cuba. Today these so-called communist economies seem to practice a strictly controlled kind of socialism. The basic four economic questions are answered through centralized government plans. Emphasis is placed on the production of goods the government needs rather than on the products that consumers might want, so there are frequent shortages of consumer goods. Workers have little choice of jobs, but special skills or talents seem to be rewarded with special privileges.

MEASURING ECONOMIC PERFORMANCE

 4 Identify the ways to measure economic performance.

Today, it is hard to turn on the radio, watch the news on television, use the Internet, or read the newspaper without hearing or seeing something about the economy. Consider for just a moment the following questions:

- Is the gross domestic product for the United States increasing or decreasing?
- Why is the unemployment rate important?
- Are U.S. workers as productive as workers in other countries?

The information needed to answer these questions, along with the answers to other similar questions, is easily obtainable from many sources. More important, the answers to these and other questions can be used to gauge the economic health of the nation. For individuals, the health of the nation's economy can affect:

- the financing you need to continue your education;
- your ability to get a job; and
- the amount of interest you pay for credit card purchases, automobiles, homes, and other credit transactions.

One way to reduce costs is to manufacture products in a foreign country. In this photo, a Chinese worker assembles an electronic keyboard. To compete with foreign competition, manufacturers in the United States use sophisticated equipment and the latest technology to reduce costs, increase profits, *and* improve productivity.

The Importance of Productivity in the Global Marketplace

One way to measure a nation's economic performance is to assess its productivity. **Productivity** is the average level of output per worker per hour. An increase in productivity results in economic growth because a larger number of goods and services are produced by a given labor force. To see how productivity affects you and the economy, consider the following three questions:

Question: *How does productivity growth affect the economy?*

Answer: Because of increased productivity, it now takes fewer workers to produce more goods and services. As a result, employers have reduced costs, earned more profits, and sold their products for less. Finally, productivity growth helps American business to compete more effectively with other nations in a competitive world.

Question: *How does a nation improve productivity?*

Answer: Reducing costs and enabling employees to work more efficiently are at the core of all attempts to improve productivity. For example, productivity in the United States is expected to improve dramatically as more economic activity is transferred onto the Internet, reducing costs for customer service and handling routine ordering functions between businesses. Other methods that can be used to increase productivity are discussed in detail in Chapter 8, Producing Quality Goods and Services.

Question: *Is productivity growth always good?*

Answer: Fewer workers producing more goods and services can lead to higher unemployment rates. In this case, increased productivity is good for employers but not good for unemployed workers seeking jobs in a very competitive work environment. Because employers had been able to produce more goods and services with fewer employees during the recent economic crisis, they did not want to increase the firm's salary expense by hiring new employees after the economy began to improve.

The Nation's Gross Domestic Product

In addition to productivity, a measure called *gross domestic product* can be used to measure the economic well-being of a nation. **Gross domestic product (GDP)** is the total dollar value of all goods and services produced by all people within the boundaries of a country during a one-year period. For example, the values of automobiles produced by employees in an American-owned General Motors plant and a Japanese-owned Toyota plant in the United States are both included in the GDP for the United States. The U.S. GDP was $15.1 trillion in 2011.[9] (*Note:* At the time of publication, 2011 was the last year for which complete statistics were available.)

The GDP figure facilitates comparisons between the United States and other countries because it is the standard used in international guidelines for economic accounting. It is also possible to compare the GDP for one nation over several different time periods. This comparison allows observers to determine the extent to which a nation is experiencing economic growth. For example, government experts project that GDP will grow to $21.8 trillion by the year 2018.[10]

To make accurate comparisons of the GDP for different years, we must adjust the dollar amounts for inflation. **Inflation** is a general rise in the level of prices. (The opposite of inflation is deflation.) **Deflation** is a general decrease in the level of prices. By using inflation-adjusted figures, we are able to measure the *real* GDP for a nation. In effect, it is now possible to compare the products and services produced by a nation in constant dollars—dollars that will purchase the same amount of goods and services. Figure 1.6 depicts the GDP of the United States in current dollars and the real GDP in

productivity the average level of output per worker per hour

gross domestic product (GDP) the total dollar value of all goods and services produced by all people within the boundaries of a country during a one-year period

inflation a general rise in the level of prices

deflation a general decrease in the level of prices

FIGURE 1.6   GDP in Current Dollars and in Inflation-Adjusted Dollars

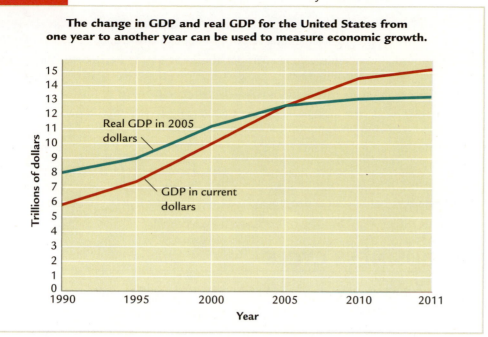

The change in GDP and real GDP for the United States from one year to another year can be used to measure economic growth.

Source: U.S. Bureau of Economic Analysis Web site at www.bea.gov (accessed January 30, 2012).

inflation-adjusted dollars. Note that between 1990 and 2011, America's real GDP grew from $8 trillion to $13.3 trillion.[11]

Important Economic Indicators that Measure a Nation's Economy

In addition to productivity, GDP, and real GDP, other economic measures exist that can be used to evaluate a nation's economy. Because of the recent economic crisis, one very important statistic that is in the news on a regular basis is the unemployment rate. The **unemployment rate** is the percentage of a nation's labor force unemployed at any time. According to the Bureau of Labor Statistics, when workers are unemployed, they, their families, and the country as a whole lose. Workers and their families lose wages, and the country loses the goods or services that could have been produced. In addition, the purchasing power of these workers is lost, which can lead to unemployment for yet other workers.[12] Although the unemployment rate for the United States is typically about 4 to 6 percent, it peaked during the recent economic crisis. Despite both federal and state programs to reduce the unemployment rate for the United States, it is still hovering around 8 percent at the time of publication. This is an especially important statistic—especially if you are unemployed.

The **consumer price index (CPI)** is a monthly index that measures the changes in prices of a fixed basket of goods purchased by a typical consumer in an urban area. Goods listed in the CPI include food and beverages, transportation, housing, clothing, medical care, recreation, education, communication, and other goods and services. Economists often use the CPI to determine the effect of inflation on not only the nation's economy but also individual consumers. Another monthly index is the producer price index. The **producer price index (PPI)** measures prices that producers receive for their finished goods. Because changes in the PPI reflect price increases or decreases at the wholesale level, the PPI is an accurate predictor of both changes in the CPI and prices that consumers will pay for many everyday necessities.

Some additional economic measures are described in Table 1.2. Like the measures for GDP, real GDP, unemployment rate, and price indexes, these measures can be used to compare one economic statistic over different periods of time.

unemployment rate the percentage of a nation's labor force unemployed at any time

consumer price index (CPI) a monthly index that measures the changes in prices of a fixed basket of goods purchased by a typical consumer in an urban area

producer price index (PPI) an index that measures prices that producers receive for their finished goods

TABLE 1.2   Common Measures Used to Evaluate a Nation's Economic Health

Economic Measure	Description
1. Balance of trade	The total value of a nation's exports minus the total value of its imports over a specific period of time.
2. Consumer confidence index	A measure of how optimistic or pessimistic consumers are about the nation's economy. This measure is usually reported on a monthly basis.
3. Corporate profits	The total amount of profits made by corporations over selected time periods.
4. Inflation rate	An economic statistic that tracks the increase in prices of goods and services over a period of time. This measure is usually calculated on a monthly or an annual basis.
5. National income	The total income earned by various segments of the population, including employees, self-employed individuals, corporations, and other types of income.
6. New housing starts	The total number of new homes started during a specific time period.
7. Prime interest rate	The lowest interest rate that banks charge their most credit-worthy customers.

© CENGAGE LEARNING 2014

Examine the different phases in the typical business cycle. **5**

THE BUSINESS CYCLE

All industrialized nations of the world seek economic growth, full employment, and price stability. However, a nation's economy fluctuates rather than grows at a steady pace every year. In fact, if you were to graph the economic growth rate for a country like the United States, it would resemble a roller coaster ride with peaks (high points) and troughs (low points). These fluctuations are generally referred to as the **business cycle**, that is, the recurrence of periods of growth and recession in a nation's economic activity. At the time of publication, many experts believed that the U.S. economy was showing signs of improvement. However, the recent economic crisis that began in fall 2007 caused a recession that will require more time before the nation experiences a complete recovery. The nation's unemployment rate is still high. People are reluctant to spend money on many consumer goods. Stock prices, although improving, are still below the record values experienced a few years ago. Although the federal government has enacted a number of stimulus plans designed to help unemployed workers, to shore up the nation's banks and Wall Street firms, to reduce the number of home foreclosures, and to free up credit for both individuals and businesses, many experts still believe that we have serious financial problems. For one, the size of the national debt—a topic described later in this section—is a concern. Another problem—the inequality of income and wealth—has also become evident as a result of the Occupy Wall Street protestors and similar groups of discontented people. To make matters worse, the recent economic crisis did not affect just the U.S. economy but also the economies of countries around the world.

The changes that result from either economic growth or economic downturn affect the amount of products and services that consumers are willing to purchase and, as a result, the amount of products and services produced by business firms. Generally, the business cycle consists of four phases: the peak (sometimes called prosperity), recession, the trough, and recovery (sometimes called expansion).

During the *peak period* (prosperity), the economy is at its highest point and unemployment is low. Total income is relatively high. As long as the economic outlook remains prosperous, consumers are willing to buy products and services. In fact, businesses often expand and offer new products and services during the peak period to take advantage of consumers' increased buying power.

Generally, economists define a **recession** as two or more consecutive three-month periods of decline in a country's GDP. Because unemployment rises during a recession, total buying power declines. The pessimism that accompanies a recession often stifles both consumer

business cycle the recurrence of periods of growth and recession in a nation's economic activity

recession two or more consecutive three-month periods of decline in a country's GDP

The dreaded pink slip. During the recent economic crisis, unemployment rates were over 10 percent and millions of Americans got a "pink slip" and lost their jobs. While economists still debate if we were in a recession or a depression, the economy is now improving and the unemployment rate is beginning to decline.

© ANDREW COMBERT/EPA/LANDOV

and business spending. As buying power decreases, consumers tend to become more value conscious and reluctant to purchase frivolous or nonessential items. And companies and government at all levels often postpone or go slow on major projects during a recession. In response to a recession, many businesses focus on producing the products and services that provide the most value to their customers. And yet, there are still opportunities out there for business firms that are well managed and provide goods and services that their customers need. For example, Caterpillar, a global company that produces earth moving and construction equipment has profited from the ongoing building boom in developing nations, where many basic infrastructure improvements move ahead regardless of what the economic conditions are in the rest of the world.

Economists define a **depression** as a severe recession that lasts longer than a typical recession and has a larger decline in business activity when compared to a recession. A depression is characterized by extremely high unemployment rates, low wages, reduced purchasing power, lack of confidence in the economy, lower stock values, and a general decrease in business activity.

The third phase of the business cycle is the *trough*. The trough of a recession or depression is the turning point when a nation's production and employment bottom out and reach their lowest levels. To offset the effects of recession and depression, the federal government uses both monetary and fiscal policies. **Monetary policies** are the Federal Reserve's decisions that determine the size of the supply of money in the nation and the level of interest rates. Through **fiscal policy**, the government can influence the amount of savings and expenditures by altering the tax structure and changing the levels of government spending.

Although the federal government collects approximately $2 trillion in annual revenues, the government usually spends more than it receives, resulting in a **federal deficit**. For example, the government had a federal deficit for each year between 2002 and 2011. The total of all federal deficits is called the **national debt**. Today, the U.S. national debt is $15.2 trillion or approximately $49,000 for every man, woman, and child in the United States.[13]

Since World War II, business cycles have lasted from three to five years from one peak period to the next peak period. During the same time period, the average length of recessions has been 11 months.[14] Some experts believe that effective use of monetary and fiscal policies can speed up recovery and reduce the amount of time the economy is in recession. *Recovery* (or *expansion*) is the movement of the economy from recession or depression to prosperity. High unemployment rates decline, income increases, and both the ability and the willingness to buy rise.

At the time of publication, many business leaders and politicians were debating whether the U.S. economy is still in recession, in the trough, or beginning recovery. Unfortunately, many of the problems that caused the recent economic crisis are still there, and they will take years to correct and resolve.

TYPES OF COMPETITION

Our capitalist system ensures that individuals and businesses make the decisions about what to produce, how to produce it, and what price to charge for the product. Mattel, Inc., for example, can introduce new versions of its famous Barbie doll, license the Barbie name, change the doll's price and method of distribution, and attempt to produce and market Barbie in other countries or over the Internet at www.mattel.com. Our system also allows customers the right to choose between Mattel's products and those produced by competitors.

As a consumer, you get to choose which products or services you want to buy. Competition like that between Mattel and other toy manufacturers is a necessary and extremely important by-product of capitalism. Business **competition** is essentially a rivalry among businesses for sales to potential customers. In a capitalistic economy, competition also ensures that a firm will survive only if it serves its customers well by providing products and services that meet needs. Economists recognize four different degrees of competition ranging from ideal, complete competition to no competition at all. These are perfect competition, monopolistic competition, oligopoly, and

depression a severe recession that lasts longer than a typical recession and has a larger decline in business activity when compared to a recession

monetary policies Federal Reserve decisions that determine the size of the supply of money in the nation and the level of interest rates

 6 Outline the four types of competition.

fiscal policy government influence on the amount of savings and expenditures; accomplished by altering the tax structure and by changing the levels of government spending

federal deficit a shortfall created when the federal government spends more in a fiscal year than it receives

national debt the total of all federal deficits

competition rivalry among businesses for sales to potential customers

Competition often gives consumers a choice. Often wonder why there are so many soap products? It's called competition. Different manufacturers use product differentiation to develop and promote the differences between their products and all similar products. Not only does product differentiation help their products stand out from the competition, it gives you—the consumer—a choice.

monopoly. For a quick overview of the different types of competition, including numbers of firms and examples for each type, look at Table 1.3.

Perfect Competition

Perfect (or pure) competition is the market situation in which there are many buyers and sellers of a product, and no single buyer or seller is powerful enough to affect the price of that product. For perfect competition to exist, there are five very important concepts.

- We are discussing the market for a single product, such as bushels of wheat.
- There are no restrictions on firms entering the industry.
- All sellers offer essentially the same product for sale.
- All buyers and sellers know everything there is to know about the market (including, in our example, the prices that all sellers are asking for their wheat).
- The overall market is not affected by the actions of any one buyer or seller.

When perfect competition exists, every seller should ask the same price that every other seller is asking. Why? Because if one seller wanted 50 cents more per bushel of wheat than all the others, that seller would not be able to sell a single bushel. Buyers could—and would—do better by purchasing wheat from the competition. On the other hand, a firm willing to sell below the going price would sell all its wheat quickly. However, that seller would lose sales revenue (and profit) because buyers are actually willing to pay more.

In perfect competition, then, sellers—and buyers as well—must accept the going price. The price of each product is determined by the actions of all buyers and all sellers together through the forces of supply and demand.

The Basics of Supply and Demand The **supply** of a particular product is the quantity of the product that producers are willing to sell at each of various prices. Producers are rational people, so we would expect them to offer more of a product for sale at higher prices and to offer less of the product at lower prices, as illustrated by the supply curve in Figure 1.7.

The **demand** for a particular product is the quantity that buyers are willing to purchase at each of various prices. Buyers, too, are usually rational, so we would expect them—as a group—to buy more of a product when its price is low and to buy less of the product when its price is high, as depicted by the demand curve in Figure 1.7.

The Equilibrium, or Market, Price There is always one certain price at which the demand for a product is exactly equal to the quantity of that product produced. Suppose that producers are willing to *supply* two million bushels of wheat at a price of $7 per bushel and that buyers are willing to *purchase* two million bushels at a price of $7 per bushel.

perfect (or pure) competition the market situation in which there are many buyers and sellers of a product, and no single buyer or seller is powerful enough to affect the price of that product

supply the quantity of a product that producers are willing to sell at each of various prices

demand the quantity of a product that buyers are willing to purchase at each of various prices

TABLE 1.3	Four Different Types of Competition	
The number of firms determines the degree of competition within an industry.		
Type of Competition	**Number of Business Firms or Suppliers**	**Real-World Examples**
1. Perfect	Many	Corn, wheat, peanuts
2. Monopolistic	Many	Clothing, shoes
3. Oligopoly	Few	Automobiles, cereals
4. Monopoly	One	Software protected by copyright, many local public utilities

© CENGAGE LEARNING 2014

In other words, supply and demand are in balance, or in equilibrium, at the price of $7. Economists call this price the *market price*. The **market price** of any product is the price at which the quantity demanded is exactly equal to the quantity supplied.

In theory and in the real world, market prices are affected by anything that affects supply and demand. The *demand* for wheat, for example, might change if researchers suddenly discovered that it offered a previously unknown health benefit. Then buyers would demand more wheat at every price. Or the *supply* of wheat might change if new technology permitted the production of greater quantities of wheat from the same amount of acreage. Other changes that can affect competitive prices are shifts in buyer tastes, the development of new products, fluctuations in income owing to inflation or recession, or even changes in the weather that affect the production of wheat.

Perfect competition is quite rare in today's world. Many real markets, however, are examples of monopolistic competition.

Monopolistic Competition

Monopolistic competition is a market situation in which there are many buyers along with a relatively large number of sellers. The various products available in a monopolistically competitive market are very similar in nature, and they are all intended to satisfy the same need. However, each seller attempts to make its product different from the others by providing unique product features, an attention-getting brand name, unique packaging, or services such as free delivery or a lifetime warranty.

Product differentiation is the process of developing and promoting differences between one's products and all competitive products. It is a fact of life for the producers of many consumer goods, from soaps to clothing to furniture to shoes. A furniture manufacturer such as Thomasville sees what looks like a mob of competitors, all trying to chip away at its share of the market. By differentiating each of its products from all

Personal APPS

Why do consumers choose one product instead of another? The next time you go to the discount store, supermarket, or drug store, notice all the products competing for your dollars. No two canned vegetables, shampoos, or candies are exactly alike. Thanks to product differentiation, you have a lot of choices when you shop.

FIGURE 1.7 Supply Curve and Demand Curve

The intersection of a supply curve and a demand curve is called the *equilibrium*, or *market price*. This intersection indicates a single price and quantity at which suppliers will sell products and buyers will purchase them.

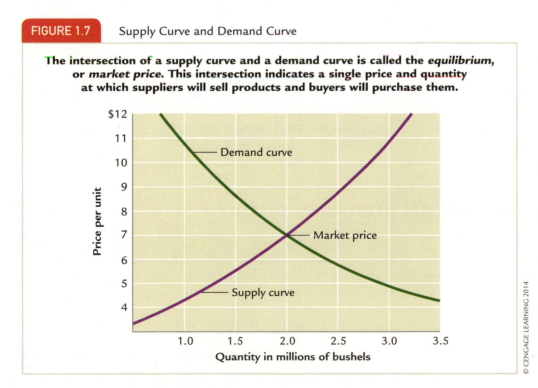

market price the price at which the quantity demanded is exactly equal to the quantity supplied

monopolistic competition a market situation in which there are many buyers along with a relatively large number of sellers who differentiate their products from the products of competitors

product differentiation the process of developing and promoting differences between one's products and all competitive products

similar products produced by competitors, Thomasville obtains some limited control over the market price of its product.

Oligopoly

An **oligopoly** is a market (or industry) situation in which there are few sellers. Generally, these sellers are quite large, and sizable investments are required to enter into their market. Examples of oligopolies are the automobile, airline, car rental, cereal, and farm implement industries.

Because there are few sellers in an oligopoly, the market actions of each seller can have a strong effect on competitors' sales and prices. If General Motors, for example, reduces its automobile prices, Ford, Honda, Toyota, and Nissan usually do the same to retain their market shares. In the absence of much price competition, product differentiation becomes the major competitive weapon; this is very evident in the advertising of the major automobile manufacturers. For instance, when Toyota was faced with declining sales as a result of quality and safety issues, it began offering buyer incentives to attract new-car buyers. Quickly, both Ford and General Motors began offering similar incentives and for the same reason—to attract new-car buyers.

Monopoly

A **monopoly** is a market (or industry) with only one seller, and there are barriers to keep other firms from entering the industry. In a monopoly, there is no close substitute for the product or service. Because only one firm is the supplier of a product, it would seem that it has complete control over price. However, no firm can set its price at some astronomical figure just because there is no competition; the firm would soon find that it has no customers or sales revenue either. Instead, the firm in a monopoly position must consider the demand for its product and set the price at the most profitable level.

Classic examples of monopolies in the United States are public utilities, including companies that provide local gas, water, or electricity. Each utility firm operates in a **natural monopoly,** an industry that requires a huge investment in capital and within which any duplication of facilities would be wasteful. Natural monopolies are permitted to exist because the public interest is best served by their existence, but they operate under the scrutiny and control of various state and federal agencies. Although many public utilities are still classified as natural monopolies, there is increased competition in many areas of the country. For example, there have been increased demands for consumer choice when selecting a company that provides electrical service to both homes and businesses.

A legal monopoly—sometimes referred to as a *limited monopoly*—is created when a government entity issues a franchise, license, copyright, patent, or trademark. For example, a copyright exists for a specific period of time and can be used to protect the owners of written materials from unauthorized use by competitors that have not shared in the time, effort, and expense required for their development. Because Microsoft owns the copyright on its popular Windows software, it enjoys a legal-monopoly position. Except for natural monopolies and legal monopolies, federal antitrust laws prohibit both monopolies and attempts to form monopolies.

AMERICAN BUSINESS TODAY

Although our economic system is far from perfect, it provides Americans with a high standard of living compared with people in other countries throughout the world. **Standard of living** is a loose, subjective measure of how well off an individual or a society is, mainly in terms of want satisfaction through goods and services. Also, our economic system offers solutions to many of the problems that plague society and provides opportunities for people who are willing to work and to continue learning.

To understand the current business environment and the challenges ahead, it helps to understand how business developed.

oligopoly a market (or industry) in which there are few sellers

monopoly a market (or industry) with only one seller, and there are barriers to keep other firms from entering the industry

natural monopoly an industry requiring huge investments in capital and within which any duplication of facilities would be wasteful and thus not in the public interest

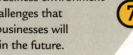

Summarize the factors that affect the business environment and the challenges that American businesses will encounter in the future.

standard of living a loose, subjective measure of how well off an individual or a society is, mainly in terms of want satisfaction through goods and services

Early Business Development

Our American business system has its roots in the knowledge, skills, and values that the earliest settlers brought to this country. The first settlers in the United States were concerned mainly with providing themselves with basic necessities—food, clothing, and shelter. Almost all families lived on farms, and the entire family worked at the business of surviving. They used their surplus for trading, mainly by barter, among themselves and with the English trading ships that called at the colonies. **Barter** is a system of exchange in which goods or services are traded directly for other goods or services without using money. As this trade increased, small businesses began to appear. Some settlers were able to use their skills and their excess time to work under the domestic system of production. The **domestic system** was a method of manufacturing in which an entrepreneur distributed raw materials to various homes, where families would process them into finished goods. The merchant entrepreneur then offered the goods for sale.

Gas shortages—could it happen again? For an industrialized economy like the United States, crude oil is an essential natural resource. When the nation experienced a shortage of crude oil during the mid-1970s, it was common to see signs like the one in this photo. Even now, both the supply and price for a gallon of gasoline are still concerns as the nation begins to rebound from the recent economic crisis.

Then, in 1793, a young English apprentice mechanic named Samuel Slater set up a textile factory in Pawtucket, Rhode Island, to spin raw cotton into thread. Slater's ingenuity resulted in America's first use of the **factory system** of manufacturing, in which all the materials, machinery, and workers required to manufacture a product are assembled in one place. The Industrial Revolution in America was born. A manufacturing technique called *specialization* was used to improve productivity. **Specialization** is the separation of a manufacturing process into distinct tasks and the assignment of the different tasks to different individuals.

The years from 1820 to 1900 were the golden age of invention and innovation in machinery. At the same time, new means of transportation greatly expanded the domestic markets for American products. Certainly, many basic characteristics of our modern business system took form during this time period.

Business Development in the 1900s

Industrial growth and prosperity continued well into the 20th century. Henry Ford's moving automotive assembly line, which brought the work to the worker, refined the concept of specialization and helped spur on the mass production of consumer goods. Fundamental changes occurred in business ownership and management as well. No longer were the largest businesses owned by one individual; instead, ownership was in the hands of thousands of corporate shareholders who were willing to invest in—but not to operate—a business.

The Roaring Twenties ended with the sudden crash of the stock market in 1929 and the near collapse of the economy. The Great Depression that followed in the 1930s was a time of misery and human suffering. People lost their faith in business and its ability to satisfy the needs of society without government involvement. After Franklin D. Roosevelt became president in 1933, the federal government devised a number of programs to get the economy moving again. In implementing these programs, the government got deeply involved in business for the first time.

To understand the major events that shaped the United States during the remainder of the 20th century, it helps to remember that the economy was compared to a roller coaster ride earlier in this chapter—periods of economic growth followed by periods of economic slowdown. The following are major events that shaped the nation's economy during the period from 1940 to 2000:

- World War II, the Korean War, and the Vietnam War
- Rapid economic growth and higher standard of living during the 1950s and 1960s
- The social responsibility movement during the 1960s
- A shortage of crude oil and higher prices for most goods in the mid-1970s
- High inflation, high interest rates, and reduced business profits during the early 1980s
- Sustained economic growth in the 1990s

During the last part of the 20th century, the Internet became a major force in the economy. e-Business—a topic we will continue to explore throughout this text—became

barter a system of exchange in which goods or services are traded directly for other goods or services without using money

domestic system a method of manufacturing in which an entrepreneur distributes raw materials to various homes, where families process them into finished goods to be offered for sale by the merchant entrepreneur

factory system a system of manufacturing in which all the materials, machinery, and workers required to manufacture a product are assembled in one place

specialization the separation of a manufacturing process into distinct tasks and the assignment of the different tasks to different individuals

an accepted method of conducting business. **e-Business** is the organized effort of individuals to produce and sell *through the Internet,* for a profit, the products and services that satisfy society's needs.

Unfortunately, by the last part of the 20th century, a larger number of business failures and declining stock values were initial signs that larger economic problems were on the way.

A New Century: 2000 and Beyond

According to many economic experts, the first part of the 21st century might be characterized as the best of times and the worst of times rolled into one package. On the plus side, technology became available at an affordable price. Both individuals and businesses could now access information with the click of a button. They also could buy and sell merchandise online.

In addition to information technology, the growth of service businesses also changed the way American firms do business in the 21st century. Because service businesses employ approximately 85 percent of the nation's workforce, we now have a service economy.[15] A **service economy** is an economy in which more effort is devoted to the production of services than to the production of goods. Typical service businesses include restaurants, laundries and dry cleaners, real estate, movie theaters, repair companies, and other services that we often take for granted. More information about how service businesses affect the economy is provided in Chapter 8, Producing Quality Goods and Services.

On the negative side, it is hard to watch television, surf the Web, listen to the radio, or read the newspaper without hearing some news about the economy. Because many of the economic indicators described in Table 1.2 on page 20 indicate troubling economic problems, there is still a certain amount of pessimism surrounding the economy.

The Current Business Environment

Before reading on, answer the following question:

In today's competitive business world, which of the following environments affects business?

 a. The competitive environment
 b. The global environment
 c. The technological environment
 d. The economic environment
 e. All of the above

Correct Answer: e. All the environments listed affect business today.

The Competitive Environment Businesses operate in a competitive environment. As noted earlier in this chapter, competition is a basic component of capitalism. Every day, business owners must figure out what makes their businesses successful and how the goods and services they provide are different from the competition. Often, the answer is contained in the basic definition of business provided on page 10. Just for a moment, review the definition:

Business is the organized effort of individuals to produce and sell, for a profit, the goods and services that satisfy society's needs.

In the definition of business, note the phrase *satisfy society's needs.* These three words say a lot about how well a successful firm competes with competitors. If you meet customer needs, then you have a better chance at success.

The Global Environment Related to the competitive environment is the global environment. Not only do American businesses have to compete with other American businesses, but they also must compete with businesses from all over the globe. According to global experts, China is one of the fastest-growing economies in the world. And China is not alone. Other countries around the world also compete with U.S. firms. There was once

e-business the organized effort of individuals to produce and sell *through the Internet,* for a profit, the products and services that satisfy society's needs

service economy an economy in which more effort is devoted to the production of services than to the production of goods

a time when the label "Made in the United States" gave U.S. businesses an inside edge both at home and in the global marketplace. Now, other countries manufacture and sell goods. According to Richard Haass, president of the Council on Foreign Relations, "There will be winners and losers from globalization. We win every time we go shopping because prices are lower. Choice is greater because of globalization. But there are losers. There are people who will lose their jobs either to foreign competition or [to] technological innovation."[16]

While many foreign firms are attempting to sell goods and services to U.S. customers, U.S. firms are also increasing both sales and profits by selling goods and services to customers in other countries. In fact there are many "potential" customers in developing nations that will buy goods and services manufactured by U.S. firms. For example, Procter & Gamble sells laundry detergent, soap, and diapers in Nigeria and has plans to do business in more than 50 African countries.[17] And Procter & Gamble is not alone. Unilever, DuPont, Johnson & Johnson, General Motors, and many more U.S. companies are also selling goods and services to customers in countries all over the globe. The world is, in fact, a much smaller place than many U.S. business leaders once thought.

The Technology Environment Although increased global competition and technological innovation has changed the way we do business, the technology environment for U.S. businesses has never been more challenging. Changes in manufacturing equipment, distribution of products, and communication with customers are all examples of how technology has changed everyday business practices. For example, many businesses are now using social media to provide customers with information about products and services. If you ask different people, you will often find different definitions for social media, but for our purposes **social media** is defined as online interaction that allows people and businesses to communicate and share ideas, personal information, and information about products or services. To illustrate how popular social media is, consider that Facebook with 800 million current users was launched in 2004 and Twitter with 300 million current users was launched in 2006. Because of rapid developments in social media and the increased importance of technology and information, businesses will need to spend additional money to keep abreast of an ever-changing technology environment and even more money to train employees to use the new technology.

The Economic Environment The economic environment must always be considered when making business decisions. This fact is especially important when the nation's economy takes a nosedive or an individual firm's sales revenue and profits are declining. For example, both small and large business firms reduced both spending and hiring new employees over the last four years because of the recent economic crisis.

In addition to economic pressures, today's socially responsible managers and business owners must be concerned about the concept of sustainability. According to the U.S. Environmental Protection Agency, **sustainability** means meeting the needs of the present without compromising the ability of future generations to meet their own needs.[18] Although the word *green* used to mean a color in a box of crayons, today green means a new way of doing business. As a result, a combination of forces, including economic factors, growth in population, increased energy use, and concerns for the environment, is changing the way individuals live and businesses operate.

When you look back at the original question we asked at the beginning of this section, clearly, each different type of environment—competitive, global, technological, and economic—affects the way a business does *business*. As a result, there are always opportunities for improvement and challenges that must be considered.

The Challenges Ahead

There it is—the American business system in brief.

When it works well, it provides jobs for those who are willing to work, a standard of living that few countries can match, and many opportunities for personal advancement. However, like every other system devised by humans, it is not perfect. Our business system may give us prosperity, but it also gave us the Great Depression of the

social media the online interaction that allows people and businesses to communicate and share ideas, personal information, and information about products or services

sustainability meeting the needs of the present without compromising the ability of future generations to meet their own needs

1930s, the economic problems of the 1970s and the early 1980s, and the economic crisis that began in the fall of 2007.

Obviously, the system can be improved. Certainly, there are plenty of people who are willing to tell us exactly what they think the American economy needs. However, these people often provide us only with conflicting opinions. Who is right and who is wrong? Even the experts cannot agree.

The experts do agree, however, that several key issues will challenge our economic system (and our nation) over the next decade. Some of the questions to be resolved include:

- How can we create a more stable economy and create new jobs for the unemployed?
- How can we regulate banks, savings and loan associations, credit unions, and other financial institutions to prevent the type of abuses that led to the recent economic crisis?
- How do we reduce the national debt and still maintain a healthy economy and stimulate business growth?
- How can we use technology to make American workers more productive and American firms more competitive in the global marketplace?
- How can we preserve the benefits of competition and small business in our American economic system?
- How can we encourage economic growth and at the same time continue to conserve natural resources and sustain our environment?
- How can we meet the needs of two-income families, single parents, older Americans, and the less fortunate who need health care and social programs to exist?
- How can we defeat terrorism and resolve conflict with Iran, North Korea, and other countries throughout the world?

The answers to these questions are anything but simple. In the past, Americans have always been able to solve their economic problems through ingenuity and creativity. Now, as we continue the journey through the 21st century, we need that same ingenuity and creativity not only to solve our current problems but also to compete in the global marketplace and build a nation and economy for future generations.

The American business system is not perfect by any means, but it does work reasonably well. We discuss some of its problems in Chapter 2 as we examine the topics of social responsibility and business ethics.

return to Inside BUSINESS

Zynga

Online games have become big business. In just a few years—and during a difficult economic period—founder Mark Pincus has transformed Zynga from a start-up game company into a profitable, 3,000-employee corporation with shares traded on the Nasdaq stock exchange. Social media games are about more than winning and losing: "We're giving a reliable 15 minutes a day that lets them not only play but also connect with people in their lives with some level of meaning," Pincus explains.

Competing against established rival firms such as Electronic Arts and Activision Blizzard, Zynga must continually introduce new games to retain player loyalty and keep revenues growing through the sale of virtual goods and advertising. Pincus and his management team keep a close eye on Zynga's business health by measuring how many people play each game, how many buy virtual goods, and which game features are the most popular. Can Zynga keep clicking ahead?

Questions

1. Of the four resources (material, human, informational, and financial) that businesses combine and organize to be successful, which have had the most significant effect on Zynga's growth—and why?

2. Of the four environments that affect business (competitive, global, technological, and economic), which do you think will help and hurt Zynga's long-term profitability?

Discuss what you must do to be successful in the world of business.

For many years, people in business—both employees and managers—assumed that prosperity would continue. When faced with both economic problems and increased competition, a large number of these people began to ask the question: What do we do now? Although this is a fair question, it is difficult to answer. Certainly, for a college student taking business courses or an employee just starting a career, the question is even more difficult to answer. And yet there are still opportunities out there for people who are willing to work hard, continue to learn, and possess the ability to adapt to change. The kind of career you choose ultimately will depend on your own values and what you feel is most important in life. By studying business, you can become a better employee or manager or you may decide to start your own business. You can also become a better consumer and investor.

 Define *business* and identify potential risks and rewards.

Business is the organized effort of individuals to produce and sell, for a profit, the goods and services that satisfy society's needs. Four kinds of resources—material, human, financial, and informational—must be combined to start and operate a business. The three general types of businesses are service businesses, manufacturers, and marketing intermediaries. Profit is what remains after all business expenses are deducted from sales revenue. It is the payment that owners receive for assuming the risks of business—primarily the risks of not receiving payment and of losing whatever has been invested in the firm. Although many people believe that profit is literally the bottom line or most important goal for a business, many corporations are careful to point out their efforts to sustain the planet, participate in the green ecological movement, and help people to live better lives.

 Define *economics* and describe the two types of economic systems: capitalism and command economy.

Economics is the study of how wealth is created and distributed. An economic system must answer four questions: *What* goods and services will be produced? *How* will they be produced? *For whom* will they be produced? *Who* owns and who controls the major factors of production? Capitalism (on which our economic system is based) is an economic system in which individuals own and operate the majority of businesses that provide goods and services. Capitalism stems from the theories of Adam Smith. Smith's pure laissez-faire capitalism is an economic system in which the factors of production are owned by private entities and

all individuals are free to use their resources as they see fit; prices are determined by the workings of supply and demand in competitive markets; and the economic role of government is limited to rule maker and umpire.

Our economic system today is a mixed economy. In the circular flow that characterizes our business system (see Figure 1.5), households and businesses exchange resources for goods and services, using money as the medium of exchange. In a similar manner, the government collects taxes from businesses and households and purchases products and resources with which to provide services.

In a command economy, government, rather than individuals, owns many of the factors of production and provides the answers to the three other economic questions. Socialist and communist economies are—at least in theory—command economies.

 Identify the ways to measure economic performance.

One way to evaluate the performance of an economic system is to assess changes in productivity, which is the average level of output per worker per hour. Gross domestic product (GDP) can also be used to measure a nation's economic well-being and is the total dollar value of all goods and services produced by all people within the boundaries of a country during a one-year period. It is also possible to adjust GDP for inflation and thus to measure real GDP. In addition to GDP, other economic indicators include a nation's balance of trade, consumer confidence index, consumer price index (CPI), corporate profits, inflation rate, national income, new housing starts, prime interest rate, producer price index (PPI), and unemployment rate.

 Examine the different phases in the typical business cycle.

A nation's economy fluctuates rather than grows at a steady pace every year. These fluctuations are generally referred to as the business cycle. Generally, the business cycle consists of four states: the peak (sometimes called prosperity), recession, the trough, and recovery (sometimes called expansion). Some experts believe that effective use of monetary policy (the Federal Reserve's decisions that determine the size of the supply of money and the level of interest rates) and fiscal policy (the government's influence on the amount of savings and expenditures) can speed up recovery.

A federal deficit occurs when the government spends more than it receives in taxes and other revenues. At the time of publication, the national debt is over $15 trillion or approximately $49,000 for every man, woman, and child in the United States.

 Outline the four types of competition.

Competition is essentially a rivalry among businesses for sales to potential customers. In a capitalist economy, competition works to ensure the efficient and effective operation of business. Competition also ensures that a firm will survive only if it serves its customers well by providing products and services that meet their needs. Economists recognize four degrees of competition. Ranging from most to least competitive, the four degrees are perfect competition, monopolistic competition, oligopoly, and monopoly. The factors of supply and demand generally influence the price that customers pay producers for goods and services.

 7 **Summarize the factors that affect the business environment and the challenges that American businesses will encounter in the future.**

From the beginning of the Industrial Revolution to the phenomenal expansion of American industry in the 19th and early 20th centuries, our government maintained an essentially laissez-faire attitude toward business. However, during the Great Depression of the 1930s, the federal government began to provide a number of social services to its citizens.

To understand the major events that shaped the United States during the remainder of the 20th and 21st century, it helps to remember that the economy was compared to a roller coaster ride earlier in this chapter—periods of economic growth followed by periods of economic slowdown. Events and a changing business environment including wars, rapid economic growth, the social responsibility movement, a shortage of crude oil, high inflation, high interest rates, reduced business profits, increased use of technology, e-business, and social media all have shaped business and the economy.

Now more than ever before, the way a business operates is affected by the competitive environment, global environment, technological environment, and economic environment. As a result, business has a number of opportunities for improvement and challenges for the future.

KEY TERMS

You should now be able to define and give an example relevant to each of the following terms:

free enterprise (4)
cultural (or workplace) diversity (6)
business (10)
profit (11)
stakeholders (12)
economics (13)
microeconomics (13)
macroeconomics (13)
economy (13)
factors of production (13)
entrepreneur (14)
capitalism (14)
invisible hand (14)

market economy (15)
mixed economy (15)
consumer products (16)
command economy (16)
productivity (18)
gross domestic product (GDP) (18)
inflation (18)
deflation (18)
unemployment rate (19)
consumer price index (CPI) (19)
producer price index (PPI) (19)
business cycle (20)

recession (20)
depression (21)
monetary policies (21)
fiscal policy (21)
federal deficit (21)
national debt (21)
competition (21)
perfect (or pure) competition (22)
supply (22)
demand (22)
market price (23)
monopolistic competition (23)

product differentiation (23)
oligopoly (24)
monopoly (24)
natural monopoly (24)
standard of living (24)
barter (25)
domestic system (25)
factory system (25)
specialization (25)
e-business (26)
service economy (26)
social media (27)
sustainability (27)

REVIEW QUESTIONS

1. What reasons would you give if you were advising someone to study business?
2. What factors affect a person's choice of careers?
3. Describe the four resources that must be combined to organize and operate a business. How do they differ from the economist's factors of production?
4. Describe the relationship among profit, business risk, and the satisfaction of customers' needs.
5. What are the four basic economic questions? How are they answered in a capitalist economy?
6. Describe the four basic assumptions required for a laissez-faire capitalist economy.
7. Based on Figure 1.5, outline the economic interactions between business and households in our business system.
8. How does capitalism differ from socialism and communism?

9. How is productivity related to the unemployment rate?
10. Define gross domestic product. Why is this economic measure significant?
11. How is the producer price index related to the consumer price index?
12. What are the four phases in a typical business cycle? How are monetary and fiscal policies related to the business cycle?
13. Identify and compare the four forms of competition.
14. Explain how the equilibrium, or market, price of a product is determined.
15. Four different environments that affect business were described in this chapter. Choose one of the environments and explain how it affects a small electronics manufacturer located in Oregon. Why?

DISCUSSION QUESTIONS

1. In what ways have the problems caused by the recent economic crisis affected business firms? In what ways have these problems affected employees and individuals?
2. What factors caused American business to develop into a mixed economic system rather than some other type of economic system?
3. Does an individual consumer really have a voice in answering the basic four economic questions?
4. Is gross domestic product a reliable indicator of a nation's economic health? What might be a better indicator?
5. Discuss this statement: "Business competition encourages efficiency of production and leads to improved product quality."
6. Is government participation in our business system good or bad? What factors can be used to explain your position.
7. Choose one of the challenges listed on page 28 and describe possible ways in which business and society could help to solve or eliminate the problem in the future.

Video Case 1.1

Entertainment Means Profits for Nederlander Concerts

Nederlander Concerts is based in Los Angeles, one of the two biggest markets in the U.S. concert industry (New York is the other). The company, which is one of the few remaining family-owned businesses in the entertainment industry, specializes in booking and promoting musical artists like the Goo Goo Dolls, Maroon 5, and Cyndi Lauper for events in the western United States. It owns or operates some of the theaters, amphitheaters, and arenas—including the Greek Theatre in Los Angeles, the Santa Barbara Bowl, and the Grove in Anaheim—and it rents space for concerts and events in other cities along the West Coast. Nederlander Concerts also partners with some of California's major cities such as Santa Monica and San Jose to manage or operate their civic theaters and present events there.

Since Nederlander Concerts deliberately focuses on small- to mid-sized events, it can offer a unique concert experience that brings audiences and performers closer together. It can therefore sell a high-quality experience at a higher price than seats in a bigger theater yield. Because of this high-quality experience, it can also count on selling out the house, which helps the company and the artists to profit. According to the concert company's chief operating officer, "The key areas or departments of the company include talent-buying and marketing, operations, finance, and business development. . . . I have a talent-buying team, I have a marketing team, we have a general manager of the building, we have a substantial team of people who take care of the fans, take care of the artist, and look after the shows that we buy. We're in a competitive market, and it's pretty interesting what we do."

Although it might seem odd that the concert business is a competitive one, in fact Nederlander Concerts competes with other promoters (like Live Nation) not just for audiences at its events but for bookings by popular artists. Therefore, it must keep both music lovers and performers happy. Musicians are especially concerned with the financial deal they are getting. As Nederlander's chief operating officer explains, "It's not always easy to get the show; there is competition. . . . We have a great reputation with the artist. But also there's one other factor, and

that's making the deal. That's making your best offer. That's trying to think about whether the agent is . . . telling you that your competition is paying more, willing to go more. You have to get your own 'I won't go above' number and stop bidding (for the act), or you have to say, 'Okay, I'll pay a little bit more and try to get the show.' So there's a real gamesmanship between agent and buyer. . . . The art of the deal is something we live with every day."

Given the talent, how does Nederlander get music lovers to its events? Says its vice president of marketing, "It's learning about the market, and picking up every newspaper you can find, listening to every radio station you can find, watching all of the TV, all the news programming. . . . It still comes back to, who is the artist, and who is their audience? And how do you find them? . . . The number one reason why people don't go to a show, so they say, is that they don't know about it. Which is infuriating. But we just try to make that percentage of people . . . smaller, and smaller, and smaller."

When everything is going well, the company profits. "Where we like to do most of our business, and in fact is where we probably do 90 percent of our business, is in the venues that we own or operate, so that the risk profile of those shows goes down . . . we have more revenues coming in to ensure that we're able to cover the cost, including the cost of talent, and then walk away with a greater profit."[19]

Questions

1. Nederlander Concerts competes for music lovers with other concert arenas and promoters. Do you think it also competes with TV, movies, CDs, DVDs, streaming video, and sports events? If yes, what implications does this type of competition have for Nederlander's business?
2. How many different groups can you think of whose needs Nederlander Concerts must satisfy in order to be a successful business?
3. Give an example showing how Nederlander Concerts uses each of the four factors of production.

The company that brought Mickey and Minnie Mouse into the public eye has been entertaining families for 90 years. Although animation was the Walt Disney Company's original focus, its entertainment empire now spans four main business groups: studio entertainment (including movies, stage shows, and recorded music), parks and resorts (such as Disney World and the Disney Cruise Line), consumer products (toys, books, and other merchandise), and media (including broadcast television, cable television, and online media). Disney has its headquarters in Burbank, California, but its operations are spread around the world, with $41 billion in annual revenues and a workforce of 156,000 employees.

Over the years, Disney has acquired other businesses and started new businesses to further strengthen its competitive position and its profits. It owns Pixar, the movie studio responsible for *Toy Story* and many other animated films, and it established Touchstone Pictures to produce and distribute movies for wider audiences. It acquired the ABC television networks and the ESPN sports channels as part of its drive for global growth in multiple media. To expand into interactive media for children, Disney bought the popular Club Penguin site and began creating online and video games, many featuring its popular movie and television characters.

Founder Walt Disney didn't invent the theme park, but he did transform the industry with the 1955 opening of Disneyland in California. The magic continued with the 1971 opening of Disney World in Florida. Both theme parks were drawing crowds from every continent when the company opened Tokyo Disneyland in 1983, at the height of the Japanese economic boom. Later, it worked with international partners to create Disneyland Paris and Hong Kong Disneyland. Shanghai Disney Resort will be the next to open, the result of a $3.7 billion joint business venture with a Chinese company. In all, more than 120 million people visit Disney theme parks and resorts over the course of one year.

Disney sees great growth potential in China. Thanks to economic and political changes, Chinese consumers have more disposable income than ever before and more opportunities to exercise their higher buying power. Box-office receipts from Chinese movie theaters are growing at double-digit rates, and many of Disney's Hollywood blockbusters have also been big hits in China. At the same time, competition to get movies into Chinese theaters is enormous, because the government limits the number of foreign movies that can be distributed nationwide. With an eye toward the future, Disney worked with a local partner to co-produce *Iron Man 3* with a Chinese plot twist. It has also been lending its movie-making expertise to help develop the Chinese animation industry.

All these years of serving customers with a smile have given Disney considerable insight into how to meet the needs of people of all ages. The company set up the Disney Institute in 1986 to teach businesses, schools, hospitals, and other organizations how to deliver good customer service with the famous Disney touch. Its experts have trained National Football League staff members in preparation for Super Bowl events and given Chevrolet dealer employees tips about working with car buyers. When Florida Hospital asked for help in improving patient satisfaction, Disney experts conducted studies and recommended a number of steps, such as having a friendly greeter to put young patients at ease and replacing the glare of fluorescent bulbs with recessed lighting. These and other changes helped push the hospital's patient satisfaction scores into the top 10 percent across America. The Disney Institute's revenues have doubled over the past few years and are yet another reason for the company's profit momentum.[20]

Questions

1. How is the Walt Disney Company combining human, informational, material, and financial resources for business success?
2. What is Disney's competitive situation, and what are the implications for its future expansion and profitability?
3. Which of the factors in the business environment seem to be exerting the most influence on Disney's ability to grow? Explain.

Building Skills for Career Success

① SOCIAL MEDIA EXERCISE

Today, many companies have a social media presence on Facebook, Twitter, Flickr, and other sites beyond their corporate Web site. Think of three of your favorite car companies and conduct a quick search using a search engine like Google or Yahoo! Answer the following:

1. Name the social networks for each company.
2. Compare each of their Facebook pages. How many "likes" does each company have? Are there multiple pages for the company? How much interaction (or engagement) is on each Facebook page?
3. What business goals do you think each company is trying to reach through their Facebook presence?

② JOURNALING FOR SUCCESS

Much of the information in this chapter was designed to get you to think about what it takes to be a successful employee in the competitive business world.

Assignment

Assume that you are now 25 years old and are interviewing for a position as a management trainee in a large corporation. Also assume that this position pays $45,000 a year.

1. Describe what steps you would take to prepare for this interview.
2. Assuming that you get the management trainee position, describe the personal traits or skills that you have that will help you to become successful.
3. Describe the one personal skill or trait that you feel needs improvement. How would you go about improving your weakness?

③ DEVELOPING CRITICAL-THINKING SKILLS

With capitalism, competition is a driving force that allows the market economy to work. Let's see how competition works by pretending that you want to buy a new car.

Assignment

1. Brainstorm the following questions:
   a. Where would you go to get information about new cars?
   b. How will you decide on the make and model of car you want to buy, where to buy the car, and how to finance it?
   c. How is competition at work in this scenario?
   d. What are the pros and cons of competition as it affects the buyer?
2. Record your ideas.
3. Write a summary of the key points you learned about how competition works in the marketplace.

④ BUILDING TEAM SKILLS

Over the past few years, employees have been expected to function as productive team members instead of working alone. People often believe that they can work effectively in teams, but many people find working with a group of people to be a challenge.

College classes that function as teams are more interesting and more fun to attend, and students generally learn more about the topics in the course. One way to begin creating a team is to learn something about each student in the class. This helps team members to feel comfortable with each other and fosters a sense of trust.

Assignment

1. Find a partner, preferably someone you do not know.
2. Each partner has two to three minutes to answer the following questions:
   a. What is your name, and where do you work?
   b. What interesting or unusual thing have you done in your life? (Do not talk about work or college; rather, focus on such things as hobbies, travel, family, and sports.)
   c. Why are you taking this course, and what do you expect to learn? (Satisfying a degree requirement is not an acceptable answer.)
3. Introduce your partner to the class. Use one to two minutes, depending on the size of the class.

⑤ RESEARCHING DIFFERENT CAREERS

In this chapter, *entrepreneurship* is defined as the willingness to take risks and the knowledge and ability to use the other factors of production efficiently. An *entrepreneur* is a person who risks time, effort, and money to start and operate a business. Often, people believe that these terms apply only to small business. However, employees with entrepreneurial attitudes have recently advanced more rapidly in large companies as well.

Assignment

1. Go to the local library or use the Internet to research how large firms, especially corporations, are rewarding employees who have entrepreneurial skills.
2. Find answers to the following questions:
   a. Why is an entrepreneurial attitude important in large corporations today?
   b. What makes an entrepreneurial employee different from other employees?
   c. How are these employees being rewarded, and are the rewards worth the effort?
3. Write a two-page report that summarizes your findings.

ENDNOTES

1. Sources: Based on information from the Zynga Web site at www.zynga.com accessed January 12, 2012; Jon Swartz, "CEO Calls Zynga His 'Crowning Achievement,'" *USA Today*, December 18, 2011, www.usatoday.com; Evelyn M. Rusli, "Zynga's Tough Culture Risks a Talent Drain," *New York Times*, November 27, 2011, www.nytimes.com; Miguel Helft, "Check Out Zynga's Zany New Offices," *Fortune*, November 7, 2011, pp. 59–60; "The World's 50 Most Innovative Companies: #9, Zynga," *Fast Company*, n.d., www.fastcompany.com.
2. The Horatio Alger Web site at www.horatioalger.org (accessed January 5, 2012).
3. Ibid.
4. The 66Apps Web site at www.66apps.com (accessed January 11, 2012).
5. Idy Fernandez, "Julie Stav," *Hispanic*, June–July 2005, 204.
6. The Walmart stores Web site at www.walmartstores.com (accessed January 9, 2012).
7. The General Mills Web site at www.generalmills.com (accessed January 9, 2012).
8. The Bureau of Economic Analysis Web site at www.bea.gov (accessed January 9, 2012).
9. The Bureau of Economic Analysis Web site at www.bea.gov (accessed January 30, 2012).
10. The Bureau of Labor Statistics Web site at www.bls.gov (accessed January 9, 2011).
11. The Bureau of Economic Analysis Web site at www.bea.gov (accessed January 30, 2012).
12. The Bureau of Labor Statistics Web site at www.bls.gov (accessed January 8, 2012).
13. The Treasury Direct Web site at www.treasurydirect.gov (accessed January 9, 2012) and the U.S. Census Bureau Web site at www.census.gov (accessed January 9, 2012).
14. The Investopedia Web site at www.investopedia.com (accessed January 9, 2012).
15. The Bureau of Labor Statistics Web site at www.bls.gov (accessed January 12, 2011).
16. Bill Weir, "Made in China: Your Job, Your Future, Your Fortune," ABC News Web site at www.abcnews.com (accessed September 20, 2005).

17. Les Dlabay, "The Future of Global Business at 'Base of the Pyramid,'" *The Daily Herald Business Ledger*, November 29, 2011, p. 22.

18. The Environmental Protection Agency Web site at www.epa.gov (accessed January 9, 2012).

19. Company Web site www.nederlanderconcerts.com (accessed January 14, 2012); "Nederlander Organization company overview," *BusinessWeek*, August 20, 2010, www.businessweek.com; Hannah Heineman, "Moving Forward on Capital Improvement Projects," *Santa Monica Mirror*, July 28, 2010, www.smmirror.com; Steve Knopper, "Tour Biz Strong in Weak Economy," *Rolling Stone*, October 2, 2008, 11–12; Ray Waddell, "Nederlander/Viejas Deal Offers Touring Opportunities," *Billboard*, January 10, 2008, www.billboard.com; interviews with Nederlander employees and the video "For Nederlander Concerts, Entertainment Is a Profitable Business."

20. Sources: Based on information in Brooks Barnes, "In Customer Service Consulting, Disney's Small World Is Growing," *New York Times*, April 23, 2012, www.nytimes.com; David Pierson and Richard Verrier, "Disney to Join Animation Initiative," *Los Angeles Times*, April 11, 2012, www.latimes.com; "Disney Making 'Iron Man 3' with Chinese Partner as Hollywood Expands China Ties," *Washington Post*, April 16, 2012, www.washingtonpost.com; Jason Garcia, "Cruise Line, Theme Parks Propel Disney Profit," *Orlando Sentinel*, February 7, 2012, www.orlandosentinel.com; http://corporate.disney.go.com.

© RYAN MILLER/GETTY IMAGES

Being Ethical and Socially Responsible

2

LEARNING OBJECTIVES

Once you complete this chapter, you will be able to:

1 Understand what is meant by *business ethics*.

2 Identify the types of ethical concerns that arise in the business world.

3 Discuss the factors that affect the level of ethical behavior in organizations.

4 Explain how ethical decision making can be encouraged.

5 Describe how our current views on the social responsibility of business have evolved.

6 Explain the two views on the social responsibility of business and understand the arguments for and against increased social responsibility.

7 Discuss the factors that led to the consumer movement and list some of its results.

8 Analyze how present employment practices are being used to counteract past abuses.

9 Describe the major types of pollution, their causes, and their cures.

10 Identify the steps a business must take to implement a program of social responsibility.

Did You Know?

Menu boards posted at Panera Cares cafés show "suggested funding levels" instead of prices, and customers pay by putting money into a donation box.

Panera Cares About Its Communities

Out of 1,500 Panera bakery-cafés spread across the United States and Canada, a handful are slightly different from the rest of the chain. These Panera Cares cafés are owned by the nonprofit division of Panera Bread, and the posted menus show "suggested funding levels" rather than specific prices. After customers place their orders, they don't pay at the cash register. Instead, they drop money into a donation box, contributing whatever amount they wish to pay for their meals. People who can't afford to pay are encouraged to do their part by volunteering some time at the café.

Welcome to Panera Cares, the next phase of an ongoing effort to "make a contribution to the community in a real, substantive way," says Ron Shaich, Panera's founder. Although his company has a long history of donating money and food to charitable causes, Shaich wanted to do more. His idea was to open pay-what-you-wish cafés where people struggling to make ends meet could enjoy a regular restaurant meal with dignity.

When the first three cafés opened (in Clayton, Missouri; Dearborn, Michigan; and Portland, Oregon), Shaich wasn't sure whether customers who could afford to pay would donate as much as expected or how many people with money to spend would take advantage by paying too little or not at all. The goal is for Panera Cares to be self-supporting so it can give back to the community with more than meals. So far, approximately 60 percent of the customers are donating the suggested amount, 20 percent are donating more, and 20 percent are donating less. The largest single donation ever made for a meal was $500.

As long as each location brings in about 80 percent of the suggested funding level, the cafes will generate enough profit to keep going and pay for extras such as providing job training for teenagers in the local area. "This is not about a handout," Shaich explains. "This is about a hand up, and every one of us has a need for that at some point in our lives."[1]

O bviously, organizations like Panera want to be recognized as responsible corporate citizens. Such companies recognize the need to harmonize their operations with environmental demands and other vital social concerns. Not all firms, however, have taken steps to encourage a consideration of social responsibility and ethics in their decisions and day-to-day activities. Some managers still regard such business practices as a poor investment, in which the cost is not worth the return. Other managers—indeed, most managers—view the cost of these practices as a necessary business expense, similar to wages or rent.

Most managers today, like those at Panera, are finding ways to balance a growing agenda of socially responsible activities with the drive to generate profits. This also happens to be a good way for a company to demonstrate its values and to attract like-minded employees, customers, and stockholders. In a highly competitive business environment, an increasing number of companies are, like Panera, seeking to set themselves apart by developing a reputation for ethical and socially responsible behavior.

We begin this chapter by defining *business ethics* and examining ethical issues. Next, we look at the standards of behavior in organizations and how ethical behavior can be encouraged. We then turn to the topic of social responsibility. We compare and contrast two present-day models of social responsibility and present arguments for and against increasing the social responsibility of business. We then examine the major elements of the consumer movement. We discuss how social responsibility in business has affected employment practices and environmental concerns. Finally, we consider the commitment, planning, and funding that go into a firm's program of social responsibility.

BUSINESS ETHICS DEFINED

1 Understand what is meant by *business ethics*.

Ethics is the study of right and wrong and of the morality of the choices individuals make. An ethical decision or action is one that is "right" according to some standard of behavior. **Business ethics** is the application of moral standards to business situations. Recent court cases involving unethical behavior have helped to make business ethics a matter of public concern. In one such case, Copley Pharmaceutical, Inc., pled guilty to federal criminal charges (and paid a $10.65 million fine) for falsifying drug manufacturers' reports to the Food and Drug Administration. In another much-publicized case, lawsuits against tobacco companies have led to $246 billion in settlements, although there has been only one class-action lawsuit filed on behalf of all smokers. The case, *Engle v. R. J. Reynolds*, could cost tobacco companies an estimated $500 billion. In yet another case, Adelphia Communications Corp., the nation's fifth-largest cable television company, agreed to pay $715 million to settle federal investigations stemming from rampant earnings manipulation by its founder John J. Rigas, and his son, Timothy J. Rigas. Prosecutors and government regulators charged that both father and son had misappropriated $2.3 billion of Adelphia funds for their own use and had failed to pay the corporation for securities they controlled. Consequently, investors lost more than $60 billion when Adelphia declared bankruptcy. The tax evasion charge against the Rigases was dismissed in early 2012. John Rigas and Timothy Rigas are serving 12 years and 17 years in prison, respectively. John Rigas applied for a presidential pardon in January 2009, but George W. Bush left office without making a decision on Rigas's request. Mr. Rigas is scheduled to be released from federal prison in 2018. The Rigases have appealed their convictions to the Second Court of Appeals and they are awaiting a date from the court for oral arguments.[2]

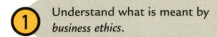

Business ethics apply to customers as well as to managers and employees. In some buying situations, the "right" thing to do isn't always clear, is it? For example, should you buy from a retail store that has been found to be unfair to its employees? Read on for tips about recognizing and resolving ethical issues.

ETHICAL ISSUES

2 Identify the types of ethical concerns that arise in the business world.

Ethical issues often arise out of a business's relationship with investors, customers, employees, creditors, or competitors. Each of these groups has specific concerns and usually exerts pressure on the organization's managers. For example, investors want management to make sensible financial decisions that will boost sales, profits, and returns on their investments. Customers expect a firm's products to be safe, reliable, and reasonably priced. Employees demand to be treated fairly in hiring, promotion, and compensation decisions. Creditors require accounts to be paid on time and the accounting information furnished by the firm to be accurate. Competitors expect the firm's competitive practices to be fair and honest. Consider TAP Pharmaceutical Products, Inc., whose sales representatives offered every urologist in the United States a big-screen TV, computers, fax machines, and golf vacations if the doctors prescribed TAP's new prostate cancer drug Lupron. Moreover, the sales representatives sold Lupron at cut-rate prices or gratis while defrauding Medicare. Recently, the federal government won an $875 million judgment against TAP when a former TAP vice president of sales, Douglas Durand, and Dr. Joseph Gerstein blew the whistle.[3]

In late 2006, Hewlett-Packard Co.'s chairman, Patricia Dunn, and general counsel, Ann Baskins, resigned amid allegations that the company used intrusive tactics in observing the personal lives of journalists and the company's directors, thus tarnishing

ethics the study of right and wrong and of the morality of the choices individuals make

business ethics the application of moral standards to business situations

Hewlett-Packard's reputation for integrity. According to Congressman John Dingell of Michigan, "We have before us witnesses from Hewlett-Packard to discuss a plunderers' operation that would make (former president) Richard Nixon blush were he still alive." Alternatively, consider Bernard Madoff, former stockbroker, financial advisor, and chairman of the NASDAQ stock exchange. In 2009, he was convicted of securities and other frauds including a Ponzi scheme that defrauded clients of $65 billion. Madoff was sentenced to 150 years in prison.

Businesspeople face ethical issues every day, and some of these issues can be difficult to assess. Although some types of issues arise infrequently, others occur regularly. Let's take a closer look at several ethical issues.

Fairness and Honesty

Fairness and honesty in business are two important ethical concerns. Besides obeying all laws and regulations, businesspeople are expected to refrain from knowingly deceiving, misrepresenting, or intimidating others. The consequences of failing to do so can be expensive. Recently, for example, Keith E. Anderson and Wayne Anderson, the leaders of an international tax shelter scheme known as Anderson's Ark and Associates, were sentenced to as many as 20 years in prison. The Andersons; Richard Marks, their chief accounting officer; and Karolyn Grosnickle, the chief administrative officer, were ordered to pay more than $200 million in fines and restitution.[4] More than 1,500 clients of Anderson's Ark and Associates lost about $31 million. In yet another case, the accounting firm PricewaterhouseCoopers LLP agreed to pay the U.S. government $42 million to resolve allegations that it made false claims in connection with travel reimbursements it collected for several federal agencies.[5]

Deere & Company requires each employee to deal fairly with its customers, suppliers, competitors, and employees. "No employee should take unfair advantage of anyone through manipulation, concealment, abuse of privileged information, misrepresentation of material facts or any other unfair dealing practice." Employees are encouraged to report possible violations of company ethics policies using a 24-hour hotline or anonymous e-mails. Reporting is not only encouraged; it is an accepted and protected behavior.[6]

Personal data security breaches have become a major threat to personal privacy in the new millennium. Can businesses keep your personal data secure?

Organizational Relationships

A businessperson may be tempted to place his or her personal welfare above the welfare of others or the welfare of the organization. For example, in late 2002, former CEO of Tyco International, Ltd, Leo Dennis Kozlowski, was indicted for misappropriating $43 million in corporate funds to make philanthropic contributions in his own name, including $5 million to Seton Hall University, which named its new business-school building Kozlowski Hall. Furthermore, according to Tyco, the former CEO took $61.7 million in interest-free relocation loans without the board's permission. He allegedly used the money to finance many personal luxuries, including a $15 million yacht and a $3.9 million Renoir painting, and to throw a $2 million party for his wife's birthday. Mr. Kozlowski, currently serving up to 25 years in prison, paid $134 million in restitution to Tyco and criminal fines of $70 million. In 2009, the U.S. Supreme Court denied his petition for a judicial review.[7]

Relationships with customers and co-workers often create ethical problems. Unethical behavior in these areas includes taking credit for others' ideas or work, not meeting one's commitments in a mutual agreement, and pressuring others to behave unethically.

© GUS CHAN/THE PLAIN DEALER/LANDOV

Violating ethics can be humiliating and costly. Former Cuyahoga County Sheriff Gerald McFaul listens to his attorney after McFaul pleaded guilty to theft in office and ethics violation.

Conflict of Interest

Conflict of interest results when a businessperson takes advantage of a situation for his or her own personal interest rather than for the employer's interest. Such conflict may occur when payments and gifts make their way into business deals. A wise rule to remember is that anything given to a person that might unfairly influence that person's business decision is a bribe, and all bribes are unethical.

For example, Nortel Networks Corporation does not permit its employees, officers, and directors to accept any gifts or to serve as directors or officers of any organization that might supply goods or services to Nortel Networks. However, Nortel employees may work part-time with firms that are not competitors, suppliers, or customers. At AT&T, employees are instructed to discuss with their supervisors any investments that may seem improper. Verizon Communications forbids its employees and executives from holding a "significant" financial stake in vendors, suppliers, or customers.

At Procter & Gamble Company (P&G), all employees are obligated to act at all times solely in the best interests of the company. A conflict of interest arises when an employee has a personal relationship or financial or other interest that could interfere with this obligation, or when an employee uses his or her position with the company for personal gain. P&G requires employees to disclose all potential conflicts of interest and to take prompt actions to eliminate a conflict when the company asks them to do so. Generally, it is not acceptable to receive gifts, entertainment, or other gratuities from people with whom P&G does business because doing so could imply an obligation on the part of the company and potentially pose a conflict of interest.

Communications

Business communications, especially advertising, can present ethical questions. False and misleading advertising is illegal and unethical, and it can infuriate customers. Sponsors of advertisements aimed at children must be especially careful to avoid misleading messages. Advertisers of health-related products also must take precautions to guard against deception when using such descriptive terms as *low fat*, *fat free*, and *light*. In fact, the Federal Trade Commission has issued guidelines on the use of these labels.

FACTORS AFFECTING ETHICAL BEHAVIOR

 Discuss the factors that affect the level of ethical behavior in organizations.

Is it possible for an individual with strong moral values to make ethically questionable decisions in a business setting? What factors affect a person's inclination to make either ethical or unethical decisions in a business organization? Although the answers to these questions are not entirely clear, three general sets of factors do appear to influence the standards of behavior in an organization. As shown in Figure 2.1, the sets consist of individual factors, social factors, and opportunities.

FIGURE 2.1   Factors that Affect the Level of Ethical Behavior in an Organization

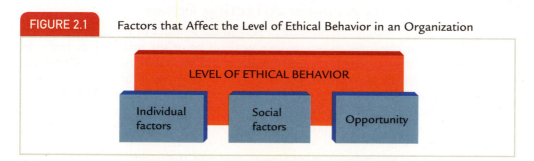

Source: Based on O. C. Ferrell and Larry Gresham, "A Contingency Framework for Understanding Ethical Decision Making in Marketing," *Journal of Marketing* (Summer 1985), 89.

Individual Factors Affecting Ethics

Several individual factors influence the level of ethical behavior in an organization.

- *Individual knowledge of an issue.* How much an individual knows about an issue is one factor. A decision maker with a greater amount of knowledge regarding a situation may take steps to avoid ethical problems, whereas a less-informed person may take action unknowingly that leads to an ethical quagmire.
- *Personal values.* An individual's moral values and central, value-related attitudes also clearly influence his or her business behavior. Most people join organizations to accomplish personal goals.
- *Personal goals.* The types of personal goals an individual aspires to and the manner in which these goals are pursued have a significant impact on that individual's behavior in an organization. The actions of specific individuals in scandal-plagued companies, such as Adelphia, Arthur Anderson, Enron, Halliburton, Qwest, and WorldCom, often raise questions about individuals' personal character and integrity.

Social Factors Affecting Ethics

- *Cultural norms.* A person's behavior in the workplace, to some degree, is determined by cultural norms, and these social factors vary from one culture to another. For example, in some countries it is acceptable and ethical for customs agents to receive gratuities for performing ordinary, legal tasks that are a part of their jobs, whereas in other countries these practices would be viewed as unethical and perhaps illegal.
- *Co-workers.* The actions and decisions of co-workers constitute another social factor believed to shape a person's sense of business ethics. For example, if your co-workers make long-distance telephone calls on company time and at company expense, you might view that behavior as acceptable and ethical because everyone does it.
- *Significant others.* The moral values and attitudes of "significant others"—spouses, friends, and relatives, for instance—also can affect an employee's perception of what is ethical and unethical behavior in the workplace.
- *Use of the Internet.* Even the Internet presents new challenges for firms whose employees enjoy easy access to sites through convenient high-speed connections at work. An employee's behavior online can be viewed as offensive to co-workers and possibly lead to lawsuits against the firm if employees engage in unethical behavior on controversial Web sites not related to their job. Interestingly, one recent survey of employees found that most workers assume that their use of technology at work will be monitored. A large majority of employees approved of most monitoring methods such as monitoring faxes and e-mail, tracking Web use, and even recording telephone calls.

"Opportunity" as a Factor Affecting Ethics

- *Presence of opportunity.* Opportunity refers to the amount of freedom an organization gives an employee to behave unethically if he or she makes that choice. In some organizations, certain company policies and procedures reduce the opportunity to be unethical. For example, at some fast-food restaurants, one employee takes your order and receives your payment, and another fills the order. This procedure reduces the opportunity to be unethical because the person handling the money is not dispensing the product, and the person giving out the product is not handling the money.
- *Ethical codes.* The existence of an ethical code and the importance management places on this code are other determinants of opportunity (codes of ethics are discussed in more detail in the next section).

- *Enforcement.* The degree of enforcement of company policies, procedures, and ethical codes is a major force affecting opportunity. When violations are dealt with consistently and firmly, the opportunity to be unethical is reduced.

Do you make personal telephone calls on company time? Many individuals do. Although most employees limit personal calls to a few minutes, some make personal calls in excess of 30 minutes. Whether you use company time and equipment to make personal calls is an example of a personal ethical decision.

Now that we have considered some of the factors believed to influence the level of ethical behavior in the workplace, let us explore what can be done to encourage ethical behavior and to discourage unethical behavior.

ENCOURAGING ETHICAL BEHAVIOR

 Explain how ethical decision making can be encouraged.

Most authorities agree that there is room for improvement in business ethics. A more problematic question is: Can business be made more ethical in the real world? The majority opinion on this issue suggests that government, trade associations, and individual firms indeed can establish acceptable levels of ethical behavior.

Government's Role in Encouraging Ethics

The government can encourage ethical behavior by legislating more stringent regulations. For example, the landmark **Sarbanes–Oxley Act of 2002** provides sweeping new legal protection for those who report corporate misconduct. At the signing ceremony, President George W. Bush stated, "The act adopts tough new provisions to deter and punish corporate and accounting fraud and corruption, ensure justice for wrongdoers, and protect the interests of workers and shareholders." Among other things, the law deals with corporate responsibility, conflicts of interest, and corporate accountability. However, rules require enforcement, and the unethical businessperson frequently seems to "slip something by" without getting caught. Increased regulation may help, but it surely cannot solve the entire ethics problem.

Sarbanes–Oxley Act of 2002 provides sweeping new legal protection for employees who report corporate misconduct

code of ethics a guide to acceptable and ethical behavior as defined by the organization

Trade Associations' Role in Encouraging Ethics

Trade associations can and often do provide ethical guidelines for their members. These organizations, which operate within particular industries, are in an excellent position to exert pressure on members who stoop to questionable business practices. For example, recently, a pharmaceutical trade group adopted a new set of guidelines to halt the extravagant dinners and other gifts sales representatives often give to physicians. However, enforcement and authority vary from association to association. Because trade associations exist for the benefit of their members, harsh measures may be self-defeating.

Individual Companies' Role in Encouraging Ethics

Codes of ethics that companies provide to their employees are perhaps the most effective way to encourage ethical behavior. A **code of ethics** is a written guide to acceptable and ethical behavior as defined by an organization; it outlines uniform policies, standards, and punishments for violations. Because employees know what is expected of them and what will happen if they violate the rules, a code of ethics goes a long way toward encouraging ethical behavior. However, codes cannot possibly

© CONGRESSIONAL QUARTERLY PHOTO BY SCOTT J. FERRELL/NEWSCOM

Meet Senators Sarbanes and Oxley. The Sarbanes–Oxley Act of 2002 adopted tough new provisions to deter and punish corporate and accounting fraud and corruption. Here, Senator Paul S. Sarbanes and John LaFalce congratulate each other as Senator Michael J. Oxley (center) looks on. The legislation passed with near unanimous support.

cover every situation. Companies also must create an environment in which employees recognize the importance of complying with the written code. Managers must provide direction by fostering communication, actively modeling and encouraging ethical decision making, and training employees to make ethical decisions.

During the 1980s, an increasing number of organizations created and implemented ethics codes. In a recent survey of *Fortune* 1000 firms, 93 percent of the companies that responded reported having a formal code of ethics. Some companies are now even taking steps to strengthen their codes. For example, to strengthen its accountability, the Healthcare Financial Management Association recently revised its code to designate contact persons who handle reports of ethics violations, to clarify how its board of directors should deal with violations of business ethics, and to guarantee a fair hearing process. S. C. Johnson & Son, makers of Pledge®, Drano®, Windex®, and many other household products, is another firm that recognizes that it must behave in ways the public perceives as ethical; its code includes expectations for employees and its commitment to consumers, the community, and society in general. As shown in Figure 2.2, the ethics code of electronics giant Texas Instruments (TI) includes issues relating to policies and procedures; laws and regulations; relationships with customers, suppliers, and competitors; conflicts of interest; handling of proprietary information; and code enforcement.

Assigning an ethics officer who coordinates ethical conduct gives employees someone to consult if they are not sure of the right thing to do. An ethics officer meets with employees and top management to provide ethical advice, establishes and maintains an anonymous confidential service to answer questions about ethical issues, and takes action on ethics code violations.

Sometimes even employees who want to act ethically may find it difficult to do so. Unethical practices can become ingrained in an organization. Employees with high personal ethics may then take a controversial step called *whistle-blowing*. **Whistle-blowing** is informing the press or government officials about unethical practices within one's organization.

The year 2002 was labeled as the "Year of the Whistle-Blower." Consider Joe Speaker, a 40-year-old acting chief financial officer (CFO) at Rite Aid Corp. in 1999. He discovered that inventories at Rite Aid had been overvalued and that millions in expenses had not been reported properly. Further digging into Rite Aid's books revealed that $541 million in earnings over the previous two years was really $1.6 billion in losses. Mr. Speaker was a main government witness when former Rite Aid Corp. Chairman and CEO Martin L. Grass went on trial. Mr. Speaker is among dozens of corporate managers who have blown the whistle. Enron's Sherron S. Watkins and WorldCom's Cynthia Cooper are now well-known whistle-blowers and *Time* magazine's persons of the year 2002. According to Linda Chatman Thomsen, deputy director for enforcement at the Securities and Exchange Commission, "Whistle-blowers give us an insider's perspective and have advanced our investigation immeasurably."

Whistle-blowing could have averted disaster and prevented needless deaths in the *Challenger* space shuttle disaster, for example. How could employees have known about life-threatening problems and let them pass? Whistle-blowing, however, can have serious repercussions for employees: Those who "blow whistles" sometimes lose their jobs. However, the Sarbanes–Oxley Act of 2002 protects whistle-blowers who report corporate misconduct. Any executive who retaliates against a whistle-blower can be held criminally liable and imprisoned for up to ten years.

Retaliations do occur, however. For example, in 2005, the U.S. Court of Appeals for the 8th Circuit unanimously upheld the right of Jane Turner, a 25-year veteran FBI agent, to obtain monetary damages and a jury trial against the FBI. The court held that Ms. Turner presented sufficient facts to justify a trial by jury based on the FBI's retaliatory transfer of Ms. Turner from her investigatory position in Minot, North Dakota, to a demeaning desk job in Minneapolis. Kris Kolesnik, executive director of the National Whistle Blower Center, said, "Jane Turner is an American hero. She refused to be silent when her co-agents committed misconduct in a child rape case. She refused to be silent when her co-agents stole property from Ground Zero. She paid the price and lost her job. The 8th Circuit Court did the right thing and insured

whistle-blowing informing the press or government officials about unethical practices within one's organization

Texas Instruments encourages ethical behavior through an extensive training program and a written code of ethics and shared values.

TEXAS INSTRUMENTS CODE OF ETHICS

"Integrity is the foundation on which TI is built. There is no other characteristic more essential to a TIer's makeup. It has to be present at all levels. Integrity is expected of managers and individuals when they make commitments. They are expected to stand by their commitments to the best of their ability.

One of TI's greatest strengths is its values and ethics. We had some early leaders who set those values as the standard for how they lived their lives. And it is important that TI grew that way. It's something that we don't want to lose. At the same time, we must move more rapidly. But we don't want to confuse that with the fact that we're ethical and we're moral. We're very responsible, and we live up to what we say."

Tom Engibous, President and CEO
Texas Instruments, 1997

We Respect and Value People By:

Treating others as we want to be treated.

- Exercising the basic virtues of respect, dignity, kindness, courtesy and manners in all work relationships.
- Recognizing and avoiding behaviors that others may find offensive, including the manner in which we speak and relate to one another and the materials we bring into the workplace, both printed and electronically.
- Respecting the right and obligation of every TIer to resolve concerns relating to ethics questions in the course of our duties without retribution and retaliation.
- Giving all TIers the same opportunity to have their questions, issues and situations fairly considered while understanding that being treated fairly does not always mean that we will all be treated the same.
- Trusting one another to use sound judgment in our use of TI business and information systems.
- Understanding that even though TI has the obligation to monitor its business information systems activity, we will respect privacy by prohibiting random searches of individual TIers' communications.
- Recognizing that conduct socially and professionally acceptable in one culture and country may be viewed differently in another.

We Are Honest By:

Representing ourselves and our intentions truthfully.

- Offering full disclosure and withdrawing ourselves from discussions and decisions when our business judgment appears to be in conflict with a personal interest.
- Respecting the rights and property of others, including their intellectual property. Accepting confidential or trade secret information only after we clearly understand our obligations as defined in a nondisclosure agreement.
- Competing fairly without collusion or collaboration with competitors to divide markets, set prices, restrict production, allocate customers or otherwise restrain competition.
- Assuring that no payments or favors are offered to influence others to do something wrong.
- Keeping records that are accurate and include all payments and receipts.
- Exercising good judgment in the exchange of business courtesies, meals and entertainment by avoiding activities that could create even the appearance that our decisions could be compromised.
- Refusing to speculate in TI stock through frequent buying and selling or through other forms of speculative trading.

Source: Courtesy of Texas Instruments, www.ti.com/corp/docs/csr/corpgov/downloads/CCR_Summary.pdf (accessed February 15, 2012).

that justice will take place in her case." In 2008, the U.S. government was ordered to pay $1 million in legal fees to Turner's lawyers. The Whistleblower Protection Act of 1989 protects federal employees who report an agency's misconduct. The Obama administration is attempting to pass a law that would further protect the government whistle-blowers.[8]

TABLE 2.1 Guidelines for Making Ethical Decisions

1. Listen and learn.	Recognize the problem or decision-making opportunity that confronts your company, team, or unit. Don't argue, criticize, or defend yourself—keep listening and reviewing until you are sure that you understand others.
2. Identify the ethical issues.	Examine how co-workers and consumers are affected by the situation or decision at hand. Examine how you feel about the situation, and attempt to understand the viewpoint of those involved in the decision or in the consequences of the decision.
3. Create and analyze options.	Try to put aside strong feelings such as anger or a desire for power and prestige and come up with as many alternatives as possible before developing an analysis. Ask everyone involved for ideas about which options offer the best long-term results for you and the company. Then decide which option will increase your self-respect even if, in the long run, things don't work out the way you hope they will.
4. Identify the best option from your point of view.	Consider it and test it against some established criteria, such as respect, understanding, caring, fairness, honesty, and openness.
5. Explain your decision and resolve any differences that arise.	This may require neutral arbitration from a trusted manager or taking "time out" to reconsider, consult, or exchange written proposals before a decision is reached.

Source: Based on information in Tom Rusk with D. Patrick Miller, "Doing the Right Thing," *Sky* (Delta Airlines), August 1993, 18–22.

When firms set up anonymous hotlines to handle ethically questionable situations, employees actually may be more likely to engage in whistle-blowing. When firms instead create an environment that educates employees and nurtures ethical behavior, fewer ethical problems arise. Ultimately, the need for whistle-blowing is greatly reduced.

It is difficult for an organization to develop ethics codes, policies, and procedures to deal with all relationships and every situation. When no company policies or procedures exist or apply, a quick test to determine if a behavior is ethical is to see if others—co-workers, customers, and suppliers—approve of it. Ethical decisions will always withstand scrutiny. Openness and communication about choices will often build trust and strengthen business relationships. Table 2.1 provides some general guidelines for making ethical decisions.

SOCIAL RESPONSIBILITY

Social responsibility is the recognition that business activities have an impact on society and the consideration of that impact in business decision making. In the first few days after Hurricane Katrina hit New Orleans, Walmart delivered $20 million in cash (including $4 million to employees displaced by the storm), 100 truckloads of free merchandise, and food for 100,000 meals. The company also promised a job elsewhere for every one of its workers affected by the catastrophe. Obviously, social responsibility costs money. It is perhaps not so obvious—except in isolated cases—that social responsibility is also good business. Customers eventually find out which firms act responsibly and which do not. Just as easily as they can purchase a product made by a company that is socially responsible, they can choose against buying from the firm that is not.

Consider the following examples of organizations that are attempting to be socially responsible:

- Social responsibility can take many forms—including flying lessons. Through Young Eagles, underwritten by S. C. Johnson, Phillips Petroleum, Lockheed Martin, Jaguar, and other corporations, 22,000 volunteer pilots have taken a half million youngsters on free flights designed to teach flying basics and inspire excitement about

social responsibility the recognition that business activities have an impact on society and the consideration of that impact in business decision making

flying careers. Young Eagles is just one of the growing number of education projects undertaken by businesses building solid records as good corporate citizens.

- The General Mills Foundation, created in 1954, is one of the nation's largest company-sponsored foundations. Since the General Mills Foundation was created, it has awarded more than $535 million to its communities.

  In the Twin Cities, the General Mills Foundation provides grants for youth nutrition and fitness, education, arts and culture, social services, and the United Way. Beyond financial resources, the General Mills Foundation also supports organizations with volunteers and mentors who share their expertise and talents. For example, General Mills plays a leadership role in supporting education, arts, and cultural organizations by matching employee and retiree contributions dollar for dollar. Recently, the Foundation donated $28.2 million in food to Feeding America, the largest hunger-relief organization in the United States. Food is also donated following natural disasters such as, devastating earthquakes in Haiti and Chile, and flood relief in Pakistan.[9]

- As part of Dell's commitment to the community, the Dell Foundation contributes significantly to the quality of life in communities where Dell employees live and work. The Dell Foundation supports innovative and effective programs that provide fundamental prerequisites to equip youth to learn and excel in a world driven by the digital economy. The Dell Foundation supports a wide range of programs that benefit children from newborn to 17 years of age in Dell's principal U.S. locations and welcomes proposals from non-profit organizations that address health and human services, education, and technology access for youth.

  Globally, the Michael and Susan Dell Foundation has contributed more than $700 million to improve student performance and increase access to education so that all children have the opportunity to achieve their dreams.[10]

- Improving public schools around the world continues to be IBM's top social priority. Its efforts are focused on preparing the next generation of leaders and workers. Through Reinventing Education and other strategic efforts, IBM is solving education's toughest problems with solutions that draw on advanced information technologies and the best minds IBM can apply. Its programs are paving the way for reforms in school systems around the world.

  IBM launched the World Community Grid in November 2004. It combines excess processing power from thousands of computers into a virtual supercomputer. This grid enables researchers to gather and analyze unprecedented quantities of data aimed at advancing research on genomics, diseases, and natural disasters. The first project, the Human Proteome Folding Project, assists in identifying cures for diseases such as malaria and tuberculosis and has registered 85,000 devices around the world to date.

  Recently, as IBM celebrated its centennial, the company announced that Africa is the destination for is 100th team and 1,000th employee involved in the company's Corporate Service Corps. Often called a "corporate version" of the Peace Corps, this program has made a direct economic impact in many of the 20 countries it has helped. Participants, who are selected from among IBM's highest performing employees, provide technology-related assistance to both local governments and community organizations. Issues they tackle include local economic development, entrepreneurship, transportation, education, citizen services, health care, and disaster recovery. Stanley S. Litow, IBM's vice president of Corporate Citizenship and Corporate Affairs, and president of IBM's Foundation stated, "Our Corporate Service Corps program epitomizes the progressive ethics of IBM's employees, both today and 100 years ago."[11]

© JACOB SILBERG/REUTERS/LANDOV

Social responsibility is good business. ICAP, the world's largest interdealer broker in Jersey City, New Jersey, hosts its 16th annual global Charity Day during which the company revenues are donated to over 100 charities around the world.

- General Electric Company (GE) has a long history of supporting the communities where its employees work and live through GE's unique combination of resources, equipment, and employees' and retirees' hearts and souls. Today GE's responsibility extends to communities around the world.

  GE applies its long-standing spirit of innovation and unique set of capabilities to take on tough challenges in its communities. For example, recently, GE awarded a five-year grant of $20 million to Milwaukee Public Schools to improve academic achievement and better prepare students for college and career opportunities, with a focus on math and science programs. This grant is a part of the GE Foundation Developing Futures™ in Education program, an initiative to ensure that U.S. students are prepared to compete in an increasingly competitive global economy.[12]

- With the help of dedicated Schwab volunteers, the Charles Schwab Foundation provides programs and funding to help individuals fill the information gap. For example, Schwab MoneyWise helps adults teach—and children learn—the basics of financial literacy. Interactive tools are available at http://schwabmoneywise.com, and local workshops cover topics such as getting kids started on a budget. In addition to these efforts, widely distributed publications and news columns by foundation President Carrie Schwab Pomerantz promote financial literacy on a wide range of topics— from saving for a child's education to bridging the health insurance gap for retirees. Since its founding in 1993, Charles Schwab Foundation has made contributions averaging $4 million a year to more than 2,300 nonprofit organizations.[13]

- Improving basic literacy skills in the United States is among the Verizon Foundation's major priorities because of its enormous impact on education, health, and economic development. Here in the United States, more than 30 million American adults have basic or below-average literacy skills. Thinkfinity.org is designed to improve education and literacy achievement. This comprehensive free Web site delivers online resources to advance student achievement. Thinkfinity delivers top-quality K–12 lesson plans, student materials, interactive tools, and connections to educational Web sites. It gives teachers, instructors, and parents the tools they need to increase student performance.

  Recently, Verizon employees and retirees donated more than 608,000 hours of service and, with the Verizon Foundation, contributed more than $25 million in combined matching gift funds, making Verizon Volunteers one of the largest corporate volunteer incentive programs in the United States.

- ExxonMobil's commitment to education spans all levels of achievement. One of its corporate primary goals is to support basic education and literacy programs in the developing world. In areas of the world where basic education levels have been met, ExxonMobil supports education programs in science, technology, engineering, and mathematics.

  ExxonMobil recognizes the essential role that proficiency in math and science plays not only in the energy business but also in fostering innovation and facilitating human progress. The company encourages new generations to pursue studies and careers in fields involving mathematics and science. Toward this goal, it supports programs focused on laying the foundation for long-term educational improvements, such as the National Math and Science Initiative and the Mickelson ExxonMobil Teachers Academy.

  In recognition of 2011 International Women's Day, ExxonMobil granted $6 million to support economic opportunities for women around the world. In announcing the grant, Suzanne McCarron, president of ExxonMobil Foundation said, "Research tells us that the success of women entrepreneurs is key to building communities. When women thrive economically, entire societies are transformed by becoming healthier, more stable and more prosperous." Recently, ExxonMobil, its employees, and retirees provided $238 million in contributions worldwide.[14]

- AT&T has built a tradition of supporting education, health and human services, the environment, public policy, and the arts in the communities it serves since Alexander Graham Bell founded the company over a century ago. Since 1984, AT&T has invested more than $600 million in support of education. Currently, more than half the company's contribution dollars, employee volunteer time, and community-service activities are directed toward education. Since 1911, AT&T has been a sponsor to the Telephone Pioneers of America, the world's largest industry-based volunteer organization consisting of nearly 750,000 employees and retirees from the telecommunications industry. Each year, the Pioneers volunteer millions of hours and raise millions of dollars for health and human services and the environment. In schools and neighborhoods, the Pioneers strengthen connections and build communities.

To respond to the high school drop-out crisis, AT&T launched Aspire, a $100 million philanthropic program that focuses on the crisis. It is the biggest and most significant investment in education in the company's history. The job shadowing program had reached more than 23,000 students in more than 200 cities. By summer of 2013, the program will provide 100,000 students with the opportunity to learn more about career options and what it takes to be successful in today's workforce.[15]

- At Merck & Co., Inc., the Patient Assistance Program makes the company's medicines available to low-income Americans and their families at no cost. When patients do not have health insurance or a prescription drug plan and are unable to afford the Merck medicines their doctors prescribe, they can work with their physicians to contact the Merck Patient Assistance Program. For more than 50 years, Merck has provided its medicines completely free of charge to people in need through this program. Patients can get information through www.merck.com; by calling a toll-free number, 1-800-727-5400; or from their physician's office. For eligible patients, the medicines are shipped directly to their home or the prescribing physician's office. Each applicant may receive up to one year of medicines, and patients may reapply to the program if their need continues.

Established in 1957, the Merck Company Foundation has contributed more than $560 million to develop and initiate programs that help improve the health and well-being of people around the world. According to Richard T. Clark, chairman, president, and CEO, "Merck established the Foundation more than 50 years ago because we knew that along with corporate success comes social responsibility."

Education programs often link social responsibility with corporate self-interest. For example, Bayer and Merck, two major pharmaceuticals firms, promote science education as a way to enlarge the pool of future employees. Students who visit the Bayer Science Forum in Elkhart, Indiana, work alongside scientists conducting a variety of experiments. Workshops created by the Merck Institute for Science Education show teachers how to put scientific principles into action through hands-on experiments.

These are just a few illustrations from the long list of companies, big and small, that attempt to behave in socially responsible ways. In general, people are more likely to want to work for and buy from such organizations.

THE EVOLUTION OF SOCIAL RESPONSIBILITY IN BUSINESS

 Describe how our current views on the social responsibility of business have evolved.

Business is far from perfect in many respects, but its record of social responsibility today is much better than that in past decades. In fact, present demands for social responsibility have their roots in outraged reactions to the abusive business practices of the early 1900s.

Historical Evolution of Business Social Responsibility

During the first quarter of the 20th century, businesses were free to operate pretty much as they chose. Government protection of workers and consumers was minimal. As a result, people either accepted what business had to offer or they did without. Working conditions often were deplorable by today's standards. The average workweek in most industries exceeded 60 hours, no minimum-wage law existed, and employee benefits were almost nonexistent. Work areas were crowded and unsafe, and industrial accidents were the rule rather than the exception. To improve working conditions, employees

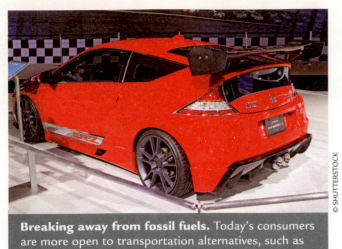

Breaking away from fossil fuels. Today's consumers are more open to transportation alternatives, such as the electric car, because they are concerned about the negative impact of gasoline-run vehicles.

organized and joined labor unions. During the early 1900s, however, businesses—with the help of government—were able to use court orders, brute force, and even the few existing antitrust laws to defeat union attempts to improve working conditions.

During this period, consumers generally were subject to the doctrine of **caveat emptor,** a Latin phrase meaning "let the buyer beware." In other words, "what you see is what you get," and if it is not what you expected, too bad. Although victims of unscrupulous business practices could take legal action, going to court was very expensive, and consumers rarely won their cases. Moreover, no consumer groups or government agencies existed to publicize their consumers' grievances or to hold sellers accountable for their actions.

Before the 1930s, most people believed that competition and the action of the marketplace would, in time, correct abuses. Government, therefore, became involved in day-to-day business activities only in cases of obvious abuse of the free-market system. Six of the more important business-related federal laws passed between 1887 and 1914 are described in Table 2.2. As you can see, these laws were aimed more at encouraging competition than at correcting abuses, although two of them did deal with the purity of food and drug products.

The collapse of the stock market on October 29, 1929, triggered the Great Depression and years of dire economic problems for the United States. Factory production fell by almost half, and up to 25 percent of the nation's workforce was unemployed. Before long, public pressure mounted for the government to "do something" about the economy and about worsening social conditions.

Soon after Franklin D. Roosevelt became president in 1933, he instituted programs to restore the economy and improve social conditions. The government passed laws to correct what many viewed as the monopolistic abuses of big business, and provided various social services for individuals. These massive federal programs became the foundation for increased government involvement in the dealings between business and society.

As government involvement has increased, so has everyone's awareness of the social responsibility of business. Today's business owners are concerned about the return on their investment, but at the same time most of them demand ethical behavior from employees. In addition, employees demand better working conditions, and consumers want safe, reliable products. Various advocacy groups echo these concerns and also call for careful consideration of Earth's delicate ecological balance. Therefore, managers must operate in a complex business environment—one in which they are just as responsible for their managerial actions as for their actions as individual citizens. Interestingly, today's high-tech and Internet-based firms fare relatively well when it comes to environmental issues, worker conditions, the representation of minorities and women in upper management, animal testing, and charitable donations.

caveat emptor a Latin phrase meaning "let the buyer beware"

TABLE 2.2	Early Government Regulations that Affected American Business
	Six of the important business-related federal laws passed between 1887 and 1914 were aimed more at encouraging competition than at correcting abuses.

Government Regulation	Major Provisions
Interstate Commerce Act (1887)	First federal act to regulate business practices; provided regulation of railroads and shipping rates
Sherman Antitrust Act (1890)	Prevented monopolies or mergers where competition was endangered
Pure Food and Drug Act (1906)	Established limited supervision of interstate sales of food and drugs
Meat Inspection Act (1906)	Provided for limited supervision of interstate sales of meat and meat products
Federal Trade Commission Act (1914)	Created the Federal Trade Commission to investigate illegal trade practices
Clayton Antitrust Act (1914)	Eliminated many forms of price discrimination that gave large businesses a competitive advantage over smaller firms

TWO VIEWS OF SOCIAL RESPONSIBILITY

6 Explain the two views on the social responsibility of business and understand the arguments for and against increased social responsibility.

Government regulation and public awareness are *external* forces that have increased the social responsibility of business. However, business decisions are made within the firm—there, social responsibility begins with the attitude of management. Two contrasting philosophies, or models, define the range of management attitudes toward social responsibility.

The Economic Model

According to the traditional concept of business, a firm exists to produce quality goods and services, earn a reasonable profit, and provide jobs. In line with this concept, the **economic model of social responsibility** holds that society will benefit most when business is left alone to produce and market profitable products that society needs. The economic model has its origins in the 18th century, when businesses were owned primarily by entrepreneurs or owner-managers. Competition was vigorous among small firms, and short-run profits and survival were the primary concerns.

To the manager who adopts this traditional attitude, social responsibility is someone else's job. After all, stockholders invest in a corporation to earn a return on their investment, not because the firm is socially responsible, and the firm is legally obligated to act in the economic interest of its stockholders. Moreover, profitable firms pay federal, state, and local taxes that are used to meet the needs of society. Thus, managers who concentrate on profit believe that they fulfill their social responsibility indirectly through the taxes paid by their firms. As a result, social responsibility becomes the problem of the government, various environmental groups, charitable foundations, and similar organizations.

The Socioeconomic Model

In contrast, some managers believe that they have a responsibility not only to stockholders but also to customers, employees, suppliers, and the general public. This broader view is referred to as the **socioeconomic model of social responsibility**, which places emphasis not only on profits but also on the impact of business decisions on society.

Recently, increasing numbers of managers and firms have adopted the socioeconomic model, and they have done so for at least three reasons. First, business is dominated by the corporate form of ownership, and the corporation is a creation of society. If a corporation does not perform as a good citizen, society can and will demand changes. Second, many firms have begun to take pride in their social responsibility records, among them Starbucks Coffee, Hewlett-Packard, Colgate-Palmolive, and Coca-Cola. Each of these companies is a winner of a Corporate Conscience Award in the areas of environmental concern, responsiveness to employees, equal opportunity, and community involvement. Of course, many other corporations are much more socially responsible today than they were ten years ago. Third, many businesspeople believe that it is in their best interest to take the initiative in this area. The alternative may be legal action brought against the firm by some special-interest group; in such a situation, the firm may lose control of its activities.

The Pros and Cons of Social Responsibility

Business owners, managers, customers, and government officials have debated the pros and cons of the economic and socioeconomic models for years. Each side seems to have four major arguments to reinforce its viewpoint.

economic model of social responsibility the view that society will benefit most when business is left alone to produce and market profitable products that society needs

socioeconomic model of social responsibility the concept that business should emphasize not only profits but also the impact of its decisions on society

Arguments for Increased Social Responsibility Proponents of the socioeconomic model maintain that a business must do more than simply seek profits. To support their position, they offer the following arguments:

1. Because business is a part of our society, it cannot ignore social issues.
2. Business has the technical, financial, and managerial resources needed to tackle today's complex social issues.
3. By helping resolve social issues, business can create a more stable environment for long-term profitability.
4. Socially responsible decision making by firms can prevent increased government intervention, which would force businesses to do what they fail to do voluntarily.

These arguments are based on the assumption that a business has a responsibility not only to its stockholders but also to its customers, employees, suppliers, and the general public.

Arguments Against Increased Social Responsibility Opponents of the socioeconomic model argue that business should do what it does best: earn a profit by manufacturing and marketing products that people want. Those who support this position argue as follows:

1. Business managers are responsible primarily to stockholders, so management must be concerned with providing a return on owners' investments.
2. Corporate time, money, and talent should be used to maximize profits, not to solve society's problems.
3. Social problems affect society in general, so individual businesses should not be expected to solve these problems.
4. Social issues are the responsibility of government officials who are elected for that purpose and who are accountable to the voters for their decisions.

These arguments obviously are based on the assumption that the primary objective of business is to earn profits and that government and social institutions should deal with social problems.

Table 2.3 compares the economic and socioeconomic viewpoints in terms of business emphasis. Today, few firms are either purely economic or purely socioeconomic in outlook; most have chosen some middle ground between the two extremes. However, our society generally seems to want—and even to expect—some degree of social responsibility from business. Thus, within this middle ground, businesses are leaning toward the socioeconomic view. In the next several sections, we look at some results of this movement in four specific areas: consumerism, employment practices, concern for the environment, and implementation of social responsibility programs.

TABLE 2.3 A Comparison of the Economic and Socioeconomic Models of Social Responsibility as Implemented in Business

Economic Model Primary Emphasis		Socioeconomic Model Primary Emphasis
1. Production		1. Quality of life
2. Exploitation of natural resources		2. Conservation of natural resources
3. Internal, market-based decisions	Middle ground	3. Market-based decisions, with some community controls
4. Economic return (profit)		4. Balance of economic return and social return
5. Firm's or manager's interest		5. Firm's and community's interests
6. Minor role for government		6. Active government

Source: Adapted from Keith Davis, William C. Frederick, and Robert L. Blomstron, *Business and Society: Concepts and Policy Issues* (New York: McGraw-Hill, 1980), 9. Used by permission of The McGraw-Hill Companies, Inc.

CONSUMERISM

7 Discuss the factors that led to the consumer movement and list some of its results.

Consumerism consists of all activities undertaken to protect the rights of consumers. The fundamental issues pursued by the consumer movement fall into three categories: environmental protection, product performance and safety, and information disclosure. Although consumerism has been with us to some extent since the early 19th century, the consumer movement became stronger in the 1960s. It was then that President John F. Kennedy declared that the consumer was entitled to a new "Bill of Rights."

The Six Basic Rights of Consumers

President Kennedy's Consumer Bill of Rights asserted that consumers have a right to safety, to be informed, to choose, and to be heard. Two additional rights added since 1975 are the right to consumer education and the right to courteous service. These six rights are the basis of much of the consumer-oriented legislation passed during the last 45 years. These rights also provide an effective outline of the objectives and accomplishments of the consumer movement.

The Right to Safety The consumers' right to safety means that the products they purchase must be safe for their intended use, must include thorough and explicit directions for proper use, and must be tested by the manufacturer to ensure product quality and reliability. There are several reasons why American business firms must be concerned about product safety.

Corrective Actions Can Be Expensive. Federal agencies, such as the Food and Drug Administration and the Consumer Product Safety Commission, have the power to force businesses that make or sell defective products to take corrective actions. Such actions include offering refunds, recalling defective products, issuing public warnings, and reimbursing consumers—all of which can be expensive.

Increasing Number of Lawsuits. Business firms also should be aware that consumers and the government have been winning an increasing number of product-liability lawsuits against sellers of defective products. Moreover, the amount of the awards in these suits has been increasing steadily. Fearing the outcome of numerous lawsuits filed around the nation, tobacco giants Philip Morris and R. J. Reynolds, which for decades had denied that cigarettes cause illness, began negotiating in 1997 with state attorneys general, plaintiffs' lawyers, and antismoking activists. The tobacco giants proposed sweeping curbs on their sales and advertising practices and the payment of hundreds of billions of dollars in compensation.

Consumer Demand. Yet another major reason for improving product safety is consumers' demand for safe products. People simply will stop buying a product they believe is unsafe or unreliable.

The Right to Be Informed The right to be informed means that consumers must have access to complete information about a product before they buy it. Detailed information about ingredients and nutrition must be provided on food containers, information about fabrics and laundering methods must be attached to clothing,

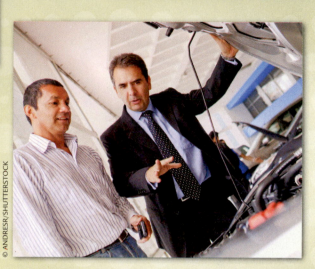

Personal APPS

Keep these consumer rights in mind when you shop around for goods or services, buy something, or have a problem with a purchase. You're entitled to be informed, to have choices, to be heard, to buy safe products, to have responsive service, and to know your rights.

consumerism all activities undertaken to protect the rights of consumers

The right to safety. The Consumer Bill of Rights asserts consumers' basic rights. The right to safety means that products must be safe for their intended use and must be tested by the processor to ensure product quality and safety.

© PICSFIVE/SHUTTERSTOCK

and lenders must disclose the true cost of borrowing the money they make available to customers who purchase merchandise on credit.

In addition, manufacturers must inform consumers about the potential dangers of using their products. Manufacturers that fail to provide such information can be held responsible for personal injuries suffered because of their products. For example, Maytag provides customers with a lengthy booklet that describes how they should use an automatic clothes washer. Sometimes such warnings seem excessive, but they are necessary if user injuries (and resulting lawsuits) are to be avoided.

The Right to Choose The right to choose means that consumers must have a choice of products, offered by different manufacturers and sellers, to satisfy a particular need. The government has done its part by encouraging competition through antitrust legislation. The greater the competition, the greater is the choice available to consumers.

Competition and the resulting freedom of choice provide additional benefits for customers by reducing prices. For example, when personal computers were introduced, they cost more than $5,000. Thanks to intense competition and technological advancements, personal computers today can be purchased for less than $500.

The Right to Be Heard This fourth right means that someone will listen and take appropriate action when customers complain. Actually, management began to listen to consumers after World War II, when competition between businesses that manufactured and sold consumer goods increased. One way that firms got a competitive edge was to listen to consumers and provide the products they said they wanted and needed. Today, businesses are listening even more attentively, and many larger firms have consumer relations departments that can be contacted easily via toll-free telephone numbers. Other groups listen, too. Most large cities and some states have consumer affairs offices to act on citizens' complaints.

Additional Consumer Rights In 1975, President Gerald Ford added to the Consumer Bill of Rights the right to consumer education, which entitles people to be fully informed about their rights as consumers. In 1994, President Bill Clinton added a sixth right, the right to service, which entitles consumers to convenience, courtesy, and responsiveness from manufacturers and sellers of consumer products.

Major Consumerism Forces

The major forces in consumerism are individual consumer advocates and organizations, consumer education programs, and consumer laws. Consumer advocates, such as Ralph Nader, take it on themselves to protect the rights of consumers. They band together into consumer organizations, either independently or under government sponsorship. Some organizations, such as the National Consumers' League and the Consumer Federation of America, operate nationally, whereas others are active at state and local levels. They inform and organize other consumers, raise issues, help businesses to develop consumer-oriented programs, and pressure lawmakers to enact consumer protection laws. Some consumer advocates and organizations encourage consumers to boycott products and businesses to which they have objections. Today, the consumer movement has adopted corporate-style marketing and addresses a broad range of issues. Current campaigns include efforts (1) to curtail the use of animals for

Ethical
SUCCESS OR FAILURE?

Is Personal Data *Really* Private?

Nearly everything you do online—from the Web sites you visit to the Facebook pages you "like"—is being tracked by a business. Advertisers want to know about your activities so they can show you appropriate online ads; retailers want to know what you buy so they can send you targeted e-mails and catalogs. But are your personal details really private?

Although privacy policies are supposed to explain which details each Web site collects and who will have access to your private data, these policies may not tell the whole story. After Facebook changed its privacy policy and then reset users' privacy controls on its own, the Federal Trade Commission charged the firm with making "deceptive privacy claims." Users believed their personal details were private, yet advertisers and others were allowed access. Now, in a settlement with the FTC, Facebook has tightened its privacy controls, and its privacy program must be monitored for the next 20 years to ensure compliance. The FTC also thinks Internet users should be able to opt out of online tracking if they choose. Meanwhile, millions of individuals have already installed anti-tracking software such as Ghostery and Do Not Track Plus for added online privacy.

Sources: Based on information in Byron Acohido, "Consumers Turn to Do-Not-Track Software to Maintain Privacy," *USA Today*, December 29, 2011, www.usatoday.com; Joel Stein, "Your Data, Yourself," *Time*, March 21, 2011, pp. 40-46; Fahmida Y. Rashid, "Facebook Settles FTC Charges about Privacy Policy Changes, Misleading Users," *EWeek*, November 29, 2011, www.eweek.com.

testing purposes, (2) to reduce liquor and cigarette billboard advertising in low-income, inner-city neighborhoods, and (3) to encourage recycling.

Educating consumers to make wiser purchasing decisions is perhaps one of the most far-reaching aspects of consumerism. Increasingly, consumer education is becoming a part of high school and college curricula and adult-education programs. These programs cover many topics—for instance, what major factors should be considered when buying specific products, such as insurance, real estate, automobiles, appliances and furniture, clothes, and food; the provisions of certain consumer-protection laws; and the sources of information that can help individuals become knowledgeable consumers.

Major advances in consumerism have come through federal legislation. Some laws enacted in the last 50 years to protect your rights as a consumer are listed and described in Table 2.4.

Here is the 2009 list of proposed legislation to protect consumers and investors:[16]

- Accountability and Transparency in Rating Agencies Act of 2009
- Consumer Financial Protection Agency Act of 2009
- Corporate and Financial Institution Compensation Fairness Act of 2009
- Credit Risk Retention Act of 2009
- Dissolution Authority for Large, Interconnected Financial Companies Act of 2009
- Federal Insurance Office Act of 2009
- Financial Stability Improvement Act of 2009
- Investor Protection Act of 2009
- Over-the-Counter Derivatives Markets Act of 2009
- Private Fund Investment Advisers Registration Act of 2009

Most businesspeople now realize that they ignore consumer issues only at their own peril. Managers know that improper handling of consumer complaints can result in lost sales, bad publicity, and lawsuits.

TABLE 2.4 Major Federal Legislation Protecting Consumers Since 1960

Legislation	Major Provisions
Federal Hazardous Substances Labeling Act (1960)	Required warning labels on household chemicals if they were highly toxic
Kefauver-Harris Drug Amendments (1962)	Established testing practices for drugs and required manufacturers to label drugs with generic names in addition to trade names
Cigarette Labeling Act (1965)	Required manufacturers to place standard warning labels on all cigarette packages and advertising
Fair Packaging and Labeling Act (1966)	Called for all products sold across state lines to be labeled with net weight, ingredients, and manufacturer's name and address
Motor Vehicle Safety Act (1966)	Established standards for safer cars
Truth in Lending Act (1968)	Required lenders and credit merchants to disclose the full cost of finance charges in both dollars and annual percentage rates
Credit Card Liability Act (1970)	Limited credit-card holder's liability to $50 per card and stopped credit-card companies from issuing unsolicited cards
Fair Credit Reporting Act (1971)	Required credit bureaus to provide credit reports to consumers regarding their own credit files; also provided for correction of incorrect information
Consumer Product Safety Commission Act (1972)	Established an abbreviated procedure for registering certain generic drugs
Fair Credit Billing Act (1974)	Amended the Truth in Lending Act to enable consumers to challenge billing errors
Equal Credit Opportunity Act (1974)	Provided equal credit opportunities for males and females and for married and single individuals
Magnuson–Moss Warranty–Federal Trade Commission Act (1975)	Provided for minimum disclosure standards for written consumer-product warranties for products that cost more than $15
Amendments to the Equal Credit Opportunity Act (1976, 1994)	Prevented discrimination based on race, creed, color, religion, age, and income when granting credit
Fair Debt Collection Practices Act (1977)	Outlawed abusive collection practices by third parties
Nutrition Labeling and Education Act (1990)	Required the Food and Drug Administration to review current food labeling and packaging focusing on nutrition label content, label format, ingredient labeling, food descriptors and standards, and health messages
Telephone Consumer Protection Act (1991)	Prohibited the use of automated dialing and prerecorded-voice calling equipment to make calls or deliver messages
Consumer Credit Reporting Reform Act (1997)	Placed more responsibility for accurate credit data on credit issuers; required creditors to verify that disputed data are accurate and to notify a consumer before reinstating the data
Children's Online Privacy Protection Act (2000)	Placed parents in control over what information is collected online from their children younger than 13 years; required commercial Web site operators to maintain the confidentiality, security, and integrity of personal information collected from children
Do Not Call Implementation Act (2003)	Directed the FCC and the FTC to coordinate so that their rules are consistent regarding telemarketing call practices including the Do Not Call Registry and other lists, as well as call abandonment
Credit Card Accountability, Responsibility, and Disclosure Act (2009)	Provided the most sweeping changes in credit card protections since the Truth in Lending Act of 1968
Dodd–Frank Wall Street Reform and Consumer Protection Act of 2010	Promoted the financial stability of the United States by improving accountability and responsibility in the financial system; established a new Consumer Financial Protection Agency to regulate home mortgages, car loans, and credit cards; became Public Law on July 21, 2010

EMPLOYMENT PRACTICES

8 Analyze how present employment practices are being used to counteract past abuses.

Managers who subscribe to the socioeconomic view of a business's social responsibility, together with significant government legislation enacted to protect the buying public, have broadened the rights of consumers. The last five decades have seen similar progress in affirming the rights of employees to equal treatment in the workplace.

Everyone should have the opportunity to land a job for which he or she is qualified and to be rewarded on the basis of ability and performance. This is an important issue for society, and it also makes good business sense. Yet, over the years, this opportunity has been denied to members of various minority groups. A **minority** is a racial, religious, political, national, or other group regarded as different from the larger group of which it is a part and that is often singled out for unfavorable treatment.

The federal government responded to the outcry of minority groups during the 1960s and 1970s by passing a number of laws forbidding discrimination in the workplace. (These laws are discussed in Chapter 9 in the context of human resources management.) Now, almost 50 years after passage of the first of these (the Civil Rights Act of 1964), abuses still exist. An example is the disparity in income levels for whites, blacks, Hispanics, and Asians, as illustrated in Figure 2.3. Lower incomes and higher unemployment rates also characterize Native Americans, handicapped persons, and women. Responsible managers have instituted a number of programs to counteract the results of discrimination.

Affirmative Action Programs

An **affirmative action program** is a plan designed to increase the number of minority employees at all levels within an organization. Employers with federal contracts of more than $50,000 per year must have written affirmative action plans. The objective of such programs is to ensure that minorities are represented within the organization in approximately the same proportion as in the surrounding community. If 25 percent of the electricians in a geographic area in which a company is located are African-Americans,

---

FIGURE 2.3   Comparative Income Levels

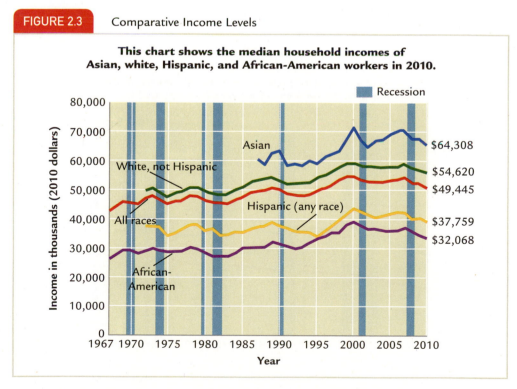

This chart shows the median household incomes of Asian, white, Hispanic, and African-American workers in 2010.

- Asian — $64,308
- White, not Hispanic — $54,620
- All races — $49,445
- Hispanic (any race) — $37,759
- African-American — $32,068

Income in thousands (2010 dollars)

Year: 1967 1970 1975 1980 1985 1990 1995 2000 2005 2010

Source: U.S. Census Bureau, Current Population Survey, 1968 to 2010 Annual Social and Economic Supplements, *Income, Poverty, and Health Insurance Coverage in the United States: 2010*, issued September 2011, U.S. Census Bureau, U.S. Department of Commerce, 8, www.census.gov/prod/2011pubs/p60-239pdf (accessed March 4, 2012).

---

minority a racial, religious, political, national, or other group regarded as different from the larger group of which it is a part and that is often singled out for unfavorable treatment

affirmative action program a plan designed to increase the number of minority employees at all levels within an organization

Meet Sam's Club president and CEO. In early 2012, Rosalind Brewer became the first African-American woman to hold a CEO position at one of the company's business units.

then approximately 25 percent of the electricians it employs also should be African-Americans. Affirmative action plans encompass all areas of human resources management: recruiting, hiring, training, promotion, and pay.

Unfortunately, affirmative action programs have been plagued by two problems. The first involves quotas. In the beginning, many firms pledged to recruit and hire a certain number of minority members by a specific date. To achieve this goal, they were forced to consider only minority applicants for job openings; if they hired nonminority workers, they would be defeating their own purpose. However, the courts have ruled that such quotas are unconstitutional even though their purpose is commendable. They are, in fact, a form of discrimination called *reverse discrimination*.

The second problem is that although most such programs have been reasonably successful, not all businesspeople are in favor of affirmative action programs. Managers not committed to these programs can "play the game" and still discriminate against workers. To help solve this problem, Congress created (and later strengthened) the **Equal Employment Opportunity Commission (EEOC)**, a government agency with the power to investigate complaints of employment discrimination and sue firms that practice it.

The threat of legal action has persuaded some corporations to amend their hiring and promotional policies, but the discrepancy between men's and women's salaries still exists, as illustrated in Figure 2.4. For more than 50 years, women have consistently earned only about 77 cents for each dollar earned by men.

Training Programs for the Hard-Core Unemployed

For some firms, social responsibility extends far beyond placing a help-wanted advertisement in the local newspaper. These firms have assumed the task of helping the **hard-core unemployed**, workers with little education or vocational training and a long history of unemployment. For example, a few years ago, General Mills helped establish Siyeza, a frozen soul-food processing plant in North Minneapolis. Through the years, Siyeza has provided stable, high-quality full-time jobs for a permanent core of 80 unemployed or underemployed minority inner-city residents. In addition, groups of up

Equal Employment Opportunity Commission (EEOC) a government agency with the power to investigate complaints of employment discrimination and the power to sue firms that practice it

hard-core unemployed workers with little education or vocational training and a long history of unemployment

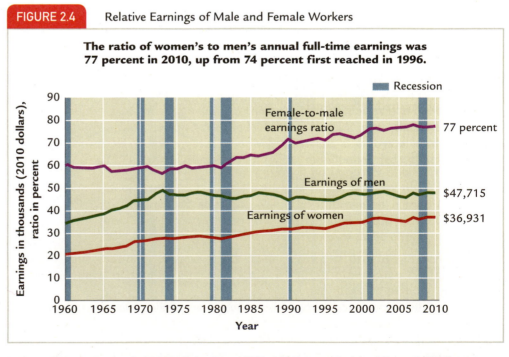

| FIGURE 2.4 | Relative Earnings of Male and Female Workers |

The ratio of women's to men's annual full-time earnings was 77 percent in 2010, up from 74 percent first reached in 1996.

Source: U.S. Census Bureau, Current Population Survey, 1960 to 2010 Annual Social and Economic Supplements, *Income, Poverty, and Health Insurance Coverage in the United States: 2010,* issued September 2011, U.S. Census Bureau, U.S. Department of Commerce, 12, www.census.gov/prod/2011pubs/p60-239.pdf (accessed March 4, 2012).

to 100 temporary employees are called in when needed. In the past, such workers often were turned down routinely by personnel managers, even for the most menial jobs.

Obviously, such workers require training; just as obviously, this training can be expensive and time-consuming. To share the costs, business and community leaders have joined together in a number of cooperative programs. One particularly successful partnership is the **National Alliance of Business (NAB)**, a joint business–government program to train the hard-core unemployed. The alliance's 5,000 members include companies of all sizes and industries, their CEOs and senior executives, as well as educators and community leaders. NAB, founded in 1968 by President Lyndon Johnson and Henry Ford II, is a major national business organization focusing on education and workforce issues.

CONCERN FOR THE ENVIRONMENT

9 Describe the major types of pollution, their causes, and their cures.

The social consciousness of responsible business managers, the encouragement of a concerned government, and an increasing concern on the part of the public have led to a major effort to reduce environmental pollution, conserve natural resources, and reverse some of the worst effects of past negligence in this area. **Pollution** is the contamination of water, air, or land through the actions of people in an industrialized society. For several decades, environmentalists have been warning us about the dangers of industrial pollution. Unfortunately, business and government leaders either ignored the problem or were not concerned about it until pollution became a threat to life and health in America. Today, Americans expect business and government leaders to take swift action to clean up our environment—and to keep it clean.

Effects of Environmental Legislation

As in other areas of concern to our society, legislation and regulations play a crucial role in pollution control. The laws outlined in Table 2.5 reflect the scope of current environmental legislation: laws to promote clean air, clean water, and even quiet work and living environments. Of major importance was the creation of the Environmental Protection Agency (EPA), the federal agency charged with enforcing laws designed to protect the environment.

When they are aware of a pollution problem, many firms respond to it rather than wait to be cited by the EPA. Other owners and managers, however, take the position that environmental standards are too strict. (Loosely translated, this means that compliance with present standards is too expensive.) Consequently, it often has been necessary for the EPA to take legal action to force firms to install antipollution equipment and to clean up waste storage areas.

Experience has shown that the combination of environmental legislation, voluntary compliance, and EPA action can succeed in cleaning up the environment and keeping it clean. However, much still remains to be done.

Water Pollution The Clean Water Act has been credited with greatly improving the condition of the waters in the United States. This success comes largely from the control of pollutant discharges from industrial and wastewater treatment plants. Although the quality of our nation's rivers, lakes, and streams has improved significantly in recent years, many of these surface waters remain severely polluted. Currently, one of the most serious water-quality problems results from the high level of toxic pollutants found in these waters.

Among the serious threats to people posed by water pollutants are respiratory irritation, cancer, kidney and liver damage, anemia, and heart failure. Toxic pollutants also damage fish and other forms of wildlife. In fish, they cause tumors or reproductive problems; shellfish and wildlife living in or drinking from toxin-laden waters also have suffered genetic defects. Recently, the Pollution Control Board of Kerala in India

National Alliance of Business (NAB) a joint business–government program to train the hard-core unemployed

pollution the contamination of water, air, or land through the actions of people in an industrialized society

TABLE 2.5 Summary of Major Environmental Laws

Legislation	Major Provisions
National Environmental Policy Act (1970)	Established the Environmental Protection Agency (EPA) to enforce federal laws that involve the environment
Clean Air Amendment (1970)	Provided stringent automotive, aircraft, and factory emission standards
Water Quality Improvement Act (1970)	Strengthened existing water pollution regulations and provided for large monetary fines against violators
Resource Recovery Act (1970)	Enlarged the solid-waste disposal program and provided for enforcement by the EPA
Water Pollution Control Act Amendment (1972)	Established standards for cleaning navigable streams and lakes and eliminating all harmful waste disposal by 1985
Noise Control Act (1972)	Established standards for major sources of noise and required the EPA to advise the Federal Aviation Administration on standards for airplanes
Clean Air Act Amendment (1977)	Established new deadlines for cleaning up polluted areas; also required review of existing air-quality standards
Resource Conservation and Recovery Act (1984)	Amended the original 1976 act and required federal regulation of potentially dangerous solid-waste disposal
Clean Air Act Amendment (1987)	Established a national air-quality standard for ozone
Oil Pollution Act (1990)	Expanded the nation's oil-spill prevention and response activities; also established the Oil Spill Liability Trust Fund
Clean Air Act Amendments (1990)	Required that motor vehicles be equipped with onboard systems to control about 90 percent of refueling vapors
Food Quality Protection Act (1996)	Amended the Federal Insecticide, Fungicide and Rodenticide Act and the Federal Food Drug and Cosmetic Act; the requirements included a new safety standard—reasonable certainty of no harm—that must be applied to all pesticides used on foods
American Recovery and Reinvestment Act (2009)	Provided $7.22 billion to the EPA to protect and promote "green" jobs and a healthier environment

© CENGAGE LEARNING 2014

ordered Coca-Cola to close its major bottling plant. For years, villagers in the nearby areas had accused Coke of depleting local groundwater and producing other local pollution. The village council president said, "We are happy that the government is finally giving justice to the people who are affected by the plant."

One of the worst environmental disasters in 2010 was the explosion of the *Deepwater Horizon*, during which 11 people died. The British Petroleum (BP) catastrophe led to an oil spill in the Gulf of Mexico that contaminated a vast area of the United States marine environment. It caused a serious impact on wildlife, the local fishing industry, and regional tourism. British Petroleum was held liable for property damaged by the oil spill and the cleanup efforts; loss of income or earning capacity; loss of income to boat owners, hotel owners, and restaurant owners; removal and cleanup costs of property; and claims of bodily injury caused by the spill. Under the settlement in early 2012, British Petroleum expected to pay out $7.8 billion to settle the claims.

The task of water cleanup has proved to be extremely complicated and costly because of pollution runoff and toxic contamination. Yet, improved water quality is not only necessary, it is also achievable. Consider Cleveland's Cuyahoga River. A few years ago, the river was so contaminated by industrial wastes that it burst into flames one hot summer day! Now, after a sustained community cleanup effort, the river is pure enough for fish to thrive in.

Another serious issue is acid rain, which is contributing significantly to the deterioration of coastal waters, lakes, and marine life in the eastern United States. Acid rain forms when sulfur emitted by smokestacks in industrialized areas combines with moisture in the atmosphere to form acids that are spread by winds. The acids eventually fall to Earth in rain, which finds its way into streams, rivers, and lakes. The acid-rain problem has spread rapidly in recent years, and experts fear that the situation will worsen if the nation begins to burn more coal to generate electricity. To solve the problem, investigators first must determine where the sulfur is being emitted. The costs of this vital investigation and cleanup are going to be high. The human costs of having ignored the problem so long may be higher still.

Air Pollution Aviation emissions are a potentially significant and growing percentage of greenhouse gases that contribute to global warming. Aircraft emissions are significant for several reasons. First, jet aircraft are the main source of human emissions deposited directly into the upper atmosphere, where they may have a greater warming effect than if they were released at Earth's surface. Second, carbon dioxide—the primary aircraft emission—is the main focus of international concern. For example, it survives in the atmosphere for nearly 100 years and contributes to global warming, according to the Intergovernmental Panel on Climate Change. The carbon dioxide emissions from worldwide aviation roughly equal those of some industrialized countries. Third, carbon dioxide emissions combined with other gases and particles emitted by jet aircraft could have two to four times as great an effect on the atmosphere as carbon dioxide alone. Fourth, the Intergovernmental Panel recently concluded that the rise in aviation emissions owing to the growing demand for air travel would not be fully offset by reductions in emissions achieved solely through technological improvements.

Usually, two or three factors combine to form air pollution in any given location. The first factor is large amounts of carbon monoxide and hydrocarbons emitted by motor vehicles concentrated in a relatively small area. The second is the smoke and other pollutants emitted by manufacturing facilities. These two factors can be eliminated in part through pollution control devices on cars, trucks, and smokestacks.

A third factor that contributes to air pollution—one that cannot be changed—is the combination of weather and geography. The Los Angeles Basin, for example, combines just the right weather and geographic conditions for creating dense smog. Los Angeles has strict regulations regarding air pollution. Even so, Los Angeles still struggles with air pollution problems because of uncontrollable conditions.

How effective is air pollution control? The EPA estimates that the Clean Air Act and its amendments will eventually result in the removal of 56 billion pounds of pollution from the air each year, thus measurably reducing lung disease, cancer, and other serious health problems caused by air pollution. Other authorities note that we have already seen improvement in air quality. A number of cities have cleaner air today than they did 30 years ago. Even in southern California, bad air-quality days have dropped to less than 40 days a year, about 60 percent lower than that observed just a decade ago. Numerous chemical companies have recognized that

Sustaining the PLANET

Social Responsibility at Xerox

Over the past 40 years, Xerox has demonstrated leadership in sustainability and corporate citizenship by designing waste-free products built in waste-free plants, investing in innovations that benefit the environment, supporting community projects, and many other initiatives. Take a look at its 2011 Report on Global Citizenship, which details its environmental sustainability initiatives, corporate donations, volunteerism and more.

www.xerox.com/about-xerox/citizenship/enus.html

Worsening water and land pollution problem. Land pollution is still a serious problem in many parts of the country. It is not just the manufacturers and service businesses that produce millions of tons of waste! We, the individuals in the United States, contribute to the waste-disposal problem, too.

they must take responsibility for operating their plants in an environmentally safe manner; some now devote considerable capital to purchasing antipollution devices. For example, 3M's pioneering Pollution Prevention Pays (3P) program, designed to find ways to avoid the generation of pollutants, marked its 30th anniversary in 2005. Since 1975, more than 5,600 employee-driven 3P projects have prevented the generation of more than 2.2 billion pounds of pollutants and produced first-year savings of nearly $1 billion.

Land Pollution Air and water quality may be improving, but land pollution is still a serious problem in many areas. The fundamental issues are (1) how to restore damaged or contaminated land at a reasonable cost and (2) how to protect unpolluted land from future damage.

The land pollution problem has been worsening over the past few years because modern technology has continued to produce increasing amounts of chemical and radioactive waste. U.S. manufacturers produce an estimated 40 to 60 million tons of contaminated oil, solvents, acids, and sludge each year. Service businesses, utility companies, hospitals, and other industries also dump vast amounts of wastes into the environment.

Individuals in the United States contribute to the waste-disposal problem, too. A shortage of landfills, owing to stricter regulations, makes garbage disposal a serious problem in some areas. Incinerators help to solve the landfill-shortage problem, but they bring with them their own problems. They reduce the amount of garbage but also leave tons of ash to be buried—ash that often has a higher concentration of toxicity than the original garbage. Other causes of land pollution include strip mining of coal, nonselective cutting of forests, and development of agricultural land for housing and industry.

To help pay the enormous costs of cleaning up land polluted with chemicals and toxic wastes, Congress created a $1.6 billion Superfund in 1980. Originally, money was to flow into the Superfund from a tax paid by 800 oil and chemical companies that produce toxic waste. The EPA was to use the money in the Superfund to finance the cleanup of hazardous waste sites across the nation. To replenish the Superfund, the EPA had two options: It could sue companies guilty of dumping chemicals at specific waste sites, or it could negotiate with guilty companies and thus completely avoid the legal system. During the 1980s, officials at the EPA came under fire because they preferred negotiated settlements. Critics referred to these settlements as "sweetheart deals" with industry. They felt that the EPA should be much more aggressive in reducing land pollution. Of course, most corporate executives believe that cleanup efficiency and quality might be improved if companies were more involved in the process. Many firms, including Delphi Automotive Systems Corporation and 3M, have modified or halted the production and sale of products that have a negative impact on the environment. For example, after tests showed that ScotchGard™ does not decompose in the environment, 3M announced a voluntary end to production of the 40-year-old product, which had generated $300 million in sales.

Noise Pollution Excessive noise caused by traffic, aircraft, and machinery can do physical harm to human beings. Research has shown that people who are exposed to loud noises for long periods of time can suffer permanent hearing loss. The Noise Control Act of 1972 established noise emission standards for aircraft and airports, railroads, and interstate motor carriers. The act also provided funding for noise research at state and local levels.

Noise levels can be reduced by two methods. The source of noise pollution can be isolated as much as possible. (Thus, many metropolitan airports are located outside the cities.) Engineers can also modify machinery and equipment to reduce noise levels. If it is impossible to reduce industrial noise to acceptable levels, workers should be required to wear earplugs to guard them against permanent hearing damage.

Entrepreneurial SUCCESS

© ELNUR/SHUTTERSTOCK

Social Entrepreneurs of Tomorrow

A growing number of young entrepreneurs are starting businesses with the goal of using their skills for a socially responsible purpose: to improve the quality of life for people all over the world. Many of these social entrepreneurs are focusing on different ways to bring reliable, inexpensive sources of electricity to poverty-stricken areas.

For example, Alan Hurt, John Harkness, Jason Schwebke, and Mike Sutarik are members of Team Light Up Africa, which won $10,000 in the first Northern Illinois University Social Venture Business Plan Competition. Their Zoom Box, currently in development, is a low-cost, lightweight generator suitable for powering electric lights and charging cell phones in Africa. "We're more than a company and more than a passing idea," says Hurt. "We're a movement."

Teenage inventor Eden Full created a rotating solar panel, the SunSaluter, that turns to follow the sun throughout the day. The improved efficiency increases the amount of solar power that can be generated in an earth-friendly manner. Her SunSaluter panels are already lighting up two villages in Kenya, with more installations on the way. Full's ingenuity has won her social enterprise additional funding to refine and manufacture the product on a larger scale.

Sources: Based on information in Jack McCarthy, "NIU Students Generate Winning Idea," *Chicago Tribune*, December 11, 2011, www.chicagotribune.com; Zachary Sniderman, "4 Young Social Good Entrepreneurs to Watch," *Mashable*, December 6, 2011, http://mashable.com; "Class Launches Social Entrepreneurs," *NIU Today (Northern Illinois University)*, December 20, 2011, www.niutoday.info; Anya Kamenetz, "Peter Thiel Gives Whiz Kids $100K to Quit College, Start Businesses," *Fast Company*, May 25, 2011, www.fastcompany.com.

Who Should Pay for a Clean Environment?

Governments and businesses are spending billions of dollars annually to reduce pollution—more than $45 billion to control air pollution, $33 billion to control water pollution, and $12 billion to treat hazardous wastes. To make matters worse, much of the money required to purify the environment is supposed to come from already depressed industries, such as the chemical industry. A few firms have discovered that it is cheaper to pay a fine than to install expensive equipment for pollution control.

Who, then, will pay for the environmental cleanup? Many business leaders offer one answer—tax money should be used to cleanup the environment and to keep it clean. They reason that business is not the only source of pollution, so business should not be forced to absorb the entire cost of the cleanup. Environmentalists disagree. They believe that the cost of proper treatment and disposal of industrial wastes is an expense of doing business. In either case, consumers probably will pay a large part of the cost—either as taxes or in the form of higher prices for goods and services.

IMPLEMENTING A PROGRAM OF SOCIAL RESPONSIBILITY

 10 Identify the steps a business must take to implement a program of social responsibility.

A firm's decision to be socially responsible is a step in the right direction—but only the first step. The firm then must develop and implement a program to reach this goal. The program will be affected by the firm's size, financial resources, past record in the area of social responsibility, and competition. Above all, however, the program must have the firm's total commitment or it will fail.

Developing a Program of Social Responsibility

An effective program for social responsibility takes time, money, and organization. In most cases, developing and implementing such a program will require four steps:

securing the commitment of top executives, planning, appointing a director, and preparing a social audit.

Commitment of Top Executives Without the support of top executives, any program will soon falter and become ineffective. For example, the Boeing Company's Ethics and Business Conduct Committee is responsible for the ethics program. The committee is appointed by the Boeing board of directors, and its members include the company chairman and CEO, the president and chief operating officer, the presidents of the operating groups, and senior vice presidents. As evidence of their commitment to social responsibility, top managers should develop a policy statement that outlines key areas of concern. This statement sets a tone of positive support and later will serve as a guide for other employees as they become involved in the program.

Planning Next, a committee of managers should be appointed to plan the program. Whatever form their plan takes, it should deal with each of the issues described in the top managers' policy statement. If necessary, outside consultants can be hired to help develop the plan.

Appointment of a Director After the social responsibility plan is established, a top-level executive should be appointed to implement the organization's plan. This individual should be charged with recommending specific policies and helping individual departments to understand and live up to the social responsibilities the firm has assumed. Depending on the size of the firm, the director may require a staff to handle the program on a day-to-day basis. For example, at the Boeing Company, the director of ethics and business conduct administers the ethics and business conduct program.

The Social Audit At specified intervals, the program director should prepare a social audit for the firm. A **social audit** is a comprehensive report of what an organization has done and is doing with regard to social issues that affect it. This document provides the information the firm needs to evaluate and revise its social responsibility program. Typical subject areas include human resources, community involvement, the quality and safety of products, business practices, and efforts to reduce pollution and improve the environment. The information included in a social audit should be as accurate and as quantitative as possible, and the audit should reveal both positive and negative aspects of the program.

Today, many companies listen to concerned individuals within and outside the company. For example, the Boeing Ethics Line listens to and acts on concerns expressed by employees and others about possible violations of company policies, laws, or regulations, such as improper or unethical business practices, as well as health, safety, and environmental issues. Employees are encouraged to communicate their concerns, as well as ask questions about ethical issues. The Ethics Line is available to all Boeing employees, including Boeing subsidiaries. It is also available to concerned individuals outside the company.

Funding the Program

We have noted that social responsibility costs money. Thus, just like any other corporate undertaking, a program to improve social responsibility must be funded. Funding can come from three sources:

1. Management can pass the cost on to consumers in the form of higher prices.
2. The corporation may be forced to absorb the cost of the program if, for example, the competitive situation does not permit a price increase. In this case, the cost is treated as a business expense, and profit is reduced.
3. The federal government may pay for all or part of the cost through tax reductions or other incentives.

social audit a comprehensive report of what an organization has done and is doing with regard to social issues that affect it

Panera Cares

Panera Cares is very much like every other Panera bakery-café, offering the same seasonal menu, the same fresh-baked bread, and the same comfortable ambiance. At Panera Cares, however, customers pay what they can afford. A mother with a toddler in tow may donate $5 for a pastry while a homeless person pays nothing for the same type of pastry. It's Panera's way of doing something for local communities, and it's starting to catch on.

Panera Cares must receive 80 percent of the suggested funding level to continue as a viable venture. Some of the cafés consistently achieve that level, while others fall short on some days. As word spreads and more customers understand what Panera is trying to achieve, the cafés are building a loyal and generous following. "The lesson here is that most people are fundamentally good," notes Panera's founder. "People step up and they do the right thing."

Questions

1. How does Panera Cares fit into the socioeconomic model of social responsibility?
2. What ethical issues are raised by the idea of expecting some people to pay more for a Panera meal so that others can pay less?

SUMMARY

1 Understand what is meant by *business ethics.*

Ethics is the study of right and wrong and of the morality of choices. Business ethics is the application of moral standards to business situations.

2 Identify the types of ethical concerns that arise in the business world.

Ethical issues arise often in business situations out of relationships with investors, customers, employees, creditors, or competitors. Businesspeople should make every effort to be fair, to consider the welfare of customers and others within the firm, to avoid conflicts of interest, and to communicate honestly.

3 Discuss the factors that affect the level of ethical behavior in organizations.

Individual, social, and opportunity factors all affect the level of ethical behavior in an organization. Individual factors include knowledge level, moral values and attitudes, and personal goals. Social factors include cultural norms and the actions and values of co-workers and significant others. Opportunity factors refer to the amount of leeway that exists in an organization for employees to behave unethically if they choose to do so.

4 Explain how ethical decision making can be encouraged.

Governments, trade associations, and individual firms can establish guidelines for defining ethical behavior. Governments can pass stricter regulations. Trade associations provide ethical guidelines for their members. Companies provide codes of ethics—written guides to acceptable and ethical behavior as defined by an organization—and create an atmosphere in which ethical behavior is encouraged. An ethical employee working in an unethical environment may resort to whistle-blowing to bring a questionable practice to light.

5 Describe how our current views on the social responsibility of business have evolved.

In a socially responsible business, management realizes that its activities have an impact on society and considers that impact in the decision-making process. Before the 1930s, workers, consumers, and government had very little influence on business activities; as a result, business leaders gave little thought to social responsibility. All this changed with the Great Depression. Government regulations, employee demands, and consumer awareness combined to create a demand that businesses act in socially responsible ways.

6 Explain the two views on the social responsibility of business and understand the arguments for and against increased social responsibility.

The basic premise of the economic model of social responsibility is that society benefits most when business is left alone to produce profitable goods and services.

According to the socioeconomic model, business has as much responsibility to society as it has to its owners. Most managers adopt a viewpoint somewhere between these two extremes.

 7 Discuss the factors that led to the consumer movement and list some of its results.

Consumerism consists of all activities undertaken to protect the rights of consumers. The consumer movement generally has demanded—and received—attention from business in the areas of product safety, product information, product choices through competition, and the resolution of complaints about products and business practices. Although concerns over consumer rights have been around to some extent since the early 19th century, the movement became more powerful in the 1960s when President John F. Kennedy initiated the Consumer Bill of Rights. The six basic rights of consumers include the right to safety, the right to be informed, the right to choose, the right to be heard, and the rights to consumer education and courteous service.

 8 Analyze how present employment practices are being used to counteract past abuses.

Legislation and public demand have prompted some businesses to correct past abuses in employment practices—mainly with regard to minority groups. Affirmative action and training of the hard-core unemployed are two types of programs that have been used successfully.

 9 Describe the major types of pollution, their causes, and their cures.

Industry has contributed to noise pollution and pollution of our land and water through the dumping of wastes, and to air pollution through vehicle and smokestack emissions. This contamination can be cleaned up and controlled, but the big question is: Who will pay? Present cleanup efforts are funded partly by government tax revenues, partly by business, and in the long run by consumers.

 10 Identify the steps a business must take to implement a program of social responsibility.

A program to implement social responsibility in a business begins with total commitment by top management. The program should be planned carefully, and a capable director should be appointed to implement it. Social audits should be prepared periodically as a means of evaluating and revising the program. Programs may be funded through price increases, reduction of profit, or federal incentives.

KEY TERMS

You should now be able to define and give an example relevant to each of the following terms:

ethics (37)
business ethics (37)
Sarbanes–Oxley Act of 2002 (41)
code of ethics (41)
whistle-blowing (42)

social responsibility (44)
caveat emptor (48)
economic model of social responsibility (49)
socioeconomic model of social responsibility (49)

consumerism (51)
minority (55)
affirmative action program (55)
Equal Employment Opportunity Commission (EEOC) (56)

hard-core unemployed (56)
National Alliance of Business (NAB) (57)
pollution (57)
social audit (62)

REVIEW QUESTIONS

1. Why might an individual with high ethical standards act less ethically in business than in his or her personal life?
2. How would an organizational code of ethics help to ensure ethical business behavior?
3. How and why did the American business environment change after the Great Depression?
4. What are the major differences between the economic model of social responsibility and the socioeconomic model?
5. What are the arguments for and against increasing the social responsibility of business?
6. Describe and give an example of each of the six basic rights of consumers.

7. There are more women than men in the United States. Why, then, are women considered a minority with regard to employment?
8. What is the goal of affirmative action programs? How is this goal achieved?
9. What is the primary function of the Equal Employment Opportunity Commission?
10. How do businesses contribute to each of the four forms of pollution? How can they avoid polluting the environment?
11. Our environment can be cleaned up and kept clean. Why haven't we simply done so?
12. Describe the steps involved in developing a social responsibility program within a large corporation.

1. When a company acts in an ethically questionable manner, what types of problems are caused for the organization and its customers?
2. How can an employee take an ethical stand regarding a business decision when his or her superior already has taken a different position?
3. Overall, would it be more profitable for a business to follow the economic model or the socioeconomic model of social responsibility?

4. Why should business take on the task of training the hard-core unemployed?
5. To what extent should the blame for vehicular air pollution be shared by manufacturers, consumers, and government?
6. Why is there so much government regulation involving social responsibility issues? Should there be less?

Video Case 2.1

Scholfield Honda—Going Green with Honda

Signs of green marketing can be found everywhere today: reusable shopping bags are the rule rather than the exception, organic and natural products fill grocers' shelves, and socially responsible companies are increasing their efforts to reduce pollution, conserve water and energy, and recycle waste paper, plastic, and other reusable materials.

Of course, some companies have always been ahead of the curve. Since the early 1970s, Honda has been producing the low-emissions, fuel-efficient Civic model, and the company has never strayed from its roots. Today's Honda line consists of four classes of vehicles: Good, Better, Best, and Ultimate. Its regular gas cars are Good, with about 30 mpg; hybrids are Better at about 45 mpg; and its Best solution is a natural gas-powered Civic GX, which gets about 220 miles to a tank. Honda also has Ultimate solutions in the works, such as the new Honda FCX Clarity—a hydrogen fuel-cell car that uses hydrogen and oxygen to create electricity. Although the Civic GX and Clarity models are available to consumers, neither vehicle is practical for the average driver as fueling stations are scarce.

Alternative energy vehicles are making their way to the Midwest. Lee Lindquist, an alternative fuels specialist at Scholfield Honda in Wichita, Kansas, was researching alternative fuel vehicles for a local Sierra Club meeting when he learned that municipalities in New York and California used the natural gas Civic GX to address air-quality issues. Although Lee recognized that his own Wichita market was not teeming with green consumers, he knew that people needed ways to combat rising fuel prices—so he proposed the Civic GX for use at his dealership.

Lee's boss was skeptical of the idea. Although management was open to clever ways to promote the dealership, owner Roger Scholfield did not want to risk muddying the waters with a new and somewhat impractical vehicle. Nevertheless, he agreed to offer the car to his fleet and corporate customers, and in time fate offered another opportunity for Scholfield Honda to go green.

In May 2007, a devastating tornado hit the nearby town of Greensburg, Kansas, leveling the area. Once again Lee Lindquist approached his boss. This time, he proposed donating both a Honda Civic GX and a natural-gas fueling station to Greensburg as a way of helping the town rebuild. Upon careful reflection, Roger realized that Lee's idea would benefit his dealership through good publicity and higher awareness of alternative fuel vehicles. Scholfield made the Civic model and fuel station available to Greensburg residents free of charge, and the dealership has been on the green bandwagon ever since.

Although there are more cost-effective ways of advertising, Roger Scholfield notes that customers are becoming more interested in alternative fuel vehicles since he donated the Civic GX. In addition, his dealership has generated plenty of goodwill in the press and among local residents—Scholfield Honda has developed a good reputation for its commitment to the environment and the people of Greensburg, even opening a "Honda Green Zone" conference room on the premises. The room can hold several hundred people. It includes a digital projector, sound system, and kitchenette and is available free to local firms and organizations for meetings and conferences. Its chairs, tables, tiles, and flooring are all made from recycled materials.[17]

Questions

1. How would you rate Scholfield Honda's sense of social responsibility? Does the dealership meet all the criteria for a socially responsible company?
2. What is Scholfield Honda's primary ethical responsibility in situations where a proposed green initiative is cost-prohibitive or even detrimental to the company's bottom line?
3. Should the government regulate companies' claims that their products are green? Should official classifications for environmental friendliness be defined?

Volkswagen Speeds Along on Global Sales

Volkswagen is shifting into high gear to become the world's largest and most profitable automaker by 2018. The company, based in Germany, sells vehicles in 150 nations under many brands, including Audi, Bentley, Bugatti, Lamborghini, Porsche, Scania, Seat, Skoda, and Volkswagen. Although Volkswagen is strongest on its home continent of Europe, it's been steering toward higher sales in Asia and the Americas for years.

Nearly 30 years ago, Volkswagen was among the first major automakers to do business in China. It has joined forces with two local partners, SAIC and FAW, to build and market cars all around the country. Originally, the cars Volkswagen made with its Chinese partners were no-frills, low-price models. Now, in addition to these basic cars, Volkswagen is introducing larger, more stylish (and more profitable) cars designed especially for China, such as the VW Lavida.

Volkswagen imports some of its cars from Germany and makes some in its new high-tech factory in Chattanooga, Tennessee. Having most of the parts supplied by United States–based companies or German firms with U.S. divisions allows Volkswagen to keep costs down, so it can price its made-in-America cars more competitively. Having a strong U.S. presence will help Volkswagen achieve its goal of becoming the industry leader by 2018, despite aggressive moves by U.S. rivals such as General Motors and global rivals such as Toyota and Hyundai. "You have to be successful in the United States if you want to be the number one in the industry," says Volkswagen's chief executive officer. "Trends are set in America, not just for consumer behavior but also for communication technology, computers, and software."

Sales are also growing in South America, where Volkswagen operates eight factories to make the compact Gol car, a popular line of minibuses, and other vehicles. The firm has an engine factory and an assembly plant in Mexico, as well, as part of its long-term plan to increase production and boost sales in both North and South America.

Two factors that might slow Volkswagen's drive for global growth are economic uncertainties and intense competition. Can the company continue accelerating toward higher sales?[1]

Volkswagen is just one of a growing number of foreign companies, large and small, that are doing business with firms in other countries. Some companies, such as Coca-Cola, sell to firms in other countries; others, such as Pier 1 Imports, buy goods around the world to import into the United States. Whether they buy or sell products across national borders, these companies are all contributing to the volume of international trade that is fueling the global economy.

Theoretically, international trade is every bit as logical and worthwhile as interstate trade between, say, California and Washington. Yet, nations tend to restrict the import of certain goods for a variety of reasons. For example, in the early 2000s, the United States restricted the import of Mexican fresh tomatoes because they were undercutting price levels of domestic fresh tomatoes.

Despite such restrictions, international trade has increased almost steadily since World War II. Many of the industrialized nations have signed trade agreements intended to eliminate problems in international business and to help less-developed nations participate in world trade. Individual firms around the world have seized the opportunity to compete in foreign markets by exporting products and increasing foreign production, as well as by other means.

Signing the Trade Act of 2002, President George W. Bush remarked, "Trade is an important source of good jobs for our workers and a source of higher growth for our economy. Free trade is also a proven strategy for building global prosperity and adding to the momentum of political freedom. Trade is an engine of economic growth. In our lifetime, trade has helped lift millions of people and whole nations out of poverty and put them on the path of prosperity."[2] In his national best seller, *The World Is Flat,* Thomas L. Friedman states, "The flattening of the world has presented us with new opportunities, new challenges, new partners but, also, alas new dangers, particularly as Americans it is imperative that we be the best global citizens that we can be—because in a flat world, if you don't visit a bad neighborhood, it might visit you."

We describe international trade in this chapter in terms of modern specialization, whereby each country trades the surplus goods and services it produces most efficiently for products in short supply. We also explain the restrictions nations place on products and services from other countries and present some of the possible advantages and disadvantages of these restrictions. We then describe the extent of international trade and identify the organizations working to foster it. We describe several methods of entering international markets and the various sources of export assistance available from the federal government. Finally, we identify some of the institutions that provide the complex financing necessary for modern international trade.

THE BASIS FOR INTERNATIONAL BUSINESS

 Explain the economic basis for international business.

International business encompasses all business activities that involve exchanges across national boundaries. Thus, a firm is engaged in international business when it buys some portion of its input from, or sells some portion of its output to, an organization located in a foreign country. (A small retail store may sell goods produced in some other country. However, because it purchases these goods from American distributors, it is not engaged in international trade.)

Absolute and Comparative Advantage

Some countries are better equipped than others to produce particular goods or services. The reason may be a country's natural resources, its labor supply, or even customs or a historical accident. Such a country would be best off if it could specialize in the production of such products so that it can produce them most efficiently. The country could use what it needed of these products and then trade the surplus for products it could not produce efficiently on its own.

Saudi Arabia thus has specialized in the production of crude oil and petroleum products; South Africa, in diamonds; and Australia, in wool. Each of these countries is said to have an absolute advantage with regard to a particular product. An **absolute advantage** is the ability to produce a specific product more efficiently than any other nation.

One country may have an absolute advantage with regard to several products, whereas another country may have no absolute advantage at all. Yet it is still worthwhile for these two countries to specialize and trade with each other. To see why this is so, imagine that you are the president of a successful manufacturing firm and that you can accurately type 90 words per minute. Your assistant can type 80 words per minute but would run the business poorly. Thus, you have an absolute advantage over your assistant in both typing and managing. However, you cannot afford to type your own letters because your time is better spent in managing the business. That is, you have a **comparative advantage** in managing. A comparative advantage is the ability to produce a specific product more efficiently than any other product.

international business all business activities that involve exchanges across national boundaries

absolute advantage the ability to produce a specific product more efficiently than any other nation

comparative advantage the ability to produce a specific product more efficiently than any other product

© KLETR/SHUTTERSTOCK

Exploiting an American advantage. The United States has long specialized in the production of wheat. Because of its natural resource, the United States and some other countries enjoy an absolute advantage— their ability to produce wheat more efficiently than countries in other parts of the world.

Your assistant, on the other hand, has a comparative advantage in typing because he or she can do that better than managing the business. Thus, you spend your time managing, and you leave the typing to your assistant. Overall, the business is run as efficiently as possible because you are each working in accordance with your own comparative advantage.

The same is true for nations. Goods and services are produced more efficiently when each country specializes in the products for which it has a comparative advantage. Moreover, by definition, every country has a comparative advantage in some product. The United States has many comparative advantages—in research and development, high-technology industries, and identifying new markets, for instance.

Exporting and Importing

Suppose that the United States specializes in producing corn. It then will produce a surplus of corn, but perhaps it will have a shortage of wine. France, on the other hand, specializes in producing wine but experiences a shortage of corn. To satisfy both needs—for corn and for wine—the two countries should trade with each other. The United States should export corn and import wine. France should export wine and import corn.

Exporting is selling and shipping raw materials or products to other nations. The Boeing Company, for example, exports its airplanes to a number of countries for use by their airlines. Figure 3.1 shows the top ten merchandise-exporting states in this country.

Importing is purchasing raw materials or products in other nations and bringing them into one's own country. Thus, buyers for Macy's department stores may purchase rugs in India or raincoats in England and have them shipped back to the United States for resale.

exporting selling and shipping raw materials or products to other nations

importing purchasing raw materials or products in other nations and bringing them into one's own country

FIGURE 3.1   The Top Ten Merchandise-Exporting States

Texas and California accounted for over one-fourth of all 2011 U.S. merchandise exports.

Billions of dollars, 2011 merchandise exports

Texas	$199.7
California	$175.2
New York	$89.2
Illinois	$79.4
Michigan	$69.9
Florida	$63.8
Washington	$54.6
Pennsylvania	$49.0
Ohio	$48.6
New Jersey	$47.0

Total 2011 U.S. exports: $876.4 billion

Source: www.census.gov/foreign-trade/statistics/state/zip/2011/12/zipstate.pdf (accessed March 7, 2012).

FIGURE 3.2   U.S. International Trade in Goods and Services

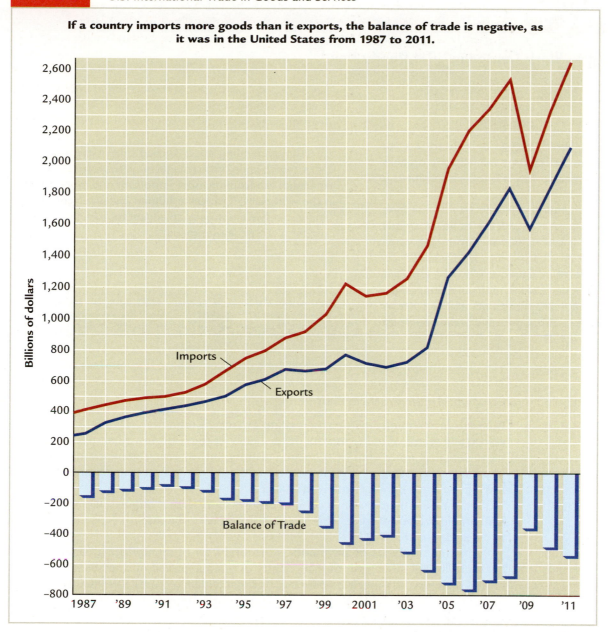

If a country imports more goods than it exports, the balance of trade is negative, as it was in the United States from 1987 to 2011.

Source: U.S. Department of Commerce, International Trade Administration, U.S. Bureau of Economic Analysis, www.census.gov/foreign-trade/Press-Release/curent_press_release/ft900.pdf (accessed March 8, 2012).

Importing and exporting are the principal activities in international trade. They give rise to an important concept called the *balance of trade*. A nation's **balance of trade** is the total value of its exports minus the total value of its imports over some period of time. If a country imports more than it exports, its balance of trade is negative and is said to be *unfavorable*. (A negative balance of trade is unfavorable because the country must export money to pay for its excess imports.)

In 2011, the United States imported $2,661 billion worth of goods and services and exported $2,103 billion worth. It thus had a trade deficit of $558 billion. A **trade deficit** is a negative balance of trade (see Figure 3.2). However, the United States has consistently enjoyed a large and rapidly growing surplus in services. For example, in 2011, the United States imported $426 billion worth of services and exported $605 billion worth, thus creating a favorable balance of $179 billion.[3]

balance of trade the total value of a nation's exports minus the total value of its imports over some period of time

trade deficit a negative balance of trade

Career SUCCESS

Want to Work Overseas? Get Ready Now!

If you'd like to work abroad for part or all of your career, start now to prepare for a successful experience by:

- *Focusing.* Which region or country do you want to work in—and why? Focusing will help you organize your job search and research the business environment in your chosen area.
- *Thinking global.* Broaden your perspective by learning more about international events as well as political trends, economic issues, and social influences in the area where you want to work.
- *Sharpening your skills.* Potential employers "will be especially interested in your language skills, either languages you already speak or your willingness and ability to learn quickly," says one expert. What other skills can you polish to show overseas employers?

- *Networking.* Talk with the professionals in your school's career office and with others who may be able to offer ideas or suggest leads to follow in locating potential jobs.

Although landing a job abroad takes time and effort, it's a worthwhile investment in your future. "Global experience is becoming more important and more valuable in the workplace," advises a human resources consultant, "and it can give employees an advantage when it comes to long-term career development."

Sources: Based on information in Anne Fisher, "Can You Get Hired for a Job Overseas?" *Fortune*, October 21, 2011, www.fortune.com; Michael Morella, "How to Find a Job Abroad," *U.S. News & World Report*, November 22, 2010, http://usnews.com/money; Michelle Goodman, "How to Find Work Outside the U.S.," ABC News, May 20, 2010, www.abcnews.go.com; Eve Tahmincioglu, "In Tough Market, Some Job Seekers Look Abroad," MSNBC, March 29, 2010, www.msnbc.msn.com.

Question: *Are trade deficits bad?*

Answer: In testimony before the Senate Finance Committee, Daniel T. Griswold, associate director of the Center for Trade Policy at the Cato Institute, remarked, "The trade deficit is not a sign of economic distress, but of rising domestic demand and investment. Imposing new trade barriers will only make Americans worse off while leaving the trade deficit virtually unchanged."

On the other hand, when a country exports more than it imports, it is said to have a favorable balance of trade. This has consistently been the case for Japan over the last two decades or so.

A nation's **balance of payments** is the total flow of money into a country minus the total flow of money out of that country over some period of time. Balance of payments, therefore, is a much broader concept than balance of trade. It includes imports and exports, of course. However, it also includes investments, money spent by foreign tourists, payments by foreign governments, aid to foreign governments, and all other receipts and payments.

A continual deficit in a nation's balance of payments (a negative balance) can cause other nations to lose confidence in that nation's economy. Alternatively, a continual surplus may indicate that the country encourages exports but limits imports by imposing trade restrictions.

Discuss the restrictions nations place on international trade, the objectives of these restrictions, and their results.

balance of payments the total flow of money into a country minus the total flow of money out of that country over some period of time

RESTRICTIONS TO INTERNATIONAL BUSINESS

Specialization and international trade can result in the efficient production of want-satisfying goods and services on a worldwide basis. As we have noted, international business generally is increasing. Yet the nations of the world continue to erect barriers to free trade. They do so for reasons ranging from internal political and economic pressures to simple mistrust of other nations. We examine first the types of restrictions that are applied and then the arguments for and against trade restrictions.

Types of Trade Restrictions

Nations generally are eager to export their products. They want to provide markets for their industries and to develop a favorable balance of trade. Hence, most trade restrictions are applied to imports from other nations.

Tariffs Perhaps the most commonly applied trade restriction is the customs (or import) duty. An **import duty** (also called a **tariff**) is a tax levied on a particular foreign product entering a country. For example, the United States imposes a 2.2 percent import duty on fresh Chilean tomatoes, an 8.7 percent duty if tomatoes are dried and packaged, and nearly 12 percent if tomatoes are made into ketchup or salsa. The two types of tariffs are revenue tariffs and protective tariffs; both have the effect of raising the price of the product in the importing nations, but for different reasons. *Revenue tariffs* are imposed solely to generate income for the government. For example, the United States imposes a duty on Scotch whiskey solely for revenue purposes. *Protective tariffs*, on the other hand, are imposed to protect a domestic industry from competition by keeping the price of competing imports level with or higher than the price of similar domestic products. Because fewer units of the product will be sold at the increased price, fewer units will be imported. The French and Japanese agricultural sectors would both shrink drastically if their nations abolished the protective tariffs that keep the price of imported farm products high. Today, U.S. tariffs are the lowest in history, with average tariff rates on all imports under 3 percent.

Some countries rationalize their protectionist policies as a way of offsetting an international trade practice called *dumping*. **Dumping** is the exportation of large quantities of a product at a price lower than that of the same product in the home market.

Thus, dumping drives down the price of the domestic item. Recently, for example, the Pencil Makers Association, which represents eight U.S. pencil manufacturers, charged that low-priced pencils from Thailand and the People's Republic of China were being sold in the United States at less than fair value prices. Unable to compete with these inexpensive imports, several domestic manufacturers had to shut down. To protect themselves, domestic manufacturers can obtain an antidumping duty through the government to offset the advantage of the foreign product. Recently, for example, the U.S. Department of Commerce imposed antidumping duties of up to 99 percent on a variety of steel products imported from China, following allegations by U.S. Steel Corp. and other producers that the products were being dumped at unfair prices.

Nontariff Barriers A **nontariff barrier** is a nontax measure imposed by a government to favor domestic over foreign suppliers. Nontariff barriers create obstacles to the marketing of foreign goods in a country and increase costs for exporters. The following are a few examples of government-imposed nontariff barriers:

- An **import quota** is a limit on the amount of a particular good that may be imported into a country during a given period of time. The limit may be set in terms of either quantity (so many pounds of beef) or value (so many dollars' worth of shoes). Quotas also may be set on individual products imported from specific countries. Once an import quota has been reached, imports are halted until the specified time has elapsed.
- An **embargo** is a complete halt to trading with a particular nation or of a particular product. The embargo is used most often as a political weapon. At present, the United States has import embargoes against Iran and North Korea—both as a result of extremely poor political relations.

import duty (tariff) a tax levied on a particular foreign product entering a country

dumping exportation of large quantities of a product at a price lower than that of the same product in the home market

nontariff barrier a nontax measure imposed by a government to favor domestic over foreign suppliers

import quota a limit on the amount of a particular good that may be imported into a country during a given period of time

embargo a complete halt to trading with a particular nation or in a particular product

Restricting the trade: The Russian style. In early 2012, Russian foreign minister Sergey Lavrov speaks at a news conference in Moscow, Russia. Mr. Lavrov threatens that Moscow will not abide by its World Trade Organization's commitments in trade with the United States unless it scraps a Cold War trade law.

What's your reaction when you see "Made in America" on a pickup truck? Would your reaction be the same if the truck had been made elsewhere? Clearly, cultural attitudes can influence how people feel about goods in the global marketplace.

- A **foreign-exchange control** is a restriction on the amount of a particular foreign currency that can be purchased or sold. By limiting the amount of foreign currency importers can obtain, a government limits the amount of goods importers can purchase with that currency. This has the effect of limiting imports from the country whose foreign exchange is being controlled.
- A nation can increase or decrease the value of its money relative to the currency of other nations. **Currency devaluation** is the reduction of the value of a nation's currency relative to the currencies of other countries.

Devaluation increases the cost of foreign goods, whereas it decreases the cost of domestic goods to foreign firms. For example, suppose that the British pound is worth $2. In this case, an American-made $2,000 computer can be purchased for £1,000. However, if the United Kingdom devalues the pound so that it is worth only $1, that same computer will cost £2,000. The increased cost, in pounds, will reduce the import of American computers—and all foreign goods—into England.

On the other hand, before devaluation, a £500 set of English bone china will cost an American $1,000. After the devaluation, the set of china will cost only $500. The decreased cost will make the china—and all English goods—much more attractive to U.S. purchasers. Bureaucratic red tape is more subtle than the other forms of nontariff barriers. Yet it can be the most frustrating trade barrier of all. A few examples are the unnecessarily restrictive application of standards and complex requirements related to product testing, labeling, and certification.

Cultural Barriers Another type of nontariff barrier is related to cultural attitudes. Cultural barriers can impede acceptance of products in foreign countries. For example, illustrations of feet are regarded as despicable in Thailand. Even so simple a thing as the color of a product or its package can present a problem. In Japan, black and white are the colors of mourning, so they should not be used in packaging. In Brazil, purple is the color of death. And in Egypt, green is never used on a package because it is the national color. When customers are unfamiliar with particular products from another country, their general perceptions of the country itself affect their attitude toward the product and help to determine whether they will buy it. Because Mexican cars have not been viewed by the world as being quality products, Volkswagen, for example, may not want to advertise that some of its models sold in the United States are made in Mexico. Many retailers on the Internet have yet to come to grips with the task of designing an online shopping site that is attractive and functional for all global customers.

Gifts to authorities—sometimes quite large ones—may be standard business procedure in some countries. In others, including the United States, they are called bribes or payoffs and are strictly illegal.

foreign-exchange control a restriction on the amount of a particular foreign currency that can be purchased or sold

currency devaluation the reduction of the value of a nation's currency relative to the currencies of other countries

Reasons for Trade Restrictions

Various reasons are given for trade restrictions either on the import of specific products or on trade with particular countries. We have noted that political considerations usually are involved in trade embargoes. Other frequently cited reasons for restricting trade include the following:

- *To equalize a nation's balance of payments.* This may be considered necessary to restore confidence in the country's monetary system and in its ability to repay its debts.

- *To protect new or weak industries.* A new, or infant, industry may not be strong enough to withstand foreign competition. Temporary trade restrictions may be used to give it a chance to grow and become self-sufficient. The problem is that once an industry is protected from foreign competition, it may refuse to grow, and "temporary" trade restrictions will become permanent. For example, a recent report by the Government Accountability Office (GAO), the congressional investigative agency, has accused the federal government of routinely imposing quotas on foreign textiles without "demonstrating the threat of serious damage" to U.S. industry. The GAO said that the Committee for the Implementation of Textile Agreements sometimes applies quotas even though it cannot prove the textile industry's claims that American companies have been hurt or jobs have been eliminated.
- *To protect national security.* Restrictions in this category generally apply to technological products that must be kept out of the hands of potential enemies. For example, strategic and defense-related goods cannot be exported to unfriendly nations.
- *To protect the health of citizens.* Products may be embargoed because they are dangerous or unhealthy (e.g., farm products contaminated with insecticides).
- *To retaliate for another nation's trade restrictions.* A country whose exports are taxed by another country may respond by imposing tariffs on imports from that country.
- *To protect domestic jobs.* By restricting imports, a nation can protect jobs in domestic industries. However, protecting these jobs can be expensive. For example, protecting 9,000 jobs in the U.S. carbon-steel industry costs $6.8 billion, or $750,000 per job. In addition, Gary Hufbauer and Ben Goodrich, economists at the Institute for International Economics, estimate that the tariffs could temporarily save 3,500 jobs in the steel industry, but at an annual cost to steel users of $2 billion, or $584,000 per job saved. Yet recently the United States imposed tariffs of up to 616 percent on steel pipes imported from China, South Korea, and Mexico. Similarly, it is estimated that we spent more than $100,000 for every job saved in the apparel manufacturing industry—jobs that seldom paid more than $35,000 a year.

Reasons Against Trade Restrictions

Trade restrictions have immediate and long-term economic consequences—both within the restricting nation and in world trade patterns. These include the following:

- *Higher prices for consumers.* Higher prices may result from the imposition of tariffs or the elimination of foreign competition, as described earlier. For example, imposing quota restrictions and import protections adds $25 billion annually to U.S. consumers' apparel costs by directly increasing costs for imported apparel.
- *Restriction of consumers' choices.* Again, this is a direct result of the elimination of some foreign products from the marketplace and of the artificially high prices that importers must charge for products that are still imported.
- *Misallocation of international resources.* The protection of weak industries results in the inefficient use of limited resources. The economies of both the restricting nation and other nations eventually suffer because of this waste.
- *Loss of jobs.* The restriction of imports by one nation must lead to cutbacks—and the loss of jobs—in the export-oriented industries of other nations. Furthermore, trade protection has a significant effect on the composition of employment. U.S. trade restrictions—whether on textiles, apparel, steel, or automobiles—benefit only a few industries while harming many others. The gains in employment accrue to the protected industries and their primary suppliers, and the losses are spread across all other industries. A few states gain employment, but many other states lose employment.

THE EXTENT OF INTERNATIONAL BUSINESS

Restrictions or not, international business is growing. Although the worldwide recessions of 1991 and 2001–2002 slowed the rate of growth, and the 2008–2009 global economic crisis caused the sharpest decline in more than 75 years, globalization is a reality of our time. In the United States, international trade now accounts for over one-fourth of GDP. As trade barriers decrease, new competitors enter the global marketplace, creating more choices for consumers and new opportunities for job seekers. International business will grow along with the expansion of commercial use of the Internet.

The World Economic Outlook for Trade

Although the global economy continued to grow robustly until 2007 economic performance was not equal: growth in the advanced economies slowed and then stopped in 2009, whereas emerging and developing economies continued to grow. Looking ahead, the International Monetary Fund (IMF), an international bank with 187 member nations, expected a gradual global growth to continue in 2012 and 2013 in both advanced and emerging developing economies.[4]

Although the U.S. economy had been growing steadily since 2000 and recorded the longest peacetime expansion in the nation's history, the worldwide recession which began in December 2007 has slowed the rate of growth. The IMF estimated that the U.S. economy grew by less than half of 1 percent in 2008 and, because of subprime mortgage lending and other global financial problems, declined 2.5 percent in 2009. However, international experts expected global economic growth of 3.3 percent in 2012 and 3.9 percent in 2013, despite the high oil prices and financial crises in the euro area economies.

Canada and Western Europe Our leading export partner, Canada, is projected to show a growth rate of 1.7 percent in 2012 and 2.0 percent in 2013. The euro area, which was projected to decline by 0.5 percent in 2012 is expected to grow 0.8 percent in 2013. The United Kingdom is expected to grow 0.6 percent and 2.0 percent in 2012 and 2013, respectively.

Mexico and Latin America Our second-largest export customer, Mexico, suffered its sharpest recession ever in 1995, and experienced another major setback in 2009. However, its growth rate in 2012 and 2013 is expected to be 3.5 percent. Brazil escaped the recent global economic crisis with only minor setbacks: Its growth in 2010 was more than 7.5 percent, and in 2011 it declined to 2.9 percent. Growth of about 3 percent and 4 percent is expected in 2012 and 2013, respectively. In general, the Latin American and the Caribbean economies are recovering at a robust pace.

Caterpillar in Saudi Arabia. Restrictions or not, international business is booming. Globalization is the reality of our time. As trade barriers decrease, ever increasing number of U.S. companies, such as Caterpillar, are selling in the global marketplace.

COURTESY, CATERPILLAR CORPORATION

Japan Japan's economy is regaining some momentum after suffering from an earthquake, tsunami, and nuclear plant disaster in 2011. Stronger consumer demand and business investment make Japan less reliant on exports for growth. The IMF estimates the growth for Japan at 1.7 percent in 2012 and 1.8 percent in 2013.

Other Asian Countries The economic growth in Asia remained strong in 2010 and 2011 despite the global recession. Growth was led by China, where its economy expanded by 9.2 percent in 2011, and is expected to grow at 8.2 percent and 8.8 percent in 2012 and 2013, respectively. Growth in India was 7.4 percent in 2011, and is predicted to grow at 7 percent and 7.3 percent in 2012 and 2013, respectively. Growth in ASEAN-5 countries—Indonesia, Malaysia, the Philippines, Thailand, and Vietnam—is expected at 5.2 percent and 5.6 percent in 2012 and 2013, respectively. In short, the key emerging economies in Asia are leading the global recovery.

China's emergence as a global economic power has been among the most dramatic economic developments of recent decades. From 1980 to

2004, China's economy averaged a real GDP growth rate of 9.5 percent and became the world's sixth-largest economy. By 2004, China had become the third-largest trading nation in dollar terms, behind the United States and Germany and just ahead of Japan. Today, China, the world's second-largest economy, generates 10 to 15 percent of world GDP, and in 2011, accounted for about 25 percent of world GDP growth. The United States now imports more goods from China than any other nation in the world. In fact, China, with almost $1.9 trillion in exports, is the world's number-one exporter. In 2012, China took steps to promote the international use of its currency, the renminbi.[5]

Commonwealth of Independent States The growth in this region is expected to be 3.7 percent in 2012 and 3.8 percent in 2013. Strong growth is expected to continue in Azerbaijan and Armenia, whereas growth is projected to remain stable in Moldova, Tajikistan, and Uzbekistan.

After World War II, trade between the United States and the communist nations of Central and Eastern Europe was minimal. The United States maintained high tariff barriers on imports from most of these countries and also restricted their exports. However, since the disintegration of the Soviet Union and the collapse of communism, trade between the United States and Central and Eastern Europe has expanded substantially.

The countries that made the transition from communist to market economies quickly have recorded positive growth for several years—those that did not continue to struggle. Among the nations that have enjoyed several years of positive economic growth are the member countries of the Central European Free Trade Association: Hungary, the Czech Republic, Poland, Slovenia, and Slovakia.

U.S. exports to Central and Eastern Europe and Russia will increase, as will U.S. investment in these countries, as demand for capital goods and technology opens new markets for U.S. products. There already has been a substantial expansion in trade between the United States and the Czech Republic, Slovakia, Hungary, and Poland. Table 3.1 shows the growth rates from 2010 to 2013 for most regions of the world.

Exports and the U.S. Economy In 2008, U.S. exports supported more than 10.3 million full- and part-time jobs during a historic time, when exports as a percentage of GDP reached the highest levels since 1916. The new record, 13.8 percent of GDP in 2011, shows that U.S. businesses have great opportunities in the global marketplace.

TABLE 3.1 Global Growth Is Picking Up Gradually

Growth has been led by developing countries and emerging markets.

		Annual Percent Change		
	2010	2011	Projected 2012	Projected 2013
World	5.2	3.8	3.3	3.9
United States	3.0	1.8	1.8	2.2
Euro area	1.9	1.6	−0.5	0.8
United Kingdom	2.1	0.9	0.6	2.0
Japan	4.4	−0.9	1.7	1.8
Canada	3.2	2.3	1.7	2.0
Other advanced economies	5.8	3.3	2.6	3.4
Newly industrialized Asian economies	8.4	4.2	3.3	4.1
Developing countries and emerging markets	7.3	6.2	5.4	5.9
Developing Asia	9.5	7.9	7.3	7.8
Commonwealth of Independent States	4.6	4.5	3.7	3.8
Middle East and North Africa	4.3	3.1	3.2	3.6
Latin America and the Caribbean	6.1	4.6	3.6	3.9

Source: *International Monetary Fund: World Economic Outlook* by International Monetary Fund. Copyright 2012 by International Monetary Fund. Reproduced with permission of International Monetary Fund via Copyright Clearance Center. www.imf.org/external/pubs/ft/weo/2012/update/01/index.htm (accessed March 10, 2012).

TABLE 3.2	Value of U.S. Merchandise Exports and Imports, 2011		
Rank/Trading Partner	**Exports ($ billions)**	**Rank/Trading Partner**	**Imports ($ billions)**
1) Canada	280.9	1) China	399.3
2) Mexico	197.5	2) Canada	316.5
3) China	103.9	3) Mexico	263.1
4) Japan	66.2	4) Japan	128.8
5) United Kingdom	55.9	5) Germany	98.4
6) Germany	49.1	6) South Korea	56.6
7) South Korea	43.5	7) United Kingdom	51.5
8) Brazil	42.9	8) Saudi Arabia	47.5
9) Netherlands	42.8	9) Venezuela	43.3
10) Hong Kong	36.5	10) Taiwan	41.3

Source: U.S. Department of Commerce, International Trade Administration, http://trade.gov/mas/ian/build/group/public/@tg_ian/documents/webcontent/tg_ian_003364.pdf (accessed March 9, 2012).

Even though the global economic crisis caused the number of jobs supported by exports to decline sharply to 8.5 million in 2009, globalization represents a huge opportunity for all countries—rich or poor. Indeed, in 2011, for the first time, the U.S. exports exceeded $2.1 trillion and supported 9.7 million jobs, an increase of $1.2 million since 2009.[6] The 15-fold increase in trade volume over the past 60 years has been one of the most important factors in the rise of living standards around the world. During this time, exports have become increasingly important to the U.S. economy. Exports as a percentage of U.S. GDP have increased steadily since 1985, except in the 2001 and 2008 recessions. Our exports to developing and newly industrialized countries are on the rise. Table 3.2 shows the value of U.S. merchandise exports to, and imports from, each of the nation's ten major trading partners. Note that Canada and Mexico are our best partners for our exports; China and Canada, for imports.

Figure 3.3 shows the U.S. goods export and import shares in 2011. Major U.S. exports and imports are manufactured goods, agricultural products, and mineral fuels.

FIGURE 3.3	U.S. Goods Export and Import Shares in 2011

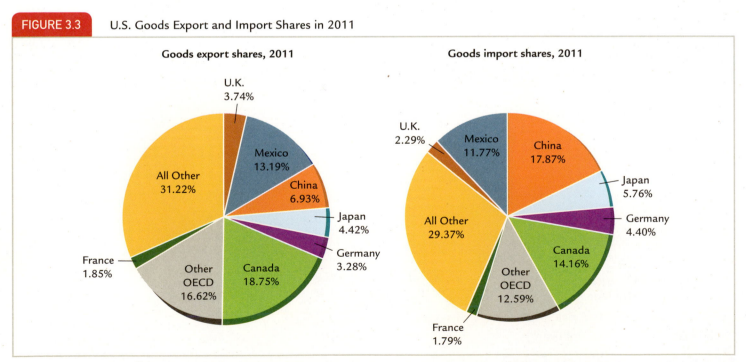

Source: Federal Reserve Bank of St. Louis, *National Economic Trends*, March 2012, 18.

INTERNATIONAL TRADE AGREEMENTS

4 Discuss international trade agreements and international economic organizations working to foster trade.

The General Agreement on Tariffs and Trade and the World Trade Organization

At the end of World War II, the United States and 22 other nations organized the body that came to be known as GATT. The **General Agreement on Tariffs and Trade (GATT)** was an international organization of 153 nations dedicated to reducing or eliminating tariffs and other barriers to world trade. These 153 nations accounted for more than 97 percent of the world's merchandise trade (see Figure 3.4). GATT, headquartered in Geneva, Switzerland, provided a forum for tariff negotiations and a means for settling international trade disputes and problems. Most-favored-nation status (MFN) was the famous principle of GATT. It meant that each GATT member nation was to be treated equally by all contracting nations. Therefore, MFN ensured that any tariff reductions or other trade concessions were extended automatically to all GATT members. From 1947 to 1994, the body sponsored eight rounds of negotiations to reduce trade restrictions. Three of the most fruitful were the Kennedy Round, the Tokyo Round, and the Uruguay Round.

The Kennedy Round (1964–1967) In 1962, the United States Congress passed the Trade Expansion Act. This law gave President John F. Kennedy the authority to negotiate reciprocal trade agreements that could reduce U.S. tariffs by as much as 50 percent. Armed with this authority, which was granted for a period of five years, President Kennedy called for a round of negotiations through GATT.

These negotiations, which began in 1964, have since become known as the Kennedy Round. They were aimed at reducing tariffs and other barriers to trade in

---

FIGURE 3.4 WTO Members Share in World Merchandise Trade, 2010

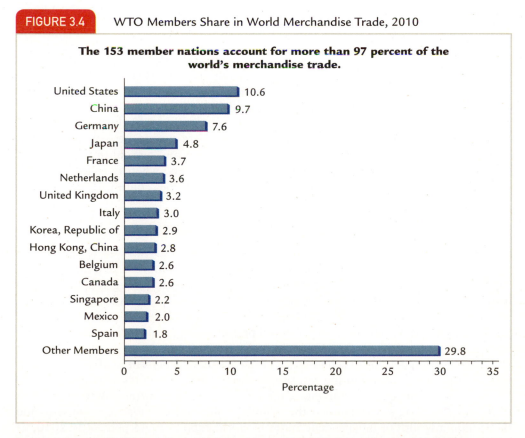

General Agreement on Tariffs and Trade (GATT) an international organization of 153 nations dedicated to reducing or eliminating tariffs and other barriers to world trade

Source: www.wto.org/english/res_e/Statis_e/its2011_e/charts_e/chart07.xls (accessed on March 7, 2012).

both industrial and agricultural products. The participants succeeded in reducing tariffs on these products by an average of more than 35 percent. However, they were less successful in removing other types of trade barriers.

The Tokyo Round (1973–1979) In 1973, representatives of approximately 100 nations gathered in Tokyo for another round of GATT negotiations. The *Tokyo Round* was completed in 1979. The participants negotiated tariff cuts of 30 to 35 percent, which were to be implemented over an eight-year period. In addition, they were able to remove or ease such nontariff barriers as import quotas, unrealistic quality standards for imports, and unnecessary red tape in customs procedures.

The Uruguay Round (1986–1993) In 1986, the *Uruguay Round* was launched to extend trade liberalization and widen the GATT treaty to include textiles, agricultural products, business services, and intellectual-property rights. This most ambitious and comprehensive global commercial agreement in history concluded overall negotiations on December 15, 1993, with delegations on hand from 109 nations. The agreement included provisions to lower tariffs by greater than one-third, to reform trade in agricultural goods, to write new rules of trade for intellectual property and services, and to strengthen the dispute-settlement process. These reforms were expected to expand the world economy by an estimated $200 billion annually.

The Uruguay Round also created the **World Trade Organization (WTO)** on January 1, 1995. The WTO was established by GATT to oversee the provisions of the Uruguay Round and resolve any resulting trade disputes. Membership in the WTO obliges 153 member nations to observe GATT rules. The WTO has judicial powers to mediate among members disputing the new rules. It incorporates trade in goods, services, and ideas and exerts more binding authority than GATT. Its main function is to ensure that trade flows as smoothly, predictably, and freely as possible.

The Doha Round (2001) On November 14, 2001, in Doha, Qatar, the WTO members agreed to further reduce trade barriers through multilateral trade negotiations over the next three years. This new round of negotiations focuses on industrial tariffs and nontariff barriers, agriculture, services, and easing trade rules. U.S. exporters of industrial and agricultural goods and services should have improved access to overseas markets. The Doha Round has set the stage for WTO members to take an important step toward significant new multilateral trade liberalization. It is a difficult task, but the rewards—lower tariffs, more choices for consumers, and further integration of developing countries into the world trading system—are sure to be worth the effort. Some experts suggest that U.S. exporters of industrial and agricultural goods and services should have improved access to overseas markets, whereas others disagree. Negotiations between the developed and developing countries continued in 2012.

World Trade and the Global Economic Crisis

After the sharpest decline in more than 72 years, world trade was set to rebound in 2010 by growing at 9.5 percent, according to the WTO economists. In a 2012 speech, WTO Director-General Pascal Lamy stated, "The multilateral trading system has been instrumental in maintaining trade openness during the crisis, thereby avoiding even worse outcomes. Members must remain vigilant. This is not the time for go-it-alone measures. This is the time to strengthen and preserve the global trading system so that it keeps performing this vital function in the future."[7]

Exports from developed economies increased nearly 13 percent in 2010, compared to a 16.5 percent increase in the rest of the world. China's exports increased in 2010 by a massive 28 percent. Furthermore, the higher prices and extraordinary growth of trade in developing Asia increased the combined share of developing economies and the Commonwealth of Independent States in world exports to 45 percent in 2010, its highest ever.

World Trade Organization (WTO) powerful successor to GATT that incorporates trade in goods, services, and ideas

FIGURE 3.5 | The Evolving European Union

The Evolving European Union: The European Union is now an economic force, with a collective economy larger than that of the United States or Japan.

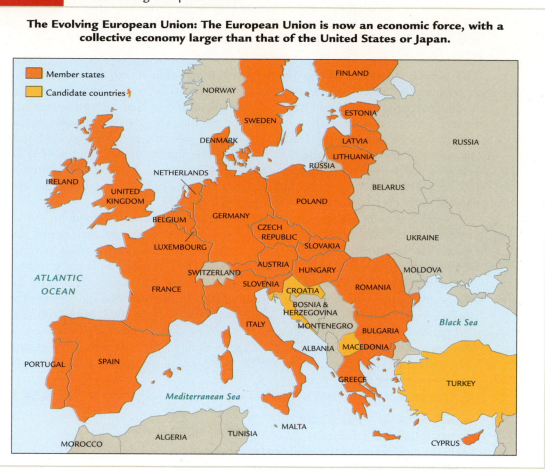

Source: http://europa.eu/abc/european_countries/index_en.htm (accessed March 14, 2012).

International Economic Organizations Working to Foster Trade

The primary objective of the WTO is to remove barriers to trade on a worldwide basis. On a smaller scale, an **economic community** is an organization of nations formed to promote the free movement of resources and products among its members and to create common economic policies. A number of economic communities now exist.

The European Union The European Union (EU), also known as the European Economic Community and the Common Market, was formed in 1957 by six countries—France, the Federal Republic of Germany, Italy, Belgium, the Netherlands, and Luxembourg. Its objective was freely conducted commerce among these nations and others that might later join. As shown in Figure 3.5, many more nations have joined the EU since then.

On January 1, 2007, the 25 nations of the EU became the EU27 as Bulgaria and Romania became new members. The EU, with a population of nearly half a billion, is now an economic force with a collective economy larger than much of the United States or Japan.

In celebrating the EU's 50th anniversary in 2007, the president of the European Commission, Jose Manuel Durao Barraso, declared, "Let us first recognize 50 years of achievement. Peace, liberty, and prosperity, beyond the dreams of even the most optimistic founding fathers of Europe. In 1957, 15 of our 27 members were either under dictatorship or were not allowed to exist as independent countries. Now we are all prospering democracies. The EU of today is around 50 times more prosperous and with three times the population of the EU of 1957."

economic community an organization of nations formed to promote the free movement of resources and products among its members and to create common economic policies

Since January 2002, 15 member nations of the EU have been participating in the new common currency, the euro. The euro is the single currency of the European Monetary Union nations. However, three EU members, Denmark, the United Kingdom, and Sweden, still maintain their own currencies.

The North American Free Trade Agreement

The North American Free Trade Agreement (NAFTA) joined the United States with its first- and second-largest export trading partners, Canada and Mexico. Implementation of NAFTA on January 1, 1994, created a market of more than 462 million people. This market consists of Canada (population 34 million), the United States (313 million), and Mexico (115 million). According to the Office of the U.S. Trade Representative, after 18 years, NAFTA has achieved its core goals of expanding trade and investment between the United States, Canada, and Mexico. For example, from 1993 to 2011, trade among the NAFTA nations more than tripled, from $297 billion to $1,058 billion.

NAFTA is built on the Canadian Free Trade Agreement, signed by the United States and Canada in 1989, and on the substantial trade and investment reforms undertaken by Mexico since the mid-1980s. Initiated by the Mexican government, formal negotiations on NAFTA began in June 1991 among the three governments. The support of NAFTA by President Bill Clinton, past U.S. Presidents Ronald Reagan and Jimmy Carter, and Nobel Prize–winning economists provided the impetus for U.S. congressional ratification of NAFTA in November 1993. By 2008, NAFTA had gradually eliminated all tariffs and quotas on goods produced and traded among Canada, Mexico, and the United States to provide for a totally free-trade area. Chile is expected to become the fourth member of NAFTA, but political forces may delay its entry into the agreement for several years.

However, NAFTA is not without its critics. Critics maintain that NAFTA:

- has not achieved its goals
- has resulted in job losses
- hurts workers by eroding labor standards and lowering wages
- undermines national sovereignty and independence
- does nothing to help the environment, and
- hurts the agricultural sector

The proponents of NAFTA call the agreement a remarkable economic success story for all three partners. They maintain that NAFTA:

- has contributed to significant increases in trade and investment
- has benefited companies in all three countries
- has resulted in increased sales, new partnerships, and new opportunities
- has created high-paying export-related jobs, and
- better prices and selection in consumer goods

The Central American Free Trade Agreement

The Central American Free Trade Agreement (CAFTA) was created in 2003 by the United States and four Central American countries—El Salvador, Guatemala, Honduras, and Nicaragua. The CAFTA became CAFTA-DR when the Dominican Republic joined the group in 2007. On January 1, 2009, Costa Rica joined CAFTA-DR as the sixth member. CAFTA-DR creates the third-largest U.S. export market in Latin America, behind only Mexico and Brazil.

The Association of Southeast Asian Nations

The Association of Southeast Asian Nations, with headquarters in Jakarta, Indonesia, was established in 1967 to promote political, economic, and social cooperation among its seven member countries: Indonesia, Malaysia, the Philippines, Singapore, Thailand, Brunei, and Vietnam. With the three new members, Cambodia, Laos, and Myanmar, this region of 600 million people is already our fifth-largest trading partner.

The Commonwealth of Independent States The Commonwealth of Independent States was established in December 1991 by the newly independent states as an association of 11 republics of the former Soviet Union.

Trans-Pacific Partnership (TPP) On November 12, 2011, the leaders of the nine countries—Australia, Brunei Darussalam, Chile, Malaysia, New Zealand, Peru, Singapore, Vietnam, and the United States—formed the Trans-Pacific Partnership. This partnership will boost economies of the member countries, lower barriers to trade and investment, increase exports, and create more jobs. Together, these eight economies would be America's fifth-largest trading partner. According to President Obama, "We already do more than $200 billion in trade with them every year, and with nearly 500 million consumers between us, there's so much more that we can do together." The Asia-Pacific region is one of the fastest growing areas in the world and TPP will open more markets to American businesses and exports.[8]

The Common Market of the Southern Cone (MERCOSUR) The Common Market of the Southern Cone (MERCOSUR) was established in 1991 under the Treaty of Asuncion to unite Argentina, Brazil, Paraguay, and Uruguay as a free-trade alliance; Colombia, Ecuador, Peru, Bolivia, and Chile joined later as associates. The alliance represents more than 267 million consumers—67 percent of South America's population, making it the third-largest trading block behind NAFTA and the EU. Like NAFTA, MERCOSUR promotes "the free circulation of goods, services and production factors among the countries" and established a common external tariff and commercial policy.

The Organization of Petroleum Exporting Countries The Organization of Petroleum Exporting Countries was founded in 1960 in response to reductions in the prices that oil companies were willing to pay for crude oil. The organization was conceived as a collective bargaining unit to provide oil-producing nations with some control over oil prices.

© PONSULAK KUNSUB/SHUTTERSTOCK

Sustaining the PLANET

2degrees: A Global Community

A new organization called 2degrees is now the world's largest community for sustainable business with around 30,000 professional members from over 90 countries. The online platform helps members (individual professionals and organizations) to improve their resource efficiency by sharing best practices and enabling them to solve common business problems together.

2degrees features webinars hosted by top experts; working groups on topics such as energy management, renewable power, greener health care and waste management; white papers; blogs; and the latest news on sustainability. Explore the site to learn more about how this organization is helping to make business more sustainable worldwide.

WWW.2DEGREESNETWORK.COM

www.2degreesnetwork.com

METHODS OF ENTERING INTERNATIONAL BUSINESS

A firm that has decided to enter international markets can do so in several ways. We will discuss several different methods. These different approaches require varying degrees of involvement in international business. Typically, a firm begins its international operations at the simplest level. Then, depending on its goals, it may progress to higher levels of involvement.

⑤ Define the methods by which a firm can organize for and enter into international markets.

Licensing

Licensing is a contractual agreement in which one firm permits another to produce and market its product and use its brand name in return for a royalty or other compensation. For example, Yoplait yogurt is a French yogurt licensed for production in the United States. The Yoplait brand maintains an appealing French image, and in return, the U.S. producer pays the French firm a percentage of its income from sales of the product.

licensing a contractual agreement in which one firm permits another to produce and market its product and use its brand name in return for a royalty or other compensation

Celebrating OPEC's 50th anniversary. Secretary General of OPEC Abdalla Salem El-Badri and Iranian Oil Minister Masoud Mir Kazemi attend a ceremony to celebrate the 50th anniversary of the founding of OPEC, in Tehran, Iran, on April 19th, 2011.

Licensing is especially advantageous for small manufacturers wanting to launch a well-known domestic brand internationally. For example, all Spalding sporting products are licensed worldwide. The licensor, the Questor Corporation, owns the Spalding name but produces no goods itself. Licensing thus provides a simple method for expanding into a foreign market with virtually no investment. On the other hand, if the licensee does not maintain the licensor's product standards, the product's image may be damaged. Another possible disadvantage is that a licensing arrangement may not provide the original producer with any foreign marketing experience.

Exporting

A firm also may manufacture its products in its home country and export them for sale in foreign markets. As with licensing, exporting can be a relatively low-risk method of entering foreign markets. Unlike licensing, however, it is not a simple method; it opens up several levels of involvement to the exporting firm.

At the most basic level, the exporting firm may sell its products outright to an *export–import merchant*, which is essentially a merchant wholesaler. The merchant assumes all the risks of product ownership, distribution, and sale. It may even purchase the goods in the producer's home country and assume responsibility for exporting the goods. An important and practical issue for domestic firms dealing with foreign customers is securing payment. This is a two-sided issue that reflects the mutual concern rightly felt by both parties to the trade deal: The exporter would like to be paid before shipping the merchandise, whereas the importer obviously would prefer to know that it has received the shipment before releasing any funds. Neither side wants to take the risk of fulfilling its part of the deal only to discover later that the other side has not. The result would lead to legal costs and complex, lengthy dealings that would waste everyone's resources. This mutual level of mistrust, in fact, makes good business sense and has been around since the beginning of trade centuries ago. The solution then was the same as it still is today—for both parties to use a mutually trusted go-between who can ensure that the payment is held until the merchandise is in fact delivered according to the terms of the trade contract. The go-between representatives employed by the importer and exporter are still, as they were in the past, the local domestic banks involved in international business.

Exporting to International Markets American companies may manufacture their products in the United States and export them for sale in foreign markets. Exporting can be a relatively low-risk method of entering foreign markets.

Here is a simplified version of how it works. After signing contracts detailing the merchandise sold and terms for its delivery, an importer will ask its local bank to issue a **letter of credit** for the amount of money needed to pay for the merchandise. The letter of credit is issued "in favor of the exporter," meaning that the funds are tied specifically to the trade contract involved. The importer's bank forwards the letter of credit to the exporter's bank, which also normally deals in international transactions. The exporter's bank then notifies the exporter that a letter of credit has been received in its name, and the exporter can go ahead with the shipment. The carrier transporting the merchandise provides the exporter with evidence of the shipment in a document called a **bill of lading**. The exporter signs over title to the merchandise (now in transit) to its bank by delivering signed copies of the bill of lading and the letter of credit.

In exchange, the exporter issues a **draft** from the bank, which orders the importer's bank to pay for the merchandise. The draft, bill of lading, and letter of credit are sent from the exporter's bank to the importer's bank. Acceptance by the importer's bank leads to return of the draft and its sale by the exporter to its bank, meaning that the exporter receives cash and the bank assumes the risk of collecting the funds from the

letter of credit issued by a bank on request of an importer stating that the bank will pay an amount of money to a stated beneficiary

bill of lading document issued by a transport carrier to an exporter to prove that merchandise has been shipped

draft issued by the exporter's bank, ordering the importer's bank to pay for the merchandise, thus guaranteeing payment once accepted by the importer's bank

foreign bank. The importer is obliged to pay its bank on delivery of the merchandise, and the deal is complete.

In most cases, the letter of credit is part of a lending arrangement between the importer and its bank. Of course, both banks earn fees for issuing letters of credit and drafts and for handling the import–export services for their clients. Furthermore, the process incorporates the fact that both importer and exporter will have different local currencies and might even negotiate their trade in a third currency. The banks look after all the necessary exchanges. For example, the vast majority of international business is negotiated in U.S. dollars, even though the trade may be between countries other than the United States. Thus, although the importer may end up paying for the merchandise in its local currency and the exporter may receive payment in another local currency, the banks involved will exchange all necessary foreign funds in order to allow the deal to take place.

Alternatively, the exporting firm may ship its products to an *export–import agent*, which arranges the sale of the products to foreign intermediaries for a commission or fee. The agent is an independent firm—like other agents—that sells and may perform other marketing functions for the exporter. The exporter, however, retains title to the products during shipment and until they are sold.

An exporting firm also may establish its own *sales offices*, or *branches*, in foreign countries. These installations are international extensions of the firm's distribution system. They represent a deeper involvement in international business than the other exporting techniques we have discussed—and thus they carry a greater risk. The exporting firm maintains control over sales, and it gains both experience in and knowledge of foreign markets. Eventually, the firm also may develop its own sales force to operate in conjunction with foreign sales offices.

Exporting to international markets. American companies may manufacture their products in the United States and export them for sale in foreign markets. Exporting can be a relatively risk-free method of entering foreign markets.

Joint Ventures

A *joint venture* is a partnership formed to achieve a specific goal or to operate for a specific period of time. A joint venture with an established firm in a foreign country provides immediate market knowledge and access, reduced risk, and control over product attributes. However, joint-venture agreements established across national borders can become extremely complex. As a result, joint-venture agreements generally require a very high level of commitment from all the parties involved.

A joint venture may be used to produce and market an existing product in a foreign nation or to develop an entirely new product. Recently, for example, Archer Daniels Midland Company (ADM), one of the world's leading food processors, entered into a joint venture with Gruma SA, Mexico's largest corn flour and tortilla company. Besides a 22 percent stake in Gruma, ADM also received stakes in other joint ventures operated by Gruma. One of them will combine both companies' U.S. corn flour operations, which account for about 25 percent of the U.S. market. ADM also has a 40 percent stake in a Mexican wheat flour mill. ADM's joint venture increased its participation in the growing Mexican economy, where ADM already produces corn syrup, fructose, starch, and wheat flour.

Totally Owned Facilities

At a still deeper level of involvement in international business, a firm may develop *totally owned facilities,* that is, its own production and marketing facilities in one or more foreign nations. This *direct investment* provides complete control over operations, but it carries a greater risk than the joint venture. The firm is really establishing a subsidiary in a foreign country. Most firms do so only after they have acquired some knowledge of the host country's markets.

Going for SUCCESS

Services Team Up to Enter India

A growing number of U.S.-based service firms are expanding into India by forming joint ventures with local firms. Both partners bring specific strengths to the joint venture, not just their brands but also the Indian firm's in-depth knowledge of customers and the U.S. firm's service concepts.

For example, Cigna, which markets health insurance, has teamed up with TTK Group to sell insurance policies in India. TTK Group operates 1,500 retail stores and sells a variety of goods and services, including insurance. The joint venture will enable Cigna to reach consumers without creating a separate network of insurance agents—and TTK Group gains another product line to diversify its offerings.

CBS and its partner in India, Reliance Broadcast Networks, recently launched English-language channels to tap into the country's burgeoning market for television entertainment. CBS provides the content (including hit programs such as CSI) and Reliance provides its expertise in distribution and advertising sales for this joint venture, known as Big CBS.

Dunkin' Donuts has a joint venture with Jubilant Foodworks to open shops featuring an all-day menu of coffee, donuts, and other foods adapted to Indian tastes. In this partnership, "Dunkin' provides flexibility in localizing recipes, and we have strengths in food and culinary which we intend to leverage," explains Jubilant's chairman.

Sources: Based on information in Vikas Bajaj, "Cigna in Deal to Sell Health Insurance in India," *New York Times*, November 21, 2011, www.nytimes.com; Sanjeev Choudhary, "Dunkin' Donuts to Enter India with Jubilant Foodworks," *Reuters*, February 25, 2011, www.reuters.com; Nyay Bhushan, "Reliance, RTL Group Plan Joint Venture for English, Local-Language Channels," *Hollywood Reporter*, March 11, 2011, www.hollywoodreporter.com.

Direct investment may take either of two forms. In the first, the firm builds or purchases manufacturing and other facilities in the foreign country. It uses these facilities to produce its own established products and to market them in that country and perhaps in neighboring countries. Firms such as General Motors, Union Carbide, and Colgate-Palmolive are multinational companies with worldwide manufacturing facilities. Colgate-Palmolive factories are becoming *Eurofactories*, supplying neighboring countries as well as their own local markets.

A second form of direct investment in international business is the purchase of an existing firm in a foreign country under an arrangement that allows it to operate independently of the parent company. When Sony Corporation (a Japanese firm) decided to enter the motion picture business in the United States, it chose to purchase Columbia Pictures Entertainment, Inc., rather than start a new motion picture studio from scratch.

strategic alliance a partnership formed to create competitive advantage on a worldwide basis

Strategic alliance for mutual benefits. Chairman and Managing Director of Air India, V. Thulasidas, and Chairman of Lufthansa AG, Wolfgang Mayrhuber, sign a strategic alliance agreement in Mumbai, India. The alliance improves their market leadership position on India–Europe–U.S. routes.

© REUTERS/LANDOV

Strategic Alliances

A **strategic alliance**, the newest form of international business structure, is a partnership formed to create competitive advantage on a worldwide basis. Strategic alliances are very similar to joint ventures. The number of strategic alliances is growing at an estimated rate of about 20 percent per year. In fact, in the automobile and computer industries, strategic alliances are becoming the predominant means of competing. International competition is so fierce and the costs of competing on a global basis are so high that few firms have all the resources needed to do it alone. Thus, individual firms that lack the internal resources essential for international success may seek to collaborate with other companies.

An example of such an alliance is the New United Motor Manufacturing, Inc. (NUMMI), formed by Toyota and General Motors to make automobiles of both firms. This enterprise united the quality engineering of Japanese cars with the marketing expertise and market access of General Motors.

Trading Companies

A **trading company** provides a link between buyers and sellers in different countries. A trading company, as its name implies, is not involved in manufacturing or owning assets related to manufacturing. It buys products in one country at the lowest price consistent with quality and sells to buyers in another country. An important function of trading companies is taking title to products and performing all the activities necessary to move the products from the domestic country to a foreign country. For example, large grain-trading companies operating out of home offices both in the United States and overseas control a major portion of the world's trade in basic food commodities. These trading companies sell homogeneous agricultural commodities that can be stored and moved rapidly in response to market conditions.

Countertrade

In the early 1990s, many developing nations had major restrictions on converting domestic currency into foreign currency. Therefore, exporters had to resort to barter agreements with importers. **Countertrade** is essentially an international barter transaction in which goods and services are exchanged for different goods and services. Examples include Saudi Arabia's purchase of ten 747 jets from Boeing with payment in crude oil and Philip Morris's sale of cigarettes to Russia in return for chemicals used to make fertilizers.

Multinational Firms

A **multinational enterprise** is a firm that operates on a worldwide scale without ties to any specific nation or region. The multinational firm represents the highest level of involvement in international business. It is equally "at home" in most countries of the world. In fact, as far as the operations of the multinational enterprise are concerned, national boundaries exist only on maps. It is, however, organized under the laws of its home country.

Table 3.3 shows the ten largest foreign and U.S. public multinational companies; the ranking is based on a composite score reflecting each company's best three out of four rankings for sales, profits, assets, and market value. Table 3.4 describes steps in entering international markets.

trading company provides a link between buyers and sellers in different countries

countertrade an international barter transaction

multinational enterprise a firm that operates on a worldwide scale without ties to any specific nation or region

TABLE 3.3	The Ten Largest Foreign and U.S. Multinational Corporations			
2011 Rank	Company	Business	Country	Revenue ($ millions)
1	Walmart Stores	General merchandiser	United States	421,849
2	Royal Dutch Shell	Energy	Netherlands/ United Kingdom	378,152
3	ExxonMobil	Energy	United States	354,674
4	BP	Energy	United Kingdom	308,928
5	Sinopec Group	Energy	China	273,422
6	China Natural Petroleum	Energy	China	240,192
7	State Grid	Power grids	China	226,294
8	Toyota Motor	Automobiles	Japan	221,760
9	Japan Post Holdings	Financial services	Japan	203,958
10	Chevron	Energy	United States	196,337

Source: From *Fortune Magazine*, "Global 500 Our Annual Ranking of the World's Largest Corporations," July 25, 2011, © 2011 Time Inc. Used under license. Fortune and Time Inc. are not affiliated with, and do not endorse products or services of, Licensee.

TABLE 3.4 Steps in Entering International Markets

Step	Activity	Marketing Tasks
1	Identify exportable products.	Identify key selling features. Identify needs that they satisfy. Identify the selling constraints that are imposed.
2	Identify key foreign markets for the products.	Determine who the customers are. Pinpoint what and when they will buy. Do market research. Establish priority, or "target," countries.
3	Analyze how to sell in each priority market (methods will be affected by product characteristics and unique features of country/market).	Locate available government and private-sector resources. Determine service and backup sales requirements.
4	Set export prices and payment terms, methods, and techniques.	Establish methods of export pricing. Establish sales terms, quotations, invoices, and conditions of sale. Determine methods of international payments, secured and unsecured.
5	Estimate resource requirements and returns.	Estimate financial requirements. Estimate human resources requirements (full- or part-time export department or operation?). Estimate plant production capacity. Determine necessary product adaptations.
6	Establish overseas distribution network.	Determine distribution agreement and other key marketing decisions (price, repair policies, returns, territory, performance, and termination). Know your customer (use U.S. Department of Commerce international marketing services).
7	Determine shipping, traffic, and documentation procedures and requirements.	Determine methods of shipment (air or ocean freight, truck, rail). Finalize containerization. Obtain validated export license. Follow export-administration documentation procedures.
8	Promote, sell, and be paid.	Use international media, communications, advertising, trade shows, and exhibitions. Determine the need for overseas travel (when, where, and how often?). Initiate customer follow-up procedures.
9	Continuously analyze current marketing, economic, and political situations.	Recognize changing factors influencing marketing strategies. Constantly re-evaluate.

Source: U.S. Department of Commerce, International Trade Administration, Washington, DC.

According to the chairman of the board of Dow Chemical Company, a multi-national firm of U.S. origin, "The emergence of a world economy and of the multinational corporation has been accomplished hand in hand." He sees multinational enterprises moving toward what he calls the "anational company," a firm that has no nationality but belongs to all countries. In recognition of this movement, there already have been international conferences devoted to the question of how such enterprises would be controlled.

Describe the various sources of export assistance.

SOURCES OF EXPORT ASSISTANCE

In August 2010, President Obama announced the *National Export Initiative* (NEI) to revitalize U.S. exports. Under the NEI, many federal agencies assist U.S. firms in developing export-promotion programs. The export services and programs of these

TABLE 3.5	U.S. Government Export Assistance Programs	
1	U.S. Export Assistance Centers, www.sba.gov/oit/export/useac.html	Provides assistance in export marketing and trade finance
2	International Trade Administration, www.ita.doc.gov/	Offers assistance and information to exporters through its domestic and overseas commercial officers
3	U.S. and Foreign Commercial Services, www.export.gov/	Helps U.S. firms compete more effectively in the global marketplace and provides information on foreign markets
4	Advocacy Center, www.ita.doc.gov/advocacy	Facilitates advocacy to assist U.S. firms competing for major projects and procurements worldwide
5	Trade Information Center, www.ita.doc.gov/td/tic/	Provides U.S. companies information on federal programs and activities that support U.S. exports
6	STAT-USA/Internet, www.stat-usa.gov/	Offers a comprehensive collection of business, economic, and trade information on the Web
7	Small Business Administration, www.sba.gov/oit/	Publishes many helpful guides to assist small- and medium-sized companies
8	National Trade Data Bank, www.stat-usa.gov/tradtest.nsf	Provides international economic and export-promotion information supplied by more than 20 U.S. agencies

© CENGAGE LEARNING 2014

agencies can help American firms to compete in foreign markets and create new jobs in the United States. For example, in 2011 the International Trade Administration coordinated 77 trade missions to 38 countries. More than 1,120 companies secured over $1.25 billion in export sales during these missions. Table 3.5 provides an overview of selected export assistance programs.

These and other sources of export information enhance the business opportunities of U.S. firms seeking to enter expanding foreign markets. Another vital energy factor is financing.

FINANCING INTERNATIONAL BUSINESS

 7 Identify the institutions that help firms and nations finance international business.

International trade compounds the concerns of financial managers. Currency exchange rates, tariffs and foreign exchange controls, and the tax structures of host nations all affect international operations and the flow of cash. In addition, financial managers must be concerned both with the financing of their international operations and with the means available to their customers to finance purchases.

Fortunately, along with business in general, a number of large banks have become international in scope. Many have established branches in major cities around the world. Thus, like firms in other industries, they are able to provide their services where and when they are needed. In addition, financial assistance is available from U.S. government and international sources.

Several of today's international financial organizations were founded many years ago to facilitate free trade and the exchange of currencies among nations. Some, such as the Inter-American Development Bank, are supported internationally and focus on developing countries. Others, such as the Export-Import Bank, are operated by one country but provide international financing.

The Export-Import Bank of the United States

The **Export-Import Bank of the United States**, created in 1934, is an independent agency of the U.S. government whose function is to assist in financing the exports of American firms. *Ex-Im Bank*, as it is commonly called, extends and guarantees credit to overseas buyers of American goods and services and guarantees short-term financing for exports. It also cooperates with commercial banks in helping American exporters to offer credit to their overseas customers.

Export-Import Bank of the United States an independent agency of the U.S. government whose function is to assist in financing the exports of American firms

If you're interested in doing business outside the United States, you'll need to know something about international finance. Currency exchange rates will affect anything you buy or sell, for example, and you'll probably want to deal with a bank experienced in global business.

According to Fred P. Hochberg, chairman and president of Ex-Im Bank, "Working with private lenders we are helping U.S. exporters put Americans to work producing the high quality goods and services that foreign buyers prefer. As part of President Obama's National Export Initiative, Ex-Im Bank's export financing is contributing to the goal of doubling of U.S. exports within the next five years."

Multilateral Development Banks

A **multilateral development bank (MDB)** is an internationally supported bank that provides loans to developing countries to help them grow. The most familiar is the World Bank, a cooperative of 187 member countries, which operates worldwide. Established in 1944 and headquartered in Washington, DC, the bank provides low-interest loans, interest-free credits, and grants to developing countries. The loans and grants help these countries to:

- supply safe drinking water
- build schools and train teachers
- increase agricultural productivity
- expand citizens' access to markets, jobs, and housing
- improve health care and access to water and sanitation
- manage forests and other natural resources
- build and maintain roads, railways, and ports, and
- reduce air pollution and protect the environment.[9]

Four other MDBs operate primarily in Central and South America, Asia, Africa, and Eastern and Central Europe. All five are supported by the industrialized nations, including the United States.

The Inter-American Development Bank The Inter-American Development Bank (IDB), the oldest and largest regional bank, was created in 1959 by 19 Latin American countries and the United States. The bank, which is headquartered in Washington, DC, makes loans and provides technical advice and assistance to countries. Today, the IDB is owned by 48 member states.

The Asian Development Bank With 67 member nations, the Asian Development Bank (ADB), created in 1966 and headquartered in the Philippines, promotes economic and social progress in Asian and Pacific regions. The U.S. government is the second-largest contributor to the ADB's capital, after Japan.

The African Development Bank The African Development Bank (AFDB), also known as *Banque Africaines de Development*, was established in 1964 with headquarters in Abidjan, Ivory Coast. Its members include 53 African and 24 non-African countries from the Americas, Europe, and Asia. The AFDB's goal is to foster the economic and social development of its African members. The bank pursues this goal through loans, research, technical assistance, and the development of trade programs.

European Bank for Reconstruction and Development Established in 1991 to encourage reconstruction and development in the Eastern and Central European countries, the London-based *European Bank for Reconstruction and Development* is owned by 61 countries and 2 intergovernmental institutions. Its loans are geared toward developing market-oriented economies and promoting private enterprise.

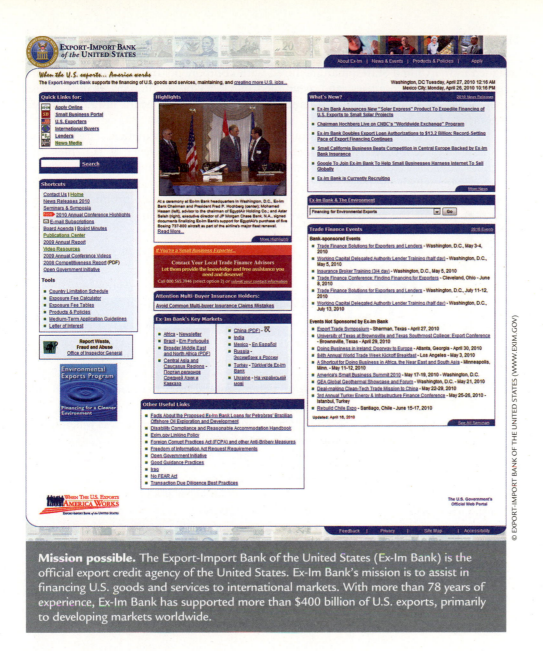

Mission possible. The Export-Import Bank of the United States (Ex-Im Bank) is the official export credit agency of the United States. Ex-Im Bank's mission is to assist in financing U.S. goods and services to international markets. With more than 78 years of experience, Ex-Im Bank has supported more than $400 billion of U.S. exports, primarily to developing markets worldwide.

The International Monetary Fund

The **International Monetary Fund (IMF)** is an international bank with 188 member nations that makes short-term loans to developing countries experiencing balance-of-payment deficits. This financing is contributed by member nations, and it must be repaid with interest. Loans are provided primarily to fund international trade. Created in 1945 and headquartered in Washington, DC, the bank's main goals are to:

- promote international monetary cooperation,
- facilitate the expansion and balanced growth of international trade,
- promote exchange rate stability,
- assist in establishing a multilateral system of payments, and
- make resources available to members experiencing balance-of-payment difficulties.

The Challenges Ahead

In a 2012 speech at Oxford University, Pascal Lamy, Director-General of the World Trade Organiztion stated, "We live in a world of ever-growing independence and interconnectedness. Our interdependence has grown beyond anyone's imagination.

multilateral development bank (MDB) an internationally supported bank that provides loans to developing countries to help them grow

International Monetary Fund (IMF) an international bank with 188 member nations that makes short-term loans to developing countries experiencing balance-of-payment deficits

The world of today is virtually unrecognizable from the world in which we lived one generation ago." The most striking example of globalization is Apple. Apple's iPod is designed in the United States, manufactured with components from Japan, Korea, and several other Asian countries, and assembled in China by a company from Chinese Taipei. Nowadays, most products are not "Made in the UK" or "Made in France"; they are in fact "Made in the World."[10]

In 2012, the global economic recovery remained sluggish. Financial challenges in some euro-area economies slowed the economic growth. However, WTO rules and principles have assisted governments in keeping markets open and they now provide a platform for which the trade can grow as the global economy improves. According to Mr. Lamy, "We see the light at the end of the tunnel and trade promises to be an important part of the recovery. But we must avoid derailing any economic revival through protectionism."

return to Inside BUSINESS

Volkswagen

If Volkswagen achieves its goal of manufacturing and selling 10 million vehicles yearly by 2018, it will move into first place as the world's largest automaker. With this in mind, Volkswagen is redesigning its vehicles so more parts fit more models, an important consideration for a company with facilities in so many countries. "We're creating a system that enables us to produce vehicles based on this architecture at any factory," explains a Volkswagen executive.

The company's joint ventures in China are also a key advantage in its expansion plans. China has the potential to be Volkswagen's largest market within just a few years because of higher demand from the ever-growing middle class. Volkswagen is already the top-selling foreign car brand in China, and building on that success will only add momentum to the company's global growth.

Questions
1. Can Volkswagen be considered a multinational firm? Explain your answer.
2. Do you agree with Volkswagen's CEO's statement that a car company has to be successful in the United States if it wants to be number one in the industry? Why or why not?

SUMMARY

Looking for Success?
Get Flashcards, Quizzes, Games, Crosswords, and more @ www.cengagebrain.com.

 Explain the economic basis for international business.

International business encompasses all business activities that involve exchanges across national boundaries. International trade is based on specialization, whereby each country produces the goods and services that it can produce more efficiently than any other goods and services. A nation is said to have a comparative advantage relative to these goods. International trade develops when each nation trades its surplus products for those in short supply.

A nation's balance of trade is the difference between the value of its exports and the value of its imports. Its balance of payments is the difference between the flow of money into and out of the nation. Generally, a negative balance of trade is considered unfavorable.

 Discuss the restrictions nations place on international trade, the objectives of these restrictions, and their results.

Despite the benefits of world trade, nations tend to use tariffs and nontariff barriers (import quotas, embargoes, and other restrictions) to limit trade. These restrictions typically are justified as being needed to protect a nation's economy, industries, citizens, or security. They can result in the loss of jobs, higher prices, fewer choices in the marketplace, and the misallocation of resources.

 Outline the extent of international business and the world economic outlook for trade.

World trade is generally increasing. Trade between the United States and other nations is increasing in dollar value but decreasing in terms of our share of the world market. Exports as a percentage of U.S. GDP have increased steadily since 1985, except in the 2001 and 2008 recessions.

 Discuss international trade agreements and international economic organizations working to foster trade.

The General Agreement on Tariffs and Trade (GATT) was formed to dismantle trade barriers and provide an environment in which international business can grow. Today, the World Trade Organization (WTO) and various economic communities carry on this mission. These world economic communities include the European Union, the NAFTA, the CAFTA, the Association of Southeast Asian Nations, the Pacific Rim, the Commonwealth of Independent States, the Caribbean Basin Initiative, the Common Market of the Southern Cone, the Organization of Petroleum Exporting Countries, and the Organization for Economic Cooperation and Development.

 Define the methods by which a firm can organize for and enter into international markets.

A firm can enter international markets in several ways. It may license a foreign firm to produce and market its products. It may export its products and sell them through foreign intermediaries or its own sales organization abroad, or it may sell its exports outright to an export–import merchant. It may enter into a joint venture with a foreign firm. It may establish its own foreign subsidiaries, or it may develop into a multinational enterprise.

Generally, each of these methods represents an increasingly deeper level of involvement in international business, with licensing being the simplest and the development of a multinational corporation the most involved.

 Describe the various sources of export assistance.

Many government and international agencies provide export assistance to U.S. and foreign firms. The export services and programs of the 19 agencies of the U.S. Trade Promotion Coordinating Committee (TPCC) can help U.S. firms to compete in foreign markets and create new jobs in the United States. Sources of export assistance include U.S. Export Assistance Centers, the International Trade Administration, U.S. and Foreign Commercial Services, Export Legal Assistance Network, Advocacy Center, National Trade Data Bank, and other government and international agencies.

 Identify the institutions that help firms and nations finance international business.

The financing of international trade is more complex than that of domestic trade. Institutions such as the Ex-Im Bank and the International Monetary Fund have been established to provide financing and ultimately to increase world trade for American and international firms.

KEY TERMS

You should now be able to define and give an example relevant to each of the following terms:

international business (71)
absolute advantage (71)
comparative advantage (71)
exporting (72)
importing (72)
balance of trade (73)
trade deficit (73)
balance of payments (74)
import duty (tariff) (75)

dumping (75)
nontariff barrier (75)
import quota (75)
embargo (75)
foreign-exchange control (76)
currency devaluation (76)
General Agreement on Tariffs and Trade (GATT) (81)

World Trade Organization (WTO) (82)
economic community (83)
licensing (85)
letter of credit (86)
bill of lading (86)
draft (86)
strategic alliance (88)
trading company (89)

countertrade (89)
multinational enterprise (89)
Export-Import Bank of the United States (91)
multilateral development bank (MDB) (93)
International Monetary Fund (IMF) (93)

REVIEW QUESTIONS

1. Why do firms engage in international trade?
2. What is the difference between an absolute and a comparative advantage in international trade? How are both types of advantages related to the concept of specialization?
3. What is a favorable balance of trade? In what way is it "favorable"?

4. List and briefly describe the principal restrictions that may be applied to a nation's imports.
5. What reasons are generally given for imposing trade restrictions?
6. What are the general effects of import restrictions on trade?

7. Define and describe the major objectives of the WTO and the international economic communities.

8. Which nations are the principal trading partners of the United States? What are the major U.S. imports and exports?

9. The methods of engaging in international business may be categorized as either direct or indirect. How would you classify each of the methods described in this chapter? Why?

10. In what ways is a multinational enterprise different from a large corporation that does business in several countries?

11. List some key sources of export assistance. How can these sources be useful to small business firms?

12. In what ways do the Ex-Im Bank, multilateral development banks, and the IMF enhance international trade?

DISCUSSION QUESTIONS

1. The United States restricts imports but, at the same time, supports the WTO and international banks whose objective is to enhance world trade. As a member of Congress, how would you justify this contradiction to your constituents?

2. What effects might the devaluation of a nation's currency have on its business firms, its consumers, and the debts it owes to other nations?

3. Should imports to the United States be curtailed by, say, 20 percent to eliminate our trade deficit? What might happen if this were done?

4. When should a firm consider expanding from strictly domestic trade to international trade? When should it consider becoming further involved in international trade? What factors might affect the firm's decisions in each case?

5. How can a firm obtain the expertise needed to produce and market its products in, for example, the EU?

Video Case 3.1   Keeping Brazil's Economy Hot

It's been hot in Brazil. No, we're not talking about the country's temperature: We're talking about its economy, which has been growing at a heated pace. In 2010, the country's GDP grew by 7.5 percent. That's a growth rate developed countries such as the United States haven't experienced for years, if not decades. Although Brazil's growth rate slowed considerably in 2011 and 2012 due to the global economic crisis, it has fared better than many other nations. Recently it surpassed the United Kingdom as the sixth-largest economy in the world.

Why has Brazil done so well economically? Increased world trade is one reason why. The country has an abundant amount of natural resources firms in other countries around the world are eager to buy—especially companies in the fast-growing nation of China. Greater exports have also helped 40 million Brazilians rise up out of poverty and into the middle class. Their massive spending power is creating new markets for multinational companies ranging from McDonald's and Whirlpool to Nestlé, Avon, and Volkswagen. Brazil has become Avon's largest market. Volkswagen now sells more cars in Brazil than it does Germany, where the company is headquartered. "China may have over a billion inhabitants, but Brazil has 200,000 consumers," explains Ivan Zurita, the president of Nestle's Brazil division.

Clouds on the horizon threaten to cool off Brazil's growth, however. To begin with, the country is concerned that its trade with China is out of balance. Although China purchases more natural resources from Brazil than any other nation, it doesn't

purchase near as many manufactured goods from Brazil as it exports to it.

A bigger issue is the appreciation of Brazil's currency, the real. Massive amounts of money have been flowing into Brazil to take advantage of the nation's high interest rates and growth opportunities. This has increased the demand for the real, causing its value to rise by nearly 50 percent relative to other currencies. The good news is that the stronger real has made imported products cheaper for Brazilians to buy. The bad news is that products made in Brazil have become more expensive for the rest of the world to purchase, slowing the country's exports and growth.

Businesses in Brazil have lobbied the government to weaken the real so their products are better able to compete against imports. Their efforts appear to have paid off. Recently, Guido Mantega, Brazil's minister of finance, said the country will take steps "as needed" to weaken the real. The government has also imposed tariffs on a number of imported products, including cars, shoes, chemicals, and textiles, and signed a trade deal with Mexico that put a quota on the number of automobiles imported from that country.

Imports and the value of the real are not the only clouds threatening Brazil, though. Businesses in the country face a great deal of bureaucratic red tape, heavy regulations, and tax rates that are some of the highest in the world. To deal with these problems, Brazilian President Dilma Rousseff has announced that her administration will eliminate payroll taxes for employers in industries hardest hit by imports. To further ease the nation's growing pains, Brazil's development bank, BDM, will subsidize business loans to boost the production of many products, including tablets and off-shore oil rigs. The goal is to stimulate technological innovations that will enable manufacturers to produce higher-value products so Brazil doesn't have to rely on natural resources to fuel its growth. "Look, a government isn't made on the second or third day," Rousseff has said about her administration's incremental efforts to keep Brazil's emerging economy moving forward. "It's made over time. Things mature."[11]

Questions

1. Do you think the efforts of Brazil's government to keep the economy growing will be successful? Why or why not?
2. What downsides might Brazil experience by implementing quotas, tariffs, and measures to devalue its currency?

Case 3.2

Global Profits Are a Menu Mainstay at McDonald's

Few U.S. businesses are as international as McDonald's, the Illinois-based fast-food giant that began as an all-American hamburger place. With $22 billion in annual revenue, McDonald's now rings the world with 32,400 restaurants and serves 60 million customers every day. Although the United States accounts for 35 percent of McDonald's global revenue, Europe accounts for 41 percent and the Asia/Pacific, Middle East, and Africa regions account for 19 percent.

Hamburgers are, of course, the main attraction in many McDonald's restaurants: Worldwide, the company sells more than four million burgers every day. However, one of McDonald's key strengths is its ability to adapt to local tastes. In Japan, McDonald's sells Cheese Katsu sandwiches, featuring fried pork and cheese. In the Middle East, it sells McArabia pita sandwiches filled with grilled chicken or spiced beef. In France, it sells Croque McDo sandwiches with melted cheese and ham. In India, it sells vegetarian McAloo Tikki burgers. In Mexico, it sells McMolletes sandwiches made with refried beans and cheese.

Being a global business also helps McDonald's weather the economic ups and downs of different regions. At one point during the recent recession, its Asian revenue grew almost twice as quickly as its European revenue, both of which balanced the smaller increase in U.S. sales. Worldwide, McDonald's owns some of its restaurants and also sells franchise licenses to firms that open restaurants under the McDonald's brand name. In some markets, the company operates restaurants in joint ventures with local firms. For example, in India, it has one joint venture with a local firm to operate restaurants in the west and south and a second joint venture with a different company to operate restaurants in the east and the north.

The company is also building its global business by attracting more customers during different "dayparts," such as at breakfast time and in the late-night hours. A growing number of its global units stay open 24 hours a day for customer convenience. McDonald's has introduced a steady stream of breakfast, beverage, snack, and sandwich items to encourage repeat visits from customers at all income levels.

On the high end, McDonald's is doing well with its McCafés, which serve mochas and other gourmet coffees in a separate area of selected McDonald's units. As the company opens new restaurants and remodels existing restaurants, it is adding more McCafés in U.S. and European markets. The Angus Burger is another popular premium menu item. Both McCafé coffees and Angus Burgers appeal to customers willing to pay a little more to splurge on high quality. At the same time, the items on McDonald's budget menus are priced to appeal to customers who keep a close rein on their wallets.

Being a major power in global business means McDonald's must think carefully about the value of the different currencies its restaurants take in. Outside the United States, much of its revenue is rung up in euros, British pounds, Australian dollars, and Canadian dollars. As a result, McDonald's pays close attention to swings in foreign-exchange rates as it manages its financial affairs.

McDonald's is stepping up its involvement in sustainability all around the world. It has increased its use of packaging made from renewable materials and boosted recycling efforts to keep waste out of landfills. It has also been building eco-friendly restaurants in North and South America as well as in Europe to test green construction methods and cut back on energy and water usage. The company's social responsibility menu includes supporting the Ronald McDonald House charities and offering a range of organic foods and beverages plus healthy snack choices.

From India to Ireland, Argentina to Australia, McDonald's is poised for continued growth in sales and profits as it expands its restaurant empire and cooks up new products for customers to enjoy around the clock and around the world.[12]

Questions

1. What are the advantages and disadvantages of McDonald's ringing up sales in so many foreign currencies worldwide?
2. Why would McDonald's use two joint ventures to operate restaurants in different regions of India?
3. Discuss how being a multinational enterprise, with a presence in more than 170 countries, helps McDonald's build its business regardless of the short-term global economic outlook.

of businesses are formed and note the advantages and disadvantages of each. Next, we consider several types of business ownership usually chosen for special purposes, including S-corporations, limited-liability companies, not-for-profit corporations, cooperatives, joint ventures, and syndicates. We conclude the chapter with a discussion of how businesses can grow through internal expansion or through mergers with other companies.

Describe the advantages and disadvantages of sole proprietorships.

SOLE PROPRIETORSHIPS

A **sole proprietorship** is a business that is owned (and usually operated) by one person. Although a few sole proprietorships are large and have many employees, most are small. Sole proprietorship is the simplest form of business ownership and the easiest to start. In most instances, the owner (the *sole* proprietor) simply decides that he or she is in business and begins operations. Some of today's largest corporations, including Walmart, JCPenney, H.J. Heinz Company, and Procter & Gamble Company, started out as tiny—and in many cases, struggling—sole proprietorships.

Often entrepreneurs with a promising idea choose the sole proprietorship form of ownership. Annie Withey, for example, created a cheddar cheese–flavored popcorn snack food. Annie's popcorn, called Smartfood, became one of the fastest-selling snack foods in U.S. history. After a few years, PepsiCo Inc.'s Frito-Lay division bought the brand for about $15 million. Ms. Withey, an organic farmer and mother of two children, went on to develop an all-natural white-cheddar macaroni and cheese product. This venture was also a success. Today even though her firm, Annie's Homegrown, has grown and become part of a larger conglomerate, Annie remains the entrepreneurial heart of the company and still thinks like a sole proprietor.

As you can see in Figure 4.1, there are approximately 23 million nonfarm sole proprietorships in the United States. They account for 72 percent of the country's business firms. Although the most popular form of ownership when compared with partnerships and corporations, they rank last in total sales revenues. As shown in Figure 4.2, sole proprietorships account for about $1.3 trillion, or about 4 percent of total annual sales.

Sole proprietorships are most common in retailing, service, and agriculture. Thus, the clothing boutique, corner grocery, television-repair shop down the street, and small, independent farmers are likely to be sole proprietorships.

sole proprietorship a business that is owned (and usually operated) by one person

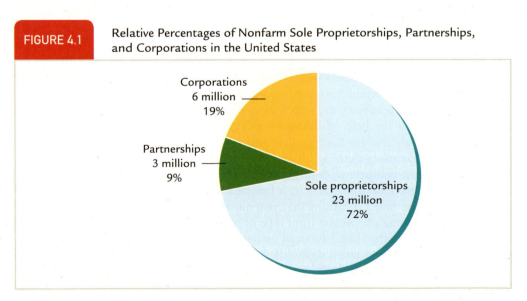

FIGURE 4.1 Relative Percentages of Nonfarm Sole Proprietorships, Partnerships, and Corporations in the United States

Corporations
6 million
19%

Partnerships
3 million
9%

Sole proprietorships
23 million
72%

Source: U.S. Bureau of the Census, *Statistical Abstract of the United States* (Washington, DC: Bureau of the Census, 2012), table 744 (www.census.gov).

FIGURE 4.2 Total Sales Receipts of American Businesses

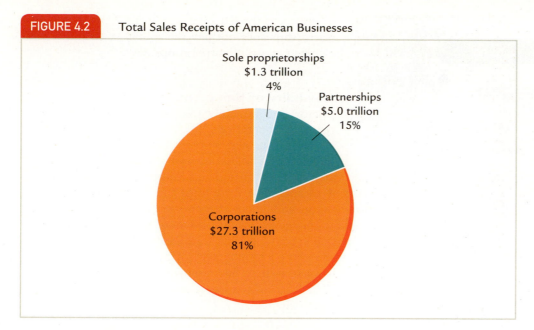

Sole proprietorships
$1.3 trillion
4%

Partnerships
$5.0 trillion
15%

Corporations
$27.3 trillion
81%

Source: U.S. Bureau of the Census, *Statistical Abstract of the United States* (Washington, DC: Bureau of the Census, 2012), table 744 (www.census.gov).

Advantages of Sole Proprietorships

Most of the advantages of sole proprietorships arise from the two main characteristics of this form of ownership: simplicity and individual control.

Ease of Start-Up and Closure Sole proprietorship is the simplest and cheapest way to start a business. Often, start-up requires no contracts, agreements, or other legal documents. Thus, a sole proprietorship can be, and most often is, established without the services of an attorney. The legal requirements often are limited to registering the name of the business and obtaining any necessary licenses or permits.

If the enterprise does not succeed, the firm can be closed as easily as it was opened. Creditors must be paid, of course, but generally, the owner does not have to go through any legal procedure before hanging up an "Out of Business" sign.

Pride of Ownership A successful sole proprietor is often very proud of her or his accomplishments—and rightfully so. In almost every case, the owner deserves a great deal of credit for solving the day-to-day problems associated with operating a sole proprietorship. Unfortunately, the reverse is also true. When the business fails, it is often the sole proprietor who is to blame.

Retention of All Profits Because all profits become the personal earnings of the owner, the owner has a strong incentive to succeed. This direct financial reward attracts many entrepreneurs to the sole proprietorship form of business and, if the business succeeds, is a source of great satisfaction.

No Special Taxes Profits earned by a sole proprietorship are taxed as the personal income of the owner. As a result, sole proprietors must report certain financial information for the business on their personal income tax returns and make estimated quarterly tax

© AP PHOTO/KATHY WILLENS

An entrepreneur with a sweet tooth! Hail a taxi anywhere in New York City and tell the driver, "Take me to the best cheesecake in New York." Odds are you will end up at a Junior's Restaurant. Founded in 1950 by Harry Rosen, the restaurant remains a family-owned business today. In this photo, Alan, a member of the Rosen family, displays some of the products that made this restaurant a New York tradition.

Do you dream of being your own boss? If you become a sole proprietor, you'll have all the flexibility that comes with making your own decisions. But remember: Although you'll have the final say, you'll also be responsible if something goes wrong.

payments to the federal government. Thus, a sole proprietorship does not pay the special state and federal income taxes that corporations pay.

Flexibility of Being Your Own Boss A sole proprietor is completely free to make decisions about the firm's operations. Without asking or waiting for anyone's approval, a sole proprietor can switch from retailing to wholesaling, move a shop's location, open a new store, or close an old one. Suppose that the sole proprietor of an appliance store finds that many customers now prefer to shop on Sunday afternoons. He or she can make an immediate change in business hours to take advantage of this information (provided that state laws allow such stores to open on Sunday). The manager of a store in a large corporate chain such as Best Buy Company may have to seek the approval of numerous managers and company officials before making such a change.

Disadvantages of Sole Proprietorships

The disadvantages of a sole proprietorship stem from the fact that these businesses are owned by one person. Some capable sole proprietors experience no problems. Individuals who start out with few management skills and little money are most at risk for failure.

Unlimited Liability **Unlimited liability** is a legal concept that holds a business owner personally responsible for all the debts of the business. There is legally no difference between the debts of the business and the debts of the proprietor. If the business fails, or if the business is involved in a lawsuit and loses, the owner's personal property—including savings and other assets—can be seized (and sold if necessary) to pay creditors.

Unlimited liability is perhaps the major factor that tends to discourage would-be entrepreneurs with substantial personal wealth from using the sole proprietor form of business organization.

Lack of Continuity Legally, the sole proprietor *is* the business. If the owner retires, dies, or is declared legally incompetent, the business essentially ceases to exist. In many cases, however—especially when the business is a profitable enterprise—the owner's heirs take it over and either sell it or continue to operate it. The business also can suffer if the sole proprietor becomes ill and cannot work for an extended period of time. If the owner, for example, has a heart attack, there is often no one who can step in and manage the business. An illness can be devastating if the sole proprietor's personal skills are what determine if the business is a success or a failure.

Lack of Money Banks, suppliers, and other lenders usually are unwilling to lend large sums of money to sole proprietorships. Only one person—the sole proprietor—can be held responsible for repaying such loans, and the assets of most sole proprietors usually are limited. Moreover, these assets may have been used already as security or collateral for personal borrowing (a home mortgage or car loan) or for short-term credit from suppliers. Lenders also worry about the lack of continuity of sole proprietorships: Who

unlimited liability a legal concept that holds a business owner personally responsible for all the debts of the business

Entrepreneurial
SUCCESS

Why Sell a Small Business to a Big Business?

Corey Capasso and Andrew Ferenci started Spinback in 2010 to help companies determine how social media connections were influencing sales. A year later, they had several large e-business customers and were ready for a major expansion, which meant raising more money. After discussing an alliance with Buddy Media, the co-founders realized that being acquired by Buddy Media was "a perfect fit," Ferenci says. "We would be able to focus more on the nuts and bolts of the business" without having to spend time looking for additional financing. But, he cautions, entrepreneurs "need to make sure the acquiring company has a solid corporate culture and will be a good place to work."

Aaron Patzer is another entrepreneur who let a big business acquire his small business, Mint.com, so he could keep improving operations and serving customers. Mint.com helps consumers manage their money online, and Patzer already had a million customers to consider when competitor Intuit approached him with an acquisition offer. The entrepreneur decided to sell, and became not only a millionaire but also a vice president at Intuit, bringing his employees to Intuit to keep running the business he had started. "They sort of left us alone to continue what we're doing," Patzer says of the post-acquisition situation.

Sources: Based on information in Aaron Shapiro, "The User-First Initiative," *Forbes,* January 4, 2012, www.forbes.com; Andrew Ferenci, "Spinback Founder: Why We Sold to Buddy Media Instead of Taking VC," *Business Insider,* June 3, 2011, www.businessinsider.com; Judith Messina, "Why Google Is the New Exit Strategy," *Crain's New York Business,* July 20, 2011, www.crainsnewyork.com; J.P. Mangalindan, "Aaron Patzer's Startups," *Fortune,* April 1, 2011, http://tech.fortune.cnn.com.

will repay a loan if the sole proprietor dies? Finally, many lenders are concerned about the large number of sole proprietorships that fail—a topic discussed in Chapter 5.

The limited ability to borrow money can prevent a sole proprietorship from growing. It is the main reason that many business owners, when in need of relatively large amounts of capital, change from a sole proprietorship to a partnership or corporate form of ownership.

Limited Management Skills The sole proprietor is often the sole manager—in addition to being the only salesperson, buyer, accountant, and, on occasion, janitor. Even the most experienced business owner is unlikely to have expertise in all these areas. Unless he or she obtains the necessary expertise by hiring employees, assistants, or consultants, the business can suffer in the areas in which the owner is less knowledgeable. For the many sole proprietors who cannot hire the help they need, there just are not enough hours in the day to do everything that needs to be done.

Difficulty in Hiring Employees The sole proprietor may find it hard to attract and keep competent help. Potential employees may feel that there is no room for advancement in a firm whose owner assumes all managerial responsibilities. And when those who *are* hired are ready to take on added responsibility, they may find that the only way to do so is to quit the sole proprietorship and go to work for a larger firm or start up their own businesses. The lure of higher salaries and increased benefits (especially health insurance) also may cause existing employees to change jobs.

Beyond the Sole Proprietorship

Like many others, you may decide that the major disadvantage of a sole proprietorship is the limited amount that one person can do in a workday. One way to reduce the effect of this disadvantage (and retain many of the advantages) is to have more than one owner.

PARTNERSHIPS

A person who would not think of starting and running a sole proprietorship business alone may enthusiastically seize the opportunity to form a business partnership. The U.S. Uniform Partnership Act defines a **partnership** as a voluntary association of two or more persons to act as co-owners of a business for profit. For example, in 1990, two young African-American entrepreneurs named Janet Smith and Gary Smith started IVY Planning Group—a company that provides strategic planning and performance measurement for clients. Today, more than 20 years later, the company has evolved into a multimillion-dollar company that has hired a diverse staff of employees and provides cultural diversity training for *Fortune* 1000 firms, large not-for-profit organizations, and government agencies. In recognition of its efforts, IVY Planning Group has been recognized by DiversityBusiness.com as one of the top 50 minority-owned companies. And both Janet Smith and Gary Smith have been named "1 of 50 Influential Minorities in Business" by Minority Business and Professionals Network.[2]

As shown in Figures 4.1 and 4.2, there are approximately 3 million partnerships in the United States, and this type of ownership accounts for about $5 trillion in sales receipts each year. Note, however, that this form of ownership is much less common than the sole proprietorship or the corporation. In fact, as Figure 4.1 shows, partnerships represent only about 9 percent of all American businesses. Although there is no legal maximum on the number of partners a partnership may have, most have only two. Regardless of the number of people involved, a partnership often represents a pooling of special managerial skills and talents; at other times, it is the result of a sole proprietor taking on a partner for the purpose of obtaining more capital.

Types of Partners

All partners are not necessarily equal. Some may be active in running the business, whereas others may have a limited role.

General Partners A **general partner** is a person who assumes full or shared responsibility for operating a business. General partners are active in day-to-day business operations, and each partner can enter into contracts on behalf of the other partners. He or she also assumes unlimited liability for all debts, including debts incurred by any other general partner without his or her knowledge or consent. A *general partnership* is a business co-owned by two or more general partners who are liable for everything the business does. To avoid future liability, a general partner who withdraws from the partnership must give notice to creditors, customers, and suppliers.

Limited Partners A **limited partner** is a person who invests money in a business but who has no management responsibility or liability for losses beyond his or her investment in the partnership. A *limited partnership* is a business co-owned by one or more general partners who manage the business and limited partners who invest money in it. Limited partnerships, for example, may be formed to finance real estate, oil and gas, motion picture, and other business ventures. Typically, the general partner or partners collect management fees and receive a percentage of profits. Limited partners receive a portion of profits and tax benefits.

Because of potential liability problems, special rules apply to limited partnerships. These rules are intended to protect customers and creditors who deal with limited partnerships. For example, prospective partners in a limited partnership must file a formal declaration, usually with the secretary of state, that describes the essential details of the partnership and the liability status of each partner involved in the business. At least one general partner must

partnership a voluntary association of two or more persons to act as co-owners of a business for profit

general partner a person who assumes full or shared responsibility for operating a business

limited partner a person who invests money in a business but has no management responsibility or liability for losses beyond the amount he or she invested in the partnership

© AP PHOTO/SHAWN BALDWIN

Sometimes it helps to have a famous partner with a proven track record. After leaving public office, former New York City Mayor Rudy Giuliani formed Giuliani Partners—a partnership with the accounting firm Ernst & Young. The objective of this partnership is to help business clients deal with the risks that stem from terrorism, crime, natural disasters, and other factors that threaten an organization's ability to survive.

be responsible for the debts of the limited partnership. Also, some states prohibit the use of the limited partner's name in the partnership's name.

A special type of partnership is referred to as a *master limited partnership*. A **master limited partnership (MLP)** (sometimes referred to as a *publicly traded partnership*, or *PTP*) is a limited partnership that has units of ownership that can be traded on security exchanges much like shares of ownership in a corporation. Generally, both general partners and limited partners are involved in an MLP. The general partners manage the business; the limited partners provide investment capital. This special ownership arrangement has two major advantages. First, units of ownership in MLPs can be sold to investors to raise capital. Because MLP units can be traded on an exchange, investors can sell their units of ownership at any time, hopefully for a profit. While there are exceptions, most MLPs typically are in natural resources, energy, or real estate-related businesses.[3] Kinder Morgan Energy Partners, for example, is one of the largest publicly traded pipeline master limited partnerships in America. For Kinder Morgan Energy Partners, ownership units are traded on the New York Stock Exchange. Second, income from MLPs is generally reported as the personal income of the owners. MLPs thus avoided the double taxation paid on corporate income. For more information on the advantages and disadvantages of the MLP form of ownership, visit the National Association of Publicly Traded Partnerships Web site at www.naptp.org.

The Partnership Agreement

Articles of partnership refers to an agreement listing and explaining the terms of the partnership. Although both oral and written partnership agreements are legal and can be enforced in the courts, a written agreement has an obvious advantage. It is not subject to lapses of memory.

Figure 4.3 shows a typical partnership agreement. The partnership agreement should state

- Who will make the final decisions
- What each partner's duties will be
- The investment each partner will make
- How much profit or loss each partner receives or is responsible for
- What happens if a partner wants to dissolve the partnership or dies

Although the people involved in a partnership can draft their own agreement, most experts recommend consulting an attorney.

When entering into a partnership agreement, partners would be wise to let a neutral third party—a consultant, an accountant, a lawyer, or a mutual friend—assist with any disputes that might arise.

ADVANTAGES AND DISADVANTAGES OF PARTNERSHIPS

 Describe the advantages and disadvantages of partnerships.

When compared to sole proprietorships and corporations, partnerships are the least popular form of business ownership. Still there are situations when forming a partnership makes perfect sense. Before you make a decision to form a partnership, all the people involved should consider both the advantages and disadvantages of a partnership.

Advantages of Partnerships

Partnerships have many advantages. The most important are described as follows.

Ease of Start-Up Partnerships are relatively easy to form. As with a sole proprietorship, the legal requirements often are limited to registering the name of the business

master limited partnership (MLP) a limited partnership that has units of ownership that can be traded on security exchanges much like shares of ownership in a corporation

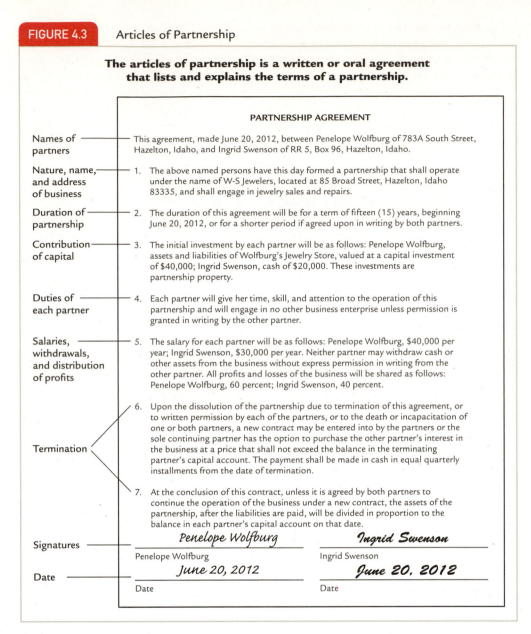

FIGURE 4.3   Articles of Partnership

The articles of partnership is a written or oral agreement that lists and explains the terms of a partnership.

PARTNERSHIP AGREEMENT

Names of partners
This agreement, made June 20, 2012, between Penelope Wolfburg of 783A South Street, Hazelton, Idaho, and Ingrid Swenson of RR 5, Box 96, Hazelton, Idaho.

Nature, name, and address of business
1. The above named persons have this day formed a partnership that shall operate under the name of W-S Jewelers, located at 85 Broad Street, Hazelton, Idaho 83335, and shall engage in jewelry sales and repairs.

Duration of partnership
2. The duration of this agreement will be for a term of fifteen (15) years, beginning June 20, 2012, or for a shorter period if agreed upon in writing by both partners.

Contribution of capital
3. The initial investment by each partner will be as follows: Penelope Wolfburg, assets and liabilities of Wolfburg's Jewelry Store, valued at a capital investment of $40,000; Ingrid Swenson, cash of $20,000. These investments are partnership property.

Duties of each partner
4. Each partner will give her time, skill, and attention to the operation of this partnership and will engage in no other business enterprise unless permission is granted in writing by the other partner.

Salaries, withdrawals, and distribution of profits
5. The salary for each partner will be as follows: Penelope Wolfburg, $40,000 per year; Ingrid Swenson, $30,000 per year. Neither partner may withdraw cash or other assets from the business without express permission in writing from the other partner. All profits and losses of the business will be shared as follows: Penelope Wolfburg, 60 percent; Ingrid Swenson, 40 percent.

Termination
6. Upon the dissolution of the partnership due to termination of this agreement, or to written permission by each of the partners, or to the death or incapacitation of one or both partners, a new contract may be entered into by the partners or the sole continuing partner has the option to purchase the other partner's interest in the business at a price that shall not exceed the balance in the terminating partner's capital account. The payment shall be made in cash in equal quarterly installments from the date of termination.

7. At the conclusion of this contract, unless it is agreed by both partners to continue the operation of the business under a new contract, the assets of the partnership, after the liabilities are paid, will be divided in proportion to the balance in each partner's capital account on that date.

Signatures
Penelope Wolfburg   *Ingrid Swenson*
Penelope Wolfburg   Ingrid Swenson

Date
June 20, 2012   *June 20, 2012*
Date   Date

Source: Adapted from Goldman and Sigismond, *Cengage Advantage Books: Business Law 8E.* © 2011 Cengage Learning.

and obtaining any necessary licenses or permits. It may not even be necessary to prepare written articles of partnership, although doing so is generally a good idea.

Availability of Capital and Credit Because partners can pool their funds, a partnership usually has more capital available than a sole proprietorship does. This additional capital, coupled with the general partners' unlimited liability, may encourage banks and suppliers to extend more credit or approve larger loans to a partnership than to a sole proprietor. This does not mean that partnerships can borrow all the money they need. Many partnerships have found it hard to get long-term financing simply because lenders worry about the possibility of management disagreements and lack of continuity.

Personal Interest General partners are very concerned with the operation of the firm—perhaps even more so than sole proprietors. After all, they are responsible for the actions of all other general partners, as well as for their own. The pride of ownership from solving the day-to-day problems of operating a business—with the help of another person(s)—is a strong motivating force and often makes all the people involved in the partnership work harder to become more successful.

Combined Business Skills and Knowledge Partners often have complementary skills. The weakness of one partner—in manufacturing, for example—may be offset by another partner's strength in that area. Moreover, the ability to discuss important decisions with another concerned individual often relieves some pressure and leads to more effective decision making.

Retention of Profits As in a sole proprietorship, all profits belong to the owners of the partnership. The partners share directly in the financial rewards and therefore are highly motivated to do their best to make the firm succeed. As noted, the partnership agreement should state how much profit or loss each partner receives or is responsible for.

No Special Taxes Although a partnership pays no income tax, the Internal Revenue Service requires partnerships to file an annual information return that states the names and addresses of all partners involved in the business. The return also must provide information about income and expenses and distributions made to each partner. Then each partner is required to report his or her share of profit (or loss) from the partnership on his or her individual tax return. Ultimately each partner's share of the partnership profit is taxed in the same way a sole proprietor is taxed.

Two entrepreneurs with one goal. There is a special pride of ownership that takes place when two people are solving problems and working together for the same purpose. Being responsible for what happens to the company—as well as your business partner—can be a motivating force for working that much harder to be successful.

Disadvantages of Partnerships

Although partnerships have many advantages when compared with sole proprietorships and corporations, they also have some disadvantages, which anyone thinking of forming a partnership should consider.

Unlimited Liability As we have noted, each *general* partner has unlimited liability for all debts of the business. Each partner is legally and personally responsible for the debts, taxes, and actions of any other partner conducting partnership business, even if that partner did not incur those debts or do anything wrong. General partners thus run the risk of having to use their personal assets to pay creditors. *Limited* partners, however, risk only their original investment.

Today, many states allow partners to form a *limited-liability partnership* (LLP), in which a partner may have limited-liability protection from legal action resulting from the malpractice or negligence of the other partners. Many states that allow LLPs restrict this type of ownership to certain types of professionals such as accountants, architects, attorneys, and similar professionals. (Note the difference between a limited partnership and a limited-liability partnership. A limited partnership must have at least one general partner that has unlimited liability. On the other hand, all partners in a limited-liability partnership may have limited liability *for the malpractice of the other partners*.)

Management Disagreements What happens to a partnership if one of the partners brings a spouse or a relative into the business? What happens if a partner wants to withdraw more money from the business? Notice that each of these situations—and for that matter, most of the other problems that can develop in a partnership—involves one partner doing something that disturbs the other partner(s). This human factor is especially important because business partners—with egos, ambitions, and money on the line—are especially susceptible to friction. When partners begin to disagree about decisions, policies, or ethics, distrust may build and get worse as time passes—often to the point where it is impossible to operate the business successfully.

Lack of Continuity Partnerships are terminated if any one of the general partners dies, withdraws, or is declared legally incompetent. However, the remaining partners can purchase that partner's ownership share. For example, the partnership agreement may permit surviving partners to continue the business after buying a deceased partner's interest from his or her estate. However, if the partnership loses an owner whose specific management or technical skills cannot be replaced, it is not likely to survive.

Frozen Investment It is easy to invest money in a partnership, but it is sometimes quite difficult to get it out. This is the case, for example, when remaining partners are unwilling to buy the share of the business that belongs to a partner who retires or wants to relocate to another city. To avoid such difficulties, the partnership agreement should include some procedure for buying out a partner.

In some cases, a partner must find someone outside the firm to buy his or her share. How easy or difficult it is to find an outsider depends on how successful the business is and how willing existing partners are to accept a new partner.

Beyond the Partnership

The main advantages of a partnership over a sole proprietorship are increased availability of capital and credit and the combined business skills and knowledge of the partners. However, some of the basic disadvantages of the sole proprietorship also plague the general partnership. One disadvantage in particular—unlimited liability—can cause problems for a partner with substantial personal wealth. A third form of business ownership, the corporation, overcomes this disadvantage.

Summarize how a corporation is formed.

CORPORATIONS

Back in 1837, William Procter and James Gamble—two sole proprietors—formed a partnership called Procter & Gamble (P&G) and set out to compete with 14 other soap and candle makers in Cincinnati, Ohio. Then, in 1890, Procter & Gamble incorporated to raise additional capital for expansion that eventually allowed the company to become a global giant. Today, P&G brands serve over 4 billion of the 7 billion people in the world today because the corporation operates in 180 countries around the globe.[4] Like many large corporations, P&G's market capitalization is greater than the gross domestic product of many countries. Although this corporation is a corporate giant, the firm's executives and employees believe it also has a responsibility to be an ethical corporate citizen. For example, P&G's purpose statement (or mission) is

> *We will provide branded products and services of superior quality and value that improve the lives of the world's consumers, now and for generations to come. As a result, consumers will reward us with leadership sales, profit and value creation, allowing our people, our shareholders and the communities in which we live and work to prosper.[5]*

In today's competitive environment, it's common to hear of large companies that are profitable. It is less common to hear of profitable companies that are held in high regard because they are good corporate citizens.

While not all sole proprietorships and partnerships become corporations, there are reasons why business owners choose the corporate form of ownership. Let's begin with a definition of a corporation. Perhaps the best definition of a corporation was given by Chief Justice John Marshall in a famous Supreme Court decision in 1819.

A corporation, he said, "is an artificial person, invisible, intangible, and existing only in contemplation of the law." In other words, a **corporation** (sometimes referred to as a *regular* or *C-corporation*) is an artificial person created by law, with most of the legal rights of a real person. These include:

- The right to start and operate a business
- The right to buy or sell property
- The right to borrow money
- The right to sue or be sued
- The right to enter into binding contracts

Unlike a real person, however, a corporation exists only on paper. There are approximately 6 million corporations in the United States. They comprise about 19 percent of all businesses, but they account for 81 percent of sales revenues (see Figures 4.1 and 4.2).

© AP PHOTO/AL BEHRMAN

Procter & Gamble: Once a sole proprietorship, then a partnership, and now a very large corporation. Although one of the largest corporations in the world, P&G was started when two sole proprietors formed a partnership to sell soap and candles. Today the corporation's product line has expanded and it now operates in 180 different countries around the globe.

Corporate Ownership

The shares of ownership of a corporation are called **stock**. The people who own a corporation's stock—and thus own part of the corporation—are called **stockholders**. Once a corporation has been formed, it may sell its stock to individuals or other companies that want to invest in the corporation. It also may issue stock as a reward to key employees in return for certain services or as a return to investors in place of cash payments.

A **closed corporation** is a corporation whose stock is owned by relatively few people and is not sold to the general public. As an example, Mars—the company famous for M&Ms, Snickers, Dove, Milky Way, Twix, and other chocolate candy—is a privately held, family-owned, closed corporation. Although many people think that a closed corporation is a small company, there are exceptions. Mars, for example, has annual sales of more than $30 billion, employs more than 65,000 associates worldwide, and operates in 70 different countries.[6]

An **open corporation** is one whose stock can be bought and sold by any individual. Examples of open corporations include General Electric, Microsoft, Apple, and Sony.

Forming a Corporation

Although you may think that incorporating a business guarantees success, it does not. There is no special magic about placing the word *Incorporated* or the abbreviation *Inc.* after the name of a business. Unfortunately, like sole proprietorships or partnerships, corporations can go broke. The decision to incorporate a business therefore should be made only after carefully considering whether the corporate form of ownership suits your needs better than the sole proprietorship or partnership forms.

If you decide that the corporate form is the best form of organization for you, most experts recommend that you begin the incorporation process by consulting a lawyer to be sure that all legal requirements are met. While it may be possible to incorporate a business without legal help, it is well to keep in mind the old saying, "A man who acts as his own attorney has a fool for a client." Table 4.1 lists some aspects of starting and running a business that may require legal help.

Where to Incorporate A business is allowed to incorporate in any state that it chooses. Most small- and medium-sized businesses are incorporated in the state where they do the most business. The founders of larger corporations or of those that will do business nationwide often compare the benefits that various states provide to corporations. The decision on where to incorporate usually is based on two factors: (1) the cost of incorporating in one state compared with the cost in another state and

corporation an artificial person created by law with most of the legal rights of a real person, including the rights to start and operate a business, to buy or sell property, to borrow money, to sue or be sued, and to enter into binding contracts

stock the shares of ownership of a corporation

stockholder a person who owns a corporation's stock

closed corporation a corporation whose stock is owned by relatively few people and is not sold to the general public

open corporation a corporation whose stock can be bought and sold by any individual

TABLE 4.1	Ten Aspects of Business That May Require Legal Help
1.	Choosing either the sole proprietorship, partnership, corporate, or some special form of ownership
2.	Constructing a partnership agreement
3.	Incorporating a business
4.	Registering a corporation's stock
5.	Obtaining a trademark, patent, or copyright
6.	Filing for licenses or permits at the local, state, and federal levels
7.	Purchasing an existing business or real estate
8.	Creating valid contracts
9.	Hiring employees and independent contractors
10.	Extending credit and collecting debts

© CENGAGE LEARNING 2014

(2) the advantages and disadvantages of each state's corporate laws and tax structure. Some states are more hospitable than others, and some offer fewer restrictions, lower taxes, and other benefits to attract new firms. Delaware, Nevada, and Wyoming are often chosen by corporations that do business in more than one state because of their corporation-friendly laws and pro-business climate.[7]

An incorporated business is called a **domestic corporation** in the state in which it is incorporated. In all other states where it does business, it is called a **foreign corporation**. Sears Holdings Corporation, the parent company of Sears and Kmart, is incorporated in Delaware, where it is a domestic corporation. In the remaining 49 states, Sears is a foreign corporation. Sears must register in all states where it does business and also pay taxes and annual fees to each state. A corporation chartered by a foreign government and conducting business in the United States is an **alien corporation**. Volkswagen AG, Sony Corporation, and the Royal Dutch/Shell Group are examples of alien corporations.

The Corporate Charter Once a home state has been chosen, the incorporator(s) submits *articles of incorporation* to the secretary of state. When the articles of incorporation are approved, they become a contract between a corporation and the state in which the state recognizes the formation of the artificial person that is the corporation. Usually, the articles of incorporation include the following information:

- The firm's name and address
- The incorporators' names and addresses
- The purpose of the corporation
- The maximum amount of stock and types of stock to be issued
- The rights and privileges of stockholders
- The length of time the corporation is to exist

To help you to decide if the corporate form of organization is the right choice, you may want to visit the library for more information on the incorporation process. You can also use an Internet search engine and enter the term "business incorporation" for useful Web sites. In addition, before making a decision to organize your business as a corporation, you may want to consider two additional areas: stockholders' rights and the importance of the organizational meeting.

Stockholders' Rights There are two basic types of stock. Owners of **common stock** may vote on corporate matters. Generally, an owner of common stock has one vote for each share owned. However, any claims of common-stock owners on profits, dividends, and assets of the corporation are paid after the claims of others. The owners

domestic corporation a corporation in the state in which it is incorporated

foreign corporation a corporation in any state in which it does business except the one in which it is incorporated

alien corporation a corporation chartered by a foreign government and conducting business in the United States

common stock stock owned by individuals or firms who may vote on corporate matters but whose claims on profits and assets are subordinate to the claims of others

preferred stock stock owned by individuals or firms who usually do not have voting rights but whose claims on dividends are paid before those of common-stock owners

of **preferred stock** usually have no voting rights, but their claims on dividends are paid before those of common-stock owners. Although large corporations may issue both common and preferred stock, generally small corporations issue only common stock.

Perhaps the most important right of owners of both common and preferred stock is to share in the profit earned by the corporation through the payment of dividends. A **dividend** is a distribution of earnings to the stockholders of a corporation. Other rights include receiving information about the corporation, voting on changes to the corporate charter, and attending the corporation's annual stockholders' meeting, where they may exercise their right to vote.

Because common stockholders usually live all over the nation, very few actually may attend a corporation's annual meeting. Instead, they vote by proxy. A **proxy** is a legal form listing issues to be decided at a stockholders' meeting and enabling stockholders to transfer their voting rights to some other individual or individuals. The stockholder can register a vote and transfer voting rights simply by signing and returning the form. Today, most corporations also allow stockholders to exercise their right to vote by proxy by accessing the Internet or using a toll-free phone number.

Organizational Meeting As the last step in forming a corporation, the incorporators and original stockholders meet to adopt corporate by-laws and elect their first board of directors. (Later, directors will be elected or reelected at the corporation's annual meetings by the firm's stockholders.) The board members are directly responsible to the stockholders for the way they operate the firm.

Personal APPS

Even if you own a single share of common stock, you're legally a part-owner of the corporation. You're entitled to receive any dividends paid to shareholders and you can vote on important matters such as electing the board of directors. Your vote is counted—and it counts.

Corporate Structure

The organizational structure of most corporations is more complicated than that of a sole proprietorship or partnership. In a corporation, both the board of directors and the corporate officers are involved in management.

Board of Directors As an artificial person, a corporation can act only through its directors, who represent the corporation's stockholders. The **board of directors** is the top governing body of a corporation and is elected by the stockholders. In theory, then, the stockholders are able to control the activities of the entire corporation through its directors because they are the group that elects the board of directors (see Figure 4.4)

Board members can be chosen from within the corporation or from outside it. *Note:* For a small corporation, only one director is required in many states although you can choose to have more. Directors who are elected from within the corporation are usually its top managers—the president and executive vice presidents, for

dividend a distribution of earnings to the stockholders of a corporation

proxy a legal form listing issues to be decided at a stockholders' meeting and enabling stockholders to transfer their voting rights to some other individual or individuals

board of directors the top governing body of a corporation, the members of which are elected by the stockholders

---

FIGURE 4.4   Hierarchy of Corporate Structure

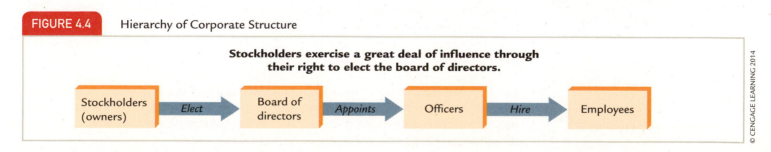

Stockholders exercise a great deal of influence through their right to elect the board of directors.

| Stockholders (owners) | → *Elect* → | Board of directors | → *Appoints* → | Officers | → *Hire* → | Employees |

Do We Need More Women in the Board Room?

Half of the world is female, yet only 16 percent of the directors on the boards of *Fortune* 500 U.S. corporations are women—and more than 20 percent of those corporations have no women directors. By comparison, Norway has the world's highest percentage of women directors (more than 30 percent), followed by Sweden (more than 25 percent). Then again, Norway's laws require that 40 percent of director's seats on corporate boards be reserved for women. Spain and France have also set quotas for women directors on corporate boards.

Should more women be serving on U.S. corporate boards? From a business perspective, women directors tend to be in tune with the views of female customers, employees, and managers. In many cases, women handle negotiations differently than men do, their careers follow slightly different paths, and their leadership styles may differ, as well. All these differences can be strengths as boards grapple with internal and external issues.

On the other hand, few women have risen to the top management ranks of U.S. corporations, which means that boards must widen their search to find women directors. Also, boards scouting for directors generally look for the best candidates with top-notch skills, education, and achievements, putting much less weight on gender. Should U.S. corporations take deliberate steps to bring more women into the board room?

Sources: Based on information in "Too Many Suits," *Economist*, November 26, 2011, pp. 11-14; "Still Lonely at the Top," *Economist*, July 23, 2011, pp. 61-62; Judy B. Rosener, "The 'Terrible Truth' About Women On Corporate Boards," *Forbes*, June 7, 2011, www.forbes.com.

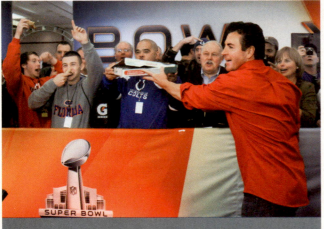

Free pizza! It helps if a corporation has a CEO that believes in the firm's products. In this photo, John Schnatter, founder, chairman of the board, and CEO of Papa John's Pizza, is sharing some of the firm's famous pizza with Super Bowl fans.

example. Those elected from outside the corporation generally are experienced managers or entrepreneurs with proven leadership ability and/or specific talents the organization seems to need. In smaller corporations, majority stockholders usually serve as board members.

The major responsibilities of the board of directors are to set company goals and develop general plans (or strategies) for meeting those goals. The board also is responsible for the firm's overall operation and appointing corporate officers.

Corporate Officers Corporate officers are appointed by the board of directors. Although a small corporation may not have all of the following officers, the chairman of the board, president, executive vice presidents, corporate secretary, and treasurer are all corporate officers. They help the board to make plans, carry out strategies established by the board, hire employees, and manage day-to-day business activities. Periodically (usually each month), they report to the board of directors. And at the annual meeting, the directors report to the stockholders.

ADVANTAGES AND DISADVANTAGES OF CORPORATIONS

 Describe the advantages and disadvantages of a corporation. (5)

corporate officers the chairman of the board, president, executive vice presidents, corporate secretary, treasurer, and any other top executive appointed by the board of directors

Back in October 2000, Manny Ruiz decided that it was time to start his own company. With the help of a team of media specialists, he founded Hispanic PR Wire. In a business where hype is the name of the game, Hispanic PR Wire is the real thing and has established itself as the nation's premier news distribution service reaching U.S. Hispanic media and opinion leaders. Today, the business continues to build on its early success.[8] Mr. Ruiz chose to incorporate this business because it provided a number of advantages that other forms of business ownership did not offer. Typical advantages include limited liability, ease of raising capital, ease of transfer of ownership, perpetual life, and specialized management.

Advantages of Corporations

Limited Liability One of the most attractive features of corporate ownership is **limited liability**. With few exceptions, each owner's financial liability is limited to the amount of money he or she has paid for the corporation's stock. This feature arises from the fact that the corporation is itself a legal person, separate from its owners. If a corporation fails or is involved in a lawsuit and loses, creditors have a claim only on the corporation's assets, not on the stockholders' (owners') personal assets. Because it overcomes the problem of unlimited liability connected with sole proprietorships and general partnerships, limited liability is one of the chief reasons why entrepreneurs often choose the corporate form of organization.

Ease of Raising Capital The corporation is one of the most effective forms of business ownership for raising capital. Like sole proprietorships and partnerships, corporations can borrow from lending institutions. However, they also can raise additional sums of money by selling stock. Individuals are more willing to invest in corporations than in other forms of business because of limited liability, and they can generally sell their stock easily—hopefully for a profit.

Would you buy stock in Facebook? Facebook—the company that started in a Harvard University dorm room back in 2004—finally sold stock to the general public in 2012. The money raised from the public stock offering can be used to "grow" the company. For investors, it was a chance to "cash in" on the phenomenal success of the world's most recognized social media company.

© AP PHOTO/PAUL SAKUMA

Ease of Transfer of Ownership Accessing a brokerage firm Web site or a telephone call to a stockbroker is all that is required to put most stock up for sale. Willing buyers are available for most stocks at the market price. Ownership is transferred when the sale is made, and practically no restrictions apply to the sale and purchase of stock issued by an open corporation.

Perpetual Life Since it is essentially a legal "person," a corporation exists independently of its owners and survives them. The withdrawal, death, or incompetence of a key executive or owner does not cause the corporation to be terminated. Sears, Roebuck and Co. incorporated in 1893 and is one of the nation's largest retailing corporations, even though its original co-founders, Richard Sears and Alvah Roebuck, have been dead for decades.

Specialized Management Typically, corporations are able to recruit more skilled, knowledgeable, and talented managers than proprietorships and partnerships. This is so because they pay bigger salaries, offer excellent employee benefits, and are large enough to offer considerable opportunity for advancement. Within the corporate structure, administration, human resources, finance, marketing, and operations are placed in the charge of experts in these fields.

Disadvantages of Corporations

Like its advantages, many of a corporation's disadvantages stem from its legal definition as an artificial person or legal entity. The most serious disadvantages are described in the following text. (See Table 4.2 for a comparison of some of the advantages and disadvantages of a sole proprietorship, general partnership, and corporation.)

Difficulty and Expense of Formation Forming a corporation can be a relatively complex and costly process. The use of an attorney is usually necessary to complete the legal forms that are submitted to the secretary of state. Application fees, attorney's fees, registration costs associated with selling stock, and other organizational costs can amount to thousands of dollars for even a medium-sized corporation.

limited liability a feature of corporate ownership that limits each owner's financial liability to the amount of money that he or she has paid for the corporation's stock

The costs of incorporating, in terms of both time and money, discourage many owners of smaller businesses from forming corporations.

Government Regulation and Increased Paperwork A corporation must meet various government standards before it can sell its stock to the public. Then it must file many reports on its business operations and finances with local, state, and federal governments. In addition, the corporation must make periodic reports to its stockholders about various aspects of the business. To prepare all the necessary reports, even small corporations often need the help of an attorney, certified public accountant, and other professionals on a regular basis. In addition, a corporation's activities are restricted by law to those spelled out in its charter.

Conflict Within the Corporation Because a large corporation may employ thousands of employees, some conflict is inevitable. For example, the pressure to increase sales revenue, reduce expenses, and increase profits often leads to increased stress and tension for both managers and employees. This is especially true when a corporation operates in a competitive industry, attempts to develop and market new products, or must downsize the workforce to reduce employee salary expense during an economic crisis.

Double Taxation Corporations must pay a tax on their profits. In addition, stockholders must pay a personal income tax on profits received as dividends. Corporate profits thus are taxed twice—once as corporate income and a second time as the personal income of stockholders. *Note:* Both the S-corporation and the limited-liability company discussed in the next section eliminate the disadvantage of double taxation because they are taxed like a partnership.

Lack of Secrecy Because open corporations are required to submit detailed reports to government agencies and to stockholders, they cannot keep their operations confidential. Competitors can study these corporate reports and then use the information to compete more effectively. In effect, every public corporation has to share some of its secrets with its competitors.

TABLE 4.2 Some Advantages and Disadvantages of a Sole Proprietorship, Partnership, and Corporation

	Sole Proprietorship	General Partnership	Regular C-Corporaton
Protecting against liability for debts	Difficult	Difficult	Easy
Raising money	Difficult	Difficult	Easy
Ownership transfer	Difficult	Difficult	Easy
Preserving continuity	Difficult	Difficult	Easy
Government regulations	Few	Few	Many
Formation	Easy	Easy	Difficult
Income taxation	Once	Once	Twice

© CENGAGE LEARNING 2014

SPECIAL TYPES OF BUSINESS OWNERSHIP

6 Examine special types of corporations, including S-corporations, limited-liability companies, and not-for-profit corporations.

In addition to the sole proprietorship, partnership, and the regular corporate form of organization, some entrepreneurs choose other forms of organization that meet their special needs. Additional organizational options include S-corporations, limited-liability companies, and not-for-profit corporations.

S-Corporations

If a corporation meets certain requirements, its directors may apply to the Internal Revenue Service for status as an S-corporation. An **S-corporation** is a corporation that is taxed as though it were a partnership. In other words, the corporation's income is taxed only as the personal income of its stockholders. Corporate profits or losses "pass through" the business and are reported on the owners' personal income tax returns.

To qualify for the special status of an S-corporation, a firm must meet the following criteria:[9]

1. No more than 100 stockholders are allowed.
2. Stockholders must be individuals, estates, or certain trusts.
3. There can be only one class of outstanding stock.
4. The firm must be a domestic corporation eligible to file for S-corporation status.
5. There can be no partnerships, corporations, or nonresident-alien stockholders.
6. All stockholders must agree to the decision to form an S-corporation.

Becoming an S-corporation can be an effective way to avoid double taxation while retaining the corporation's legal benefit of limited liability.

Limited-Liability Companies

A new form of ownership called a *limited-liability company* has been approved in all 50 states—although each state's laws may differ. A **limited-liability company (LLC)** is a form of business ownership that combines the benefits of a corporation and a partnership while avoiding some of the restrictions and disadvantages of those forms of ownership. Chief advantages of an LLC are as follows:

1. Like a sole proprietorship or partnership, an LLC enjoys pass-through taxation. This means that owners report their share of profits or losses in the company on their individual tax returns and avoid the double taxation imposed on most corporations. LLCs with at least two members are taxed like a partnership. LLCs with just one member are taxed like a sole proprietorship. LLCs can even elect to be taxed as a corporation if there are benefits to offset the corporate double taxation.
2. Like a corporation, it provides limited-liability protection for acts and debts of the LLC. An LLC thus extends the concept of personal-asset protection to small business owners.
3. The LLC type of organization provides more management flexibility when compared with corporations. A corporation, for example, is required to hold annual meetings and record meeting minutes; an LLC is not.

Although many experts believe that the LLC is nothing more than a variation of the S-corporation, there is a difference. An LLC is not restricted to 100 stockholders—a common drawback of the S-corporation. LLCs are also less restricted and have more flexibility than S-corporations in terms of who can become an owner. Although the owners of an LLC may file the required articles of organization in any state, most choose to file in their home state—the state where they do most of their business.

S-corporation a corporation that is taxed as though it were a partnership

limited-liability company (LLC) a form of business ownership that combines the benefits of a corporation and a partnership while avoiding some of the restrictions and disadvantages of those forms of ownership

© AP PHOTO/WICHITA FALLS TIMES RECORD NEWS, TORIN HALSEY

Edible Arrangements: A limited-liability company. A limited-liability company doesn't have to be small. Edible Arrangements has over 1,100 stores around the world and is ranked as one of America's top 5,000 fastest growing private companies. It chose the limited-liability form of ownership to avoid some of the restrictions and disadvantages of other forms of business ownership.

Even though most LLCs are small to medium-sized businesses, a limited-liability company doesn't have to be small. American Girl Brands—a limited-liability company that sells dolls, clothing, furniture, books, and magazines for the popular American Girl product lines—chose the LLC type of business ownership because it provided limited liability for investors and avoided some of the restrictions and disadvantages of other forms of business ownership.

Because of the increased popularity of the LLC form of organization, experts are predicting that LLCs may become one of the most popular forms of business ownership available. For more information about the benefits of forming an LLC, go to www.llc.com/LLC_Benefits.html. For help in understanding the differences between a regular corporation, S-corporation, and limited-liability company, see Table 4.3.

Not-for-Profit Corporations

A **not-for-profit corporation** (sometimes referred to as *non-profit*) is a corporation organized to provide a social, educational, religious, or other service rather than to earn a profit. Various charities, museums, private schools, colleges, and charitable organizations are organized in this way, primarily to ensure limited liability.

While the process used to organize a not-for-profit corporation is similar to the process used to create a regular corporation, each state does have different laws. In fact, many of the requirements are different than the requirements for establishing a regular corporation. Once approved by state authorities, not-for-profit corporations must meet specific Internal Revenue Service guidelines in order to obtain tax-exempt status.

Today, there is a renewed interest in not-for-profits because these organizations are formed to improve communities and change lives. For example, Habitat for Humanity is a not-for-profit corporation and was formed to provide homes for qualified lower income people who cannot afford housing. Even though this corporation may receive more money than it spends, any surplus funds are "reinvested" in building activities to provide low-cost housing to qualified individuals. Other examples of not-for-profit corporations include the SeaWorld and Busch Gardens Conservation Fund, the Girl Scouts, the Bill and Melinda Gates Foundation, and many local not-for-profits designed to meet specific needs within a community.

not-for-profit corporation a corporation organized to provide a social, educational, religious, or other service rather than to earn a profit

TABLE 4.3	Some Advantages and Disadvantages of a Regular Corporation, S-Corporation, and Limited-Liability Company		
	Regular C-Corporation	S-Corporation	Limited-Liability Company
Double taxation	Yes	No	No
Limited liability and personal asset protection	Yes	Yes	Yes
Management flexibility	No	No	Yes
Restrictions on the number of owners/ stockholders	No	Yes	No
Internal Revenue Service tax regulations	Many	Many	Fewer

© CENGAGE LEARNING 2014

Many not-for-profit corporations operate in much the same way as for-profit businesses. Employees of not-for-profit businesses are responsible for making sure the organization achieves its goals and objectives, ensuring accountability for finances and donations, and monitoring activities to improve performance of both paid employees and volunteers. If you are interested in a business career, don't rule out the non-profit sector. You might consider volunteering your time and effort in a local not-for-profit organization to see if you enjoy this type of challenge.

COOPERATIVES, JOINT VENTURES, AND SYNDICATES

 7 Discuss the purpose of a cooperative, joint venture, and syndicate.

Today, three additional types of business organizations—cooperatives, joint ventures, and syndicates—are used for special purposes. Each of these forms of organization is unique when compared with more traditional forms of business ownership.

Cooperatives

A **cooperative** is an association of individuals or firms whose purpose is to perform some business function for its members. The cooperative can perform its function more effectively than any member could by acting alone. For example, cooperatives purchase goods in bulk and distribute them to members; thus, the unit cost is lower than it would be if each member bought the goods in a much smaller quantity.

Although cooperatives are found in all segments of our economy, they are most prevalent in agriculture. Farmers use cooperatives to purchase supplies, to buy services such as trucking and storage, and to process and market their products. Ocean Spray Cranberries, Inc., for example, is a cooperative of some 700 cranberry growers and about 50 citrus growers spread throughout the country and is North America's leading producer of canned and bottled juices and juice drinks.[10]

Joint Ventures

A **joint venture** is an agreement between two or more groups to form a business entity in order to achieve a specific goal or to operate for a specific period of time. Both the scope of the joint venture and the liabilities of the people or businesses involved usually are limited to one project. Once the goal is reached, the period of time elapses, or the project is completed, the joint venture is dissolved.

Corporations, as well as individuals, may enter into joint ventures. Major oil producers often have formed a number of joint ventures to share the extremely high cost of exploring for offshore petroleum deposits. And many U.S. companies are forming joint ventures with foreign firms in order to enter new markets around the globe. For example, Walmart has joined forces with India's Bharti Enterprises to establish wholesale cash-and-carry stores that sell directly to local retailers in different cities and towns in India. Plans are for each store to offer an assortment of approximately 6,000 items including food and nonfood items at competitive wholesale prices, allowing retailers and small business owners to lower their cost of operation. By the beginning of 2012, the Bharti Walmart joint venture had opened 14 cash-and-carry stores and employed over 3,000 associates.[11]

Syndicates

A **syndicate** is a temporary association of individuals or firms organized to perform a specific task that requires a large amount of capital. The syndicate is formed because no one person or firm is willing to put up the entire amount required for the undertaking. Like a joint venture, a syndicate is dissolved as soon as its purpose has been accomplished.

cooperative an association of individuals or firms whose purpose is to perform some business function for its members

joint venture an agreement between two or more groups to form a business entity in order to achieve a specific goal or to operate for a specific period of time

syndicate a temporary association of individuals or firms organized to perform a specific task that requires a large amount of capital

Syndicates are used most commonly to underwrite large insurance policies, loans, and investments. To share the risk of default, banks have formed syndicates to provide loans to developing countries. Stock brokerage firms usually join together in the same way to market a new issue of stock. In May 2012 and after years of anticipation in the investment world, Facebook sold stock to investors. Facebook—the world's leading social media Web site—raised $16 billion with the help of a syndicate of Wall Street firms including Bank of America Merrill Lynch, JPMorgan Chase & Co., Morgan Stanley, and Goldman Sachs.[12] This initial public offering, often referred to as an IPO, is one of the largest in recent history. (An *initial public offering* is the term used to describe the first time a corporation sells stock to the general public.)

Explain how growth from within and growth through mergers can enable a business to expand.

CORPORATE GROWTH

Growth seems to be a basic characteristic of business. One reason for seeking growth has to do with profit: A larger firm generally has greater sales revenue and thus greater profit. Another reason is that in a growing economy, a business that does not grow is actually shrinking relative to the economy. A third reason is that business growth is a means by which some executives boost their power, prestige, and reputation.

Growth poses new problems and requires additional resources that first must be available and then must be used effectively. The main ingredient in growth is capital—and as we have noted, capital is most readily available to corporations.

Growth from Within

Most corporations grow by expanding their present operations. Some introduce and sell new but related products. Others expand the sale of present products to new geographic markets or to new groups of consumers in geographic markets already served. Although Walmart was started by Sam Walton in 1962 with one discount store, today Walmart has over 10,000 stores in the United States and 27 other countries and has long-range plans for expanding into additional international markets.[13]

Growth from within, especially when carefully planned and controlled, can have relatively little adverse effect on a firm. For the most part, the firm continues to do what it has been doing, but on a larger scale. For instance, Larry Ellison, co-founder and CEO of Oracle Corporation of Redwood Shores, California, built the firm's annual revenues up from a mere $282 million in 1988 to approximately $36 billion today.[14] Much of this growth has taken place over the last 15 years as Oracle capitalized on its global leadership in information management software.

Growth Through Mergers and Acquisitions

Another way a firm can grow is by purchasing another company. The purchase of one corporation by another is called a **merger**. An *acquisition* is essentially the same thing as a merger, but the term usually is used in reference to a large corporation's purchases of other corporations. Although most mergers and acquisitions are friendly, hostile takeovers also occur. A **hostile takeover** is a situation in which the management and board of directors of a firm targeted for acquisition disapprove of the merger.

When a merger or acquisition becomes hostile, a corporate raider—another company or a wealthy investor—may make a tender offer or start a proxy fight to gain control of the target company. A **tender offer** is an offer to purchase the stock of a firm targeted for acquisition at a price just high enough to tempt stockholders to sell their shares. Corporate raiders also may initiate a proxy fight. A **proxy fight** is

merger the purchase of one corporation by another

hostile takeover a situation in which the management and board of directors of a firm targeted for acquisition disapprove of the merger

tender offer an offer to purchase the stock of a firm targeted for acquisition at a price just high enough to tempt stockholders to sell their shares

proxy fight a technique used to gather enough stockholder votes to control a targeted company

a technique used to gather enough stockholder votes to control a targeted company.

If the corporate raider is successful and takes over the targeted company, existing management usually is replaced. Faced with this probability, existing management may take specific actions, sometimes referred to as "poison pills," "shark repellents," or "porcupine provisions," to maintain control of the firm and avoid the hostile takeover. Whether mergers are friendly or hostile, they are generally classified as *horizontal, vertical,* or *conglomerate* (see Figure 4.5).

Horizontal Mergers A *horizontal merger* is a merger between firms that make and sell similar products or services in similar markets. The proposed merger between AT&T and T-Mobile was an example of a horizontal merger because both firms provide cell phone service to their customers. This type of merger tends to reduce the number of firms in an industry—and thus may reduce competition. As a result most horizontal mergers are reviewed carefully by federal agencies before they are approved in order to protect competition in the marketplace. In fact, the AT&T merger with T-Mobile was effectively blocked when the U.S. Department of Justice filed a law suit to block the merger. According to the Department of Justice, the main reason behind the government's legal action was to protect the competitive environment and the consumers' right to choose. Rather than fight the government's attempt to block the merger, AT&T withdrew its offer to acquire T-Mobile.

Growth through global joint ventures. General Electric, which owns many businesses that fortify the world's infrastructure, recently formed two joint ventures in Russia. Here is Russian president Vladimir Putin meeting with GE executives.

Vertical Mergers A *vertical merger* is a merger between firms that operate at different but related levels in the production and marketing of a product. Generally, one of the merging firms is either a supplier or a customer of the other. A vertical

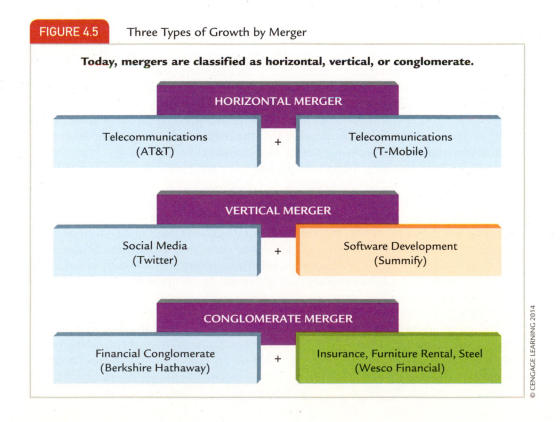

FIGURE 4.5	Three Types of Growth by Merger

Today, mergers are classified as horizontal, vertical, or conglomerate.

HORIZONTAL MERGER

Telecommunications (AT&T) + Telecommunications (T-Mobile)

VERTICAL MERGER

Social Media (Twitter) + Software Development (Summify)

CONGLOMERATE MERGER

Financial Conglomerate (Berkshire Hathaway) + Insurance, Furniture Rental, Steel (Wesco Financial)

© CENGAGE LEARNING 2014

merger occurred when social media giant Twitter acquired Summify. At the time of the 2012 merger, Summify, based in Vancouver, was a startup technology company in the process of building the next generation of news-reader software that had a unique approach to summarizing the most important information from social media feeds from Google, Facebook, and Twitter. Rather than develop its own software to summarize the most important information, Twitter simply purchased the Summify company.[15]

Conglomerate Mergers A *conglomerate* merger takes place between firms in completely different industries. A conglomerate merger occurred when financial conglomerate Berkshire Hathaway acquired Wesco Financial Corporation. While both companies were recognized as successful companies that have a history of increasing sales revenues and profits, they operate in different industries. Berkshire Hathaway, led by its CEO Warren Buffett, has a long history of acquiring firms that have great financial potential. Wesco, on the other hand, is a smaller company with its main business interests in insurance, furniture rental, and steel.[16] The Berkshire Hathaway–Wesco merger was friendly because it was beneficial for both firms. (Note: For more information on the Berkshire Hathaway Corporation and its merger activities, read Case 4.2 on page 130.)

Merger and Acquisition Trends for the Future

While there have always been mergers and acquisitions, the recent economic crisis has changed the dynamics of how and why firms merge. Recently, mergers and acquisitions have been fueled by the desire of financially secure firms to take over firms in financial trouble. For a firm experiencing financial difficulties, a merger or acquisition is often a better option than bankruptcy. During the recent economic crisis, this trend was especially evident in the financial services and banking industry. For example, Wachovia was purchased by Wells Fargo in order to avoid a Wachovia bank failure or a government takeover of Wachovia's assets and loan portfolio. In other situations, a financially secure firm will purchase a company experiencing financial problems because it is a good investment.

Economists, financial analysts, corporate managers, and stockholders still hotly debate whether mergers and acquisitions are good for the economy—or for individual companies—in the long run. Takeover advocates argue that for companies that have been taken over, the purchasers have been able to make the company more profitable and productive by installing a new top-management team, by reducing expenses, and by forcing the company to concentrate on one main business.

Takeover opponents argue that takeovers do nothing to enhance corporate profitability or productivity. These critics argue that the only people who benefit from takeovers are investment bankers, brokerage firms, and takeover "artists," who receive financial rewards by manipulating corporations rather than by producing tangible products or services.

Most experts now predict that mergers and acquisitions after the economic crisis will be the result of cash-rich companies looking to acquire businesses that will enhance their position in the marketplace. Analysts also anticipate more mergers that involve companies or investors from other countries. Regardless of the companies involved or where the companies are from, future mergers and acquisitions will be driven by solid business logic and the desire to compete in the international marketplace.

Whether they are sole proprietorships, partnerships, corporations, or some other form of business ownership, most U.S. businesses are small. In the next chapter, we focus on these small businesses. We examine, among other things, the meaning of the word *small* as it applies to business and the place of small business in the American economy.

Kimpton Hotel & Restaurant Group

While Kimpton's chef partners use their culinary talents to build the restaurant side of the business, its hotel experts focus on delivering personalized customer service, which requires a knowledgeable, dedicated workforce. Kimpton grooms future managers through a formal training program and matches promising employees with experienced mentors to further develop their skills. Based on its many employee development and motivation programs, it has twice been named to the *Fortune* magazine list of "Best Companies to Work For."

The company has also made environmental protection one of its top priorities. Following its Kimpton EarthCare plan, it has installed water-conservation systems in its hotels, expanded its recycling programs, and invested in energy-efficient equipment to save power. Going further,

Kimpton works with the Nature Conservancy and the Trust for Public Land to raise money for environmental projects. The company isn't finished growing—watch for more boutique hotels and restaurants to open in the coming years.

Questions

1. Do you think Kimpton should switch from the LLC form of ownership to an open corporation to be able to raise money by selling shares of stock? Explain your answer.
2. Kimpton sometimes buys individual hotels from other companies, renovates them, and reopens them under a new name. Why would Kimpton do this rather than grow through a merger with a larger, more recognized hotel?

SUMMARY

Looking for Success?
Get Flashcards, Quizzes, Games, Crosswords, and more @ www.cengagebrain.com.

 Describe the advantages and disadvantages of sole proprietorships.

In a sole proprietorship, all business profits become the property of the owner, but the owner is also personally responsible for all business debts. A successful sole proprietorship can be a great source of pride for the owner. When comparing different types of business ownership, the sole proprietorship is the simplest form of business to enter, control, and leave. It also pays no special taxes. Perhaps for these reasons, 72 percent of all American business firms are sole proprietorships. Sole proprietorships nevertheless have disadvantages, such as unlimited liability and limits on one person's ability to borrow or to be an expert in all fields. As a result, this form of ownership accounts for only 4 percent of total revenues when compared with partnerships and corporations.

 Explain the different types of partners and the importance of partnership agreements.

Like sole proprietors, general partners are responsible for running the business and for all business debts. Limited partners receive a share of the profit in return for investing in the business. However, they are not responsible for

business debts beyond the amount they have invested. It is also possible to form a master limited partnership (MLP) and sell units of ownership to raise capital. Regardless of the type of partnership, it is always a good idea to have a written agreement (or articles of partnership) setting forth the terms of a partnership.

 Describe the advantages and disadvantages of partnerships.

Although partnership eliminates some of the disadvantages of sole proprietorship, it is the least popular of the major forms of business ownership. The major advantages of a partnership include ease of start-up, availability of capital and credit, personal interest, combined skills and knowledge, retention of profits, and possible tax advantages. The effects of management disagreements are one of the major disadvantages of a partnership. Other disadvantages include unlimited liability (in a general partnership), lack of continuity, and frozen investment. By forming a limited partnership, the disadvantage of unlimited liability may be eliminated for the limited partner(s). This same disadvantage may be eliminated for partners that form a limited-liability partnership (LLP). Of course, special requirements must be met if partners form either the limited partnership or the limited-liability partnership.

Summarize how a corporation is formed.

A corporation is an artificial person created by law, with most of the legal rights of a real person, including the right to start and operate a business, to buy or sell property, to borrow money, to be sued or sue, and to enter into contracts. With the corporate form of ownership, stock can be sold to individuals to raise capital. The people who own a corporation's common or preferred stock are called stockholders. Stockholders are entitled to receive any dividends paid by the corporation, and common stockholders can vote either in person or by proxy. Generally, corporations are classified as closed corporations (few stockholders) or open corporations (many stockholders).

The process of forming a corporation is called incorporation. Most experts believe that the services of a lawyer are necessary when making decisions about where to incorporate and about obtaining a corporate charter, issuing stock, holding an organizational meeting, and all other legal details involved in incorporation. In theory, stockholders are able to control the activities of the corporation because they elect the board of directors who appoint the corporate officers.

 Describe the advantages and disadvantages of a corporation.

Perhaps the major advantage of the corporate form is limited liability—stockholders are not liable for the corporation's debts beyond the amount they paid for its stock. Other important advantages include ease of raising capital, ease of transfer of ownership, perpetual life, and specialized management. A major disadvantage of a large corporation is double taxation: All profits are taxed once as corporate income and again as personal income because stockholders must pay a personal income tax on the profits they receive as dividends. Other disadvantages include difficulty and expense of formation, government regulation, conflict within the corporation, and lack of secrecy.

6 **Examine special types of corporations, including S-corporations, limited-liability companies, and not-for-profit corporations.**

S-corporations are corporations that are taxed as though they were partnerships but that enjoy the benefit of limited liability. To qualify as an S-corporation, a number of criteria must be met. A limited-liability company (LLC) is a form of business ownership that provides limited liability and has fewer restrictions when compared to a regular corporation or an S-corporation. LLCs with at least two members are taxed like a partnership and thus avoid the double taxation imposed on most corporations. LLCs with just one member

are taxed like a sole proprietorship. When compared with a regular corporation or an S-corporation, an LLC is more flexible. Not-for-profit corporations are formed to provide social services and to improve communities and change lives rather than to earn profits.

 Discuss the purpose of a cooperative, joint venture, and syndicate.

Three additional forms of business ownership—the cooperative, joint venture, and syndicate—are used by their owners to meet special needs. A cooperative is an association of individuals or firms whose purpose is to perform some business function for its members. A joint venture is formed when two or more groups form a business entity in order to achieve a specific goal or to operate for a specific period of time. Once the goal is reached, the period of time elapses, or the project is completed, the joint venture is dissolved. A syndicate is a temporary association of individuals or firms organized to perform a specific task that requires large amounts of capital. Like a joint venture, a syndicate is dissolved as soon as its purpose has been accomplished.

 Explain how growth from within and growth through mergers can enable a business to expand.

A corporation may grow by expanding its present operations or through a merger or an acquisition. Although most mergers are friendly, hostile takeovers also occur. A hostile takeover is a situation in which the management and board of directors of a firm targeted for acquisition disapprove of the merger. Mergers generally are classified as horizontal, vertical, or conglomerate.

During the recent economic crisis, mergers and acquisitions have been fueled by the desire of financially secure firms to take over firms in financial trouble. For a firm experiencing financial trouble, a merger or acquisition is often a better option than bankruptcy. In other situations, a financially secure firm will purchase a company experiencing financial problems because it is a good investment.

While economists, financial analysts, corporate managers, and stockholders debate the merits of mergers, some trends should be noted. First, experts predict that future mergers will be the result of cash-rich companies looking to acquire businesses that will enhance their position in the marketplace. Second, more mergers are likely to involve foreign companies or investors. Third, mergers will be driven by business logic and the desire to compete in the international marketplace.

KEY TERMS

You should now be able to define and give an example relevant to each of the following terms:

preferred stock (116)
dividend (117)
proxy (117)
board of directors (117)
corporate officers (118)

limited liability (119)
S-corporation (121)
limited-liability company
   (LLC) (121)

not-for-profit corporation
   (122)
cooperative (123)
joint venture (123)
syndicate (123)

merger (124)
hostile takeover (124)
tender offer (124)
proxy fight (125)

REVIEW QUESTIONS

1. What is a sole proprietorship? What are the major advantages and disadvantages of this form of business ownership?
2. How does a partnership differ from a sole proprietorship? Which disadvantages of sole proprietorship does the partnership tend to eliminate or reduce?
3. What is the difference between a general partner and a limited partner?
4. What issues should be included in a partnership agreement? Why?
5. Explain the difference between
   a. an open corporation and a closed corporation.
   b. a domestic corporation, a foreign corporation, and an alien corporation.
6. Outline the incorporation process, and describe the basic corporate structure.

7. What rights do stockholders have?
8. What are the primary duties of a corporation's board of directors? How are directors selected?
9. What are the major advantages and disadvantages associated with the corporate form of business ownership?
10. How do an S-corporation and a limited-liability company differ?
11. Why are not-for-profit corporations and cooperatives formed? Explain how they operate.
12. In what ways are joint ventures and syndicates alike? In what ways do they differ?
13. What is a hostile takeover? How is it related to a tender offer and a proxy fight?
14. Describe the three types of mergers.

DISCUSSION QUESTIONS

1. If you were to start a business, which ownership form would you choose? What factors might affect your choice?
2. Why might an investor choose to become a partner in a limited partnership instead of purchasing the stock of an open corporation?
3. Discuss the following statement: "Corporations are not really run by their owners."

4. What kinds of services do not-for-profit corporations provide? Would a career in a not-for-profit corporation appeal to you?
5. Is growth a good thing for all firms? How does management know when a firm is ready to grow?

Video Case 4.1
AT&T and T-Mobile: What Went Wrong with Their Merger?

When it tried to buy T-Mobile for $39 billion in 2011, AT&T went so far as to offer the company a "break up" fee of $4 billion if the deal fell through. Why was AT&T so determined to purchase T-Mobile? AT&T was no. 2 in the wireless phone-service market. T-Mobile was no. 4. By merging, they would have become the nation's largest wireless provider, surpassing Verizon. The deal would also have given AT&T access to the spectrum (airwaves) T-Mobile owned but couldn't afford to upgrade to 4G (state-of-the art, fourth-generation technology).

Executives at the companies said that in addition to creating jobs, the merger would result in fewer dropped calls and faster connection times for customers. The merged company would also be able to immediately expand wireless service to rural areas that lacked it. "AT&T will immediately gain cell sites

equivalent to what would have taken on average five years to build without the transaction," the two companies said in their merger announcement. The announcement also referred to a government report that showed that despite many mergers in the industry over the past decade, the price of wireless service had declined.

Investors cheered when they heard about the merger. However, many consumers, the Department of Justice, and the Federal Communications Commission (FCC) were wary of the deal. The merged company would have controlled nearly half of the market. The only remaining big players in the industry would have been Verizon and Sprint. Some industry experts thought Sprint might get forced out of the market because it held the least market share. They also believed few new companies would enter

business is now growing, and you have decided to add a full line of catering services. This means more work and responsibility. You will need someone to help you, but you are undecided about what to do. Should you hire an employee or find a partner? If you add a partner, what type of decisions should be made to create a partnership agreement?

Assignment

In a group, discuss the following questions:

a. What are the advantages and disadvantages of adding a partner versus hiring an employee?

b. Assume that you have decided to form a partnership. What articles should be included in a partnership agreement?

c. How would you go about finding a partner?

Summarize your group's answers to these questions, and present them to your class. As a group, prepare an articles-of-partnership agreement. Be prepared to discuss the pros and cons of your group's agreement with other groups from your class, as well as to examine their agreements.

⑤ RESEARCHING DIFFERENT CAREERS

Many people spend their entire lives working in jobs that they do not enjoy. Why is this so? Often, it is because they have taken the first job they were offered without giving it much thought.

How can you avoid having this happen to you? First, you should determine your "personal profile" by identifying and analyzing your own strengths, weaknesses, things you enjoy, and things you dislike. Second, you should identify the types of jobs that fit your profile. Third, you should identify and research the companies that offer those jobs.

Assignment

a. Take two sheets of paper and draw a line down the middle of each sheet, forming two columns on each page. Label column 1 "Things I Enjoy or Like to Do," column 2 "Things I Do Not Like Doing," column 3 "My Strengths," and column 4 "My Weaknesses."

b. Record data in each column over a period of at least one week. You may find it helpful to have a relative or friend give you input.

c. Summarize the data, and write a profile of yourself.

d. Take your profile to a career counselor at your college or to the public library and ask for help in identifying jobs that fit your profile. Your college may offer testing to assess your skills and personality. The Internet is another resource.

e. Research the companies that offer the types of jobs that fit your profile.

f. Write a report on your findings.

ENDNOTES

1. Sources: Based on information from the Kimpton Hotel and Restaurant Group, LLC Web site at www.kimptonhotels.com (accessed February 9, 2012); Tim McKeough, "Putting Nemo to Work," *New York Times*, November 17, 2011, p. D4; Robert Klara, "Boutique Chic," *Adweek*, September 26, 2011, p. 32; "5 Questions for Niki Leondakis," *Hospitality Design*, July 2011, p. 76; Len Vermillion, "Kimpton's 30-Year Journey," *Lodging*, April 13, 2011, www.lodgingmagazine.com; Paris Wolfe, "Kimpton Reaches 51 Hotels in 30 Years," *Lodging Hospitality Online*, June 15, 2011, http://lhon-line.com; Lisa Fickenscher, "Crain's 2011 Best Places to Work in NYC," *Crain's New York Business*, December 5, 2011, p. 22.

2. The IVY Planning Group Web site at www.ivygroupllc.com (accessed February 2, 2012).

3. The National Association of Publicly Traded Partnerships Web site at www.naptp.com (accessed February 5, 2012).

4. The Procter & Gamble Web site at www.pg.com (accessed February 5, 2012).

5. Ibid.

6. The Mars Corporate Web site at www.mars.com (accessed February 5, 2012).

7. The My New Company Web site at www.mynewcompany.com (accessed February 2, 2012).

8. The Hispanic PR Wire Web site at www.hispanicprwire.com (accessed February 3, 2012).

9. The Internal Revenue Service Web site at www.irs.gov (accessed February 2, 2012).

10. The Ocean Spray Cranberries, Inc. Web site at www.oceanspray.com (accessed January 30, 2012).

11. The Walmart Corporate Web site at www.walmartstores.com (accessed December 31, 2011).

12. "Facebook, Banks Sued Over Pre-IPO Analyst Calls," The Reuters Web site at www.reuters.com (accessed May 23, 2012).

13. The Walmart Corporate Web site at www.walmartstores.com (accessed February 4, 2012).

14. The Oracle Web site at www.oracle.com (accessed June 23, 2011).

15. "Twitter Acquires Social Media Feed Condenser Summify," The Tech World Web site at www.techworld.com (accessed February 4, 2012).

16. Maria Aspen, "Berkshire Hathaway to Buy Rest of Wesco," The Thomson Reuters Web site at www.reuters.com (accessed February 4, 2012).

17. Based on information from Amy Schatz and Greg Bensinger, "FCC Blasts AT&T Deal," *Wall Street Journal*, November 30, 2011; http://online.wsj.com; David Goldman, "DOJ Files Antitrust Suit to Block AT&T Merger with T-Mobile, *CNNMoney*, August 31, 2011, http://money.cnn.com; Russ Wiles, "AT&T Merger with T-Mobile May Cut Competition," *Arizona Republic*, March 11, 2011, www.azcentral.com/arizonarepublic.

18. Based on information from the Berkshire Hathaway Corporate Web site at www.berkshirehathaway.com (accessed February 6, 2012); Becky Quick, "Who Says the Economy Is Rebounding?" *Fortune*, May 3, 2010, www.fortune.com; Angela Greiling Keane and Ed Dufner, "CSX's Ward Calls Buffett's Rail Purchase 'Brilliant,'" *BusinessWeek*, April 14, 2010, www.businessweek.com; Alice Schroeder, *The Snowball: Warren Buffett and the Business of Life* (New York: Bantam Dell, 2008), Chapters 22 and 44, www.BerkshireHathaway.com.

© MANGOSTOCK/SHUTTERSTOCK

Small Business, Entrepreneurship, and Franchises

5

Once you complete this chapter, you will be able to:

1 Define what a small business is and recognize the fields in which small businesses are concentrated.

2 Identify the people who start small businesses and the reasons why some succeed and many fail.

3 Assess the contributions of small businesses to our economy.

4 Describe the advantages and disadvantages of operating a small business.

5 Explain how the Small Business Administration helps small businesses.

6 Explain the concept and types of franchising.

7 Analyze the growth of franchising and its advantages and disadvantages.

Locker Lookz Looks for Higher Sales

Texas entrepreneurs Christi Sterling and JoAnn Brewer started Locker Lookz in 2008 with $50,000 in personal savings and an idea based on their daughters' interest in personalizing their school lockers. Shopping for fun accessories before the start of school, the mothers and their daughters found very little ready-made for dressing up a locker, in stores or online. Eventually, they bought materials at local craft stores to create wallpaper and carpeting for the girls' lockers. When friends started asking where they could buy these decorations, "We had a light-bulb moment," Brewer says. "There's a real need for something that's cute, easy, and one-stop shopping."

The co-founders designed a limited line of locker decorations, all styled for middle-school tastes, and priced at $10 and up. Next, they connected with a sales expert who specializes in distributing products through local and national retailers. With his help, Sterling and Brewer arranged for overseas manufacturers to produce the items, found a packager to ready the products for retail display, and completed a successful sales test in several dozen stores. Soon, JCPenney and Hallmark were placing orders, followed by Learning Express and other retail chains.

By mid-2011, more than 1,200 stores were signed up to carry Locker Lookz accessories for the back-to-school selling season. Now Sterling and Brewer had a few weeks to raise $1 million to pay for manufacturing and shipping the goods from factories in China to stores across the United States. Just in time, they raised cash from relatives and from a church investment group. The containers filled with Locker Lookz merchandise arrived on schedule, and soon the co-founders began crisscrossing the country to publicize their expanding product line.

Today, Locker Lookz is an entrepreneurial multimillion-dollar company facing increased competition from other firms that see locker decor as a profitable business opportunity. Although the preferences of preteen girls can change rapidly and without warning, Brewer and Sterling are paying close attention to fashion trends and asking their daughters' advice about new product ideas. How much room does Locker Lookz have to grow?[1]

As is in the case of Christie Sterling's and JoAnn Brewer's Locker Lookz, most businesses start small and those that survive usually stay small. They provide a solid foundation for our economy—as employers, as suppliers and purchasers of goods and services, and as taxpayers.

In this chapter, we do not take small businesses for granted. Instead, we look closely at this important business sector—beginning with a definition of small business, a description of industries that often attract small businesses, and a profile of some of the people who start small businesses. Next, we consider the importance of small businesses in our economy. We also present the advantages and disadvantages of smallness in business. We then describe services provided by the Small Business Administration, a government agency formed to assist owners and managers of small businesses. We conclude the chapter with a discussion of the pros and cons of franchising, an approach to small-business ownership that has become very popular in the last 50 years.

SMALL BUSINESS: A PROFILE

1 Define what a small business is and recognize the fields in which small businesses are concentrated.

The Small Business Administration (SBA) defines a **small business** as "one which is independently owned and operated for profit and is not dominant in its field." How small must a firm be not to dominate its field? That depends on the particular industry it is in. The SBA has developed the following specific "smallness" guidelines for the various industries, as shown in Table 5.1.[2] The SBA periodically revises and simplifies its small-business size regulations.

Annual sales in millions of dollars may not seem very small. However, for many firms, profit is only a small percentage of total sales. Thus, a firm may earn only $40,000 or $50,000 on yearly sales of $1 million—and that is small in comparison with the profits earned by most medium-sized and large firms. Moreover, most small firms have annual sales well below the maximum limits in the SBA guidelines.

Small businesses are very important to the U.S. economy. For example, small businesses

- represent 99.7 percent of all employer firms;
- employ about half of all private sector employees;
- pay 43 percent of total U.S. private payroll;
- have generated 65 percent of net new jobs over the past 17 years;
- create more than half of the nonfarm private GDP;
- hire 43 percent of high-tech workers (scientists, engineers, computer programmers, and others);
- are 52 percent home-based and 2 percent franchises;
- made up 97.5 percent of all identified exporters and produced 31 percent of export value in FY 2008; and
- produced 16.5 times more patents per employee than large patenting firms.[3]

The Small-Business Sector

In the United States, it typically takes less than a week and $500 to establish a business as a legal entity. The steps include registering the name of the business, applying for

TABLE 5.1   Industry Group-Size Standards

Small-business size standards are usually stated in number of employees or average annual sales. In the United States, 99.7 percent of all businesses are considered small.	
Industry Group	**Size Standard**
Manufacturing, mining industries	500 employees
Wholesale trade	100 employees
Agriculture	$750,000
Retail trade	$7 million
General and heavy construction (except dredging)	$33.5 million
Dredging	$20 million
Special trade contractors	$14 million
Travel agencies	$3.5 million (commissions and other income)
Business and personal services except	$7 million
• Architectural, engineering, surveying, and mapping services	$4.5 million
• Dry cleaning and carpet cleaning services	$4.5 million

Source: www.sba.gov/content/summary-size-standards-industry (accessed March 19, 2012).

small business one that is independently owned and operated for profit and is not dominant in its field

tax IDs, and setting up unemployment and workers' compensation insurance. In Japan, however, a typical entrepreneur spends more than $3,500 and 31 days to follow 11 different procedures.

A surprising number of Americans take advantage of their freedom to start a business. There are, in fact, about 27.5 million businesses in this country. Only just 18,469 of these employ more than 500 workers—enough to be considered large.

Interest in owning or starting a small business has never been greater than it is today. During the last decade, the number of small businesses in the United States has increased 49 percent. For the last few years, new-business formation in the United States has broken successive records, except during the 2001–2002 and 2008 recessions. Recently, nearly 552,600 new businesses were incorporated. Furthermore, part-time entrepreneurs have increased fivefold in recent years; they now account for one-third of all small businesses.[4]

According to a recent study, 69 percent of new businesses survive at least two years, about 50 percent survive at least five years, and 31 percent survive at least ten years.[5] The primary reason for these failures is mismanagement resulting from a lack of business know-how. The makeup of the small-business sector thus is constantly changing. Despite the high failure rate, many small businesses succeed modestly. Some, like Apple Computer, Inc., are extremely successful—to the point where they can no longer be considered small. Taken together, small businesses are also responsible for providing a high percentage of the jobs in the United States. According to some estimates, the figure is well over 50 percent.

Industries That Attract Small Businesses

Some industries, such as auto manufacturing, require huge investments in machinery and equipment. Businesses in such industries are big from the day they are started—if an entrepreneur or group of entrepreneurs can gather the capital required to start one.

By contrast, a number of other industries require only a low initial investment and some special skills or knowledge. It is these industries that tend to attract new businesses. Growing industries, such as outpatient-care facilities, are attractive because of their profit potential. However, knowledgeable entrepreneurs choose areas with which they are familiar, and these are most often the more established industries.

Small enterprise spans the gamut from corner newspaper vending to the development of optical fibers. The owners of small businesses sell gasoline, flowers, and coffee to go. They publish magazines, haul freight, teach languages, and program computers. They make wines, movies, and high-fashion clothes. They build new homes and restore old ones. They fix appliances, recycle metals, and sell used cars. They drive cabs and fly planes. They make us well when we are ill, and they sell us the products of corporate giants. In fact, 74 percent of real estate, rental, and leasing industries; 61 percent of the businesses in the leisure and hospitality services; and 86 percent of the construction industries are dominated by small businesses. The various kinds of businesses generally fall into three broad categories of industry: distribution, service, and production.

Distribution Industries This category includes retailing, wholesaling, transportation, and communications—industries concerned with the movement of goods from producers to consumers. Distribution industries account for approximately 33 percent of all small businesses. Of these, almost three-quarters are involved in retailing, that is, the sale of goods directly to consumers. Clothing and jewelry stores, pet shops, bookstores, and grocery stores, for example, are all retailing firms. Slightly less than one-quarter of the small distribution firms are wholesalers. Wholesalers purchase products in quantity from manufacturers and then resell them to retailers.

Service Industries This category accounts for more than 48 percent of all small businesses. Of these, about three-quarters provide such nonfinancial services as medical and dental care; watch, shoe, and TV repairs; haircutting and styling; restaurant meals; and dry cleaning. About 8 percent of the small service firms offer financial services, such as accounting, insurance, real estate, and investment counseling. An increasing number of self-employed Americans are running service businesses from home.

Production Industries This last category includes the construction, mining, and manufacturing industries. Only about 19 percent of all small businesses are in this group, mainly because these industries require relatively large initial investments. Small firms that do venture into production generally make parts and subassemblies for larger manufacturing firms or supply special skills to larger construction firms.

THE PEOPLE IN SMALL BUSINESSES: THE ENTREPRENEURS

 Identify the people who start small businesses and the reasons why some succeed and many fail.

The entrepreneurial spirit is alive and well in the United States. One study revealed that the U.S. population is quite entrepreneurial when compared with those of other countries. More than 70 percent of Americans would prefer being an entrepreneur to working for someone else. This compares with 46 percent of adults in Western Europe and 58 percent of adults in Canada. Another study on entrepreneurial activity for 2002 found that of 36 countries studied, the United States was in the top third in entrepreneurial activity and was the leader when compared with Japan, Canada, and Western Europe.[6]

Small businesses typically are managed by the people who started and own them. Most of these people have held jobs with other firms and still could be so employed if they wanted. Yet owners of small businesses would rather take the risk of starting and operating their own firms, even if the money they make is less than the salaries they otherwise might earn.

Researchers have suggested a variety of personal factors as reasons why people go into business for themselves. These are discussed next.

Characteristics of Entrepreneurs

Entrepreneurial spirit is the desire to create a new business. For example, Nikki Olyai always knew that she wanted to create and develop her own business. Her father, a successful businessman in Iran, was her role model. She came to the United States at the age of 17 and lived with a host family in Salem, Oregon, attending high school there. Undergraduate and graduate degrees in computer science led her to start Innovision Technologies while she held two other jobs to keep the business going and took care of her four-year-old son. Recently, Nikki Olyai's business was honored by the Women's Business Enterprise National Council's "Salute to Women's Business Enterprises" as one of 11 top successful firms. For three consecutive years, her firm was selected as a "Future 50 of Greater Detroit Company."

Other Personal Factors

Other personal factors in small-business success include

- independence;
- a desire to determine one's own destiny;

©AP PHOTO/NATI HARNIK

Meet Sam Altman, co-founder and CEO of Loopt. In 2004, Altman co-founded a location-based social networking mobile application when he was a sophomore majoring in computer science at Stanford University. *BusinessWeek* named him one of the "Best Young Entrepreneurs in Technology" and *Inc.* magazine ranked him number 4 among the top 30 entrepreneurs under the age of 30. In 2012, prepaid money card issuer Green Dot Corp. agreed to acquire Loopt Inc. for $43.4 million.

- a willingness to find and accept a challenge;
- family background (in particular, researchers think that people whose families have been in business, successfully or not, are most apt to start and run their own businesses); and
- age (those who start their own businesses also tend to cluster around certain ages—more than 70 percent are between 24 and 44 years of age; see Figure 5.1).

Motivation

There must be some motivation to start a business. A person may decide that he or she simply has "had enough" of working and earning a profit for someone else. Another may lose his or her job for some reason and decide to start the business he or she has always wanted rather than to seek another job. Still another person may have an idea for a new product or a new way to sell an existing product. Or the opportunity to go into business may arise suddenly, perhaps as a result of a hobby. For example, Cheryl Strand started baking and decorating cakes from her home while working full time as a word processor at Clemson University. Her cakes became so popular that she soon found herself working through her lunch breaks and late into the night to meet customer demand.

Women as Small-Business Owners

According to the latest 2012 data available from the Small Business Administration:

- Women are 51 percent of the U.S. population, and according to the SBA, they owned at least 50 percent of all small businesses in 2008.
- Women already own 66 percent of the home-based businesses in this country, and the number of men in home-based businesses is growing rapidly.
- About 7.8 million women-owned businesses in the United States provide almost 7.6 million jobs and generate $1.2 trillion in sales.
- Women-owned businesses in the United States have proven that they are more successful; more than 40 percent have been in business for 12 years or more.
- Women-owned businesses are financially sound and credit-worthy, and their risk of failure is lower than average.
- Compared to other working women, self-employed women are older, better educated, and have more managerial experience.
- Just over one-half of small businesses are home based, and 91 percent have no employees. About 60 percent of home-based businesses are in service industries, 16 percent in construction, 14 percent in retail trade, and the rest in manufacturing, finance, transportation, communications, wholesaling, and other industries.[7]

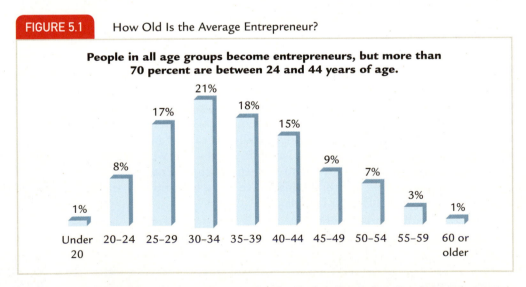

FIGURE 5.1 How Old Is the Average Entrepreneur?

People in all age groups become entrepreneurs, but more than 70 percent are between 24 and 44 years of age.

Under 20	20–24	25–29	30–34	35–39	40–44	45–49	50–54	55–59	60 or older
1%	8%	17%	21%	18%	15%	9%	7%	3%	1%

Source: Data developed and provided by the National Federation of Independent Business Foundation and sponsored by the American Express Travel Related Services Company, Inc.

Career SUCCESS

Is Entrepreneurship in Your Future?

Some entrepreneurs realize early that they want to start a business. Others become entrepreneurs after working for other people. You can take a number of tests to assess whether you have the drive, temperament, and attitude to be your own boss. No test can tell whether your business will be successful, but you can get a sense of your own skills and capabilities as a future entrepreneur.

Stop by the career center on campus, which may offer an entrepreneurship self-test. For another perspective on your entrepreneurial potential, take at least one more test. For example, the informal questions on the Isenberg Entrepreneur Test, created by Professor Daniel Isenberg of Babson College, are designed to get you thinking about what you like and why.

Do you like to challenge yourself? Would you prefer to fail at something you've chosen rather than succeed at something chosen by someone else?

The U.S. Small Business Administration (www.sba.gov) offers an online self-assessment to determine whether you're ready to start your own business. In addition, compare what you know about yourself to the SBA's listing of entrepreneur characteristics to see how well you match up. Similarly, the Business Development Bank of Canada's online test shows whether your attitudes, aptitudes, and motivations would be a good fit with the entrepreneurial life.

Sources: Based on information in Daniel Isenberg, "Should You Be an Entrepreneur? Take This Test," *Harvard Business Review*, February 12, 2010, www.hbr.org; U.S. Small Business Administration, www.sba.gov; Business Development Bank of Canada, www.bdc.ca.

Teenagers as Small-Business Owners

High-tech teen entrepreneurship is definitely exploding. "There's not a period in history where we've seen such a plethora of young entrepreneurs," comments Nancy F. Koehn, associate professor of business administration at Harvard Business School. Still, teen entrepreneurs face unique pressures in juggling their schoolwork, their social life, and their high-tech workload. Some ultimately quit school, whereas others quit or cut back on their business activities. Consider Brian Hendricks at Winston Churchill High School in Potomac, Maryland. He is the founder of StartUpPc and VB Solutions, Inc. StartUpPc, founded in 2001, sells custom-built computers and computer services for home users, home offices, small businesses, and students. Brian's services include design, installation of systems, training, networking, and on-site technical support. In October 2002, Brian founded VB Solutions, Inc., which develops and customizes Web sites and message boards. The firm sets up advertising contracts and counsels Web site owners on site improvements. The company has designed corporate ID kits, logos, and Web sites for clients from all over the world. Brian learned at a very young age that working for yourself is one of the best jobs available. According to Brian, a young entrepreneur must possess "the five P's of entrepreneurship"—planning, persistence, patience, people, and profit. Brian knows what it takes to be a successful entrepreneur. His accolades include Junior Achievement's "National Youth Entrepreneur of the Year" and SBA's 2005 "Young Entrepreneur of the Year" awards.[8]

In some people, the motivation to start a business develops slowly as they gain the knowledge and ability required for success as a business owner. Knowledge and ability—especially, management ability—are probably the most important factors involved. A new firm is very much built around the entrepreneur. The owner must be able to manage the firm's finances, its personnel (if there are any employees), and its day-to-day operations. He or she must handle sales, advertising, purchasing, pricing, and a variety of other business functions. The knowledge and ability to do so are acquired most often through experience working for other firms in the same area of business.

Mary Rodas, a child entrepreneur. At age 13, Mary scored an instant success with the 'Balzac,' a ball made by blowing up a balloon inside a fabric sack, jazzed up with vivid colors and designs. At Catco, Inc., she became vice president of marketing at age 14, earning $200,000 a year. Balzac Balloon Ball sales have exceeded $100 million per year.

TABLE 5.2 U.S. Business Start-ups, Closures, and Bankruptcies

	New	Closures	Bankruptcies
2010	NA	NA	56,282
2009	552,600e	660,990e	60,837
2008	597,074	641,400	43,546
2007	668,395	592,410	28,322
2006	670,058	599,333	19,695
2005	644,122	565,745	39,201

e = Advocacy estimate. For a discussion of methodology, see Brian Headd, 2005 (www.sba.gov/advo/research/rs258tot.pdf).
NA = Not available.

Source: U.S. Small Business Administration, Office of Advocacy, *Small Business Economy 2011*, www.sba.gov/advocacy (accessed March 21, 2012).

Why Some Entrepreneurs and Small Businesses Fail

Small businesses are prone to failure. Capital, management, and planning are the key ingredients in the survival of a small business, as well as the most common reasons for failure. Businesses can experience a number of money-related problems. It may take several years before a business begins to show a profit. Entrepreneurs need to have not only the capital to open a business but also the money to operate it in its possibly lengthy start-up phase. One cash flow obstacle often leads to others. Moreover, a series of cash flow predicaments usually ends in a business failure. This scenario is played out all too often by small and not-so-small start-up Internet firms that fail to meet their financial backers' expectations and so are denied a second wave of investment dollars to continue their drive to establish a profitable online firm. According to Maureen Borzacchiello, co-owner of Creative Display Solutions, a trade show products company, "Big businesses such as Bear Stearns, Fannie Mae and Freddie Mac, and AIG can get bailouts, but small-business owners are on their own when times are tough and credit is tight."

Many entrepreneurs lack the management skills required to run a business. Money, time, personnel, and inventory all need to be managed effectively if a small business is to succeed. Starting a small business requires much more than optimism and a good idea.

Success and expansion sometimes lead to problems. Frequently, entrepreneurs with successful small businesses make the mistake of overexpansion. Fast growth often results in dramatic changes in a business. Thus, the entrepreneur must plan carefully and adjust competently to new and potentially disruptive situations.

Every day, and in every part of the country, people open new businesses. For example, 552,600 new businesses recently opened their doors. At the same time, however, 660,900 businesses closed their business and 60,837 businesses (in 2009) declared bankruptcy (see Table 5.2).[9] Although many fail, others represent well-conceived ideas developed by entrepreneurs who have the expertise, resources, and determination to make their businesses succeed. As these well-prepared entrepreneurs pursue their individual goals, our society benefits in many ways from their work and creativity. Billion-dollar companies such as Apple Computer, McDonald's Corporation, and Procter & Gamble are all examples of small businesses that expanded into industry giants.

THE IMPORTANCE OF SMALL BUSINESSES IN OUR ECONOMY

This country's economic history abounds with stories of ambitious men and women who turned their ideas into business dynasties. The Ford Motor Company started as a one-man operation with an innovative method for industrial production. L.L.Bean, Inc., can

Assess the contributions of small businesses to our economy.

trace its beginnings to a basement shop in Freeport, Maine. Both Xerox and Polaroid began as small firms with a better way to do a job. Indeed, every year since 1963, the President of the United States has proclaimed National Small Business Week to recognize the contributions of small businesses to the economic well-being of America.

Providing Technical Innovation

Invention and innovation are part of the foundations of our economy. The increases in productivity that have characterized the past 200 years of our history are all rooted in one principal source: new ways to do a job with less effort for less money. Studies show that the incidence of innovation among small-business workers is significantly higher than among workers in large businesses. Small firms produce two-and-a-half times as many innovations as large firms relative to the number of persons employed. In fact, small firms employ 40 percent of all high-tech workers such as scientists, engineers, and computer specialists. No wonder small firms produce 13 to 14 times more patents per employee than large patenting firms.

Consider Waymon Armstrong, the owner of a small business that uses computer simulations to help government and other clients prepare for and respond to natural disasters, medical emergencies, and combat. In presenting the 2010 National Small Business Person of the Year award, Karen Mills, Administrator of the U.S. Small Business Administration, said, "Waymon Armstrong is a perfect example of the innovation, inspiration, and determination that exemplify America's most successful entrepreneurs. He believed in his brainchild to the point where he deferred his own salary for three years to keep it afloat. When layoffs loomed for his staff after 9/11, their loyalty and belief in the company was so great that they were willing to work without pay for four months.

"Waymon's commitment to his employees and to his business—Engineering & Computer Simulations, Inc.—demonstrates the qualities that make small businesses such a powerful force for job creation in the American economy and in their local communities," said Mills. "It's the same qualities that will lead us to economic recovery. We are especially proud that his company benefited from two grants under SBA's Small Business Innovation and Research Program."[10]

According to the U.S. Office of Management and Budget, more than half the major technological advances of the 20th century originated with individual inventors and small companies. Even just a sampling of those innovations is remarkable:

- Air conditioning
- Airplane
- Automatic transmission
- FM radio
- Heart valve
- Helicopter
- Instant camera
- Insulin
- Jet engine
- Penicillin
- Personal computer
- Power steering

Perhaps even more remarkable—and important—is that many of these inventions sparked major new U.S. industries or contributed to an established industry by adding some valuable service.

Providing Employment

Small firms traditionally have added more than their proportional share of new jobs to the economy. Seven out of the ten industries that added the most new jobs were small-business-dominated industries. Small businesses creating the most new jobs recently included business services, leisure and hospitality services, and special trade

©WIREIMAGE/GETTY IMAGES

Providing technical innovation. Meet *Time* magazine's 2010 Person of the Year, entrepreneur Mark Zuckerberg, who founded Facebook while still a student at Harvard. In 2008, Zuckerberg became the world's youngest billionaire at age 25.

contractors. Small firms hire a larger proportion of employees who are younger workers, older workers, women, or workers who prefer to work part time.

Furthermore, small businesses provide 67 percent of workers with their first jobs and initial on-the-job training in basic skills. According to the SBA, small businesses represent 99.7 percent of all employers, employ more than 50 percent of the private workforce, and provide about two-thirds of the net new jobs added to our economy.[11] Small businesses thus contribute significantly to solving unemployment problems.

The business cycle, as discussed in Chapter 1, is an important factor in the net creation or loss of jobs. During the 2008–2009 recession, businesses with fewer than 20 employees began losing jobs as early as mid-2007. From 2008 to mid-2009, these smallest businesses accounted for 24 percent of the net job losses, while those with 20–499 employees accounted for 36 percent; the remaining 40 percent of job losses were in larger firms with more than 500 employees.[12]

Providing Competition

Small businesses challenge larger, established firms in many ways, causing them to become more efficient and more responsive to consumer needs. A small business cannot, of course, compete with a large firm in all respects. However, a number of small firms, each competing in its own particular area and its own particular way, together have the desired competitive effect. Thus, several small janitorial companies together add up to reasonable competition for the no-longer-small ServiceMaster.

Filling Needs of Society and Other Businesses

Small firms also provide a variety of goods and services to each other and to much larger firms. Sears, Roebuck & Co. purchases merchandise from approximately 12,000 suppliers—and most of them are small businesses. General Motors relies on more than 32,000 companies for parts and supplies and depends on more than 11,000 independent dealers to sell its automobiles and trucks. Large firms generally buy parts and assemblies from smaller firms for one very good reason: It is less expensive than manufacturing the parts in their own factories. This lower cost eventually is reflected in the price that consumers pay for their products.

It is clear that small businesses are a vital part of our economy and that, as consumers and as members of the labor force, we all benefit enormously from their existence. Now let us look at the situation from the viewpoint of the owners of small businesses.

Describe the advantages and disadvantages of operating a small business.

THE PROS AND CONS OF SMALLNESS

Do most owners of small businesses dream that their firms will grow into giant corporations—managed by professionals—while they serve only on the board of directors? Or would they rather stay small, in a firm where they have the opportunity (and the responsibility) to do everything that needs to be done? The answers depend on the personal characteristics and motivations of the individual owners. For many, the advantages of remaining small far outweigh the disadvantages.

Advantages of Small Business

Small-business owners with limited resources often must struggle to enter competitive new markets. They also have to deal with increasing international competition. However, they enjoy several unique advantages.

Personal Relationships with Customers and Employees

For those who like dealing with people, small business is the place to be. The owners of retail shops get to know many of their customers by name and deal with them on a personal basis. Through such relationships, small-business owners often become involved in the social, cultural, and political life of the community.

Relationships between owner-managers and employees also tend to be closer in smaller businesses. In many cases, the owner is a friend and counselor as well as the boss.

These personal relationships provide an important business advantage. The personal service small businesses offer to customers is a major competitive weapon—one that larger firms try to match but often cannot. In addition, close relationships with employees often help the small-business owner to keep effective workers who might earn more with a larger firm.

Getting personal. For those who like dealing with people, small business is the place to be. Here a business owner provides personalized service to a happy customer.

Ability to Adapt to Change

Being his or her own boss, the owner-manager of a small business does not need anyone's permission to adapt to change. An owner may add or discontinue merchandise or services, change store hours, and experiment with various price strategies in response to changes in market conditions. And through personal relationships with customers, the owners of small businesses quickly become aware of changes in people's needs and interests, as well as in the activities of competing firms.

Simplified Record Keeping

Many small firms need only a simple set of records. Record keeping might consist of a checkbook, a cash-receipts journal in which to record all sales, and a cash-disbursements journal in which to record all amounts paid out. Obviously, enough records must be kept to allow for producing and filing accurate tax returns.

Independence

Small-business owners do not have to punch in and out, bid for vacation times, take orders from superiors, or worry about being fired or laid off. They are the masters of their own destinies—at least with regard to employment. For many people, this is the prime advantage of owning a small business.

Other Advantages

According to the SBA, the most profitable companies in the United States are small firms that have been in business for more than ten years and employ fewer than 20 people. Small-business owners also enjoy all the advantages of sole proprietorships, which were discussed in Chapter 4. These include being able to keep all profits, the ease and low cost of going into business and (if necessary) going out of business, and being able to keep business information secret.

Disadvantages of Small Business

Personal contacts with customers, closer relationships with employees, being one's own boss, less cumbersome record-keeping chores, and independence are the bright side of small business. In contrast, the dark side reflects problems unique to these firms.

Risk of Failure

As we have noted, small businesses (especially new ones) run a heavy risk of going out of business—about 50 percent survive at least five years.

Older, well-established small firms can be hit hard by a business recession mainly because they do not have the financial resources to weather an extended difficult period.

Limited Potential Small businesses that survive do so with varying degrees of success. Many are simply the means of making a living for the owner and his or her family. The owner may have some technical skill—as a hair stylist or electrician, for example—and may have started a business to put this skill to work. Such a business is unlikely to grow into big business. In addition, employees' potential for advancement is limited.

Limited Ability to Raise Capital Small businesses typically have a limited ability to obtain capital. Figure 5.2 shows that most small-business financing comes out of the owner's pocket. Personal loans from lending institutions provide only about one-fourth of the capital required by small businesses. About 50 percent of all new firms begin with less than $30,000 in total capital, according to Census Bureau and Federal Reserve surveys. In fact, almost 36 percent of new firms begin with less than $20,000, usually provided by the owner or family members and friends.[13]

Although every person who considers starting a small business should be aware of the hazards and pitfalls we have noted, a well-conceived business plan may help to avoid the risk of failure. The U.S. government is also dedicated to helping small businesses make it. It expresses this aim most actively through the SBA.

The Importance of a Business Plan

Lack of planning can be as deadly as lack of money to a new small business. Planning is important to any business, large or small, and never should be overlooked or taken lightly. A **business plan** is a carefully constructed guide for the person starting a business. Consider it as a tool with three basic purposes: communication, management,

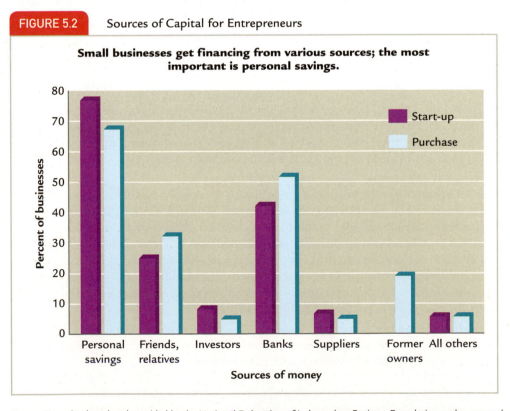

FIGURE 5.2   Sources of Capital for Entrepreneurs

Small businesses get financing from various sources; the most important is personal savings.

Source: Data developed and provided by the National Federation of Independent Business Foundation and sponsored by the American Express Travel Related Services Company, Inc.

business plan a carefully constructed guide for the person starting a business

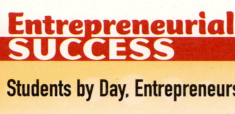

Entrepreneurial SUCCESS

Students by Day, Entrepreneurs by Night

A growing number of students are becoming entrepreneurs even before they graduate, gaining valuable business experience and taking advantage of the many resources on campus. Brandt Page, who started a company while at Brigham Young University and has since founded or co-founded two more, explains that as a student entrepreneur, "you have free access to libraries, free access to mentors, to professors, to business competitions, to really being recognized and mentored."

Corinne Prevot had already earned $8,000 from her ski apparel business, Skida, before she entered college. After taking an entrepreneurship course as a freshman at Middlebury College, she rethought her approach to business. She researched competitors, looked at distribution, repriced her products, and formalized her branding. Now Skida's yearly sales are more than $100,000, and Prevot is ready to expand.

Partners Noah Chilton, Harry Kelley, Jackson Kroopf, and Misha Epstein like gourmet coffee, so they created a rolling cart to bring their favorite brews to classmates at Vassar through a business they called Tree City. The entrepreneurs buy from growers who use eco-friendly agricultural methods and they discuss good coffee while they brew a fresh cup for each customer. "Part of what we love about coffee is the way it brings people together," Kroopf says.

Sources: Based on information in Rebecca Palmer, "The College of Hard Knocks," *Utah Business*, January 11, 2012, www.utahbusiness.com; Joanna Hamer, "Tree City Serves Up Ethical Coffee, Enticing Conversation," *Miscellany News* (Poughkeepsie, New York), October 25, 2011, www.miscellanynews.com; Helen Coster, "All Star Student Entrepreneurs," *Forbes*, August 3, 2011, www.forbes.com; Brian Nichols, "Know-How for Hire," *New York Times Education Life*, November 6, 2011, p. 34.

---

and planning. As a communication tool, a business plan serves as a concise document that potential investors can examine to see if they would like to invest or assist in financing a new venture. It shows whether a business has the potential to make a profit. As a management tool, the business plan helps to track, monitor, and evaluate the progress. The business plan is a living document; it is modified as the entrepreneur gains knowledge and experience. It also serves to establish time lines and milestones and allows comparison of growth projections against actual accomplishments. Finally, as a planning tool, the business plan guides a businessperson through the various phases of business. For example, the plan helps to identify obstacles to avoid and to establish alternatives. According to Robert Krummer, Jr., chairman of First Business Bank in Los Angeles, "The business plan is a necessity. If the person who wants to start a small business can't put a business plan together, he or she is in trouble."

Components of a Business Plan

Table 5.3 shows the 12 sections that a business plan should include. Each section is further explained at the end of each of the seven major parts in the text. The goal of each end-of-the-part exercise is to help a businessperson create his or her own business plan. When constructing a business plan, the businessperson should strive to keep it easy to read, uncluttered, and complete. Like other busy executives, officials of financial institutions do not have the time to wade through pages of extraneous data. The business plan should answer the four questions banking officials and investors are most interested in: (1) What exactly is the nature

Personal APPS

Although writing a business plan won't guarantee your success, it will help you think through many of the issues that can trip up entrepreneurs. And if you work for a big company, you may find yourself writing a kind of business plan for a product or project.

TABLE 5.3   Components of a Business Plan

1. *Introduction.* Basic information such as the name, address, and phone number of the business; the date the plan was issued; and a statement of confidentiality to keep important information away from potential competitors.

2. *Executive Summary.* A one- to two-page overview of the entire business plan, including a justification why the business will succeed.

3. *Benefits to the Community.* Information on how the business will have an impact on economic development, community development, and human development.

4. *Company and Industry.* The background of the company, choice of the legal business form, information on the products or services to be offered, and examination of the potential customers, current competitors, and the business's future.

5. *Management Team.* Discussion of skills, talents, and job descriptions of management team, managerial compensation, management training needs, and professional assistance requirements.

6. *Manufacturing and Operations Plan.* Discussion of facilities needed, space requirements, capital equipment, labor force, inventory control, and purchasing requirement.

7. *Labor Force.* Discussion of the quality of skilled workers available and the training, compensation, and motivation of workers.

8. *Marketing Plan.* Discussion of markets, market trends, competition, market share, pricing, promotion, distribution, and service policy.

9. *Financial Plan.* Summary of the investment needed, sales and cash flow forecasts, breakeven analysis, and sources of funding.

10. *Exit Strategy.* Discussion of a succession plan or going public. Who will take over the business?

11. *Critical Risks and Assumptions.* Evaluation of the weaknesses of the business and how the company plans to deal with these and other business problems.

12. *Appendix.* Supplementary information crucial to the plan, such as résumés of owners and principal managers, advertising samples, organization chart, and any related information.

Source: From HATTEN, *Small Business Management,* 5E. © 2012 Cengage Learning.

and mission of the new venture? (2) Why is this new enterprise a good idea? (3) What are the businessperson's goals? (4) How much will the new venture cost?

The great amount of time and consideration that should go into creating a business plan probably will end up saving time later. For example, Sharon Burch, who was running a computer software business while earning a degree in business administration, had to write a business plan as part of one of her courses. Burch has said, "I wish I'd taken the class before I started my business. I see a lot of things I could have done differently. But it has helped me since because I've been using the business plan as a guide for my business." Table 5.4 provides a business plan checklist. Accuracy and realistic expectations are crucial to an effective business plan. It is unethical to deceive loan officers, and it is unwise to deceive yourself.

TABLE 5.4	Business Plan Checklist

1. Does the executive summary grab the reader's attention and highlight the major points of the business plan?

2. Does the business-concept section clearly describe the purpose of the business, the customers, the value proposition, and the distribution channel and convey a compelling story?

3. Do the industry and market analyses support acceptance and demand for the business concept in the marketplace and define a first customer in depth?

4. Does the management team plan persuade the reader that the team could implement the business concept successfully? Does it assure the reader that an effective infrastructure is in place to facilitate the goals and operations of the company?

5. Does the product/service plan clearly provide details on the status of the product, the time line for completion, and the intellectual property that will be acquired?

6. Does the operations plan prove that the product or service could be produced and distributed efficiently and effectively?

7. Does the marketing plan successfully demonstrate how the company will create customer awareness in the target market and deliver the benefit to the customer?

8. Does the financial plan convince the reader that the business model is sustainable—that it will provide a superior return on investment for the investor and sufficient cash flow to repay loans to potential lenders?

9. Does the growth plan convince the reader that the company has long-term growth potential and spin-off products and services?

10. Does the contingency and exit-strategy plan convince the reader that the risk associated with this venture can be mediated? Is there an exit strategy in place for investors?

Source: From ALLEN, *Launching New Ventures,* 6E. © 2012 Cengage Learning.

THE SMALL BUSINESS ADMINISTRATION

 Explain how the Small Business Administration helps small businesses.

The **Small Business Administration (SBA)**, created by Congress in 1953, is a governmental agency that assists, counsels, and protects the interests of small businesses in the United States. It helps people get into business and stay in business. The agency provides assistance to owners and managers of prospective, new, and established small businesses. Through more than 1,000 offices and resource centers throughout the nation, the SBA provides both financial assistance and management counseling. Recently, the SBA provided training, technical assistance, and education to more than 3 million small businesses. It helps small firms to bid for and obtain government contracts, and it helps them to prepare to enter foreign markets.

SBA Management Assistance

Statistics show that most failures in small business are related to poor management. For this reason, the SBA places special emphasis on improving the management ability of the owners and managers of small businesses. The SBA's Management Assistance Program is extensive and diversified. It includes free individual counseling, courses, conferences, workshops, and a wide range of publications. Recently, the SBA provided management and technical assistance to nearly 1 million small businesses through its

Small Business Administration (SBA) a governmental agency that assists, counsels, and protects the interests of small businesses in the United States

1,100 Small Business Development Centers and 13,000 volunteers from the Service Corps of Retired Executives.[14]

Management Courses and Workshops The management courses offered by the SBA cover all the functions, duties, and roles of managers. Instructors may be teachers from local colleges and universities or other professionals, such as management consultants, bankers, lawyers, and accountants. Fees for these courses are quite low. The most popular such course is a general survey of eight to ten different areas of business management. In follow-up studies, businesspeople may concentrate in depth on one or more of these areas depending on their particular strengths and weaknesses. The SBA occasionally offers one-day conferences. These conferences are aimed at keeping owner-managers up-to-date on new management developments, tax laws, and the like. The Small Business Training Network (SBTN) is an online training network consisting of 83 SBA-run courses, workshops, and resources. Some of the most requested courses include Entrepreneurship, Starting and Managing Your Own Business, Developing a Business Plan, Managing the Digital Enterprise, Identify Your Target Market, and Analyze Profitability. Find out more at www.sba.gov/training. Recently, more than 240,000 small-business owners benefited from SBA's free online business courses.

SCORE The **Service Corps of Retired Executives (SCORE)**, created in 1964, is a group of more than 13,000 retired and active businesspeople including more than 2,000 women who volunteer their services to small businesses through the SBA. The collective experience of SCORE volunteers spans the full range of American enterprise. These volunteers have worked for such notable companies as Eastman Kodak, General Electric, IBM, and Procter & Gamble. Experts in areas of accounting, finance, marketing, engineering, and retailing provide counseling and mentoring to entrepreneurs.

A small-business owner who has a particular problem can request free counseling from SCORE. An assigned counselor visits the owner in his or her establishment and, through careful observation, analyzes the business situation and the problem. If the problem is complex, the counselor may call on other volunteer experts to assist. Finally, the counselor offers a plan for solving the problem and helping the owner through the critical period.

Consider the plight of Elizabeth Halvorsen, a mystery writer from Minneapolis. Her husband had built up the family advertising and graphic arts firm for 17 years when he was called in 1991 to serve in the Persian Gulf War. The only one left behind to run the business was Mrs. Halvorsen, who admittedly had no business experience. Enter SCORE. With a SCORE management expert at her side, she kept the business on track. Recently, SCORE volunteers served more than 523,800 small-business people like Mrs. Halvorsen through its 389 offices. The 13,000 counselors provided 203,000 face-to-face counseling sessions, 119,000 online counseling sessions, and more than 49,500 online workshops to more than 201,000 workshop participants. Since its inception, SCORE has assisted more than 9 million small-business people with online and face-to-face small business counseling.[15]

Service Corps of Retired Executives (SCORE) a group of businesspeople who volunteer their services to small businesses through the SBA

Banking on the Banks. Meet Marilyn and Dwayne Banks, owners of Marilyn's Gift Gallery and Sound World Music, in their East Waco, TX, gift shop. Since opening their business in 1989, they have helped start many community projects including an association to help minority business owners in the area.

Help for Minority-Owned Small Businesses

Americans who are members of minority groups have had difficulty entering the nation's economic mainstream. Raising money is a nagging problem for minority business owners, who also may lack adequate training. Members of minority groups are, of course, eligible for all SBA programs, but the SBA makes a special effort to assist those minority groups who want to start small businesses or expand existing ones. For example, the Minority Business Development Agency awards grants to develop and increase business opportunities for members of racial and ethnic minorities.

Helping women become entrepreneurs is also a special goal of the SBA. Emily Harrington, one of nine children, was born in Manila, the Philippines. She arrived in the United States in 1972 as a foreign-exchange student. Convinced that there was a market for hard-working, dedicated minorities and women, she launched Qualified Resources, Inc., a professional staffing services firm. *Inc.* magazine selected her firm as one of "America's Fastest Growing Private Companies" just six years later. Harrington credits the SBA with giving her the technical support that made her first loan possible. Finding a SCORE counselor to work directly with her, she refined her business plan until she got a bank loan. Before contacting the SBA, Harrington was turned down for business loans "by all the banks I approached," even though she worked as a manager of loan credit and collection for a bank. Later, Emily Harrington was SBA's winner of the local, regional, and national Small Business Entrepreneurial Success Award for Rhode Island, the New England region, and the nation! For several years in a row, Qualified Resources, Inc., was named one of the fastest growing private companies in Rhode Island. Now with more than 100 Women's Business Centers, entrepreneurs like Harrington can receive training and technical assistance, access to credit and capital, federal contracts, and international markets. The SBA's Online Women's Business Center (www.sba.gov/aboutsba/sbaprograms/onlinewbc/index.html) is a state-of-the-art Internet site to help women expand their businesses. This free, interactive Web site offers women information about business principles and practices, management techniques, networking, industry news, market research and technology training, online counseling, and hundreds of links to other sites, as well as information about the many SBA services and resources available to them.

Small-Business Institutes

Small-business institutes (SBIs), created in 1972, are groups of senior and graduate students in business administration who provide management counseling to small businesses. SBIs have been set up on more than 520 college campuses as another way to help business owners. The students work in small groups guided by faculty advisers and SBA management-assistance experts. Like SCORE volunteers, they analyze and help solve the problems of small-business owners at their business establishments.

Small-Business Development Centers

Small-business development centers (SBDCs) are university-based groups that provide individual counseling and practical training to owners of small businesses. SBDCs draw from the resources of local, state, and federal governments, private businesses, and universities. These groups can provide managerial and technical help, data from research studies, and other types of specialized assistance of value to small businesses. In 2011, there were more than 1,000 SBDC locations, primarily at colleges and universities, assisting people such as Kathleen DuBois. After scribbling a list of her abilities and the names of potential clients on a napkin in a local restaurant, Kathleen DuBois decided to start her own marketing firm. Beth Thornton launched her engineering firm after a discussion with a colleague in the ladies room of the Marriott. When Richard Shell was laid off after 20 years of service with Nisource (Columbia Gas), he searched the Internet tirelessly before finding the right franchise option. Introduced by mutual friends, Jim Bostic and Denver McMillion quickly connected, built a high level of trust, and combined their diverse professional backgrounds to form a manufacturing company. Although these entrepreneurs took different routes in starting their new businesses in West Virginia, all of them turned to the West Virginia Small Business Development Center for the technical assistance to make their dreams become a reality.

SBA Publications

The SBA issues management, marketing, and technical publications dealing with hundreds of topics of interest to present and prospective managers of small firms. Most of these publications are available from the SBA free of charge. Others can be obtained for a small fee from the U.S. Government Printing Office.

small-business institutes (SBIs) groups of senior and graduate students in business administration who provide management counseling to small businesses

small-business development centers (SBDCs) university-based groups that provide individual counseling and practical training to owners of small businesses

SBA Financial Assistance

Small businesses seem to be constantly in need of money. An owner may have enough capital to start and operate the business. But then he or she may require more money to finance increased operations during peak selling seasons, to pay for required pollution control equipment, to finance an expansion, or to mop up after a natural disaster such as a flood or a terrorist attack. For example, the Supplemental Terrorist Activity Relief program has made $3.7 billion in loans to 8,202 small businesses harmed or disrupted by the September 11 terrorist attacks. In October 2005, the SBA guaranteed loans of up to $150,000 to small businesses affected by Hurricanes Katrina and Rita. Since the 2005 hurricanes, SBA has made more than $4.9 billion in disaster loans to 102,903 homeowners and renters in the Gulf region. Businesses in the area received 16,828 business disaster loans with disbursements worth $1.5 billion.[16] In 2010, the SBA offered economic injury loans to fishing and fishing-dependent small businesses as a result of the Deepwater BP spill that shut down commercial and recreational fishing waters. According to the SBA Administrator Karen Mills, "SBA remains committed to taking every step to help small businesses deal with the financial challenges they are facing as a result of the Deepwater BP oil spill."[17] The SBA offers special financial-assistance programs that cover all these situations. However, its primary financial function is to guarantee loans to eligible businesses.

Regular Business Loans Most of the SBA's business loans are actually made by private lenders such as banks, but repayment is partially guaranteed by the agency. That is, the SBA may guarantee that it will repay the lender up to 90 percent of the loan if the borrowing firm cannot repay it. Guaranteed loans approved on or after October 1, 2002, may be as large as $1.5 million (this loan limit may be increased in the future). The average size of an SBA-guaranteed business loan is about $300,000, and its average duration is about eight years.

Small-Business Investment Companies Venture capital is money that is invested in small (and sometimes struggling) firms that have the potential to become very successful. In many cases, only a lack of capital keeps these firms from rapid and solid growth. The people who invest in such firms expect that their investments will grow with the firms and become quite profitable.

The popularity of these investments has increased over the past 30 years, but most small firms still have difficulty obtaining venture capital. To help such businesses, the SBA licenses, regulates, and provides financial assistance to **small-business investment companies (SBICs)**.

An SBIC is a privately owned firm that provides venture capital to small enterprises that meet its investment standards. Such firms as America Online, Apple Computer, Federal Express, Compaq Computer, Intel Corporation, Outback Steakhouse, and Staples, Inc., all were financed through SBICs during their initial growth period. SBICs are intended to be profit-making organizations. The aid that SBA offers allows them to invest in small businesses that otherwise would not attract venture capital. Since Congress created the program in 1958, SBICs have financed more than 107,000 small businesses for a total of about $60 billion. Recently, SBIC benefited 1,477 businesses, and 24 percent of these firms were less than two years old.[18]

State of Small Business During the Recession

Celebrating the 47th annual observance of National Small Business Week in May 2010, President Obama stated,

Our nation is still emerging from one of the worst recessions in our history, and small businesses were among the hardest hit. From mom-and-pop stores to high tech start-ups, countless small businesses have been forced to lay off employees or shut their doors entirely. In these difficult times, we must do all we can to help these firms recover from the recession and put Americans back to work. Our

venture capital money that is invested in small (and sometimes struggling) firms that have the potential to become very successful

small-business investment companies (SBICs) privately owned firms that provide venture capital to small enterprises that meet their investment standards

government cannot guarantee a company's success, but it can help create market conditions that allow small businesses to thrive.

My Administration is committed to helping small businesses drive our economy toward recovery and long-term growth. The American Recovery and Reinvestment Act has supported billions of dollars in loans and Federal contracts for small businesses across the country. The Affordable Care Act makes it easier for small business owners to provide health insurance to their employees, and gives entrepreneurs the security they need to innovate and take risks. We have enacted new tax cuts and tax credits for small firms. Still, we must do more to empower these companies. Small businesses are the engine of our prosperity and a proud reflection of our character. A healthy small business sector will give us vibrant communities, cutting-edge technology, and an American economy that can compete and win in the 21st century.[19]

As if the recession was not enough, in the states near the Gulf of Mexico, many small businesses suffered financial losses following the April 20, 2010, Deepwater Horizon BP oil spill that shut down commercial and recreational fishing along the coasts. According to the SBA Administrator Karen Mills, "With the region still recovering from previous devastation and the national recession of the last couple of years, it's critical that we take every step we can to provide small businesses with resources to make it through this latest crisis so that they can continue to drive local economic growth and provide good-paying jobs." The SBA offered working capital loans up to $2 million at an interest rate of 4 percent with terms up to 30 years.[20]

We have discussed the importance of the small-business segment of our economy. We have weighed the advantages and drawbacks of operating a small business as compared with a large one. But is there a way to achieve the best of both worlds? Can one preserve one's independence as a business owner and still enjoy some of the benefits of "bigness"? Let's take a close look at franchising.

FRANCHISING

 6 Explain the concept and types of franchising.

A **franchise** is a license to operate an individually owned business as if it were part of a chain of outlets or stores. Often, the business itself is also called a *franchise*. Among the most familiar franchises are McDonald's, H&R Block, AAMCO Transmissions, GNC (General Nutrition Centers), and Dairy Queen. Many other franchises carry familiar names; this method of doing business has become very popular in the last 30 years or so. It is an attractive means of starting and operating a small business.

What Is Franchising?

Franchising is the actual granting of a franchise. A **franchisor** is an individual or organization granting a franchise. A **franchisee** is a person or organization purchasing a franchise. The franchisor supplies a known and advertised business name, management skills, the required training and materials, and a method of doing business. The franchisee supplies labor and capital, operates the franchised business, and agrees to abide by the provisions of the franchise agreement. Table 5.5 lists the basic franchisee rights and obligations that would be covered in a typical franchise agreement.

Types of Franchising

Franchising arrangements fall into three general categories. In the first approach, a manufacturer authorizes a number of retail stores to sell a certain brand-name item. This type of franchising arrangement, one of the oldest, is prevalent in sales of passenger cars and trucks, farm equipment, shoes, paint, earth-moving equipment, and petroleum. About 90 percent of all gasoline is sold through franchised, independent retail service stations, and franchised dealers handle virtually all sales of new cars and trucks. In the second type of franchising arrangement, a producer licenses distributors to sell a

franchise a license to operate an individually owned business as though it were part of a chain of outlets or stores

franchising the actual granting of a franchise

franchisor an individual or organization granting a franchise

franchisee a person or organization purchasing a franchise

TABLE 5.5 Basic Rights and Obligations Delineated in a Franchise Agreement

Franchisee rights include:

1. use of trademarks, trade names, and patents of the franchisor;

2. use of the brand image and the design and decor of the premises developed by the franchisor;

3. use of the franchisor's secret methods;

4. use of the franchisor's copyrighted materials;

5. use of recipes, formulae, specifications, processes, and methods of manufacture developed by the franchisor;

6. conducting the franchised business upon or from the agreed premises strictly in accordance with the franchisor's methods and subject to the franchisor's directions;

7. guidelines established by the franchisor regarding exclusive territorial rights; and

8. rights to obtain supplies from nominated suppliers at special prices.

Franchisee obligations include:

1. to carry on the business franchised and no other business upon the approved and nominated premises;

2. to observe certain minimum operating hours;

3. to pay a franchise fee;

4. to follow the accounting system laid down by the franchisor;

5. not to advertise without prior approval of the advertisements by the franchisor;

6. to use and display such point-of-sale advertising materials as the franchisor stipulates;

7. to maintain the premises in good, clean, and sanitary condition and to redecorate when required to do so by the franchisor;

8. to maintain the widest possible insurance coverage;

9. to permit the franchisor's staff to enter the premises to inspect and see if the franchisor's standards are being maintained;

10. to purchase goods or products from the franchisor or his designated suppliers;

11. to train the staff in the franchisor's methods to ensure that they are neatly and appropriately clothed; and

12. not to assign the franchise contract without the franchisor's consent.

Source: Excerpted from the SBA's "Is Franchising for Me?" www.sba.gov (accessed March 12, 2012).

given product to retailers. This arrangement is common in the soft drink industry. Most national manufacturers of soft drink syrups—The Coca-Cola Company, Dr. Pepper/Seven-Up Companies, PepsiCo, Royal Crown Companies, Inc.—franchise independent bottlers who then serve retailers. In a third form of franchising, a franchisor supplies brand names, techniques, or other services instead of a complete product. Although the franchisor may provide certain production and distribution services, its primary role is the careful development and control of marketing strategies. This approach to franchising, which is the most typical today, is used by Holiday Inns, Howard Johnson Company, AAMCO Transmissions, McDonald's, Dairy Queen, Avis, Hertz Corporation, KFC (Kentucky Fried Chicken), and SUBWAY, to name but a few.

THE GROWTH OF FRANCHISING

7 Analyze the growth of franchising and its advantages and disadvantages.

Franchising, which began in the United States around the time of the Civil War, was used originally by large firms, such as the Singer Sewing Company, to distribute their products. Franchising has been increasing steadily in popularity since the early 1900s, primarily for filling stations and car dealerships; however, this retailing strategy has experienced enormous growth since the mid-1970s. The franchise proliferation generally has paralleled the expansion of the fast-food industry.

Of course, franchising is not limited to fast foods. Hair salons, tanning parlors, and dentists and lawyers are expected to participate in franchising arrangements in growing numbers. Franchised health clubs, pest exterminators, and campgrounds are already widespread, as are franchised tax preparers and travel agencies. The real estate industry also has experienced a rapid increase in franchising.

Also, franchising is attracting more women and minority business owners in the United States than ever before. One reason is that special outreach programs designed to encourage franchisee diversity have developed. Consider Angela Trammel, a young mother of two. She had been laid off from her job at the Marriott after 9/11. Since she was a member of a Curves Fitness Center and liked the concept of empowering women to become physically fit, she began researching the cost of purchasing a Curves franchise and ways to finance the business. "I was online looking for financing, and I linked to Enterprise Development Group in Washington, DC. I knew that they had diverse clients." The cost for the franchise was $19,500, but it took $60,000 to open the doors to her fitness center. "Applying for a loan to start the business was much harder than buying a house," said Trammel. Just three years later, Angela and her husband, Ernest, own three Curves Fitness Centers with 12 employees. Recently, since giving birth to her third child, she has found the financial freedom and flexibility needed to care for her busy family. In fact, within a three-year period, the Trammels grew their annual household income from $80,000 to $250,000.[21] Franchisors such as Wendy's, McDonald's, Burger King, and Church's Chicken all have special corporate programs to attract minority and women franchisees. Just as important, successful women and minority franchisees are willing to get involved by offering advice and guidance to new franchisees.

Herman Petty, the first African-American McDonald's franchisee, remembers that the company provided a great deal of help while he worked to establish his first units. In turn, Petty traveled to help other black franchisees, and he invited new franchisees to gain hands-on experience in his Chicago restaurants before starting their own establishments. In 1972, Petty also organized a support group, the National Black McDonald's Operators Association, to help black franchisees in other areas. Today, members of this association own nearly 1,400 McDonald's restaurants throughout the United States, South Africa, and the Caribbean with annual sales of more than $3.2 billion. "We are really concentrating on helping our operators to be successful both operationally and financially," says Craig Welburn, the McDonald's franchisee who leads the group.

Dual-branded franchises, in which two franchisors offer their products together, are a new small-business trend. For example, in 1993, pleased with the success of its first cobranded restaurant with Texaco in Beebe, Arkansas, McDonald's now has more than 400 cobranded restaurants in the United States. Also, an agreement between franchisors Doctor's Associates, Inc., and TCBY Enterprises, Inc., now allows franchisees to sell SUBWAY sandwiches and TCBY yogurt in the same establishment.

PR NEWSFOTO/SIGNS BY TOMORROW

Getting ad value from your car. Joe McGuinness founded Signs By Tomorrow in 1986. Today, with over 180 locations nationwide, the Columbia, Md.-based franchise company turns hundreds of autos into rolling billboards each year, much like this one for 1-800-GOT-JUNK. Some companies may compensate your gas costs to use your car.

Are Franchises Successful?

Franchising is designed to provide a tested formula for success, along with ongoing advice and training. The success rate for businesses owned and operated by franchisees is significantly higher than the success rate for other independently owned small businesses. In a recent nationwide Gallup poll of 944 franchise owners, 94 percent of franchisees indicated that they were very or somewhat successful, only 5 percent believed that they were very unsuccessful or somewhat unsuccessful, and 1 percent did not know. Despite these impressive statistics, franchising is not a guarantee of success for either franchisees or franchisors. Too rapid expansion, inadequate capital or management skills, and a host of other problems can cause failure for both franchisee and franchisor. Thus, for example, the Dizzy Dean's Beef and Burger franchise is no longer in business. Timothy Bates, a Wayne State University economist, warns, "Despite the hype that franchising is the safest way to go when starting a new business, the research just doesn't bear that out." Just consider Boston Chicken, which once had more than 1,200 restaurants before declaring bankruptcy in 1998.

Advantages of Franchising

Franchising plays a vital role in our economy and soon may become the dominant form of retailing. Why? Because franchising offers advantages to both the franchisor and the franchisee.

To the Franchisor
The franchisor gains fast and well-controlled distribution of its products without incurring the high cost of constructing and operating its own outlets. The franchisor thus has more capital available to expand production and to use for advertising. At the same time, it can ensure, through the franchise agreement, that outlets are maintained and operated according to its own standards.

The franchisor also benefits from the fact that the franchisee—a sole proprietor in most cases—is likely to be very highly motivated to succeed. The success of the franchise means more sales, which translate into higher royalties for the franchisor.

To the Franchisee
The franchisee gets the opportunity to start a business with limited capital and to make use of the business experience of others. Moreover, an outlet with a nationally advertised name, such as RadioShack, McDonald's, or Century 21, has guaranteed customers as soon as it opens.

If business problems arise, the franchisor gives the franchisee guidance and advice. This counseling is primarily responsible for the very high degree of success enjoyed by franchises. In most cases, the franchisee does not pay for such help.

The franchisee also receives materials to use in local advertising and can take part in national promotional campaigns sponsored by the franchisor. McDonald's and its franchisees, for example, constitute one of the nation's top 20 purchasers of advertising. Finally, the franchisee may be able to minimize the cost of advertising, supplies, and various business necessities by purchasing them in cooperation with other franchisees.

Disadvantages of Franchising

The main disadvantage of franchising affects the franchisee, and it arises because the franchisor retains a great deal of control. The franchisor's contract can dictate every aspect of the business: decor, design of employee uniforms, types of signs, and all the details of business operations. All Burger King French fries taste the same because all Burger King franchisees have to make them the same way.

Contract disputes are the cause of many lawsuits. For example, Rekha Gabhawala, a Dunkin' Donuts franchisee in Milwaukee, alleged that the franchisor was forcing her out of business so that the company could profit by reselling the downtown franchise to someone else; the company, on the other hand, alleged that

The growth of franchising. Franchising is designed to provide a tested formula for success, along with ongoing advice and training. The franchisor, such as Wendy's or Burger King, supplies a known and advertised business name, management skills, the required training and materials, and a method of doing business. Franchising, however, is not a guarantee of success for either franchisees or franchisors.

Gabhawala breached the contract by not running the business according to company standards. In another case, Dunkin' Donuts sued Chris Romanias, its franchisee in Pennsylvania, alleging that Romanias intentionally underreported gross sales to the company. Romanias, on the other hand, alleged that Dunkin' Donuts, Inc., breached the contract because it failed to provide assistance in operating the franchise. Other franchisees claim that contracts are unfairly tilted toward the franchisors. Yet others have charged that they lost their franchise and investment because their franchisor would not approve the sale of the business when they found a buyer.

To arbitrate disputes between franchisors and franchisees, the National Franchise Mediation Program was established in 1993 by 30 member firms, including Burger King Corporation, McDonald's Corporation, and Wendy's International, Inc. Negotiators have since resolved numerous cases through mediation. Recently, Carl's Jr. brought in one of its largest franchisees to help set its system straight, making most franchisees happy for the first time in years. The program also helped PepsiCo settle a long-term contract dispute and renegotiate its franchise agreements.

Because disagreements between franchisors and franchisees have increased in recent years, many franchisees have been demanding government regulation of franchising. In 1997, to avoid government regulation, some of the largest franchisors proposed a new self-policing plan to the Federal Trade Commission.

Franchise holders pay for their security, usually with a one-time franchise fee and continuing royalty and advertising fees, collected as a percentage of sales. A SUBWAY franchisee pays an initial franchise fee of $15,000 and an annual fee of 8 percent of gross sales. In some fields, franchise agreements are not uniform. One franchisee may pay more than another for the same services.

Even success can cause problems. Sometimes a franchise is so successful that the franchisor opens its own outlet nearby, in direct competition—although franchisees may fight back. For example, a court recently ruled that Burger King could not enter into direct competition with the franchisee because the contract was not specific on the issue. A spokesperson for one franchisor contends that the company "gives no geographical protection" to its franchise holders and thus is free to move in on them. Franchise operators work hard. They often put in 10- and 12-hour days, six days a week. The International Franchise Association advises prospective franchise purchasers to investigate before investing and to approach buying a franchise cautiously. Franchises vary widely in approach as well as in products. Some, such as Dunkin' Donuts and Baskin-Robbins, demand long hours. Others, such as Great Clips hair salons and Albert's Family Restaurants, are more appropriate for those who do not want to spend many hours at their stores.

GLOBAL PERSPECTIVES IN SMALL BUSINESS

For small American businesses, the world is becoming smaller. National and international economies are growing more and more interdependent as political leadership and national economic directions change and trade barriers diminish or disappear. Globalization and instant worldwide communications are rapidly shrinking distances at the same time that they are expanding business opportunities. According to a recent study, the Internet is increasingly important to small-business strategic thinking, with more than 50 percent of those surveyed indicating that the Internet represented their most favored strategy for growth. This was more than double the next-favored choice, strategic alliances reflecting the opportunity to reach both global and domestic customers. The Internet and online payment systems enable even very small businesses to serve international customers. In fact, technology now gives small businesses the leverage and power to reach markets that were once limited solely to large corporations. No wonder the number of businesses exporting their goods and services has tripled since 1990, with two-thirds of that boom coming from companies with fewer than 20 employees.[22]

The SBA offers help to the nation's small-business owners who want to enter the world markets. The SBA's efforts include counseling small firms on how and where to market overseas, matching U.S. small-business executives with potential overseas customers, and helping exporters to secure financing. The agency brings small U.S. firms into direct contact with potential overseas buyers and partners. The SBA International Trade Loan program provides guarantees of up to $5 million in loans to small-business owners. These loans help small firms in expanding or developing new export markets. The U.S. Commercial Service, a Commerce Department division, aids small and medium-sized businesses in selling overseas. The division's global network includes more than 100 offices in the United States and 151 others in 75 countries around the world.[23]

Consider Daniel J. Nanigian, President of Nanmac Corporation in Framingham, Massachusetts. This company manufactures temperature sensors used in a wide range of industrial applications. With an export strategy aimed at growing revenues in diverse foreign markets including China, the Nanmac Corporation experienced explosive growth in 2009. The company nearly doubled its sales from $2.7 million in 2008 to $5.1 million in 2009. The company's international sales, at $300,000 in 2004, reached $700,000 in 2009 and $1.7 million in 2010. Its administrative, sales, and manufacturing employees have increased by 80 percent.

The company has a strong presence in China and is expanding in other markets, as well, including Latin America, Singapore, and Russia. Under Nanigian's guidance, the company has developed creative solutions and partnerships to help maximize its presence internationally. As part of its China strategy, Nanmac partners with distributors, recruits European and in-country sales representatives, uses a localized Chinese Web site, and relies for advice on the export assistance programs of the Massachusetts Small Business Development Center Network's Massachusetts Export Center. The strategy, along with travel to China to conduct technical training seminars and attend trade shows and technical conferences, has helped to grow Nanmac's Chinese client list from 1 in 2003 to more than 30 accounts today. Mr. Nanigian received SBA's 2010 Small Business Exporter of the Year Award.[24]

International trade will become more important to small-business owners as they face unique challenges in the new century. Small businesses, which are expected to remain the dominant form of organization in this country, must be prepared to adapt to significant demographic and economic changes in the world marketplace.

This chapter ends our discussion of American business today. From here on, we shall be looking closely at various aspects of business operations. We begin, in the next chapter, with a discussion of management—what management is, what managers do, and how they work to coordinate the basic economic resources within a business organization.

return to Inside BUSINESS

Locker Lookz

JoAnn Brewer and Christi Sterling had never run a company before they teamed up to found Locker Lookz. After helping their preteen daughters create accessories to dress up their school lockers as a way to show off their personal style, they recognized a viable business opportunity. "Self-expression is such a huge, huge thing at this age," explains Sterling. "Not everybody gets to see your bedroom at home, but everyone gets to see your locker."

Part of the fun for customers is mixing and matching products for a unique look. For this reason, Locker Lookz's Web site has an interactive design feature to help girls visualize how different products go together. The site also offers instructional videos so customers know how to install and remove accessories without damaging the locker. Coming soon: Accessories to personalize boys' lockers.

Questions
1. When Locker Lookz needed to raise money quickly, why do you think the founders sought financing from family, friends, and a church investment group rather than talking with banks?
2. If you were writing a business plan for Locker Lookz, what would you recommend as an exit strategy? Explain your answer.

SUMMARY

 Define what a small business is and recognize the fields in which small businesses are concentrated.

A small business is one that is independently owned and operated for profit and is not dominant in its field. There are about 27.5 million businesses in this country, and more than 99.7 percent of them are small businesses. Small businesses employ more than half the nation's workforce. About 69 percent of small businesses survive at least two years and about 50 percent survive at least five years. More than half of all small businesses are in retailing and services.

 Identify the people who start small businesses and the reasons why some succeed and many fail.

Such personal characteristics as independence, desire to create a new enterprise, and willingness to accept a challenge may encourage individuals to start small businesses. Various external circumstances, such as special expertise or even the loss of a job, also can supply the motivation to strike out on one's own. Poor planning and lack of capital and management experience are the major causes of small-business failures.

 Assess the contributions of small businesses to our economy.

Small businesses have been responsible for a wide variety of inventions and innovations, some of which have given rise to new industries. Historically, small businesses have created the bulk of the nation's new jobs. Further, they have mounted effective competition to larger firms. They provide things that society needs, act as suppliers to larger firms, and serve as customers of other businesses, both large and small.

 Describe the advantages and disadvantages of operating a small business.

The advantages of smallness in business include the opportunity to establish personal relationships with customers and employees, the ability to adapt to changes quickly, independence, and simplified record keeping. The major disadvantages are the high risk of failure, the limited potential for growth, and the limited ability to raise capital.

 Explain how the Small Business Administration helps small businesses.

The Small Business Administration (SBA) was created in 1953 to assist and counsel the nation's millions of small-business owners. The SBA offers management courses and workshops; managerial help, including one-to-one counseling through SCORE; various publications; and financial assistance through guaranteed loans and SBICs. It places special emphasis on aid to minority-owned businesses, including those owned by women.

 Explain the concept and types of franchising.

A franchise is a license to operate an individually owned business as though it were part of a chain. The franchisor provides a known business name, management skills, a method of doing business, and the training and required materials. The franchisee contributes labor and capital, operates the franchised business, and agrees to abide by the provisions of the franchise agreement. There are three major categories of franchise agreements.

 Analyze the growth of franchising and its advantages and disadvantages.

Franchising has grown tremendously since the mid-1970s. The franchisor's major advantage in franchising is fast and well-controlled distribution of products with minimal capital outlay. In return, the franchisee has the opportunity to open a business with limited capital, to make use of the business experience of others, and to sell to an existing clientele. For this, the franchisee usually must pay both an initial franchise fee and a continuing royalty based on sales. He or she also must follow the dictates of the franchise with regard to operation of the business.

Worldwide business opportunities are expanding for small businesses. The SBA assists small-business owners in penetrating foreign markets. The next century will present unique challenges and opportunities for small-business owners.

KEY TERMS

You should now be able to define and give an example relevant to each of the following terms:

small business (135)
business plan (144)
Small Business Administration (SBA) (147)
Service Corps of Retired Executives (SCORE) (148)

small-business institutes (SBIs) (149)
small-business development centers (SBDCs) (149)
venture capital (150)
small-business investment companies (SBICs) (150)

franchise (151)
franchising (151)
franchisor (151)
franchisee (151)

1. What information would you need to determine whether a particular business is small according to SBA guidelines?
2. Which two areas of business generally attract the most small businesses? Why are these areas attractive to small business?
3. Distinguish among service industries, distribution industries, and production industries.
4. What kinds of factors encourage certain people to start new businesses?
5. What are the major causes of small-business failure? Do these causes also apply to larger businesses?
6. Briefly describe four contributions of small business to the American economy.
7. What are the major advantages and disadvantages of small-ness in business?
8. What are the major components of a business plan? Why should an individual develop a business plan?
9. Identify five ways in which the SBA provides management assistance to small businesses.
10. Identify two ways in which the SBA provides financial assistance to small businesses.
11. Why does the SBA concentrate on providing management and financial assistance to small businesses?
12. What is venture capital? How does the SBA help small businesses to obtain it?
13. Explain the relationships among a franchise, the franchisor, and the franchisee.
14. What does the franchisor receive in a franchising agreement? What does the franchisee receive? What does each provide?
15. Cite one major benefit of franchising for the franchisor. Cite one major benefit of franchising for the franchisee.

1. Most people who start small businesses are aware of the high failure rate and the reasons for it. Why, then, do some take no steps to protect their firms from failure? What steps should they take?
2. Are the so-called advantages of small business really advantages? Wouldn't every small-business owner like his or her business to grow into a large firm?
3. Do average citizens benefit from the activities of the SBA, or is the SBA just another way to spend our tax money?
4. Would you rather own your own business independently or become a franchisee? Why?

Video Case 5.1

**Murray's Cheese:
More Cheese Please**

Murray's Cheese began in New York's Greenwich Village in 1940, as a wholesale butter and egg shop owned by a Jewish veteran of the Spanish Civil War named Murray Greenberg. When the current president Rob Kaufelt purchased the shop in 1991, it was little more than a local hole-in-the-wall. Kaufelt and his staff made the decision to focus on high-quality gourmet cheeses from around the world. Today, people come from all over to sample Murray's cheeses and to take classes or attend its Cheese U boot camp to learn about cheese. Although Murray's has extended its product line to include gourmet meats, crackers, olives, and dried fruit, cheese remains its core product. In fact, Murray's Cheese has been voted by *Forbes* as "the best cheese shop" and it is expanding to three other stores. Its success prompted Kroger to seek it out as a partner in its chain of supermarkets, a step that included intensively training Kroger employees in the fine points of selling Murray's products and the creation of a 300-page cheese service guide for them.

"We are little and they are very big," says Murray's managing director, Liz Thorpe, in speaking of Kroger. "So it's a very interesting model for us. We've begun operating cheese shops in Kroger delis that are similar to our New York shops. This allows us to bring our knowledge and expertise on sourcing, production selection, education, and customer service to a different format. . . . We're actually going to be opening 50 of these shops in the next 36 months."

Murray's is still small, with about 70 employees, and has an advertising budget of zero dollars. Instead of advertising, Murray's relies on providing great customer service and creating positive word of mouth to promote its products and to secure its reputation. Personal selling is key. The company recruits salespeople who are passionate about both cheese and people and trains them carefully. The key is to inform customers about the store's many unique products and persuade them to taste and then purchase. The staff enjoys listening to customers, gaining an understanding of their interests, and trying to find the right product to satisfy their needs. Their efforts often succeed in getting customers to purchase more and to make repeat buys.

All customers get to taste free samples of cheese before they buy it. "We like knowing the folks who walk in our door and having everyone taste the cheese," said the managing director. "It's part of the shopping experience. That said, we are getting more sophisticated about how we communicate with people. E-mail marketing continues to be really critical, and we're starting to take advantage of social networking outlets like Twitter. For people who are into cheese and into Murray's, it's a great way for them to be directly tapped into knowing what's going on right this second."

What continues to appeal to sophisticated shoppers about Murray's is that cheese is an affordable luxury. A wine and cheese party for a dozen people, for instance, can fit almost any budget, and Murray's salespeople are happy to provide suggestions and samples to assist in the selection. Murray's manager also credits popular media like the Food Network with helping to popularize food in general, and cheese in particular. After all, he says, cheeses "don't have to be improved upon or fortified. They are naturally good for you."[25]

Questions

1. How does Murray's overcome one of the most common limitations facing small companies: its nonexistent advertising budget?
2. What are some of the advantages of being a small business that Murray's can (or does) take advantage of? What disadvantages might it face as a small firm?
3. Do you think the partnership with Kroger will have a negative or a positive effect on the unique experience customers expect from Murray's? Why?

Case 5.2 — Warby Parker's Business Vision

Fashionable, affordable prescription eyeglasses sold directly to customers—that's the business vision of Warby Parker, a fast-growing small firm based in New York City. Founded by four friends from the Wharton business school, Warby Parker uses easy-on-the-eyes styling and easy-on-the-budget pricing to compete with national chains such as LensCrafters as well as with neighborhood optical shops. Its exclusive retro-style prescription glasses are priced under $100, with prescription sunglasses priced at $150. Warby Parker's affordable prices include extras such as free shipping, free in-home frame try-ons, and a money-back guarantee. Just as important is that, for every pair of glasses purchased, the company donates one pair to someone in need.

Rather than pay to license famous brand names for its frames, Warby Parker designs its own, inspired by styles from the 1950s and 1960s and manufactured in China. Based on each customer's individual prescription, the company has the optical lenses made to order by a U.S. lab. After the lenses are set in place, the finished product is inspected twice before glasses are shipped to customers.

Because Warby Parker's prices are significantly lower than those of traditional eyeglass providers, customers can afford to buy frames as fashion accessories, not just for vision correction. Co-founder David Gilboa points out that while U.S. consumers typically buy new eyeglasses every other year, many Warby Parker customers "are buying six, seven, eight pairs at a time." They choose different frames for different occasions, such as one pair for going to work and another pair for going out with friends, and they buy frames to fit with particular outfits. The largest single order Warby Parker ever received was from a customer who ordered 14 pairs at once.

Warby Parker operates a showroom at its headquarters in the hip SoHo section of New York, plus seven other showrooms inside fashion boutiques across the country. It also invites customers to call a toll-free number for information and ordering. The main focus, however, is on the interactive Web site, where customers can browse more than two dozen frames, narrow down the choice by color, shape, and size, and upload a digital headshot for a virtual "try on" before ordering. Customers can order up to five frames and try them on at home for five days—enough time to post photos on Warby Parker's Facebook page, if they choose, and ask for feedback on which frames are the most flattering. Shipping and returns are paid by the company, which takes the risk out of trying and buying.

Customers feel good about buying from Warby Parker because they save money and they know each purchase covers a donation of eyeglasses. The company's "buy one, give one" policy allows it to donate more than 100,000 pairs of eyeglasses a year to people in need worldwide through a connection with the nonprofit organization VisionSpring. Now, with the help of venture capital funding, Warby Parker is expanding. It has more than 50 employees and uses social media such as Twitter, Tumblr, and Pinterest to publicize its business vision. Because satisfied customers tell friends and relatives about their experiences, "over 50 percent of our sales are driven by word of mouth," says co-founder Neil Blumenthal.[26]

Questions

1. If you were writing a business plan for Warby Parker, what critical risks and challenges would you mention? What are the business implications of each risk or challenge?
2. Why would Warby Parker have eyeglass frames made in China but optical lenses made in America?
3. Do you agree with Warby Parker's decision to open showrooms inside trendy boutiques in addition to operating on the Internet? Explain your answer.

Personal APPS

Maybe you've never thought of yourself as a manager. But if you've ever headed a committee or organized a new school club, you've actually been involved in management. Understanding more about the way management works can make you more successful in the daily business of *your* life.

Material resources are the tangible, physical resources an organization uses. For example, General Motors uses steel, glass, and fiberglass to produce cars and trucks on complex machine-driven assembly lines. A college or university uses books, classroom buildings, desks, and computers to educate students. And the Mayo Clinic uses operating room equipment, diagnostic machines, and laboratory tests to provide health care.

Perhaps the most important resources of any organization are its *human resources*—people. In fact, some firms live by the philosophy that their employees are their most important assets. Some managers believe that the way employees are developed and managed may have more impact on an organization than other vital components such as marketing, sound financial decisions about large expenditures, production, or use of technology. One such firm that takes pride in its employees is Southwest Airlines. Southwest treats its employees with the same respect and attention it gives its passengers. Southwest selectively seeks employees with upbeat attitudes and promotes from within 80 percent of the time. In decision making, everyone who will be affected is encouraged to get involved in the process. In an industry in which deregulation, extreme price competition, and fluctuating fuel costs have eliminated several major competitors, Southwest keeps growing and making a profit because of its employees. Many experts would agree with Southwest's emphasis on employees.

Financial resources are the funds an organization uses to meet its obligations to investors and creditors. A 7-Eleven convenience store obtains money from customers at the checkout counter and uses a portion of that money to pay its suppliers. Your college obtains money in the form of tuition, income from its endowments, and state and federal grants. It uses the money to pay utility bills, insurance premiums, and professors' salaries.

Finally, many organizations increasingly find that they cannot afford to ignore *information*. External environmental conditions—including the economy, consumer markets, technology, politics, and cultural forces—are all changing so rapidly that a business that does not adapt probably will not survive. To adapt to change, the business must know what is changing and how it is changing. Most companies gather information about their competitors to increase their knowledge about changes in their industry and to learn from other companies' failures and successes.

It is important to realize that the four types of resources described earlier are only general categories of resources. Within each category are hundreds or thousands of more specific resources. It is this complex mix of specific resources—and not simply "some of each" of the four general categories—that managers must coordinate to produce goods and services.

Another interesting way to look at management is in terms of the different functions managers perform. These functions have been identified as planning, organizing, leading and motivating employees, and controlling. We look at each of these management functions in the next section.

FIGURE 6.1 The Four Main Resources of Management

BASIC MANAGEMENT FUNCTIONS

Describe the four basic management functions: planning, organizing, leading and motivating, and controlling.

When pharmaceutical company Eli Lilly decided to focus on the emerging market of China, the company reorganized its structure so that one of its six units would handle emerging markets, doubled its employee count from 1,100 to 2,200, and began construction on a second manufacturing plant in Suzhou, China. The company also implemented a partnering strategy in China to handle research and development. Eli Lilly's key strategies include maximizing their core assets, accelerating new product launches, capitalizing on longer product life-cycles in areas like China, and establishing local alliances to access fast-growing market segments.[2]

Management functions such as those just described do not occur according to some rigid, preset timetable. Managers do not plan in January, organize in February, lead and motivate in March, and control in April. At any given time, managers may engage in a number of functions simultaneously. However, each function tends to lead naturally to others. Figure 6.2 provides a visual framework for a more detailed discussion of the four basic management functions. How well managers perform these key functions determines whether a business is successful.

© KURHAN/SHUTTERSTOCK

Superior human resources management can set a firm apart. Do you have a great business plan or product? A competitor can easily copy both. Great employees, however, are much harder to duplicate. That's why being able to attract, train, and retain talented workers can give a firm a competitive advantage over its rivals.

Planning

Planning, in its simplest form, is establishing organizational goals and deciding how to accomplish them. It is often referred to as the "first" management function because all other management functions depend on planning. Organizations such as Starbucks, Houston Community College system, and Facebook begin the planning process by developing a mission statement.

An organization's **mission** is a statement of the basic purpose that makes that organization different from others. Starbucks' mission statement, for example, is "to inspire and nurture the human spirit—one person, one cup, and one neighborhood at a time." Houston Community College's mission is to provide an education for local citizens. Facebook's mission statement is "to give people the power to share and make the world more open and connected."[3] Once an organization's mission has been described in a mission statement, the next step is to engage in strategic planning.

Strategic Planning Process The **strategic planning process** involves establishing an organization's major goals and objectives and allocating resources to achieve them. Top management is responsible for strategic planning, although customers, products, competitors, and company resources are some of the factors that are analyzed in the strategic planning process.

> ✳ **planning** establishing organizational goals and deciding how to accomplish them
>
> ✳ **mission** a statement of the basic purpose that makes an organization different from others
>
> ✳ **strategic planning process** the establishment of an organization's major goals and objectives and the allocation of resources to achieve them

---

FIGURE 6.2	The Management Process

Note that management is not a step-by-step procedure but a process with a feedback loop that represents a flow.

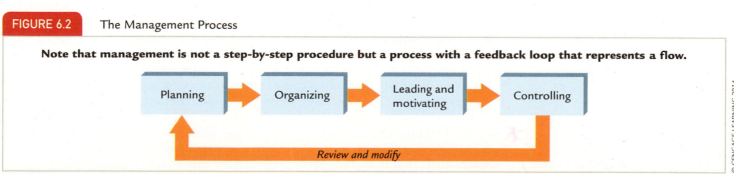

Planning → Organizing → Leading and motivating → Controlling

Review and modify

© CENGAGE LEARNING 2014

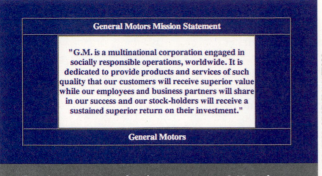

General Motors Mission Statement

"G.M. is a multinational corporation engaged in socially responsible operations, worldwide. It is dedicated to provide products and services of such quality that our customers will receive superior value while our employees and business partners will share in our success and our stock-holders will receive a sustained superior return on their investment."

General Motors

What is your organization's purpose? How is it different than other organizations? Those are the questions a firm's mission statement like the one shown here should answer. Mission statements are meant for multiple audiences, including a company's customers, investors, the general public, and employees. Most firms familiarize their personnel with their mission statements so they know what's expected of them and what they should strive for.

In today's rapidly changing business environment, constant internal or external changes may necessitate changes in a company's goals, mission, or strategy. The time line for strategic plans is generally one to two years and can be as long as ten years. Strategic plans should be flexible and include action items, such as outlining how plans will be implemented.

Establishing Goals and Objectives A **goal** is an end result that an organization is expected to achieve over a one- to ten-year period. An **objective** is a specific statement detailing what the organization intends to accomplish over a shorter period of time.

Goals and objectives can deal with a variety of factors, such as sales, company growth, costs, customer satisfaction, and employee morale. Whereas a small manufacturer may focus primarily on sales objectives for the next six months, a large firm may be more interested in goals that impact several years in the future. Starbucks, for example, has established several goals under its "Shared Planet" program to be completed in the next few years, specifically in the areas of ethical sourcing, environmental stewardship, and community involvement. By 2015, Starbucks hopes to purchase 100 percent of its coffee from ethical sources or farmers who grow their coffee responsibly without permanently harming the environment. The company also hopes to combat climate change by encouraging farmers to prevent deforestation through the use of incentive programs. Starbucks hopes to make 100% of its cups reusable or recyclable by 2015. Also, the company hopes to use their stores to lead volunteer programs in each store's community.[4] Finally, goals are set at every level of an organization. Every member of an organization—the president of the company, the head of a department, and an operating employee at the lowest level—has a set of goals that he or she hopes to achieve.

The goals developed for these different levels must be consistent. However, it is likely that some conflict will arise. A production department, for example, may have a goal of minimizing costs. One way to do this is to produce only one type of product and offer "no frills." Marketing may have a goal of maximizing sales. One way to implement this goal is to offer customers a wide range of products and options. As part of goal setting, the manager who is responsible for *both* departments must achieve some sort of balance between conflicting goals. This balancing process is called *optimization*.

The optimization of conflicting goals requires insight and ability. Faced with the marketing-versus-production conflict just described, most managers probably would not adopt either viewpoint completely. Instead, they might decide on a reasonably diverse product line offering only the most widely sought-after options. Such a compromise would seem to be best for the whole organization.

SWOT Analysis **SWOT analysis** is the identification and evaluation of a firm's strengths, weaknesses, opportunities, and threats. Strengths and weaknesses are internal factors that affect a company's capabilities. Strengths refer to a firm's favorable characteristics and core competencies. **Core competencies** are approaches and processes that a company performs well that may give it an advantage over its competitors. These core competencies may help the firm attract financial and human resources and be more capable of producing products that better satisfy customers. Weaknesses refer to any internal limitations a company faces in developing or implementing plans. At times, managers have difficulty identifying and understanding the negative effects of weaknesses in their organizations.

External opportunities and threats exist independently of the firm. Opportunities refer to favorable conditions in the environment that could produce rewards for the organization. That is, opportunities are situations that exist but must be exploited for

goal an end result that an organization is expected to achieve over a one- to ten-year period

objective a specific statement detailing what an organization intends to accomplish over a shorter period of time

SWOT analysis the identification and evaluation of a firm's strengths, weaknesses, opportunities, and threats

core competencies approaches and processes that a company performs well that may give it an advantage over its competitors

Ethical
SUCCESS OR FAILURE?

Digging Deep to Research Competitors

When preparing a SWOT analysis, how far can companies go in researching their competition? Many firms carefully monitor social media comments in search of tidbits about their rivals, for example. What are the ethical limits of competitive research?

In general, companies are going too far when they rummage through a competitor's trash cans, tap its phone lines, hack into its computer systems, or try to obtain proprietary information such as customer lists and product blueprints. On the other hand, visiting competitors' publicly-available Web sites and Facebook pages, shopping their stores or showrooms, and watching for announcements of new products and price changes are all good ways to map the competitive landscape. One biotechnology firm pays close attention to how quickly competitors' pharmaceutical products are moving through regulatory channels, clues that help it plan the timing of its own introductions and its marketing campaigns.

No matter how much a company learns about its competitors' strengths and weaknesses, the information is useless unless the right people see it. That's why Egencia, a travel agency that serves business customers, maintains a "Know Your Enemy" internal site where employees can post and review competitive details. Then, when salespeople meet with customers, they can emphasize Egencia's competitive strengths.

Sources: Based on information in Robert L. Scheier, "Why Social Tech's Real Value Is Inside the Business," *InfoWorld*, December 19, 2011, http:// infoworld.com/d/applications/why-social-techs-real-value-inside-the-business-178336; "Crash Course in Competitive Intelligence (CI)," *Management Today*, May 1, 2011, p. 18; Judith Lamont, "Gaining Insight to Enhance Decision-Making," *KMWorld*, November–December 2011, p. 12.

the firm to benefit from them. Threats, on the other hand, are conditions or barriers that may prevent the firm from reaching its objectives. Opportunities and threats can stem from many sources within the business environment. For example, a competitor's actions, new laws, economic changes, or new technology can be threats. Threats for some firms may be opportunities for others. Examples of strengths, weaknesses, opportunities, and threats are shown in Figure 6.3.

FIGURE 6.3 Elements and Examples of SWOT Analysis

STRENGTHS
- Efficient distribution channels
- Employee education and experience
- Protected patents
- Core competencies
- Excellent facilities/equipment
- Proven management
- Economies of scale
- Cost advantages

WEAKNESSES
- High turnover, absenteeism
- Lack of strategic direction
- Obsolete production facilities
- Labor grievances
- Lack of managerial depth
- Negative public image

SWOT Analysis

OPPORTUNITIES
- New markets opening up
- New technologies
- Increased demand for new products
- Potential strategic alliances
- More favorable trade regulations in desirable foreign markets
- Competitor complacency

THREATS
- Entry of lower-cost foreign competitors
- Unfavorable changes in buyer needs and tastes
- Rising sales of substitute products
- Slowing market growth
- Costly regulatory requirements
- Vulnerability to business cycle changes
- Sole sourcing

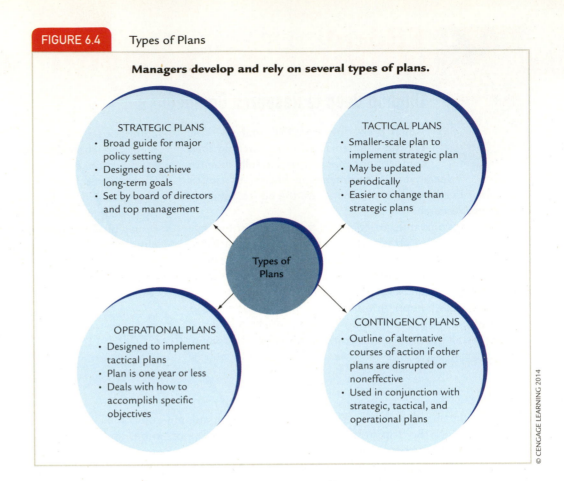

FIGURE 6.4 Types of Plans

Managers develop and rely on several types of plans.

Types of Plans

STRATEGIC PLANS
- Broad guide for major policy setting
- Designed to achieve long-term goals
- Set by board of directors and top management

TACTICAL PLANS
- Smaller-scale plan to implement strategic plan
- May be updated periodically
- Easier to change than strategic plans

OPERATIONAL PLANS
- Designed to implement tactical plans
- Plan is one year or less
- Deals with how to accomplish specific objectives

CONTINGENCY PLANS
- Outline of alternative courses of action if other plans are disrupted or noneffective
- Used in conjunction with strategic, tactical, and operational plans

© CENGAGE LEARNING 2014

Types of Plans Once goals and objectives have been set for the organization, managers must develop plans for achieving them. A **plan** is an outline of the actions by which an organization intends to accomplish its goals and objectives. Just as it has different goals and objectives, the organization also develops several types of plans, as shown in Figure 6.4.

Resulting from the strategic planning process, an organization's **strategic plan** is its broadest plan, developed as a guide for major policy setting and decision making. Strategic plans are set by the board of directors and top management and are generally designed to achieve the organization's long-term goals. Thus, a firm's strategic plan defines what business the company is in or wants to be in and the kind of company it is or wants to be. Gannett, a major publisher of 82 different newspapers, revamped its strategic plan in the face of a prolonged advertising slump. The firm's plan involved increasing sports coverage and revamping its subscriber model in an effort to boost revenues. The new strategic plan recognizes that subscribers increasingly obtain their news online in a digital format and implemented an online subscriber system. Customers can read between 5 and 15 articles per month for free, after which they have to pay.[5]

In addition to strategic plans, most organizations also employ several narrower kinds of plans. A **tactical plan** is a smaller scale plan developed to implement a strategy. Most tactical plans cover a one- to three-year period. If a strategic plan will take five years to complete, the firm may develop five tactical plans, one covering each year. Tactical plans may be updated periodically as dictated by conditions and experience. Their more limited scope permits them to be changed more easily than strategies. IKEA has a tactical plan that involves opening three stores per year in China through 2016. These stores must be located in urban areas near transit, such as train or light rail. Because Chinese infrastructure, income levels, lifestyles, and living spaces all differ from those of its customers in the west, IKEA must utilize a different tactical plan for its Chinese expansion.[6]

plan an outline of the actions by which an organization intends to accomplish its goals and objectives

strategic plan an organization's broadest plan, developed as a guide for major policy setting and decision making

tactical plan a smaller scale plan developed to implement a strategy

An **operational plan** is a type of plan designed to implement tactical plans. Operational plans are usually established for one year or less and deal with how to accomplish the organization's specific objectives.

Regardless of how hard managers try, sometimes business activities do not go as planned. Today, most corporations also develop contingency plans along with strategies, tactical plans, and operational plans. A **contingency plan** is a plan that outlines alternative courses of action that may be taken if an organization's other plans are disrupted or become ineffective. For instance, Air Canada was forced to enact its contingency plan for servicing aircraft after its normal supplier, Aveos Fleet Performance, suspended operations. Without warning, Aveos locked out 2,300 workers, filed for credit protection, and announced that it permanently closed its airframe maintenance operation. Luckily, Air Canada had a contingency plan in place to reroute aircraft to a supplier in Quebec for repairs.[7]

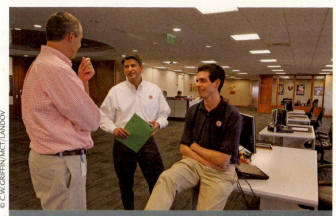

Tearing down the walls at Burger King. Burger King's top-level executives no longer have closed door offices, and employees no longer work in cubicles. The new physical arrangement facilitates better communication and collaboration among employees at all levels.

Organizing the Enterprise

After goal setting and planning, the manager's second major function is organization. **Organizing** is the grouping of resources and activities to accomplish some end result in an efficient and effective manner. Consider the case of an inventor who creates a new product and goes into business to sell it. At first, the inventor will do everything on his or her own—purchase raw materials, make the product, advertise it, sell it, and keep business records. Eventually, as business grows, the inventor will need help. To begin with, he or she might hire a professional sales representative and a part-time bookkeeper. Later, it also might be necessary to hire sales staff, people to assist with production, and an accountant. As the inventor hires new personnel, he or she must decide what each person will do, to whom each person will report, and how each person can best take part in the organization's activities. We discuss these and other facets of the organizing function in much more detail in Chapter 7.

Leading and Motivating

The leading and motivating function is concerned with the human resources within an organization. Specifically, **leading** is the process of influencing people to work toward a common goal. **Motivating** is the process of providing reasons for people to work in the best interests of an organization. Together, leading and motivating are often referred to as **directing**.

We have already noted the importance of an organization's human resources. Because of this importance, leading and motivating are critical activities. Obviously, different people do things for different reasons—that is, they have different *motivations*. Some are interested primarily in earning as much money as they can. Others may be spurred on by opportunities to get promoted. Part of a manager's job, then, is to determine what factors motivate workers and to try to provide those incentives to encourage effective performance. Jeffrey R. Immelt, GE's chairperson and CEO, has worked to transform GE into a leader in essential themes tied to world development, such as emerging markets, environmental solutions, demographics, and digital connections. He believes in giving freedom to his teams and wants them to come up with their own solutions. However, he does not hesitate to intervene if the situation demands. He believes that a leader's primary role is to teach, and he makes people feel that he is willing to share what he has learned. Immelt also laid the vision for GE's ambitious "ecomagination initiative" and has been named one of the "World's Best CEOs" three times by *Barron's*.[8] A lot of research has been done on both motivation and leadership. As you will see in Chapter 10, research on motivation has yielded very useful information. However, research on leadership has been less successful. Despite decades of study, no one has discovered a general set of personal traits or characteristics that makes a good leader. Later in this chapter, we discuss leadership in more detail.

operational plan a type of plan designed to implement tactical plans

contingency plan a plan that outlines alternative courses of action that may be taken if an organization's other plans are disrupted or become ineffective

organizing the grouping of resources and activities to accomplish some end result in an efficient and effective manner

leading the process of influencing people to work toward a common goal

motivating the process of providing reasons for people to work in the best interests of an organization

directing the combined processes of leading and motivating

FIGURE 6.5   The Control Function

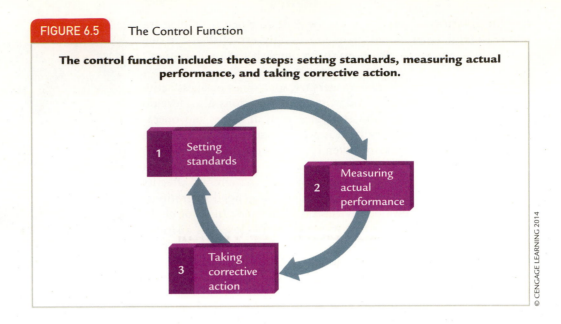

The control function includes three steps: setting standards, measuring actual performance, and taking corrective action.

1. Setting standards
2. Measuring actual performance
3. Taking corrective action

Controlling Ongoing Activities

Controlling is the process of evaluating and regulating ongoing activities to ensure that goals are achieved. To see how controlling works, consider a rocket launched by NASA to place a satellite in orbit. Do NASA personnel simply fire the rocket and then check back in a few days to find out whether the satellite is in place? Of course not. The rocket is monitored constantly, and its course is regulated and adjusted as needed to get the satellite to its destination.

The control function includes three steps (see Figure 6.5). The first is *setting standards* with which performance can be compared. The second is *measuring actual performance* and comparing it with the standard. The third is *taking corrective action* as necessary. Notice that the control function is circular in nature. The steps in the control function must be repeated periodically until the goal is achieved. For example, suppose that Southwest Airlines establishes a goal of increasing profits by 12 percent. To ensure that this goal is reached, Southwest's management might monitor its profit on a monthly basis. After three months, if profit has increased by 3 percent, management might be able to assume that plans are going according to schedule. In this case, it is likely that no action will be taken. However, if profit has increased by only 1 percent after three months, some corrective action is needed to get the firm on track. The particular action that is required depends on the reason for the small increase in profit.

KINDS OF MANAGERS

Managers can be classified in two ways: according to their level within an organization and according to their area of management. In this section, we use both perspectives to explore the various types of managers.

Levels of Management

For the moment, think of an organization as a three-story structure (as illustrated in Figure 6.6). Each story corresponds to one of the three general levels of management: top managers, middle managers, and first-line managers.

Top Managers   A **top manager** is an upper-level executive who guides and controls an organization's overall fortunes. Top managers constitute a small group. In terms of planning, they are generally responsible for developing the organization's mission. They also

---

Distinguish among the various kinds of managers in terms of both level and area of management.   ③

controlling the process of evaluating and regulating ongoing activities to ensure that goals are achieved

top manager an upper-level executive who guides and controls the overall fortunes of an organization

FIGURE 6.6 Management Levels Found in Most Companies

The coordinated effort of all three levels of managers is required to implement the goals of any company.

Top management

Middle management

First-line management

© CENGAGE LEARNING 2014

determine the firm's strategy. It takes years of hard work, long hours, and perseverance, as well as talent and no small share of good luck, to reach the ranks of top management in large companies. Common job titles associated with top managers are president, vice president, chief executive officer (CEO), and chief operating officer (COO).

Middle Managers Middle managers probably make up the largest group of managers in most organizations. A **middle manager** is a manager who implements the strategy and major policies developed by top management. Middle managers develop tactical plans and operational plans, and they coordinate and supervise the activities of first-line managers. Titles at the middle-management level include division manager, department head, plant manager, and operations manager.

First-Line Managers A **first-line manager** is a manager who coordinates and supervises the activities of operating employees. First-line managers spend most of their time working with and motivating their employees, answering questions, and solving day-to-day problems. Most first-line managers are former operating employees who, owing to their hard work and potential, were promoted into management. Many of today's middle and top managers began their careers on this first management level. Common titles for first-line managers include office manager, supervisor, and foreman.

Areas of Management Specialization

Organizational structure can also be divided into areas of management specialization (see Figure 6.7). The most common areas are finance, operations, marketing, human resources, and administration. Depending on its mission, goals, and objectives, an organization may include other areas as well—research and development (R&D), for example.

Financial Managers A **financial manager** is primarily responsible for an organization's financial resources. Accounting and investment are specialized areas within financial management. Because

middle manager a manager who implements the strategy and major policies developed by top management

first-line manager a manager who coordinates and supervises the activities of operating employees

financial manager a manager who is primarily responsible for an organization's financial resources

© AP PHOTO/MARK LENNIHAN

A top manager's out-of-this world business strategy. At the age of 16, Richard Branson, the CEO and founder of the Virgin Group, started his first business venture: a magazine called *The Student*. Today, the Virgin Group consists of over 400 companies, including Virgin Telecommunications, Virgin Radio, Virgin Cola, Virgin Wine, Virgin Spa, Virgin Airlines—and the list goes on. By 2014, Virgin Galactic, one of Branson's newest companies, aims to launch paying customers into space.

Going for SUCCESS

Steve Jobs: Futurist Extraordinaire

The late Steve Jobs was not just an inspiring leader within Apple, the company he cofounded—he was also an inspiration to many other business leaders, including Virgin Group's entrepreneur-in-chief, Richard Branson. Observing that "all true leaders go about things in their own way," Branson observes that Jobs's success as CEO was due to his ability to envision things that others could not.

With Jobs as its visionary CEO, Apple introduced now-iconic products such as the iPhone, the iPad, and iTunes. Jobs was creative, charismatic, and autocratic. He made quick and confident decisions, pushing Apple to be the very best at what it does. At his insistence, any product carrying the company logo of an apple minus a bite had to be aesthetically distinctive, intuitive to use, and top quality.

To the outside world, Jobs was the face of Apple, introducing every new product with personal pride. Inside the company, he was a relentless innovator, always thinking about the next new thing and pushing for the next breakthrough. Over the years, Jobs changed the way people use computers, make phone calls, and listen to music. His leadership legacy is a strong, successful company with can-do spirit.

Sources: Based on information in Steve Lohr, "The Yin and Yang of Corporate Innovation," *New York Times,* January 26, 2012, p. BU-3; Frederick E. Allen, "Steve Jobs Broke Every Leadership Rule. Don't Try It Yourself," *Forbes,* August 27, 2011, http://forbes.com/sites/frederickallen/2011/08/27/steve-jobs-broke-every-leadership-rule-dont-try-that-yourself/; Joe Nocera, "What Makes Steve Jobs Great," *New York Times,* August 26, 2011, http://nytimes.com/2011/08/27/opinion/nocera-what-makes-steve-jobs-great.html; Richard Branson, "Apple Boss Steve Jobs Was the Entrepreneur I Most Admired," *Telegraph (U.K.),* October 6, 2011, http://telegraph.co.uk/technology/steve-jobs/8811232/Virgins-Richard-Branson-Apple-boss-Steve-Jobs-was-the-entrepreneur-I-most-admired.html.

financing affects the operation of the entire firm, many of the CEOs and presidents of this country's largest companies are people who got their "basic training" as financial managers.

Operations Managers An **operations manager** manages the systems that convert resources into goods and services. Traditionally, operations management has been equated with manufacturing—the production of goods. However, in recent years, many of the techniques and procedures of operations management have been applied to the production of services and to a variety of nonbusiness activities. As with financial management, operations management has produced a large percentage of today's company CEOs and presidents.

Marketing Managers A **marketing manager** is responsible for facilitating the exchange of products between an organization and its customers or clients. Specific areas within marketing are marketing research, product management, advertising, promotion, sales, and distribution. A sizable number of today's company presidents have risen from the ranks of marketing management.

Human Resources Managers A **human resources manager** is charged with managing an organization's human resources programs. He or she engages in human resources planning; designs systems for hiring, training, and evaluating the performance of employees; and ensures that the organization follows government

operations manager a manager who manages the systems that convert resources into goods and services

marketing manager a manager who is responsible for facilitating the exchange of products between an organization and its customers or clients

human resources manager a person charged with managing an organization's human resources programs

---

FIGURE 6.7 Areas of Management Specialization

Other areas may have to be added, depending on the nature of the firm and the industry.

| Finance | Operations | Marketing | Human resources | Administration | Other (e.g., research and development) |

regulations concerning employment practices. Some human resources managers make effective use of technology. For example, more than 1 million job openings are posted on Monster.com, which attracts about 23 million visitors monthly.[9]

Administrative Managers An **administrative manager** (also called a *general manager*) is not associated with any specific functional area but provides overall administrative guidance and leadership. A hospital administrator is an example of an administrative manager. He or she does not specialize in operations, finance, marketing, or human resources management but instead coordinates the activities of specialized managers in all these areas. In many respects, most top managers are really administrative managers.

Whatever their level in the organization and whatever area they specialize in, successful managers generally exhibit certain key skills and are able to play certain managerial roles. However, as we shall see, some skills are likely to be more critical at one level of management than at another.

Harnessing the cooperation of an organization's specialized managers. Imagine the managers of different departments as a team of horses. If they—and their employees—don't all work together and pull in the same direction, the organization won't get to the destination it's trying to reach.

© AUREMAR/SHUTTERSTOCK

KEY SKILLS OF SUCCESSFUL MANAGERS

④ Identify the key management skills of successful managers.

As shown in Figure 6.8, managers need a variety of skills, including conceptual, analytic, interpersonal, technical, and communication skills.

Conceptual Skills

Conceptual skills involve the ability to think in abstract terms. Conceptual skills allow a manager to see the "big picture" and understand how the various parts of an organization or idea can fit together. For example, Jim Whitehurst of Red Hat, an open-source technology company, strongly believes in the advantage offered by conceptual thinkers. He believes that managers should solicit creative ideas from all levels of the

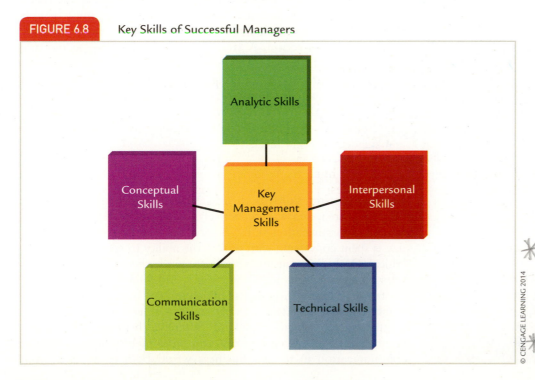

FIGURE 6.8 Key Skills of Successful Managers

Analytic Skills

Conceptual Skills

Key Management Skills

Interpersonal Skills

Communication Skills

Technical Skills

© CENGAGE LEARNING 2014

✳administrative manager a manager who is not associated with any specific functional area but who provides overall administrative guidance and leadership

✳conceptual skills the ability to think in abstract terms organization in order to help them see the big picture better and to obtain a wide variety of creative viewpoints.[10] These skills are useful in a wide range of situations, including the optimization of goals described earlier.

Analytic Skills

Employers expect managers to use **analytic skills** to identify problems correctly, generate reasonable alternatives, and select the "best" alternatives to solve problems. Top-level managers especially need these skills because they need to discern the important issues from the less important ones, as well as recognize the underlying reasons for different situations. Managers who use these skills not only address a situation but also correct the initial event or problem that caused it to occur. Thus, these skills are vital to run a business efficiently and logically.

Interpersonal Skills

Interpersonal skills involve the ability to deal effectively with other people, both inside and outside an organization. Examples of interpersonal skills are the ability to relate to people, understand their needs and motives, and show genuine compassion. Howard Schultz, founder and CEO of Starbucks, used his knowledge of interpersonal communication to save the company recently. Schultz quickly shut down 800 poorly performing stores, laid off 4,000 employees, retrained staff, modernized technology, and improved operations. Despite these drastic changes, employees are still loyal to the company and motivated for change because of Schultz's commitment to community and employee growth. For example, he refused to reduce employee health coverage because this would "sap the reservoir of trust" that employees have. While it may be obvious that a CEO such as Schultz must be able to work with employees throughout the organization, it's not so obvious that middle and first-line managers must also possess these interpersonal skills.[11]

Technical Skills

Technical skills involve specific skills needed to accomplish a specialized activity. For example, the skills engineers and machinists need to do their jobs are technical skills. First-line managers (and, to a lesser extent, middle managers) need the technical skills relevant to the activities they manage. Although these managers may not perform the technical tasks themselves, they must be able to train subordinates, answer questions, and otherwise provide guidance and direction. A first-line manager in the accounting department of the Hyatt Corporation, for example, must be able to perform computerized accounting transactions and help employees complete the same accounting task. In general, top managers do not rely on technical skills as heavily as managers at other levels. Still, understanding the technical side of a business is an aid to effective management at every level.

Communication Skills

Communication skills, both oral and written, involve the ability to speak, listen, and write effectively. Managers need both oral and written communication skills. Because a large part of a manager's day is spent conversing with others, the ability to speak *and* listen is critical. Oral communication skills are used when a manager makes sales presentations, conducts interviews, and holds press conferences. Written communication skills are important because a manager's ability to prepare letters, e-mails, memos, sales reports, and other written documents may spell the difference between success and failure. Computers, smartphones, and other high-tech devices make communication in today's business world both easier and more

analytic skills the ability to identify problems correctly, generate reasonable alternatives, and select the "best" alternatives to solve problems

interpersonal skills the ability to deal effectively with other people

technical skills specific skills needed to accomplish a specialized activity

communication skills the ability to speak, listen, and write effectively

How good are your managerial skills? To be successful, managers must master and simultaneously utilize a number of skills, including: technical skills that aid with specialized work; conceptual skills that foster abstract thinking; and interpersonal skills to help manage and motivate their employees. Which of these skills will you need to work on as you build your career?

© BLEND IMAGES/SHUTTERSTOCK

complex. To effectively manage an organization and to stay adequately informed, it is very important that managers understand how to use and maximize the potential of digital communication devices.

LEADERSHIP

5 Explain the different types of leadership.

Leadership has been defined broadly as the ability to influence others. A leader can use his or her power to affect the behavior of others. Leadership is different from management in that a leader strives for voluntary cooperation, whereas a manager may have to depend on coercion to change employee behavior.

Formal and Informal Leadership

Some experts make distinctions between formal leadership and informal leadership. Formal leaders have legitimate power of position. They have *authority* within an organization to influence others to work for the organization's objectives. Informal leaders usually have no such authority and may or may not exert their influence in support of the organization. Both formal and informal leaders make use of several kinds of power, including the ability to grant rewards or impose punishments, the possession of expert knowledge, and personal attraction or charisma. Informal leaders who identify with the organization's goals are a valuable asset to any organization. However, a business can be brought to its knees by informal leaders who turn work groups against management.

Styles of Leadership

For many years, leadership was viewed as a combination of personality traits, such as self-confidence, concern for people, intelligence, and dependability. Achieving a consensus on which traits were most important was difficult, however, so attention turned to styles of leadership behavior. In recent years, several styles of leadership have emerged, including *autocratic, participative,* and *entrepreneurial.*

Autocratic leadership is very task-oriented. Decisions are made confidently, with little concern about employee opinions. Employees are told exactly what is expected from them and given specific guidelines, rules, and regulations on how to achieve their tasks. Managers at Hyundai USA successfully employ the autocratic leadership style.[12]

Participative leadership is common in today's business organizations. Participative leaders consult workers before making decisions. This helps workers understand which goals are important and fosters a sense of ownership and commitment to reach those goals. Participative leaders can be classified into three groups: consultative, consensus, and democratic. *Consultative leaders* discuss issues with workers but retain the final authority for decision making. *Consensus leaders* seek input from almost all workers and make final decisions based on their support. *Democratic leaders* give final authority to the group. They collect opinions and base their decisions on the vote of the group. Google co-founders Larry Page and Sergey Brin are known for their democratic decision-making styles.[13] Communication is active upward and downward in participative organizations. Coaching, collaborating, and negotiating are important skills for participative leaders.

* **leadership** the ability to influence others

* **autocratic leadership** task-oriented leadership style in which workers are told what to do and how to accomplish it; workers have no say in the decision-making process

* **participative leadership** leadership style in which all members of a team are involved in identifying essential goals and developing strategies to reach those goals

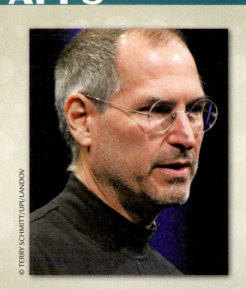

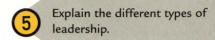

Personal APPS

Think of a leader you admire—someone in the business world or an entertainer raising awareness for a social cause, for example. Why does this person inspire you or make you want to take action? What can you learn from his or her leadership that will help you become a leader in *your* life?

A CEO who leads by example. Bill Gates's leadership style and technological know-how have helped him foster an environment at Microsoft in which top-notch products can be created. Gates's leadership style includes dimensions of both autocratic and participative leadership.

Entrepreneurial leadership is personality dependent. Although each entrepreneur is different, this leadership style is generally task-oriented, driven, charismatic, and enthusiastic.[14] The entrepreneurial personality tends to take initiative, venture into new areas, be visionary, and focus on the next deal. Their enthusiasm energizes and inspires their people. Entrepreneurial leaders tend to be very invested in their businesses, working extremely long hours trying to ensure the success of their firm. They may not understand why their employees do not have the same level of passion for their work. Steve Jobs, former CEO of Apple, was probably the preeminent example of an entrepreneurial leader. He was highly charismatic and worked tirelessly and passionately for his organization.[15]

Which Leadership Style Is the Best?

Today, most management experts agree that no "best" managerial leadership style exists. Each of the styles described—autocratic, participative, and entrepreneurial—has advantages and disadvantages. Participative leadership can motivate employees to work effectively because they are implementing their own decisions. However, the decision-making process in participative leadership takes time that subordinates could be devoting to the work itself. Table 6.1 presents tips for effective leadership. Most of these tips are consistent with the participative leadership style.

Although hundreds of research studies have been conducted to prove which leadership style is best, there are no definite conclusions. The "best" leadership seems to occur when the leader's style matches the situation. Each of the leadership styles can be effective in the right situation. The *most* effective style depends on interaction among employees, characteristics of the work situation, and the manager's personality.

TABLE 6.1	Tips for Successful Leadership
1.	Walk the talk. Make your actions consistent with your words.
2.	Be truthful, fair, and respectful, and honor confidences.
3.	Demonstrate a vision and values worth following.
4.	Co-workers make mistakes. So do you. Admit to them and learn from them.
5.	Be open to what others have to offer. Ask questions and take time to listen to co-workers.
6.	Know your weaknesses, so that you can build a team to make up for them.
7.	All work and no fun can reduce productivity.
8.	Help workers do their best by encouraging them to grow and learn.
9.	Never publicly blame anyone but yourself.
10.	Stay positive and expect it of your people. Negativity leads downhill fast.
11.	Involve people in decisions—especially those regarding change.
12.	Be open to new ways of doing things. Embrace change—it's inevitable.
13.	Recognize and celebrate individual and team successes, both big and not so big.
14.	Embrace and benefit from diversity.
15.	Empower your workers. They will have greater self-respect, responsibility, and accountability.
16.	Take your work, but not yourself, seriously.

© CENGAGE LEARNING 2014

entrepreneurial leadership personality-based leadership style in which the manager seeks to inspire workers with a vision of what can be accomplished to benefit all stakeholders

MANAGERIAL DECISION MAKING

6 Discuss the steps in the managerial decision-making process.

Decision making is the act of choosing one alternative from a set of alternatives.[16] In ordinary situations, decisions are made casually and informally. We encounter a problem, mull it over, settle on a solution, and go on. Managers, however, require a more systematic method for solving complex problems. As shown in Figure 6.9, managerial decision making involves four steps: (1) identifying the problem or opportunity, (2) generating alternatives, (3) selecting an alternative, and (4) implementing and evaluating the solution.

Identifying the Problem or Opportunity

A **problem** is the discrepancy between an actual condition and a desired condition—the difference between what is occurring and what one wishes would occur. For example, a marketing manager at Campbell's Soup Company has a problem if sales revenues for Campbell's Hungry Man frozen dinners are declining (the actual condition). To solve this problem, the marketing manager must take steps to increase sales revenues (desired condition). Most people consider a problem to be "negative"; however, a problem also can be "positive." A positive problem should be viewed as an "opportunity."

Although accurate identification of a problem is essential before it can be solved or turned into an opportunity, this stage of decision making creates many difficulties for managers. Sometimes managers' preconceptions of the problem prevent them from seeing the actual situation. They produce an answer before the proper question has been asked. In other cases, managers overlook truly significant issues by focusing on unimportant matters. Also, managers may mistakenly analyze problems in terms of symptoms rather than underlying causes.

Effective managers learn to look ahead so that they are prepared when decisions must be made. They clarify situations and examine the causes of problems, asking whether the presence or absence of certain variables alters a situation. Finally, they consider how individual behaviors and values affect the way problems or opportunities are defined.

Generating Alternatives

After a problem has been defined, the next task is to generate alternatives. The more important the decision, the more attention must be devoted to this stage. Managers should be open to fresh, innovative ideas as well as obvious answers.

Certain techniques can aid in the generation of creative alternatives. Brainstorming, commonly used in group discussions, encourages participants to produce many new ideas. During brainstorming, other group members are not permitted to criticize or ridicule. Another approach, developed by the U.S. Navy, is called "Blast! Then Refine." Group members tackle a recurring problem by erasing all previous solutions and procedures. The group then re-evaluates its original objectives, modifies them if necessary, and devises new solutions. Other techniques—including trial and error—are also useful in this stage of decision making.

Selecting an Alternative

Final decisions are influenced by a number of considerations, including financial constraints, human and informational resources, time limits, legal obstacles, and political

---

FIGURE 6.9   Major Steps in the Managerial Decision-Making Process

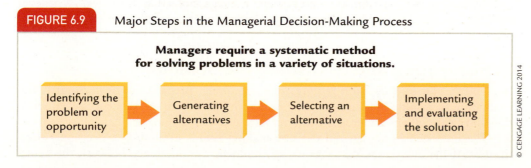

Managers require a systematic method for solving problems in a variety of situations.

Identifying the problem or opportunity → Generating alternatives → Selecting an alternative → Implementing and evaluating the solution

© CENGAGE LEARNING 2014

decision making the act of choosing one alternative from a set of alternatives

problem the discrepancy between an actual condition and a desired condition

Social MEDIA

Through Social Media, Do Workers Create Problems for Their Employers?

How should managers handle employee use of social media? Despite the growing popularity of Facebook, LinkedIn, Twitter, and other sites, some companies are concerned that employees will disclose proprietary information or become involved in controversial conversations that could harm the company's image. They also worry that employees will be distracted during the workday.

Employers in a few industries—such as financial services—are required to monitor business-related messages posted by employees to ensure compliance with government regulations. In most cases, however, companies are free to set their own policies. For example, IBM's policy requires employees to use respectful language, obey copyright laws, and indicate that their views are personal.

A growing number of firms are encouraging employees to interact with each other and with customers and suppliers using social media, as long as they follow specific guidelines. Kodak's employees must disclose their affiliation when discussing anything related to the company's business and are not allowed to reveal any confidential information. The social-media policy of online retailer Zappos is short and to the point: "Be real and use your best judgment."

Sources: Tamara Schweitzer, "Do You Need a Social Media Policy?" *Inc.*, January 25, 2010, www.inc.com/articles/2010/01/need-a-social-media-policy.html; David Scheer, "Brokers' Facebook, Twitter Posts Must Be Tracked by Employers," *BusinessWeek*, January 25, 2010, www.businessweek.com; Charlene Li, *Open Leadership* (San Francisco, CA: Jossey-Bass, 2010), chap. 5; Stephen Baker, "Beware Social Media Snake Oil," *BusinessWeek*, December 14, 2009, 48–51.

© JUAN CAMILO BERNAL/SHUTTERSTOCK

Sources: Melinda J. Caterine, "Your Business: Make Your Social Media Policy Clear," *Portland Press Herald* (Maine), January 25, 2011, www.pressherald.com; Tamara Schweitzer, "Do You Need a Social Media Policy?" *Inc.*, January 25, 2010, www.inc.com; David Scheer, "Brokers' Facebook, Twitter Posts Must Be Tracked by Employers," *BusinessWeek*, January 25, 2010, www.businessweek.com.

factors. Managers must select the alternative that will be most effective and practical. Long known for its simple menu of fast food, McDonald's has been forced recently to choose between different alternatives in order to accommodate changing consumer tastes. A few years ago, McDonald's was faced with a problem of slumping sales and had to make decisions regarding business structure and the type of food offerings that would attract customers. Management outlined its alternatives selection in the "Plan to Win," which involved changing the fast food chain's menu to include more salads, smoothies, and other healthier items; as well as acquiring other companies, such as Chipotle, which offers healthy Mexican fast food. Management also implemented a careful leadership succession plan in order to make leadership transfers as smooth as possible.[17]

At times, two or more alternatives or some combination of alternatives will be equally appropriate. Managers may choose solutions to problems on several levels. The coined word *satisfice* describes solutions that are only adequate and not ideal. When lacking time or information, managers often make decisions that "satisfice." Whenever possible, managers should try to investigate alternatives carefully and select the ideal solution.

Implementing and Evaluating the Solution

Implementation of a decision requires time, planning, preparation of personnel, and evaluation of results. Managers usually deal with unforeseen consequences even when they have carefully considered the alternatives.

The final step in managerial decision making entails evaluating a decision's effectiveness. If the alternative that was chosen removes the difference between the actual condition and the desired condition, the decision is considered effective. If the problem still exists, managers may select one of the following choices:

- Decide to give the chosen alternative more time to work.
- Adopt a different alternative.
- Start the problem identification process all over again.

Failure to evaluate decisions adequately may have negative consequences. After the recent Wall Street financial meltdown, stakeholders and regulators spent years debating what happened and how to prevent a similar financial system breakdown in the future. Derivatives were largely blamed for the meltdown. At the time, organizational management, gatekeepers, and regulators all failed to adequately assess the risks of using derivatives. Recently, regulators came together to approve new rules that they hope will reduce the likelihood of widespread derivatives problems in the future.[18]

MANAGING TOTAL QUALITY

 7 Describe how organizations benefit from total quality management.

The management of quality is a high priority in some organizations today. Major reasons for a greater focus on quality include foreign competition, more demanding customers, and poor financial performance resulting from reduced market shares and higher costs. Over the last few years, several U.S. firms have lost the dominant competitive positions they had held for decades.

Total quality management is a much broader concept than just controlling the quality of the product itself (which is discussed in Chapter 8). **Total quality management (TQM)** is the coordination of efforts directed at improving customer satisfaction, increasing employee participation, strengthening supplier partnerships, and facilitating an organizational atmosphere of continuous quality improvement. For TQM programs to be effective, management must address each of the following components:

- *Customer satisfaction.* Ways to improve include producing higher-quality products, providing better customer service, and showing customers that the company cares.
- *Employee participation.* This can be increased by allowing employees to contribute to decisions, develop self-managed work teams, and assume responsibility for improving the quality of their work.
- *Strengthening supplier partnerships.* Developing good working relationships with suppliers can ensure that the right supplies and materials will be delivered on time at lower costs.
- *Continuous quality improvement.* A program based on continuous improvement has proven to be the most effective long-term approach.

One tool that is used for TQM is called benchmarking. **Benchmarking** is the process of evaluating the products, processes, or management practices of another organization for the purpose of improving quality. The focal organization may be superior in safety, customer service, productivity, innovativeness, or in some other way.

For example, competitors' products might be disassembled and evaluated, or wage and benefit plans might be surveyed to measure compensation packages against the labor market. The four basic steps of benchmarking are identifying objectives, forming a benchmarking team, collecting data, analyzing data, and acting on the results. Best practices may be discovered in any industry or organization.

Although many factors influence the effectiveness of a TQM program, two issues are crucial. First, top management must make a strong commitment to a TQM program by treating quality improvement as a top priority and giving it frequent attention. Firms that establish a TQM program but then focus on other priorities will find that their quality-improvement initiatives will fail.

total quality management (TQM) the coordination of efforts directed at improving customer satisfaction, increasing employee participation, strengthening supplier partnerships, and facilitating an organizational atmosphere of continuous quality improvement

benchmarking a process used to evaluate the products, processes, or management practices of another organization that is superior in some way in order to improve quality

© EVERETT KENNEDY BROWN/EPA/LANDOV

Total quality management accelerates Toyota's competitiveness. Prior to the 1970s, products "Made in Japan" were often considered shoddy. Not anymore. Toyota Motor Company worked hard to change that image by pioneering the use of total quality management practices. As a part of its total quality management practices, Toyota meticulously inspects its products and continuously strives to improve them.

Second, management must coordinate the specific elements of a TQM program so that they work in harmony with each other.

Although not all U.S. companies have TQM programs, these programs provide many benefits. Overall financial benefits include lower operating costs, higher return on sales and on investments, and an improved ability to use premium pricing rather than competitive pricing. Firms that do not implement TQM are sometimes afraid that the costs of doing so will be prohibitive. While implementing TQM can be high initially, the savings from preventing future problems and integrating systems usually make up for the expense. The long-term costs of not implementing TQM can involve damage to a company's reputation and lost productivity and time from fixing mistakes after they have happened.[19]

return to Inside BUSINESS

IBM

As Virginia Rometty rose through the ranks of IBM, she earned the experience and skills needed to head this pioneering technology company. She worked closely with the previous CEO on implementing the current strategic plan, which aims to accelerate growth of IBM's global sales and profits. On her first day as CEO, she announced top-management changes to support IBM's international activities and its services division, two key groups important to the company's future.

Although IBM is more than 100 years old, its CEO wants it to be as innovative as a young start-up. For more than 15 years, IBM has been awarded more U.S. patents than any other company, and Rometty plans to maintain this technological leadership as she positions the company for aggressive growth in the years ahead.

Questions

1. Virginia Rometty worked for IBM for more than 30 years before she was named CEO. How do you think this experience affects her ability to plan, organize, lead, and control as CEO? Explain your answer.

2. Would you recommend that IBM use its closest competitors as the models for benchmarking technological innovation? Why or why not?

SUMMARY

Looking for Success?
Get Flashcards, Quizzes, Games, and more at @ www.cengagebrain.com.

 Define what management is.

Management is the process of coordinating people and other resources to achieve an organization's goals. Managers are concerned with four types of resources—material, human, financial, and informational.

 Describe the four basic management functions: planning, organizing, leading and motivating, and controlling.

Managers perform four basic functions. Management functions do not occur according to some rigid, preset timetable, though. At any time, managers may engage in a number of functions simultaneously. However, each function tends to lead naturally to others. First, managers engage in planning—determining where the firm should be going and how best to get there. One method of planning that can be used is SWOT analysis, which identifies and evaluates a firm's strengths, weaknesses, opportunities, and threats. Three types of plans, from the broadest to the most specific, are strategic plans, tactical plans, and operational plans. Managers also organize resources and activities to accomplish results in an efficient and effective manner, and they lead and motivate others to work in the best interests of the organization. In addition, managers control ongoing activities to keep the organization on course. There are three steps in the control function: setting standards, measuring actual performance, and taking corrective action.

 Distinguish among the various kinds of managers in terms of both level and area of management.

Managers—or management positions—may be classified from two different perspectives. From the perspective of level within the organization, there are top managers, who control the fortunes of the organization; middle managers, who implement strategies and major policies; and first-line managers, who supervise the activities of operating employees. From the viewpoint of area of management, managers most often deal with the areas of finance, operations, marketing, human resources, and administration.

 Identify the key management skills of successful managers.

Managers need a variety of skills in order to run a successful and efficient business. Conceptual skills are used to think in abstract terms or see the "big picture." Analytic skills are used to identify problems correctly, generate reasonable alternatives, and select the "best" alternatives to solve problems. Interpersonal skills are used to deal effectively with other people, both inside and outside an organization. Technical skills are needed to accomplish a specialized activity, whether they are used to actually do the task or used to train and assist employees. Communication skills are used to speak, listen, and write effectively.

 Explain the different types of leadership.

Managers' effectiveness often depends on their styles of leadership—that is, their ability to influence others, either formally or informally. Autocratic leaders are very task oriented; they tell their employees exactly what is expected from them and give them specific instructions on how to do their assigned tasks. Participative leaders consult their employees before making decisions and can be classified into three groups: consultative, consensus, and democratic. Entrepreneurial leaders are different depending on their personalities, but they are generally enthusiastic and passionate about their work and tend to take initiative.

 Discuss the steps in the managerial decision-making process.

Decision making, an integral part of a manager's work, is the process of developing a set of possible alternative solutions to a problem and choosing one alternative from among the set. Managerial decision making involves four steps: Managers must accurately identify problems, generate several possible solutions, choose the solution that will be most effective under the circumstances, and implement and evaluate the chosen course of action.

 Describe how organizations benefit from total quality management.

Total quality management (TQM) is the coordination of efforts directed at improving customer satisfaction, increasing employee participation, strengthening supplier partnerships, and facilitating an organizational atmosphere of continuous quality improvement. Another tool used for TQM is benchmarking, which is used to evaluate the products, processes, or management practices of another organization that is superior in some way in order to improve quality. The five basic steps in benchmarking are identifying objectives, forming a benchmarking team, collecting data, analyzing data, and acting on the results. To have an effective TQM program, top management must make a strong, sustained commitment to the effort and must be able to coordinate all the program's elements so that they work in harmony. Overall financial benefits of TQM include lower operating costs, higher return on sales and on investment, and an improved ability to use premium pricing rather than competitive pricing.

KEY TERMS

You should now be able to define and give an example relevant to each of the following terms:

management (165)
planning (167)
mission (167)
strategic planning process (167)
goal (168)
objective (168)
SWOT analysis (168)
core competencies (168)
plan (170)
strategic plan (170)

tactical plan (170)
operational plan (171)
contingency plan (171)
organizing (171)
leading (171)
motivating (171)
directing (171)
controlling (172)
top manager (172)
middle manager (173)
first-line manager (173)

financial manager (173)
operations manager (174)
marketing manager (174)
human resources manager (174)
administrative manager (175)
conceptual skills (175)
analytic skills (176)
interpersonal skills (176)
technical skills (176)
communication skills (176)

leadership (177)
autocratic leadership (177)
participative leadership (177)
entrepreneurial leadership (178)
decision making (179)
problem (179)
total quality management (TQM) (181)
benchmarking (181)

REVIEW QUESTIONS

1. Define the term *manager* without using the word *management* in your definition.
2. Identify and describe the basic management functions.
3. What are the major elements of SWOT analysis?

4. How do a strategic plan, a tactical plan, and an operational plan differ? What do they all have in common?
5. What exactly does a manager organize and for what reason?

6. Why are leadership and motivation necessary in a business in which people are paid for their work?
7. Explain the steps involved in the control function.
8. How are the two perspectives on kinds of managers—that is, level and area—different from each other?
9. What skills should a manager possess in order to be successful?
10. Compare and contrast the major styles of leadership.
11. Discuss what happens during each of the four steps of the managerial decision-making process.
12. What are the major benefits of a total quality management program?

DISCUSSION QUESTIONS

1. Does a healthy firm (one that is doing well) have to worry about effective management? Explain.
2. What might be the mission of a neighborhood restaurant? Of the Salvation Army? What might be reasonable objectives for these organizations?
3. Which of the management functions and skills do not apply to the owner-operator of a sole proprietorship?
4. Which leadership style might be best suited to each of the three general levels of management within an organization?
5. According to this chapter, the leadership style that is *most* effective depends on interaction among the employees, characteristics of the work situation, and the manager's personality. Do you agree or disagree? Explain your answer.
6. Do you think that people are really as important to an organization as this chapter seems to indicate?
7. As you learned in this chapter, managers often work long hours at a hectic pace. Would this type of career appeal to you? Explain your answer.

Video Case 6.1

L.L.Bean Relies on Its Core Values and Effective Leadership

L.L.Bean's first product was a waterproof boot, designed by Maine outdoorsman Leon Leonwood Bean, who promised complete customer satisfaction. One hundred pairs were sold—and 90 pairs were returned because of a defect. Bean refunded the customers' money and went to work perfecting the product, now one of the most popular in the firm's long and successful history.

L.L.Bean began in 1912 as a tiny mail-order company and has grown to include 14 retail stores in ten states, an online store, and a popular catalog showcasing many of the company's 20,000 items, including high-quality clothing, accessories, outdoor gear, luggage, linens, and furniture. It is still privately owned and family run and has had just three presidents in its history—L.L.Bean himself, his grandson Leon Gorman, and now Chris McCormick, the first nonfamily member to lead the firm. New England is the core of L.L.Bean's market, and its selling cycle accelerates sharply every year around the winter holidays. Headquartered in Freeport, Maine, near its original store, the company reports annual sales of over $1.5 billion.

Managers at L.L.Bean today have many opportunities for using their planning, organizing, leading, and controlling skills. During the preholiday selling season, for instance, temporary workers hired to handle the increased workload bring the regular staff of about 4,600 to almost double its size, so managers have to reorganize the teams of 25 to 30 front-line employees who work in the call centers. Regular employees not currently in leadership positions are asked to head the teams

of temps, ensuring they have an experienced person to help them develop their skills and perform to expectations. This organizing strategy works so well that many temps return year after year.

Planning skills come to the fore when top management decides when and where to open new retail stores, whether to expand the number of outlet stores offering discontinued items and overstocks, and how much to invest in ensuring that L.L.Bean buildings meet the highest standards of environmental stewardship. One recent strategic planning project resulted in the creation of a new clothing and accessories collection called L.L.Bean Signature, featuring updated versions of classic items from the company's 100-year heritage.

With respect to the control function, managers assess employee performance with a continuous evaluation process. Corporate-level goals are broken down to the level of the individual store and employee. If something isn't on track, the supervisor is expected to let the employee know and help figure out a solution. However, control at L.L.Bean is not entirely a top-down process. Employees are encouraged to develop their own personal goals, such as learning a new skill or gaining a better appreciation of the way L.L.Bean makes business decisions. Managers help them find ways to meet these personal objectives as well, through a temporary reassignment within the firm or participation in a special company project.

L.L.Bean has a strong collaborative work culture in which it is equally important to work through your supervisor, your co-workers, and your subordinates. That means everyone is a leader to some extent. Formal management candidates are asked to demonstrate both analytical and interpersonal skills and to model the company's six core values: outdoor heritage, integrity, service, respect, perseverance, and safe and healthy living. In the early days of the company, L.L.Bean lived above the store and would come downstairs in the middle of the night to help a customer who rang the bell. "A customer is the most important person ever in this office—in person or by mail," he was fond of saying. So, true to his beliefs, leadership style continues to revolve around serving the customer's needs. As one L.L.Bean manager said, the company is all about salespeople and customer service representatives so that they can better serve customers.[20]

Questions

1. What style of leadership do you think most L.L.Bean managers probably employ?
2. To produce hot water in L.L.Bean's flagship store, the company recently installed a solar hot water system that will offset almost 11,000 pounds of carbon dioxide emissions every year. Suggest some of the questions the company's managers might have asked at each level of planning (strategic, tactical, operational, and contingency) for this project.
3. Which managerial role or roles do you think the leaders of L.L.Bean's temp teams fill?

Case 6.2

What's Next for "Earth's Biggest Bookstore"?

When CEO Jeff Bezos founded the pioneering online retailer Amazon.com in 1995, his goal was to build "Earth's biggest bookstore." Amazon now rings up $48 billion in annual sales and offers "Earth's biggest selection" of merchandise, everything from cameras and clothing to lamps and luggage. What began as a virtual bookstore has become a multifaceted, multinational business serving 164 million consumers and business customers, thanks to the founder's visionary leadership and relentless focus on customer satisfaction.

Sitting around the conference table with his top managers, Bezos often leaves one chair empty to represent "the most important person in the room"—the customer. Although many CEOs keep a close eye on the earnings they must report to shareholders every three months, Bezos has always paid more attention to long-term customer needs than to short-term financial results. Amazon's strategic plans look ahead a decade or more, and cover innovations that take advantage of the company's technology strengths. "We are comfortable planting seeds and waiting for them to grow into trees," he says. Bezos and his executives have the patience and conviction to make far-reaching decisions about future investments and actions, watch how things unfold during implementation, and adjust the plans as needed while the world catches up.

The Kindle is a good example of how Amazon's strategic planning pays off. When electronic book readers were in their infancy, Bezos was convinced that Amazon could upend the market by making an easy-to-use device capable of downloading and displaying any book in one minute or less. Company engineers invested years (and millions of dollars) inventing the original Kindle, which immediately sold out when introduced in 2007. Since then, newer models with additional features and functionality, including the Kindle Fire, have attracted a huge wave of new customers as well as new "content creators"—authors who use the Kindle platform to publish their own books. Electronic books now outsell printed books, a development that has driven

Borders and other book stores into bankruptcy while Amazon profits from the surge in digital downloads that its Kindle helped to stimulate.

To ensure that Amazon is doing what it should be doing to satisfy customers, management sets standards for hundreds of everyday activities and constantly measures actual performance. For example, it times how quickly its web pages load and finds ways to speed things up, because it has learned that even a split-second delay can cause customers to click away. The company maintains minimum inventory levels to avoid running out of merchandise, presorts packages to add to its shipping partners' efficiency, and tracks down the cause of any delivery delays so customers will know they can rely on Amazon's delivery promises. No wonder Amazon routinely comes out on top in customer-satisfaction surveys.

Today, the company's Web site serves as an online marketplace where individuals and businesses can sell their products, paying Amazon a small percentage every time they make a sale. Major corporations like Netflix pay for access to Amazon's sophisticated Internet software and data storage systems. Still, because Amazon's roots are in retailing, Bezos continues his habit of reading customers' letters to see what they like and what they don't like, seeking clues that will lead him to the next big opportunity.[21]

Questions

1. Knowing that Amazon.com's strength is technology, which can change rapidly and unpredictably, do you agree with Jeff Bezos's method of looking up to a decade ahead for strategic planning purposes? Explain your answer.
2. Does Jeff Bezos appear to be an autocratic, a participative, or an entrepreneurial leader? What are the implications for Amazon.com?
3. How does Amazon.com apply total quality management, and why?

Understand what an organization is and identify its characteristics.

WHAT IS AN ORGANIZATION?

We used the term *organization* throughout Chapter 6 without really defining it mainly because its everyday meaning is close to its business meaning. Here, however, let us agree that an **organization** is a group of two or more people working together to achieve a common set of goals. A neighborhood dry cleaner owned and operated by a husband-and-wife team is an organization. IBM and Home Depot, which employ thousands of workers worldwide, are also organizations in the same sense. Although each corporation's organizational structure is more complex than the dry-cleaning establishment, all must be organized to achieve their goals.

An inventor who goes into business to produce and market a new invention hires people, decides what each will do, determines who will report to whom, and so on. These activities are the essence of organizing, or creating, the organization. One way to create this "picture" is to create an organization chart.

Developing Organization Charts

An **organization chart** is a diagram that represents the positions and relationships within an organization. An example of an organization chart is shown in Figure 7.1. Each rectangle represents a particular position or person in the organization. At the top is the president, at the next level are the vice presidents. The solid vertical lines connecting

organization a group of two or more people working together to achieve a common set of goals

organization chart a diagram that represents the positions and relationships within an organization

---

FIGURE 7.1 A Typical Corporate Organization Chart

A company's organization chart represents the positions and relationships within the organization and shows the managerial chains of command.

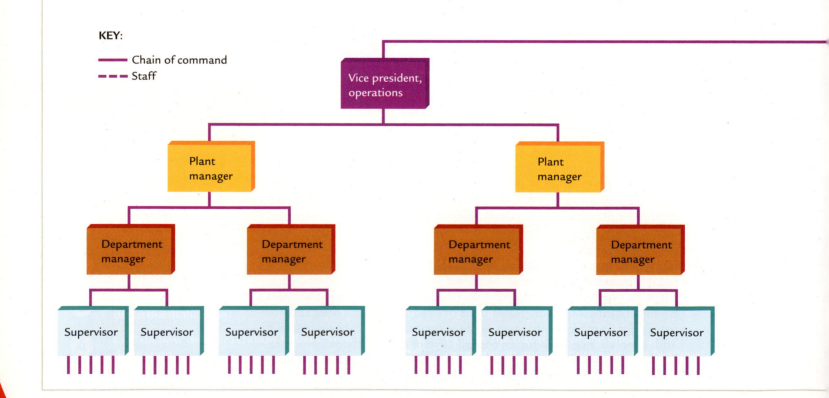

the vice presidents to the president indicate that the vice presidents are in the chain of command. The **chain of command** is the line of authority that extends from the highest to the lowest levels of the organization. Moreover, each vice president reports directly to the president. Similarly, the plant managers, regional sales managers, and accounting department manager report to the vice presidents. The chain of command can be short or long. A small local restaurant may have a very short chain of command consisting of the owner at the top and employees below. Large multinational corporations, on the other hand, may have very long chains of command. No matter what the length of the chain of command, organizations must make certain that communication along the chain is clear. In the chart, the connections to the directors of legal services, public affairs, and human resources are shown as broken lines; these people are not part of the direct chain of command. Instead, they hold *advisory,* or *staff,* positions. This difference will be examined later in this chapter when we discuss line-and-staff positions.

Most smaller organizations find organization charts useful. They clarify positions and report relationships for everyone in the organization, and they help managers to track growth and change in the organizational structure. However, many large organizations, such as ExxonMobil, Kellogg's, and Procter & Gamble, do not maintain complete, detailed charts. There are two reasons for this. First, it is difficult to chart even a few dozen positions accurately, much less the thousands that characterize larger firms. Second, larger organizations are almost always changing parts of their structure. An organization chart would be outdated before it was completed. However, organizations

chain of command the line of authority that extends from the highest to the lowest levels of an organization

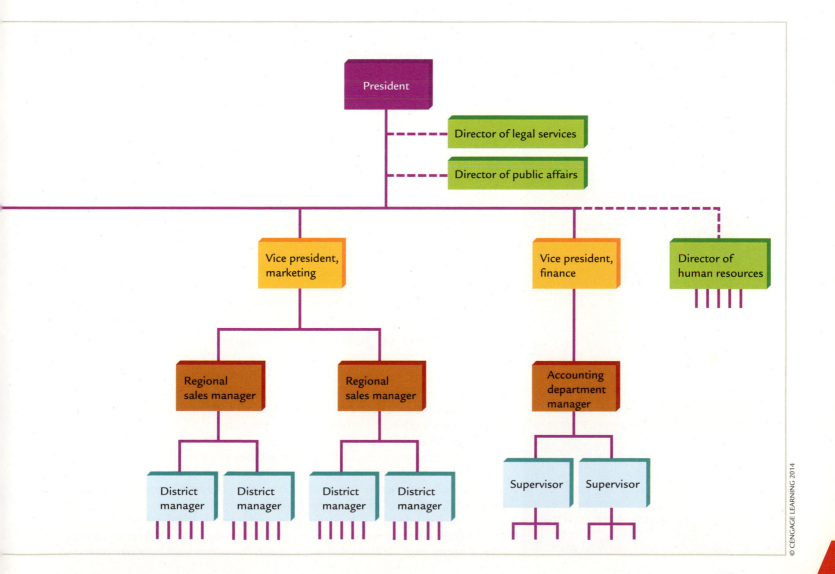

© CENGAGE LEARNING 2014

must exist without a chart in order for the business to be successful. Technology is helping large companies implement up-to-date organization charts.

Major Considerations for Organizing a Business

When a firm is started, management must decide how to organize the firm. These decisions focus on job design, departmentalization, delegation, span of management, and chain of command. In the next several sections, we discuss major issues associated with these dimensions.

Explain why job specialization is important. ②

job specialization the separation of all organizational activities into distinct tasks and the assignment of different tasks to different people

job rotation the systematic shifting of employees from one job to another

JOB DESIGN

In Chapter 1, we defined *specialization* as the separation of a manufacturing process into distinct tasks and the assignment of different tasks to different people. Here we are extending that concept to *all* the activities performed within an organization.

Job Specialization

Job specialization is the separation of all organizational activities into distinct tasks and the assignment of different tasks to different people. Adam Smith, the 18th-century economist whose theories gave rise to capitalism, was the first to emphasize the power of specialization in his book, *The Wealth of Nations*. According to Smith, the various tasks in a particular pin factory were arranged so that one worker drew the wire for the pins, another straightened the wire, a third cut it, a fourth ground the point, and a fifth attached the head. Smith claimed that 10 men were able to produce 48,000 pins per day. Before specialization, they could produce only 200 pins per day because each worker had to perform all five tasks!

The Rationale for Specialization

For a number of reasons, some job specialization is necessary in every organization because the "job" of most organizations is too large for one person to handle. In a firm such as Ford Motor Company, thousands of people are needed to manufacture automobiles. Others are needed to sell the cars, control the firm's finances, and so on.

Second, when a worker has to learn one specific, highly specialized task, that individual should be able to learn it very efficiently. Third, a worker repeating the same job does not lose time changing from operations, as the pin workers did when producing complete pins. Fourth, the more specialized the job, the easier it is to design specialized equipment. And finally, the more specialized the job, the easier the job training.

Alternatives to Job Specialization

Unfortunately, specialization can have negative consequences as well. The most significant drawback is the boredom and dissatisfaction employees may feel when repeating the same job. Bored employees may be absent from work frequently, may not put much effort into their work, and may even sabotage the company's efforts to produce quality products.

To combat these problems, managers often turn to job rotation. **Job rotation** is the systematic shifting of employees from one job to another. For example, a worker may be assigned a different job every week for a four-week period and then return to the first job in the fifth week. Job rotation provides a variety of tasks so that workers are less likely to become bored and dissatisfied. Intel, for instance, offers an internal database of short-term assignments for employees. Job rotation helps workers stay interested in their jobs, develop new skills, and identify new roles where they may like to focus

© OLAF SPELER/SHUTTERSTOCK

Specialization has its drawbacks. This employee has a specialized job that includes cutting out leather components that will be used to produce handbags. Specialization is efficient for the firm, but it can leave employees bored and dissatisfied. What do you think a firm can do to offset these problems?

their energies in the future. According to a Society for Human Resource Management survey, 43% of firms offer some sort of cross-training for workers.[2]

Two other approaches—job enlargement and job enrichment—also can provide solutions to the problems caused by job specialization. These topics, along with other methods used to motivate employees, are discussed in Chapter 10.

DEPARTMENTALIZATION

3 Identify the various bases for departmentalization.

After jobs are designed, they must be grouped together into "working units," or departments. This process is called *departmentalization*. More specifically, **departmentalization** is the process of grouping jobs into manageable units. Several departmentalization bases are used commonly. In fact, most firms use more than one. Today, the most common bases for organizing a business into effective departments are by function, by product, by location, and by customer.

By Function

Departmentalization by function groups jobs that relate to the same organizational activity. Under this scheme, all marketing personnel are grouped together in the marketing department, all production personnel in the production department, and so on.

Most smaller and newer organizations departmentalize by function. Supervision is simplified because everyone is involved in the same activities, and coordination is easy. The disadvantages of this method of grouping jobs are that it can lead to slow decision making and that it tends to emphasize the department over the whole organization.

By Product

Departmentalization by product groups activities related to a particular good or service. This approach is used often by older and larger firms that produce and sell a variety of products. Each department handles its own marketing, production, financial management, and human resources activities.

Departmentalization by product makes decision making easier and provides for the integration of all activities associated with each product. However, it causes some duplication of specialized activities—such as finance—from department to department. Moreover, the emphasis is placed on the product rather than on the whole organization.

By Location

Departmentalization by location groups activities according to the defined geographic area in which they are performed. Departmental areas may range from whole countries (for international firms) to regions within countries (for national firms) to areas of several city blocks (for police departments organized into precincts). Departmentalization by location allows the organization to respond readily to the unique demands or requirements of different locations. Nevertheless, a large administrative staff and an elaborate control system may be needed to coordinate operations in many locations.

By Customer

Departmentalization by customer groups activities according to the needs of various customer populations. A local Chevrolet dealership, for example, may have one sales staff to deal with individual consumers and a different sales staff to work with

departmentalization the process of grouping jobs into manageable units

departmentalization by function grouping jobs that relate to the same organizational activity

departmentalization by product grouping activities related to a particular product or service

departmentalization by location grouping activities according to the defined geographic area in which they are performed

departmentalization by customer grouping activities according to the needs of various customer populations

How is your school organized? These call center employees are organized by their function. Some businesses are organized by more than their functions, though. For example, if your university has more than one campus, they are organized by location but also by function such as by their business, social sciences, and math departments. Your school also might be organized by customer such as by undergraduate, graduate, and continuing education students.

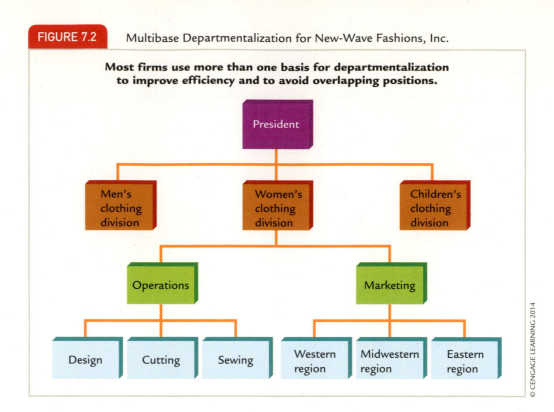

FIGURE 7.2   Multibase Departmentalization for New-Wave Fashions, Inc.

Most firms use more than one basis for departmentalization to improve efficiency and to avoid overlapping positions.

President

Men's clothing division · Women's clothing division · Children's clothing division

Operations · Marketing

Design · Cutting · Sewing · Western region · Midwestern region · Eastern region

© CENGAGE LEARNING 2014

corporate fleet buyers. The obvious advantage of this approach is that it allows the firm to deal efficiently with unique customers or customer groups. The biggest drawback is that a larger-than-usual administrative staff is needed.

Combinations of Bases

Many organizations use more than one of these departmentalization bases. PepsiCo, for instance, is divided by product and location. It has product divisions such as Beverages, Frito-Lay, Quaker, and Latin American Foods, as well as divisions based on location such as Asia, Europe, the Middle East, and Africa.[3]

Take a moment to examine Figure 7.2. Notice that departmentalization by customer is used to organize New-Wave Fashions, Inc., into three major divisions: men's, women's, and children's clothing. Then functional departmentalization is used to distinguish the firm's production and marketing activities. Finally, location is used to organize the firm's marketing efforts.

DELEGATION, DECENTRALIZATION, AND CENTRALIZATION

 Explain how decentralization follows from delegation.

The third major step in the organizing process is to distribute power in the organization. **Delegation** assigns part of a manager's work and power to other workers. The degree of centralization or decentralization of authority is determined by the overall pattern of delegation within the organization.

Delegation of Authority

Because no manager can do everything, delegation is vital to completion of a manager's work. Delegation is also important in developing the skills and abilities of subordinates. It allows those who are being groomed for higher-level positions to play increasingly important roles in decision making.

delegation assigning part of a manager's work and power to other workers

Going for SUCCESS

Dell Restructures to Jump–Start Innovation

With more than $60 billion in global revenue from computers, cloud computing, and other high-tech offerings, Dell is hardly a scrappy startup. To recapture market share and create the hot new products of tomorrow, the Texas-based company is decentralizing to encourage speedier innovation. As an example, it maintains a separate research-and-development group in Silicon Valley to identify, develop, and market new offerings in networking and other technologies.

As another example, one of Dell's business units—located just eight miles from headquarters—comes up with its own designs for data storage centers. The business acts like a firm founded in somebody's garage, rather than one of many units in a multinational corporation's portfolio. In fact, one of its engineers actually built a piece of equipment in his garage

when the unit was young. The head of this unit says "you need a crayon drawing on a napkin," not layers of bureaucracy and strict guidelines, to fuel entrepreneurial innovation. In just five years, this unit has blossomed into a $1 billion business with 500 employees—and more growth is on the horizon.

Restructuring to nurture innovation doesn't guarantee a product hit, as Dell knows from its unsuccessful first experience with a separate smartphone division. Still, decentralization is giving Dell an opportunity to recapture the nimble, innovative spirit of its early days.

Sources: Based on information in Shara Tibken, "Dell Plans to Expand Silicon Valley Staff for R&D," *Marketwatch,* January 31, 2012, http://marketwatch.com/story/dell-plans-to-expand-silicon-valley-staff-for-rd-2012-01-31; Christopher Calnan, "Dell to Up Staff in Santa Clara, Calif.," *Austin Business Journal,* January 31, 2012, http://bizjournals.com/austin/news/2012/01/31/dell-to-up-staff-in-santa-clara-calif.html; Anne VanderMey, "Dell Gets in Touch with Its Inner Entrepreneur," *Fortune,* December 12, 2011, p. 58.

Steps in Delegation The delegation process generally involves three steps (see Figure 7.3). First, the manager must *assign responsibility*. **Responsibility** is the duty to do a job or perform a task. In most job settings, a manager simply gives the worker a job to do. Typical job assignments might range from having a worker prepare a report on the status of a new quality control program to placing the person in charge of a task force. Second, the manager must *grant authority*. **Authority** is the power, within the organization, to accomplish an assigned job or task. This might include the power to obtain specific information, order supplies, authorize relevant expenditures, or make certain decisions. Finally, the manager must *create accountability*. **Accountability** is the obligation of a worker to accomplish an assigned job or task.

Note that accountability is created, but it cannot be delegated. Suppose that you are an operations manager for Target and are responsible for performing a specific task. You, in turn, delegate this task to someone else. You nonetheless remain accountable to your immediate supervisor for getting the task done properly. If the other person fails to complete the assignment, you—not the person to whom you delegated the task—will be held accountable.

Barriers to Delegation For several reasons, managers may be unwilling to delegate work. Many managers are reluctant to delegate because they want to be sure that the work gets done. Another reason for reluctance stems from the opposite situation. The manager fears that the worker will do the work well and attract the approving notice of higher-level managers. Finally, some managers do not delegate because they are so disorganized that they simply are not able to plan and assign work effectively.

Decentralization of Authority

The pattern of delegation throughout an organization determines the extent to which that organization is decentralized or centralized. In a **decentralized organization**, management consciously attempts to spread authority widely across various organization levels. A

responsibility the duty to do a job or perform a task

authority the power, within an organization, to accomplish an assigned job or task

accountability the obligation of a worker to accomplish an assigned job or task

decentralized organization an organization in which management consciously attempts to spread authority widely in the lower levels of the organization

Delegate, delegate, delegate. The industrialist Andrew Carnegie once said, "No person will make a great business who wants to do it all himself or get all the credit." Delegating gives employees different tasks to do, which can enrich and enlarge their jobs. It also enables both employees and their superiors to learn new skills required for higher-level positions.

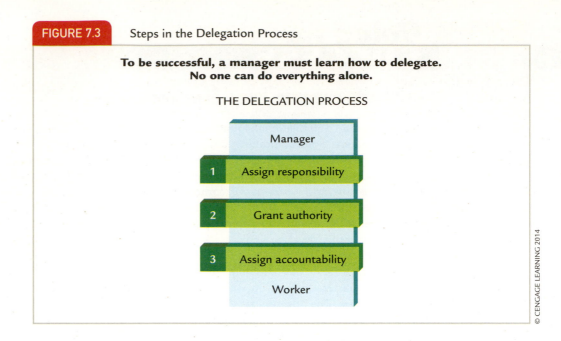

FIGURE 7.3   Steps in the Delegation Process

To be successful, a manager must learn how to delegate.
No one can do everything alone.

THE DELEGATION PROCESS

Manager

1 Assign responsibility

2 Grant authority

3 Assign accountability

Worker

centralized organization, on the other hand, systematically works to concentrate authority at the upper levels. For example, many publishers of college-level textbooks are centralized organizations, with authority concentrated at the top. Large organizations may have characteristics of both decentralized and centralized organizations.

A number of factors can influence the extent to which a firm is decentralized. One is the external environment in which the firm operates. The more complex and unpredictable this environment, the more likely it is that top management will let lower-level managers make important decisions. After all, lower-level managers are closer to the problems. Another factor is the nature of the decision itself. The riskier or more important the decision, the greater is the tendency to centralize decision making. A third factor is the abilities of lower-level managers. If these managers do not have strong decision-making skills, top managers will be reluctant to decentralize. And, in contrast, strong lower-level decision-making skills encourage decentralization. Finally, a firm that traditionally has practiced centralization or decentralization is likely to maintain that posture in the future.

In principle, neither decentralization nor centralization is right or wrong. What works for one organization may or may not work for another. Kmart Corporation and McDonald's are very successful—and both practice centralization. But decentralization has worked very well for General Electric and Sears. Every organization must assess its own situation and then choose the level of centralization or decentralization that will work best.

Understand how the span of management describes an organization.

centralized organization an organization that systematically works to concentrate authority at the upper levels of the organization

span of management (or **span of control**) the number of workers who report directly to one manager

THE SPAN OF MANAGEMENT

The fourth major step in organizing a business is establishing the **span of management** (or **span of control**), which is the number of workers who report directly to one manager. For hundreds of years, theorists have searched for an ideal span of management. When it became apparent that there is no perfect number of subordinates for a manager to supervise, they turned their attention to the general issue of whether the span should be wide or narrow. This issue is complicated because the span of management may change by department within the same organization. A highly mechanized factory where all operations are standardized may allow for a fairly wide span of management. An advertising agency, where new problems and opportunities arise every day and where teamwork is a constant necessity, will have a much narrower span of management.

Wide and Narrow Spans of Management

A *wide* span of management exists when a manager has a larger number of subordinates. A *narrow* span exists when the manager has only a few subordinates. Several factors determine the span that is better for a particular manager (see Figure 7.4). Generally, the span of control may be wide when (1) the manager and the subordinates are very competent, (2) the organization has a well-established set of standard operating procedures, and (3) few new problems are expected to arise. The span should be narrow when (1) workers are physically located far from one another, (2) the manager has much work to do in addition to supervising workers, (3) a great deal of interaction is required between supervisor and workers, and (4) new problems arise frequently.

Organizational Height

The span of management has an obvious impact on relations between managers and workers. It has a more subtle but equally important impact on the height of the organization. **Organizational height** is the number of layers, or levels, of management in a firm. The span of management plays a direct role in determining the height of the organization (see Figure 7.4). If spans of management are wider, fewer levels are needed, and the organization is *flat*. If spans of management generally are narrow, more levels are needed, and the resulting organization is *tall*.

In a taller organization, administrative costs are higher because more managers are needed. Communication among levels may become distorted because information has to pass up and down through more people. When companies are cutting costs, one option is to decrease organizational height in order to reduce related administrative expenses. For example, when cosmetics provider Avon experienced declining sales, the company began a series of long and extensive restructuring programs. The programs focused on increasing efficiency and organizational effectiveness. The restructuring

Narrow versus wide spans of management: Which is better? The manager on the right side of the photo supervises only a handful of employees. Consequently, he has a narrow span of management. Companies are constantly searching for the ideal number of employees their supervisors should manage.

organizational height the number of layers, or levels, of management in a firm

---

FIGURE 7.4	The Span of Management

Several criteria determine whether a firm uses a wide span of management, in which a number of workers report to one manager, or a narrow span, in which a manager supervises only a few workers.

WIDE SPAN
- High level of competence in managers and workers
- Standard operating procedures
- Few new problems

Flat organization

NARROW SPAN
- Physical dispersion of subordinates
- Manager has additional tasks
- High level of interaction required between manager and workers
- High frequency of new problems

Tall organization

© CENGAGE LEARNING 2014

program is expected to save the company an estimated $200 million per year upon full implementation.[4] Although flat organizations avoid these problems, their managers may perform more administrative duties simply because there are fewer managers. Wide spans of management also may require managers to spend considerably more time supervising and working with subordinates.

Describe the four basic forms of organizational structure. 6

FORMS OF ORGANIZATIONAL STRUCTURE

Up to this point, we have focused our attention on the major characteristics of organizational structure. In many ways, this is like discussing the parts of a jigsaw puzzle one by one. It is now time to put the puzzle together. In particular, we discuss four basic forms of organizational structure: line, line-and-staff, matrix, and network.

The Line Structure

line structure an organizational structure in which the chain of command goes directly from person to person throughout the organization

The simplest and oldest form of organizational structure is the **line structure**, in which the chain of command goes directly from person to person throughout the organization. Thus, a straight line could be drawn down through the levels of management, from the chief executive down to the lowest level in the organization. In a small retail store, for example, an hourly employee might report to an assistant manager, who reports to a store manager, who reports to the owner.

line manager a position in which a person makes decisions and gives orders to subordinates to achieve the organization's goals

Managers within a line structure, called **line managers**, make decisions and give orders to subordinates to achieve the organization's goals. A line structure's simplicity and clear chain of command allow line managers to make decisions quickly with direct accountability because the decision-maker only has one supervisor to report to.

line-and-staff structure an organizational structure that utilizes the chain of command from a line structure in combination with the assistance of staff managers

The downside of a line structure, however, is that line managers are responsible for many activities, and therefore must have a wide range of knowledge about all of them. While this may not be a problem for small organizations with a lower volume of activities, in a larger organization, activities become more numerous and complex, thus making it more difficult for line managers to fully understand what they are in charge of. Therefore, line managers in a larger organization would have a hard time making an educated decision without expert advice from outside sources. As a result, line structures are not very effective in medium- or large-sized organizations, but are very popular in small organizations.

staff manager a position created to provide support, advice, and expertise within an organization

The Line-and-Staff Structure

A **line-and-staff structure** not only utilizes the chain of command from a line structure but also provides line managers with specialists, called staff managers. Therefore, this structure works much better for medium- and large-sized organizations than line management alone. **Staff managers** provide support, advice, and expertise to line managers, thus eliminating the previous drawback of line structures. Staff managers are not part of the chain of command like line managers are, but they do have authority over their assistants (see Figure 7.5).

Both line and staff managers are needed for effective management, but the two positions differ in important ways. The basic difference is in terms of authority. Line managers have *line authority*, which means that they can make decisions and issue directives relating to the organization's goals. Staff managers seldom have this kind of authority. Instead, they usually have either advisory authority or functional authority. *Advisory*

Personal APPS

© VJOM/SHUTTERSTOCK

© DAVID YOUNG-WOLFF/PHOTOEDIT

If you're looking to move up, try to get some advice from co-workers in both line and staff positions. Not only will this broaden your understanding of the organization, it will also help you bridge the gaps between line and staff and connect with both groups.

FIGURE 7.5   Line and Staff Managers

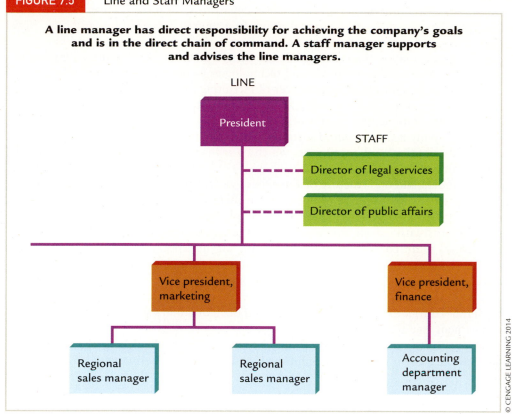

A line manager has direct responsibility for achieving the company's goals and is in the direct chain of command. A staff manager supports and advises the line managers.

LINE

President

STAFF

Director of legal services

Director of public affairs

Vice president, marketing

Vice president, finance

Regional sales manager

Regional sales manager

Accounting department manager

© CENGAGE LEARNING 2014

---

authority is the expectation that line managers will consult the appropriate staff manager when making decisions. Functional authority is stronger. *Functional authority* is the authority of staff managers to make decisions and issue directives about their areas of expertise. For example, a legal adviser for Nike can decide whether to retain a particular clause in a contract but not product pricing.

Staff managers in a line-and-staff structure tend to have more access to information than line managers. This means that line managers must rely on the staff managers for information. This is usually not an issue, unless the staff manager makes a wrong decision and there is no one else to catch his or her mistake.[5] For a variety of reasons, conflict between line managers and staff managers is fairly common in business. Staff managers often have more formal education and sometimes are younger (and perhaps more ambitious) than line managers. Line managers may perceive staff managers as a threat to their own authority and thus may resent them. For their part, staff managers may become annoyed or angry if their expert recommendations—for example, in public relations or human resources management—are not adopted by line management.

Fortunately, there are several ways to minimize the likelihood of such conflict. One way is to integrate line and staff managers into one team. Another is to ensure that the areas of responsibility of line and staff managers are clearly defined. Finally, line and staff managers both can be held accountable for the results of their activities.

The Matrix Structure

When the matrix structure is used, individuals report to more than one superior at the same time. The **matrix structure** combines

matrix structure an organizational structure that combines vertical and horizontal lines of authority, usually by superimposing product departmentalization on a functionally departmentalized organization

© AP PHOTO

Line-and-staff organization structure. Ronald McDonald occupies a staff position and does not have direct authority over other employees at McDonald's. The other individuals shown here occupy line positions and do have direct authority over some of the other McDonald's employees.

vertical and horizontal lines of authority, which is why it is called a matrix structure. The matrix structure occurs when product departmentalization is superimposed on a functionally departmentalized organization. In a matrix organization, authority flows both down and across.

Since information flows are more complicated in a matrix structure, many organizations choose to utilize software and technologies to help them manage information. For instance, Aqayo, a leading producer of recruiting and talent management software and programs, offers features especially for organizations utilizing a matrix structure.

Another example of a matrix organization could be an automobile manufacturer whose company is divided into functional departments, such as production, sales, marketing, distribution, and accounting, which co-manage with product departments (the vehicle models).

To understand the structure of a matrix organization, consider the usual functional arrangement, with people working in departments such as engineering, finance, and marketing. Now suppose that we assign people from these departments to a special group that is working on a new project as a team—a cross-functional team. A **cross-functional team** consists of individuals with varying specialties, expertise, and skills that are brought together to achieve a common task. Frequently, cross-functional teams are charged with the responsibility of developing new products. The manager in charge of a team is usually called a *project manager*. Any individual who is working with the team reports to *both* the project manager and the individual's superior in the functional department (see Figure 7.6).

Cross-functional team projects may be temporary, in which case the team is disbanded once the mission is accomplished, or they may be permanent. GE employs a

cross-functional team a team of individuals with varying specialties, expertise, and skills that are brought together to achieve a common task

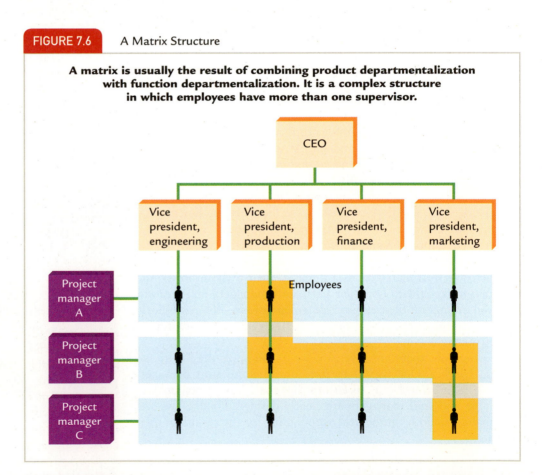

| FIGURE 7.6 | A Matrix Structure |

A matrix is usually the result of combining product departmentalization with function departmentalization. It is a complex structure in which employees have more than one supervisor.

Source: Ricky W. Griffin, *Management,* 11th ed. Copyright © 2012 by South-Western/Cengage Learning, Mason, OH. Adapted with permission.

permanent cross-functional team within its Appliances division, called the Lean Big Room, which works to identify and remove wastefulness from its production processes, while developing exciting new products for the market.[6]

These teams often are empowered to make major decisions. When a cross-functional team is employed, prospective team members may receive special training because effective teamwork can require different skills. For cross-functional teams to be successful, team members must be given specific information on the job each performs. The team also must develop a sense of cohesiveness and maintain good communications among its members.

Matrix structures offer advantages over other organizational forms. Added flexibility is probably the most obvious advantage. The matrix structure also can increase productivity, raise morale, and nurture creativity and innovation. In addition, employees experience personal development through doing a variety of jobs.

The matrix structure also has disadvantages. Having employees report to more than one supervisor can cause confusion about who is in charge. Like committees, teams may take longer to resolve problems and issues than individuals working alone. Other difficulties include personality clashes, poor communication, undefined individual roles, unclear responsibilities, and finding ways to reward individual and team performance simultaneously. Because more managers and support staff may be needed, a matrix structure may be more expensive to maintain.

The Network Structure

In a **network structure** (sometimes called a *virtual organization*), administration is the primary function performed, and other functions such as engineering, production, marketing, and finance are contracted out to other organizations. Frequently, a network organization does not manufacture the products it sells. This type of organization has a few permanent employees consisting of top management and hourly clerical workers. Leased facilities and equipment, as well as temporary workers, are increased or decreased as the organization's needs change. Thus, there is rather limited formal structure associated with a network organization.

An obvious strength of a network structure is flexibility that allows the organization to adjust quickly to changes. Network structures consist of a lot of teams working together, rather than relying on one centralized leader. This also means that network structures may be more likely to survive if an important leader or member leaves because there is no power vacuum left at the top.[7] Some of the challenges faced by managers in network-structured organizations include controlling the quality of work performed by other organizations, low morale and high turnover among hourly workers, and the vulnerability associated with relying on outside contractors.

CORPORATE CULTURE

 7 Describe the effects of corporate culture.

Most managers function within a corporate culture. A **corporate culture** is generally defined as the inner rites, rituals, heroes, and values of a firm. An organization's culture has a powerful influence on how employees think and act. It also can determine public perception of the organization.

Corporate culture generally is thought to have a very strong influence on a firm's performance over time. Hence, it is useful to be able to assess a firm's corporate culture. Common indicators include the physical setting (building or office layouts), what the company says about its corporate culture (in advertising or news releases), how the company greets guests (formal or informal reception areas), and how employees spend their time (working alone in an office or working with others).

network structure an organizational structure in which administration is the primary function, and most other functions are contracted out to other firms

corporate culture the inner rites, rituals, heroes, and values of a firm

FIGURE 7.7   Types of Corporate Cultures

Which corporate culture would you choose?

High

Sociability

Networked Culture
- Extrovert energized by relationships
- Tolerant of ambiguities and have low needs for structure
- Can spot politics and act to stop "negative" politics
- Consider yourself easygoing, affable, and loyal to others

Communal Culture
- You consider yourself passionate
- Strong need to identify with something bigger than yourself
- You enjoy being in teams
- Prepared to make sacrifices for the greater good

Fragmented Culture
- Are a reflective and self-contained introvert
- Have a high autonomy drive and strong desire to work independently
- Have a strong sense of self

Mercenary Culture
- Goal-oriented and have an obsessive desire to complete tasks
- Thrive on competitive energy
- Keep "relationships" out of work—develop them

Source: "Types of Corporate Culture," in Rob Goffee and Gareth Jones, *The Character of a Corporation* (New York: HarperCollins, 1998). Copyright © 1998 by Rob Goffee and Gareth Jones. Permission granted by Rob Goffee and Gareth Jones.

Goffee and Jones have identified four distinct types of corporate cultures (see Figure 7.7). One is called the *networked culture,* characterized by a base of trust and friendship among employees, a strong commitment to the organization, and an informal environment. A small nonprofit organization may seek to build a networked culture where employees look out for each other and believe strongly in the organizational mission. Building a networked culture in such an organization is important because employees may have to work long hours for little pay, and a strong sense of community and commitment helps to keep productivity high and turnover low.

The *mercenary culture* embodies the feelings of passion, energy, sense of purpose, and excitement for one's work. Large banks and investment firms often have mercenary cultures because the environment is fast-paced, the stakes are high, and winning is important. Ever since the Wall Street failures in 2008, many stakeholders internal and external to firms have been calling on the major players of the financial industry to change their excessively mercenary corporate cultures. This kind of culture can be very stressful for an employee with an incompatible personality.[8] The term *mercenary* does not imply that employees are motivated to work only for the money, but this is part of it. In this culture, employees are very intense, focused, and determined to win. In the *fragmented culture,* employees do not become friends, and they work "at" the organization, not "for" it. Employees have a high degree of autonomy, flexibility, and equality. The *communal culture* combines the positive traits of the networked culture and the mercenary culture—those of friendship, commitment, high focus on performance, and high energy. People's lives revolve around the product in this culture, and success by anyone in the organization is celebrated by all.[9]

Some experts believe that cultural change is needed when a company's environment changes, when the industry becomes more competitive, the company's performance is mediocre, and when the company is growing or is about to become a truly large

© AP PHOTO/TED S. WARREN

Food and fun are a part of the corporate culture at Google. This company believes satisfied employees produce the best and most innovative ideas. How would you describe Google's corporate culture in Goffee and Jones's terms—as networked, mercenary, fragmented, or communal? Why?

Ethical
SUCCESS OR FAILURE?

Internships—Who Benefits?

Are businesses and nonprofits recruiting college students and recent graduates for low-paying or unpaid internships instead of hiring and paying employees? How do interns benefit from these internships?

According to estimates, as many as three out of four college graduates have been interns during their 21st-century college careers. Through internships, students gain real-world experience and polish their skills to shine in today's highly competitive job market. In some cases, internships carry college credit, another plus. Many, however, are unpaid or pay a small amount that barely covers commuting costs.

"They're giving me a ton of experience and a ton of responsibility, so I'm happy to have that," says one recent grad who interns with a nonprofit group. "But at the same time, it's really frustrating to not get paid for your work."

The U.S. Department of Labor says that unpaid internships are legal if they meet specific guidelines. For example, interns must benefit from the internship, and must receive training similar to what they would receive in an educational setting. The intern is not supposed to displace an employee or be entitled to a job after the internship ends. Finally, the employer should not gain an "immediate advantage" from the intern's work—meaning the intern should be the one to benefit, not the employer.

Sources: Based on information in Beenish Ahmed, "Unpaid Interns; Real World Work or Just Free Labor?" *NPR*, November 16, 2011, http://npr.org/2011/11/16/142224360/unpaid-interns-real-world-work-or-just-free-labor; Alexis Grant, "The Ethics of Unpaid Internships," *U.S. News & World Report*, July 19, 2011, http://money.usnews.com/money/careers/articles/2011/07/19/the-ethics-of-unpaid-internships; Andrea Sachs, "Intern Nation," *Time*, September 12, 2011, http://time.com/time/magazine/article/0,9171,2091366,00.html.

---

organization. An example of a company that some believe is due for a culture change is the investment giant Goldman Sachs. The organization was placed under scrutiny when a manager at its London office wrote a scathing op-ed piece for *The New York Times,* calling out its highly negative corporate culture.[10]

Organizations in the future will look quite different. Experts predict that tomorrow's businesses will comprise small, task-oriented work groups, each with control over its own activities. These small groups will be coordinated through an elaborate computer network and held together by a strong corporate culture. Businesses operating in fast-changing industries will require leadership that supports trust and risk taking. Creating a culture of trust in an organization can lead to increases in growth, profit, productivity, and job satisfaction. A culture of trust can retain the best people, inspire customer loyalty, develop new markets, and increase creativity.

Another area where corporate culture plays a vital role is the integration of two or more companies. Business leaders often cite the role of corporate cultures in the integration process as one of the primary factors affecting the success of a merger or acquisition. Experts note that corporate culture is a way of conducting business both within the company and externally. If two merging companies do not address differences in corporate culture, they are setting themselves up for missed expectations and possibly failure.

Sustaining the
PLANET

Take the "R" For Tomorrow

P&G clearly communicates sustainability as part of its corporate culture. Employees are sent a clear message to focus on sustainability both at work and at home. The program entitled "Take the R for Tomorrow" encourages responsibility (R) when it comes to making decisions that impact the environment. Employees are reminded at meetings to build sustainability into everyday decisions. The company vision includes goals for packaging, eliminating consumer and manufacturing waste, and resource conservation by 2020. www.pg.com/en_US/sustainability/employee_engagement.shtml.

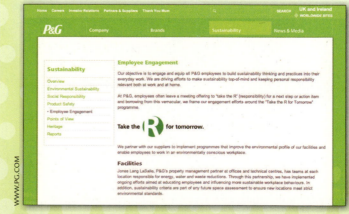

Understand how committees and task forces are used. 8

ad hoc committee a committee created for a specific short-term purpose

standing committee a relatively permanent committee charged with performing some recurring task

task force a committee established to investigate a major problem or pending decision

informal organization the pattern of behavior and interaction that stems from personal rather than official relationships

Explain the functions of the informal organization and the grapevine in a business. 9

informal group a group created by the members themselves to accomplish goals that may or may not be relevant to an organization

grapevine the informal communications network within an organization

Personal APPS

When you are searching for a new job, look for clues that reveal the inner workings of the firm's corporate culture. You'll want to be in step with the culture, understand what the organization values, and if those values fit your own.

COMMITTEES AND TASK FORCES

Today, business firms use several types of committees that affect organizational structure. An **ad hoc committee** is created for a specific short-term purpose, such as reviewing the firm's employee benefits plan. Once its work is finished, the ad hoc committee disbands. A **standing committee** is a relatively permanent committee charged with performing a recurring task. A firm might establish a budget review committee, for example, to review departmental budget requests on an ongoing basis. Finally, a **task force** is a committee established to investigate a major problem or pending decision. A firm contemplating a merger with another company might form a task force to assess the pros and cons of the merger.

Committees offer some advantages over individual action. Their several members are able to bring information and knowledge to the task at hand. Furthermore, committees tend to make more accurate decisions and to transmit their results through the organization more effectively. However, committee deliberations take longer than individual actions. In addition, unnecessary compromise may take place within the committee, or the opposite may occur, as one person dominates (and thus negates) the committee process.

THE INFORMAL ORGANIZATION AND THE GRAPEVINE

So far, we have discussed the organization as a formal structure consisting of interrelated positions. This is the organization that is shown on an organization chart. There is another kind of organization, however, that does not show up on any chart. We define this **informal organization** as the pattern of behavior and interaction that stems from personal rather than official relationships. Firmly embedded within every informal organization are informal groups and the notorious grapevine.

An **informal group** is created by the group members themselves to accomplish goals that may or may not be relevant to the organization. Workers may create an informal group to go bowling, form a union, get a particular manager fired or transferred, or meet for lunch. The group may last for several years or a few hours.

Informal groups can be powerful forces in organizations. They can restrict output, or they can help managers through tight spots. They can cause disagreement and conflict, or they can help to boost morale and job satisfaction. They can show new people how to contribute to the organization, or they can help people to get away with substandard performance. Clearly, managers should be aware of these informal groups. Those who make the mistake of fighting the informal organization have a major obstacle to overcome.

The **grapevine** is the informal communications network within an organization. It is completely separate from—and sometimes much faster than—the organization's formal channels of communication. Formal communications usually follow a path that parallels the organizational chain of command. Information can be transmitted through the grapevine in any direction—up, down, diagonally, or horizontally across the organizational structure. Subordinates may pass information to their bosses, an executive may relay something to a maintenance worker, or there may be an exchange of information between people who work in totally unrelated departments.

Grapevine information may be concerned with topics ranging from the latest management decisions to gossip.

How should managers treat the grapevine? Certainly, it would be a mistake to try to eliminate it. People working together, day in and day out, are going to communicate. A more rational approach is to recognize its existence. For example, managers should respond promptly and aggressively to inaccurate grapevine information to minimize the damage that such misinformation might do. Moreover, the grapevine can come in handy when managers are on the receiving end of important communications from the informal organization.

In the next chapter, we apply these and other management concepts to an extremely important business function: the production of goods and services.

There is power in numbers. It's common for employees to befriend one another and form informal groups within an organization. The groups provide their members with camaraderie and information but can create both challenges and benefits for the organization.

return to **Inside**
BUSINESS

Kraft Foods

When Kraft Foods announced it was splitting into two companies, the grapevine buzzed for months over who would wind up in which positions on the new organization charts. Little by little, announcements filled in the blanks, with senior managers from the parent predecessor firm taking the top spots in each spinoff. About 1,600 jobs were cut as each side consolidated offices and streamlined its structure.

Kraft needed more than a year to plan the split, because of the complexity of separating the two companies' operations and getting each business ready to stand on its own. To ease the transition, the company created a high-level management group to resolve issues related to the structural changes. Even during the reorganization period, sales were up—especially outside the United States—giving the two spinoffs momentum as they left their former parent, Kraft Foods.

Questions

1. Would you expect the two spinoffs to be flatter or taller, compared with the structure of Kraft Foods before the split? Why?

2. The structure of the two spinoffs is geared toward location, for responsiveness to local needs. How can each of the spinoffs use this structure as a global strength, not just a local strength?

SUMMARY

 Understand what an organization is and identify its characteristics.

An organization is a group of two or more people working together to achieve a common set of goals. The relationships among positions within an organization can be illustrated by means of an organization chart. Five specific characteristics—job design, departmentalization, delegation, span of management, and chain of command—help to determine what an organization chart and the organization itself look like.

 Explain why job specialization is important.

Job specialization is the separation of all the activities within an organization into smaller components and the assignment of those different components to different people. Several factors combine to make specialization a useful technique for designing jobs, but high levels of specialization may cause employee dissatisfaction and boredom. One technique for overcoming these problems is job rotation.

 Identify the various bases for departmentalization.

Departmentalization is the grouping of jobs into manageable units. Typical bases for departmentalization are by function, product, location, or customer. Because each of these bases provides particular advantages, most firms—especially larger ones—use a combination of different bases in different organizational situations.

 Explain how decentralization follows from delegation.

Delegation is the assigning of part of a manager's work to other workers. It involves the following three steps: (1) assigning responsibility, (2) granting authority, and (3) creating accountability. A decentralized firm is one that delegates as much power as possible to people in the lower management levels. In a centralized firm, on the other hand, power is systematically retained at the upper levels.

 Understand how the span of management describes an organization.

The span of management is the number of workers who report directly to a manager. Spans generally are characterized as wide (many workers per manager) or narrow (few workers per manager). Wide spans generally result in flat organizations (few layers of management); narrow spans generally result in tall organizations (many layers of management).

 Describe the four basic forms of organizational structure.

There are four basic forms of organizational structure. The line structure is the oldest and most simple structure, in which the chain of command goes in a straight line from person to person down through the levels of management. The line-and-staff structure is similar to the line structure, but adds specialists called staff managers to assist the line managers in decision making. The line structure works most efficiently for smaller organizations, whereas the line-and-staff structure is used by medium- and large-sized organizations. The matrix structure may be visualized as product departmentalization superimposed on functional departmentalization. With the matrix structure, an employee on a cross-functional team reports to both the project manager and the individual's supervisor in a functional department. In an organization with a network structure, the primary function performed internally is administration, and other functions are contracted out to other firms.

 Describe the effects of corporate culture.

Corporate culture has both internal and external effects on an organization. An organization's culture can influence the way employees think and act, and it can also determine the public's perception of the organization. Corporate culture can affect a firm's performance over time, either negatively or positively. Creating a culture of trust, for example, can lead to increased growth, profits, productivity, and job satisfaction, while retaining the best employees, inspiring customer loyalty, developing new markets, and increasing creativity. In addition, when two or more companies undergo the integration process, their different or similar corporate cultures can affect the success of a merger or acquisition.

 Understand how committees and task forces are used.

Committees and task forces are used to develop organizational structure within an organization. An ad hoc committee is created for a specific short-term purpose, whereas a standing committee is relatively permanent. A task force is created to investigate a major problem or pending decision.

 Explain the functions of the informal organization and the grapevine in a business.

Informal groups are created by group members to accomplish goals that may or may not be relevant to the organization, and they can be very powerful forces. The grapevine—the informal communications network within an organization—can be used to transmit information (important or gossip) through an organization much faster than through the formal communication network. Information transmitted through the grapevine can go in any direction across the organizational structure, skipping up or down levels of management and even across departments.

KEY TERMS

You should now be able to define and give an example relevant to each of the following terms:

organization (190)
organization chart (190)
chain of command (191)
job specialization (192)
job rotation (192)
departmentalization (193)

departmentalization by function (193)
departmentalization by product (193)
departmentalization by location (193)

departmentalization by customer (193)
delegation (194)
responsibility (195)
authority (195)
accountability (195)

decentralized organization (195)
centralized organization (196)
span of management (or span of control) (196)
organizational height (197)

REVIEW QUESTIONS

1. In what way do organization charts create a picture of an organization?
2. What is the chain of command in an organization?
3. What determines the degree of specialization within an organization?
4. Describe how job rotation can be used to combat the problems caused by job specialization.
5. What are the major differences among the four departmentalization bases?
6. Why do most firms employ a combination of departmentalization bases?
7. What three steps are involved in delegation? Explain each.
8. How does a firm's top management influence its degree of centralization?
9. How is organizational height related to the span of management?
10. What are the key differences between line and staff positions?
11. Contrast line-and-staff and matrix forms of organizational structure.
12. What is corporate culture? Describe the major types.
13. Which form of organizational structure probably would lead to the strongest informal organization? Why?
14. What is the role of the informal organization?

DISCUSSION QUESTIONS

1. How does the corporate culture of a local Best Buy store compare to that of a local McDonald's?
2. Which kinds of firms probably would operate most effectively as centralized firms? As decentralized firms?
3. How do decisions concerning span of management and the use of committees affect organizational structure?
4. How might a manager go about formalizing the informal organization?

Video Case 7.1   At Numi Organic Tea, Teams and Organizational Culture Are Critical

You might expect a company specializing in marketing organic teas to have a distinctive corporate culture. In the case of Numi Organic Tea, a progressive seller of premium organic and Fair Trade teas based in Oakland, California, you'd be right.

With a relatively small staff of about 50 people and a recent growth rate of 180 percent a year, Numi needs to remain nimble and responsive. Its founders, the brother-and-sister team of Ahmed and Reem Rahim, were inspired to create a tea company after Ahmed had spent some years operating tea houses in Europe while Reem studied art in the United States. Combining both their interests led to a unique firm dedicated to quality, sustainability, and community. Numi occupies offices that include a tea garden where employees often gather to relax, and it has won awards for many achievements including its unique teas, its innovative packaging, and its commitment to the environment. Numi's 25 different tea and flowering tea products and gift packs are sold in Whole Foods and Safeway markets, as well as in individual natural food and grocery stores throughout the United States, and in 20 other countries overseas.

The prevailing attitude in the company, which maintains a blog and a presence on Facebook and MySpace, is a can-do, team-oriented spirit. Because it's a small firm where everyone works hard, Numi can't afford rapid employee turnover and the time that would be lost in recruiting, interviewing, and training. Employees are thus carefully chosen for their willingness to do whatever it takes to get the job done and to remain upbeat and positive despite the occasional stress of working for a small company with customers around the world. Workers must also be able to devote long hours when necessary and share the company's goals.

Employees in Numi's distribution center, for instance, recently found themselves under pressure because it was taking nearly two weeks to fill international orders. However, with a new manager and a new focus on everyone understanding how each job fit into the big picture, a sense of teamwork began to grow. Soon each employee had been trained to perform all the critical tasks in order fulfillment, so instead of working in isolation they were able to pitch in during crunch times. Their new flexibility reduced lead times for overseas orders to about five days and cut the time for domestic orders in half. In fact, sometimes the team can ship orders the same day.

At Numi, managers who communicate well and who are out working alongside their staff are the norm. They must also communicate well with customers and demonstrate a high level of emotional maturity. Some meet with their teams on a regular basis, to review project status against deadlines and due dates and to make changes in workload and procedures where necessary. The company offers flextime to help employees retain a balance between their work and personal life, and when things get overwhelming at the office, there's always the tea garden and a freshly brewed cup of organic tea.[11]

Questions

1. Numi's customer service manager, Cindy Graffort, says the company is like a "living, breathing organism." What does she mean? How does the company's culture reflect this belief?
2. Numi's distribution manager, Dannielle Oviedo, says her philosophy of management means she gets involved in what her team is doing: "I do what I ask folks to do." Do you think she is a good delegator? Why or why not?
3. What can you infer about Numi's basis for departmentalization and its chain of command?

Case 7.2

HP's Corporate Challenge: To Remain Agile and Responsive in an Ever-Changing Environment

Hewlett-Packard (HP) is the original "started in a garage" technology company, founded by Bill Hewlett and Dave Packard in 1939. Over the years, HP has grown into a market leader, with $114 billion in annual revenue, 300,000 employees worldwide, and tens of millions of customers on six continents. Its rivals, multinationals such as Apple, Dell, Acer, and Lenovo, never stop looking for the next big tech breakthrough. No wonder HP, approaching its 75th birthday, uses its organizational structure for competitive advantage in the 21st-century race for higher sales and profits.

The company has seven divisions, organized according to product or function: Services, Enterprise Storage and Servers, HP Software, the Personal Systems Group, the Imaging and Printing Group, HP Financial Services, and Corporate Investments. Within each division are business units organized by product. For example, the services division contains four main units (infrastructure technology outsourcing, applications services, business process outsourcing, and technology services). Each unit hires managers and employees with the particular skills, experience, and training appropriate for the services it offers.

Some HP business units are organized by customer and by product within a division. The Personal Systems Group, for example, includes one unit that focuses on commercial PCs and one that focuses on consumer PCs. Establishing these as separate business units allows HP to address differences in products and customers' needs while sharing expertise within the division. For efficiency, some functions straddle divisions and serve multiple units. The company recently consolidated its data-center operations and now has six megacenters instead of 85 smaller centers for data management.

Through its organizational structure, HP seeks to achieve two key objectives. First, knowing that technological change can occur at any time and move in unexpected directions, the company is determined to remain agile and adaptable. Its structure leaves day-to-day planning, decisions, and implementation in the hands of each unit's managers, allowing them to satisfy customers, initiate projects, and respond to environmental shifts

without delay. Major decisions that affect the overall organization, such as whether to acquire another company, are made at higher levels.

Second, the company uses its structure to support growth. Eyeing a larger share of the $1.7 trillion global market for information technology, HP has been steadily adding to its portfolio of goods and services. Some of this expansion has occurred through acquisition. During the past few years, HP has bought EDS, 3Com, and Palm, among other businesses, and merged their operations into the appropriate corporate divisions. Palm, a pioneer of handheld computing devices and maker of smartphones, was integrated into HP's Personal Systems Group to enhance that division's technical capabilities in preparation for future growth.

Innovation has been woven into the fabric of HP's corporate culture since the early days. The company is famous for investing billions of dollars annually to research new technology and develop new products. Although senior managers don't want to stifle innovation by imposing too many limits, they have very clear expectations for research projects. "The key change we made was to take our brilliant scientists and sharpen their focus around a much smaller pool of big bets," explains the head of HP Labs. Researchers know that "every single [project] must have the potential to [generate] $1 billion-plus in revenue for HP." As a result, instead of pursuing as many as 150 projects at any given time, researchers now concentrate their efforts on the most promising two dozen projects.

Top managers are also involved in coordinating the overall efforts of employees that serve their very largest customers. For example, HP has a $3 billion contract to handle information technology operations for Procter & Gamble on an outsourcing basis. The head of the HP division visits with Procter & Gamble's senior managers six times a year to jointly evaluate performance. HP's CEO also joins the conversation at least twice a year. "When you have the CEO of a company sitting across the table saying, 'We're going to deliver this,' you know they're going to deliver," says a senior Procter & Gamble executive.[12]

Questions

1. How is corporate culture likely to affect HP's ability to integrate acquired companies into its organizational structure?
2. Analyze HP's use of departmentalization. Why are its choices appropriate for a technology company?
3. Analyze HP's approach to delegation and decentralization. Are its choices appropriate for a technology company? Why or why not?

Building Skills for Career Success

① SOCIAL MEDIA EXERCISE

Zappo's is a company that embraces the notion that customers come first. It is well known that this company is customer-centered. One of the ways that it allows employees to communicate with customers is through its blog www.zapposinsights.com/blog.

1. Take a look at this blog. What can you tell about the corporate culture of Zappo's?
2. How do they approach customer service? Do you think it works? Why or why not?

② JOURNALING FOR SUCCESS

Discovery statement: This chapter described the powerful influence that a corporate culture has on an organization.

Assume that after leaving school, you are hired by your "dream company."

Assignment

1. What are the major corporate culture dimensions of your dream company?
2. Before accepting a job at your "dream company," how will you find out about the company's corporate culture?
3. From Figure 7.7, identify the type of corporate culture that you prefer and explain why.
4. Thinking back to previous jobs that you have had, describe the worst corporate culture you have ever experienced.

③ DEVELOPING CRITICAL-THINKING SKILLS

A firm's culture is a reflection of its most basic beliefs, values, customs, and rituals. Because it can have a powerful influence on how employees think and act, this culture also can have a powerful influence on a firm's performance. The influence may be for the better, of course, as in the case of Kraft Foods, or it may be for the worse, as in the case of a bureaucratic organization whose employees feel hopelessly mired in red tape. When a company is concerned about mediocre performance and declining sales figures, its managers would do well to examine the cultural environment to see what might be in need of change.

Assignment

1. Analyze the cultural environment in which you work. (If you have no job, consider your school as your workplace and your instructor as your supervisor.) Ask yourself and your co-workers (or classmates) the following questions and record the answers:

a. Do you feel that your supervisors welcome your ideas and respect them even when they may disagree with them? Do you take pride in your work? Do you feel that your work is appreciated? Do you think that the amount of work assigned to you is reasonable? Are you compensated adequately for your work?

b. Are you proud to be associated with the company? Do you believe what the company says about itself in its advertisements? Are there any company policies or rules, written or unwritten, that you feel are unfair? Do you think that there is an opportunity for you to advance in this environment?

c. How much independence do you have in carrying out your assignments? Are you ever allowed to act on your own, or do you feel that you have to consult with your supervisor on every detail?

d. Do you enjoy the atmosphere in which you work? Is the physical setting pleasant? How often do you laugh in an average workday? How well do you get along with your supervisor and co-workers?

e. Do you feel that the company cares about you? Will your supervisor give you time off when you have some pressing personal need? If the company had to downsize, how do you think you would be treated?

2. Using the responses to these questions, write a two-page paper describing how the culture of your workplace affects your performance and the overall performance of the firm. Point out the cultural factors that have the most beneficial and negative effects. Include your thoughts on how negative effects could be reversed.

④ BUILDING TEAM SKILLS

An organization chart is a diagram showing how employees and tasks are grouped and how the lines of communication and authority flow within an organization. These charts can look very different depending on a number of factors, including the nature and size of the business, the way it is departmentalized, its patterns of delegating authority, and its span of management.

Assignment

1. Working in a team, use the following information to draw an organization chart: The KDS Design Center works closely with two home-construction companies, ACME Homebuilders and Highmass. KDS's role is to help customers select materials for

Unilever: Producing Quality Goods the Green Way

Unilever, with headquarters in London and Rotterdam, aims to double sales worldwide and slash its environmental footprint in half by 2020. These are aggressive goals even for a $62 billion company with 170,000 employees and more than 120 years of experience producing high quality skin-care products, foods, and other consumer goods. Some of the most famous brands in Unilever's pantry are Axe, Bertolli, Ben & Jerry's, Dove, Knorr, Lipton, Vaseline, and Sunlight. The Dove brand alone accounts for $3.7 billion in annual global sales.

To compete with local firms as well as with multinational giants such as Nestlé and Procter & Gamble, Unilever spends $1.3 billion each year on research and development. More than 6,000 Unilever researchers worldwide work closely with experts from the company's Safety and Environmental Assurance Center to develop new products and production processes that are safe, effective, and innovative. In particular, the company is focused on improving the nutritional value of its food products, and it has invested heavily to create healthy new foods with lower fat and salt content, fewer calories, and less sugar.

Unilever is also building greener, more energy-efficient production facilities to support sustainable growth in international markets, which account for 56 percent of sales. For example, it recently opened a new manufacturing plant in South Africa to produce Knorr soup mixes and other packaged foods. This is Unilever's most environmentally-friendly factory: it recycles rainwater for plant use, composts unneeded materials in local gardens, and reuses packaging so nothing lands in landfills. Once fully expanded, this factory—the size of three soccer fields—will have the largest production capacity of any of Unilever's dry-food facilities.

Although large corporations often try to improve their profit margins by squeezing suppliers for more savings, Unilever prefers a partnership approach. Instead of seeking to buy at the lowest cost, it shares its long-term goals with key suppliers of raw materials, packaging, and services, inviting them to jointly develop product and process innovations for mutual benefit. As a result, suppliers have provided the inspiration for hundreds of items that are currently in Unilever's new-product pipeline.[1]

There's a good chance when you saw the name Unilever in the Inside Business opening case for this chapter you didn't recognize a company that operates in 190 countries around the globe and employs 170,000 people. And yet, this company generates annual sales exceeding $62 billion by producing consumer products that you may use on a regular basis including Axe, Bertolli, Ben & Jerry's, Dove, Knorr, Lipton, Vaseline, and Sunlight. In fact, on any given day, more than two billion people use Unilever products to look good, feel good, and get more out of life. Although the company was founded more than 120 years ago and has been extremely profitable, Unilver continues to innovate and introduce new products to compete with not only local firms but also global giants including Procter & Gamble and Nestle. At the same time, it is a company known for its efforts to sustain the planet. Today, Unilever is an excellent example of what this chapter's content—the production of quality goods and services—is all about.

We begin this chapter with an overview of operations management—the activities required to produce goods and services that meet the needs of customers. In this section, we also discuss the role of manufacturing in the U.S. economy, competition in the global marketplace, and careers in operations management. Next, we describe the conversion process that makes production possible and also note the growing role of services in our economy. Then we examine more closely three important aspects of operations management: developing ideas for new products, planning for production, and effectively controlling operations after production has begun. We close the chapter with a look at the productivity trends and the ways that manufacturing can be improved through the use of technology.

WHAT IS PRODUCTION?

1 Explain the nature of production.

Have you ever wondered where a new pair of Levi's jeans comes from? Or an Apple iPhone, or a Uniroyal tire for your car? Even factory service on a Hewlett-Packard computer or a Maytag clothes dryer would be impossible if it weren't for the activities described in this chapter. In fact, these products and services and millions of others like them would not exist if it weren't for production activities.

Let's begin this chapter by reviewing what an operating manager does. In Chapter 6, we described an *operations manager* as a person who manages the systems that convert resources into goods and services. This area of management is usually referred to as **operations management**, which consists of all the activities required to produce goods and services.

To produce a product or service successfully, a business must perform a number of specific activities. For example, suppose that Toyota (the parent company of Lexus automobiles) has an idea for a new, sport version of the Lexus GS 350 that will cost approximately $50,000. Marketing research must determine not only if customers are willing to pay the price for this product but also what special features they want. Then Toyota's operations managers must turn the idea into reality.

Toyota's managers cannot just push the "start button" and immediately begin producing the new automobile. Production must be planned. As you will see, planning takes place both *before* anything is produced and *during* the production process.

Managers also must concern themselves with the control of operations to ensure that the organization's goals are achieved. For a product such as the Lexus GS 350, control of operations involves a number of important issues, including product quality, performance standards, the amount of inventory of both raw materials and finished products, and production costs.

We discuss each of the major activities of operations management later in this chapter. First, however, let's take a closer look at American manufacturers and how they compete in the global marketplace.

operations management all the activities required to produce goods and services

How American Manufacturers Compete in the Global Marketplace

After World War II, the United States became the most productive country in the world. For almost 30 years, until the late 1970s, its leadership was never threatened. By then, however, manufacturers in Japan, Germany, Taiwan, Korea, Singapore, Sweden, and other industrialized nations were offering U.S. firms increasing competition. Now the Chinese are manufacturing everything from sophisticated electronic equipment and automobiles to less expensive everyday items—often at a lower cost than the same goods can be manufactured in other countries. And yet, in the face of increasing competition, there is both good and bad news for U.S. manufacturers. First the bad news.

The Bad News for Manufacturers The number of Americans employed in the manufacturing sector has decreased. Currently, approximately 12 million U.S. workers are employed in manufacturing jobs—down from just over 19 million back in 1979.[2] While there are many additional factors, three major factors explain why employment in this economic sector has declined.

- Many of the manufacturing jobs that were lost were outsourced to low-wage workers in nations where there are few labor and environmental regulations.

©AP PHOTO/APPLE

Why is the product in this photo important?
While it may be hard to tell at this stage of production, the product at this work station is one of the most successful products in recent history—the Apple iPhone. On the left, the man in the yellow coat is Apple CEO Tim Cook who is talking with lab technicians that produce the product in this Chinese factory.

- It costs about 20 percent more to manufacture goods in the United States than it does anywhere else in the world.[3]
- The number of unemployed factory workers increased during the recent economic crisis because of decreased consumer demand for manufactured goods.

As a result, manufacturing accounts for only about 9 percent of the current workforce.[4] Since 1979, 7 million jobs have been lost, and many of those jobs aren't coming back.

The Good News for Manufacturers The United States remains one of the largest manufacturing countries in the world. While some people would argue that "Made in America" doesn't mean what it used to mean, consider the following:

- U.S. manufacturers produce approximately 20 percent of total global manufacturing output.[5]
- Every year, manufacturing contributes approximately $2 trillion to the U.S. economy.[6]
- Manufacturing exports are nearly 60 percent of all U.S. exports.[7]
- Between now and 2018, it is anticipated that there will be 2 million job openings in manufacturing.[8]
- For every new manufacturing job created, there are another three new jobs created in the supply chain, the trucking industry, and other related areas of the economy.[9]

As a result, the manufacturing sector is still a very important part of the U.S. economy. Although the number of manufacturing jobs has declined, productivity has increased. At least two very important factors account for increases in productivity: First, innovation—finding a better way to produce products—is the key factor that has enabled American manufacturers to compete in the global marketplace. Often, innovation is the result of manufacturers investing money to purchase new, state-of-the-art equipment that helps employees improve productivity. Second, today's workers in the manufacturing sector are highly skilled in order to operate sophisticated equipment. Simply put, Americans are making more goods, but with fewer employees.

Even more good news is that many American manufacturers that outsourced work to factories in foreign nations are once again beginning to manufacture goods in the United States. For our purposes, the term **reshoring** (sometimes referred to as onshoring or insourcing) describes a situation where U.S. manufacturers bring manufacturing jobs back to the United States. For example, General Electric (GE) opened a new plant in Louisville, Kentucky, to manufacture hybrid electric water heaters in 2012.[10] Before the Kentucky plant was built, the water heaters were manufactured in China.[11] Ford, Procter & Gamble, NCR, Caterpillar, Honda, Intel, and Master Lock and many other U.S. firms are involved in reshoring. The primary reasons why U.S. firms are "coming back home" include increasing labor costs in foreign nations, higher shipping costs, significant quality and safety issues, faster product development when goods are produced in the United States, and federal and state subsidies to encourage manufactures to produce products in the United States.

Although there are many challenges facing U.S. manufacturers, experts predict that there could be a significant resurgence for manufacturers that can meet current and future challenges. The bottom line: The global marketplace has never been more competitive and successful U.S. firms will focus on the following:

1. Meeting the needs of customers and improving product quality.
2. Motivating employees to cooperate with management and improve productivity.
3. Reducing costs by selecting suppliers that offer higher quality raw materials and components at reasonable prices.
4. Using computer-aided and flexible manufacturing systems that allow a higher degree of customization.
5. Improving control procedures to help ensure lower manufacturing costs.
6. Using green manufacturing to conserve natural resources and sustain the planet.

For most firms, competing in the global marketplace is not only profitable but also an essential activity that requires the cooperation of everyone within the organization.

reshoring a situation in which U.S. manufacturers bring manufacturing jobs back to the United States

Careers in Operations Management

Although it is hard to provide information about specific career opportunities in operations management, some generalizations do apply to this management area. First, you must appreciate the manufacturing process and the steps required to produce a product or service. A basic understanding of mass production and the difference between an analytical process and a synthetic process is essential. **Mass production** is a manufacturing process that lowers the cost required to produce a large number of identical or similar products over a long period of time. An **analytical process** breaks raw materials into different component parts. For example, a barrel of crude oil refined by Marathon Oil Corporation—a Texas-based oil and chemical refiner—can be broken down into gasoline, oil, lubricants, and many other petroleum by-products. A **synthetic process** is just the opposite of the analytical one; it combines raw materials or components to create a finished product. Black & Decker uses a synthetic process when it combines plastic, steel, rechargeable batteries, and other components to produce a cordless drill.

Once you understand that operations managers are responsible for producing tangible products or services that customers want, you must determine how you fit into the production process. Today's successful operations managers must:

1. Be able to motivate and lead people.
2. Understand how technology can make a manufacturer more productive and efficient.
3. Appreciate the control processes that help lower production costs and improve product quality.
4. Understand the relationship between the customer, the marketing of a product, and the production of a product.

If operations management seems like an area you might be interested in, why not do more career exploration?

mass production a manufacturing process that lowers the cost required to produce a large number of identical or similar products over a long period of time

analytical process a process in operations management in which raw materials are broken into different component parts

synthetic process a process in operations management in which raw materials or components are combined to create a finished product

utility the ability of a good or service to satisfy a human need

form utility utility created by people converting raw materials, finances, and information into finished products

THE CONVERSION PROCESS

> **2** Outline how the conversion process transforms raw materials, labor, and other resources into finished goods or services.

The purpose of manufacturing or a service business is to provide utility to customers. **Utility** is the ability of a good or service to satisfy a human need. Although there are four types of utilities—form, place, time, and possession—operations management focuses primarily on form utility. **Form utility** is created by people converting raw materials, finances, and information into finished products. The other types of utility—place, time, and possession—are discussed in Chapter 12.

But how does the conversion take place? How does Kellogg's convert grain, sugar, salt, and other ingredients; money from previous sales and stockholders' investments; production workers and managers; and economic and marketing forecasts into Frosted Flakes cereal products? How does H&R Block employ more than 100,000 tax preparers and convert retail locations, computers and software, and advertising and promotion into tax services for its clients. They do so through the use of a conversion process like the one illustrated in Figure 8.1. As indicated by our H&R Block example, the conversion process can be used to produce services.

©PASCAL LAUENER/REUTERS/LANDOV

Pretty expensive product! The worker in this photo is creating *gold* bars. Although the original resource comes from the ground, the final product—100 gram gold bars—is often used by some people as a means of retaining and accumulating wealth—especially when they are concerned about a downturn in the economy or a decline in the value of other investments.

Factors That Affect a Conversion Process

The conversion of resources into products and services can be described in several ways. We limit our discussion here to three: the focus or major resource used in the conversion process, its magnitude of change, and the number of production processes employed.

Focus By the *focus* of a conversion process, we mean the resource or resources that make up the major or most important *input*. The resources are financial, material, information, and people—the same resources discussed in Chapters 1 and 6. For a bank such as Citibank, financial resources are the major resource. A chemical and energy company such as Chevron concentrates on material resources. Your college or university is concerned primarily with information. And temporary employment services, such as Manpower, focus on the use of human resources.

Magnitude of Change The *magnitude* of a conversion process is the degree to which the resources are physically changed. At one extreme lie such processes as the one by

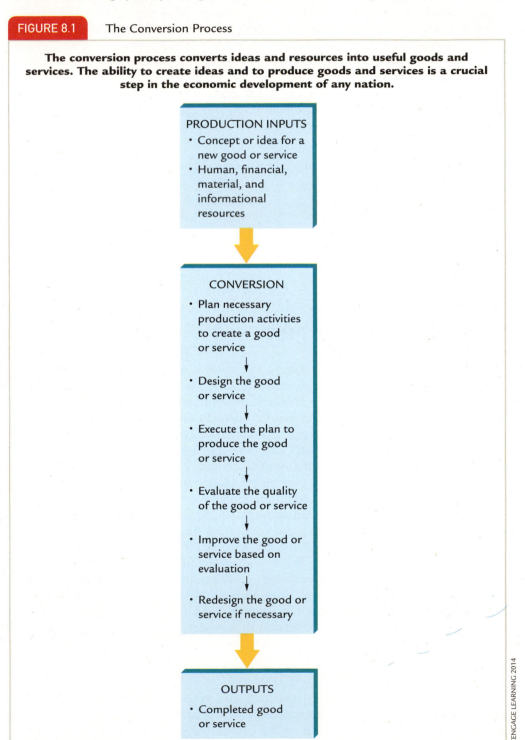

FIGURE 8.1   The Conversion Process

The conversion process converts ideas and resources into useful goods and services. The ability to create ideas and to produce goods and services is a crucial step in the economic development of any nation.

PRODUCTION INPUTS

- Concept or idea for a new good or service
- Human, financial, material, and informational resources

CONVERSION

- Plan necessary production activities to create a good or service
- Design the good or service
- Execute the plan to produce the good or service
- Evaluate the quality of the good or service
- Improve the good or service based on evaluation
- Redesign the good or service if necessary

OUTPUTS

- Completed good or service

which the Glad Products Company produces Glad® Cling Wrap. Various chemicals in liquid or powder form are combined to produce long, thin sheets of plastic Glad Cling Wrap. Here, the original resources are totally unrecognizable in the finished product. At the other extreme, Southwest Airlines produces no physical change in its original resources. The airline simply provides a service and transports people from one place to another.

Number of Production Processes A single firm may employ one production process or many. In general, larger firms that make a variety of products use multiple production processes. For example, GE manufactures some of its own products, buys other merchandise from suppliers, and operates multiple divisions including a finance division, a lighting division, an appliance division, a healthcare division, and other divisions responsible for the products and services that customers associate with the GE name. Smaller firms, by contrast, may use one production process. For example, Texas-based Advanced Cast Stone, Inc., manufactures one basic product: building materials made from concrete.

THE INCREASING IMPORTANCE OF SERVICES

3 Understand the importance of service businesses to consumers, other business firms, and the nation's economy.

The application of the basic principles of operations management to the production of services has coincided with a dramatic growth in the number and diversity of service businesses. In 1900, only 28 percent of American workers were employed in service firms. By 1950, this figure had grown to 40 percent, and by 2011, it had risen to 87 percent.[12] In fact, the American economy is now characterized as a service economy (see Figure 8.2). A **service economy** is one in which more effort is devoted to the production of services than to the production of goods.

Planning Quality Services

Today, the managers of restaurants, laundries, real estate agencies, banks, movie theaters, airlines, travel bureaus, and other service firms have realized that they can benefit from the experience of manufacturers. And while service firms are different from manufacturing firms, both types of businesses must complete many of the same activities in order to be successful. For example, as illustrated in the middle section of Figure 8.1, service businesses must plan, design, execute, evaluate, improve, and redesign their services in order to provide the services that their customers want.

For a service firm, planning often begins with determining who the customer is and what needs the customer has. After customer needs are identified, the next step for

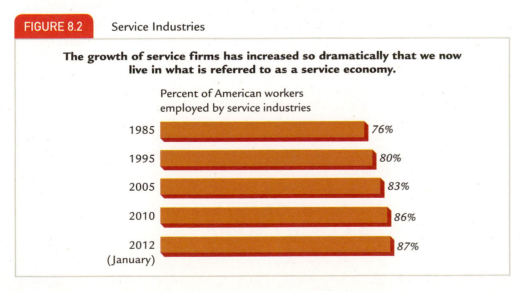

FIGURE 8.2 Service Industries

The growth of service firms has increased so dramatically that we now live in what is referred to as a service economy.

Percent of American workers employed by service industries

Year	Percent
1985	76%
1995	80%
2005	83%
2010	86%
2012 (January)	87%

Source: U.S. Bureau of Labor Statistics Web site, www.bls.gov (accessed February 13, 2012).

service economy an economy in which more effort is devoted to the production of services than to the production of goods

successful service firms is to develop a plan that will enable the firm to deliver the services that their customers want or need. For example, a swimming pool repair business must develop a business plan that includes a process for hiring and training qualified employees, obtaining necessary parts and supplies, marketing the firm's services, and creating management and accounting systems to control the firm's activities. Once the firm provides a service to a customer, successful firms evaluate their operating systems and measure customer satisfaction. And if necessary, redesign their operating systems and their services to improve the customer's experience.

Evaluating the Quality of a Firm's Services

The production of services is very different from the production of manufactured goods in the following five ways:

1. When compared to manufactured goods, customers are much more involved in obtaining the service they want or need.
2. Services are consumed immediately and, unlike manufactured goods, cannot be stored. For example, a hair stylist cannot store completed haircuts.
3. Services are provided when and where the customer desires the service. In many cases, customers will not travel as far to obtain a service.
4. Services are usually labor-intensive because the human resource is often the most important resource used in the production of services.
5. Services are intangible, and it is therefore more difficult to evaluate customer satisfaction.[13]

Although it is often more difficult to measure the customer's level of satisfaction, today's successful service firms work hard to exceed the customer's expectations. To make their guests feel at home, Affinia Hotels has developed a revolutionary new customer service program that allows guests to customize every aspect of their stay. Using the new online service, guests of this upscale hotel chain can pre-select not only the type of pillow they want, but also amenities including a guitar, golf ball and putter, a fitness kit, or even a rubber ducky to help make their stay perfect and at the same time build repeat business.[14]

Compared with manufacturers, service firms often listen more carefully to customers and respond more quickly to the market's changing needs. For example, Maggiano's Little Italy restaurant is a chain of eating establishments owned by Brinker International. In order to continuously improve customer service, the restaurant encourages diners to complete online surveys that prompt diners to evaluate the food, atmosphere, service, and other variables. The information from the surveys is then used to fine-tune the way Maggiano's meets its customers' needs.

In addition, many service firms are now using social media to build relationships with their customers. Coldwell Banker, one of the largest real estate companies in the United States sponsors an Internet blog that can be used not only to provide information about the current housing market, but also as a method to encourage comments and questions from customers. And Olive Garden, the restaurant chain owned by the Darden family of restaurants, uses the Internet to provide recipes for many of its menu items so customers can try their hand at creating the "perfect" Italian meal in their own kitchens.

Now that we understand something about the production process that is used to transform resources into goods and services, we can consider three major activities involved in operations management: research and development, planning for production, and operations control.

WHERE DO NEW PRODUCTS AND SERVICES COME FROM?

Describe how research and development lead to new products and services. 4

No firm can produce a product or service until it has an idea. Both Apple's iPad and Ford's Electric Focus automobile began as an idea. Although no one can predict with 100 percent accuracy what types of products and services will be available in the next five years, it is safe to say that companies will continue to introduce new products and services that will change our everyday lives.

Research and Development

How did we get the Apple iPad or the Electric Ford Focus automobile? We got them as a result of people working with new ideas that developed into useful products. These activities generally are referred to as research and development. For our purposes, **research and development (R&D)** involves a set of activities intended to identify new ideas that have the potential to result in new goods and services.

Today, business firms use three general types of R&D activities. *Basic research* consists of activities aimed at uncovering new knowledge. The goal of basic research is scientific advancement, without regard for its potential use in the development of goods and services. *Applied research*, in contrast, consists of activities geared toward discovering new knowledge with some potential use. *Development and implementation* involves research activities undertaken specifically to put new or existing knowledge to use in producing goods and services. For many companies, R&D is a very important part of their business operations. The 3M company, for example, has always been known for its development and implementation research activities. Currently, 3M employs 7,350 researchers worldwide and has invested more than $7 billion over the last five years to develop new products designed to make people's lives easier and safer.[15]

Personal APPS

Your idea for a new good or service may be your ticket to a small business of your own, if you have entrepreneurial spirit. But don't forget that big corporations also value people with new product ideas.

Product Extension and Refinement

When a brand-new product is first marketed, its sales start at zero and slowly increase from that point. If the product is successful, annual sales increase more and more rapidly until they reach some peak. Then, as time passes, annual sales begin to decline, and they continue to decline until it is no longer profitable to manufacture the product. (This rise-and-decline pattern, called the *product life-cycle*, is discussed in more detail in Chapter 13.)

If a firm sells only one product, when that product reaches the end of its life-cycle, the firm will die, too. To stay in business, the firm must, at the very least, find ways to refine or extend the want-satisfying capability of its product. Consider television sets. Since they were introduced in the late 1930s, television sets have been constantly *refined* so that they now provide clearer, sharper pictures with less dial adjusting. During the same time, television sets also were *extended*. There are basic flat-screen televisions without added features, and many others that include DVD or Blu-Ray players and Internet streaming options. The latest development—high-definition television—has already become the standard.

For most firms, extension and refinement are expected results of their research, development, and implementation activities. Each refinement or extension results in an essentially "new" product whose sales make up for the declining sales of a product that was introduced earlier. When consumers were introduced to the original five varieties of Campbell's Soup, they discovered that these soups were of the highest quality, as well as inexpensive, and the soups were an instant success. Although one of the most successful companies at the beginning of the 1900s, Campbell's had to continue to innovate, refine, and extend its product line. For example, many consumers in

research and development (R&D) a set of activities intended to identify new ideas that have the potential to result in new goods and services

A pill a day keeps the doctor away. Schering GmbH and Company, a subsidiary of Bayer Schering Pharmaceutical, produces over 7 billion tablets and pills each year. While the company already produces over 40 different drug products sold in over 100 countries, research and development is constantly working to identify new products to treat illness and disease.

the United States live in what is called an on-the-go society. To meet this need, Campbell's Soup has developed ready-to-serve products that can be popped into a microwave at work or school.

Discuss the components involved in planning the production process.

HOW DO MANAGERS PLAN PRODUCTION?

Only a few of the many ideas for new products, refinements, and extensions ever reach the production stage. For those ideas that do, however, the next step is planning for production. Once a new idea for a product or service has been identified, planning for production involves three different phases: design planning, facilities planning, and operational planning (see Figure 8.3).

Design Planning

design planning the development of a plan for converting an idea into an actual product or service

product line a group of similar products that differ only in relatively minor characteristics

When the R&D staff at Samsung recommended to top management that the firm manufacture and market a "Smart Fridge" with an LCD screen, Wi-Fi connectivity, and apps that allow consumers to update their calendars, leave notes to family members, or listen to music, the company could not simply swing into production the next day. Instead, a great deal of time and energy had to be invested in determining what the new refrigerator would look like, where and how it would be produced, and what options would be included. These decisions are a part of design planning. **Design planning** is the development of a plan for converting an idea into an actual product or service. The major decisions involved in design planning deal with product line, required capacity, and use of technology.

A product that has been around for a long time. Building on a rich (and profitable) history, Campbell's Soup continues to listen to customers to develop new products and to adapt and to refine existing products to meet customer needs.

Product Line A **product line** is a group of similar products that differ only in relatively minor characteristics. During the design-planning stage, a manufacturer like Samsung must determine how many different models to produce and what major options to offer. Likewise, a restaurant chain such as Pizza Hut must decide how many menu items to offer.

FIGURE 8.3   Planning for Production

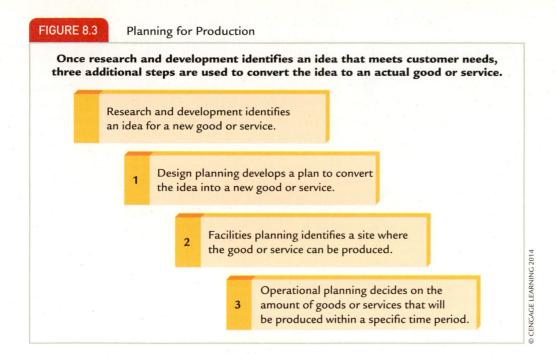

Once research and development identifies an idea that meets customer needs, three additional steps are used to convert the idea to an actual good or service.

Research and development identifies an idea for a new good or service.

1   Design planning develops a plan to convert the idea into a new good or service.

2   Facilities planning identifies a site where the good or service can be produced.

3   Operational planning decides on the amount of goods or services that will be produced within a specific time period.

© CENGAGE LEARNING 2014

An important issue in deciding on the product line is to balance customer preferences and production requirements. For this reason, marketing managers play an important role in making product-line decisions. Typically, marketing personnel want a "long" product line that offers customers many options. Because a long product line with more options gives customers greater choice, it is easier to sell products that meet the needs of individual customers. On the other hand, production personnel generally want a "short" product line with fewer options because products are easier to produce.

Once the product line has been determined, each distinct product within the product line must be designed. **Product design** is the process of creating a set of specifications from which a product can be produced. When designing a new product, specifications are extremely important. For example, product engineers for Samsung must make sure that their new "Smart Fridge" keeps food frozen in the freezer compartment. At the same time, they must make sure that lettuce and tomatoes do not freeze in the crisper section of the refrigerator. The need for a complete product design is fairly obvious; products that work cannot be manufactured without it. But services should be designed carefully as well—and *for the same reason*.

Required Production Capacity **Capacity** is the amount of products or services that an organization can produce in a given period of time. (For example, the capacity of a Panasonic assembly plant might be 1.3 million high-definition televisions per year.) Operations managers—again working with the firm's marketing managers—must determine the required capacity. This, in turn, determines the size of the production facility. If the facility is built with too much capacity, valuable resources (plant, equipment, and money) will lie idle. If the facility offers insufficient capacity, additional capacity may have to be added later when it is much more expensive than in the initial building stage.

Capacity means about the same thing to service businesses. For example, the capacity of a restaurant such as the Hard Rock Cafe in Nashville, Tennessee, is the number of customers it can serve at one time. As with the Panasonic manufacturing facility described earlier, if the restaurant is built with too much capacity—too many tables and chairs—valuable resources will be wasted. If the restaurant is too small, customers may have to wait for service; if the wait is too long, they may leave and choose another restaurant.

product design the process of creating a set of specifications from which a product can be produced

capacity the amount of products or services that an organization can produce in a given time

Saving Energy—And the Environment

The industrial sector uses approximately 40% of the world's total delivered energy, so it's fertile ground for energy optimization efforts. By working with their customers on energy resource management and reducing emissions and waste, Rockwell Automation, a manufacturer of industrial automation control and information solutions, is helping make their customers' operations cleaner, more energy efficient, and more competitive. In short, they're showing their customers ways they can save money and energy while saving the environment. Take a closer look at how Rockwell is helping their customers meet their lean objectives while still meeting their green objectives at www.rockwellautomation.com.

Sources: www.rockwellautomation.com/solutions/sustainability; Presher, A. (August 8, 2011), "Energy Optimization as Productivity Enhancer," *DesignNews*. Retrieved from www.designnews.com/document.asp?doc_id=231868; "Rockwell Automation named to Dow Jones Sustainability North America Index," *ReliablePlant*, retrieved February 22, 2012 from www.reliableplant.com/Read/26680/Rockwell-Automation-sustainability-index.

labor-intensive technology a process in which people must do most of the work

capital-intensive technology a process in which machines and equipment do most of the work

Use of Technology During the design-planning stage, management must determine the degree to which *automation* and *technology* will be used to produce a product or service. Here, there is a trade-off between high initial costs and low operating costs (for automation) and low initial costs and high operating costs (for human labor). Ultimately, management must choose between a labor-intensive technology and a capital-intensive technology. A **labor-intensive technology** is a process in which people must do most of the work. Housecleaning services and the New York Yankees baseball team, for example, are labor-intensive. A **capital-intensive technology** is a process in which machines and equipment do most of the work. A Sony automated assembly plant is capital intensive.

Site Selection and Facilities Planning

Generally, a business will choose to produce a new product in an existing factory as long as (1) the existing factory has enough capacity to handle customer demand for both the new product and established products and (2) the cost of refurbishing an existing factory is less than the cost of building a new one.

After exploring the capacity of existing factories, management may decide to build a new production facility. In determining where to locate production facilities, management must consider a number of variables, including the following:

- Locations of major customers and suppliers.
- Availability and cost of skilled and unskilled labor.
- Quality of life for employees and management in the proposed location.
- The cost of land and construction to build a new facility.
- Local and state taxes, environmental regulations, and zoning laws.
- The amount of financial support and subsidies, if any, offered by local and state governments.
- Special requirements, such as great amounts of energy or water used in the production process.

Before making a final decision about where a proposed plant will be located and how it will be organized, two other factors—human resources and plant layout—should be examined.

Human Resources Several issues involved in site selection and facilities planning fall within the province of human resources managers. When Nestlé built its new 900,000-square-foot production facility to make liquid Nesquik® and Coffee-Mate® products in Anderson, Indiana, human resources managers were involved to make sure the necessary managers and employees needed to staff the plant were available. And when a company decides to build a new facility in a foreign country, again human resources managers are involved. For example, suppose that a U.S. firm like AT&T wants to lower labor costs by importing products from China. It has two choices. It can build its own manufacturing facility in a foreign country or it can outsource production to local firms. In either case, human resources become involved in the decision. If the decision is made to build its own plant, human resources managers will have to recruit managers and employees with the appropriate skills who are willing to relocate to a foreign country, develop training programs for local Chinese workers, or both. On the other hand, if the decision is made to outsource production to local suppliers, human resources managers must make sure that local suppliers are complying with the U.S. company's human rights policies and with all applicable national and local wage and hour laws.

Plant Layout Plant layout is the arrangement of machinery, equipment, and personnel within a production facility. Three general types of plant layout are used (see Figure 8.4).

The *process layout* is used when different operations are required for creating small batches of different products or working on different parts of a product. The plant is arranged so that each operation is performed in its own particular area. An auto repair facility at a local automobile dealership provides an example of a process layout. The various operations may be engine repair, bodywork, wheel alignment, and safety inspection. If you take your Lincoln Navigator for a wheel alignment, your car "visits" only the area where alignments are performed.

A *product layout* (sometimes referred to as an *assembly line*) is used when all products undergo the same operations in the same sequence. Workstations are arranged to match the sequence of operations, and work flows from station to station. An assembly line is the best example of a product layout. For example, California-based Maxim Integrated Products, Inc., uses a product layout to manufacture components for consumer and business electronic products. A *fixed-position layout* is used when a very large product is produced. Aircraft manufacturers and shipbuilders apply this method because of the difficulty of moving a large product such as an airliner or a ship. The product remains stationary, and people and machines are moved as needed to assemble the product. Boeing, for example, uses the fixed-position layout to build 787 Dreamliner jet aircraft at its Everett, Washington, manufacturing facility.

Operational Planning

The objective of operational planning is to decide on the amount of products or services each facility will produce during a specific period of time. Four steps are required.

Step 1: Selecting a Planning Horizon A **planning horizon** is simply the time period during which an operational plan will be in effect. A common planning horizon for production plans is one year. Then, before each year is up, management must plan for the next. A planning horizon of one year generally is long enough to average out seasonal increases and decreases in sales. At the same time, it is short enough for planners to adjust production to accommodate long-range sales trends.

Step 2: Estimating Market Demand The *market demand* for a product is the quantity that customers will purchase at the going price. This quantity must be estimated for the time period covered by the planning horizon. Sales projections developed by marketing managers are the basis for market-demand estimates.

Step 3: Comparing Market Demand with Capacity The third step in operational planning is to compare the estimated

Ice cream that tastes as good as homemade. The goal for Roundy's Supermarkets is to make their ice cream taste just like Mom's—but production is on a much larger scale. To accomplish the task, the Wisconsin-based company uses a stainless steel assembly line that snakes through the company's food manufacturing and processing plant in Kenosha, Wisconsin.

plant layout the arrangement of machinery, equipment, and personnel within a production facility

planning horizon the period during which an operational plan will be in effect

A big product! The British Royal Navy's aircraft carrier HMS Queen Elizabeth was constructed using a fixed-position layout. To see how large the ship is, compare its size with the people at the bottom of this photo. When a product is this large, it is easier to move people, machinery, and parts to where they are needed instead of moving the ship.

FIGURE 8.4   Facilities Planning

The process layout is used when small batches of different products are created or when working on different parts of a product. The product layout (assembly line) is used when all products undergo the same operations in the same sequence. The fixed-position layout is used in producing a product too large to move.

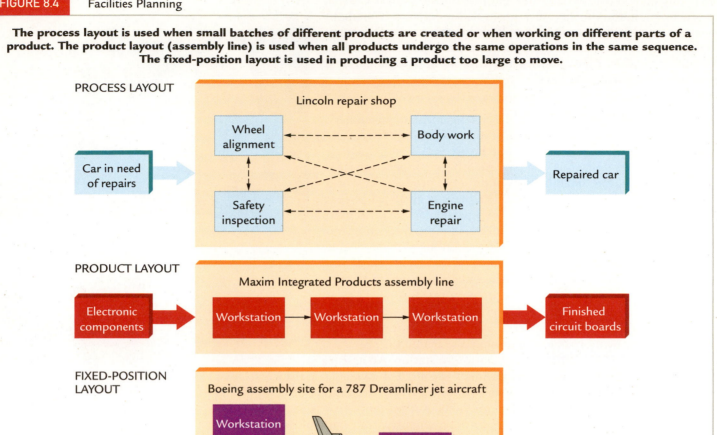

PROCESS LAYOUT

Lincoln repair shop

Car in need of repairs → Wheel alignment ⇄ Body work ⇄ Safety inspection ⇄ Engine repair → Repaired car

PRODUCT LAYOUT

Maxim Integrated Products assembly line

Electronic components → Workstation → Workstation → Workstation → Finished circuit boards

FIXED-POSITION LAYOUT

Boeing assembly site for a 787 Dreamliner jet aircraft

Resources and components → Workstation / Workstation / Workstation / Workstation / Workstation → Finished plane

© CENGAGE LEARNING 2014

market demand with the facility's capacity to satisfy that demand. (Remember that capacity is the amount of products or services that an organization can produce in a given time period.) One of three outcomes may result: Demand may exceed capacity, capacity may exceed demand, or capacity and demand may be equal. If they are equal, the facility should be operated at full capacity. However, if market demand and capacity are not equal, adjustments may be necessary.

Step 4: Adjusting Products or Services to Meet Demand The biggest reason for changes to a firm's production schedule is changes in the amount of products or services that a company sells to its customers. For example, Indiana-based Berry Plastics produces all kinds of plastic products. One particularly successful product line for Berry Plastics is drink cups that can be screen-printed to promote a company or its products or services.[16] If Berry Plastics obtains a large contract to provide promotional cups to a large fast-food chain such as Whataburger or McDonald's, the company may need to work three shifts a day, seven days a week, until the contract is fulfilled. Unfortunately, the reverse is also true. If the company's sales force does not generate new sales, there may be only enough work for the employees on one shift.

When market demand exceeds capacity, several options are available to a firm. Production of products or services may be increased by operating the facility overtime with existing personnel or by starting a second or third work shift. For manufacturers, another response is to subcontract or outsource a portion of the work to other manufacturers. If the excess demand is likely to be permanent, the firm may expand the current facility or build another facility.

What happens when capacity exceeds market demand? Again, there are several options. To reduce output temporarily, workers may be laid off and part of the facility shut down, or the facility may be operated on a shorter-than-normal workweek for as long as the excess capacity persists. To adjust to a permanently decreased demand, management may shift the excess capacity of a manufacturing facility to the production of other goods or services. The most radical adjustment is to eliminate the excess capacity by selling unused manufacturing facilities.

OPERATIONS CONTROL

6 Explain how purchasing, inventory control, scheduling, and quality control affect production.

We have discussed the development of an idea for a product or service and the planning that translates that idea into the reality. Now we are ready to begin the actual production process. In this section, we examine four important areas of operations control: purchasing, inventory control, scheduling, and quality control (see Figure 8.5).

Purchasing

Purchasing consists of all the activities involved in obtaining required materials, supplies, components (or subassemblies), and parts from other firms. Levi Strauss, for example, must purchase denim cloth, thread, and zippers before it can produce a single pair of jeans. For all firms, the purchasing function is far from routine, and its importance should not be underestimated. For some products, purchased materials make up more than 50 percent of their wholesale costs.

The objective of purchasing is to ensure that required materials are available when they are needed, in the proper amounts, and at minimum cost. Generally, the company with purchasing needs and suppliers must develop a working relationship built on trust. In addition to a working relationship built on trust, many companies believe that purchasing is one area where they can promote diversity. For example, AT&T developed a Supplier Diversity Program in 1968. Today, more than 40 years later, goals for the AT&T program include purchasing a total of 21.5 percent of all products and services from minorities, women, and disabled veteran business enterprises.[17]

Purchasing personnel should constantly be on the lookout for new or backup suppliers, even when their needs are being met by their present suppliers, because problems

---

FIGURE 8.5   Four Aspects of Operations Control

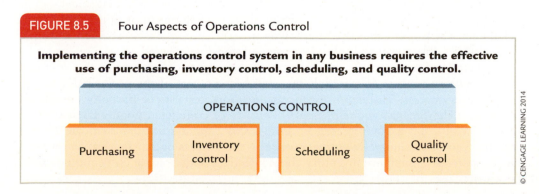

Implementing the operations control system in any business requires the effective use of purchasing, inventory control, scheduling, and quality control.

OPERATIONS CONTROL

Purchasing   Inventory control   Scheduling   Quality control

© CENGAGE LEARNING 2014

purchasing all the activities involved in obtaining required materials, supplies, components, and parts from other firms

Entrepreneurial SUCCESS

Africa's New Role in Socially-Responsible Production

From boots to chocolate bars, Africa is attracting socially-responsible manufacturing firms that want to make good use of the continent's abundance of raw materials. Tal Dehtiar started Oliberte with the goal of bringing good-paying jobs to Africa while selling high-quality fashion shoes in the world marketplace. Rather than build facilities from scratch, he partnered with local leather suppliers and small factories in Ethiopia, Liberia, and Kenya. Although output is relatively low—the company makes and sells about 18,000 pairs of shoes per year—it is steadily increasing production capacity and expanding distribution as the Oliberte brand becomes better known.

Madecasse Chocolate, founded by former Peace Corps volunteers Tim McCollum and Brett Beach, transforms locally-grown cocoa beans into premium chocolate bars for export from the company's base in Madagascar. The entrepreneurs began by contracting with farming cooperatives that grow top-quality cocoa. Next, they figured out how to transport a ton of cocoa beans to a contract manufacturing plant downriver, where the beans are roasted and turned into chocolate bars. Finally, they arranged for stores like Whole Foods Market to sell the chocolate bars. With annual sales topping $2 million, Madecasse Chocolate is about to expand its storage facilities to prepare for future growth.

Sources: Based on information in Peter Wonacott, "Small Factories Take Root in Africa," *Wall Street Journal*, September 24, 2011, www.wsj.com; Lisa Desai and Sarah Gross, "Shoe Company Hopes to Kick-Start Manufacturing in Africa," *CNN*, February 1, 2011, www.cnn.com; Barry Silverstein, "Madecasse, Rich," *Brand Channel*, March 17, 2010, www.brandchannel.com; and telephone interview with Tim McCollum, Madecasse Chocolate, May 4, 2012.

such as strikes and equipment breakdowns can cut off the flow of purchased materials from a primary supplier at any time.

The choice of suppliers should result from careful analysis of a number of factors. The following are especially critical:

- *Price*. Comparing prices offered by different suppliers is always an essential part of selecting a supplier.
- *Quality*. Purchasing specialists always try to buy materials at a level of quality in keeping with the type of product being manufactured. The lowest acceptable quality is usually specified by product designers.
- *Reliability*. An agreement to purchase high-quality materials at a low price is the purchaser's dream. However, the dream becomes a nightmare if the supplier does not deliver.
- *Credit terms*. Purchasing specialists should determine if the supplier demands immediate payment or will extend credit.
- *Shipping costs*. The question of who pays the shipping costs should be answered before any supplier is chosen.

Inventory Control

Can you imagine what would happen if a Coca-Cola manufacturing plant ran out of the company's familiar red-and-white aluminum cans? It would be impossible to complete the manufacturing process and ship the cases of Coke to retailers. Management would be forced to shut the assembly line down until the next shipment of cans arrived from a supplier. The simple fact is that shutdowns are expensive because costs such as wages, rent, utilities, insurance, and other expenses still must be covered.

Operations managers are concerned with three types of inventories. A *raw-materials inventory* consists of materials that will become part of the product during the production process. The *work-in-process inventory* consists of partially completed products. The *finished-goods inventory* consists of completed goods. Each type of inventory also has a *holding cost*, or storage cost, and a *stock-out cost*, the cost of running out of inventory. **Inventory control** is the process of managing inventories in such a way as to minimize inventory costs, including both holding costs and potential stock-out costs.

inventory control the process of managing inventories in such a way as to minimize inventory costs, including both holding costs and potential stock-out costs

Today, computer systems are being used to keep track of inventories and alert managers to impending stock-outs. One of the most sophisticated methods of inventory control used today is materials requirements planning. **Materials requirements planning (MRP)** is a computerized system that integrates production planning and inventory control. One of the great advantages of an MRP system is its ability to juggle delivery schedules and lead times effectively. For a complex product such as an automobile with 4,000 or more individual parts, it is virtually impossible for individual managers to oversee the hundreds of parts that go into the finished product. However, a manager using an MRP system can arrange both order and delivery schedules so that materials, parts, and supplies arrive when they are needed.

Today a popular extension of MRP is known as *enterprise resource planning (ERP)*. The primary difference between ERP and MRP is that ERP software is more sophisticated and can monitor not only inventory and production processes but also quality, sales, and even such variables as inventory at a supplier's location.

Because large firms can incur huge inventory costs, much attention has been devoted to inventory control. The just-in-time system being used by some businesses is one result of all this attention. A **just-in-time inventory system** is designed to ensure that materials or supplies arrive at a facility just when they are needed so that storage and holding costs are minimized. The customer must specify what will be needed, when, and in what amounts. The supplier must be sure that the right supplies arrive at the agreed-upon time and location. For example, managers using a just-in-time inventory system at a Toyota assembly plant determine the number of automobiles that will be assembled in a specified time period. Then Toyota purchasing personnel order just the parts needed to produce those automobiles. In turn, suppliers deliver the parts in time or when they are needed on the assembly line.

Without proper inventory control, it is impossible for operations managers to schedule the work required to produce goods that can be sold to customers.

Tracking inventory can be a tedious, but necessary chore. For a wholesaler or retailer, running out of inventory means a business has nothing to sell. For a manufacturer, no inventory can lead to shutting down a production facility and no finished products. In either case, no inventory equals no sales and can lead to no profits.

Scheduling

Scheduling is the process of ensuring that materials and other resources are at the right place at the right time. The materials and resources may be moved from a warehouse to the workstations, they may move from station to station along an assembly line, or they may arrive at workstations "just in time" to be made part of the work-in-process there.

As our definition implies, both place and time are important to scheduling. The *routing* of materials is the sequence of workstations that the materials will follow. Assume that Drexel-Heritage—one of America's largest and oldest furniture manufacturers—is scheduling production of an oval coffee table made from cherry wood. Operations managers route the needed materials (wood, screws, packaging materials, etc.) through a series of individual workstations along an assembly line. At each workstation, a specific task is performed, and then the partially finished coffee table moves to the next workstation. When routing materials, operations managers are especially concerned with the sequence of each step of the production process. For the coffee table, the top and legs must be cut to specifications before the wood is finished. (If the wood were finished before being cut, the finish would be ruined, and the coffee table would have to be stained again.)

When scheduling production, managers also are concerned with timing. The *timing* function specifies when the materials will arrive at each station and how long they will remain there. For the cherry coffee table, it may take workers 30 minutes to cut the table top and legs and another 30 minutes to drill the holes and assemble the table. Before packaging the coffee table for shipment, it must be finished with cherry stain

materials requirements planning (MRP) a computerized system that integrates production planning and inventory control

just-in-time inventory system a system designed to ensure that materials or supplies arrive at a facility just when they are needed so that storage and holding costs are minimized

scheduling the process of ensuring that materials and other resources are at the right place at the right time

and allowed to dry. This last step may take as long as three days depending on weather conditions and humidity.

Regardless of whether the finished product requires a simple or complex production process, operations managers are responsible for monitoring schedules—called *follow-up*—to ensure that the work flows according to a timetable. For some products, operations managers often prefer to use Gantt charts or the PERT technique to schedule production activities.

Scheduling Through Gantt Charts Developed by Henry L. Gantt, a **Gantt chart** is a graphic scheduling device that displays the tasks to be performed on the vertical axis and the time required for each task on the horizontal axis. Gantt charts do the following:

- Allow you to determine how long a project should take.
- Lay out the order in which tasks need to be completed.
- Determine the resources needed.
- Monitor progress of different activities required to complete the project.

A Gantt chart that describes the activities required to build three dozen golf carts is illustrated in Figure 8.6. Gantt charts usually are not suitable for scheduling extremely complex situations. Nevertheless, using them forces a manager to plan the steps required to get a job done and to specify time requirements for each part of the job.

Gantt chart a graphic scheduling device that displays the tasks to be performed on the vertical axis and the time required for each task on the horizontal axis

PERT (Program Evaluation and Review Technique) a scheduling technique that identifies the major activities necessary to complete a project and sequences them based on the time required to perform each one

Scheduling via PERT A technique for scheduling a complex project and maintaining control of the schedule is **PERT (Program Evaluation and Review Technique)**. To use PERT, you begin by identifying all the major *activities* involved in the project. For example, the activities involved in producing your textbook are illustrated in Figure 8.7.

All events are arranged in a sequence. In doing so, we must be sure that an event that must occur before another event in the actual process also occurs before that event on the PERT chart. The manuscript, for example, must be edited before the type is set. Next, we use arrows to connect events that must occur in sequence. We then estimate the time required for each activity and mark it near the corresponding arrow. The

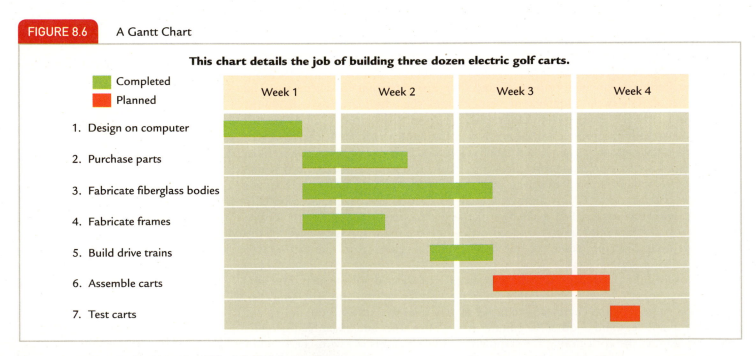

FIGURE 8.6   A Gantt Chart

This chart details the job of building three dozen electric golf carts.

	Week 1	Week 2	Week 3	Week 4
1. Design on computer	Completed			
2. Purchase parts	Completed			
3. Fabricate fiberglass bodies	Completed			
4. Fabricate frames	Completed			
5. Build drive trains		Completed		
6. Assemble carts			Planned	
7. Test carts				Planned

Legend: ▮ Completed   ▮ Planned

Source: From Kreitner/Cassidy, *Management*, 12th ed. © 2013 Cengage Learning.

FIGURE 8.7   Simplified PERT Diagram for Producing This Book

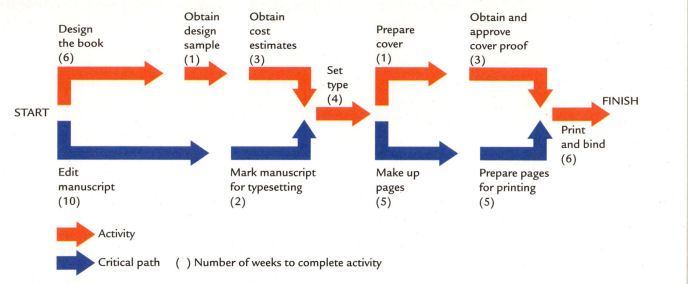

A PERT diagram identifies the activities necessary to complete a given project and arranges the activities based on the total time required for each to become an event. The activities on the critical path determine the minimum time required.

sequence of production activities that take the longest time from start to finish is called the *critical path*. The activities on this path determine the minimum time in which the process can be completed. These activities are the ones that must be scheduled and controlled carefully. A delay in any one of them will cause a delay in completion of the project as a whole.

Quality Control

Over the years, more and more managers have realized that quality is an essential "ingredient" of the good or service being produced. This view of quality provides several benefits. The number of defects decreases, which causes profits to increase. Furthermore, making products or completing services right the first time reduces many of the rejects and much of the rework.

As mentioned earlier in this chapter, American business firms that compete in the very competitive global marketplace have taken another look at the importance of improving quality. Today, there is even a national quality award. The **Malcolm Baldrige National Quality Award** is given by the President of the United States to organizations judged to be outstanding in specific managerial tasks that lead to improved quality for both products and services. Past winners include Ritz-Carlton Hotels, Boeing Aerospace, Motorola, Nestlé Purina Petcare, Cargill Corn Milling North America, and Richland Community College (part of the Dallas Community College District), among many others. For many organizations, using the Baldrige criteria results in

- better employee relations,
- higher productivity,
- greater customer satisfaction,
- increased market share, and
- improved profitability.[18]

All Baldrige winners have one factor in common: They use quality control to improve their firm's products or services.

Malcolm Baldrige National Quality Award an award given by the President of the United States to organizations judged to be outstanding in specific managerial tasks that lead to improved quality for both products and services

Quality matters! In this photo, an employee inspects a custom-made shoe to make sure small details like the quality of leather and stitching meet the company's design specifications. Products that are not within design specifications and don't pass inspection are removed from production.

Quality control is the process of ensuring that goods and services are produced in accordance with design specifications. The major objective of quality control is to see that the organization lives up to the standards it has set for itself on quality. Some firms, such as Mercedes-Benz, have built their reputations on quality. Other firms adopt a strategy of emphasizing lower prices along with reasonable (but not particularly high) quality. Today, many firms use the techniques described in Table 8.1 to gather information and statistics that can be used to improve the quality of a firm's products or services.

Although the techniques described in Table 8.1 can provide information and statistics, it is people who must act on the information and make changes to improve the production process. And the firm's employees are often the most important component needed to improve quality.

Improving Quality Through Employee Participation One of the first steps needed to improve quality is employee participation. Simply put: Successful firms encourage employees to accept full responsibility for the quality of their work. When Toyota, once the role model for world-class manufacturing, faced a quality crisis, the company announced a quality-improvement plan based on its famous "Toyota Way." One tenet of the Toyota Way is the need to solve problems at their source, which allows factory workers to stop the production line if necessary to address a problem. Another tenet that enabled Toyota to resolve quality problems was the use of quality circles designated to deal with difficulties as they arise. A **quality circle** is a team of employees who meet on company time to solve problems of product quality. This level of employee participation allowed Toyota to correct the problems and improve the firm's automobiles. Today, Toyota is once again recognized as one of the most reliable automobile brands. Quality circles have also been used successfully in companies such as IBM, Northrop Grumman Corporation, Lockheed Martin, and GE.

Increased effort is also being devoted to **inspection,** which is the examination of the quality of work-in-process. Employees perform inspections at various times during production. Purchased materials may be inspected when they arrive at the production facility. Subassemblies and manufactured parts may be inspected before they become part of a finished product. In addition, finished goods may be inspected before they are shipped to customers. Items that are within design specifications continue on their way. Those that are not within design specifications are removed from production.

Total quality management (TQM) can also be used to improve quality of a firm's products or services. As noted in Chapter 6, a TQM program coordinates the efforts directed at improving customer satisfaction, increasing employee participation, strengthening supplier partnerships, and facilitating an organizational atmosphere of continuous quality improvement. Firms such as American Express, AT&T, Motorola,

quality control the process of ensuring that goods and services are produced in accordance with design specifications

quality circle a team of employees who meet on company time to solve problems of product quality

inspection the examination of the quality of work-in-process

TABLE 8.1	Four widely used techniques to improve the quality of a firm's products.
Technique	**Description**
Benchmarking	A process of comparing the way a firm produces products or services to the methods used by organizations known to be leaders in an industry in order to determine the "best practices" that can be used to improve quality.
Continuous Improvement	Continuous improvement is a never-ending effort to eliminate problems and improve quality. Often this method involves many small changes or steps designed to improve the production process on an ongoing basis.
Statistical Process Control (SPC)	Sampling to obtain data that are plotted on control charts and graphs to see if the production process is operating as it should and to pinpoint problem areas.
Statistical Quality Control (SQC)	A detailed set of specific statistical techniques used to monitor all aspects of the production process to ensure that both work-in-process and finished products meet the firm's quality standards.

and Hewlett-Packard all have used TQM to improve product quality and, ultimately, customer satisfaction.

Another technique that businesses may use to improve not only quality but also overall performance is Six Sigma. **Six Sigma** is a disciplined approach that relies on statistical data and improved methods to eliminate defects for a firm's products and services. Although many experts agree that Six Sigma is similar to TQM, Six Sigma often has more top-level support, much more teamwork, and a new corporate attitude or culture. The companies that developed, refined, and have the most experience with Six Sigma are Motorola, GE, and Honeywell. Although each of these companies is a corporate giant, the underlying principles of Six Sigma can be used by any firm, regardless of size.[19]

World Quality Standards: ISO 9000 and ISO 14000

Without a common standard of quality, customers may be at the mercy of manufacturers and vendors. As the number of companies competing in the global marketplace has increased, so has the seriousness of this problem. To deal with the problem of standardization, the International Organization for Standardization, a nongovernmental organization with headquarters in Geneva, Switzerland, was created. The **International Organization for Standardization (ISO)** is a network of national standards institutes and similar organizations from over 160 different countries that is charged with developing standards for quality products and services that are traded throughout the globe. According to the organization,

> *ISO's work makes a positive difference to the world we live in. ISO standards add value to all types of business operations. They contribute to making the development, manufacturing and supply of products and services more efficient, safer and cleaner. They make trade between countries easier and fairer. ISO standards also serve to safeguard consumers and users of products and services in general, as well as making their lives simpler.*[20]

Standardization is achieved through consensus agreements between national delegations representing all the economic stakeholders—suppliers, customers, and often governments. The member organization for the United States is the American National Standards Institute located in Washington, D.C.

In 1987, the panel published ISO 9000 (*iso* is Greek for "equal"), which sets the guidelines for quality management procedures that manufacturers and service providers must use to receive certification. Certification by independent auditors and laboratory testing services serves as evidence that a company meets the standards for quality control procedures in design, production processes, and product testing.

Although certification is not a legal requirement to conduct business globally, the organization's member countries have approved the ISO standards. In fact, ISO standards are so prevalent around the globe that many customers refuse to do business with noncertified companies. As an added bonus, companies completing the certification process often discover new, cost-efficient ways to improve their existing quality-control programs.

As a continuation of this standardization process, the International Organization for Standardization has developed ISO 14000. ISO 14000 is a family of international standards for incorporating environmental concerns into operations and product standards. Both the ISO 9000 and ISO 14000 family of standards are updated periodically. For example, ISO 9001:2008 includes important clarifications and addresses issues of compatibility with ISO's other quality standards.

Personal APPS

©TYLER OLSON/SHUTTERSTOCK

You don't want to buy a shoddy product, and any company you work for doesn't want to gain a reputation for poor quality. That's why strict quality control is so important.

Six Sigma a disciplined approach that relies on statistical data and improved methods to eliminate defects for a firm's products and services

International Organization for Standardization (ISO) a network of national standards institutes and similar organizations from over 160 different countries that is charged with developing standards for quality products and services that are traded throughout the globe

Summarize how technology can make American firms more productive and competitive in the global marketplace.

7

IMPROVING PRODUCTIVITY WITH TECHNOLOGY

No coverage of operations management would be complete without a discussion of productivity and technology. Productivity concerns all managers, but it is especially important to operations managers, the people who must oversee the creation of a firm's goods or services. In Chapter 1, *productivity* was defined as the average level of output per worker per hour. Hence, if each worker at plant A produces 75 units per day and each worker at plant B produces only 70 units per day, the workers at plant A are more productive. If one bank teller serves 25 customers per hour and another serves 28 per hour, the second teller is more productive.

Productivity Trends

For U.S. businesses, overall productivity growth for output per hour averaged 4.1 percent for the period 1979–2010.[21] More specifically, 2010 output per hour for U.S. firms increased 5.8 percent.[22] (*Note:* At the time of publication, 2010 was the last year that complete statistics were available.) While the 5.8 increase in output per hour in 2010 was impressive when compared with our average productivity growth, 12 other nations that the U.S. Bureau Labor Statistics tracks each year had larger growth in productivity than the United States—as illustrated in Figure 8.8.[23]

Improving Productivity Growth

In an effort to improve productivity, an increasingly large number of business firms are adopting the concept of lean manufacturing. **Lean manufacturing** is a concept built on the idea of eliminating waste from all of the activities required to produce a product or service. Benefits of lean manufacturing include a reduction in the amount of resources required to produce a product or service, more efficient use of employee time, improved quality, and increased profits. In addition to lean manufacturing, several other factors must be considered if U.S. firms are going to increase productivity *and* their ability to compete in the global marketplace. For example:

- The United States must stabilize its economy so that firms will invest more money in new facilities, equipment, technology and employee training.

lean manufacturing a concept built on the idea of eliminating waste from all of the activities required to produce a product or service

FIGURE 8.8   Productivity Growth Rates

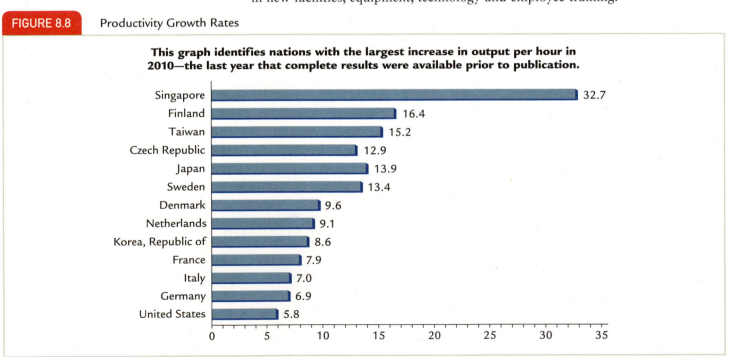

This graph identifies nations with the largest increase in output per hour in 2010—the last year that complete results were available prior to publication.

Singapore	32.7
Finland	16.4
Taiwan	15.2
Czech Republic	12.9
Japan	13.9
Sweden	13.4
Denmark	9.6
Netherlands	9.1
Korea, Republic of	8.6
France	7.9
Italy	7.0
Germany	6.9
United States	5.8

Source: Based on information in "International Comparisons of Manufacturing Productivity and Unit Labor Cost Trends News Release," The Bureau of Labor Statistics Web site at www.bls.gov (accessed October 13, 2011).

- Business firms must cooperate with employees to increase employee motivation and participation in the workplace.
- All government policies must be examined to ensure that unreasonable regulations that may be hindering productivity growth are eliminated.
- Successful techniques that have been used in manufacturing firms must be used to increase productivity in the service industry.
- Increased use of automation, robotics, and computer manufacturing systems must be used to lower production costs.
- There must be more emphasis on satisfying the customer's needs with quality goods and services.

Finally, innovation and research and development efforts to create new products and services must be increased in order for U.S. firms to compete in the global marketplace.

The Impact of Automation, Robotics, and Computers on Productivity

Automation is the total or near-total use of machines to do work. The rapid increase in automated procedures has been made possible by the microprocessor, a silicon chip that led to the production of desktop computers for businesses, homes, and schools. In factories, microprocessors are used in robotics and in computer manufacturing systems.

Robotics Robotics is the use of programmable machines to perform a variety of tasks by manipulating materials and tools. Robots work quickly, accurately, and steadily. For example, Illumina, Inc., a San Diego company, sells robotic equipment that performs medical laboratory tests. Available information then is sold to some of the world's largest pharmaceutical companies where it is used to alter existing prescription drugs, develop new drug therapies, and customize treatments for all kinds of serious diseases. As an added bonus, Illumina's robotic equipment can work 24 hours a day at much lower costs than if human lab workers performed the same tests.[24]

Robots are especially effective in tedious, repetitive assembly-line jobs, as well as in handling hazardous materials. Lincoln Electric, for example, provides robotic arc welders that eliminate the hot, dirty job of welding, which is key to many manufacturing tasks. As an added bonus, robotic arc welders are often quicker and are more precise than old-fashioned welding machines. Robots are also useful as artificial "eyes" that can check the quality of products as they are being processed on assembly lines. To date, the automotive industry has made the most extensive use of robotics, but robots also have been used to mine coal, inspect the inner surfaces of pipes, assemble computer components, provide certain kinds of patient care in hospitals, and clean and guard buildings at night.

Computer Manufacturing Systems People are quick to point out how computers have changed their everyday lives, but most people do not realize the impact computers have had on manufacturing. In simple terms, the factory of the future has already arrived. For most manufacturers, the changeover began with the use of computer-aided design and computer-aided manufacturing. **Computer-aided design (CAD)** is the use of computers to aid in the development of products. Ford speeds up car design, Canon designs new photocopiers, and American Greetings creates new birthday cards by using CAD.

Computer-aided manufacturing (CAM) is the use of computers to plan and control manufacturing processes. A well-designed

automation the total or near-total use of machines to do work

robotics the use of programmable machines to perform a variety of tasks by manipulating materials and tools

computer-aided design (CAD) the use of computers to aid in the development of products

computer-aided manufacturing (CAM) the use of computers to plan and control manufacturing processes

©NATALIYA HORA/SHUTTERSTOCK

Robotics can be a manufacturer's best friend. One of the first industries to use robotics to increase the number of products produced and improve employee productivity was the automobile industry. In this photo, robotics are used to move the right side of a sport utility vehicle (SUV) from one workstation on an assembly line to the next station.

CAM system allows manufacturers to become much more productive. Not only are a greater number of products produced, but speed and quality also increase. Using CAM systems, Toyota produces automobiles, Hasbro manufactures toys, and Apple Computer creates electronic products.

If you are thinking that the next logical step is to combine the CAD and CAM computer systems, you are right. Today, the most successful manufacturers use CAD and CAM together to form a computer-integrated manufacturing system. Specifically, **computer-integrated manufacturing (CIM)** is a computer system that not only helps to design products but also controls the machinery needed to produce the finished product. For example, Fifth & Pacific Companies (formerly Liz Claiborne), uses CIM to design clothing, to establish patterns for new fashions, and then to cut the cloth needed to produce the finished product. Other advantages of using CIM include improved flexibility, more efficient scheduling, and higher product quality—all factors that make a production facility more competitive in today's global economy.

Flexible Manufacturing Systems Manufacturers have known for a number of years that the mass-production and traditional assembly lines used to manufacture products present a number of problems. For example, although traditional assembly lines turn out extremely large numbers of identical products economically, the system requires expensive, time-consuming retooling of equipment whenever a new product is to be manufactured. This type of manufacturing is often referred to as a continuous process. **Continuous process** is a manufacturing process in which a firm produces the same product(s) over a long period of time. Now it is possible to use flexible manufacturing systems to solve such problems. A **flexible manufacturing system (FMS)** combines electronic machines and computer-integrated manufacturing in a single production system. Instead of having to spend large amounts of time and effort to retool the traditional mechanical equipment on an assembly line for each new product, an FMS is rearranged simply by reprogramming electronic machines. Because FMSs require less time and expense to reprogram than traditional systems, manufacturers can produce smaller batches of a variety of products without raising the production cost. Flexible manufacturing is sometimes referred to as an intermittent process. An **intermittent process** is a manufacturing process in which a firm's manufacturing machines and equipment are changed to produce different products.

For most manufacturers, the driving force behind FMSs is the customer. In fact, the term *customer-driven production* is often used to describe a manufacturing system that is driven by customer needs and what customers want to buy. For example, advanced software and a flexible manufacturing system have enabled Dell Computer to change to a more customer-driven manufacturing process. The process starts when a customer phones a sales representative on a toll-free line or accesses Dell's Web site. Then the representative or the customer enters the specifications for the new product directly into a computer. The order then is sent to a nearby plant. Once the order is received, a team of employees, with the help of a reprogrammable assembly line, can build the product just the way the customer wants it. Products include desktop computers, notebook computers, and other Dell equipment. [25] Although the costs of designing and installing an FMS such as this are high, the electronic equipment is used more frequently and efficiently than the machinery on a traditional assembly line.

Sustainability and Technological Displacement

In Chapter 1, *sustainability* was defined as meeting the needs of the present without compromising the ability of future generations to meet their own needs. While sustainability affects all aspects of a nation, its people, and the economy, the concept is especially important for manufacturers and service providers. Because of the amount of resources required to produce goods and services, these businesses must conserve

computer-integrated manufacturing (CIM) a computer system that not only helps to design products but also controls the machinery needed to produce the finished product

continuous process a manufacturing process in which a firm produces the same product(s) over a long period of time

flexible manufacturing system (FMS) a single production system that combines electronic machines and computer-integrated manufacturing

intermittent process a manufacturing process in which a firm's manufacturing machines and equipment are changed to produce different products

resources whenever possible. As an added bonus, efforts to reduce waste and sustain the planet can often improve a firm's bottom-line profit amount.

In the future, most experts agree that, because U.S. manufacturers will continue to innovate, workers who have manufacturing jobs will be highly skilled and can work with the automated and computer-assisted manufacturing systems. Those that don't possess high-tech skills will be dispensable and unemployed. Many workers will be faced with the choice of retraining for new jobs or seeking jobs in other sectors of the economy. Government, business, and education will have to cooperate to prepare workers for new roles in an automated workplace.

The next chapter discusses many of the issues caused by technological displacement. In addition, a number of major components of human resources management are described, and we see how managers use various reward systems to boost motivation, productivity, and morale.

return to Inside BUSINESS

Unilever

Store shelves all over the world are packed with foods, skin-care products, household cleaners, and other consumer products made by Unilever. In fact, more than two billion consumers in 190 countries use a Unilever product every day. Over the years, the company has been awarded 20,000 patents to protect product innovations resulting from research conducted at its centers in Asia, Europe, and the Americas. Scientists, chemists, nutritionists, and other specialists work closely with market researchers, quality assurance experts, and safety professionals to create and refine new products and meet the everyday needs of consumers in the countries where Unilever does business.

Unilever has set goals for minimizing the environmental impact of its products at all stages, from sourcing raw materials to the production process to packaging and beyond. For example, as one of the world's largest buyers of tea leaves, Unilever recognizes that if it can encourage customers to compost used teabags, they will keep thousands of tons of waste out of landfills and make the planet greener for future generations.

Questions

1. How do the concepts of focus, magnitude of change, and number of production processes, describe the way Unilever produces products?

2. Why would a large multinational company like Unilever with established products that consumers purchase on a regular basis continue to invest money in research and development?

SUMMARY

Looking for Success?
Get Flashcards, Quizzes, Games, Crosswods, and more @ www.cengagebrain.com.

 Explain the nature of production.

Operations management consists of all the activities that managers engage in to create goods and services. Operations are as relevant to service organizations as to manufacturing firms. Today, U.S. companies are forced to compete in an ever-smaller world to meet the needs of more-demanding customers. As a result, U.S. manufacturers have used innovation to improve productivity. Because of innovation, fewer workers are needed, but those workers who are needed possess the skills to use automation and technology. In an attempt to regain a competitive edge, manufacturers have taken another look at the importance of improving quality and meeting the needs of their customers. They also have used new techniques to motivate employees, reduced costs, used computer-aided and flexible manufacturing systems, improved control procedures, and used green manufacturing. Competing in the global economy is not only profitable but also an essential activity that requires the cooperation of everyone within an organization. A number of career options are available for employees in operations management.

Outline how the conversion process transforms raw materials, labor, and other resources into finished goods or services.

A business transforms resources into goods and services in order to provide utility to customers. Utility is the ability of a good or service to satisfy a human need. Form utility is created by people converting raw materials, finances, and information into finished products. Conversion processes vary in terms of the major resources used to produce goods and services (focus), the degree to which resources are changed (magnitude of change), and the number of production processes that a business uses.

 Understand the importance of service businesses to consumers, other business firms, and the nation's economy.

The application of the basic principles of operations management to the production of services has coincided with the growth and importance of service businesses in the United States. Today 87 percent of American workers are employed in the service industry. In fact, the American economy is now characterized as a service economy. For a service firm, planning often begins with determining who the customer is and what needs the customer has. After customer needs are identified the next step is to develop a plan that will enable the firm to deliver the services that their customers want or need. Although it is often more difficult to measure customer satisfaction, today's successful service firms work hard at providing the services customers want. For example, compared with manufacturers, service firms often listen more carefully to customers and respond more quickly to the market's changing needs.

 Describe how research and development lead to new products and services.

Operations management often begins with product research and development and often referred to as R&D. The results of R&D may be entirely new products or services or extensions and refinements of existing products or services. R&D activities are classified as basic research (aimed at uncovering new knowledge), applied research (discovering new knowledge with some potential use), and development and implementation (using new or existing knowledge to produce goods and services). If a firm sells only one product or provides only one service, when that product or service reaches the end of its life-cycle, the firm will die, too. To stay in business, the firm must, at the very least, find ways to refine or extend the want-satisfying capability of its product or service.

 Discuss the components involved in planning the production process.

Planning for production involves three major phases: design planning, site selection and facilities planning, and operational planning. First, design planning is undertaken to address questions related to the product line, required production capacity, and the use of technology. Then production facilities, human resources, and plant layout must be considered. Operational planning focuses on the use of production facilities and resources. The steps for operational planning include (1) selecting a planning horizon, (2) estimating market demand, (3) comparing market demand with capacity, and (4) adjusting production of products or services to meet demand.

 Explain how purchasing, inventory control, scheduling, and quality control affect production.

The major areas of operations control are purchasing, inventory control, scheduling, and quality control. Purchasing involves selecting suppliers. The choice of suppliers should result from careful analysis of a number of factors, including price, quality, reliability, credit terms, and shipping costs. Inventory control is the management of stocks of raw materials, work-in-process, and finished goods to minimize the total inventory cost. Scheduling ensures that materials and other resources are at the right place at the right time. Both Gantt charts and PERT can be used to improve a firm's ability to schedule the production of products. Quality control guarantees that products and services are produced in accordance with design specifications. The major objective of quality control is to see that the organization lives up to the standards it has set for itself on quality. A number of different activities can be used to improve quality.

 Summarize how technology can make American firms more productive and competitive in the global marketplace.

Productivity is the average level of output per worker per hour. From 1979 to 2010, U.S. productivity growth averaged a 4.1 percent increase. More specifically, productivity in 2010 increased 5.8 percent. Although a 5.8 percent was impressive when compared to our average productivity growth, 12 other nations that the U.S. Bureau of Labor Statistics tracks each year had larger growth in productivity than the United States. Several factors must be considered if U.S. firms are going to increase productivity and their ability to compete in the global marketplace.

Automation, the total or near-total use of machines to do work, has for some years been changing the way work is done in factories. A growing number of industries are using programmable machines called robots. Computer-aided design, computer-aided manufacturing, and computer-integrated manufacturing use computers to help design and manufacture products. FMS combines electronic machines and computer-integrated manufacturing to produce smaller batches of products more efficiently than on the traditional assembly line. Instead of having to spend vast amounts of time and effort to retool the traditional mechanical equipment on an assembly line for each new product, an FMS is rearranged simply by reprogramming electronic machines.

KEY TERMS

You should now be able to define and give an example relevant to each of the following terms:

operations management (213)
reshoring (214)
mass production (215)
analytical process (215)
synthetic process (215)
utility (215)
form utility (215)
service economy (217)
research and
    development (R&D) (219)
design planning (220)
product line (220)

product design (221)
capacity (221)
labor-intensive technology (222)
capital-intensive technology (222)
plant layout (223)
planning horizon (223)
purchasing (225)
inventory control (226)
materials requirements
    planning (MRP) (227)
just-in-time inventory system (227)
scheduling (227)

Gantt chart (228)
PERT (Program Evaluation and
    Review Technique) (228)
Malcolm Baldrige National
    Quality Award (229)
quality control (230)
quality circle (230)
inspection (230)
Six Sigma (231)
International Organization for
    Standardization (ISO) (231)
lean manufacturing (232)

automation (233)
robotics (233)
computer-aided
    design (CAD) (233)
computer-aided manufacturing
    (CAM) (233)
computer-integrated
    manufacturing (CIM) (234)
continuous process (234)
flexible manufacturing
    system (FMS) (234)
intermittent process (234)

REVIEW QUESTIONS

1. List all the activities involved in operations management.
2. What is the difference between an analytical and a synthetic manufacturing process? Give an example of each type of process.
3. In terms of focus, magnitude, and number, characterize the production processes used by a local pizza parlor, a dry-cleaning establishment, and an auto repair shop.
4. Describe how research and development leads to new products and product extension and refinement.
5. What are the major elements of design planning?
6. What factors should be considered when selecting a site for a new manufacturing facility?
7. If you were an operations manager, what would you do if market demand exceeded the production capacity of your manufacturing facility? What action would you take if the production capacity of your manufacturing facility exceeded market demand?

8. Why is selecting a supplier so important?
9. What costs must be balanced and minimized through inventory control?
10. How can materials requirements planning (MRP), enterprise resource planning (ERP), and the just-in-time inventory system help to control inventory and a company's production processes?
11. Explain in what sense scheduling is a *control* function of operations managers.
12. In what ways can employees help to improve the quality of a firm's products?
13. How might productivity be measured in a restaurant? In a department store? In a public school system?
14. How can CIM and FMS help a manufacturer to produce products?

DISCUSSION QUESTIONS

1. Why would Rubbermaid—a successful U.S. company—need to expand and sell its products to customers in foreign countries?
2. What steps have U.S. firms taken to regain a competitive edge in the global marketplace?
3. Do certain kinds of firms need to stress particular areas of operations management? Explain.

4. Is it really necessary for service firms to engage in research and development? In planning for production and operations control?
5. How are the four areas of operations control interrelated?
6. Is operations management relevant to nonbusiness organizations such as colleges and hospitals? Why or why not?

Video Case 8.1   Burton Snowboards' High-Quality Standards

"The people at Burton are a powerful, inspiring, and fun group, and I will miss that," said the former CEO of Vermont's fabled Burton Snowboards upon departure. In fact, the company's nearly 900 employees are some of the many reasons the firm

has grown to be the world's leading snowboard and accessories company. Many are snowboard enthusiasts, not least among them Jake Burton Carpenter, founder and currently interim CEO. Despite his management responsibilities, Jake still rides a

HUMAN RESOURCES MANAGEMENT: AN OVERVIEW

The human resource is not only unique and valuable but also an organization's most important resource. It seems logical that an organization would expend a great deal of effort to acquire and make full use of such a resource. This effort is known as *human resources management*. It also has been called *staffing* and *personnel management*.

Human resources management (HRM) consists of all the activities involved in acquiring, maintaining, and developing an organization's human resources. As the definition implies, HRM begins with acquisition—getting people to work for the organization. The acquisition process can be quite competitive for certain types of qualified employees. Next, steps must be taken to keep these valuable resources. (After all, they are the only business resources that can leave an organization.) Finally, the human resources should be developed to their full capacity.

HRM Activities

Each of the three phases of HRM—acquiring, maintaining, and developing human resources—consists of a number of related activities. Acquisition, for example, includes planning, as well as the various activities that lead to hiring new personnel. Altogether this phase of HRM includes five separate activities:

- *Human resources planning*—determining the firm's future human resources needs
- *Job analysis*—determining the exact nature of the positions
- *Recruiting*—attracting people to apply for positions
- *Selection*—choosing and hiring the most qualified applicants
- *Orientation*—acquainting new employees with the firm

Maintaining human resources consists primarily of encouraging employees to remain with the firm and to work effectively by using a variety of HRM programs, including the following:

- *Employee relations*—increasing employee job satisfaction through satisfaction surveys, employee communication programs, exit interviews, and fair treatment
    - *Compensation*—rewarding employee effort through monetary payments
    - *Benefits*—providing rewards to ensure employee well-being

The development phase of HRM is concerned with improving employees' skills and expanding their capabilities. The two important activities within this phase are:

- *Training and development*—teaching employees new skills, new jobs, and more effective ways of doing their present jobs
- *Performance appraisal*—assessing employees' current and potential performance levels

These activities are discussed in more detail shortly, when we have completed this overview of HRM.

Responsibility for HRM

In general, HRM is a shared responsibility of line managers and staff HRM specialists. In very small organizations, the owner handles all or most HRM activities. As a firm grows in size, a human resources manager is hired to take over staff responsibilities. In firms as large as Disney, HRM activities tend to be very highly specialized. There are separate groups to

human resources management (HRM) all the activities involved in acquiring, maintaining, and developing an organization's human resources

The power of people. Many firms believe their employees are their most important assets. However, unlike other assets such as machinery, capital, and products, employees can pick up and leave an organization. Carefully designing compensation and reward packages can help a firm attract and retain valuable employees.

©MORGAN LANE PHOTOGRAPHY/SHUTTERSTOCK

CULTURAL DIVE...

Today's workforce is made u...
that every employee has si...
white males may believe in c...
it. In Hispanic cultures, peop...
a custom that U.S. businesses...
not make eye contact during...
when, according to his or he...

Because a larger number c...
workforce, the workplace is...
47 percent of the U.S. workfo...
12 and 15 percent of U.S. w...
white-collar jobs than men in...
lege graduates. After the mos...
of employment. Male employ...

Cultural (or workplace...
workforce owing to race, eth...
managers to learn to supervis...
tems. The high proportion of...
on participative parenting by...
place. Today's more educated...
In return for their efforts, the...

Although cultural divers...
opportunity rather than a l...
can provide advantages for...

TABLE 9.1 Advantages of ...
Economic Measure
Cost
Resource acquisition
Marketing edge
Flexibility
Creativity
Problem solving
Bilingual skills

Sources: Taylor H. Cox and Stacy Bla...
1991; Ricky Griffin and Gregory Mo...
(Mason, OH: South-Western/Cenga...

deal with compensation, benefits, training and development, and other staff activities. GE, for example, has many divisions and offices all over the world. Because of the size and complexity of the organization, GE has hundreds of different HR managers to cover different geographic areas and departments within the firm.[2]

Specific HRM activities are assigned to those who are in the best position to perform them. Human resources planning and job analysis usually are done by staff specialists, with input from line managers. Similarly, recruiting and selection are handled by staff experts, although line managers are involved in hiring decisions. Orientation programs are devised by staff specialists and carried out by both staff specialists and line managers. Compensation systems (including benefits) most often are developed and administered by the HRM staff. However, line managers recommend pay increases and promotions. Training and development activities are the joint responsibility of staff and line managers. Performance appraisal is the job of the line manager, although HRM personnel design the firm's appraisal system in many organizations.

Personal APPS

The more skills you develop, the more valuable you are to any employer. Do your own personal skills inventory before you write a résumé or interview for a job. Then you'll be prepared to explain the special skills you can bring to an employer.

HUMAN RESOURCES PLANNING

Human resources planning is the development of strategies to meet a firm's future human resources needs. The starting point is the organization's overall strategic plan. From this, human resources planners can forecast future demand for human resources. Next, the planners must determine whether the needed human resources will be available. Finally, they have to take steps to match supply with demand.

Forecasting Human Resources Demand

Planners should base forecasts of the demand for human resources on as much relevant information as available. The firm's overall strategic plan will provide information about future business ventures, new products, and projected expansions or contractions of specific product lines. Information on past staffing levels, evolving technologies, industry staffing practices, and projected economic trends also can be helpful. Technological advances are creating new opportunities in forecasting and planning for human resources demand. A survey released by Deloitte Consulting found that new technologies such as social media, cloud computing, and analytics have increased the speed of doing business, which increases the importance of international growth and strong leadership in organizations. Firms must hire HR talent that is fluent in using these new technologies in order to take advantage of opportunities and be aware of threats.[3]

HRM managers use this information to determine both the number of employees required and their qualifications. Planners use a wide range of methods to forecast specific personnel needs. For example, with one simple method, personnel requirements are projected to increase or decrease in the same proportion as sales revenue. Thus, if a 30 percent increase in sales volume is projected over the next two years, then up to a 30 percent increase in personnel requirements may be expected for the same period. (This method can be applied to specific positions as well as to the workforce in general. It is not, however, a very precise forecasting method.) At the other extreme are elaborate, computer-based personnel planning models used by some large firms such as ExxonMobil Corporation.

2 Identify the steps in human resources planning.

human resources planning the development of strategies to meet a firm's future human resources needs

Chapter 9 Attracting and Retaini...

Chapter 9 Attracting and Retaining the Best Employees

247

Going for SUCCESS

What Does a Chief Diversity Officer Do?

Hundreds of America's largest corporations have named a chief diversity officer (CDO) to enhance diversity recruiting and training initiatives. But what, exactly, does a CDO do? At Ingersoll Rand, the CDO has implemented a leadership training program for women employees and started internal networking groups for women, military veterans, and African Americans, aiming to increase innovation and support global growth. In addition to training, the CDO of Caesars Entertainment, which runs hotels and casinos, forms "Diverse by Design" teams to tackle difficult challenges. He picks employees from different cultural, geographical, demographic, and professional backgrounds to bring new insights and perspectives to solving each problem.

At Sodexho, the CDO is applying diversity principles to its suppliers as well as to its workforce, so the company can better serve customers in the food and facilities management industry. A Diversity and Inclusion Advisory Board identifies diversity trends that affect Sodexho and represents the company in its communities. American Express's CDO has implemented a series of leadership and mentoring programs to improve diversity at the senior management level. And, like Sodexho, American Express looks beyond its workforce to promote "a supplier base that is reflective of our diverse customer base, employees, and shareholders."

Sources: Based on information in Leslie Kwoh, "Firms Hail New Chiefs (of Diversity)," *Wall Street Journal*, January 5, 2012, http://online.wsj.com/article/SB10001424052970203899504577129261732884578.html; Eric Baca, Mariana Gutierrez Briones, and Jorge Ferraez, "From the Mouths of the Leaders: Conversations with Four Chief Diversity Officers," *Latino Leaders*, December 2011, pp. 24; Todd Henneman, "Making the Pieces Fit," *Workforce Management*, August 1, 2011, p. 12.

✳ replacement chart a list of key personnel and their possib... replacements within a firm

✳ skills inventory a computer... data bank containing informa... on the skills and experience o... present employees

**The demand for labor vers...
supply: A balancing act.** Th... and demand for employees wi... different skills is constantly sh... In some industries, qualified v... are plentiful. In others, they a... hard to find, even when the na... unemployment rate is high.

---

creative management of cultural diversity can offer. A firm that manages diversity properly can develop cost advantages over other firms. Moreover, organizations that manage diversity creatively are in a much better position to attract the best personnel. A culturally diverse organization may gain a marketing edge because it understands different cultural groups. Proper guidance and management of diversity in an organization also can improve the level of creativity. People who embrace cultural diversity frequently are more flexible in the types of positions they will accept and are more comfortable working with culturally diverse co-workers.

Because cultural diversity creates challenges along with advantages, it is important for an organization's employees to understand it. To accomplish this goal, numerous U.S. firms have trained their managers to respect and manage diversity. Diversity training programs may include recruiting minorities, training minorities to be managers, training managers to view diversity positively, teaching English as a second language, and facilitating support groups for immigrants. Many companies are realizing the necessity of having diversity training span beyond just racial issues. For example, companies such as PricewaterhouseCoopers and Sodexo require annual diversity training and use company-sanctioned global employee-resource groups.[8] Companies such as these are continuously expanding their business worldwide and therefore need to meld a cohesive workforce from a labor pool whose demographics are constantly becoming more diverse.

A diversity program will be successful only if it is systematic, is ongoing, and has a strong, sustained commitment from top leadership. Cultural diversity is here to stay. Its impact on organizations is widespread and will continue to grow within corporations. Management must learn to overcome the obstacles and capitalize on the advantages associated with culturally diverse human resources.

Why hiring a diverse group of employees can benefit your business. Organizations that hire diverse types of employees benefit from their different skills and life experiences. The different points of view of these workers can help a firm find new opportunities and ways of doing things. In addition, diverse employees often have a greater understanding of diverse customers and the goods and services they prefer.

JOB ANALYSIS

4 Explain the objectives and uses of job analysis.

There is no sense in hiring people unless we know what we are hiring them for. In other words, we need to know the nature of a job before we can find the right person to do it.

Job analysis is a systematic procedure for studying jobs to determine their various elements and requirements. Consider the position of a clerk, for example. In a large corporation, there may be 50 kinds of clerk positions. They all may be called "clerks," but each position may differ from the others in the activities performed, the level of proficiency required for each activity, and the particular set of qualifications that the position demands. These distinctions are the focus of job analysis. HRTMS is a leader in job description management. The company recently unveiled the Job Description Project, which combines one-on-one consulting, online support, with access to HRTMS programs that help craft job descriptions and ensure that they are in compliance with existing laws and regulations.[9]

The job analysis for a particular position typically consists of two parts—a job description and a job specification. A **job description** is a list of the elements that make up a particular job. It includes the duties to be performed, the working conditions, the responsibilities, and the tools and equipment that must be used on the job (see Figure 9.1).

A **job specification** is a list of the qualifications required to perform a particular job, such as certain skills, abilities, education, and experience. When attempting to hire a financial analyst, the Bank of America might use the following job specification: "Requires eight to ten years of financial experience, a broad-based financial background, strong customer focus, the ability to work confidently with the client's management team, strong analytical skills. Must have strong Excel and Word skills. Personal characteristics should include strong desire to succeed, impact performer

job analysis a systematic procedure for studying jobs to determine their various elements and requirements

job description a list of the elements that make up a particular job

job specification a list of the qualifications required to perform a particular job

---

FIGURE 9.1 Job Description and Job Specification

This job description explains the job of sales coordinator and lists the responsibilities of the position. The job specification is contained in the last paragraph.

> SOUTH-WESTERN
> JOB DESCRIPTION
>
> | | | | |
> |---|---|---|---|
> | **TITLE:** | Georgia Sales Coordinator | **DATE:** | 3/26/12 |
> | **DEPARTMENT:** | College, Sales | **GRADE:** | 12 |
> | **REPORTS TO:** | Regional Manager | **EXEMPT/NONEXEMPT:** | Exempt |
>
> **BRIEF SUMMARY:**
> Supervise one other Georgia-based sales representative to gain supervisory experience. Captain the four members of the outside sales rep team that are assigned to territories consisting of colleges and universities in Georgia. Oversee, coordinate, advise, and make decisions regarding Georgia sales activities. Based upon broad contact with customers across the state and communication with administrators of schools, the person will make recommendations regarding issues specific to the needs of higher education in the state of Georgia such as distance learning, conversion to the semester system, potential statewide adoptions, and faculty training.
>
> **PRINCIPAL ACCOUNTABILITIES:**
> 1. Supervises/manages/trains one other Atlanta-based sales rep.
> 2. Advises two other sales reps regarding the Georgia schools in their territories.
> 3. Increases overall sales in Georgia as well as his or her individual sales territory.
> 4. Assists regional manager in planning and coordinating regional meetings and Atlanta conferences.
> 5. Initiates a dialogue with campus administrators, particularly in the areas of the semester conversion, distance learning, and faculty development.
>
> **DIMENSIONS:**
> This position will have one direct report in addition to the leadership role played within the region. Revenue most directly impacted will be within the individually assigned territory, the supervised territory, and the overall sales for the state of Georgia.
>
> **KNOWLEDGE AND SKILLS:**
> Must have displayed a history of consistently outstanding sales in personal territory. Must demonstrate clear teamwork and leadership skills and be willing to extend beyond the individual territory goals. Should have a clear understanding of the company's systems and product offerings in order to train and lead other sales representatives. Must have the communication skills and presence to communicate articulately with higher education administrators and to serve as a bridge between the company and higher education in the state.

(individually and as a member of a team), positive attitude, high energy level and ability to influence others."

The job analysis is not only the basis for recruiting and selecting new employees; it is also used in other areas of HRM, including evaluation and the determination of equitable compensation levels.

Describe the processes of recruiting, employee selection, and orientation.

RECRUITING, SELECTION, AND ORIENTATION

In an organization with jobs waiting to be filled, HRM personnel need to (1) find candidates for the jobs and (2) match the right candidate with each job. Three activities are involved: recruiting, selection, and new employee orientation.

Recruiting

Recruiting is the process of attracting qualified job applicants. Because it is a vital link in a costly process (the cost of hiring an employee can be several thousand dollars), recruiting needs to be a systematic process. One goal of recruiters is to attract the "right number" of applicants. The right number is enough to allow a good match between applicants and open positions but not so many that matching them requires too much time and effort. For example, if there are five open positions and five applicants, the firm essentially has no choice. It must hire those five applicants (qualified or not), or the positions will remain open. At the other extreme, if several hundred job seekers apply for the five positions, HRM personnel will have to spend weeks processing their applications.

Recruiters may seek applicants outside the firm, within the firm, or both. The source used depends on the nature of the position, the situation within the firm, and sometimes the firm's established or traditional recruitment policies.

External Recruiting **External recruiting** is the attempt to attract job applicants from outside an organization. External recruiting may include recruiting via newspaper advertising, employment agencies, and online employment organizations; recruiting on college campuses; soliciting recommendations from present employees; and conducting "open houses." Increasingly, people utilize the Internet to conduct their job searches. Social networking sites like LinkedIn or TweetMyJobs help match employers with interested potential employees. Online job search sites, like Monster.com or MediaBistro, help job seekers search for jobs by a variety of criteria like location and industry.[10]

* **recruiting** the process of attracting qualified job applicants

* **external recruiting** the attempt to attract job applicants from outside an organization

Clearly, it is best to match the recruiting means with the kind of applicant being sought. Technology is helping organizations with this matching process. TweetMyJobs, a more recent addition to the social networking HRM arsenal, is a new means of matching job seekers with available positions. It is a service that alerts people via Twitter when a job opens up for which they are qualified. Web sites like LinkedIn allow employees to post their résumés, skills, and experiences; and employers can search for qualified employees. Technologies like these allow employers and employees to more easily locate positions that are a good fit.[11]

External recruiting has both advantages and disadvantages. A primary advantage of external recruiting is that it brings in people with new perspectives and varied business backgrounds. Some firms prefer to hire recruits directly out of college because they believe that these candidates will be more trainable to fit with the corporate culture and the needs of the company. An additional benefit of hiring younger talent is that they tend to be more technologically savvy than their older counterparts, a characteristic that is highly desirable in today's fast-moving workplace. A disadvantage

©FENG YU/SHUTTERSTOCK

Don't just search the classified ads to find a job. Potential employees are being recruited in increasingly different ways today. Companies often keep statistics on their recruiting sources so they can determine which methods are the best for finding good employees.

of external recruiting is that it is often expensive, especially if private employment agencies must be used. External recruiting also may provoke resentment among present employees.

Internal Recruiting **Internal recruiting** means considering present employees as applicants for available positions. Generally, current employees are considered for *promotion* to higher-level positions. However, employees may be considered for *transfer* from one position to another at the same level. Among leading companies, 85 percent of CEOs are promoted from within. In the companies that hire CEOs from outside, 60 to 80 percent of the CEOs are gone after 18 months.[12]

Promoting from within provides strong motivation for current employees and helps the firm to retain quality personnel. General Electric and ExxonMobil are companies dedicated to promoting from within. The practice of *job posting*, or informing current employees of upcoming openings, may be a company policy or required by union contract. The primary disadvantage of internal recruiting is that promoting a current employee leaves another position to be filled. Not only does the firm still incur recruiting and selection costs, but it also must train two employees instead of one.

In many situations it may be impossible to recruit internally. For example, a new position may be such that no current employee is qualified, or the firm may be growing so rapidly that there is no time to reassign positions that promotion or transfer requires.

Selection

Selection is the process of gathering information about applicants for a position and then using that information to choose the most appropriate applicant. Note the use of the word *appropriate*. In selection, the idea is not to hire the person with the *most* qualifications but rather the applicant who is *most appropriate*. The selection of an applicant is made by line managers responsible for the position. However, HRM personnel usually help by developing a pool of applicants and by expediting the assessment of these applicants. Common means of obtaining information about applicants' qualifications are employment applications, interviews, references, and assessment centers.

Employment Applications An employment application is useful in collecting factual information on a candidate's education, work experience, and personal history (see Figure 9.2). The data obtained from applications usually are used for two purposes: to identify applicants who are worthy of further scrutiny and to familiarize interviewers with their backgrounds. Many firms offer online applications, which help to streamline the process and improve data gathering capabilities for the firm. In fact, paper applications are becoming increasingly rare.

Many job candidates submit résumés, and some firms require them. A *résumé* is a one- or two-page summary of the candidate's background and qualifications. It may include a description of the type of job the applicant is seeking. A résumé may be sent to a firm to request consideration for available jobs, or it may be submitted along with an employment application.

To improve the usefulness of information, HRM specialists ask current employees about factors in their backgrounds most related to their current jobs. Then these factors are included on the applications and may be weighted more heavily when evaluating new applicants' qualifications.

Employment Tests Tests administered to job candidates usually focus on aptitudes, skills, abilities, or knowledge relevant to the job. Such tests (basic computer skills tests, for example) indicate how well the applicant will do the job. Occasionally, companies use general intelligence or personality tests, but these are seldom helpful in predicting specific job performance. Many organizations, from the very small up to *Fortune 500* companies, use predictive behavior tests. Improved technology has brought down substantially the costs of administering such tests.

internal recruiting considering present employees as applicants for available positions

selection the process of gathering information about applicants for a position and then using that information to choose the most appropriate applicant

FIGURE 9.2 Typical Employment Application

Employers use applications to collect factual information on a candidate's education, work experience, and personal history.

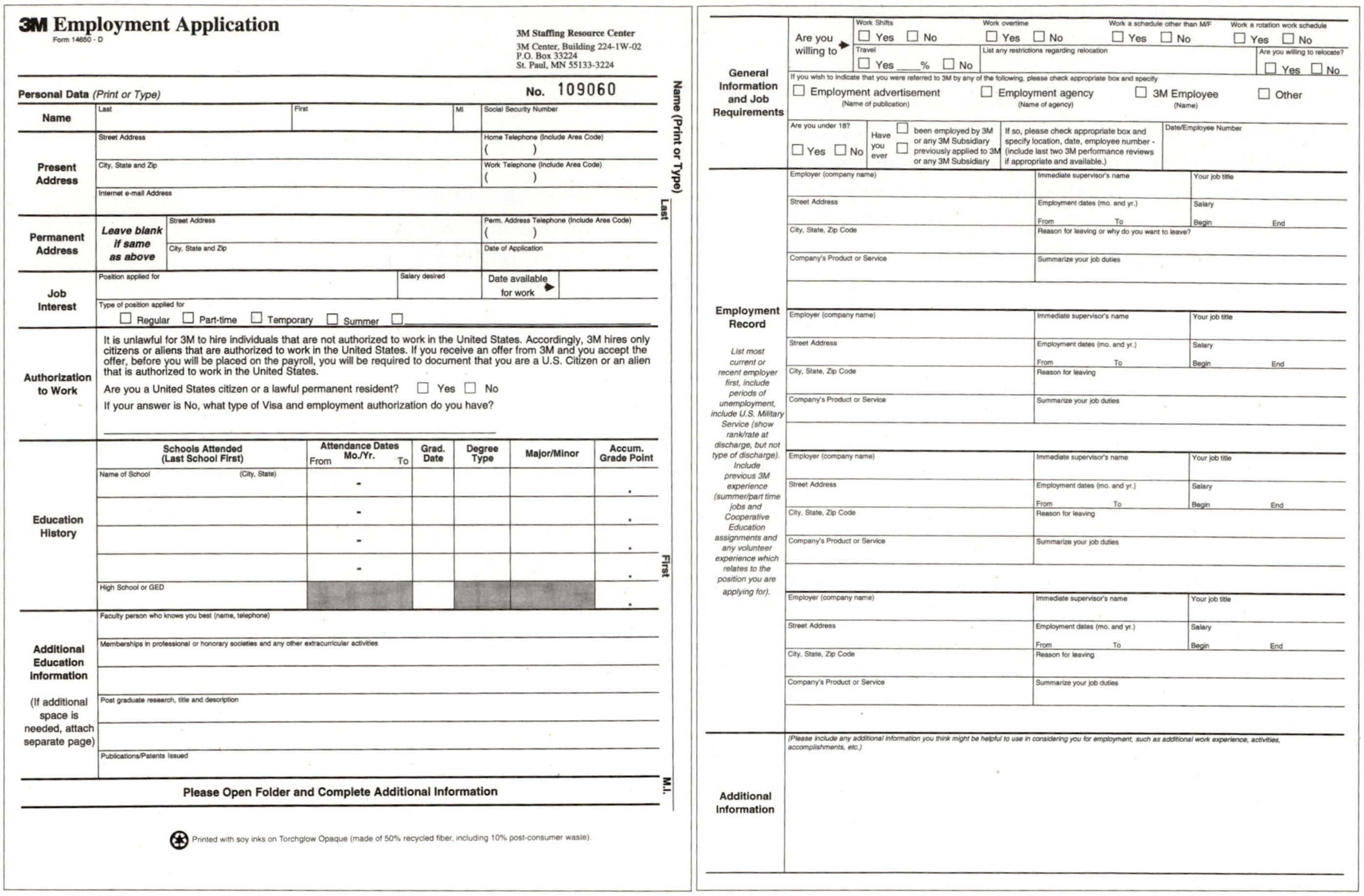

3M Employment Application
Form 14650 - D

3M Staffing Resource Center
3M Center, Building 224-1W-02
P.O. Box 33224
St. Paul, MN 55133-3224

Personal Data (Print or Type) — No. 109060

Name: Last / First / MI / Social Security Number

Present Address: Street Address / Home Telephone (Include Area Code) ( ) / City, State and Zip / Work Telephone (Include Area Code) ( ) / Internet e-mail Address

Permanent Address: *Leave blank if same as above* / Street Address / Perm. Address Telephone (Include Area Code) ( ) / City, State and Zip / Date of Application

Job Interest: Position applied for / Salary desired / Date available for work / Type of position applied for ☐ Regular ☐ Part-time ☐ Temporary ☐ Summer ☐

Authorization to Work: It is unlawful for 3M to hire individuals that are not authorized to work in the United States. Accordingly, 3M hires only citizens or aliens that are authorized to work in the United States. If you receive an offer from 3M and you accept the offer, before you will be placed on the payroll, you will be required to document that you are a U.S. Citizen or an alien that is authorized to work in the United States.
Are you a United States citizen or a lawful permanent resident? ☐ Yes ☐ No
If your answer is No, what type of Visa and employment authorization do you have?

Education History:

Schools Attended (Last School First)	Attendance Dates Mo./Yr. From – To	Grad. Date	Degree Type	Major/Minor	Accum. Grade Point
Name of School (City, State)	-				.
	-				.
	-				.
	-				.
High School or GED					.

Additional Education Information (If additional space is needed, attach separate page): Faculty person who knows you best (name, telephone) / Memberships in professional or honorary societies and any other extracurricular activities / Post graduate research, title and description / Publications/Patents Issued

Name (Print or Type) Last / First / M.I.

Please Open Folder and Complete Additional Information

Printed with soy inks on Torchglow Opaque (made of 50% recycled fiber, including 10% post-consumer waste).

General Information and Job Requirements:
Are you willing to → Work Shifts ☐ Yes ☐ No / Work overtime ☐ Yes ☐ No / Work a schedule other than M/F ☐ Yes ☐ No / Work a rotation work schedule ☐ Yes ☐ No / Travel ☐ Yes ___% ☐ No / List any restrictions regarding relocation / Are you willing to relocate? ☐ Yes ☐ No
If you wish to indicate that you were referred to 3M by any of the following, please check appropriate box and specify: ☐ Employment advertisement (Name of publication) ☐ Employment agency (Name of agency) ☐ 3M Employee (Name) ☐ Other
Are you under 18? ☐ Yes ☐ No / Have you ever ☐ been employed by 3M or any 3M Subsidiary ☐ previously applied to 3M or any 3M Subsidiary / If so, please check appropriate box and specify location, date, employee number - (include last two 3M performance reviews if appropriate and available.) / Date/Employee Number

Employment Record (*List most current or recent employer first, include periods of unemployment, include U.S. Military Service (show rank/rate at discharge, but not type of discharge). Include previous 3M experience (summer/part time jobs and Cooperative Education assignments and any volunteer experience which relates to the position you are applying for).*):
Employer (company name) / Immediate supervisor's name / Your job title / Street Address / Employment dates (mo. and yr.) From To / Salary Begin End / City, State, Zip Code / Reason for leaving or why do you want to leave? / Company's Product or Service / Summarize your job duties
Employer (company name) / Immediate supervisor's name / Your job title / Street Address / Employment dates (mo. and yr.) From To / Salary Begin End / City, State, Zip Code / Reason for leaving / Company's Product or Service / Summarize your job duties
Employer (company name) / Immediate supervisor's name / Your job title / Street Address / Employment dates (mo. and yr.) From To / Salary Begin End / City, State, Zip Code / Reason for leaving / Company's Product or Service / Summarize your job duties
Employer (company name) / Immediate supervisor's name / Your job title / Street Address / Employment dates (mo. and yr.) From To / Salary Begin End / City, State, Zip Code / Reason for leaving / Company's Product or Service / Summarize your job duties

Additional Information: *(Please include any additional information you think might be helpful to use in considering you for employment, such as additional work experience, activities, accomplishments, etc.)*

Source: Courtesy of 3M.

Interviews The interview is perhaps the most widely used selection technique. Job candidates are interviewed by at least one member of the HRM staff and by the person for whom they will be working. Candidates for higher-level jobs may meet with a department head or vice president over several interviews.

Interviews provide an opportunity for applicants and the firm to learn more about each other. Interviewers can pose problems to test the candidate's abilities, probe employment history, and learn something about the candidate's attitudes and motivation. The candidate has a chance to find out more about the job and potential co-workers. In some instances, companies are able to use video conferencing software like Skype or Oovoo. This has made the interviewing process easier for companies. Some companies have been able to reduce the number of applicants being flown in for interviews.[13]

Unfortunately, interviewing may be the stage at which discrimination begins. For example, suppose that a female applicant mentions that she is the mother of small children. Her interviewer may assume that she would not be available for job-related travel. In addition, interviewers may be unduly influenced by such factors as appearance, or they may ask different questions of different applicants so that it becomes impossible to compare candidates' qualifications. Table 9.2 contains interview questions that are difficult to answer.

Some of these problems can be solved through better interviewer training and use of structured interviews. In a *structured interview,* the interviewer asks only a prepared

Career SUCCESS

Click Here to Be Tested

Paper and pencil testing has given way to online tests that enable companies to assess your skills, attitudes, and personality before making a hiring decision—and, in many cases, before scheduling an interview. Pre-employment testing helps companies screen out people who lack the necessary skills and focus on candidates who may have what it takes to succeed in a particular position. For example, St. Luke's Hospital in Bethlehem, Pennsylvania, doesn't just look for top-notch medical skills—it also uses a pre-employment test to determine whether job applicants have a positive attitude toward customer service.

When Bon-Ton Stores wants to fill a sales position in the cosmetics department, it requires applicants to complete an online test with 80 questions. The test helps the department store identify people who are good problem-solvers, who can think logically, and who have strong math skills. Since Bon-Ton began using this test, it has significantly reduced turnover in the cosmetics department while improving sales results.

Brown Shoe, a footwear retailer, began using pre-employment assessments as part of a broader shift toward more personalized customer service. Then, in testing the test for store managers, it wound up fine-tuning questions that evaluate verbal reasoning, because those skills are particularly important for good on-the-job performance.

Sources: Based on information in Bill Roberts, "Hire Intelligence," *HR Magazine*, May 2011, p.63; "The Buyer's Guide to . . . Skills Testing," *Recruiter*, September 15, 2010, p.28; Ruth Mantell, "Job Seekers Are Getting Tested," *Wall Street Journal*, September 11, 2011, online.wsj .com/article/SB10001424053111904836104576563350928693850.html

TABLE 9.2   Interview Questions That May Be Difficult to Answer

1. Tell me about yourself.
2. What do you know about our organization?
3. What can you do for us? Why should we hire you?
4. What qualifications do you have that make you feel that you will be successful in your field?
5. What have you learned from the jobs that you have held?
6. Where do you see yourself in five years?
7. What are your special skills, and how did you acquire them?
8. Have you had any special accomplishments in your lifetime that you are particularly proud of?
9. Why did you leave your most recent job?
10. How do you spend your spare time? What are your hobbies?
11. What are your strengths and weaknesses?
12. Discuss five major accomplishments.
13. What kind of boss would you like? Why?
14. If you could spend a day with someone you have known or known of, who would it be?
15. What personality characteristics rub you the wrong way?
16. How do you show your anger? What type of things make you angry?
17. With what type of person do you spend the majority of your time?
18. What activities have you ever quit?
19. Define cooperation.
20. Do you have any questions for me?

Sources: From GREENE/MARTEL, *The Ultimate Job Hunter's Guidebook*, 6E. © 2012 Cengage Learning.

A job interview is similar to a first date. Like a date, interviews can occur in a variety of locations and through several formats. The purpose is to give the candidate and the company the opportunity to find out about each other. Can you think of any other selection methods that benefit *both* parties in the recruiting process?

set of job-related questions. The firm also may consider using several different interviewers for each applicant, but this is likely to be costly.

References A job candidate generally is asked to furnish the names of references—people who can verify background information and provide personal evaluations. Naturally, applicants tend to list only references who are likely to say good things. Thus, personal evaluations obtained from references may not be of much value. However, references are often contacted to verify such information as previous job responsibilities and the reason an applicant left a former job. In some instances, online social networking has changed the order in which employers receive information. Usually, references come after interviews. However, applicants may have former employers and colleagues post recommendations to their LinkedIn accounts so that potential employers see positive reviews about their work even before interviewing them.

Assessment Centers An assessment center is used primarily to select current employees for promotion to higher-level positions. Typically, a group of employees is sent to the center for a few days. While there, they participate in activities designed to simulate the management environment and to predict managerial effectiveness. Trained observers make recommendations regarding promotion possibilities. Although this technique is gaining popularity, the expense involved limits its use.

Orientation

Once all information about job candidates has been collected and analyzed, the company extends a job offer. If it is accepted, the candidate becomes an employee.

Soon after a candidate joins a firm, he or she goes through the firm's orientation program. **Orientation** is the process of acquainting new employees with an organization. Orientation topics range from the location of the company cafeteria to career paths within the firm. The orientation itself may consist of a half-hour informal presentation by a human resources manager, or it may be an elaborate program involving dozens of people and lasting several days or weeks.

 Discuss the primary elements of employee compensation and benefits. **6**

COMPENSATION AND BENEFITS

An effective employee reward system must (1) enable employees to satisfy basic needs, (2) provide rewards comparable with those offered by other firms, (3) be distributed fairly within the organization, and (4) recognize that different people have different needs.

A firm's compensation system can be structured to meet the first three of these requirements. The fourth is more difficult because it must account for many variables. Most firms offer a number of benefits that, taken together, generally help to provide for employees' varying needs.

Compensation Decisions

Compensation is the payment employees receive in return for their labor. Its importance to employees is obvious. Because compensation can account for a significant percentage of a firm's operating costs, it is equally important to the management. For example, health care services have the highest ratio of salaries to operating expenses—salaries account for 54 percent of operating costs.[14] Therefore, the firm's **compensation system**, the policies and strategies that determine employee compensation, must be designed

orientation the process of acquainting new employees with an organization

compensation the payment employees receive in return for their labor

compensation system the policies and strategies that determine employee compensation carefully to provide for employees' needs while keeping labor costs within reasonable limits. For most firms, designing an effective compensation system requires three separate management decisions—wage level, wage structure, and individual wages.

Wage Level Management first must position the firm's general pay level relative to pay levels of comparable firms. Most firms choose a pay level near the industry average. However, a firm that is not in good financial shape may pay less than average, and large, prosperous organizations may pay more than average.

To determine the average pay for a job, the firm may use wage surveys. A **wage survey** is a collection of data on prevailing wage rates within an industry or a geographic area. Such surveys are compiled by industry associations, local governments, personnel associations, and (occasionally) individual firms.

Wage Structure Next, management must decide on relative pay levels for all the positions within the firm. Will managers be paid more than secretaries? Will secretaries be paid more than custodians? The result of this set of decisions is often called the firm's *wage structure*.

The wage structure almost always is developed on the basis of a job evaluation. **Job evaluation** is the process of determining the relative worth of the various jobs within a firm. Most observers probably would agree that a secretary should make more money than a custodian, but how much more? Job evaluation should provide the answer to this question.

A number of techniques may be used to evaluate jobs. The simplest is to rank all the jobs within the firm according to value. A more frequently used method is based on the job analysis. Points are allocated to each job for each of its elements and requirements. For example, "college degree required" might be worth 50 points, whereas the need for a high school education might count for only 25 points. The more points a job is allocated, the more important it is presumed to be (and the higher its level in the firm's wage structure).

Individual Wages Finally, the company must determine the specific payments individual employees will receive. Consider the case of two secretaries working side by side. Job evaluation has been used to determine the relative level of secretarial pay within the firm's wage structure. However, suppose that one secretary has 15 years of experience and can type 80 words per minute accurately and the other has two years of experience and can type only 55 words per minute; in most firms, these two people would not receive the same pay. Instead, a wage range would be established for the secretarial position. In this case, the range might be $8.50 to $12.50 per hour. The more experienced and proficient secretary then would be paid an amount near the top of the range (say, $12.25 per hour); the less experienced secretary would receive an amount that is lower but still within the range (say, $8.75 per hour).

Two wage decisions come into play here. First, the employee's initial rate must be established. It is based on experience, other qualifications, and expected performance. Later, the employee may be given pay increases based on seniority and performance.

Comparable Worth

One reason women in the workforce are paid less may be that a proportion of women occupy female-dominated jobs—nurses, secretaries, and medical records analysts, for example—that require education, skills, and training equal to higher-paid positions but are undervalued. **Comparable worth** is a concept that seeks equal compensation for jobs that require about the same level of education, training, and skill. In recent decades, many states have taken steps to ensure that all workers have equal pay for comparable worth, but the issue remains contentious. Wisconsin, for example, has mulled passing a bill that would remove workers' ability to sue employers for many types of discrimination. Legal moves like this prove that the issue of equal pay for equal

wage survey a collection of data on prevailing wage rates within an industry or a geographic area

job evaluation the process of determining the relative worth of the various jobs within a firm

comparable worth a concept that seeks equal compensation for jobs requiring about the same level of education, training, and skills

work is far from settled. Critics of comparable worth believe that the market should determine the worth of jobs and laws should not tamper with the market's pricing mechanisms.[15] The Equal Pay Act, discussed later in this chapter, does not address the issue of comparable worth. Critics also argue that inflating salaries artificially for female-dominated occupations encourages women to keep these jobs rather than seek out higher-paying jobs.

Types of Compensation

Compensation can be paid in a variety of forms. Most forms of compensation fall into the following categories: hourly wage, weekly or monthly salary, commissions, incentive payments, lump-sum salary increases, and profit sharing.

Hourly Wage An **hourly wage** is a specific amount of money paid for each hour of work. People who earn wages are paid their hourly wage for the first 40 hours worked in any week. They are then paid one-and-one-half times their hourly wage for time worked in excess of 40 hours (i.e., they are paid "time-and-a-half" for overtime). Workers in retail and fast-food chains, on assembly lines, and in clerical positions usually are paid an hourly wage.

Weekly or Monthly Salary A **salary** is a specific amount of money paid for an employee's work during a set calendar period, regardless of the actual number of hours worked. Salaried employees receive no overtime pay, but they do not lose pay when they are absent from work. Most professional and managerial positions are salaried.

Commissions A **commission** is a payment that is a percentage of sales revenue. Sales representatives and sales managers often are paid entirely through commissions or through a combination of commissions and salary.

Incentive Payments An **incentive payment** is a payment in addition to wages, salary, or commissions. Incentive payments are really extra rewards for outstanding job performance. They may be distributed to all employees or only to certain employees. Some firms distribute incentive payments to all employees annually. The size of the payment depends on the firm's earnings and, at times, on the particular employee's length of service with the firm. Firms sometimes offer incentives to employees who exceed specific sales or production goals, a practice called *gain sharing*.

To avoid yearly across-the-board salary increases, some organizations reward outstanding workers individually through *merit pay*. This pay-for-performance approach allows management to control labor costs while encouraging employees to work more efficiently. An employee's merit pay depends on his or her achievements relative to those of others.

Lump-Sum Salary Increases In traditional reward systems, an employee who receives an annual pay increase is given part of the increase in each pay period. For example, suppose that an employee on a monthly salary gets a 10 percent annual pay hike. He or she actually receives 10 percent of the former monthly salary added to each month's paycheck for a year. Companies that offer a **lump-sum salary increase** give the employee the option of taking the entire pay raise in one lump sum. The employee then draws his or her "regular" pay for the rest of the year. The lump-sum payment typically is treated as an interest-free loan that must be repaid if the employee leaves the firm during the year.

Profit-Sharing **Profit-sharing** is the distribution of a percentage of a firm's profit among its employees. The idea is to motivate employees to work effectively by giving them a stake in the company's financial success. General Motors employees participate in employee profit-sharing plans. Workers have benefited from this perk recently, as the

hourly wage a specific amount of money paid for each hour of work

salary a specific amount of money paid for an employee's work during a set calendar period, regardless of the actual number of hours worked

commission a payment that is a percentage of sales revenue

incentive payment a payment in addition to wages, salary, or commissions

lump-sum salary increase an entire pay raise taken in one lump sum

profit-sharing the distribution of a percentage of a firm's profit among its employees

company recovered after the auto bailouts. Recently, it reported profits of over $400 million and was able to cut profit-sharing checks of up to $7,000 to its hourly wage earners.[16]

Employee Benefits

An **employee benefit** is a reward in addition to regular compensation that is provided indirectly to employees. Employee benefits consist mainly of services (such as insurance) that are paid for partially or totally by employers and employee expenses (such as college tuition) that are reimbursed by employers. Currently, the average cost of these benefits is nearly 30 percent of an employee's total compensation, which includes wages plus benefits.[17] Thus, a person who received total compensation (including benefits) of $50,000 a year earned $35,300 in wages and received an additional $14,700 in benefits.

Types of Benefits Employee benefits take a variety of forms. *Pay for time not worked* covers such absences as vacation time, holidays, and sick leave. *Insurance packages* may include health, life, and dental insurance for employees and their families. Some firms pay the entire cost of the insurance package, and others share the cost with the employee. The costs of *pension and retirement programs* also may be borne entirely by the firm or shared with the employee.

Some benefits are required by law. For example, employers must maintain *workers' compensation insurance,* which pays medical bills for injuries that occur on the job and provides income for employees who are disabled by job-related injuries. Employers must also pay for *unemployment insurance* and contribute to each employee's federal *Social Security* account.

Other benefits provided by employers include tuition-reimbursement plans, credit unions, child-care services, company cafeterias, exercise rooms, and broad stock-option plans available to all employees. Some companies offer special benefits to U.S. military reservists who are called up for active duty.

Some companies offer unusual benefits to attract and retain employees. Zappos.com has on-site "laughter yoga" classes. Wegmans Food Markets offer a free smoking-cessation program and a 24/7 health hotline. Google is known for its unusual perks and fun activities, which include bocce courts, a bowling alley, eyebrow shaping, and free food in companywide cafes. Employees at Autodesk can bring their dogs to work and can take a six-week paid sabbatical every four years. FactSet Research System offers employees free lunches, summer barbecues, an on-site Pie Truck, Cheese Truck, Cupcake Truck, and a gym.[18]

Flexible Benefit Plans Through a **flexible benefit plan**, an employee receives a predetermined amount of benefit dollars and may allocate those dollars to various categories of benefits in the mix that best fits his or her needs. Some flexible benefit plans offer a broad array of benefit options, including health care, dental care, life insurance, accidental death and dismemberment coverage for both the worker and dependents, long-term disability coverage, vacation benefits, retirement savings, and dependent-care benefits.

Personal APPS

When you're applying for a new job, wait to ask about benefits until you've been offered the position. During your first interview, stay focused on the company and how you can be an asset in this position, not on the benefits or compensation.

employee benefit a reward in addition to regular compensation that is provided indirectly to employees

What job benefits are crucial to you? The benefits companies provide vary widely. Large companies are often able to offer employees more benefits than small ones. However, in small firms, employees are more likely to do a broader range of tasks and advance to higher positions more quickly.

Explain the purposes and techniques of employee training and development.

Other firms offer limited options, primarily in health and life insurance and retirement plans.

Although the cost of administering flexible plans is high, a number of organizations, including Quaker Oats and Coca-Cola, have implemented this option for several reasons. Because employees' needs are so diverse, flexible plans help firms to offer benefit packages that more specifically meet their employees' needs. Flexible plans can, in the long run, help a company to contain costs because a specified amount is allocated to cover the benefits of each employee. Furthermore, organizations that offer flexible plans with many choices may be perceived as being employee-friendly. Thus, they are in a better position to attract and retain qualified employees.

TRAINING AND DEVELOPMENT

Training and development are extremely important at the Container Store. Because great customer service is so important, every first-year full-time salesperson receives about 185 hours of formal training as opposed to the industry standard, which is approximately seven hours. Training and development continue throughout a person's career. Each store has a full-time trainer called the *super sales trainer*. This trainer provides product training, sales training, and employee-development training. A number of top managers believe that the financial and human resources invested in training and development are well worth it.

Both training and development are aimed at improving employees' skills and abilities. However, the two are usually differentiated as either employee training or management development. **Employee training** is the process of teaching operations and technical employees how to do their present jobs more effectively and efficiently. **Management development** is the process of preparing managers and other professionals to assume increased responsibility in both present and future positions. Thus, training and development differ in who is being taught and the purpose of the teaching. However, both are necessary for personal and organizational growth. Companies that hope to stay competitive typically make huge commitments to employee training and development. Internet-based e-learning is growing. Driven by cost, travel, and time savings, online learning alone (and in conjunction with face-to-face situations) is a strong alternative strategy. Development of a training program usually has three components: analysis of needs, determination of training and development methods, and creation of an evaluation system to assess the program's effectiveness.

Some employers are using new approaches to train and certify workers. They have found that having a good education may not provide an employee with necessary skills to do a job well, so some organizations have developed a system that works similarly to the Boy Scouts merit badge. A potential employee completes a certification course geared toward a certain line of work and receives a "badge" upon successful completion. Programs like this cut down on the additional on-the-job training required after being hired because they are geared toward training in a specific field. Having such certification provides an employer with a better idea of the exact skill set of a potential employee. Once hired, employees undergo additional training, which varies a great deal from firm to firm and between industries.[19]

Analysis of Training Needs

When thinking about developing a training program, managers first must determine if training is needed and, if so, what types of training needs exist. At times, what at first appears to be a need for training is actually, on assessment, a need for motivation. Training needs can vary considerably. For example, some employees may need training to improve their technical skills, or they may need

© ADAM GREGOR/SHUTTERSTOCK

What job training methods have you experienced, and how effective were they? Organizations train employees using a variety of methods and locations. Depending on the type of business, the training may take just a few hours or more than a year.

training about organizational procedures. Training also may focus on business ethics, product information, or customer service. Because training is expensive, it is critical that the correct training needs be identified.

Training and Development Methods

A number of methods are available for employee training and management development. Some of these methods may be more suitable for one or the other, but most can be applied to both training and management development.

- *On-the-job methods.* The trainee learns by doing the work under the supervision of an experienced employee.
- *Simulations.* The work situation is simulated in a separate area so that learning takes place away from the day-to-day pressures of work.
- *Classroom teaching and lectures.* You probably already know these methods quite well.
- *Conferences and seminars.* Experts and learners meet to discuss problems and exchange ideas.
- *Role-playing.* Participants act out the roles of others in the organization for better understanding of those roles (primarily a management development tool).

Evaluation of Training and Development

Training and development are very expensive. The training itself costs quite a bit, and employees are usually not working—or are working at a reduced load and pace—during training sessions. To ensure that training and development are cost-effective, the managers responsible should evaluate the company's efforts periodically.

The starting point for this evaluation is a set of verifiable objectives that are developed before the training is undertaken. Suppose that a training program is expected to improve the skills of machinists. The objective of the program might be stated as follows: "At the end of the training period, each machinist should be able to process 30 parts per hour with no more than one defective part per 90 parts completed." This objective clearly specifies what is expected and how training results may be measured or verified. Evaluation then consists of measuring machinists' output and the ratio of defective parts produced after the training.

The results of training evaluations should be made known to all those involved in the program—including trainees and upper management. For trainees, the results of evaluations can enhance motivation and learning. For upper management, the results may be the basis for making decisions about the training program itself.

Social MEDIA

Nuts About Southwest

Southwest Airlines employees celebrated the company's entrance into the Atlanta market with a Flash Mob, which they posted on the company blog and YouTube. The blog, Nuts About Southwest, was launched in 2006, well before many companies were blogging. The company's Facebook and Twitter accounts were created in 2007. Southwest has had a significant social media presence even though a formal social media policy, with clearly communicated social media guidelines, was not put in place until 2010. The following URL links to Twitter, Facebook, Flickr, LinkedIn, YouTube, and other social media. According to the Web site, the core blogging team of 30 is comprised of employees, customers, and business partners.

www.blogsouthwest.com

WWW.BLOGSOUTHWEST.COM

See also the following sites:

www.facebook.com/Southwest The Facebook page contains live streaming content, posts promotions and special fares and builds community through interaction between Southwest employees and customers.

http://twitter.com/southwestair This site encourages one-on-one interaction with current and future customers.

www.flickr.com/groups/southwestairlines/ This site encourages anyone to share photos which are randomly fed into the blog and share videos through YouTube at www.youtube.com/nutsaboutsouthwest

PERFORMANCE APPRAISAL

 8 Discuss performance appraisal techniques and performance feedback.

Performance appraisal is the evaluation of employees' current and potential levels of performance to allow managers to make objective human resources decisions. The process has three main objectives. First, managers use performance appraisals to let

FIGURE 9.3 Performance Appraisal

3M Contribution and Development Summary
FORM 37450 - B

Employee Name	Employee Number	Job Title
Department		Location
Coach/Supervisor(s) Name(s)		Review Period
		From : To :

Major Job Responsibilities

Goals/Expectations | **Contributions/Results**

Contribution (To be completed by coach/supervisor)

☐ Good Level of Contribution for this year   ☐ Exceptional Level of Contribution for this year

☐ Unsatisfactory Level of Contribution for this year

page 3

Development Summary
Areas of Strength | Development Priorities

Career Interests
Next job | Longer Range

Current Mobility

☐ 0 - Currently Unable to Relocate   ☐ 3 - Position Within O.U.S. Area (ex: Europe, Asia)
☐ 1 - Position In Home Country Only (Use if Home   ☐ 4 - Position In U.S.
     Country is Outside U.S.)
☐ 2 - Position Within O.U.S. Region (e: Nordic,   ☐ 5 - Position Anywhere In The World
     SEA...)

Development

☐ W - Well placed. Development plans achievable in   ☐ X - Not well placed. Action required to resolve
       current role for at least the next year   placement issues.
☐ C - Ready now for a move to a different job for   **Comments on Development**
       career broadening experience
☐ I - Ready now for a move to a different job
       involving increased responsibility

Employee Comments

Coach/Supervisor Comments | **Other Supervisor (if applicable) and/or Reviewer**

Signatures

| Coach/Supervisor | Date | Other Coach/Supervisor or Reviewer | Date |
| Employee | | | Date |

page 4

Source: Courtesy of 3M.

performance appraisal the evaluation of employees' current and potential levels of performance to allow managers to make objective human resources decisions

workers know how well they are doing and how they can do better in the future. Second, a performance appraisal provides an effective basis for distributing rewards, such as pay raises and promotions. Third, performance appraisal helps the organization monitor its employee selection, training, and development activities. If large numbers of employees continually perform below expectations, the firm may need to revise its selection process or strengthen its training and development activities. Most performance appraisal processes include a written document. An example appears in Figure 9.3.

Common Evaluation Techniques

The various techniques and methods for appraising employee performance are either objective or judgmental in nature.

Objective Methods Objective appraisal methods use some measurable quantity as the basis for assessing performance. Units of output, dollar volume of sales, number of defective products, and number of insurance claims processed are all objective, measurable quantities. Thus, an employee who processes an average of 26 insurance claims per week is given a higher evaluation than one whose average is 19 claims per week.

Such objective measures may require some adjustment for the work environment. Suppose that the first of our insurance claims processors works in New York City and the second works in rural Iowa. Both must visit each client because they are processing homeowners' insurance claims. The difference in their average weekly output may be entirely because of the long distances the Iowan must travel to visit clients. In this case, the two workers may very well be equally competent and motivated. Thus, a manager must take into account circumstances that may be hidden by a purely statistical measurement.

Judgmental Methods Judgmental appraisal methods are used much more frequently than objective methods. They require that the manager judge or estimate the employee's performance level. However, judgmental methods are not capricious. These methods are based on employee ranking or rating scales. When ranking is used, the manager ranks subordinates from best to worst. This approach has a number of drawbacks, including the lack of any absolute standard. Use of rating scales is the most popular judgmental appraisal technique. A *rating scale* consists of a number of statements; each employee is rated on the degree to which the statement applies. For example, one statement might be, "This employee always does high-quality work." The supervisor would give the employee a rating, from 5 down to 1, corresponding to gradations ranging from "strongly agree" to "strongly disagree." The ratings on all the statements are added to obtain the employee's total evaluation.

Avoiding Appraisal Errors Managers must be cautious if they are to avoid making mistakes when appraising employees. It is common to overuse one portion of an evaluation instrument, thus overemphasizing some issues and underemphasizing others. A manager must guard against allowing an employee's poor performance on one activity to influence his or her judgment of that subordinate's work on other activities. Similarly, putting too much weight on recent performance distorts an employee's evaluation. For example, if the employee is being rated on performance over the last year, a manager should not permit last month's disappointing performance to overshadow the quality of the work done in the first 11 months of the year. Finally, a manager must guard against discrimination on the basis of race, age, gender, religion, national origin, or sexual orientation.

Performance Feedback

No matter which appraisal technique is used, the results should be discussed with the employee soon after the evaluation is completed. The manager should explain the basis for present rewards and should let the employee know what he or she can do to be recognized as a better performer in the future. The information provided to an employee in such discussions is called *performance feedback,* and the process is known as a *performance feedback interview.*

There are three major approaches to performance feedback interviews: tell-and-sell, tell-and-listen, and problem solving. In a *tell-and-sell* feedback interview, the superior tells the employee how good or bad the employee's performance has been and then attempts to persuade the employee to accept the evaluation. Because the employee has no input into the evaluation, the tell-and-sell interview can lead to defensiveness, resentment, and frustration on the part of the subordinate. The employee may not accept the results of the interview and may not be committed to achieving the goals that are set.

With the *tell-and-listen* approach, the supervisor tells the employee what has been right and wrong with the employee's performance and then gives the employee a chance to respond. The subordinate may simply be given an opportunity to react to the supervisor's statements or may be permitted to offer a full self-appraisal, challenging the supervisor's assessment.

In the *problem-solving* approach, employees evaluate their own performance and set their own goals for future performance. The supervisor is more a colleague than a judge and offers comments and advice in a noncritical manner. An active and open dialogue ensues in which goals for improvement are mutually established. The problem-solving interview is most likely to result in the employee's commitment to the established goals.

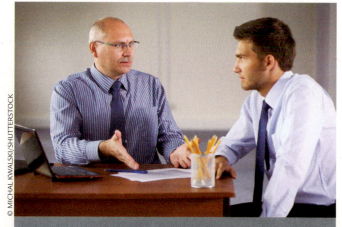

Performance feedback can help employees progress within an organization. A business usually evaluates its employees on an annual basis, but sometimes it does so quarterly and even monthly, especially when they are newly hired. Performance reviews that gather feedback about an employee from his or her peers, subordinates, and supervisors can help the person get a realistic view of his or her strengths and weaknesses.

To avoid some of the problems associated with the tell-and-sell interview, supervisors sometimes use a mixed approach. The mixed interview uses the tell-and-sell approach to communicate administrative decisions and the problem-solving approach to discuss employee-development issues and future performance goals.

An appraisal approach that has become popular is called a *360-degree evaluation*. A 360-degree evaluation collects anonymous reviews about an employee from his or her peers, subordinates, and supervisors and then compiles these reviews into a feedback report that is given to the employee. Companies that invest significant resources in employee-development efforts are especially likely to use 360-degree evaluations. An employee should not be given a feedback report without first having a one-on-one meeting with his or her supervisor. The most appropriate way to introduce a 360-degree evaluation system in a company is to begin with upper-level management. Then managers should be trained on how to interpret feedback reports so that they can coach their employees on how to use the feedback to achieve higher-level job-related skills and behaviors.

Finally, we should note that many managers find it difficult to discuss the negative aspects of an appraisal. Unfortunately, they may ignore performance feedback altogether or provide it in a very weak and ineffectual manner. In truth, though, most employees have strengths that can be emphasized to soften the discussion of their weaknesses. An employee may not even be aware of the weaknesses and their consequences. If such weaknesses are not pointed out through performance feedback, they cannot possibly be eliminated. Only through tactful, honest communication can the results of an appraisal be fully used.

Outline the major legislation affecting human resources management.

THE LEGAL ENVIRONMENT OF HRM

Legislation regarding HRM practices has been passed mainly to protect the rights of employees, to promote job safety, and to eliminate discrimination in the workplace. The major federal laws affecting HRM are described in Table 9.3.

National Labor Relations Act and Labor–Management Relations Act

These laws are concerned with dealings between business firms and labor unions. This general area is, in concept, a part of HRM. However, because of its importance, it is often treated as a separate set of activities. We discuss both labor–management relations and these two acts in detail in Chapter 11.

Fair Labor Standards Act

This act, passed in 1938 and amended many times since, applies primarily to wages. It established minimum wages and overtime pay rates. Many managers and other professionals, however, are exempt from this law. Managers, for example, seldom get paid overtime when they work more than 40 hours a week.

Equal Pay Act

Passed in 1963, this law overlaps somewhat with Title VII of the Civil Rights Act (see next section). The Equal Pay Act specifies that men and women who are doing equal jobs must be paid the same wage. Equal jobs are jobs that demand equal effort, skill, and responsibility and are performed under the same conditions. Differences in pay are legal if they can be attributed to differences in seniority, qualifications, or performance. However, women cannot be paid less (or more) for the same work solely because they are women. In spite of having this law on the books for 50 years, women and men are not treated equally in the workplace. For example, only 3 percent of CEOs of *Fortune* 500 companies are women, and women still only earn 77 cents for every dollar earned by men. In order to better gauge and track this issue, the Department of Labor called on technology gurus to help. It created the Equal Pay App Challenge, which asks the general public to help develop an app that will educate people about persistent pay inequality issues.[20]

TABLE 9.3 Federal Legislation Affecting Human Resources Management

Law	Purpose
National Labor Relations Act (1935)	Established a collective-bargaining process in labor–management relations as well as the National Labor Relations Board (NLRB).
Fair Labor Standards Act (1938)	Established a minimum wage and an overtime pay rate for employees working more than 40 hours per week.
Labor–Management Relations Act (1947)	Provides a balance between union power and management power; also known as the Taft–Hartley Act.
Equal Pay Act (1963)	Specifies that men and women who do equal jobs must be paid the same wage.
Title VII of the Civil Rights Act (1964)	Prohibits discrimination in employment practices based on sex, race, color, religion, or national origin.
Age Discrimination in Employment Act (1967–1986)	Prohibits personnel practices that discriminate against people aged 40 years and older; the 1986 amendment eliminated a mandatory retirement age.
Occupational Safety and Health Act (1970)	Regulates the degree to which employees can be exposed to hazardous substances and specifies the safety equipment that the employer must provide.
Employment Retirement Income Security Act (1974)	Regulates company retirement programs and provides a federal insurance program for retirement plans that go bankrupt.
Worker Adjustment and Retraining Notification (WARN) Act (1988)	Requires employers to give employees 60 days notice regarding plant closure or layoff of 50 or more employees.
Americans with Disabilities Act (1990)	Prohibits discrimination against qualified individuals with disabilities in all employment practices, including job-application procedures, hiring, firing, advancement, compensation, training, and other terms, conditions, and privileges of employment.
Civil Rights Act (1991)	Facilitates employees' suing employers for sexual discrimination and collecting punitive damages.
Family and Medical Leave Act (1993)	Requires an organization with 50 or more employees to provide up to 12 weeks of leave without pay on the birth (or adoption) of an employee's child or if an employee or his or her spouse, child, or parent is seriously ill.
Affordable Care Act (2010)	Requires an organization with 50 or more employees to make health insurance available to employees or pay an assessment and gives employees the right to buy health insurance from another provider if an organization's health insurance is too expensive.

© CENGAGE LEARNING 2014

Civil Rights Acts

Title VII of the Civil Rights Act of 1964 applies directly to selection and promotion. It forbids organizations with 15 or more employees to discriminate in those areas on the basis of sex, race, color, religion, or national origin. The purpose of Title VII is to ensure that employers make personnel decisions on the basis of employee qualifications only. As a result of this act, discrimination in employment (especially against African Americans) has been reduced in this country.

The EEOC is charged with enforcing Title VII. A person who believes that he or she has been discriminated against can file a complaint with the EEOC. The commission then investigates the complaint and, if it finds that the person has, in fact, been the victim of discrimination, the commission can take legal action on his or her behalf.

The Civil Rights Act of 1991 facilitates an employee's suing and collecting punitive damages for sexual discrimination. Discriminatory promotion and termination decisions as well as on-the-job issues, such as sexual harassment, are covered by this act.

Age Discrimination in Employment Act

The general purpose of this act, which was passed in 1967 and amended in 1986, is the same as that of Title VII—to eliminate discrimination. However, as the name implies, the Age Discrimination in Employment Act is concerned only with discrimination based on age. It applies to companies with 20 or more employees. In particular, it outlaws personnel practices that discriminate against people aged 40 years or older. (No federal law forbids discrimination against people younger than 40 years, but several states have adopted age discrimination laws that apply to a variety of age groups.) Also outlawed are company policies that specify a mandatory retirement age. Employers must base employment decisions on ability and not on a number.

Occupational Safety and Health Act

Passed in 1970, this act is mainly concerned with issues of employee health and safety. For example, the act regulates the degree to which employees can be exposed to hazardous substances. It also specifies the safety equipment that the employer must provide.

The Occupational Safety and Health Administration (OSHA) was created to enforce this act. Inspectors from OSHA investigate employee complaints regarding unsafe working conditions. They also make spot checks on companies operating in particularly hazardous industries, such as chemical and mining industries, to ensure compliance with the law. A firm found to be in violation of federal standards can be heavily fined or shut down. Nonetheless, many people feel that issuing OSHA violations is not enough to protect workers from harm.

Employee Retirement Income Security Act

This act was passed in 1974 to protect the retirement benefits of employees. It does not require that firms provide a retirement plan. However, it does specify that if a retirement plan is provided, it must be managed in such a way that the interests of employees are protected. It also provides federal insurance for retirement plans that go bankrupt.

Affirmative Action

Affirmative action is not one act but a series of executive orders issued by the President of the United States. These orders established the requirement for affirmative action in personnel practices. This stipulation applies to all employers with 50 or more employees holding federal contracts in excess of $50,000. It prescribes that such employers (1) actively encourage job applications from members of minority groups and (2) hire qualified employees from minority groups who are not fully represented in their organizations. Many firms that do not hold government contracts voluntarily take part in this affirmative action program.

© AUREMAR/SHUTTERSTOCK

Focus on what employees and job candidates can do—not what they can't. The American Disabilities Act (ADA) requires businesses to make reasonable accommodations for applicants and employees with disabilities. The law isn't the only reason why firms should hire and retain the disabled, though. Studies have shown that firms that do so experience positive business outcomes. Many manual and electronic devices are available today that can help the disabled work safely and productively. Simply redesigning a workstation slightly can make it possible for someone to work at a job he or she couldn't before.

Americans with Disabilities Act

The Americans with Disabilities Act (ADA) prohibits discrimination against qualified individuals with disabilities in all employment practices—including job-application procedures, hiring, firing, advancement, compensation, training, and other terms and conditions of employment. All private employers and government agencies with 15 or more employees are covered by the ADA. Defining who is a qualified individual with a disability is, of course, difficult. Depending on how *qualified individual with a disability* is interpreted, more than 50 million Americans can be included under this law.[21] This law also mandates that all businesses that serve the public must make their facilities accessible to people with disabilities.

The ADA not only protects individuals with obvious physical disabilities but also safeguards those with less visible conditions, such as heart disease, diabetes, epilepsy, cancer, AIDS, and mental illnesses. Because of this law, many organizations no longer require job applicants to pass physical examinations as a condition of employment.

Employers are required to provide disabled employees with reasonable accommodation. *Reasonable accommodation* is any modification or adjustment to a job or work environment that will enable a qualified employee with a disability to perform a central job function. Examples of reasonable accommodation include making existing facilities readily accessible to and usable by an individual confined to a wheelchair. Reasonable accommodation also might mean restructuring a job, modifying work schedules, acquiring or modifying equipment, providing qualified readers or interpreters, or changing training programs.

return to Inside BUSINESS

LinkedIn

When LinkedIn launched in 2003, its founders could never have imagined that less than a decade later, it would attract 120 new members per minute, around the clock and around the world. This social media site for professionals has grown into an important networking tool for connecting companies and job candidates at all levels. In the words of one LinkedIn executive, the site is a "global talent marketplace" where individual members are "entrepreneurs of their own lives."

To get noticed by potential employers on LinkedIn, members need to post and keep their professional profiles updated. The more people in their network of contacts, the more possibilities for connecting with someone at a company that's hiring. Joining industry or specialized groups helps members stay on top of new developments and new openings in their chosen fields. Finally, LinkedIn is a good place to research possible employers and make one-to-one connections with a company recruiter.

Questions

1. What are the advantages and disadvantages of asking employees to alert their LinkedIn member networks when a job opening is available?

2. Do you think a company should be able to view the LinkedIn profiles of members who work for its competitors and even contact them about job openings? Explain your answer.

SUMMARY

Looking for Success?
Get Flashcards, Quizzes, Games, Crosswords, and more @ www.cengagebrain.com.

 Describe the major components of human resources management.

Human resources management (HRM) is the set of activities involved in acquiring, maintaining, and developing an organization's human resources. Responsibility for HRM is shared by specialized staff and line managers. HRM activities include human resources planning, job analysis, recruitment, selection, orientation, compensation, benefits, training and development, and performance appraisal.

 Identify the steps in human resources planning.

Human resources planning consists of forecasting the human resources that a firm will need and those that it will have available and then planning a course of action to match supply with demand. Layoffs, attrition, early retirement, and (as a last resort) firing are ways to reduce the size of the workforce. Supply is increased through hiring.

 Describe cultural diversity and understand some of the challenges and opportunities associated with it.

Cultural diversity refers to the differences among people in a workforce owing to race, ethnicity, and gender. With an increasing number of women, minorities, and immigrants entering the U.S. workforce, management is faced with both challenges and competitive advantages. Some organizations are implementing diversity-related training programs and working to make the most of cultural diversity. With proper guidance and management, a culturally diverse organization can prove beneficial to all involved.

 Explain the objectives and uses of job analysis.

Job analysis provides a job description and a job specification for each position within a firm. A job description is a list of the elements that make up a particular job. A job specification is a list of qualifications required to perform a particular job. Job analysis is used in evaluation and in the determination of compensation levels and serves as the basis for recruiting and selecting new employees.

Describe the processes of recruiting, employee selection, and orientation.

Recruiting is the process of attracting qualified job applicants. Candidates for open positions may be recruited from within or outside a firm. In the selection process, information about candidates is obtained from applications, résumés, tests, interviews, references, or assessment centers. This information then is used to select the most appropriate candidate for the job. Newly hired employees will then go through a formal or an informal orientation program to acquaint themselves with the firm.

 Discuss the primary elements of employee compensation and benefits.

Compensation is the payment employees receive in return for their labor. In developing a system for paying employees, management must decide on the firm's general wage level (relative to other firms), the wage structure within the firm, and individual wages. Wage surveys and job analyses are useful in making these decisions. Employees may be paid hourly wages, salaries, or commissions. They also may receive incentive payments, lump-sum salary increases, and profit-sharing payments. Employee benefits, which are nonmonetary rewards to employees, add about 28 percent to the cost of compensation.

 Explain the purposes and techniques of employee training and development.

Employee-training and management-development programs enhance the ability of employees to contribute to a firm. When developing a training program, the company should analyze training needs and then select training methods. Because training is expensive, an organization should periodically evaluate the effectiveness of its training programs.

 Discuss performance appraisal techniques and performance feedback.

Performance appraisal, or evaluation, is used to provide employees with performance feedback, to serve as a basis for distributing rewards, and to monitor selection and training activities. Both objective and judgmental appraisal techniques are used. Their results are communicated to employees through three performance feedback approaches: tell-and-sell, tell-and-listen, and problem solving.

 Outline the major legislation affecting human resources management.

A number of laws have been passed that affect HRM practices and that protect the rights and safety of employees. Some of these are the National Labor Relations Act of 1935, the Labor–Management Relations Act of 1947, the Fair Labor Standards Act of 1938, the Equal Pay Act of 1963, Title VII of the Civil Rights Act of 1964, the Age Discrimination in Employment Acts of 1967 and 1986, the Occupational Safety and Health Act of 1970, the Employment Retirement Income Security Act of 1974, the Worker Adjustment and Retraining Notification Act of 1988, the Americans with Disabilities Act of 1990, the Civil Rights Act of 1991, and the Family and Medical Leave Act of 1993.

KEY TERMS

You should now be able to define and give an example relevant to each of the following terms:

human resources management (HRM) (246)	job description (251)	compensation system (256)	lump-sum salary increase (258)
human resources planning (247)	job specification (251)	wage survey (257)	profit-sharing (258)
replacement chart (248)	recruiting (252)	job evaluation (257)	employee benefit (259)
skills inventory (248)	external recruiting (252)	comparable worth (257)	flexible benefit plan (259)
cultural (workplace) diversity (249)	internal recruiting (253)	hourly wage (258)	employee training (260)
	selection (253)	salary (258)	management development (260)
job analysis (251)	orientation (256)	commission (258)	
	compensation (256)	incentive payment (258)	performance appraisal (261)

REVIEW QUESTIONS

1. List the three main HRM activities and their objectives.
2. In general, on what basis is responsibility for HRM divided between staff and line managers?
3. How is a forecast of human resources demand related to a firm's organizational planning?
4. How do human resources managers go about matching a firm's supply of workers with its demand for workers?
5. What are the major challenges and benefits associated with a culturally diverse workforce?
6. How are job analysis, job description, and job specification related?
7. What are the advantages and disadvantages of external recruiting and of internal recruiting?
8. In your opinion, what are the two best techniques for gathering information about job candidates?

9. Why is orientation an important HRM activity?
10. Explain how the three wage-related decisions result in a compensation system.
11. How is a job analysis used in the process of job evaluation?
12. Suppose that you have just opened a new Ford sales showroom and repair shop. Which of your employees would be paid wages, which would receive salaries, and which would receive commissions?
13. What is the difference between the objective of employee training and the objective of management development?
14. Why is it so important to provide feedback after a performance appraisal?

DISCUSSION QUESTIONS

1. How accurately can managers plan for future human resources needs?
2. How might an organization's recruiting and selection practices be affected by the general level of employment?
3. Are employee benefits really necessary? Why?
4. As a manager, what actions would you take if an operations employee with six years of experience on the job refused ongoing training and ignored performance feedback?
5. Why are there so many laws relating to HRM practices? Which are the most important laws, in your opinion?

Video Case 9.1 — Whirlpool's Award-Winning Diversity Program Is Facilitated Through Employee Network

In today's global marketplace, managers interact with people of different cultures, languages, beliefs, and values. Whirlpool Corporation has shown that a diverse workforce can be a powerful advantage.

Since its establishment in 1911, Whirlpool, headquartered in Michigan, has grown into a global corporation with manufacturing locations on every major continent and annual revenues in excess of $19 billion. Approximately 60 percent of Whirlpool's 70,000 employees work outside North America. The development of this broad workforce is aided by the company's award-winning diversity program, which gathers workers into support groups based on personal affiliations. To enter the program, workers join a particular employee network of their choosing, such as the Hispanic network, the young professionals network, the Asian or African American networks, the women's network, the Native American network, or the Pride network, which includes gay, lesbian, bisexual, and transgender (GLBT) employees.

These networks give employees access to a world of new career resources and training opportunities. For instance, according to the company's Web site, "Our primary objective is to become the employer of choice for GLBT and affirming employees." Despite the program's obvious focus on employee well-being, leaders at Whirlpool say the networks also offer a competitive advantage in global marketing. "Having diverse people making decisions and giving input to the factors that we consider on a daily basis is extremely important to the business," according to the company's vice president of consumer and appliance care, Kathy Nelson. "It's important because we need to make sure that the people who are making business decisions are reflective of who our consumers are."

This belief is fully in keeping with the company's Diversity Mission Statement, expressed by Chairman and CEO Jeff Fettig: "We best serve the unique needs of our customers through diverse, inclusive, and engaged employees who truly reflect our global customer base."[22]

Questions

1. What are the three main objectives of Whirlpool's diversity networks?
2. What challenges do managers face in establishing a diverse workplace, and how might they respond to these challenges?
3. Do you think formation of Whirlpool's employee networks is the best way to promote a positive culture of diversity? Explain.

Case 9.2 — High Tech Recruiting Is a No-Brainer at Intel

When the California-based company Intel was founded in 1968, computers were room-sized machines, and most people thought that chips were made of chocolate. Today, Intel rings up $54 billion in annual sales from the production of chips that put computing power into all kinds of digital products for home, office, and factory use. The company also creates cloud computing systems for banks, businesses, and educational institutions.

To stay ahead of demand for its chips and services, Intel adds 1,000 new positions annually to its worldwide workforce, currently at 43,000 employees. It uses a variety of high-tech and in-person recruiting methods to recruit candidates who have what it takes to succeed in Intel's fast-paced work environment. On campus, recruiters carry iPads with special software so that they can input key details for each student they meet, including name,

REI Remains True to Its Roots

Since 1998, when the annual ranking began, REI has appeared on every one of *Fortune* magazine's lists of "100 Best Companies to Work For." REI—short for Recreational Equipment Inc.—sells outdoor equipment and clothing through two e-commerce sites and 122 stores in 29 states. Founded in the 1930s by a group of mountain climbers, REI has remained true to its roots by promoting responsible enjoyment of the outdoors, from the peak of Mount Everest to the dunes of Manhattan Beach. This is only one reason why REI's 10,400 employees—whether they're climbers, kayakers, skiers, or campers—are so enthusiastic about their jobs.

Working for REI brings outdoor-minded employees into daily contact with dozens of like-minded colleagues and customers, as well as everyday opportunities to test and sell the best equipment for their sports. The company also offers employees generous discounts on merchandise and adventure travel, and encourages them to volunteer for conservation programs and other community activities. Before opening a new store, REI hires local guides to give employees a taste of nearby outdoor activities. For example, employees of the New York City megastore hiked parks and waterfront inlets in northern Manhattan, far greener areas than the busy downtown district where the store is located—forging closer team ties in the process.

All REI staff members are eligible for health-care benefits, whether they work full- or part-time, a rarity in the retail industry but in keeping with the firm's tradition of caring for its employees. "We truly believe that our employees are our greatest asset," explains REI's senior vice president of human resources. "Whether they work five hours a week or they work 40 hours a week, they create the customer experience and they create the success for the organization."

Another way REI boosts satisfaction is by helping employees balance their personal and professional lives, through options such as telecommuting and flexible work schedules. And the longer employees remain with REI, the longer their vacation period. Finally, employees can apply for a company grant to realize their dreams of tackling personal outdoor challenges such as climbing in the Himalayas.[1]

To achieve its goals, any organization—whether it is REI, Google, or a local convenience store—must be sure that its employees have more than the right raw materials, adequate facilities, and equipment that works. The organization also must ensure that its employees are *motivated*. To some extent, a high level of employee motivation derives from effective management practices.

In this chapter, after first explaining what motivation is, we present several views of motivation that have influenced management practices over the years: Taylor's ideas of scientific management, Mayo's Hawthorne Studies, Maslow's hierarchy of needs, Herzberg's motivation–hygiene theory, McGregor's Theory X and Theory Y, Ouchi's Theory Z, and reinforcement theory. Then, turning our attention to contemporary ideas, we examine equity theory, expectancy theory, and goal-setting theory. Finally, we discuss specific techniques managers can use to foster employee motivation and satisfaction.

WHAT IS MOTIVATION?

1 Explain what motivation is.

A *motive* is something that causes a person to act. A successful athlete is said to be "highly motivated." A student who avoids work is said to be "unmotivated." We define **motivation** as the individual internal process that energizes, directs, and sustains behavior. It is the personal "force" that causes you or me to act in a particular way. For example, although job rotation may increase your job satisfaction and your enthusiasm for your work so that you devote more energy to it, job rotation may not have the same impact on me.

Morale is an employee's attitude or feelings about the job, about superiors, and about the firm itself. To achieve organizational goals effectively, employees need more than the right raw materials, adequate facilities, and efficient equipment. High morale results mainly from the satisfaction of needs on the job or as a result of the job. One need that might be satisfied on the job is the need *to be recognized* as an important contributor to the organization. A need satisfied as a result of the job is the need for *financial security*. High morale, in turn, leads to dedication and loyalty, as well as to the desire to do the job well. Low morale, however, can lead to shoddy work, absenteeism, and high turnover rates as employees leave to seek more satisfying jobs with other firms. After the most recent recession, job turnover rates lowered as many people considered themselves lucky to have work. As the economy continues to recover, job turnover is again rising.[2] To offset this turnover trend, companies are creating work environments focused on increasing employee satisfaction. One obvious indicator of satisfaction at a specific organization is whether employees like working there and whether other people want to work there. In a recent list of *Fortune* magazine's "Top 100 Companies to Work For," the top ten best companies to work for were Google, Boston Consulting Group, SAS, Wegmans Food Markets, Edward Jones, Netapp, Camden Property Trust, REI Recreational Equipment, CHG Healthcare Services, and Quicken Loans.[3] Motivation, morale, and the satisfaction of employees' needs are thus intertwined. Along with productivity, they have been the subject of much study since the end of the 19th century. We continue our discussion of motivation by outlining some landmarks of the early research.

motivation the individual internal process that energizes, directs, and sustains behavior; the personal "force" that causes you or me to behave in a particular way

morale an employee's feelings about his or her job and superiors and about the firm itself

scientific management the application of scientific principles to management of work and workers

HISTORICAL PERSPECTIVES ON MOTIVATION

2 Understand some major historical perspectives on motivation.

Researchers often begin a study with a fairly narrow goal in mind. After they develop an understanding of their subject, however, they realize that both their goal and their research should be broadened. This is exactly what happened when early research into productivity blossomed into the more modern study of employee motivation.

Scientific Management

Toward the end of the 19th century, Frederick W. Taylor became interested in improving the efficiency of individual workers. This interest, which stemmed from his own experiences in manufacturing plants, eventually led to **scientific management**, the application of scientific principles to management of work and workers.

One of Taylor's first jobs was with the Midvale Steel Company in Philadelphia, where he developed a strong distaste for waste and inefficiency. He also observed a practice he called "soldiering." Workers "soldiered," or worked slowly, because they feared that if they worked faster, they would run out of work and lose their jobs. Taylor realized that managers were not aware of this practice because they had no idea what the workers' productivity levels *should* be.

Is anyone happy? A century ago, most businesses in the United States weren't overly concerned about employee satisfaction. This is not the case today. Why do you think attitudes about employee motivation and satisfaction have changed?

Taylor later left Midvale and spent several years at Bethlehem Steel. While there, he made his most significant contribution to the field of motivation. He suggested that each job should be broken down into separate tasks. Then management should determine (1) the best way to perform each task and (2) the job output to expect when employees performed the tasks properly. Next, management should carefully choose the best person for each job and train that person in how to do the job properly. Finally, management should cooperate with workers to ensure that jobs were performed as planned.

Taylor also developed the idea that most people work only to earn money. He therefore reasoned that pay should be tied directly to output. The more a person produced, the more he or she should be paid. This gave rise to the **piece-rate system**, under which employees are paid a certain amount for each unit of output they produce. Under Taylor's piece-rate system, each employee was assigned an output quota. Those exceeding the quota were paid a higher per-unit rate for all units they produced (see Figure 10.1). Today, the piece-rate system is still used by some manufacturers and by farmers who grow crops that are harvested by farm laborers.

When Taylor's system was put into practice at Bethlehem Steel, the results were dramatic. Average earnings per day for steel handlers rose from $1.15 to $1.88. (Do not let the low wages that prevailed at the time obscure the fact that this was an increase of more than 60 percent!) The average amount of steel handled per day increased from 16 to 57 tons.

Taylor's revolutionary ideas had a profound impact on management practice. However, his view of motivation was soon recognized as overly simplistic and narrow. It is true that most people expect to be paid for their work, but it is also true that people work for a variety of reasons other than pay. Therefore, simply increasing a person's pay may not increase that person's motivation or productivity.

The Hawthorne Studies

Between 1927 and 1932, Elton Mayo conducted two experiments at the Hawthorne plant of the Western Electric Company in Chicago. The original objective of these studies, now referred to as the *Hawthorne Studies,* was to determine the effects of the work environment on employee productivity.

In the first set of experiments, lighting in the workplace was varied for one group of workers but not for a second group. Then the productivities of both groups were measured to determine the effect of light. To the amazement of the researchers, productivity increased for both groups. For the group whose lighting was varied, productivity remained high until the light was reduced to the level of moonlight!

piece-rate system a compensation system under which employees are paid a certain amount for each unit of output they produce

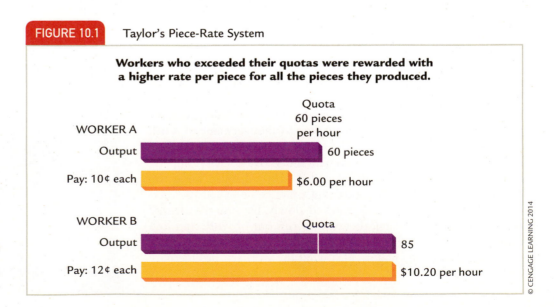

FIGURE 10.1   Taylor's Piece-Rate System

Workers who exceeded their quotas were rewarded with a higher rate per piece for all the pieces they produced.

Quota
60 pieces
per hour

WORKER A

Output — 60 pieces

Pay: 10¢ each — $6.00 per hour

WORKER B

Quota

Output — 85

Pay: 12¢ each — $10.20 per hour

© CENGAGE LEARNING 2014

The second set of experiments focused on the effectiveness of the piece-rate system in increasing the output of groups of workers. Researchers expected that output would increase because faster workers would put pressure on slower workers to produce more. Again, the results were not as expected. Output remained constant no matter what "standard" rates management set.

The researchers came to the conclusion that *human factors* were responsible for the results of the two experiments. In the lighting experiments, researchers had given both groups of workers a *sense of involvement* in their jobs merely by asking them to participate in the research. These workers—perhaps for the first time—felt as though they were an important part of the organization. In the piece-rate experiments, each group of workers informally set the acceptable rate of output for the group. To gain or retain the *social acceptance* of the group, each worker had to produce at that rate. Slower or faster workers were pressured to maintain the group's pace.

The Hawthorne Studies showed that such human factors are at least as important to motivation as pay rates. From these and other studies, the *human relations movement* in management was born. Its premise was simple: Employees who are happy and satisfied with their work are motivated to perform better. Hence, management is best served by providing a work environment that maximizes employee satisfaction.

Maslow's Hierarchy of Needs

Abraham Maslow, an American psychologist whose best-known works were published in the 1960s and 1970s, developed a theory of motivation based on a hierarchy of needs. A **need** is a personal requirement. Maslow assumed that humans are "wanting" beings who seek to fulfill a variety of needs. He observed that these needs can be arranged according to their importance in a sequence now known as **Maslow's hierarchy of needs** (see Figure 10.2).

At the most basic level are **physiological needs**, the things we require to survive. They include food and water, clothing, shelter, and sleep. In the employment context, these needs usually are satisfied through adequate wages.

At the next level are **safety needs**, the things we require for physical and emotional security. Safety needs may be satisfied through job security, health insurance, pension plans, and safe working conditions. Many companies are facing increasing insurance premiums for employee health care. The rising costs of providing health care and retirement benefits are major issues for many firms and many have reduced medical coverage in order to keep costs low. These changes affect younger employees disproportionately. While previous generations often counted on relatively secure retirement packages, young people entering the workforce have no such guarantee.[4]

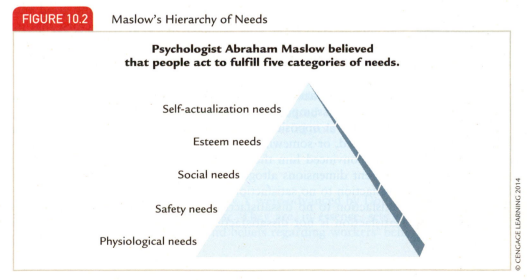

FIGURE 10.2 Maslow's Hierarchy of Needs

Psychologist Abraham Maslow believed that people act to fulfill five categories of needs.

- Self-actualization needs
- Esteem needs
- Social needs
- Safety needs
- Physiological needs

© CENGAGE LEARNING 2014

need a personal requirement

Maslow's hierarchy of needs a sequence of human needs in the order of their importance

physiological needs the things we require for survival

safety needs the things we require for physical and emotional security

Theory X is a concept of employee motivation generally consistent with Taylor's scientific management. Theory X assumes that employees dislike work and will function effectively only in a highly controlled work environment.

Theory X is based on the following assumptions:

1. People dislike work and try to avoid it.
2. Because people dislike work, managers must coerce, control, and frequently threaten employees to achieve organizational goals.
3. People generally must be led because they have little ambition and will not seek responsibility; they are concerned mainly about security.

The logical outcome of such assumptions will be a highly controlled work environment—one in which managers make all the decisions and employees take all the orders.

On the other hand, **Theory Y** is a concept of employee motivation generally consistent with the ideas of the human relations movement. Theory Y assumes that employees accept responsibility and work toward organizational goals, and by doing so they also achieve personal rewards. Theory Y is based on the following assumptions:

1. People do not naturally dislike work; in fact, work is an important part of their lives.
2. People will work toward goals to which they are committed.
3. People become committed to goals when it is clear that accomplishing the goals will bring personal rewards.
4. People often seek out and willingly accept responsibility.
5. Employees have the potential to help accomplish organizational goals.
6. Organizations generally do not make full use of their human resources.

Obviously, this view is quite different from—and much more positive than—that of Theory X. McGregor argued that most managers behave in accordance with Theory X, but he maintained that Theory Y is more appropriate and effective as a guide for managerial action (see Table 10.1).

The human relations movement and Theories X and Y increased managers' awareness of the importance of social factors in the workplace. However, human motivation is a complex and dynamic process to which there is no simple key. Neither money nor social factors alone can provide the answer. Rather, a number of factors must be considered in any attempt to increase motivation.

Theory Z

William Ouchi, a management professor at UCLA, studied business practices in American and Japanese firms. He concluded that different types of management systems dominate in these two countries.[6] In Japan, Ouchi found what he calls *type J* firms. They are characterized by lifetime employment for employees, collective (or group) decision making, collective responsibility for the outcomes of decisions, slow

Theory X a concept of employee motivation generally consistent with Taylor's scientific management; assumes that employees dislike work and will function only in a highly controlled work environment

Theory Y a concept of employee motivation generally consistent with the ideas of the human relations movement; assumes responsibility and work toward organizational goals, and by doing so they also achieve personal rewards

TABLE 10.1	Theory X and Theory Y Contrasted	
Area	**Theory X**	**Theory Y**
Attitude toward work	Dislike	Involvement
Control systems	External	Internal
Supervision	Direct	Indirect
Level of commitment	Low	High
Employee potential	Ignored	Identified
Use of human resources	Limited	Not limited

© CENGAGE LEARNING 2014

FIGURE 10.4   The Features of Theory Z

The best aspects of Japanese and American management theories combine to form the nucleus of Theory Z.

TYPE J FIRMS
(Japanese)
- Lifetime employment
- Collective decision making
- Collective responsibility
- Slow promotion
- Implied control mechanisms
- Nonspecialized career paths
- Holistic concern for employees

TYPE Z FIRMS
(Best choice for American firms)
- Long-term employment
- Collective decision making
- Individual responsibility
- Slow promotion
- Informal control
- Moderately specialized career paths
- Holistic concern for employees

TYPE A FIRMS
(American)
- Short-term employment
- Individual decision making
- Individual responsibility
- Rapid promotion
- Explicit control mechanisms
- Specialized career paths
- Segmented concern for employees

© CENGAGE LEARNING 2014

evaluation and promotion, implied control mechanisms, nonspecialized career paths, and a holistic concern for employees as people.

American industry is dominated by what Ouchi calls *type A* firms, which follow a different pattern. They emphasize short-term employment, individual decision making, individual responsibility for the outcomes of decisions, rapid evaluation and promotion, explicit control mechanisms, specialized career paths, and a segmented concern for employees only as employees.

A few very successful American firms represent a blend of the type J and type A patterns. These firms, called *type Z* organizations, emphasize long-term employment, collective decision making, individual responsibility for the outcomes of decisions, slow evaluation and promotion, informal control along with some formalized measures, moderately specialized career paths, and a holistic concern for employees.

Ouchi's **Theory Z** is the belief that some middle ground between his type A and type J practices is best for American business (see Figure 10.4). A major part of Theory Z is the emphasis on participative decision making. The focus is on "we" rather than on "us versus them." Theory Z employees and managers view the organization as a family. This participative spirit fosters cooperation and the dissemination of information and organizational values.

Reinforcement Theory

Reinforcement theory is based on the premise that behavior that is rewarded is likely to be repeated, whereas behavior that is punished is less likely to recur. A *reinforcement* is an action that follows directly from a particular behavior. It may be a pay raise after a particularly large sale to a new customer or a reprimand for coming to work late.

Reinforcements can take a variety of forms and can be used in a number of ways. A *positive reinforcement* is one that strengthens desired behavior by providing a reward. For example, many employees respond well to praise; recognition from their supervisors for a job done well increases (strengthens) their willingness to perform well in the future. A *negative reinforcement* strengthens desired behavior by eliminating an undesirable task or situation. Suppose that a machine shop must be cleaned thoroughly every month—a dirty, miserable task. During one particular month when the workers do a less-than-satisfactory job at their normal work assignments, the boss requires the workers to clean the factory rather than bringing in the usual private maintenance service. The employees will be motivated to work harder the next month to avoid the unpleasant cleanup duty again.

Theory Z the belief that some middle ground between type A and type J practices is best for American business

reinforcement theory a theory of motivation based on the premise that rewarded behavior is likely to be repeated, whereas punished behavior is less likely to recur

You'll see reinforcement theory at work in many situations. When a sports team receives recognition for winning a championship game, that's positive reinforcement. When a student receives a low mark for a paper and must redo it, that's negative reinforcement.

Punishment is an undesired consequence of undesirable behavior. Common forms of punishment used in organizations include reprimands, reduced pay, disciplinary layoffs, and termination (firing). Punishment often does more harm than good. It tends to create an unpleasant environment, fosters hostility and resentment, and suppresses undesirable behavior only until the supervisor's back is turned.

Managers who rely on *extinction* hope to eliminate undesirable behavior by not responding to it. The idea is that the behavior eventually will become "extinct." Suppose, for example, that an employee writes memo after memo to his or her manager about insignificant events. If the manager does not respond to any of these memos, the employee probably will stop writing them, and the behavior will be squelched.

The effectiveness of reinforcement depends on which type is used and how it is timed. One approach may work best under certain conditions, although some situations lend themselves to the use of more than one approach. Generally, positive reinforcement is considered the most effective, and it is recommended when the manager has a choice.

Continual reinforcement can become tedious for both managers and employees, especially when the same behavior is being reinforced over and over again in the same way. At the start, it may be necessary to reinforce a desired behavior every time it occurs. However, once a desired behavior has become more or less established, occasional reinforcement seems to be most effective.

Describe three contemporary views of motivation: equity theory, expectancy theory, and goal-setting theory.

CONTEMPORARY VIEWS ON MOTIVATION

Maslow's hierarchy of needs and Herzberg's motivation–hygiene theory are popular and widely known theories of motivation. Each is also a significant step up from the relatively narrow views of scientific management and Theories X and Y. However, they do have one weakness: each attempts to specify *what* motivates people, but neither explains *why* or *how* motivation develops or is sustained over time. In recent years, managers have begun to explore three other models that take a more dynamic view of motivation. These are equity theory, expectancy theory, and goal-setting theory.

Equity Theory

The **equity theory** of motivation is based on the premise that people are motivated to obtain and preserve equitable treatment for themselves. As used here, *equity* is the distribution of rewards in direct proportion to each employee's contribution to the organization. Everyone need not receive the same rewards, but the rewards should be in accordance with individual contributions.

According to this theory, we tend to implement the idea of equity in the following way. First, we develop our own input-to-outcome ratio. *Inputs* are the time, effort, skills, education, experience, and so on, that we contribute to the organization. *Outcomes* are the rewards we get from the organization, such as pay, benefits, recognition, and promotions. Next, we compare this ratio with what we perceive as the input-to-outcome ratio for some other person. It might be a co-worker, a friend who works for another firm, or even an average of all the people in our organization. This person is called the *comparison other*. Note that our perception of this person's input-to-outcome ratio may be absolutely correct or completely wrong. However, we believe that it is correct.

equity theory a theory of motivation based on the premise that people are motivated to obtain and preserve equitable treatment for themselves

© DOORQ/SHUTTERSTOCK

Going for SUCCESS

The Gamification of Motivation

Gamification—adapting elements of video games to challenge and reward employees—is changing the way businesses motivate employees. Target, for example, lets cashiers compete against each other for bragging rights about who delivers the speediest checkout service. Employees at LiveOps, which provides call-center software, earn badges and other intangible rewards playing an ongoing virtual game that encourages friendly competition while sharpening work skills. The game is so popular that 75 percent of LiveOps employees play at least twice a month, and employee performance has improved, as well.

IBM has created a number of games that only employees can play, some directly related to work situations and others indirectly related. In one game, employees try to improve the efficiency of systems that keep a virtual city running. Chuck Hamilton, who leads IBM's virtual learning department, says these games help far-flung employees feel more connected to each other and the company.

The U.K. Department of Work and Pensions has a Web-browser game called Idea Street that rewards employees for submitting and fine-tuning ideas for higher effectiveness and efficiency. Employees earn points when they send in an idea, comment on ideas submitted by others, or sign up to implement someone else's idea. A leader board tracks the highest-ranked players—and the department expects to save $30 million by implementing the top ideas.

Sources: Based on information in Fiona Graham, "What If You Got Paid to Play Games at Work?" BBC News, February 28, 2012, http://bbc.co.uk/news/business-17160118; Rachel Emma Silverman, "Latest Game Theory: Mixing Work and Play," Wall Street Journal, October 10, 2011, http://online.wsj.com/article/SB10001424052970204294504576615371783795248.html; Kenrick Vezina, "Using Games to Get Employees Thinking," MIT Technology Review, August 17, 2011, http://technologyreview.com/business/38191/.

If the two ratios are roughly the same, we feel that the organization is treating us equitably. In this case, we are motivated to leave things as they are. However, if our ratio is the higher of the two, we feel under-rewarded and are motivated to make changes. We may (1) decrease our own inputs by not working so hard, (2) try to increase our total outcome by asking for a raise in pay, (3) try to get the comparison other to increase some inputs or receive decreased outcomes, (4) leave the work situation, or (5) do a new comparison with a different comparison other.

Equity theory is most relevant to pay as an outcome. Because pay is a very real measure of a person's worth to an organization, comparisons involving pay are a natural part of organizational life. Managers can try to avoid problems arising from inequity by making sure that rewards are distributed on the basis of performance and that everyone clearly understands the basis for his or her own pay.

Expectancy Theory

Expectancy theory, developed by Victor Vroom, is a very complex model of motivation based on a deceptively simple assumption. According to expectancy theory, motivation depends on how much we want something and on how likely we think we are to get it (see Figure 10.5). Consider, for example, the case of three sales representatives who are candidates for promotion to one sales manager's job. Bill has had a very good sales year and always gets good performance evaluations. However, he is not sure that he wants the job because it involves a great deal of travel, long working hours, and much stress and pressure. Paul wants the job badly, but does not think he has much chance of getting it. He has had a terrible sales year and gets only mediocre performance evaluations from his present boss. Susan wants the job as much as Paul, and she thinks that she has a pretty good shot at it. Her sales have improved significantly this past year, and her evaluations are the best in the company.

Expectancy theory would predict that Bill and Paul are not very motivated to seek the promotion. Bill does not really want it, and Paul does not

expectancy theory a model of motivation based on the assumption that motivation depends on how much we want something and on how likely we think we are to get it

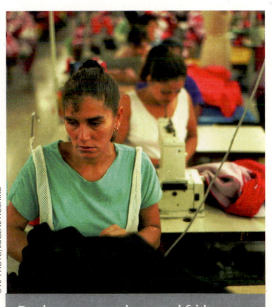
© AP PHOTO/EUGENE HOSHIKO

Employees want to be treated fairly. Employees compare the amount of effort they put into their jobs and the outcomes they get to that of their coworkers. This is the idea behind equity theory. At sweatshops such as this one, though, all employees are treated unfairly. Does equity theory come into play in this instance?

Chapter 10 Motivating and Satisfying Employees and Teams

283

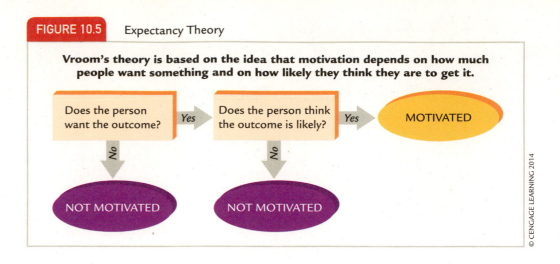

FIGURE 10.5 Expectancy Theory

Vroom's theory is based on the idea that motivation depends on how much people want something and on how likely they think they are to get it.

Does the person want the outcome? — *Yes* → Does the person think the outcome is likely? — *Yes* → MOTIVATED

Does the person want the outcome? — *No* → NOT MOTIVATED

Does the person think the outcome is likely? — *No* → NOT MOTIVATED

© CENGAGE LEARNING 2014

think that he has much of a chance of getting it. Susan, however, is very motivated to seek the promotion because she wants it and thinks that she can get it.

Expectancy theory is complex because each action we take is likely to lead to several different outcomes; some we may want, and others we may not want. For example, a person who works hard and puts in many extra hours may get a pay raise, be promoted, and gain valuable new job skills. However, that person also may be forced to spend less time with his or her family and be forced to cut back on his or her social life.

For one person, the promotion may be paramount, the pay raise and new skills fairly important, and the loss of family and social life of negligible importance. For someone else, the family and social life may be most important, the pay raise of moderate importance, the new skills unimportant, and the promotion undesirable because of the additional hours it would require. The first person would be motivated to work hard and put in the extra hours, whereas the second person would not be motivated at all to do so. In other words, it is the entire bundle of outcomes—and the individual's evaluation of the importance of each outcome—that determines motivation.

goal-setting theory a theory of motivation suggesting that employees are motivated to achieve goals that they and their managers establish together

Expectancy theory is difficult to apply, but it does provide several useful guidelines for managers. It suggests that managers must recognize that (1) employees work for a variety of reasons; (2) these reasons, or expected outcomes, may change over time; and (3) it is necessary to clearly show employees how they can attain the outcomes they desire.

Goal-Setting Theory

Goal-setting theory suggests that employees are motivated to achieve goals that they and their managers establish together. The goal should be very specific, moderately difficult, and one that the employee will be committed to achieve.[7] Rewards should be tied directly to goal achievement. Using goal-setting theory, a manager can design rewards that fit employee needs, clarify expectations, maintain equity, and provide reinforcement. For example, a manager might discover that one of her employees is very motivated by the occasional day off. Therefore, the manager and the employee may work out a plan together that involves giving the employee a free day as a reward after he completes a project satisfactorily and ahead of schedule, as long as he is up-to-date in his other work. A major benefit of this theory is that it provides a good understanding of the goal the employee has to achieve and the rewards that will accrue for the employee if the goal is accomplished.

©YURI ARCURS/SHUTTERSTOCK

What do employees want? That's what their managers need to determine. Different employees are motivated by different rewards. Figuring out which rewards motivate each is key step in goal setting.

KEY MOTIVATION TECHNIQUES

4 Explain several techniques for increasing employee motivation.

Today, it takes more than a generous salary to motivate employees. Increasingly, companies are trying to provide motivation by satisfying employees' less-tangible needs. At times, businesses use simple, low- or no-cost approaches such as those listed in Table 10.2 to motivate workers. Organizations also use more complex approaches. In this section, we discuss several specific techniques that help managers to boost employee motivation and job satisfaction.

Management by Objectives

Management by objectives (MBO) is a motivation technique in which managers and employees collaborate in setting goals. The primary purpose of MBO is to clarify the roles employees are expected to play in reaching the organization's goals.

By allowing individuals to participate in goal setting and performance evaluation, MBO increases their motivation. Most MBO programs consist of a series of five steps. The first step in setting up an MBO program is to secure the acceptance of top management. It is essential that top managers endorse and participate in the program if others in the firm are to accept it. The commitment of top management also provides a natural starting point for educating employees about the purposes and mechanics of MBO.

Next, preliminary goals must be established. Top management also plays a major role in this activity because the preliminary goals reflect the firm's mission and strategy. The intent of an MBO program is to have these goals filter down through the organization.

The third step, which actually consists of several smaller steps, is the heart of MBO:

1. The manager explains to each employee that he or she has accepted certain goals for the group (the manager as well as the employees) and asks the individual to think about how he or she can help to achieve these goals.
2. The manager later meets with each employee individually. Together they establish goals for the employee. Whenever possible, the goals should be measurable and should specify the time frame for completion (usually one year).
3. The manager and the employee decide what resources the employee will need to accomplish his or her goals.

As the fourth step, the manager and each employee meet periodically to review the employee's progress. They may agree to modify certain goals during these meetings if circumstances have changed. For example, a sales representative may have accepted a goal of increasing sales by 20 percent. However, an aggressive competitor may have entered the marketplace, making this goal unattainable. In light of this circumstance, the goal may be revised downward to 10 or 15 percent.

The fifth step in the MBO process is evaluation. At the end of the designated time period, the manager and each employee meet again to determine which of the individual's goals were met and which were not met, and why. The employee's reward (in the form of a pay raise, praise, or promotion) is based primarily on the degree of goal attainment.

As with every other management method, MBO has advantages and disadvantages. MBO can motivate employees by involving them actively in the life of the firm. The collaboration on goal setting and performance appraisal improves communication and makes employees feel that they are an important part of the organization. Periodic review of progress also enhances control within an organization. A major problem with MBO is that it does not work unless the process begins at the top of an organization. In some cases, MBO results in excessive paperwork. Also, a manager may not like sitting down and working out goals with subordinates and may instead just assign them goals. Finally, MBO programs prove difficult to implement unless goals are quantifiable.

management by objectives (MBO) a motivation technique in which managers and employees collaborate in setting goals

TABLE 10.2 No-Cost/Low-Cost Motivation Techniques

1.	Acknowledge and celebrate birthdays and other important events.
2.	Allow an employee to choose his or her next assignment.
3.	Call an employee to your office to thank him or her (do not discuss any other issue).
4.	In the department newsletter, publish a "kudos" column and ask for nominations throughout the department.
5.	Nominate the employee for a formal award program.
6.	Plan a surprise achievement celebration for an employee or group of employees.
7.	Pop in at the first meeting of a special project team and express your appreciation for their involvement.
8.	Send a letter to all team members at the conclusion of a project, thanking them for their participation.
9.	When you hear a positive remark about someone, repeat it to that person as soon as possible in person or electronically.
10.	Widely publicize suggestions used and their positive impact on your department.
11.	Support flexible work schedules.
12.	Ask the employee to be a mentor to a new hire.
13.	Put up a bulletin board in your department and post letters of thanks from customers.
14.	Take the opportunity to learn what your people are working on and recognize their efforts.
15.	Interview your people and capture their wisdom. Compile the quotes and stories in a booklet and hand it out to employees.
16.	Send a letter of praise to the employee's spouse or family.
17.	Honor employee subgroups in your department with their own day or week (e.g., Administrative Staff Week, Custodian Week) and present them with flowers, candy, breakfast, and so on.
18.	Recognize highly skilled employees with increased responsibility that will develop new skills that may be helpful for advancement.
19.	Pass around an office trophy to the employee of the week or other traveling awards.
20.	Volunteer to do an employee's least favorite task.
21.	Wash the employee's car.
22.	Give the person tickets to a ball game, golf lessons, movie tickets, a book by his or her favorite author, "Lunch on me" coupons, and so on.
23.	Reserve the best parking spot for employees who have done something truly worthwhile.
24.	Send a handwritten note or praise about a specific action, not "thanks for all you do."
25.	Create a yearbook for your team with pictures and stories of accomplishments during the year.
26.	Copy senior management on your thank-you note to the employee, to advise them of an employee's efforts or accomplishments.
27.	Introduce employees to key suppliers, customers, or someone in senior management.
28.	Reward good ideas even if they fail.
29.	Set aside a public space inside your firm as a "wall of fame" and place photos of employees who have accomplished something truly special along with the details of what they did to earn that space.
30.	Say, "Thank you."

Sources: Texas A&M University Human Resources Department, http://employees.tamu.edu/docs/employment/classComp/614recognitionIdeas.pdf; HRWorld, www.hrworld.com/features/25-employee-rewards/; Michigan Office of Great Workplace Development, www.michigan.gov/documents/firstgentleman/50_242400_7.pdf.

Career SUCCESS

Are You Ready for Frequent Feedback?

Will the usual yearly or twice-yearly employee performance review evolve into monthly or even daily feedback sessions to reinforce good performance and discourage less-productive actions? Some businesses find that employees actually welcome more frequent and less formal feedback than most organizations provide. Younger employees, in particular, are accustomed to texting, Tweeting, and other brief spurts of conversation, and they bring their expectations of quick response into the workplace. And in today's rapidly changing business environment, companies don't want employees to have to wait weeks or months for comments that will help them do a better job.

For example, managers at the social media site Facebook formally review employee performance two times a year. In addition, employees ask colleagues and managers for feedback and offer their own opinions when projects wrap up, after meetings, and after presentations. "You don't have to schedule time with someone," explains Facebook's vice president of human resources. "It's a 45-second conversation: 'How did that go? What could be done better?'"

At Atlassian, an Australian software company, managers and employees discuss goals and performance every week, prompted by questions such as "How often have you stretched yourself?" As these firms know, getting a compliment or a suggestion for improvement at the right moment can make all the difference in reinforcing effective behavior.

Sources: Based on information in Adriana Gardella, "Beyond Annual Performance Reviews," *New York Times*, February 27, 2012, http://boss.blogs.nytimes.com/2012/02/27/beyond-annual-performance-reviews/; Rachel Emma Silverman, "Yearly Reviews? Try Weekly," *Wall Street Journal*, September 6, 2011, http://online.wsj.com/article/SB1000142405311190389590457654296203041987 4.html; Rachel Emma Silverman, "Performance Reviews Lose Steam," *Wall Street Journal*, December 19, 2011, http://online.wsj.com/article/SB10001424052970204319004577088810100916828.html; "Should Performance Reviews Be Fired?" *Knowledge@Wharton*, April 27, 2011, http://knowledge.wharton.upenn.edu.

Job Enrichment

Job enrichment is a method of motivating employees by providing them with variety in their tasks while giving them some responsibility for, and control over, their jobs. At the same time, employees gain new skills and acquire a broader perspective about how their individual work contributes to the goals of the organization. Earlier in this chapter, we noted that Herzberg's motivation–hygiene theory is one rationale for the use of job enrichment; that is, the added responsibility and control that job enrichment confers on employees increases their satisfaction and motivation. For example, engineers at Google get to spend 20 percent of their time at work on projects of their choosing.[8] This type of enrichment can motivate employees and create a variety of benefits for the company. At times, **job enlargement**, expanding a worker's assignments to include additional but similar tasks, can lead to job enrichment. Job enlargement might mean that a worker on an assembly line who used to connect three wires to components moving down the line now connects five wires. Unfortunately, the added tasks often are just as routine as those the worker performed before the change. In such cases, enlargement may not be effective.

Whereas job enlargement does not really change the routine and monotonous nature of jobs, job enrichment does. Job enrichment requires that added tasks give an employee more responsibility for what he or she does. It provides workers with both more tasks to do and more control over how they perform them. In particular, job enrichment removes many controls from jobs, gives workers more authority, and assigns work in complete, natural units. Moreover, employees frequently are given fresh and challenging job assignments. By blending more planning and decision making into jobs, job enrichment gives work more depth and complexity.

job enrichment a motivation technique that provides employees with more variety and responsibility in their jobs

job enlargement expanding a worker's assignments to include additional but similar tasks

© OLIVER BUNIC/BLOOMBERG VIA GETTY IMAGES

Job enlargement versus job enrichment. It's no secret. Doing the same task over and over at your job is boring. Being able to do a variety of tasks helps. Having more responsibility over how you do your job is even better.

Job redesign is a type of job enrichment in which work is restructured in ways that cultivate the worker–job match. Job redesign can be achieved by combining tasks, forming work groups, or establishing closer customer relationships. Employees often are more motivated when jobs are combined because the increased variety of tasks presents more challenge and therefore more reward. Work groups motivate employees by showing them how their jobs fit within the organization as a whole and how they contribute to its success. Establishing client relationships allows employees to interact directly with customers. This type of redesign adds a personal dimension to employment. Another motivation for job redesign is to reduce employees' stress at work. A job redesign that carefully matches worker to job can prevent stress-related injuries. Employees can sometimes play an active role in redesigning their jobs more to their liking. If an employee recognizes an opportunity at work to rework his or her job in such a way as to improve efficiency or productivity, he or she may want to approach a superior with the idea. Redesigning a position based around organizational needs may help improve employee satisfaction and reduce employee turnover—all while improving efficiency at the firm.[9]

Job enrichment works best when employees seek more challenging work. Of course, not all workers respond positively to job-enrichment programs. Employees must desire personal growth and have the skills and knowledge to perform enriched jobs. Lack of self-confidence, fear of failure, and distrust of management's intentions are likely to lead to ineffective performance on enriched jobs. In addition, some workers do not view their jobs as routine and boring, and others even prefer routine jobs because they find them satisfying. Companies that use job enrichment as an alternative to specialization also face extra expenses, such as the cost of retraining.

Behavior Modification

Behavior modification is a systematic program of reinforcement to encourage desirable behavior. Behavior modification involves both rewards to encourage desirable actions and punishments to discourage undesirable actions. However, studies have shown that rewards, such as compliments and expressions of appreciation, are much more effective behavior modifiers than punishments, such as reprimands and scorn.

When applied to management, behavior modification strives to encourage desirable organizational behavior. Use of this technique begins with identification of a *target behavior*—the behavior that is to be changed. (It might be low production levels or a high rate of absenteeism, for example.) Existing levels of this behavior are then measured. Next, managers provide positive reinforcement in the form of a reward when employees exhibit the *desired behavior* (such as increased production or less absenteeism). The reward might be praise or a more tangible form of recognition, such as a gift, meal, or trip. Apple created the Corporate Gifting and Rewards Program in order to give companies the ability to reward their staff with iPods, iPhones, iPads, Mac computers, or iTunes gift cards.[10] Finally, the levels of the target behavior are measured again to determine whether the desired changes have been achieved. If they have been achieved, the reinforcement is maintained. However, if the target behavior has not changed significantly in the desired direction, the reward system must be changed to one that is likely to be more effective. The key is to devise effective rewards that will not only modify employees' behavior in desired ways but also motivate them. To this end, experts suggest that management should reward quality, loyalty, and productivity.

Flextime

Flextime is a system in which employees set their own work hours within certain limits determined by employers. Typically, the firm establishes two bands of time: the *core time*, when all employees must be at work, and the *flexible time*, when employees may choose whether to be at work. The only condition is that every employee must work a total of eight hours each day. For example, the hours between 9 and 11 a.m. and 1 and 3 p.m. might be core times, and the hours between 6 and 9 a.m., 11 a.m. and 1 p.m., and 3 and 6 p.m. might be flexible times. This would give employees the

job redesign a type of job enrichment in which work is restructured to cultivate the worker–job match

behavior modification a systematic program of reinforcement to encourage desirable behavior

flextime a system in which employees set their own work hours within employer-determined limits

option of coming in early and getting off early, coming in later and leaving later, or taking a long lunch break. But flextime also ensures that everyone is present at certain times, when conferences with supervisors and department meetings can be scheduled. Another type of flextime allows employees to work a 40-hour work week in four days instead of five. Workers who put in ten hours a day instead of eight get an extra day off each week. Offering flextime can be a low-cost way for a firm to show an employee that it cares about his or her well-being through offering a better work–life balance.[11] The needs and lifestyles of today's workforce are changing. Dual-income families make up a much larger share of the workforce than ever before, and women are one of its fastest-growing sectors. In addition, more employees are responsible for the care of elderly relatives. Recognizing that these changes increase the demand for family time, many employers are offering flexible work schedules that not only help employees to manage their time better but also increase employee motivation and job satisfaction. The sense of independence and autonomy employees gain from having a say in what hours they work can be a motivating factor. In addition, employees who have enough time to deal with non-work issues often work more productively and with greater satisfaction when they are on the job. Two common problems associated with using flextime are (1) supervisors sometimes find their jobs complicated by having employees who come and go at different times and (2) employees without flextime sometimes resent co-workers who have it.

To most people, a work schedule means the standard nine-to-five, 40-hour work week. In reality, though, some people have work schedules that are quite different from this. Flexible schedules are becoming much more common as improvements in technology allow people to stay connected, no matter where they are or what time it is. However, some industries are more likely to offer their workers flexible schedules than others. Medical and health, education and training, administrative jobs, and accounting are all likely to offer flexible schedule options. For example, many high-pressure accounting firms, such as Ernst & Young, have implemented flextime as a reward for working in an intense industry that requires some long hours during busy times. In order to offset the 60- or 70-hour work weeks during tax season, some accounting firms allow their employees to work 3-day weeks or take extended breaks during the summer. Flex policies like this help to reduce employee burnout and keep turnover low in what can be a stressful industry.[12]

part-time work permanent employment in which individuals work less than a standard work week

job sharing an arrangement whereby two people share one full-time position

Part-Time Work and Job Sharing

Part-time work is permanent employment in which individuals work less than a standard work week. The specific number of hours worked varies, but part-time jobs are structured so that all responsibilities can be completed in the number of hours an employee works. Part-time work is of special interest to parents who want more time with their children and people who simply desire more leisure time. One disadvantage of part-time work is that it often does not provide the benefits that come with a full-time position. However, working without benefits is not always the case. A few large retailers do offer good benefit packages to part-time employees. Among the best firms for part-timers are REI, Land's End, Starbucks, and Barnes & Noble. All of these organizations offer insurance packages to nearly all of their employees. Outfitter chain REI even offers its part-time employees incentive pay and the option to participate in a retirement and profit-sharing plan.[13]

Job sharing (sometimes referred to as *work sharing*) is an arrangement whereby two people share one full-time position. One job sharer may work from 8 a.m. to noon, and the other may work from 1 to 5 p.m., or they may alternate workdays. Job sharing is different than part-time work because two people share one single position, which is generally more skilled than a

©AP PHOTO/DAMIAN DOVARGANES

Part-time pay, full-time benefits. Many employees want to work part-time but can't afford not to have benefits such as health insurance. Companies known for hiring part-time employees with full benefits include UPS, REI, Land's End, Starbucks, and Barnes & Noble.

union–management partnerships and summarizing important labor-relations laws. We discuss the unionization process, why employees join unions, how a union is formed, and what the National Labor Relations Board does. Then, collective-bargaining procedures are explained. Next, we consider issues in union–management contracts, including employee pay, working hours, security, management rights, and grievance procedures. We close with a discussion of various labor and management negotiating techniques: strikes, slowdowns and boycotts, lockouts, mediation, and arbitration.

Explain how and why labor unions came into being.

THE HISTORICAL DEVELOPMENT OF UNIONS

Until the middle of the 19th century, there was very little organization of labor in this country. Groups of workers occasionally did form a **craft union**, an organization of skilled workers in a single craft or trade. These alliances were usually limited to a single city, and they often lasted only a short time. In 1786, the first-known strike in the United States involved a group of Philadelphia printers who stopped working over demands for higher wages. When the employers granted the printers a pay increase, the group disbanded.

Life before unions. Working conditions 100 years ago were often crowded, unpleasant, unsafe, and in some cases, lethal. In many less-developed nations, they still are.

Early History

In the mid-1800s, improved transportation opened new markets for manufactured goods. Improved manufacturing methods made it possible to supply those markets, and American industry began to grow. The Civil War and the continued growth of the railroads after the war led to further industrial expansion.

Large-scale production required more and more skilled industrial workers. As the skilled labor force grew, craft unions emerged in the more industrialized areas. From these craft unions, three significant labor organizations evolved. (See Figure 11.1 for a historical overview of unions and their patterns of membership.)

Knights of Labor The first significant national labor organization to emerge was the Knights of Labor, which was formed as a secret society in 1869 by Uriah Stephens, a utopian reformer and abolitionist from Philadelphia. Membership reached approximately 700,000 by 1886. One major goal of the Knights was to eliminate the depersonalization of the worker, which resulted from mass-production technology. Another was to improve the moral standards of both employees and society. To the detriment of the group, its leaders concentrated so intently on social and economic change that they did not recognize the effects of technological change. Moreover, they assumed that all employees had the same goals as the Knights' leaders: social and moral reform. The major reason for the demise of the Knights was the Haymarket riot of 1886.

At a rally (called to demand a reduction in the length of a work day from ten to eight hours) in Chicago's Haymarket Square, a bomb exploded. Several police officers and civilians were killed or wounded. The Knights were not implicated directly, but they quickly lost public favor.

American Federation of Labor In 1886, several leaders of the Knights of Labor joined with independent craft unions to form the *American Federation of Labor* (AFL). Samuel Gompers, one of AFL's founders, became its first president. Gompers believed that the goals of the union should be those of its members rather than those of its leaders. The AFL did not seek to change the existing business system, as the Knights of Labor had. Instead, its goal was to improve its members' living standards within the system.

Another major difference between the Knights of Labor and the AFL was in their positions regarding strikes. A **strike** is a temporary work stoppage by employees,

craft union an organization of skilled workers in a single craft or trade

strike a temporary work stoppage by employees, calculated to add force to their demands

FIGURE 11.1 Historical Overview of Unions

The total number of members for all unions generally rose between 1869, when the first truly national union was organized, and 1980. The dates of major events in the history of labor unions are singled out along the line of membership change.

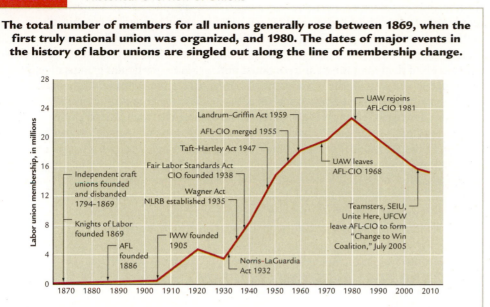

Source: "Union Membership (Annual)," U.S. Department of Labor, Bureau of Labor Statistics, www.bls.gov/news. release/union2.toc.htm (accessed January 6, 2012)

calculated to add force to their demands. The Knights did not favor the use of strikes, whereas the AFL strongly believed that striking was an effective labor weapon. The AFL also believed that organized labor should play a major role in politics. As we will see, the AFL is still very much a part of the American labor scene.

Industrial Workers of the World The *Industrial Workers of the World* (IWW) was created in 1905 as a radical alternative to the AFL. Among its goals was the overthrow of capitalism. This revolutionary stance prevented the IWW from gaining much of a foothold. Perhaps its major accomplishment was to make the AFL seem, by comparison, less threatening to the general public and to business leaders.

Evolution of Contemporary Labor Organizations

Between 1900 and 1920, both business and government attempted to keep labor unions from growing. This period was plagued by strikes and violent confrontations between management and unions. In steelworks, garment factories, and auto plants, clashes took place in which striking union members fought bitterly against non-union workers, police, and private security guards.

The AFL continued to be the major force in organized labor. By 1920, its membership included 75 percent of all those who had joined unions. Throughout its existence, however, the AFL had been unsure of the best way to deal with unskilled and semiskilled workers. Most of its members were workers skilled in specific crafts or trades. However, technological changes during World War I had brought about a significant increase in the number of unskilled and semiskilled employees in the workforce. These people sought to join the AFL, but they were not well received by its established membership.

Some unions within the AFL did recognize the need to organize unskilled and semiskilled workers, and they began to penetrate the auto and steel industries. The type of union they formed was an **industrial union**, an organization of both skilled and unskilled workers in a single industry. Soon workers in the rubber, mining, newspaper, and communications industries were also organized into unions. Eventually, these unions left the AFL and formed the *Congress of Industrial Organizations* (CIO).

industrial union an organization of both skilled and unskilled workers in a single industry

During the same time (the late 1930s), there was a major upswing in rank-and-file membership in the AFL, the CIO, and independent unions. Strong union leadership, the development of effective negotiating tactics, and favorable legislation combined to increase total union membership to 9 million in 1940. At that point, the CIO began to rival the AFL in size and influence. There was another bitter rivalry: The AFL and CIO often clashed over which of them had the right to organize and represent particular groups of employees.

Since World War II, the labor scene has gone through a number of changes. For one thing, during and after the war years there was a downturn in public opinion regarding unions. A few isolated but very visible strikes during the war caused public sentiment to shift against unionism. Perhaps the most significant occurrence, however, was the merger of the AFL and the CIO. After years of bickering, the two groups recognized that they were wasting effort and resources by fighting each other and that a merger would greatly increase the strength of both. The merger took place on December 5, 1955. The resulting organization, called the *AFL–CIO*, had a membership of as many as 16 million workers, which made it the largest labor organization of its kind in the world. Its first president was George Meany, who served until 1979.

 Discuss the sources of unions' negotiating power and trends in union membership

ORGANIZED LABOR TODAY

The power of unions to negotiate effectively with management is derived from two sources. The first is their membership. The more workers a union represents within an industry, the greater is its clout in dealing with firms operating in that industry. The second source of union power is the group of laws that guarantee unions the right to negotiate and, at the same time, regulate the negotiating process.

Union Membership

Approximately 11.8 percent of the nation's workers belong to unions.[2] Union membership is concentrated in a few industries and job categories. Within these industries, though, unions wield considerable power.

The AFL–CIO is still the largest union organization in this country, boasting approximately 12 million members.[3] Those represented by the AFL–CIO include actors, barbers, construction workers, carpenters, retail clerks, musicians, teachers, postal workers, painters, steel and iron workers, firefighters, bricklayers, and newspaper reporters.

One of the largest unions not associated directly with the AFL–CIO is the *Teamsters Union*. The Teamsters originally were part of the AFL–CIO, but in 1957 they were expelled for corrupt and illegal practices. The union started out as an organization of professional drivers, but it has begun recently to recruit employees in a wide variety of jobs. Current membership is about 1.4 million workers.[4]

The *United Steelworkers* (USW) and the *United Auto Workers* (UAW) are two of the largest industrial unions. The USW membership has risen to over 1 million workers. It is known as the dominant union in paper and forestry products, steel, aluminum, tire and rubber, mining, glass, chemicals, petroleum, and other basic resource industries. The UAW represents employees in the automobile industry. The UAW, too, originally was part of the AFL–CIO, but it left the parent union—of its own accord—in 1968. Currently, the UAW has about 376,000 members.[5] The UAW rejoined the AFL–CIO in 1981.

PROTECT AMERICA WITH STRONG UNIONS

8 REASONS TO JOIN A UNION

1. **BETTER WAGE COMPENSATION**
2. **STRONGER BENEFIT PACKAGES**
3. **ENHANCED RETIREMENT OPTIONS**
4. **HEALTH & SAFETY IN THE WORK PLACE**
5. **BETTER WORKING CONDITIONS**
6. **PROTECTION OF WORKERS RIGHTS**
7. **SUPPORTS EDUCATION FOR MEMBERS**
8. **STRENGTHENS WORKER & MANAGEMENT**

© SUSAN VAN ETTEN

Want to join a union? There are several general reasons why workers join unions. Clearly, there are additional reasons for joining a union related to the characteristics of a specific company, industry practices, and a worker's individual needs.

Social **MEDIA**

Union Tweeting

Labor unions are increasingly using social media to promote their causes. A growing number of union organizations and members are already represented on Facebook and other social networking sites. It is also common for workers to set up community sites and blogs where they can openly discuss their concerns without having to worry about doing so on the job. Organizing 2.0 is an organization that is dedicated to helping labor organizers use social media more effectively. They also encourage users to join them on Twitter. Organizing 2.0 utilizes social media to connect people from many types of organizations, including labor, progressives, nonprofits, tech firms, faith communities, and information technologists.

Sources: Marissa Oberlander, "An Unlikely Union: Social Media and Labor Relations," January 12, 2011, http://news.medill.northwestern.edu/chicago/news.aspx?id=176075; "Unions Labor to Embrace Social Media," November 13, 2011, www.newlabormedia.com/; www.organizing20.org/; http://twitter.com/#!/organize20.

The proportion of union members relative to the size of the nation's workforce has declined over the last 30 years. Moreover, total union membership has dropped since 1980 despite steadily increasing membership in earlier years (see Figure 11.1).

To a great extent, this decline in membership is caused by several factors. Heavily unionized industries either have been decreasing in size or have not been growing as fast as non-unionized industries. For example, cutbacks in the steel industry have tended to reduce union membership. At the same time, the growth of high-tech industries has increased the ranks of non-union workers. Many firms have moved from the heavily unionized Northeast and Great Lakes regions to the less-unionized southeast and southwest regions—the so-called Sunbelt. At the relocated plants, formerly unionized firms tend to hire non-union workers. The largest growth in employment is occurring in the service industries, and these industries typically are not unionized. Some U.S. companies have moved their manufacturing operations to other countries where less-unionized labor is employed.

A recent study on union participation rates found a negative correlation between union participation and wage inequality. Decades ago, when unions were strong and roughly 1 in 3 men were union members, they were able to exert a powerful influence over maintaining high wages. The study found that the largest factor contributing to union decline has been the growth of jobs outside of traditionally unionized industries, such as manufacturing and construction. The study also found that, even in unionized industries, managers have increasingly grown opposed to union activity.[6]

Union–Management Partnerships

For most of the 20th century, unions represented workers with respect to wages and working conditions. To obtain rights for workers and recognition for themselves, unions engaged in often-antagonistic collective-bargaining sessions and strikes. At the same time, management traditionally protected its own rights of decision making, workplace organization, and strategic planning. Increasingly, however, management has become aware that this traditionally adversarial relationship does not result in the kind of high-performance workplace and empowered workforce necessary to succeed in today's highly competitive markets. For their part, unions and their members acknowledge that most major strikes result in failures that cost members thousands of jobs and reduce the unions' credibility. Today, instead of maintaining an "us versus them" mentality, many unions are becoming partners with management and cooperating to enhance the workplace, empower workers, increase production, improve quality, and reduce costs. According to the Department of Labor, the number of union–management partnerships in the United States is increasing.

Union–management partnerships can be initiated by union leaders, employees, or management. *Long-range strategic partnerships* focus on sharing decision-making power for a whole range of workplace and business issues. Long-range partnerships sometimes begin as limited ones and develop slowly over time. *Limited partnerships* center on accomplishing one specific task or project, such as the introduction of teams or the design of training programs. Education remains an industry that has relatively high union participation rates. Yale University, for instance, has a long-range strategic partnership with employees who belong to the Unite Here Locals 34 and 35 labor unions. This arrangement helps the two parties to develop best practices, as well as provides a forum to solve disputes and agree on contracts.[7]

From conflict to cooperation. A union leader and a top executive at Chrysler group LLC are leading their organization toward a partnership that will expand Chrysler's operations and the number of workers it needs. Traditionally, labor-management relations have been contentious. However, over the years, many firm and unions have learned that cooperation is the key to the success of both groups.

Although strategic union–management partnerships vary, most of them have several characteristics in common. First, strategic partnerships focus on developing cooperative relationships between unions and management instead of arguing over contractual rights. Second, partners work toward mutual gain, in which the organization becomes more competitive, employees are better off, and unions are stronger as a result of the partnership. Finally, as already noted, strategic partners engage in joint decision making on a broad array of issues. These issues include performance expectations, organizational structure, strategic alliances, new technology, pay and benefits, employee security and involvement, union–management roles, product development, and education and training.

Good labor–management relations can help everyone to deal with new and difficult labor issues as they develop. For example, many companies hope that their union–management partnerships will be strong enough to deal with the critical issue of rising health care costs. Unions work hard to protect their members from having to pay an increased percentage of health care costs, and they have experienced some success, in that an average union worker pays about 17 percent of his or her health care premiums compared with a non-union worker's contribution of about 33 percent.[8] Strong union–management partnerships will play a vital role in resolving health care issues.

Union–management partnerships have many potential benefits for management, workers, and unions. For management, partnerships can result in lower costs, increased revenue, improved product quality, and greater customer satisfaction. For workers, benefits may include increased response to their needs, more decision-making opportunities, less supervision, more responsibility, and increased job security. Unions can gain credibility, strength, and increased membership.

Among the many organizations that have found union-management partnerships beneficial is the Ford Motor Company. It has currently signed a union-management partnership agreement with the UAW. This partnership was created to increase the number of jobs and to make Ford more completive. The partnership will result in a better communications network throughout the company's management system as well as improvement in quality performance.[9]

LABOR–MANAGEMENT LEGISLATION

3 Identify the main focus of several major pieces of labor–management legislation.

As we have noted, business opposed early efforts to organize labor. The federal government generally supported anti-union efforts through the court system, and in some cases federal troops were used to end strikes. Gradually, however, the government began to correct this imbalance through the legislative process.

Norris–LaGuardia Act

The first major piece of legislation to secure rights for unions, the *Norris–LaGuardia Act* of 1932, was considered a landmark in labor–management relations. This act made it difficult for businesses to obtain court orders that banned strikes, picketing, or union membership drives. Previously, courts had issued such orders readily as a means of curbing these activities.

National Labor Relations Act

The *National Labor Relations Act,* also known as the *Wagner Act,* was passed by Congress in 1935. It established procedures by which employees decide whether they want to be represented by a union. If workers choose to be represented, the Wagner Act requires management to negotiate with union representatives. Before this law was passed, union efforts sometimes were interpreted as violating the Sherman Act (1890) because they were viewed as attempts to monopolize. The Wagner Act also forbid certain unfair labor practices on the part of management, such as firing or punishing workers because they were pro-union, spying on union meetings, and bribing employees to vote against unionization.

Finally, the Wagner Act established the **National Labor Relations Board (NLRB)** to enforce the provisions of the law. The NLRB is concerned primarily with (1) overseeing the elections in which employees decide whether they will be represented by a union and (2) investigating complaints lodged by unions or employees. Recently, the NLRB passed a ruling that most U.S. employers must post a notice informing employees of their right to join a union and bargain collectively. The decision has proved divisive, spurring more than 7,000 comments when it was first posted online. Pro-labor groups applaud it for keeping workers informed of their rights, while some managers and lawyers complain that the NLRB has become too pro-union.[10]

Fair Labor Standards Act

In 1938, Congress enacted the *Fair Labor Standards Act*. One major provision of this act permits the federal government to set a minimum wage. The first minimum wage, which was set in the late 1930s and did not include farm workers and retail employees, was $0.25 an hour. Today, the national minimum wage is $7.25 an hour, although many states and cities set their own minimum wages to account for differences in costs of living. Washington state has the highest minimum wage in the nation at $9.04 an hour.[11] Some employees, such as wait persons and farm workers, are still exempt from the minimum-wage provisions in

National Labor Relations Board (NLRB) the federal agency that enforces the provisions of the Wagner Act

Ethical
SUCCESS OR FAILURE?

Should Public-Sector Unions Have Collective Bargaining Rights?

Government employees in many states have long been represented by unions empowered to bargain on their behalf. In recent years, however, officials in some cash-strapped states have sought to curtail or eliminate collective bargaining rights for public-sector unions. Wisconsin, for example, passed a law that limits unions representing public employees to bargaining for wages only. This led to a recall effort aimed at unseating the governor who spearheaded the law. The Ohio legislature also voted to limit collective bargaining by public-sector unions—although that law was repealed the following year.

Those arguing for limitations on public-sector unions are worried about budget shortfalls and the size of public payrolls as states try to recover from a long, difficult recession. People who favor such restrictions are looking to improve the future financial condition of their state.

Public-sector employees oppose limitations on their collective bargaining rights. They see limitations as one step toward preventing unions from representing their interests in negotiations over working conditions and other issues, not just pay. Many also feel that public-sector unions are being unfairly blamed for states' budget problems. So should the collective-bargaining rights of public-sector unions be curtailed?

Sources: Based on information in Monica Davey, "'Right to Work' Bills Face Uncertain Future in an Election Year," *New York Times*, March 20, 2012, www.nytimes.com; "Unions Risk Their Future at Ballot Box," *Times Herald (Port Huron, MI)*, March 19, 2012, www.thetimesherald.com; Tom LoBianco, "Indiana Joins Right-to-Work Ranks, Gov. Signs Bill," *Associated Press*, February 1, 2012, www.ap.org; Michael A. Memoli and Alana Semuels, "Ohio Votes to Overturn New Collective Bargaining Law," *Los Angeles Times*, November 8, 2011, www.latimes.com.

most states. The act also requires that employees be paid overtime rates for work in excess of 40 hours a week. Finally, it prohibits the use of child labor.

Labor–Management Relations Act

The legislation of the 1930s sought to discourage unfair practices on the part of employers. Recall from Figure 11.1 that union membership grew from approximately 2 million in 1910 to almost 12 million by 1945. Unions represented over 35 percent of all nonagricultural employees in 1945. As union membership and power grew, however, the federal government began to examine the practices of labor. Several long and bitter strikes in the 1940s, mainly in the coal mining and trucking industries, led to a demand for legislative restraint on unions. As a result, in 1947 Congress passed the *Labor–Management Relations Act*, also known as the *Taft–Hartley Act*, over President Harry Truman's veto.

The Taft–Hartley Act's objective is to provide a balance between union power and management authority. It lists unfair labor practices that unions are forbidden to use. These include refusal to bargain with management in good faith, charging excessive membership dues, harassing non-union workers, and using various means of coercion against employers.

The Taft–Hartley Act also gives management more rights during union organizing campaigns. For example, management may outline for employees the advantages and disadvantages of union membership, as long as the information it presents is accurate. The act gives the President of the United States the power to obtain a temporary injunction to prevent or stop a strike that endangers national health and safety. An **injunction** is a court order requiring a person or group either to perform some act or to refrain from performing some act. Finally, the Taft–Hartley Act authorized states to enact laws to allow employees to work in a unionized firm without joining the union. Currently, 22 states (many in the south) have passed such *right-to-work laws*.[12]

Landrum–Griffin Act

In the 1950s, Senate investigations and hearings exposed racketeering in unions and uncovered cases of bribery, extortion, and embezzlement among union leaders. It was discovered that a few union leaders had taken union funds for personal use and accepted

injunction a court order requiring a person or group either to perform some act or to refrain from performing some act

payoffs from employers for union protection. Some were involved in arson, blackmail, and murder. Public pressure for reform resulted in the 1959 *Landrum–Griffin Act*.

This law was designed to regulate the internal functioning of labor unions. Provisions of the law require unions to file annual reports with the U.S. Department of Labor regarding their finances, elections, and various decisions made by union officers. The Landrum–Griffin Act also ensures that each union member has the right to seek, nominate, and vote for each elected position in his or her union. It provides safeguards governing union funds, and it requires management and unions to report the lending of management funds to union officers, union members, or local unions.

The various pieces of legislation we have reviewed here effectively regulate much of the relationship between labor and management after a union has been established. The next section demonstrates that forming a union is also a carefully regulated process.

THE UNIONIZATION PROCESS

Enumerate the steps involved in forming a union and show how the National Labor Relations Board is involved in the process.

Before a union can be formed at a particular firm, some employees of the firm must be interested in being represented by a union. Then, they must take a number of steps to formally declare their desire for a union. To ensure fairness, most of the steps in this unionization process are supervised by the NLRB.

Why Some Employees Join Unions

Obviously, employees start or join a union for a variety of reasons.

In many industries, such as teaching, union membership is so prevalent that new employees may feel compelled to join. In some states, even those employees who choose not to join a union are required to pay union dues, which is a serious incentive to join. Another commonly cited reason for joining a union is to combat a feeling of alienation.[13] Some employees—especially those whose jobs are dull and repetitive— may perceive themselves as merely parts of a machine. They may feel that they lose their individual or social identity at work. Union membership is one way to establish contact with others in a firm.

Another common reason for joining a union is the perception that union membership increases job security. No one wants to live in fear of arbitrary or capricious dismissal from a job. Unions actually have only limited ability to guarantee a member's job, but they can help to increase job security by enforcing seniority rules.

Employees may also join a union because of dissatisfaction with one or more elements of their jobs. If they are unhappy with their pay, benefits, or working conditions, they may look to a union to correct the perceived deficiencies.

Some people join unions because of their personal backgrounds. For example, a person whose parents are strong believers in unions might be inclined to feel just as positive about union membership.

In some situations, employees must join a union to keep their jobs. Many unions try, through their labor contracts, to require that a firm's new employees join the union after a specified probationary period. Under the Taft–Hartley Act, states may pass right-to-work laws prohibiting this practice.

Steps in Forming a Union

The first step in forming a union is the *organizing campaign* (see Figure 11.2). Its primary objective is to develop widespread employee interest in having a union. To kick off the campaign, a national union may send organizers to the firm to stir this interest. Alternatively, the employees themselves may decide that they want a union. Then they contact the appropriate national union and ask for organizing assistance.

The organizing campaign can be quite emotional, and it may lead to conflict between employees and management. On the one hand, the employees who want the union will be dedicated to its creation. On the other hand, management will be extremely sensitive to what it sees as a potential threat to its power and control.

FIGURE 11.2 Steps in Forming a Union

The unionization process consists of a campaign, signing of authorization cards, a formal election, and certification of the election by the NLRB.

1. Organizing campaign
2. Authorization cards
3. Election
4. NLRB certification

© CENGAGE LEARNING 2014

FIGURE 11.3   Sample Authorization Card

Unions must have written authorization to represent employees.

OBLIGATION OF

"I _____ , in the presence of
(PLEASE PRINT NAME)

members of the _____

promise and agree to conform to and abide by the Constitution

and laws of the _____ and its Local Unions. I will further the

purpose for which the _____ is instituted. I will bear true

allegiance to it and will not sacrifice its interest in any manner."

_____
(TO BE SIGNED BY APPLICANT – PLEASE DO NOT PRINT)

PRINT OR TYPE IN BLACK INK ONLY

SEX – MALE ☐ FEMALE ☐

LAST NAME	FIRST	INITIAL	SOCIAL SECURITY NO.
ADDRESS (STREET & NUMBER)			DATE OF BIRTH
CITY & STATE (OR PROVINCE)		POSTAL CODE	TELEPHONE NO.
PRESENT EMPLOYER			DATE HIRED
CLASSIFICATION			DATE OF THIS APPLICATION

Have you ever been   YES ☐
a member of   ?   NO ☐   If so, where? _____ LOCAL NO. _____ STATE _____

PORTION BELOW TO BE FILLED IN BY L.U. SECRETARY

LOCAL UNION NO.	DATE OF INITIATION	TYPE OF MEMBERSHIP	CARD NO.

At some point during the organizing campaign, employees are asked to sign *authorization cards* (see Figure 11.3) to indicate—in writing—their support for the union. Because of various NLRB rules and regulations, both union organizers and company management must be very careful in their behavior during this authorization drive. For example, employees cannot be asked to sign the cards when they are supposed to be working. Management may not indicate in any way that employees' jobs or job security will be in jeopardy if they do sign the cards.

If at least 30 percent of the eligible employees sign authorization cards, the organizers generally request that the firm recognize the union as the employees' bargaining representative. Usually the firm rejects this request, and a *formal election* is held to decide whether to have a union. This election usually involves secret ballots and is conducted by the NLRB. The outcome of the election is determined by a simple majority of eligible employees who choose to vote.

If the union obtains a majority, it becomes the official bargaining agent for its members, and the final step, *NLRB certification,* takes place. The union may immediately begin the process of negotiating a labor contract with management. If the union is voted down, the NLRB will not allow another election for one year.

Several factors can complicate the unionization process. For example, the **bargaining unit**, which is the specific group of employees that the union is to represent, must be defined. Union organizers may want to represent all hourly employees at a particular site (such as all workers at a manufacturing plant), or they may wish to represent only a specific group of employees (such as all electricians in a large manufacturing plant).

bargaining unit the specific group of employees represented by a union

Another issue that may have to be resolved is that of **jurisdiction**, which is the right of a particular union to organize particular groups of workers (such as nurses). When jurisdictions overlap or are unclear, the employees themselves may decide who will represent them. In some cases, two or more unions may be trying to organize some or all of the employees of a firm. Then, the election choices may be union A, union B, or no union at all.

The Role of the NLRB

As we have demonstrated, the NLRB is heavily involved in the unionization process. Generally, the NLRB is responsible for overseeing the organizing campaign, conducting the election (if one is warranted), and certifying the election results.

During the organizing campaign, both employers and union organizers can take steps to educate employees regarding the advantages and disadvantages of having a union. However, neither is allowed to use underhanded tactics or to distort the truth. If violations occur, the NLRB can stop the questionable behavior, postpone the election, or set aside the results of an election that has already taken place.

The NLRB usually conducts the election within 45 days of receiving the required number of signed authorization cards from the organizers. A very high percentage of the eligible voters generally participate in the election, and it is held at the workplace during normal working hours. In certain cases, however, a mail ballot or some other form of election may be called for.

Certification of the election involves counting the votes and considering challenges to the election. After the election results are announced, management and the union organizers have five days to challenge the election. The basis for a challenge might be improper conduct before the election or participation by an ineligible voter. After considering any challenges, the NLRB passes final judgment on the election results.

When union representation is established, union and management get down to the serious business of contract negotiations.

Unions are facing new challenges. Compensation and employee benefits are often the major issues a company and union leaders discuss during contract negotiations. Other issues include the working conditions and hours employees face and their right to organize and bargain with their employers in the first place. For example, to save money, the state of Wisconsin recently stripped away the bargaining rights of state government workers, who are union members.

COLLECTIVE BARGAINING

5 Describe the basic elements of the collective-bargaining process.

Once certified by the NLRB, a new union's first task is to establish its own identity and structure. It immediately signs up as many members as possible. Then, in an internal election, members choose officers and representatives. A negotiating committee is also chosen to begin **collective bargaining**, the process of negotiating a labor contract with management.

The First Contract

To prepare for its first contract session with management, the negotiating committee decides on its position on the various contract issues and determines the issues that are most important to the union's members. For example, the two most pressing concerns might be a general wage increase and an improved benefits package.

The union then informs management that it is ready to begin negotiations, and the two parties agree on a time and location. Both sides continue to prepare for the session up to the actual date of the negotiations.

Negotiations are occasionally held on company premises, but it is more common for the parties to meet away from the workplace—perhaps in a local hotel. The union typically is represented by the negotiating committee and one or more officials from the regional or national union office. The firm normally is represented by managers from the industrial-relations, operations, human resources management, and legal

jurisdiction the right of a particular union to organize particular groups of workers

collective bargaining the process of negotiating a labor contract with management

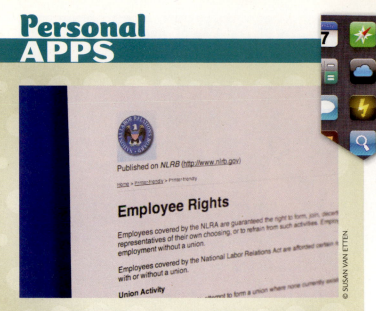
departments. Each side is required by law to negotiate in good faith and not to stall or attempt to extend the bargaining proceedings unnecessarily.

The union normally presents its contract demands first. Management then responds to the demands, often with a counterproposal. The bargaining may move back and forth, from proposal to counterproposal, over a number of meetings. Throughout the process, union representatives constantly keep their members informed of what is going on and how the negotiating committee feels about the various proposals and counterproposals.

Each side clearly tries to "get its own way" as much as possible, but each also recognizes the need for compromise. For example, the union may begin the negotiations by demanding a wage increase of $1 per hour but may be willing to accept 60 cents per hour. Management initially may offer 40 cents but may be willing to pay 75 cents. Eventually, the two sides will agree on a wage increase of between 60 and 75 cents per hour.

If an agreement cannot be reached, the union may strike. However, strikes are rare during a union's first contract negotiations. In most cases, the negotiating teams are able to agree on an initial contract without recourse to a strike.

The final step in collective bargaining is **ratification**, which is approval of the contract by a vote of the union membership. If the membership accepts the terms of the contract, it is signed and becomes a legally binding agreement. If the contract is not ratified, the negotiators must go back and try to iron out a more acceptable agreement.

Later Contracts

A labor contract may cover a period of one to three years or more, but every contract has an expiration date. As that date approaches, both management and the union begin to prepare for new contract negotiations. Now, however, the entire process is likely to be much thornier than the first negotiation.

For one thing, the union and the firm have "lived with each other" for several years, during which some difficulties may have emerged. Each side may see certain issues as being of critical importance—issues that provoke a great deal of emotion at the bargaining table and often are difficult to resolve. Also, each side has learned from the earlier negotiations. Each may take a harder line on certain issues and be less willing to compromise.

The contract deadline itself also produces tension. As the expiration date of the existing contract draws near, each side feels a pressure—real or imagined—to reach an agreement. This pressure may nudge the negotiators toward an agreement, but it also can have the opposite effect, making an accord more difficult to reach. Moreover, at some point during the negotiations, union leaders are likely to take a *strike vote*. This vote reveals whether union members are willing to strike in the event that a new contract is not negotiated before the old one expires. In almost all cases, this vote supports a strike. Thus, the threat of a strike may add to the pressure mounting on both sides as they go about the business of negotiating.

UNION–MANAGEMENT CONTRACT ISSUES

6 Identify the major issues covered in a union–management contract.

As you might expect, many diverse issues are negotiated by unions and management and are incorporated into a labor contract. Unions tend to emphasize issues related to members' income, their standard of living, and the strength of the union. Management's primary goals are to retain as much control as possible over the firm's operations and to maximize its strength relative to that of the union. The balance of power between union and management varies from firm to firm.

ratification approval of a labor contract by a vote of the union membership

Going for SUCCESS

Arbitration Down Under

On every continent, airlines are feeling squeezed by gyrating fuel prices and global competition. So when Australia's Qantas Airways wanted to restructure to get ready for expansion, unions representing its engineers, pilots, and ground staff worried about job security and pay. Airline management and union representatives negotiated for months to resolve their differences, without success. After a series of strikes by unionized ground crew, Qantas took the very unusual step of halting all flights, domestic and international, for nearly two days.

Then the country's labor relations tribunal, Fair Work Australia, intervened to prevent further strikes and get Qantas flying again. It allowed three weeks for the airline and its

unions come to agreement. When the deadline passed without a resolution, the tribunal ruled that the disputes would be settled by binding arbitration. During the next few months, while the airline and its engineers worked out an agreement that the tribunal approved, negotiations with ground crew and long-haul pilots continued toward arbitration. Neither the unions nor the airline knew what the tribunal would decide about pay and security.

Sources: Based on information in "Qantas Pay Dispute to Go to Arbitration," *Brisbane Times (Australia)*, March 26, 2012, www.brisbanetimes.com.au; "Qantas: 'Book with Confidence,'" *Airports International*, December 2011, p. 23; Kim Arlington with Matt O'Sullivan, "Qantas, Engineers Settle First Leg of Dispute Route," *The Age (Melbourne, Australia)*, December 19, 2011, p. 3; John Walton, "Govt Terminates Qantas Strike," *Australian Business Traveller*, October 31, 2011, www.ausbt.com.au; Ben Schneiders, "Work Tribunal Endorses Qantas Engineers' Deal," *The Age (Melbourne, Australia)*, January 24, 2012, p. 5.

Employee Pay

An area of bargaining central to union–management relations is employee pay. Three separate issues are usually involved: the forms of pay, the magnitude of pay, and the means by which the magnitude of pay will be determined.

Forms of Pay The primary form of pay is direct compensation—the wage or salary and benefits an employee receives in exchange for his or her contribution to the organization. Because direct compensation is a fairly straightforward issue, negotiators often spend much more of their time developing a benefits package for employees. Because the range of benefits and their costs have escalated over the years, this element of pay has become increasingly important and complex.

We discussed various employee benefits in Chapter 9. Of these, health, life, disability, and dental insurance are important benefits that unions try to obtain for their members. As the costs of health care continue to increase, insurance benefits are costing employers more, and many are trying to pass a higher portion of this increased cost on to their employees. Deferred compensation, in the form of pension or retirement programs, is also a common focal point. Decisions about deferred compensation can have a long-lasting impact on a company.

Other benefits commonly dealt with in the bargaining process include paid vacation time, holidays, and a policy on paid sick leave. Obviously, unions argue for as much paid vacation and holiday time as possible and for liberal sick-leave policies. Management naturally takes the opposite position. After decades of generous benefits packages, most firms have been forced to cut back due to decreased revenues or increased expenses. Especially as more baby boomers retire, pensions have become too expensive to be sustainable. Even heavily unionized industries, such as automobile manufacturing and utilities, have had to reduce their pensions and benefits for younger workers.[14]

Magnitude of Pay Of considerable importance is the *magnitude*, or amount, of pay that employees receive as both direct and indirect compensation. The union attempts to ensure that pay is on par with that received by other employees in the same or similar industries, both locally and nationally. The union also attempts to include in the contract clauses that provide pay increases over the life of the agreement. The most common is the *cost-of-living clause*, which ties periodic pay increases to increases in the cost of living, as defined by various economic statistics or indicators.

Of course, the magnitude of pay is also affected by the organization's ability to pay. If the firm has posted large profits recently, the union may expect large pay increases for its members. If the firm has not been very profitable, the union may agree to smaller pay hikes or even to a pay freeze. In an extreme situation (e.g., when the firm is bordering on bankruptcy), the union may agree to pay cuts. Very stringent conditions usually are included in any agreement to a pay cut.

Bargaining with regard to magnitude also revolves around employee benefits. At one extreme, unions seek a wide range of benefits, entirely or largely paid for by the firm. At the other extreme, management may be willing to offer the benefits package but may want its employees to bear most of the cost. Again, factors such as equity (with similar firms and jobs) and ability to pay enter into the final agreement.

Pay Determinants Negotiators also address the question of how individual pay will be determined. For management, the ideal arrangement is to tie wages to each employee's productivity. As we have seen, this method of payment tends to motivate and reward effort. Unions, on the other hand, feel that this arrangement can create unnecessary competition among employees. They generally argue that employees should be paid—at least in part—according to seniority. **Seniority** is the length of time an employee has worked for an organization.

Determinants regarding benefits are also negotiated. For example, management may want to provide profit-sharing benefits only to employees who have worked for the firm for a specified number of years. The union may want these benefits provided to all employees. Members of the Chicago police union receive large portions of their pay in the form of perks and benefits. For example, the union has an incredibly generous sick leave package. Police officers are allowed to take off up to 365 days of sick leave every two years. They also receive an annual allowance of $1,800 to compensate them for uniform costs and $2,800 in compensation for on-call time. Mayor Rahm Emanuel has been searching for ways to reduce the generous and expensive police benefits package.[15]

Working Hours

The number of working hours is another important issue in contract negotiations. The matter of overtime is of special interest. Federal law defines **overtime** as time worked in excess of 40 hours in one week. It also specifies that overtime pay must be at least one-and-one-half times the normal hourly wage. Unions may also attempt to negotiate overtime rates for all hours worked beyond eight hours in a single day. Similarly, the union may attempt to obtain higher overtime rates (say, twice the normal hourly wage) for weekend or holiday work. Still another issue is an upper limit to overtime, beyond which employees can refuse to work.

In firms with two or more work shifts, workers on less desirable shifts are paid a premium for their time. Both the amount of the premium and the manner in which workers are chosen for (or choose) particular shifts are negotiable issues. Other issues related to working hours are the work starting times and the length of lunch periods and coffee breaks.

Security

Security actually covers two issues. One is the job security of the individual worker; the other is the security of the union as the bargaining representative of the firm's employees.

Job security is protection against the loss of employment. It is a major concern of individuals. As we noted earlier, the desire for increased job security is a major reason for joining unions in the first place. In the typical labor contract, job security is based on seniority. If employees must be laid off or dismissed, those with the least seniority are the first to go. Some of the more senior employees may have to move to lower-level jobs, but they remain employed.

seniority the length of time an employee has worked for an organization

overtime time worked in excess of 40 hours in one week (under some union contracts, time worked in excess of eight hours in a single day)

job security protection against the loss of employment

Union security is protection of the union's position as the employees' bargaining agent. Union security is frequently a more volatile issue than job security. Unions strive for as much security as possible, but management tends to see an increase in union security as an erosion of its control.

Union security arises directly from its membership. The greater the ratio of union employees to non-union employees, the more secure the union is. In contract negotiations, unions thus attempt to establish various union membership conditions. The most restrictive of these is the **closed shop**, in which workers must join the union before they are hired. This condition was outlawed by the Taft–Hartley Act, but several other arrangements, including the following, are subject to negotiation:

- The **union shop**, in which new employees must join the union after a specified probationary period
- The **agency shop**, in which employees can choose not to join the union but must pay dues to the union anyway (The idea is that non-union employees benefit from union activities and should help to support them.)
- The **maintenance shop**, in which an employee who joins the union must remain a union member as long as he or she is employed by the firm

Management Rights

Of particular interest to the firm are those rights and privileges that are to be retained by management. For example, the firm wants as much control as possible over whom it hires, how work is scheduled, and how discipline is handled. The union, in contrast, would like some control over these and other matters affecting its members. It is interesting that some unions are making progress toward their goal of playing a more direct role in corporate governance. Some union executives have, in fact, been given seats on corporate boards of directors. In the wake of negative publicity related to an allegedly toxic corporate culture, Goldman Sachs CEO Lloyd Blankfein agreed to a union deal with the American Federation of State, County and Municipal Employees (AFSCME), which represents 1.6 million members. The deal creates more independent oversight of the firm and its board, but allows CEO Blankfein to retain much of his previous power.[16]

Grievance Procedures

A **grievance procedure** is a formally established course of action for resolving employee complaints against management. Virtually every labor contract contains a grievance procedure. Procedures vary in scope and detail, but they may involve the four steps described as follows (see Figure 11.4).

Original Grievance The process begins with an employee who believes that he or she has been treated unfairly in violation of the labor contract. For example, an employee may be entitled to a formal performance review after six months on the job. If no such review is conducted, the employee may file a grievance. To do so, the employee explains the grievance to a **shop steward**, an employee elected by union members to serve as their representative. The employee and the steward then discuss the grievance with the employee's immediate supervisor. Both the grievance and the supervisor's response are put in writing.

Broader Discussion In most cases, the problem is resolved during the initial discussion with the supervisor. If it is not, a second discussion is held. Now the participants include the original parties (employee, supervisor, and steward), a representative from the union's grievance committee, and the firm's industrial-relations representative. Again, a record is kept of the discussion and its results.

Full-Scale Discussion If the grievance is still not resolved, a full-scale discussion is arranged. This discussion includes everyone involved in the broader discussion, as well as all remaining members of the union's grievance committee and another high-level

union security protection of the union's position as the employees' bargaining agent

closed shop a workplace in which workers must join the union before they are hired; outlawed by the Taft–Hartley Act

union shop a workplace in which new employees must join the union after a specified probationary period

agency shop a workplace in which employees can choose not to join the union but must pay dues to the union anyway

maintenance shop a workplace in which an employee who joins the union must remain a union member as long as he or she is employed by the firm

grievance procedure a formally established course of action for resolving employee complaints against management

shop steward an employee elected by union members to serve as their representative

FIGURE 11.4   Steps in Resolving a Grievance

The employee grievance procedure for most organizations consists of four steps. Each ensuing step involves all the personnel from the preceding step plus at least one higher-level person. The final step is to go to a neutral third party, the arbitrator.

1 ORIGINAL GRIEVANCE

Employee takes grievance to shop steward.

Employee, shop steward, and supervisor discuss grievance and put grievance and response in writing.

E S
SS

2 BROADER DISCUSSION

Employee, shop steward, supervisor, representative from union's grievance committee, and firm's industrial-relations representative discuss grievance.

E S R U
SS

3 FULL-SCALE DISCUSSION

All of the people included in the broader discussion plus the remaining members of the union's grievance committee and a high-level manager discuss grievance.

E S R U
SS M U

4 ARBITRATION

Neutral third party hears both sides of grievance, reviews written documentation, and resolves matter.

E A S

E Employee   S Supervisor   A Arbitrator   U Union representative

SS Shop steward   M Manager   R Industrial-relations representative

© CENGAGE LEARNING 2014

manager. As usual, all proceedings are put in writing. All participants are careful not to violate the labor contract during this attempt to resolve the complaint.

Arbitration The final step in a grievance procedure is **arbitration**, in which a neutral third party hears the two sides of a dispute and renders a binding decision. As in a court hearing, each side presents its case and has the right to cross-examine witnesses. In addition, the arbitrator reviews the written documentation of all previous steps in the grievance procedure. Both sides may then give summary arguments and/or present briefs. The arbitrator then decides whether a provision of the labor contract has been violated and proposes a remedy. The arbitrator cannot make any decision that would add to, detract from, or modify the terms of the contract. If it can be proved that the arbitrator exceeded the scope of his or her authority, either party may appeal the decision to the courts.

What actually happens when union and management "lock horns" over all the issues we have mentioned? We can answer this question by looking now at the negotiating tools each side can wield.

UNION AND MANAGEMENT NEGOTIATING TOOLS

> Explain the primary bargaining tools available to unions and management. ⑦

Management and unions can draw on certain tools to influence each other during contract negotiations. Both sides may use advertising and publicity to gain support for their respective positions. The most extreme tools are strikes and lockouts, but there are other, milder techniques as well.

Strikes

Unions only go out on strike in a very few instances. These almost always occur after an existing labor contract has expired. Generally speaking, strikes have been on the decline. There were only five major strikes in 2009, which was the lowest

arbitration the step in a grievance procedure in which a neutral third party hears the two sides of a dispute and renders a binding decision

documented annual number since the U.S. government started tracking in 1947. The following year, 2010, had only 11 major strikes. There were 19 major strikes and lockouts in 2011, which represented a significant increase over the previous year.[17] Even then, if new contract negotiations seem to be proceeding smoothly, a union does not actually start a strike. The union does take a strike vote, but the vote may be used primarily to show members' commitment to a strike if negotiations fail.

The main objective of a strike is to put financial pressure on the company to encourage management to meet union demands. When union members do go out on strike, it is usually because negotiations seem to be stalled. A strike is simply a work stoppage: The employees do not report for work. In addition, striking workers engage in **picketing**, marching back and forth in front of a place of employment with signs informing the public that a strike is in progress. In doing so, they hope that (1) the public will be sympathetic to the strikers and will not patronize the struck firm, (2) nonstriking employees of the firm will honor the picket line and not report to work, and (3) members of other unions will not cross the picket line (e.g., to make deliveries) and thus will further restrict the operations of the struck firm. Unions may also engage in informational picketing to let companies know of their dissatisfaction.

In March 2012, union members of Allied Waste and Republic picketed in cities around Washington, Alabama, New York, and Ohio over complaints regarding changes to their health care coverage. The picketing and waste service stoppages affected over 60,000 customers.[18]

Obviously, strikes are expensive to both the firm and the strikers. The firm loses business and earnings during the strike, and the striking workers lose the wages they would have earned if they had been at their jobs. During a strike, unions try to provide their members with as much support as possible. Larger unions are able to put a portion of their members' dues into a *strike fund*. The fund is used to provide financial support for striking union members. At times, workers may go out on a **wildcat strike**, which is a strike that has not been approved by the union. In this situation, union leaders typically work with management to convince the strikers to return to work.

Slowdowns and Boycotts

Almost every labor contract contains a clause that prohibits strikes during the life of the contract. (This is why strikes, if they occur, usually take place after a contract has expired.) However, a union may strike a firm while the contract is in force if members believe that management has violated its terms. Workers also may engage in a **slowdown**, a technique whereby workers report to their jobs but work at a pace that is slower than normal.

A **boycott** is a refusal to do business with a particular firm. Unions occasionally bring this strategy to bear by urging members (and sympathizers) not to purchase the products of a firm with which they are having a dispute. The Major League Baseball players' union released a statement condemning the Arizona state law that gives police unprecedented powers to determine anyone's immigration status. In addition to expressing their disapproval of the law, many big-league players vowed they would not attend the All-Star Game, which was held in Arizona, but everything went according to plan, despite the dispute over the law.[19] A *primary boycott,* aimed at the employer directly involved in the dispute, can be a powerful weapon. A *secondary boycott,* aimed at a firm doing business with the employer, is prohibited by the Taft–Hartley Act. Cesar Chavez, a migrant worker who founded the United Farm Workers Union, used boycotts to draw attention to the low pay and awful conditions endured by produce pickers.

To strike or not to strike? A strike can increase the public's support for a union and hamper a firm's ability to operate effectively. But strikes are risky. They can cost their members a lot of money and even their jobs. The public isn't always sympathetic to strikers either—especially during period of high unemployment when it's hard for people to find even low-paying jobs with few or no benefits

Picketing is used to publicize that a strike is occurring. In this illustration, airline pilots are picketing to inform the public that they are on strike.

Have you ever worked at a business that was involved in a strike? It is likely that the strike involved compensation and benefits. Did you want to continue working instead of striking? Did you want to be a part of a picket line? Would you suggest that others participate in a strike?

picketing marching back and forth in front of a place of employment with signs informing the public that a strike is in progress

wildcat strike a strike not approved by the strikers' union

slowdown a technique whereby workers report to their jobs but work at a slower pace than normal

boycott a refusal to do business with a particular firm

lockout a firm's refusal to allow employees to enter the workplace

strikebreaker a non-union employee who performs the job of a striking union member

mediation the use of a neutral third party to assist management and the union during their negotiations

Lockouts and Strikebreakers

Management's most potent weapon is the **lockout**. In a **lockout,** the firm refuses to allow employees to enter the workplace. Like strikes, lockouts are expensive for both the firm and its employees. For this reason, they are only used rarely and in certain circumstances. A firm that produces perishable goods, for example, may use a lockout if management believes that its employees will soon go on strike. The idea is to stop production in time to ensure minimal spoilage of finished goods or work-in-process.

Management also may attempt to hire strikebreakers. A **strikebreaker** is a non-union employee who performs the job of a striking union member. Hiring strikebreakers can result in violence when picketing employees confront the non-union workers at the entrance to the struck facility. The firm also faces the problem of finding qualified replacements for the striking workers. Sometimes management personnel take over the jobs of strikers. Managers at telephone companies have had to get actively involved in phone repair services.

Mediation and Arbitration

Strikes, strikebreaking, lockouts, and boycotts all pit one side against the other. Ultimately, one side "wins" and the other "loses." Unfortunately, the negative effects of such actions—including resentment, fear, and distrust—may linger for months or years after a dispute has been resolved.

More productive techniques that are being used increasingly are mediation and arbitration. Either one may come into play before a labor contract expires or after some other strategy, such as a strike, has proved ineffective.

Mediation is the use of a neutral third party to assist management and the union during their negotiations. This third party (the mediator) listens to both sides, trying to find common ground for agreement. The mediator also tries to facilitate communication between the two sides, to promote compromise, and generally to keep the negotiations moving. At first the mediator may meet privately with each side. Eventually, however, his or her goal is to get the two to settle their differences. The Federal Mediation and Conciliation Service (FMCS) is an independent government agency that handles mediation for labor disputes. The agency handles 4,700 collective-bargaining negotiations per year, with 75 percent of those mediations reaching an agreement from both parties. The agency reports to have saved businesses and workers approximately $20 billion during 1999–2011, showing the benefits of mediation for both parties.[20]

Unlike mediation, the *arbitration* step is a formal hearing. Just as it may be the final step in a grievance procedure, it also may be used in contract negotiations (perhaps after mediation attempts) when the two sides cannot agree on one or more issues. Here, the arbitrator hears the formal positions of both parties on outstanding, unresolved issues. The arbitrator then analyzes these positions and makes a decision on the possible resolution of the issues. If both sides have agreed in advance that the arbitration will be *binding,* they must accept the arbitrator's decision.

This chapter ends our discussion of human resources. Next, we examine the marketing function of business. We begin in Chapter 12 by discussing the meaning of the term *marketing.*

return to **Inside BUSINESS**

Return to Inside Business: National Basketball Association

On the Friday after Thanksgiving in 2011, when representatives for the basketball players met with representatives for the team owners and the league, the fate of the NBA's 2011-12 season was at stake. The NBA had imposed a lockout after the previous collective bargaining agreement expired. Now the owners were negotiating to improve team profitability and the players were negotiating to avoid giving up basketball-related income.

Talks stretched from Friday into Saturday, and before dawn, the two sides came to agreement. The players would receive at least 50 percent and possibly more of the basketball-related income, according to a complex formula. The owners would have some spending restrictions and make payments for better competitive and financial balance

between teams. The players withdrew their lawsuits and applied to have their union recertified so they could ratify the new contract. Owners began signing players, and the shortened season got underway on December 25.

Questions

1. After mediation failed to help resolve the issues between players and owners, do you think arbitration should have been the next step? Explain your answer.
2. What are the advantages and disadvantages of using a lockout when lengthy talks don't lead to an agreement and both players and owners will face heavy financial losses if games aren't played?

SUMMARY

Looking for Success?
Get Flashcards, Quizzes, Games, Crosswords, and More at **www.cengagebrain.com**.

 Explain how and why labor unions came into being.

A labor union is an organization of workers who act together to negotiate wages and working conditions with their employers. Labor relations are the dealings between labor unions and business management.

The first major union in the United States was the Knights of Labor, formed in 1869 to eliminate the depersonalization of workers. The Knights were followed in 1886 by the American Federation of Labor (AFL). The goal of the AFL was to improve its members' living standards without changing the business system. In 1905, the radical Industrial Workers of the World (IWW) was formed; its goal was to overthrow capitalism. Of these three, only the AFL remained when the Congress of Industrial Organizations (CIO) was founded as a body of industrial unions between World War I and World War II. After years of competing, the AFL and CIO merged in 1955. The largest union not affiliated with the AFL–CIO is the Teamsters Union.

 Discuss the sources of unions' negotiating power and trends in union membership.

The power of unions to negotiate with management comes from two sources. The first is the size of their membership. The second is the groups of laws that guarantee unions the right to negotiate and that regulate the negotiation process. At present, union membership accounts for less than 15 percent

of the American workforce, and it seems to be decreasing for various reasons. Nonetheless, unions wield considerable power in many industries—those in which their members comprise a large proportion of the workforce.

Many unions today are entering into partnerships with management rather than maintaining their traditional adversarial position. Unions and management cooperate to increase production, improve quality, lower costs, empower workers, and enhance the workplace. Limited partnerships center on accomplishing one specific task or project. Long-range strategic partnerships focus on sharing decision-making power for a range of workplace and business matters.

 Identify the main focus of several major pieces of labor–management legislation.

Important laws that affect union power are the Norris–LaGuardia Act (limits management's ability to obtain injunctions against unions), the Wagner Act (forbids certain unfair labor practices by management), the Fair Labor Standards Act (allows the federal government to set the minimum wage and to mandate overtime rates), the Taft–Hartley Act (forbids certain unfair practices by unions), and the Landrum–Griffin Act (regulates the internal functioning of labor unions). The National Labor Relations Board (NLRB), a federal agency that oversees union–management relations, was created by the Wagner Act.

 Enumerate the steps involved in forming a union and show how the National Labor Relations Board is involved in the process.

Attempts to form a union within a firm begin with an organizing campaign to develop widespread employee interest in having a union. Next, employees sign authorization cards, indicating in writing their support for the union. The third step is to hold a formal election to decide whether to have a union. Finally, if the union obtains a majority, it receives NLRB certification, making it the official bargaining agent for its members. The entire process is supervised by the NLRB, which oversees the organizing campaign, conducts the election, and certifies the election results.

 Describe the basic elements of the collective-bargaining process.

Once a union is established, it may negotiate a labor contract with management through the process of collective bargaining. First, the negotiating committee decides on its position on the various contract issues. The union informs management that it is ready to begin negotiations, and a time and place are set. The union is represented by the negotiating committee, and the organization is represented by managers from several departments in the company. Each side is required to negotiate in good faith and not to stall or attempt to extend the bargaining unnecessarily. The final step is ratification, which is approval of the contract by a vote of the union membership.

 Identify the major issues covered in a union–management contract.

As the expiration date of an existing contract approaches, management and the union begin to negotiate a new contract. Contract issues include employee pay and benefits, working hours, job and union security, management rights, and grievance procedures.

 Explain the primary bargaining tools available to unions and management.

Management and unions can use certain tools to sway one another—and public opinion—during contract negotiations. Advertising and publicity help each side to gain support. When contract negotiations do not run smoothly, unions may apply pressure on management through strikes, slowdowns, or boycotts. Management may counter by imposing lockouts or hiring strikebreakers. Less drastic techniques for breaking contract deadlocks are mediation and arbitration. In both, a neutral third party is involved in the negotiations.

KEY TERMS

You should now be able to define and give an example relevant to each of the following terms:

labor union (303)
union-management (labor) relations (303)
craft union (304)
strike (304)
industrial union (305)
National Labor Relations Board (NLRB) (309)

injunction (310)
bargaining unit (312)
jurisdiction (313)
collective bargaining (313)
ratification (314)
seniority (316)
overtime (316)
job security (316)

union security (317)
closed shop (317)
union shop (317)
agency shop (317)
maintenance shop (317)
grievance procedure (317)
shop steward (317)
arbitration (318)

picketing (319)
wildcat strike (319)
slowdown (319)
boycott (319)
lockout (320)
strikebreaker (320)
mediation (320)

REVIEW QUESTIONS

1. Briefly describe the history of unions in the United States.
2. Describe the three characteristics common to most union-management partnerships. Discuss the benefits of union-management partnerships to management, unions, and workers.
3. How has government regulation of union-management relations evolved during this century?
4. For what reasons do employees start or join unions?
5. Describe the process of forming a union, and explain the role of the National Labor Relations Board (NLRB) in this process.
6. List the major areas that are negotiated in a labor contract.
7. Explain the three issues involved in negotiations concerning employee pay.
8. What is the difference between job security and union security? How do unions attempt to enhance union security?
9. What is a grievance? Describe the typical grievance procedure.
10. What are the steps involved in collective bargaining?
11. Why are strikes and lockouts relatively rare nowadays?
12. What are the objectives of picketing?
13. In what ways do the techniques of mediation and arbitration differ?

DISCUSSION QUESTIONS

1. Do unions really derive their power mainly from their membership and labor legislation? What are some other sources of union power?
2. Which labor contract issues are likely to be the easiest to resolve? Which are likely to be the most difficult?
3. Discuss the following statement: Union security means job security for union members.
4. How would you prepare for labor contract negotiations as a member of management? As head of the union negotiating committee?
5. Under what circumstances are strikes and lockouts justified in place of mediation or arbitration?

Most people probably don't think "Hollywood" when they think "unions." Perhaps they think of truck drivers, teachers, autoworkers, electricians, and other members of powerful and well-known labor unions. But in fact, the Writers Guild of America (WGA) is a long-standing and potent force in the media business and has been protecting and advocating for creative workers across the United States for over 50 years.

The Guild consists of two separate unions that are loosely linked but often act together—the Writers Guild East and the Writers Guild West. It's a not-for-profit organization whose members include thousands of graphic artists and writers for motion pictures, television, radio, newscasts, and increasingly the Internet. One direct result of the three-month writers' strike in 2008 was the Guild's extension of its jurisdiction to include Internet content, and the organization is now in the process of developing rules to protect and govern its members' work online. The Guild has created the position of New Media Project Manager for this purpose.

As one writer associated with a late-night TV talk show observed, in the entertainment business "all ideas start with the writer. Without writers you don't have a business at all—we start the ball rolling." That's the kind of pride in authorship that members of the Guild readily feel with the power of their union behind them.

The main purpose of the Writers Guild union is to protect its members, ensuring they get proper credit for their work and are properly paid. Compensation for scriptwriters consists of two parts: up-front money, which is paid on delivery of the work, and residuals, which are continuing payments made when the work is reused—for instance, when a show is rerun or goes into syndication. One way the Guild protects members is by receiving their residuals directly from the networks and other broadcasters, so it can check their accuracy before turning the money over to the individual writer who earned it. The Guild maintains a complex monitoring system that allows it to track reruns and verify payments and crediting. When something goes wrong—if someone isn't properly paid or credited—the Guild will step in on the writer's behalf. In the event of disagreements, the Guild will take the case to arbitration to ensure the writer gets what he or she has earned.

Most networks are closed shops, meaning writers must belong to the union to work there. In return, the Guild provides benefits like health care plans and pensions. Members' income can range widely, so the Guild makes special efforts to draw them together and develop the kind of solidarity that can make picketing and strikes effective. Recently, for instance, almost 1,000 WGA members filed a class-action lawsuit against two leading talent agencies claiming age discrimination. A $4.5 million settlement fund was the result.

Picketing has been successful, too. WGA picket lines recently won members protection against employers' ability to fire workers at will (employment at will means an employee can be fired at any time for almost any reason and with few legal rights). And strikes, while costly to all parties, can get good, if imperfect, results for union members. The 2008 writers' strike, for instance, sought a penny increase in the fee writers earned from the sale of movie videos and a percentage of the income from foreign sales of films (many U.S. films earn even more money abroad than they do at home). After three long months of a strike that disrupted the fall seasons of many top-rated TV shows and left other workers associated with those shows temporarily out of work, the strike ended with the achievement of only one of the goals—the percentage of foreign sales. Union officials were satisfied that the deal made everyone at least a little bit happy, and from that perspective it was a good outcome.

The WGA continues to support creative workers in the entertainment area. Writers Guild West recently came out in support of Hollywood's composers and lyricists, who are currently not unionized but are seeking entry to Teamsters Local 399. "We're very supportive," said a Guild spokesperson. "We consider composers and lyricists our colleagues, and we believe they deserve the benefits of a union contract."[21]

Questions

1. Should union members in nonessential industries like entertainment have the right to strike when their actions may put others out of work as well?
2. Do you think a labor dispute outcome that leaves both sides partly satisfied is a good outcome? Why or why not?
3. Union membership in the United States has been on a slow decline for about 30 years. What factors do you think account for this drop?

Case 11.2

When Nurses and Hospitals Don't Agree

What happens when unionized nurses and hospital administrators do not agree? Not long ago, the California Nurses Association threatened a one-day strike against dozens of California hospitals. The union wanted to call attention to its serious concerns about hospitals' preparations for protecting nurses against the potentially deadly H1N1 swine flu. At the time, 200 people in California had died from the flu strain, and hospitals around the state were coping with an influx of patients suffering from swine flu. The union was also in the middle of negotiating a new contract for its members, seeking higher pay and higher staffing levels than specified in the previous contract, which had expired months earlier.

Only days before the strike was scheduled to take place, however, it was called off as union negotiators and hospital administrators sat down with a federal mediator and worked to resolve their differences. The two sides were able to reach an agreement, and the union's members ratified the contract, which included extra safety precautions to protect nurses against swine flu.

This is only one example of how complex the negotiations can be when nurses' unions and hospital management disagree. Adding to the challenge, the U.S. health care system is currently facing two conflicting issues: a shortage of nurses and pressure to contain costs while providing proper medical care. The quality of care is, in fact, an important consideration for both sides, especially in light of research published by the National Bureau of Economic Research. Covering 50 nurses' strikes in New York state hospitals over 20 years, the study found higher mortality rates and higher readmission rates among patients hospitalized during the strikes, even when hospitals hired replacement nurses to cover for those on the picket line.

Because the stakes are so high, some nurses' unions are banding together to boost their advocacy efforts. In 2009, the California Nurses Association, the Massachusetts Nurses Association, and the United American Nurses merged to create National Nurses United, a union with 150,000 members across the nation. The union's top priority is to lobby for a higher ratio of nurses to patients.

Strikes are not the only way a nurses' union can put the spotlight on their concerns. When members of the Washington State Nursing Association were unhappy with proposed contract changes that could limit rest breaks, the nurses walked an informational picket line outside the Providence Sacred Heart Medical Center. The nurses were worried about fatigue affecting the quality of care, and they wanted to ensure that they had a full ten minutes of break time every four hours to rest. Rather than call a strike, nurses carried explanatory picket signs outside the hospital before and after their regular shifts. This nurses' union also set up an informational picket line when its contract negotiations with Tacoma General Hospital were stalled over pay increases and changes to retirement programs.

Sometimes nurses' unions and hospital administrators disagree on other issues. The Pennsylvania Association of Staff Nurses and Allied Professionals decided to strike Temple University Hospital in Pennsylvania after working without a contract for months. One of the key reasons was to protest a clause preventing union leaders and members from publicly criticizing hospital administration and staff. The hospital's CEO said the "non-disparagement" clause would not prevent nurses from alerting administrators to concerns about patient care. Other issues included pay, retirement programs, and college-tuition benefits for the children of hospital workers. The hospital hired 850 temporary nurses to maintain staffing levels during the strike, which lasted for a month. At the end, union and hospital negotiators bargained for days about the issues that had divided them, reached an agreement acceptable to both sides, and the union promptly ratified the new multiyear contract.[22]

Questions

1. Identify the major issues that have led to disagreements between nurses' unions and hospitals. Which do you think are most important for each side, and why?
2. Why would a nurses' union choose an informational picket instead of a strike when it wants to call attention to important contract issues?
3. Should U.S. lawmakers forbid nurses' unions from striking unless mediation and arbitration fail to settle their disputes with management?

Building Skills for Career Success

① SOCIAL MEDIA EXERCISE

Social media influencer, Glen Gilmore, wrote an interesting post on how unions are using Twitter and what they can do better. Visit his post at http://socialmediavoice.com/2011/03/14-ways-unions-are-using-twitter-labor.html.

1. After reviewing the article, do you think unions are using social media effectively? Why or why not?
2. Can you think of other ways that unions can benefit by using social media? If you have difficulty answering this question, consider doing a quick search in Google or Bing to find articles that may be useful.

② JOURNALING FOR SUCCESS

Discovery statement: This chapter focused on the unionization process and why employees join unions.

Assignment

1. What are the major reasons for joining and being a part of a labor union?
2. Under what conditions would you like to be a union member?
3. Are there any circumstances under which a striking union member should cross a picket line and go back to work? Explain.
4. Will the unions in the United States grow or decline over the next decade? Why?

③ DEVELOPING CRITICAL-THINKING SKILLS

Recently, while on its final approach to an airport in Lubbock, Texas, a commercial airliner encountered a flock of ducks. The flight crew believed that one or more of the ducks hit the aircraft and were ingested into the plane's main engine. The aircraft landed safely and taxied to the terminal. The flight crew advised the maintenance and operations crews of the incident. Operations grounded the plane until it could be inspected, but because of the time of day, maintenance personnel available to perform the inspection were in short supply. A supervisor, calling from an overtime list, made calls until contacting two available off-duty mechanics. They worked on overtime pay to perform the inspection and return the aircraft to a safe flying status. Several days after the inspection, a mechanic on the overtime list who was not home when the supervisor called complained that she had been denied overtime. This union member believed that the company owed her overtime pay for the same number of hours worked by a mechanic who performed the actual inspection. The company disagreed. What options are available to resolve this conflict?

Assignment

1. Using the following questions as guidelines, determine how this dispute can be resolved.
   a. What options are available to the unhappy mechanic? What process must she pursue? How does this process work?
   b. Do you believe that the mechanic should receive pay for the time she did not work? Justify your answer.
   c. What do you think was the final outcome of this conflict?
2. Prepare a report describing how you would resolve this situation.

④ BUILDING TEAM SKILLS

For more than a century, American unions have played an important role in the workplace, striving to improve the working conditions and quality of life of employees. Today, federal laws cover many of the workers' rights that unions first championed. For this reason, some people believe that unions are no longer necessary. According to some experts, however, as technology changes the workplace and as cultural diversity and the number of part-time workers increase, unions will increase their memberships and become stronger as we move into the new century. What do you think?

Assignment

1. Form a "pro" group and a "con" group and join one of them.
2. Debate whether unions will be stronger or weaker in the next century.
3. Record the key points for each side.
4. Summarize what you learned about unions and their usefulness in a report, and state your position on the debated issue.

⑤ RESEARCHING DIFFERENT CAREERS

When applying for a job, whether mailing or faxing in your résumé, you should always include a letter of application, or a cover letter, as it is often called. A well-prepared cover letter should convince the prospective employer to read your résumé and to phone you for an interview. The letter should describe the job you want and your qualifications for the job. It should also let the firm know where you can be reached to set up an appointment for an interview.

Assignment

1. Prepare a letter of application to use with the résumé you prepared in Chapter 9. (An example appears in Appendix A online.)
2. After having several friends review your letter, edit it carefully.
3. Ask your instructor to comment on your letter.

Running a Business PART 4   Graeter's

At Graeter's, Tenure Is "a Proud Number"

Although you might think working for an ice-cream company would be motivating under almost any circumstances, Graeter's doesn't take its employees' commitment for granted. Including full-time and part-time seasonal workers, the company employs about 800 people in three production facilities and dozens of ice-cream shops. Teenagers who take a summer job at a Graeter's shop often return to help out during the winter holidays and then come back to work the following summer, and the summer after that. Production employees tend to remain with the company for long periods, as well, and Graeter's is relying on their experience and expertise as it expands its national distribution and opens new stores far from the Cincinnati base.

PROFESSIONAL PROCEDURES WITH PERSONAL TOUCHES

Over the last few years, Graeter's has benefitted from tightening up some of its long-standing human resource management

© MAITREE LAPITAKSIN/SHUTTERSTOCK

12 Building Customer Relationships Through Effective Marketing

LEARNING OBJECTIVES

Once you complete this chapter, you will be able to:

1. Understand the meaning of *marketing* and the importance of management of customer relationships.

2. Explain how marketing adds value by creating several forms of utility.

3. Trace the development of the marketing concept and understand how it is implemented.

4. Understand what markets are and how they are classified.

5. Identify the four elements of the marketing mix and be aware of their importance in developing a marketing strategy.

6. Explain how the marketing environment affects strategic market planning.

7. Understand the major components of a marketing plan.

8. Describe how market measurement and sales forecasting are used.

9. Distinguish between a marketing information system and marketing research.

10. Identify the major steps in the consumer buying decision process and the sets of factors that may influence this process.

At $62 a Pound, Single-Serve Coffee is Hot!

Nespresso knows that what makes single-serve coffee so hot is the ability to brew one very good cup of coffee in a very short time. Owned by the Swiss food giant Nestlé, Nespresso focuses on convenience and quality when it markets machines and coffee capsules to consumers and businesses. Now its annual sales of $3 billion are growing at a rate of nearly 20 percent per year as the company introduces dozens of new coffeemakers and compatible capsules for consumers, small businesses, and corporate use.

Although Nespresso's machines and capsules are especially popular in Europe, where they were first introduced, the firm also targets coffee lovers in other countries where the "coffee culture" is strong. Customers view single-serve coffee or espresso as an affordable luxury, whether the economy is up or down. Nespresso makes it easy to reorder replacement capsules online, by phone, or in one of 300 branded boutiques in 50 countries. For the convenience of premeasured, premium coffee in their choice of flavors and strengths, customers pay about 55 cents per capsule. This works out to about $62 per pound, and earns Nespresso a healthy profit margin from every cup.

As the single-serve coffee market heats up, Nespresso faces an increasingly competitive marketing environment. For example, Vermont's Green Mountain Coffee Roasters holds a sizable share of the U.S. market, thanks to its fast-selling Keurig coffee machines and individual K-Cup portions. In addition to marketing a variety of flavors under its own brand, Green Mountain makes K-Cups prefilled with Starbucks, Dunkin' Donuts, and Newman's Own coffees.

The competitive stakes are particularly high because Nespresso's capsules don't work in Keurig machines, and K-Cups don't work in Nespresso machines. This is generally the case for other brands, as well. So when customers buy a single-serve coffeemaker, they're also making a choice about the replacement capsules they will buy in the future. As a result, Nespresso's marketers aren't just selling a machine—they're vying for the opportunity to sell each customer thousands of coffee, tea, and cocoa capsules at a sizable profit, year after year after year.[1]

Did You Know?

Nespresso has sold more than 100 million single-serve coffee capsules since being founded in 1986.

Numerous organizations, like Nepresso, use marketing efforts to provide customer satisfaction and value. Understanding customers' needs, such as "what's cool," is crucial to provide customer satisfaction. Although marketing encompasses a diverse set of decisions and activities, marketing always begins and ends with the customer. The American Marketing Association defines **marketing** as "The activity, set of institutions, and processes for creating, communicating, delivering, and exchanging offerings that have value for customers, clients, partners, and society at large."[2] The marketing process involves eight major functions and numerous related activities (see Table 12.1). All of these are essential if the marketing process is to be effective.

In this chapter, we examine marketing activities that add value to products. We trace the evolution of the marketing concept and describe how organizations practice it. Next, our focus shifts to market classifications and marketing strategy. We analyze the four elements of a marketing mix and discuss uncontrollable factors in the marketing environment. Then we examine the major components of a marketing plan. We consider tools for strategic market planning, including market measurement, sales forecasts, marketing information systems, and marketing research. Last, we look at the forces that influence consumer and organizational buying behavior.

marketing the activity, set of institutions, and processes for creating, communicating, delivering, and exchanging offerings that have value for customers, clients, partners, and society at large

TABLE 12.1 Eight Major Marketing Functions

Exchange functions: All companies—manufacturers, wholesalers, and retailers—buy and sell to market their merchandise.

1. Buying includes obtaining raw materials to make products, knowing how much merchandise to keep on hand, and selecting suppliers.

2. Selling creates possession utility by transferring the title of a product from seller to customer.

Physical distribution functions: These functions involve the flow of goods from producers to customers. Transportation and storage provide time utility and place utility and require careful management of inventory.

3. Transporting involves selecting a mode of transport that provides an acceptable delivery schedule at an acceptable price.

4. Storing goods is often necessary to sell them at the best selling time.

Facilitating functions: These functions help the other functions to take place.

5. Financing helps at all stages of marketing. To buy raw materials, manufacturers often borrow from banks or receive credit from suppliers. Wholesalers may be financed by manufacturers, and retailers may receive financing from the wholesaler or manufacturer. Finally, retailers often provide financing to customers.

6. Standardization sets uniform specifications for products or services. Grading classifies products by size and quality, usually through a sorting process. Together, standardization and grading facilitate production, transportation, storage, and selling.

7. Risk taking—even though competent management and insurance can minimize risks—is a constant reality of marketing because of such losses as bad-debt expense, obsolescence of products, theft by employees, and product-liability lawsuits.

8. Gathering market information is necessary for making all marketing decisions.

> **Understand the meaning of *marketing* and the importance of management of customer relationships.**

MANAGING CUSTOMER RELATIONSHIPS

Marketing relationships with customers are the lifeblood of all businesses. Maintaining positive relationships with customers is an important goal for marketers. The term **relationship marketing** refers to "marketing decisions and activities focused on achieving long-term, satisfying relationships with customers." Relationship marketing continually deepens the buyer's trust in the company, which, as the customer's loyalty grows, increases a company's understanding of the customer's needs and desires. Successful marketers respond to customers' needs and strive to continually increase value to buyers over time. Eventually, this interaction becomes a solid relationship that allows for cooperation and mutual trust. The Internet has expanded and improved relationship marketing options for many firms by making targeted communication faster, cheaper, and easier. New digital technologies allow firms to connect to consumers and have a dialogue with them in real-time. This not only improves the speed at which firms can innovate, but it gives consumers a feeling that they are being listened to. Some firms specialize in cultivating this relationship. Sparks and Honey, for example, is a trend-spotting agency started by advertising holding company Omnicom Group. Sparks and Honey seeks to take advantage of the technological forces that are remaking the advertising industry through utilizing social media, Twitter, and YouTube to identify and market the products that consumers currently like and want.[3]

To build long-term customer relationships, marketers are increasingly turning to marketing research and information technology. **Customer relationship management (CRM)** focuses on using information about customers to create marketing strategies that develop and sustain desirable customer relationships. By increasing customer value over time, organizations try to retain and increase long-term profitability through customer loyalty. Because CRM is such an important part of creating and building customer loyalty, many companies offer high-tech products aimed at helping firms to identify good customers and to manage relations with them over the long-term. The accessibility of technology has contributed to a more even playing field for firms of all

© SUSAN VAN ETTEN

Who do customers want? Like many other organizations, airline companies spend a considerable amount of money on marketing programs to develop and maintain long-term relationships with their customers—especially the valuable ones. Sometimes it's more profitable to retain these customers by offering them big rewards than attracting new customers who may never develop the same loyalty.

Ethical
SUCCESS OR FAILURE?

The Customer Is Always Right—Or Not

Is the customer *always* right? When customers return a broken product to Kohler, which makes kitchen and bathroom fixtures, the company nearly always offers a replacement, to maintain good customer relations. Still, "there are times you've got to say 'no,'" explains a Kohler warranty expert, such as when a product is undamaged or has been abused. Entrepreneur Lauren Thorp, who owns the e-commerce company Umba Box, says, "While the customer is 'always' right, sometimes you just have to fire a customer." When Thorp has tried everything to resolve a complaint and realizes that the customer will be dissatisfied no matter what, she returns her attention to the rest of her customers, who she says are "the reason for my success."

What about customers who hurt other customers? On Black Friday, at the start of the Christmas gift-buying season, some customers waiting for bargains have started fights or broken store fixtures. What about customers who abuse marketers' policies? Costco traditionally offered a money-back guarantee on everything. A few years ago, however, the retailer noticed that some customers were returning older televisions, receiving refunds, and then buying newer models at lower prices. To stop these practices, Costco now offers a 90-day return policy on electronics and invites customers to call a toll-free hotline for technical assistance.

Sources: Based on information in Leslie Bradshaw, "Lauren Thorp on Taking the Plunge," *Forbes*, March 6, 2012, www.forbes.com; "Warranty Success Stories," *Warranty Week*, March 1, 2012, www.warrantyweek.com; Laarni A. Ragaza, "Costco Laptops and Desktops for the Holidays," *PC Magazine*, November 19, 2010, www.pcmag.com; Nick Carbone, "Black and Blue Friday," *Time*, November 26, 2011, www.time.com; www.costco.com.

---

sizes. Software and programs such as Batchbook and Mailchimp allow even very small companies to manage customers and maintain consistent communication with them.[4]

Managing customer relationships requires identifying patterns of buying behavior and using this information to focus on the most promising and profitable customers. Companies must be sensitive to customers' requirements and desires and establish communication to build customers' trust and loyalty. In some instances, it may be more profitable for a company to focus on satisfying a valuable existing customer than to attempt to attract a new one who may never develop the same level of loyalty. This involves determining how much the customer will spend over his or her lifetime. The **customer lifetime value** (CLV) is a measure of a customer's worth (sales minus costs) to a business during one's lifetime.[5] However, there are also intangible benefits of retaining lifetime-value customers, such as their ability to provide feedback to a company and refer new customers of similar value. The amount of money a company is willing to spend to retain such customers is also a factor. In general, when marketers focus on customers chosen for their lifetime value, they earn higher profits in future periods than when they focus on customers selected for other reasons.[6] Thanks to technological innovations and improved research, it is a fairly straightforward task to calculate CLV these days. In fact there are many online calculators that companies can utilize, including one created by Harvard University.[7] Because the loss of a potential lifetime customer can result in lower profits, managing customer relationships has become a major focus of marketers.

relationship marketing establishing long-term, mutually satisfying buyer–seller relationships

customer relationship management (CRM) using information about customers to create marketing strategies that develop and sustain desirable customer relationships

customer lifetime value a measure of a customer's worth (sales minus costs) to a business over one's lifetime

utility the ability of a good or service to satisfy a human need

UTILITY: THE VALUE ADDED BY MARKETING

As defined in Chapter 8, **utility** is the ability of a good or service to satisfy a human need. The latest iPad, Nike Zoom running shoes, or Mercedes Benz luxury car all satisfy human needs. Thus, each possesses utility. There are four kinds of utility.

Form utility is created by converting production inputs into finished products. Marketing efforts may influence form utility indirectly because the data gathered as part of marketing research are frequently used to determine the size, shape, and features of a product.

The three kinds of utility that are created directly by marketing are place, time, and possession utility. **Place utility** is created by making a product available at a location

2 Explain how marketing adds value by creating several forms of utility.

form utility utility created by converting production inputs into finished products

place utility utility created by making a product available at a location where customers wish to purchase it

TABLE 12.3	Common Bases of Market Segmentation		
Demographic	**Psychographic**	**Geographic**	**Behavioristic**
Age	Personality attributes	Region	Volume usage
Gender	Motives	Urban, suburban, rural	End use
Race	Lifestyles	Market density	Benefit expectations
Ethnicity		Climate	Brand loyalty
Income		Terrain	Price sensitivity
Education		City size	
Occupation		County size	
Family size		State size	
Family life cycle			
Religion			
Social class			

Source: William M. Pride and O. C. Ferrell, *Marketing: Concepts and Strategies,* 17th ed. (Mason, OH: South-Western/Cengage Learning, 2014). Adapted with permission.

lines and a spiced-up catalog. OfficeMax has made a huge effort to separate itself from other office supply stores by further defining its target market based on research data that women are responsible for over 85 percent of office purchases.[12]

Identify the four elements of the marketing mix and be aware of their importance in developing a marketing strategy.

Creating a Marketing Mix

A business firm controls four important elements of marketing that it combines in a way that reaches the firm's target market. These are the *product* itself, the *price* of the product, the means chosen for its *distribution*, and the *promotion* of the product. When combined, these four elements form a marketing mix (see Figure 12.3). Marketers for Toyota's Scion brand automobiles developed a marketing mix to target consumers who are young and hip. Scion aims much of its marketing efforts at the 18 to 34 demographic. Around 75% of Scion purchasers are new to the Scion brand. Many Scion customers are buying a car for the first time. Scion's most recent advertising campaign, called iQ Therefore I Am, surrounded the release of the new Scion model, the iQ, and included a variety of online content, such as racy videos, an interactive car brochure to highlight features of the vehicle, and even an online museum of underground cultural movements. Also included in the Scion iQ marketing mix is a test drive program in major cities around the country and collaborative events with artists to underscore Scion's affiliation with arts and music.[13]

A firm can vary its marketing mix by changing any one or more of these ingredients. Thus, a firm may use one marketing mix to reach one target market and a second, somewhat different, marketing mix to reach another target market. For example, most automakers produce several different types and models of vehicles and aim them at different market segments based on the potential customers' age, income, and other factors.

The *product* ingredient of the marketing mix includes decisions about the product's design, brand name, packaging, warranties, and the like. When McDonald's decides on brand names, package designs, sizes of orders, flavors of sauces, and recipes, these choices are all part of the product ingredient.

The *pricing* ingredient is concerned with both base prices and discounts of various kinds. Pricing decisions are intended to achieve particular goals, such as to maximize profit or even to make room for new models. The rebates offered by automobile manufacturers are a pricing strategy developed to boost low auto sales. Product and pricing are discussed in detail in Chapter 13.

The *distribution* ingredient involves not only transportation and storage but also the selection of intermediaries. How many levels of intermediaries should be used

FIGURE 12.3   The Marketing Mix and the Marketing Environment

The marketing mix consists of elements that the firm controls—product, price, distribution, and promotion. The firm generally has no control over forces in the marketing environment.

- Marketing mix
- Marketing environment

Source: William M. Pride and O. C. Ferrell, *Marketing: Concepts and Strategies,* 17th ed. (Mason, OH: South-Western/ Cengage Learning, 2014). Adapted with permission.

in the distribution of a particular product? Should the product be distributed as widely as possible or should distribution be restricted to a few specialized outlets in each area? Video rental retailers have had to make numerous decisions regarding distribution. Currently, Redbox, owned by Coinstar, has 24 percent of the video rental market share, Dish Network Corporation, who recently took over Blockbuster, has 14 percent, and Netflix has 5 percent.[14] Fifteen years ago, almost all videos were distributed through brick-and-mortar stores. Distribution decisions and activities are discussed in more detail in Chapter 14.

The *promotion* ingredient focuses on providing information to target markets. The major forms of promotion are advertising, personal selling, sales promotion, and public relations. These four forms are discussed in Chapter 15.

These ingredients of the marketing mix are controllable elements. A firm can vary each of them to suit its organizational goals, marketing goals, and target markets. As we extend our discussion of marketing strategy, we will see that the marketing environment includes a number of *uncontrollable* elements.

MARKETING STRATEGY AND THE MARKETING ENVIRONMENT

The marketing mix consists of elements that a firm controls and uses to reach its target market. In addition, the firm has control over such organizational resources as finances and information. These resources may be used to accomplish marketing goals,

Developing the right marketing mix. Firms have little control over the marketing environment. However, they *can* control the marketing mixes for their products—that is, the nature of the products themselves and how they are priced, distributed, and promoted. The maker of All Small & Mighty has developed a specific marketing mix for the detergent. Who do you think the product is aimed at?

 6 Explain how the marketing environment affects strategic market planning.

KEY TERMS

You should now be able to define and give an example relevant to each of the following terms:

marketing (331)
relationship marketing (332)
customer relationship
    management (CRM) (332)
customer lifetime value (333)
utility (333)
form utility (333)
place utility (333)

time utility (334)
possession utility (334)
marketing concept (334)
market (336)
marketing
    strategy (337)
marketing mix (337)
target market (337)

undifferentiated approach
    (337)
market segment (339)
market segmentation (339)
marketing plan (342)
sales forecast (343)
marketing information system
    (344)

marketing research (344)
buying behavior (348)
consumer buying behavior
    (348)
business buying behavior (348)
personal income (349)
disposable income (349)
discretionary income (349)

REVIEW QUESTIONS

1. How, specifically, does marketing create place, time, and possession utility?
2. What is relationship marketing?
3. How is a marketing-oriented firm different from a production-oriented firm or a sales-oriented firm?
4. What are the major requirements for a group of individuals and organizations to be a market? How does a consumer market differ from a business-to-business market?
5. What are the major components of a marketing strategy?
6. What is the purpose of market segmentation? What is the relationship between market segmentation and the selection of target markets?
7. What are the four elements of the marketing mix? In what sense are they "controllable"?
8. Describe the forces in the marketing environment that affect an organization's marketing decisions.

9. What is a marketing plan, and what are its major components?
10. What major issues should be specified before conducting a sales forecast?
11. What is the difference between a marketing information system and a marketing research project? How might the two be related?
12. What new information technologies are changing the ways that marketers keep track of business trends and customers?
13. What are the major sources of secondary information?
14. Why do marketers need to understand buying behavior?
15. How are personal income, disposable income, and discretionary income related? Which is the best indicator of consumer purchasing power?

DISCUSSION QUESTIONS

1. What problems might face a company that focuses mainly on its most profitable customers?
2. In what way is each of the following a marketing activity?
   a. The provision of sufficient parking space for customers at a suburban shopping mall.
   b. The purchase by a clothing store of seven dozen sweaters in assorted sizes and colors.
   c. The inclusion of a longer and more comprehensive warranty on an automobile.

3. How might adoption of the marketing concept benefit a firm? How might it benefit the firm's customers?
4. Is marketing information as important to small firms as it is to larger firms? Explain.
5. How does the marketing environment affect a firm's marketing strategy?

Video Case 12.1
Raleigh Wheels Out Steel Bicycle Marketing

From its 19th-century roots as a British bicycle company, Raleigh has developed a worldwide reputation for marketing sturdy, comfortable, steel-frame bicycles. The firm, named for the street in Nottingham, England, where it was originally located, was

a trend-setter in designing and manufacturing bicycles. When Raleigh introduced steel-frame bicycles equipped with three-speed gear hubs in 1903, it revolutionized the industry and set off a never-ending race to improve the product's technology. In the pre-auto era, its bicycles became a two-wheeled status symbol for British consumers, and the brand maintained its cachet for decades. Although Raleigh's chopper-style bicycles were hugely popular in the 1970s, international competition and changing consumer tastes have taken a toll during the past few decades.

Now Raleigh markets a wide variety of bicycles to consumers in Europe, Canada, and the United States. Its U.S. division, based in Kent, Washington, has been researching new bicycles for contemporary consumers and developing models that are lighter, faster, and better. Inspired by the European lifestyle and tradition of getting around on bicycles, and its long history in the business, Raleigh is looking to reinvigorate sales and capture a larger share of the $6 billion U.S. bicycle market.

Raleigh's U.S. marketers have been observing the "messenger market," customers who ride bicycles through downtown streets to deliver documents and small packages to businesses and individuals. They have also noted that many everyday bicycle riders dress casually, in T-shirts and jeans, rather than in special racing outfits designed for speed. Targeting consumers who enjoy riding bicycles as a lifestyle, Raleigh's marketers are focusing on this segment's specific needs and preferences as they develop, price, promote, and distribute new models.

In recent years, Raleigh's marketers have stepped up the practice of bringing demonstration fleets to public places where potential buyers can hop on one of the company's bicycles and pedal for a few minutes. The idea is to allow consumers who enjoy bicycling to actually experience the fun feeling of riding a Raleigh. The marketers are also fanning out to visit bicycle races and meet bicyclists in cities and towns across America, encourag-

ing discussions about Raleigh and about bicycling in general and seeking feedback about particular Raleigh products.

Listening to consumers, Raleigh's marketers recognized that many had misperceptions about the weight of steel-frame bicycles. Although steel can be quite heavy, Raleigh's bicycles are solid yet light, nimble, and easy to steer. Those who have been on bicycles with steel frames praise the quality of the ride, saying that steel "has a soul," according to market research.

To stay in touch with its target market, Raleigh is increasingly active in social media. It has several thousand fans who visit its Facebook page to see the latest product concepts and post their own photos and comments about Raleigh bicycles. It also uses Twitter to keep customers informed and answer questions about its bicycles and upcoming demonstration events. The company's main blog communicates the latest news about everything from frame design and new bike colors under consideration to product awards and racing activities. It has a separate blog about both the fun and the challenges of commuting on bicycle, a topic in which its customers are intensely interested because so many do exactly that. By listening to customers and showing that it understands the daily life of its target market, Raleigh is wheeling toward higher sales in a highly competitive marketplace.[24]

Questions for Discussion

1. Is Raleigh using the marketing concept? Explain.
2. What type of approach does Raleigh use to select target markets?
3. Of the four categories of segmentation variables, which is most important to Raleigh's segmentation strategy, and why?

Case 12.2

PepsiCo Tailors Tastes to Tantalize Tastebuds of Target Markets

PepsiCo, the world's leading snack marketer, aims to gobble up more market share through careful targeting and creative marketing. Most of PepsiCo's sales come from North and South America, where it has traditionally been a strong competitor. Among its ever-expanding pantry of brands, 19 are already billion-dollar businesses, including Pepsi-Cola, Diet Pepsi, and Mountain Dew soft drinks; Lay's, Doritos, and Tostitos chips; Lipton teas; Tropicana fruit drinks; Gatorade sports drinks; Quaker foods; and Aquafina bottled waters.

The company faces aggressive competition from Coca-Cola and Draft Foods, both of which are making marketing waves in the Americas, across Europe, and in Asia. It must also deal with a variety of local brands that, in some cases, have large and loyal customer bases. Therefore, PepsiCo's marketers constantly research customers' needs and study the influence of environmental forces so that they can develop the right marketing mix for the right market.

One global trend that PepsiCo's marketers have identified is increased interest in healthier eating. Several years ago, the U.K. government mounted a campaign warning consumers of the dangers of high salt intake and urged them to change their diets. In response, PepsiCo slashed the amount of sodium in its locally

popular Walkers snacks by 25 percent. With U.S. health experts also calling for lower salt in processed foods, PepsiCo is now reducing the level of salt in many other snacks worldwide. It is also lightening up on fats and sugar and making nutrition labeling more prominent so that consumers can make educated choices. "What we want to do with our 'fun for you' products is to make them the healthiest 'fun for you' products," says the CEO.

Another trend that PepsiCo's marketers noticed is sharply higher use of digital media among teenagers and young adults, a large and lucrative target market for snacks and beverages. As a result, PepsiCo has stepped up its use of the Internet, blogs, Twitter, Facebook, and YouTube to communicate with and influence these consumers. Its Dewmocracy campaigns, for example, invite customers to vote online for their favorite new Mountain Dew flavors. It has also run contests asking customers to create and submit homemade television commercials for Doritos chips. After posting the finalists online for public viewing and voting, PepsiCo airs the winning advertisements during the Super Bowl, giving winners cash prizes and their 30 seconds of fame.

PepsiCo's recent Refresh Project, one of its more unusual marketing efforts, combined digital marketing with social responsibility.

PepsiCo's Pantry of Billion-Dollar Brands

From Cheetos and Doritos to Aquafina and Gatorade, PepsiCo's pantry is bulging with billion-dollar brands as the snack and beverage company launches innovative new products and sets prices for products purchased in different places. With $30 billion in annual sales, PepsiCo increasingly plans joint promotions of two or more brands because "consumers think about our beverage and snack brands together," says a senior executive. For example, the company targets young men with convenience-store displays featuring Hot Doritos chips and Pepsi Max cola and reaches out to baseball fans with "Double Play" promotions starring Lay's chips and specific Pepsi colas.

PepsiCo has a nonstop schedule for launching new products. Targeting customers who crave bold new flavors, its Frito-Lay division has created smokier, spicier versions of Doritos and Tostitos chips, among other snacks. Meanwhile, its Tropicana business has been developing good-tasting, good-for-you juice blends. The Trop50 product line consists of premium fruit-juice blends with Stevia, a natural sweetener, to reduce the sugar and calorie content. Every few months, Tropicana adds a new flavor, such as red orange or peach with white tea, to provide more variety and please buyers' taste buds. Since Trop50 first landed on store shelves in 2009, sales have skyrocketed by as much as 50 percent every year, giving PepsiCo a major new product success. Just as important, these unique blends help PepsiCo compete with Coca-Cola's Minute Maid and Simply Orange premium juices.

The company's knowledge of consumer behavior is especially vital for price setting. PepsiCo offers 99-cent soft drinks in grab-and-go bottle sizes for customers who stop into convenience stores and gas stations. It also offers 99-cent 1.5 liter bottles for mealtimes in small households and volume-priced 20-packs of 12-ounce cans for parties and other occasions. And customers who want a smaller size pay a little more per ounce for PepsiCo's 7.5-ounce cans. Meanwhile, PepsiCo has to pay more for sugar and some other ingredients, but it can't always pass these higher costs along in the form of higher prices because of competition, customer resistance, and economic conditions. Looking ahead, how will the company manage its profits as it puts new products into its pantry?[1]

A **product**, like a Diet Pepsi, is everything one receives in an exchange, including all tangible and intangible attributes and expected benefits. An Apple iPod purchase, for example, includes not only the iPod itself but also earbuds, a power adapter, instructions, and a warranty. A new car includes a warranty, an owner's manual, and perhaps free emergency road service for a year. Some of the intangibles that may go with an automobile include the status associated with ownership and the memories generated from past rides. Developing and managing products effectively are crucial to an organization's ability to maintain successful marketing mixes.

A product may be a good, a service, or an idea. A *good* is a real, physical thing that we can touch, such as a Dell laptop computer. A *service* is the result of applying human or mechanical effort to a person or thing. Basically, a *service* is a change we pay others to make for us. A real estate agent's services result in a change in the ownership of real property. A barber's services result in a change in your appearance. An *idea* may take the form of philosophies, lessons, concepts, or advice. Often ideas are included with a good or service. Thus, we might buy a book (a good) that provides ideas on how to lose weight. Alternatively, we might join Weight Watchers for ideas on how to lose weight and for help (services) in doing so.

product everything one receives in an exchange, including all tangible and intangible attributes and expected benefits; it may be a good, a service, or an idea

We look at products first in this chapter. We examine product classifications and describe the four stages, or life-cycles, through which every product moves. Next, we illustrate how firms manage products effectively by modifying or deleting existing products and by developing new products. We also discuss branding, packaging, and labeling of products. Then our focus shifts to pricing. We explain competitive factors that influence sellers' pricing decisions and also explore buyers' perceptions of prices. After considering organizational objectives that can be accomplished through pricing, we outline several methods for setting prices. Finally, we describe pricing strategies by which sellers can reach target markets successfully.

CLASSIFICATION OF PRODUCTS

1 Explain what a product is and how products are classified.

Different classes of products are directed at particular target markets. A product's classification largely determines what kinds of distribution, promotion, and pricing are appropriate in marketing the product.

Products can be grouped into two general categories: consumer and business (the latter are also called *business-to-business* or *industrial products*). A product purchased to satisfy personal and family needs is a **consumer product**. A product bought for resale, for making other products, or for use in a firm's operations is a **business product**. The buyer's use of the product determines the classification of an item. Note that a single item can be both a consumer and a business product. Light bulbs are a consumer product when you use them in your home, but the same light bulbs are a business product if you purchase them for use in a business.

Consumer Product Classifications

The traditional and most widely accepted system of classifying consumer products consists of three categories: convenience, shopping, and specialty products. These groupings are based primarily on characteristics of buyers' purchasing behavior.

A **convenience product** is a relatively inexpensive, frequently purchased item for which buyers want to exert only minimal effort. Examples include bread, gasoline, newspapers, soft drinks, and chewing gum. The buyer spends little time in planning the purchase of a convenience item or in comparing available brands or sellers.

A **shopping product** is an item for which buyers are willing to expend considerable effort on planning and making the purchase. Buyers allocate ample time for comparing stores and brands with respect to prices, product features, qualities, services, and perhaps warranties. Appliances, upholstered furniture, men's suits, bicycles, and mobile phones are examples of shopping products. These products are expected to last for a fairly long time and thus are purchased less frequently than convenience items.

A **specialty product** possesses one or more unique characteristics for which a group of buyers is willing to expend considerable purchasing effort. Buyers actually plan the purchase of a specialty product; they know exactly what they want and will not accept a substitute. While searching for specialty products, purchasers do not compare alternatives. Examples include unique sports cars, a specific type of antique dining table, a rare imported beer, or perhaps special handcrafted stereo speakers.

Business Product Classifications

Based on their characteristics and intended uses, business products can be classified into the following categories: raw materials, major equipment, accessory equipment, component parts, process materials, supplies, and services.

A **raw material** is a basic material that actually becomes part of a physical product. It usually comes from mines, forests, oceans, or recycled solid wastes. Raw materials are usually bought and sold according to grades and specifications.

Major equipment includes large tools and machines used for production purposes. Examples of major equipment are lathes, cranes, and stamping machines. Some major

consumer product a product purchased to satisfy personal and family needs

business product a product bought for resale, for making other products, or for use in a firm's operations

convenience product a relatively inexpensive, frequently purchased item for which buyers want to exert only minimal effort

shopping product an item for which buyers are willing to expend considerable effort on planning and making the purchase

specialty product an item that possesses one or more unique characteristics for which a significant group of buyers is willing to expend considerable purchasing effort

raw material a basic material that actually becomes part of a physical product; usually comes from mines, forests, oceans, or recycled solid wastes

major equipment large tools and machines used for production purposes

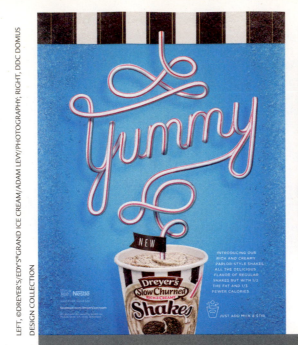

Convenience product or shopping product? Dreyer's ice cream is a convenience product. It's an item you are likely to grab off the shelf without much thought as you walk through the frozen-food aisle of a store. By contrast, people may spend considerable amount of time and effort when buying a shopping product, like furniture.

accessory equipment standardized equipment used in a firm's production or office activities

component part an item that becomes part of a physical product and is either a finished item ready for assembly or a product that needs little processing before assembly

process material a material that is used directly in the production of another product but is not readily identifiable in the finished product

supply an item that facilitates production and operations but does not become part of a finished product

business service an intangible product that an organization uses in its operations

equipment is custom-made for a particular organization, but other items are standardized products that perform one or several tasks for many types of organizations.

Accessory equipment is standardized equipment used in a firm's production or office activities. Examples include hand tools, fax machines, fractional horsepower motors, and calculators. Compared with major equipment, accessory items are usually much less expensive and are purchased routinely with less negotiation.

A **component part** becomes part of a physical product and is either a finished item ready for assembly or a product that needs little processing before assembly. Although it becomes part of a larger product, a component part can often be identified easily. Clocks, tires, computer chips, and switches are examples of component parts.

A **process material** is used directly in the production of another product. Unlike a component part, however, a process material is not readily identifiable in the finished product. Like component parts, process materials are purchased according to industry standards or to the specifications of the individual purchaser. Examples include industrial glue and food preservatives.

A **supply** facilitates production and operations but does not become part of a finished product. Paper, pencils, oils, and cleaning agents are examples.

A **business service** is an intangible product that an organization uses in its operations. Examples include financial, legal, online, janitorial, and marketing research services. Purchasers must decide whether to provide their own services internally or to hire them from outside the organization.

THE PRODUCT LIFE-CYCLE

Discuss the product life-cycle and how it leads to new-product development. ②

product life-cycle a series of stages in which a product's sales revenue and profit increase, reach a peak, and then decline

In a way, products are like people. They are born, they live, and they die. Every product progresses through a **product life-cycle**, a series of stages in which a product's sales revenue and profit increase, reach a peak, and then decline. A firm must be able to launch, modify, and delete products from its offering of products in response to changes in product life-cycles. Otherwise, the firm's profits will disappear, and the firm will fail. Depending on the product, life-cycle stages will vary in length. In this section, we discuss the stages of the life-cycle and how marketers can use this information.

Stages of the Product Life-Cycle

Generally, the product life-cycle is assumed to be composed of four stages—introduction, growth, maturity, and decline—as shown in Figure 13.1. Some products progress through these stages rapidly, in a few weeks or months. Others may take years to go through each stage. The Rubik's Cube had a relatively short life-cycle. In contrast, Parker Brothers' Monopoly game, which was introduced nearly a century ago, is still going strong.

Introduction In the *introduction stage*, customer awareness and acceptance of the product are low. Sales rise gradually as a result of promotion and distribution activities; initially, however, high development and marketing costs result in low profit or even in a loss. There are no competitors. The price is sometimes high, and purchasers are primarily people who want to be "the first" to own the new product. The marketing challenge at this stage is to make potential customers aware of the product's existence and its features, benefits, and uses.

A new product is seldom an immediate success. Marketers must watch early buying patterns carefully and be prepared to modify the new product promptly if necessary. The product should be priced to attract the particular market segment that has the greatest desire and ability to buy the product. Plans for distribution and promotion should suit the targeted market segment. As with the product itself, the initial price, distribution channels, and promotional efforts may need to be adjusted quickly to maintain sales growth during the introduction stage.

Growth In the *growth stage*, sales increase rapidly as the product becomes well known. Other firms have probably begun to market competing products. The competition and lower unit costs (owing to mass production) result in a lower price, which reduces the profit per unit. Note that industry profits reach a peak and begin to decline during this stage. To meet the needs of the growing market, the originating firm offers modified versions of its product and expands its distribution.

| FIGURE 13.1 | Product Life-Cycle |

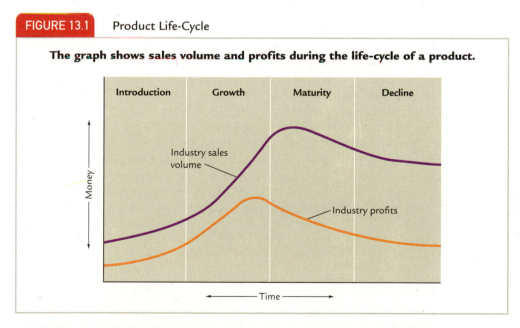

The graph shows sales volume and profits during the life-cycle of a product.

Source: William M. Pride and O. C. Ferrell, *Marketing: Concepts and Strategies*, 17th ed. (Mason, OH: South-Western/Cengage Learning, 2014). Adapted with permission.

Personal APPS

Think back to toys that were wildly popular when you were younger, such as Furby and Tickle Me Elmo dolls. How many do you still see in stores? This shows how quickly some products can pass through the stages of the product life-cycle.

Saying "goodbye" to the pay telephone. The pay telephone is in the decline stage of the product life cycle. Do you recall seeing one? If so, when and where? You might have a hard time remembering.

Management's goal in the growth stage is to stabilize and strengthen the product's position by encouraging brand loyalty. To beat the competition, the company may further improve the product or expand the product line to appeal to additional market segments. Apple, for example, has introduced several variations of its wildly popular iPod MP3 player. The iPod Shuffle is the smallest and most affordable version, whereas the iPod Nano offers song, photo, and video support in a thin, lightweight version that has a built-in video camera. The iPod Classic provides up to 160 GB of hard drive space, the most of any of the versions. The iPod Touch has a large, vibrant touch screen and an additional Wi-Fi connection that can use GPS technology and download applications. Apple has expanded its iTunes Music Store to include downloadable versions of popular TV shows (to be purchased per episode or as an entire season), exclusive music video downloads, and movies that can be purchased or rented online. Apple greatly expanded its product mix with the release of the iPhone, a combination iPod Touch and mobile phone. Continuous product innovation and service expansion have helped to expand Apple's market penetration in the competitive MP3 player market.[2]

Management also may compete by lowering prices if increased production efficiency has resulted in savings for the company. As the product becomes more widely accepted, marketers may be able to broaden the network of distributors. Marketers can also emphasize customer service and prompt credit for defective products. During this period, promotional efforts attempt to build brand loyalty among customers.

Maturity Sales are still increasing at the beginning of the *maturity stage*, but the rate of increase has slowed. Later in this stage, the sales curve peaks and begins to decline. Industry profits decline throughout this stage. Product lines are simplified, markets are segmented more carefully, and price competition increases. The increased competition forces weaker competitors to leave the industry. Refinements and extensions of the original product continue to appear on the market.

During a product's maturity stage, its market share may be strengthened by redesigned packaging or style changes. Barq's root beer, a popular soda for more than a century, recently unveiled a package redesign and new slogan that pay homage to its Gulf Coast roots. The bottles and cans sport a diamond design reminiscent of the beverage's original 1898 glass bottles (which are still available in the Gulf Coast area) and the new slogan reads "It's good. Since 1898." The company hopes to capitalize on customers' feelings of solidarity with the Gulf region after the catastrophic BP oil spill, while attracting new attention to the mature brand.[3] In addition, consumers may be encouraged to use the product more often or in new ways. Pricing strategies are flexible during this stage. Markdowns and price incentives are not uncommon, although price increases may work to offset production and distribution costs. Marketers may offer incentives and assistance of various kinds to dealers to encourage them to support mature products, especially in the face of competition from private-label brands. New promotional efforts and aggressive personal selling may be necessary during this period of intense competition.

Decline During the *decline stage*, sales volume decreases sharply. Profits continue to fall. The number of competing firms declines, and the only survivors in the marketplace are firms that specialize in marketing the product. Production and marketing costs become the most important determinant of profit.

When a product adds to the success of the overall product line, the company may retain it; otherwise, management must determine when to eliminate the product. A product usually declines because of technological advances or environmental factors or because consumers have switched to competing brands. Therefore, few changes are made in the product itself during this stage. Instead, management may raise the price to cover costs, reprice to maintain market share, or lower the price to reduce inventory. Similarly, management will narrow distribution of the declining product to the most profitable existing markets. During this period, the company probably will not spend heavily on promotion, although it may use some advertising and sales incentives to slow the product's decline. The company may choose to eliminate less-profitable versions of the product from the product line or may decide to drop the product entirely. Google actively discontinues products. Last year, Google discontinued ten products that failed to take off, including Google Desktop, Aardvark, and Google Pack. Some of these products were dropped immediately and some were phased out.[4]

©NEWSCAST/ALAMY

How companies use product lines to expand. Firms use the knowledge and expertise they develop producing one product line to develop others. It's much a like a tree in a forest that grows new branches to find sunlight and thrive. This photo shows only a few of Kellogg Company's 20 different cereal brands. Cereals aren't Kellogg's only product line, though. The company also produces a wide variety of crackers, bars, beverages, toaster pastries, waffles, pancakes, syrups, and fruit-flavored snacks.

Using the Product Life-Cycle

Marketers should be aware of the life-cycle stage of each product for which they are responsible. Moreover, they should try to estimate how long the product is expected to remain in that stage. Both must be taken into account in making decisions about the marketing strategy for a product. If a product is expected to remain in the maturity stage for a long time, a replacement product might be introduced later in the maturity stage. If the maturity stage is expected to be short, however, a new product should be introduced much earlier. In some cases, a firm may be willing to take the chance of speeding up the decline of existing products. In other situations, a company will attempt to extend a product's life-cycle. Extending its life can be an importance tool in maintaining a product's profitability. Developed over 150 years ago, Kraft has extended the life of Jell-O through frequently developing new flavors, uses, and recipes, including seasonal desserts and even baked goods.[5]

PRODUCT LINE AND PRODUCT MIX

 Define product line and product mix and distinguish between the two.

A **product line** is a group of similar products that differ only in relatively minor characteristics. Generally, the products within a product line are related to each other in the way they are produced, marketed, or used. Procter & Gamble, for example, manufactures and markets several shampoos, including Prell, Head & Shoulders, and Ivory.

Many organizations tend to introduce new products within existing product lines. This permits them to apply the experience and knowledge they have acquired to the production and marketing of new products. Other firms develop entirely new product lines.

An organization's **product mix** consists of all the products the firm offers for sale. For example, Procter & Gamble, which acquired Gillette, has over 85 brands that fall into one of two product line categories: beauty and grooming and household care.[6] Two "dimensions" are often applied to a firm's product mix. The *width* of the mix is the number of product lines it contains. The *depth* of the mix is the average number of individual products within each line. These are general measures; we speak of a *broad* or a *narrow* mix rather than a mix of exactly three or five product lines. Some organizations provide broad product mixes in order to be competitive.

product line a group of similar products that differ only in relatively minor characteristics

product mix all the products a firm offers for sale

MANAGING THE PRODUCT MIX

To provide products that satisfy people in a firm's target market or markets and that also achieve the organization's objectives, a marketer must develop, adjust, and maintain an effective product mix. Seldom can the same product mix be effective for long. Because customers' product preferences and attitudes change, their desire for a product may diminish or grow. In some cases, a firm needs to alter its product mix to adapt to competition. A marketer may have to eliminate a product from the mix because one or more competitors dominate that product's specific market segment. Similarly, an organization may have to introduce a new product or modify an existing one to compete more effectively. A marketer may also expand the firm's product mix to take advantage of excess marketing and production capacity. For example, General Mills has a wide product mix consisting of many different brands. It frequently expands its product mix by adding new offerings to its different product lines, such as breakfast cereals. The breakfast cereals product line consists of different familiar brands, such as Fiber One, Cascadian Farms, and Wheaties. General Mills takes advantage of production capacity for the Cheerios line by increasing its depth with new flavors, such as peanut butter, chocolate, and dulce de leche.[7] For whatever reason a product mix is altered, the product mix must be managed to bring about improvements in the mix. There are three major ways to improve a product mix: change an existing product, delete a product, or develop a new product.

Managing Existing Products

A product mix can be changed by deriving additional products from existing ones. This can be accomplished through product modifications and by line extensions.

Product Modifications **Product modification** refers to changing one or more of a product's characteristics. For this approach to be effective, several conditions must be met. First, the product must be modifiable. Second, existing customers must be able to perceive that a modification has been made, assuming that the modified item is still directed at the same target market. Third, the modification should make the product more consistent with customers' desires so that it provides greater satisfaction. For example, General Motors upgraded the structure and cooling systems in the battery for its Chevrolet Volt hybrid car in order to address some consumer hesitations over the battery's safety. Volt owners were encouraged to bring their vehicles to a dealership to receive the new modified battery. In order to publicize the improvement, GM made widespread announcements regarding the change, including on the National Highway Safety Administration Web site.[8]

Existing products can be altered in three primary ways: in quality, function, and aesthetics. *Quality modifications* are changes that relate to a product's dependability and durability and are usually achieved by alterations in the materials or production process. *Functional modifications* affect a product's versatility, effectiveness, convenience, or safety; they usually require redesign of the product. Typical product categories that have undergone extensive functional modifications include home appliances, office and farm equipment, and consumer electronics. *Aesthetic modifications* are directed at changing the sensory appeal of a product by altering its taste, texture, sound, smell, or visual characteristics. Because a buyer's purchasing decision is affected by how a product looks, smells, tastes, feels, or sounds, an aesthetic modification may have a definite impact on purchases. Through aesthetic modifications, a firm can differentiate its product from competing brands and perhaps gain a sizable market share if customers find the modified product more appealing.

product modification the process of changing one or more of a product's characteristics

line extension development of a new product that is closely related to one or more products in the existing product line but designed specifically to meet somewhat different customer needs

Line Extensions A **line extension** is the development of a product closely related to one or more products in the existing product line but designed specifically to meet somewhat different customer needs. WD-40, maker of the multi-use lubricant, recently launched its first-ever line extension. The WD-40 Specialist line consists of five different products for industrial and home use, including a rust remover and a waterproofer.[9]

Many of the so-called new products introduced each year are in fact line extensions. Line extensions are more common than new products because they are a less-expensive, lower-risk alternative for increasing sales. A line extension may focus on a different market segment or be an attempt to increase sales within the same market segment by more precisely satisfying the needs of people in that segment. Line extensions are also used to take market share from competitors.

Deleting Products

To maintain an effective product mix, an organization often has to eliminate some products. This is called **product deletion**. A weak product costs a company time, money, and resources that could be used to modify other products or develop new ones. In addition, when a weak product generates an unfavorable image among customers, the negative image may rub off on other products sold by the firm.

Most organizations find it difficult to delete a product. Some firms drop weak products only after they have become severe financial burdens. A better approach is to conduct some form of systematic review of the product's impact on the overall effectiveness of a firm's product mix. Such a review should analyze a product's contribution to a company's sales for a given period. It should include estimates of future sales, costs, and profits associated with the product and a consideration of whether changes in the marketing strategy could improve the product's performance.

A product-deletion program can definitely improve a firm's performance. For example, T-Mobile recently decided to delete the Sidekick 4G smartphone due to declining sales and customer interest. However, the company announced that it had no plans to discontinue the entire Sidekick line.[10]

©SUSAN VAN ETTEN

A product-line extension with staying power: Oreo Fudge Cremes. Nabisco, the maker of Oreos, developed a product line extension when it launched Oreo Fudge Cremes. The product, which consists of fudge atop Oreo cream filling, was originally supposed to be produced for just a short time. However, it was so popular Nabisco kept it in its product lineup and later launched mint, peanut butter, and other versions of the treat.

Developing New Products

Developing and introducing new products is frequently time consuming, expensive, and risky. Thousands of new products are introduced annually. The overall failure rate for new products is around 50 percent, although the failure rate in some industries can be much higher.[11] Although developing new products is risky, failing to introduce new products can be just as hazardous. Successful new products bring a number of benefits to an organization, including survival, profits, a sustainable competitive advantage, and a favorable public image. Consider the numerous ways that the producers of the products in Table 13.1 have benefited.

TABLE 13.1	Top Ten New Products Since 2000	
Rank	**Product Name**	**Year Introduced**
1	iPod	2001
2	Wii	2006
3	Axe	2002
4	$5 Footlong	2008
5	Activia	2006
6	Mini Cooper	2002
7	Crest Whitestrips	2000
8	Guitar Hero	2005
9	Toyota Prius	2000
10	7 For All Mankind	2000

Source: *Advertising Age*, December 14, 2009, 16. http://adage.com/article?article_id=141032 (accessed February 21, 2012).

product deletion the elimination of one or more products from a product line

Fan blades 'chop' the airflow, causing buffeting. The new Dyson fan works differently. An annular jet accelerates the surrounding air and amplifies it fifteen times. There are no blades to chop the air so the airflow is smooth – it cools without the unpleasant buffeting.

Blades cause buffeting.

No blades means no buffeting.

dyson air multiplier
No blades. No buffeting.

Learn more at www.dyson.co.uk
Or experience in-store.

Not your grandparents'old fan. You probably won't find a fan like this one in your grandparents' attic. This new type of bladeless fan, developed by Dyson,is called the Air Multiplier. What new-product category do you think the Air Multiplier falls into? Is it an imitation, innovation, or adaptation?

New products are generally grouped into three categories on the basis of their degree of similarity to existing products. *Imitations* are products designed to be similar to—and to compete with—existing products of other firms. Examples are the various brands of whitening toothpastes that were developed to compete with those offered by Rembrandt. *Adaptations* are variations of existing products that are intended for an established market. Product refinements and extensions are the adaptations considered most often, although imitative products may also include some refinement and extension. *Innovations* are entirely new products. They may give rise to a new industry or revolutionize an existing one. The introduction of digital music, for example, has brought major changes to the recording industry. Innovative products take considerable time, effort, and money to develop. They are therefore less common than adaptations and imitations. Google recently announced an innovative new product dubbed Project Glass. It involves a futuristic and ambitious plan to merge online technology with spectacles that users wear. Once finalized, the product will perform the function of many common electronic items. The product will act as a smartphone, day planner, navigation system, and even camera—all in wearable glasses with information showing up as small icons on the lenses. Because this product idea is so new, it has been the target of considerable consumer scrutiny, although many technophiles and early adopters are excited by the possibilities such a product can offer.[12] As shown in Figure 13.2, the process of developing a new product consists of seven phases.

Idea Generation Idea generation involves looking for product ideas that will help a firm to achieve its objectives. Although some organizations get their ideas almost by chance, firms trying to

Entrepreneurial SUCCESS

Yak to the Future: From the Himalayas to the World

Julian Wilson and Aaron Pattillo, the cofounders of Khunu, market high-quality sweaters made of an unusual material: fine wool from yaks raised by Himalayan herders. The entrepreneurs met while on a mountain-biking tour outside Beijing and quickly discovered a shared interest in expanding economic opportunities for Himalayan herders. They noticed herders making coarse yak fiber into ropes, while the softer yak wool blew away. Wilson and Pattillo reasoned that if yak wool keeps animals warm high in the Himalayas, it would be good for cold-weather clothing.

As pioneers of yak-wool clothing, the entrepreneurs had to educate retailers and consumers about their products' benefits while dispelling the misperception that yak wool is stiff and heavy. They also had to explain that their products

carry premium prices because of the high quality and the fair-market cost of raw yak wool bought from nomadic herders. For its associations with the area's ancient Mongolian tribes, they chose Khunu as their brand name.

Wilson and Pattillo are currently riding the wave of two trends: using natural materials and ethical sourcing of raw materials. Yak wool is still a novelty, but not for long, says Wilson: "Global fashion brands are always on the lookout for new fibers, and they're the ones most likely to take yak hair into the mainstream."

Sources: Based on information in Mark Graham, "Yak-to-Back Success," *China Daily*, January 4, 2012, www.chinadaily.com; Leah Hyslop, "The Expats Introducing the World to Yak Wool," *Telegraph (UK)*, October 26, 2011, www.telegraph.co.uk; John Stroud, "Glenwood Springs Man Helps Launch Adventure Wear Line Using Yak Wool from Himalayas," *Post Independent (Colorado)*, March 2, 2010, www.postindependent.com; "Racing Start for Pioneers of Yak-Hair Clothing," *Financial Times*, February 11, 2010, www.ft.com.

FIGURE 13.2   Phases of New-Product Development

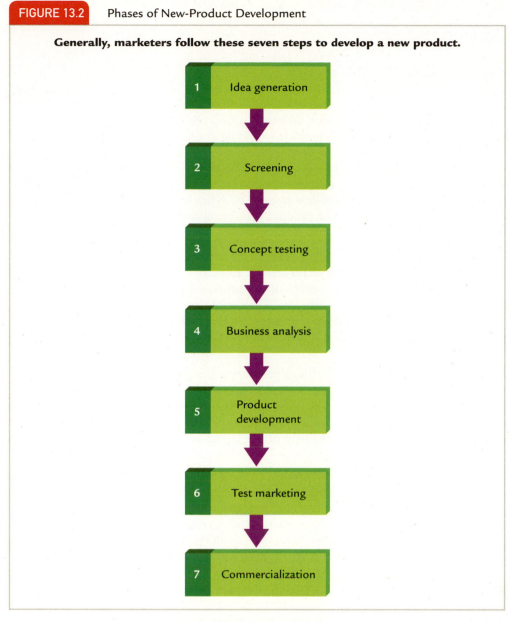

Generally, marketers follow these seven steps to develop a new product.

1 Idea generation

2 Screening

3 Concept testing

4 Business analysis

5 Product development

6 Test marketing

7 Commercialization

Source: William M. Pride and O. C. Ferrell, *Marketing: Concepts and Strategies*, 17th ed. (Mason, OH: South-Western/ Cengage Learning, 2014). Adapted with permission.

maximize product-mix effectiveness usually develop systematic approaches for generating new-product ideas. Ideas may come from managers, researchers, engineers, competitors, advertising agencies, management consultants, private research organizations, customers, salespersons, or top executives. Sometimes, large firms with superior experience and resources may mentor small firms and help them generate ideas to help their businesses grow. Business incubators sprung up around the country that pair new small businesses with large established ones so that the new business can learn about marketing and branding from experts at established firms. Cincinnati-based Brandery is one such incubator. It pairs tech start-ups with marketers from firms like Procter & Gamble or with major branding agencies. The entrepreneurs can get ideas, help hone their image, and improve marketing strategy.[13]

Screening During screening, ideas that do not match organizational resources and objectives are rejected. In this phase, a firm's managers consider whether the organization has personnel with the expertise to develop and market the proposed product.

Management may reject a good idea because the company lacks the necessary skills and abilities. The largest number of product ideas are rejected during the screening phase.

Concept Testing Concept testing is a phase in which a product idea is presented to a small sample of potential buyers through a written or oral description (and perhaps a few drawings) to determine their attitudes and initial buying intentions regarding the product. For a single product idea, an organization can test one or several concepts of the same product. Concept testing is a low-cost means for an organization to determine consumers' initial reactions to a product idea before investing considerable resources in product research and development (R&D). Product development personnel can use the results of concept testing to improve product attributes and product benefits that are most important to potential customers. The types of questions asked vary considerably depending on the type of product idea being tested. The following are typical questions:

- Which benefits of the proposed product are especially attractive to you?
- Which features are of little or no interest to you?
- What are the primary advantages of the proposed product over the one you currently use?
- If this product were available at an appropriate price, how often would you buy it?
- How could this proposed product be improved?

Business Analysis Business analysis provides tentative ideas about a potential product's financial performance, including its probable profitability. During this stage, the firm considers how the new product, if it were introduced, would affect the firm's sales, costs, and profits. Marketing personnel usually work up preliminary sales and cost projections at this point, with the help of R&D and production managers.

Product Development In the product development phase, the company must find out first if it is technically feasible to produce the product and then if the product can be made at costs low enough to justify a reasonable price. If a product idea makes it to this point, it is transformed into a working model, or prototype. For example, Aptera, a California-based vehicle manufacturer, recently developed a prototype electric vehicle called the 2e. The 2e is an innovative three-wheeled, two-seat vehicle that uses an electric motor with phosphate-based lithium-ion batteries. The 2e is expected to operate at about 200 MPG and travel about 100 miles on a single charge.[14] Often, this step is time-consuming and expensive for the organization. If a product successfully moves through this step, then it is ready for test marketing.

Test Marketing Test marketing is the limited introduction of a product in several towns or cities chosen to be representative of the intended target market. Its aim is to determine buyers' probable reactions. The product is left in the test markets long enough to give buyers a chance to repurchase the product if they are so inclined. Marketers can experiment with advertising, pricing, and packaging in different test areas and can measure the extent of brand awareness, brand switching, and repeat purchases that result from alterations in the marketing mix. Columbus, Ohio, is a very popular test marketing location because its demographics are representative of the nation as a whole. When Wendy's wanted to test market its new Black Label Burger, it turned to Columbus first. Likewise, Jeni's Ice Cream tested its cayenne pepper–flavored ice cream in Columbus and found it was a big hit.[15]

Commercialization During commercialization, plans for full-scale manufacturing and marketing must be refined and completed, and budgets for the project must be prepared. In the early part of the commercialization phase, marketing management analyzes the results of test marketing to find out what changes in the marketing mix

TABLE 13.2   Examples of Product Failures

Company	Product
Gillette	For Oily Hair shampoo
3M	Floptical storage disk
IncrEdibles Breakaway Foods	Push n' Eat
General Mills	Betty Crocker MicroRave Singles
Adams (Pfizer)	Body Smarts nutritional bars
Ford	Edsel
Anheuser-Busch	Bud Dry and Michelob Dry beer
Coca-Cola	New Coke
Heinz	Ketchup Salsa
Noxema	Noxema Skin Fitness

Sources: Robert McMath and Thom Forbes, "What Were They Thinking?," Reed Business Information, 1998; Robert M. McMath, "Copycat Cupcakes Don't Cut It," *American Demographics,* January 1997, 60; Eric Berggren and Thomas Nacher, "Why Good Ideas Go Bust," *Management Review,* February 2000, 32–36.

are needed before the product is introduced. The results of test marketing may tell the marketers, for example, to change one or more of the product's physical attributes, to modify the distribution plans to include more retail outlets, to alter promotional efforts, or to change the product's price. Products are usually not introduced nationwide overnight. Most new products are marketed in stages, beginning in selected geographic areas and expanding into adjacent areas over a period of time.

Why Do Products Fail?

Despite this rigorous process for developing product ideas, most new products end up as failures. In fact, many well-known companies have produced market failures (see Table 13.2).

Why does a new product fail? Mainly because the product and its marketing program are not planned and tested as completely as they should be. For example, to save on development costs, a firm may market-test its product but not its entire marketing mix. Alternatively, a firm may market a new product before all the "bugs" have been worked out. Or, when problems show up in the testing stage, a firm may try to recover its product development costs by pushing ahead with full-scale marketing anyway. Finally, some firms try to market new products with inadequate financing.

BRANDING, PACKAGING, AND LABELING

 5 Explain the uses and importance of branding, packaging, and labeling.

Three important features of a product (particularly a consumer product) are its brand, package, and label. These features may be used to associate a product with a successful product line or to distinguish it from existing products. They may be designed to attract customers at the point of sale or to provide information to potential purchasers. Because the brand, package, and label are very real parts of the product, they deserve careful attention during product planning.

What Is a Brand?

A **brand** is a name, term, symbol, design, or any combination of these that identifies a seller's products and distinguishes it from other sellers' products. A **brand name** is the part of a brand that can be spoken. It may include letters, words, numbers, or pronounceable symbols, such as the ampersand in *Procter & Gamble.* A **brand mark**, on the other hand, is the part of a brand that is a symbol or distinctive design, such as the Nike "swoosh." A **trademark** is a brand name or brand mark that is registered with the U.S. Patent and Trademark Office and thus is legally protected from use by

brand a name, term, symbol, design, or any combination of these that identifies a seller's products as distinct from those of other sellers

brand name the part of a brand that can be spoken

brand mark the part of a brand that is a symbol or distinctive design

trademark a brand name or brand mark that is registered with the U.S. Patent and Trademark Office and thus is legally protected from use by anyone except its owner

How low can you go? Price competition is fierce among fast food restaurants. McDonald's launched the first dollar menu in its industry in 2002. It wasn't long before many of its competitors did the same thing.

however, the price is fixed by the seller. Suppose that a seller sets a price of $10 for a particular product. In essence, the seller is saying, "Anyone who wants this product can have it here and now in exchange for $10."

Each interested buyer then makes a personal judgment regarding the product's utility, often in terms of some dollar value. A particular person who feels that he or she will get at least $10 worth of want satisfaction (or value) from the product is likely to buy it. If that person can get more want satisfaction by spending $10 in some other way, however, he or she will not buy the product.

Price thus serves the function of *allocator*. First, it allocates goods and services among those who are willing and able to buy them. (As we noted in Chapter 1, the answer to the economic question "For whom to produce?" depends primarily on prices.) Second, price allocates financial resources (sales revenue) among producers according to how well they satisfy customers' needs. Third, price helps customers to allocate their own financial resources among various want-satisfying products.

Supply and Demand Affects Prices

In Chapter 1, we defined the **supply** of a product as the quantity of the product that producers are willing to sell at each of various prices. We can draw a graph of the supply relationship for a particular product, say, a pair of jeans (see the left graph in Figure 13.3). Note that the quantity supplied by producers *increases* as the price increases along this *supply curve*.

As defined in Chapter 1, the **demand** for a product is the quantity that buyers are willing to purchase at each of various prices. We can also draw a graph of the demand relationship (see the center graph in Figure 13.3). Note that the quantity demanded by purchasers *increases* as the price decreases along the *demand curve*. The buyers and sellers of a product interact in the marketplace. We can show this interaction by superimposing the supply curve onto the demand curve for our product, as shown in the right graph in Figure 13.3. The two curves intersect at point *E*, which represents a quantity of 15 million pairs of jeans and a price of $30 per pair. Point *E* is on the *supply curve*; thus, producers are willing to supply 15 million pairs at $30 each. Point *E* is also on the demand curve; thus, buyers are willing to purchase 15 million pairs at $30 each. Point *E*

supply the quantity of a product that producers are willing to sell at each of various prices

demand the quantity of a product that buyers are willing to purchase at each of various prices

| FIGURE 13.3 | Supply and Demand Curves |

Supply curve (*left*): The upward slope means that producers will supply more jeans at higher prices. **Demand curve (*center*):** The downward slope (to the right) means that buyers will purchase fewer jeans at higher prices. **Supply and demand curves together (*right*):** Point *E* indicates equilibrium in quantity and price for both sellers and buyers.

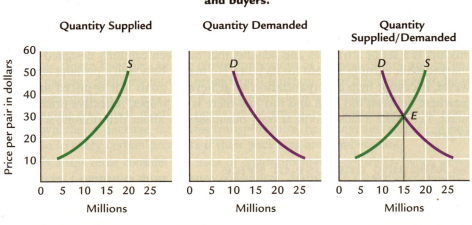

represents *equilibrium*. If 15 million pairs are produced and priced at $30, they all will be sold. In addition, everyone who is willing to pay $30 will be able to buy a pair of jeans.

Price and Non-Price Competition

Before a product's price can be set, an organization must determine the basis on which it will compete—whether on price alone or some combination of factors. The choice influences pricing decisions as well as other marketing-mix variables.

Price competition occurs when a seller emphasizes a product's low price and sets a price that equals or beats competitors' prices. To use this approach most effectively, a seller must have the flexibility to change prices often and must do so rapidly and aggressively whenever competitors change their prices. Price competition allows a marketer to set prices based on demand for the product or in response to changes in the firm's finances. Competitors can do likewise, however, which is a major drawback of price competition. They, too, can quickly match or outdo an organization's price cuts. In addition, if circumstances force a seller to raise prices, competing firms may be able to maintain their lower prices. The Internet has made it more difficult than ever for sellers to compete on the basis of price, as consumers can quickly and easily conduct comparison-shopping online. Lower-priced competitors for pricy but popular products quickly crop up. For example, the Apple iPad tablet controls nearly three-quarters of the tablet market, but less expensive tablets running on Google's Android operating system are providing consumers with different options with lower price tags.[25]

Non-price competition is competition based on factors other than price. It is used most effectively when a seller can make its product stand out from the competition by distinctive product quality, customer service, promotion, packaging, or other features. Buyers must be able to perceive these distinguishing characteristics and consider them desirable. Once customers have chosen a brand for non-price reasons, they may not be attracted as easily to competing firms and brands. In this way, a seller can build customer loyalty to its brand. A method of non-price competition, **product differentiation**, is the process of developing and promoting differences between one's product and all similar products. Vibram Five Fingers shoes, for example, are sufficiently differentiated from the competition that marketers do not have to compete on price. The shoes have highly distinct styling and are unlike any other shoe on the market. Designed in the silhouette of a foot, tracing the shape of each individual toe, they appeal to athletes who want to protect the soles of their feet while also having a barefoot experience.[26]

Buyers' Perceptions of Price

In setting prices, managers should consider the price sensitivity of people in the target market. How important is price to them? Is it always "very important"? Members of one market segment may be more influenced by price than members of another. For a particular product, the price may be a bigger factor for some buyers than for others. For example, buyers may be more sensitive to price when purchasing gasoline than when purchasing running shoes.

Buyers will accept different ranges of prices for different products; that is, they will tolerate a narrow range for certain items and a wider range for others. Consider the wide range of prices that consumers pay for soft drinks—from 15 cents per ounce at the movies down to 1.5 cents per ounce on sale at the grocery store. Management should be aware of these limits of acceptability and the products to which they apply. The firm also should take note of buyers' perceptions of a given product in relation to competing products. A premium price may be appropriate if a product is considered superior to others in its category or if the product has inspired strong brand loyalty. On the other hand, if buyers have even a hint of a negative view of a product, a lower price may be necessary.

Sometimes buyers relate price to quality. They may consider a higher price to be an indicator of higher quality. Managers involved in pricing decisions should determine whether this outlook is widespread in the target market. If it is, a higher price may improve the image of a product and, in turn, make the product more desirable.

price competition an emphasis on setting a price equal to or lower than competitors' prices to gain sales or market share

non-price competition competition based on factors other than price

product differentiation the process of developing and promoting differences between one's product and all similar products

FIGURE 13.4   Breakeven Analysis

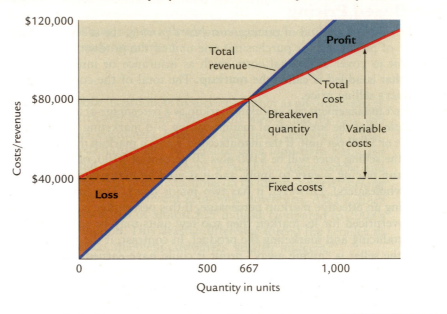

Breakeven analysis answers the question: What is the lowest level of production and sales at which a company can break even on a particular product?

© CENGAGE LEARNING 2014

when demand is weak. Some long-distance telephone companies use demand-based pricing. To use this method, a marketer estimates the amount of a product that customers will demand at different prices and then chooses the price that generates the highest total revenue. Obviously, the effectiveness of this method depends on the firm's ability to estimate demand accurately. In order to address severe problems with parking shortages, the city of San Francisco adopted a demand-based parking meter system. Rates are raised and lowered throughout the day according to demand. The city hopes that the variable fees will help smooth demand for parking spaces and traffic by encouraging people to park outside of congested areas and either walk, bike, or bus to their final destination. The plan is being watched closely by other cities, such as Boston, as a potential market-driven solution to parking and transportation problems.[28]

A firm may favor a demand-based pricing method called *price differentiation* if it wants to use more than one price in the marketing of a specific product. Price differentiation can be based on such considerations as time of the purchase, type of customer, or type of distribution channel. Sports arenas increasingly use demand-based pricing to sell tickets to events. Seats for single games are priced according to fan demand, meaning that the most popular seats sell for the highest price, no matter what the location within the stadium or arena. The St. Louis Cardinals, San Francisco Giants, and Minnesota Twins all utilize demand-based pricing. The Twins, for instance, began this practice in 2011 for two seating sections. It was so successful that the sports franchise decided to expand demand-based pricing for subsequent seasons.[29] For price differentiation to work correctly, the company first must be able to segment a market on the basis of different strengths of demand. The company must then be able to keep the segments separate enough so that those who buy at lower prices cannot sell to buyers in

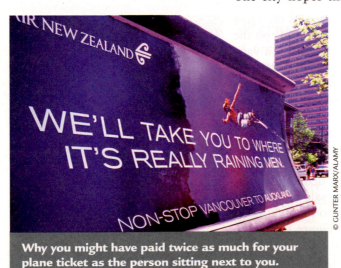

© GUNTER MARX/ALAMY

Why you might have paid twice as much for your plane ticket as the person sitting next to you.
Airlines use demand-based pricing because the number of passengers that can be put on a specific flight is limited. The sophisticated software the companies use constantly re-price seats based on the number of tickets customers are purchasing at any given time as well as historical data.

Amazon's Price-Check App: Is This OK?

Price comparisons are nothing new: Anybody with Internet access (via smartphone, tablet, or computer) can easily find out how much online retailers charge for items also sold in local stores. Still, bricks-and-mortar stores were outraged when Amazon.com first encouraged consumers to download its price-check app and use it to compare prices as they browsed in stores. Why? Because the app included a special incentive to comparison-shop and then buy from Amazon.

While standing in a store, the user would scan (or photograph) the UPC product code of an item they might buy and wait to see Amazon's price for the same item. If the user bought that item from Amazon within 24 hours, the price would be discounted by $5. Amazon promoted its app during the year-end holiday shopping season, generating a lot of downloads and a lot of controversy.

Critics said the app turned local stores into showrooms where customers examined products, asked questions, and then bought from Amazon. In fact, surveys show that 20 percent of consumers research purchases such as kitchen appliances in local stores before they buy from an Internet retailer. Meanwhile, Amazon has been getting valuable competitive pricing data and boosting its sales. What are the ethics of price-check apps?

Sources: Based on information in Allison Enright, "Online Shoppers Use Stores as 'Showrooms' Before Buying Items," *Internet Retailer*, March 8, 2012, www.internetretailer.com; Christina DesMarais, "Amazon Price Check Discount Has Competitors Crying Foul," *PC World*, December 10, 2011, www.pcworld.com; Erik Kain, "Amazon Price Check May Be Evil But It's the Future," *Forbes.com*, December 14, 2011, www.forbes.com.

---

segments that are charged a higher price. This isolation can be accomplished, for example, by selling to geographically separated segments.

Compared with cost-based pricing, demand-based pricing places a firm in a better position to attain higher profit levels, assuming that buyers value the product at levels sufficiently above the product's cost. To use demand-based pricing, however, management must be able to estimate demand at different price levels, which may be difficult to do accurately.

Competition-Based Pricing

In using *competition-based pricing,* an organization considers costs and revenue secondary to competitors' prices. The importance of this method increases if competing products are quite similar and the organization is serving markets in which price is the crucial variable of the marketing strategy. A firm that uses competition-based pricing may choose to be below competitors' prices, slightly above competitors' prices, or at the same level. The price that your bookstore paid to the publishing company of this text was determined using competition-based pricing. Competition-based pricing can help to attain a pricing objective to increase sales or market share. Competition-based pricing may also be combined with other cost approaches to arrive at profitable levels.

PRICING STRATEGIES

9 Explain the different strategies available to companies for setting prices

A *pricing strategy* is a course of action designed to achieve pricing objectives. Generally, pricing strategies help marketers to solve the practical problems of setting prices. The extent to which a business uses any of the following strategies depends on its pricing and marketing objectives, the markets for its products, the degree of product differentiation, the product's life-cycle stage, and other factors. Figure 13.5 contains a list of the major types of pricing strategies. We discuss these strategies in the remainder of this section.

FIGURE 13.5   Types of Pricing Strategies

Companies have a variety of pricing strategies available to them.

PRICING STRATEGIES

New-Product Pricing	Differential Pricing	Psychological Pricing	Product-Line Pricing	Promotional Pricing
• Price skimming • Penetration pricing	• Negotiated pricing • Secondary-market pricing • Periodic discounting • Random discounting	• Odd-number pricing • Multiple-unit pricing • Reference pricing • Bundle pricing • Everyday low prices • Customary pricing	• Captive pricing • Premium pricing • Price lining	• Price leaders • Special-event pricing • Comparison discounting

© CENGAGE LEARNING 2014

New-Product Pricing

The two primary types of new-product pricing strategies are price skimming and penetration pricing. An organization can use either one, or even both, over a period of time.

Price Skimming Some consumers are willing to pay a high price for an innovative product either because of its novelty or because of the prestige or status that owner-ship confers. **Price skimming** is the strategy of charging the highest possible price for a product during the introduction stage of its life-cycle. The seller essentially "skims the cream" off the market, which helps to recover the high costs of R&D more quickly. In addition, a skimming policy may hold down demand for the product, which is helpful if the firm's production capacity is limited during the introduction stage. A danger is that a price-skimming strategy may make the product appear more lucrative than it actually is to potential competitors.

Penetration Pricing At the opposite extreme, **penetration pricing** is the strategy of setting a low price for a new product. The main purpose of setting a low price is to build market share for the product quickly. The seller hopes that building a large market share quickly will discourage competitors from entering the market. If the low price stimulates sales, the firm also may be able to order longer production runs, which result in lower production costs per unit. A disadvantage of penetration pricing is that it places a firm in a less flexible position. It is more difficult to raise prices significantly than it is to lower them.

Differential Pricing

An important issue in pricing decisions is whether to use a single price or different prices for the same product. A single price is easily understood by both employees and customers. Since many salespeople and customers do not like having to negotiate a price, having a single price reduces the chance of a marketer developing an adversarial relationship with a customer.

Differential pricing means charging different prices to different buyers for the same quality and quantity of product. For differential pricing to be effective, the market must consist of multiple segments with different price sensitivities. When this method is employed, caution should be used to avoid confusing or antagonizing customers. Differential pricing can occur in several ways, including negotiated pricing, secondary-market pricing, periodic discounting, and random discounting.

price skimming the strategy of charging the highest possible price for a product during the introduction stage of its life-cycle

penetration pricing the strategy of setting a low price for a new product

Negotiated Pricing Negotiated pricing occurs when the final price is established through bargaining between the seller and the customer. Negotiated pricing occurs in a number of industries and at all levels of distribution. Even when there is a predetermined stated price or a price list, manufacturers, wholesalers, and retailers still may negotiate to establish the final sales price. Consumers commonly negotiate prices for houses, cars, and used equipment.

Secondary-Market Pricing Secondary-market pricing means setting one price for the primary target market and a different price for another market. Often the price charged in the secondary market is lower. However, when the costs of serving a secondary market are higher than normal, secondary-market customers may have to pay a higher price. Examples of secondary markets include a geographically isolated domestic market, a market in a foreign country, and a segment willing to purchase a product during off-peak times (such as "early bird" diners at restaurants and off-peak users of mobile phones).

Periodic Discounting Periodic discounting is the temporary reduction of prices on a patterned or systematic basis. For example, many retailers have annual holiday sales, and some women's apparel stores have two seasonal sales each year—a winter sale in the last two weeks of January and a summer sale in the first two weeks of July. From the marketer's point of view, a major problem with periodic discounting is that customers can predict when the reductions will occur and may delay their purchases until they can take advantage of the lower prices.

Random Discounting To alleviate the problem of customers' knowing when discounting will occur, some organizations employ **random discounting.** That is, they reduce their prices temporarily on a nonsystematic basis. When price reductions of a product occur randomly, current users of that brand are unlikely to predict when the reductions will occur; therefore, they will not delay their purchases in anticipation of buying the product at a lower price. Marketers also use random discounting to attract new customers.

Psychological Pricing

Psychological pricing strategies encourage purchases based on emotional responses rather than on economically rational responses. These strategies are used primarily for consumer products rather than business products.

Odd-Number Pricing Many retailers believe that consumers respond more positively to odd-number prices such as $4.99 than to whole-dollar prices such as $5. **Odd-number pricing** is the strategy of setting prices using odd numbers that are slightly below whole-dollar amounts. Nine and five are the most popular ending figures for odd-number prices.

Sellers who use this strategy believe that odd-number prices increase sales. The strategy is not limited to low-priced items. Auto manufacturers may set the price of a car at $11,999 rather than $12,000. Odd-number pricing has been the subject of various psychological studies, but the results have been inconclusive.

Multiple-Unit Pricing Many retailers (and especially supermarkets) practice **multiple-unit pricing**, setting a single price for two or more units, such as two cans for 99 cents rather than 50 cents per can. Especially for frequently purchased products, this strategy can increase sales. Customers who see the single price and who expect eventually to use more than one unit of the product regularly purchase multiple units to save money.

Reference Pricing Reference pricing means pricing a product at a moderate level and positioning it next to a more expensive model or brand in the hope that the

negotiated pricing establishing a final price through bargaining

secondary-market pricing setting one price for the primary target market and a different price for another market

periodic discounting temporary reduction of prices on a patterned or systematic basis

random discounting temporary reduction of prices on an unsystematic basis

odd-number pricing the strategy of setting prices using odd numbers that are slightly below whole-dollar amounts

multiple-unit pricing the strategy of setting a single price for two or more units

reference pricing pricing a product at a moderate level and positioning it next to a more expensive model or brand

The benefits of bundling. Companies like Verizon bundle their goods and services to entice consumers to purchase multiple products. This can increase a firm's market share as well as get consumers interested in products they might not have been willing to purchase alone. Bundling can also help a firm match or undercut its competitors' prices, especially if the competitor offers a single product or has fewer of them to bundle.

customer will use the higher price as a reference price (i.e., a comparison price). Because of the comparison, the customer is expected to view the moderate price favorably.

Bundle Pricing Bundle pricing is the packaging together of two or more products, usually of a complementary nature, to be sold for a single price. To be attractive to customers, the single price usually is considerably less than the sum of the prices of the individual products. Being able to buy the bundled combination of products in a single transaction may be of value to the customer as well. Bundle pricing is used commonly for banking and travel services, computers, and automobiles with option packages. Bundle pricing can help to increase customer satisfaction. By bundling slow-moving products with ones with a higher turnover, an organization can stimulate sales and increase its revenues. Selling products as a package rather than individually also may result in cost savings. It is common for telecommunications providers to sell service bundles of cable, Internet, and phone service for one price. AT&T, Comcast, and DirectTV all offer such services.

Everyday Low Prices (EDLPs) To reduce or eliminate the use of frequent short-term price reductions, some organizations use an approach referred to as **everyday low prices (EDLPs)**. When EDLPs are used, a marketer sets a low price for its products on a consistent basis rather than setting higher prices and frequently discounting them. EDLPs, though not deeply discounted, are set far enough below competitors' prices to make customers feel confident that they are receiving a fair price. EDLPs are employed by retailers such as Walmart and by manufacturers such as Procter & Gamble. A company that uses EDLPs benefits from reduced promotional costs, reduced losses from frequent markdowns, and more stability in its sales. A major problem with this approach is that customers have mixed responses to it. In some instances, customers simply do not believe that EDLPs are what they say they are but are instead a marketing gimmick.

Customary Pricing In **customary pricing**, certain goods are priced primarily on the basis of tradition. Examples of customary, or traditional, prices would be those set for candy bars and chewing gum.

Product-Line Pricing

Rather than considering products on an item-by-item basis when determining pricing strategies, some marketers employ product-line pricing. *Product-line pricing* means establishing and adjusting the prices of multiple products within a product line. Product-line pricing can provide marketers with flexibility in price setting. For example, marketers can set prices so that one product is quite profitable, whereas another increases market share by virtue of having a lower price than competing products.

When marketers employ product-line pricing, they have several strategies from which to choose. These include captive pricing, premium pricing, and price lining.

Captive Pricing When **captive pricing** is used, the basic product in a product line is priced low, but the price on the items required to operate or enhance it are set at a higher level. Two common examples of captive pricing are razor blades and printer ink. The razor handle and the printer are generally priced quite low, but the razor blades and the printer ink replacement cartridges are usually very expensive. Sometimes, a brand will even give away the razor handle because it knows that consumers will then be compelled to buy the requisite razor blades.

bundle pricing packaging together two or more complementary products and selling them for a single price

everyday low prices (EDLPs) setting a low price for products on a consistent basis

customary pricing pricing on the basis of tradition

captive pricing pricing the basic product in a product line low, but pricing related items at a higher level

Premium Pricing **Premium pricing** occurs when the highest-quality product or the most-versatile version of similar products in a product line is given the highest price. Other products in the line are priced to appeal to price-sensitive shoppers or to those who seek product-specific features. Marketers that use premium pricing often realize a significant portion of their profits from premium-priced products. Examples of product categories in which premium pricing is common are small kitchen appliances, beer, ice cream, and television cable service.

Price Lining **Price lining** is the strategy of selling goods only at certain predetermined prices that reflect definite price breaks. For example, a shop may sell men's ties only at $22 and $37. This strategy is used widely in clothing and accessory stores. It eliminates minor price differences from the buying decision—both for customers and for managers who buy merchandise to sell in these stores.

Promotional Pricing

Price, as an ingredient in the marketing mix, often is coordinated with promotion. The two variables sometimes are so interrelated that the pricing policy is promotion oriented. Examples of promotional pricing include price leaders, special-event pricing, and comparison discounting.

Price Leaders Sometimes a firm prices a few products below the usual markup, near cost, or below cost, which results in prices known as **price leaders**. This type of pricing is used most often in supermarkets and restaurants to attract customers by giving them especially low prices on a few items. Management hopes that sales of regularly priced products will more than offset the reduced revenues from the price leaders.

Special-Event Pricing To increase sales volume, many organizations coordinate price with advertising or sales promotions for seasonal or special situations. **Special-event pricing** involves advertised sales or price cutting linked to a holiday, season, or event. If the pricing objective is survival, then special sales events may be designed to generate the necessary operating capital.

Comparison Discounting **Comparison discounting** sets the price of a product at a specific level and simultaneously compares it with a higher price. The higher price may be the product's previous price, the price of a competing brand, the product's price at another retail outlet, or a manufacturer's suggested retail price. Customers may find comparative discounting informative, and it can have a significant impact on them. However, because this pricing strategy on occasion has led to deceptive pricing practices, the Federal Trade Commission has established guidelines for comparison discounting. If the higher price against which the comparison is made is the price formerly charged for the product, sellers must have made the previous price available to customers for a reasonable period of time. If sellers present the higher price as the one charged by other retailers in the same trade area, they must be able to demonstrate that this claim is true. When they present the higher price as the manufacturer's suggested retail price, then the higher price must be similar to the price at which a reasonable proportion of the product was sold. Some manufacturers' suggested retail prices are so high that very few products actually are sold at those prices. In such cases, it would be deceptive to use comparison discounting.

PRICING BUSINESS PRODUCTS

Many of the pricing issues discussed thus far in this chapter deal with pricing in general. However, setting prices for business products can be different from setting prices for consumer products owing to several factors such as size of purchases, transportation considerations, and geographic issues. We examine three types of pricing associated with business products: geographic pricing, transfer pricing, and discounting.

---

premium pricing pricing the highest-quality or most-versatile products higher than other models in the product line

price lining the strategy of selling goods only at certain predetermined prices that reflect definite price breaks

price leaders products priced below the usual markup, near cost, or below cost

special-event pricing advertised sales or price cutting linked to a holiday, season, or event

comparison discounting setting a price at a specific level and comparing it with a higher price

(10) Describe three major types of pricing associated with business products.

Geographic Pricing

Geographic pricing strategies deal with delivery costs. The pricing strategy that requires the buyer to pay the delivery costs is called *FOB origin pricing*. It stands for "free on board at the point of origin," which means that the price does not include freight charges, and thus the buyer must pay the transportation costs from the seller's warehouse to the buyer's place of business. *FOB destination* indicates that the price does include freight charges, and thus the seller pays these charges.

Transfer Pricing

When one unit in an organization sells a product to another unit, **transfer pricing** occurs. The price is determined by calculating the cost of the product. A transfer price can vary depending on the types of costs included in the calculations. The choice of the costs to include when calculating the transfer price depends on the company's management strategy and the nature of the units' interaction. An organization also must ensure that transfer pricing is fair to all units involved in the purchases.

Discounting

A **discount** is a deduction from the price of an item. Producers and sellers offer a wide variety of discounts to their customers, including trade, quantity, cash, and seasonal discounts as well as allowances. *Trade discounts* are discounts from the list prices that are offered to marketing intermediaries, or middlemen. *Quantity discounts* are discounts given to customers who buy in large quantities. The seller's per-unit selling cost is lower for larger purchases. *Cash discounts* are discounts offered for prompt payment. A seller may offer a discount of "2/10, net 30," meaning that the buyer may take a 2 percent discount if the bill is paid within ten days and that the bill must be paid in full within 30 days. A *seasonal discount* is a price reduction to buyers who purchase out of season. This discount lets the seller maintain steadier production during the year. An *allowance* is a reduction in price to achieve a desired goal. Trade-in allowances, for example, are price reductions granted for turning in used equipment, like aircraft, when purchasing new equipment. Table 13.4 describes some of the reasons for using these discounting techniques as well as some examples.

transfer pricing prices charged in sales between an organization's units

discount a deduction from the price of an item

TABLE 13.4	Discounts Used for Business Markets	
Type	**Reasons for Use**	**Examples**
Trade (functional)	To attract and keep effective resellers by compensating them for performing certain functions, such as transportation, warehousing, selling, and providing credit.	A college bookstore pays about one-third less for a new textbook than the retail price a student pays.
Quantity	To encourage customers to buy large quantities when making purchases and, in the case of cumulative discounts, to encourage customer loyalty.	Numerous companies serving business markets allow a 2 percent discount if an account is paid within ten days.
Seasonal	To allow a marketer to use resources more efficiently by stimulating sales during off-peak periods.	Florida hotels provide companies holding national and regional sales meetings with deeply discounted accommodations during the summer months.
Allowance	In the case of a trade-in allowance, to assist the buyer in making the purchase and potentially earn a profit on the resale of used equipment; in the case of a promotional allowance, to ensure that dealers participate in advertising and sales support programs.	A farm equipment dealer takes a farmer's used tractor as a trade-in on a new one. Nabisco pays a promotional allowance to a supermarket for setting up and maintaining a large end-of-aisle display for a two-week period.

Source: William M. Pride and O. C. Ferrell, *Foundations of Marketing* (Mason, OH: South-Western/Cengage Learning, 2013), 358.

PepsiCo

Pursuing ever-higher market share, PepsiCo continues to face head-to-head competition with Coca-Cola, Kraft, and other international and local food and beverage rivals. Although price is a big part of its marketing strategy, PepsiCo puts even more emphasis on product differentiation. This is why it has been cooking up line extensions to be introduced under its billion-dollar brands, with distinctive flavors and diverse package sizes for a range of customer preferences and budgets.

Innovative product lines such as the Trop50 reduced-calorie juices earn PepsiCo higher profit margins because customers will pay more for unique flavors and valued benefits. No wonder PepsiCo is pouring more money into developing new products and building on brand equity by marketing its beverage and snack brands together for more impact.

Questions

1. How is PepsiCo using price differentiation in marketing its soft drinks?
2. How does the product life-cycle help to explain why PepsiCo introduces so many flavor variations of Doritos snacks and Mountain Dew soft drinks?

SUMMARY

Looking for Success?

Get Flashcards, Quizzes, Games, Crosswords and More at **www.cengagebrain.com**.

 Explain what a product is and how products are classified.

A product is everything one receives in an exchange, including all attributes and expected benefits. The product may be a manufactured item, a service, an idea, or some combination of these.

Products are classified according to their ultimate use. Classification affects a product's distribution, promotion, and pricing. Consumer products, which include convenience, shopping, and specialty products, are purchased to satisfy personal and family needs. Business products are purchased for resale, for making other products, or for use in a firm's operations. Business products can be classified as raw materials, major equipment, accessory equipment, component parts, process materials, supplies, and services.

 Discuss the product life-cycle and how it leads to new-product development.

Every product moves through a series of four stages—introduction, growth, maturity, and decline—which together form the product life-cycle. As the product progresses through these stages, its sales and profitability increase, peak, and then decline. Marketers keep track of the life-cycle stage of products in order to estimate when a new product should be introduced to replace a declining one.

 Define *product line* **and** *product mix* **and distinguish between the two.**

A product line is a group of similar products marketed by a firm. The products in a product line are related to each other in the way they are produced, marketed, and used. The firm's product mix includes all the products it offers for sale. The width of a mix is the number of product lines it contains. The depth of the mix is the average number of individual products within each line.

 Identify the methods available for changing a product mix.

Customer satisfaction and organizational objectives require marketers to develop, adjust, and maintain an effective product mix. Marketers may improve a product mix by changing existing products, deleting products, and developing new products.

New products are developed through a series of seven steps. The first step, idea generation, involves the accumulation of a pool of possible product ideas. Screening, the second step, removes from consideration those product ideas that do not mesh with organizational goals or resources. Concept testing, the third step, is a phase in which a small sample of potential buyers is exposed to a proposed product through a written or oral description in order to determine their initial reaction and buying intentions. The fourth step, business analysis, generates information about the potential sales, costs, and profits. During the development step, the product idea is transformed into mock-ups and actual prototypes to determine if the product is technically feasible to build and can be produced at reasonable costs. Test marketing is an actual launch of the product in several selected cities. Finally, during commercialization, plans for full-scale production and marketing are refined and implemented. Most product failures result from inadequate product planning and development.

 Explain the uses and importance of branding, packaging, and labeling.

A brand is a name, term, symbol, design, or any combination of these that identifies a seller's products as distinct from those of other sellers. Brands can be classified as manufacturer brands, store brands, or generic brands. A firm can choose between two branding strategies—individual branding or family branding. Branding strategies are used to associate (or *not* associate) particular products with existing products, producers, or intermediaries. Packaging protects goods, offers consumer convenience, and enhances marketing efforts by communicating product features, uses, benefits, and image. Labeling provides customers with product information, some of which is required by law.

 Describe the economic basis of pricing and the means by which sellers can control prices and buyers' perceptions of prices.

Under the ideal conditions of pure competition, an individual seller has no control over the price of its products. Prices are determined by the workings of supply and demand. In our real economy, however, sellers do exert some control, primarily through product differentiation. Product differentiation is the process of developing and promoting differences between one's product and all similar products. Firms also attempt to gain some control over pricing through advertising. A few large sellers have considerable control over prices because each controls a large proportion of the total supply of the product. Firms must consider the relative importance of price to buyers in the target market before setting prices. Buyers' perceptions of prices are affected by the importance of the product to them, the range of prices they consider acceptable, their perceptions of competing products, and their association of quality with price.

 Identify the major pricing objectives used by businesses.

Objectives of pricing include survival, profit maximization, target return on investment, achieving market goals, and maintaining the status quo. Firms sometimes have to price products to survive, which usually requires cutting prices to attract customers. ROI is the amount earned as a result of the investment in developing and marketing the product. The firm sets an annual percentage ROI as the pricing goal. Some firms use pricing to maintain or increase their market share. And in industries in which price stability is important, firms often price their products by charging about the same as competitors.

 Examine the three major pricing methods that firms employ.

The three major pricing methods are cost-based pricing, demand-based pricing, and competition-based pricing. When cost-based pricing is employed, a proportion of the cost is added to the total cost to determine the selling price. When demand-based pricing is used, the price will be higher when demand is higher, and the price will be lower when demand is lower. A firm that uses competition-based pricing may choose to price below competitors' prices, at the same level as competitors' prices, or slightly above competitors' prices.

 Explain the different strategies available to companies for setting prices.

Pricing strategies fall into five categories: new-product pricing, differential pricing, psychological pricing, product-line pricing, and promotional pricing. Price skimming and penetration pricing are two strategies used for pricing new products. Differential pricing can be accomplished through negotiated pricing, secondary-market pricing, periodic discounting, and random discounting. Types of psychological pricing strategies are odd-number pricing, multiple-unit pricing, reference pricing, bundle pricing, everyday low prices, and customary pricing. Product-line pricing can be achieved through captive pricing, premium pricing, and price lining. The major types of promotional pricing are price-leader pricing, special-event pricing, and comparison discounting.

 Describe three major types of pricing associated with business products.

Setting prices for business products can be different from setting prices for consumer products as a result of several factors, such as the size of purchases, transportation considerations, and geographic issues. The three types of pricing associated with the pricing of business products are geographic pricing, transfer pricing, and discounting.

KEY TERMS

You should now be able to define and give an example relevant to each of the following terms:

product (358)	raw material (359)	business service (360)	product deletion (365)
consumer product (359)	major equipment (359)	product life-cycle (360)	brand (369)
business product (359)	accessory equipment (360)	product line (363)	brand name (369)
convenience product (359)	component part (360)	product mix (363)	brand mark (369)
shopping product (359)	process material (360)	product modification (364)	trademark (369)
specialty product (359)	supply (360)	line extension (364)	trade name (370)

manufacturer (or producer) brand (370)
store (or private) brand (370)
generic product (or brand) (370)
brand loyalty (371)
brand equity (371)
individual branding (373)
family branding (373)
brand extension (373)
packaging (373)
labeling (375)
express warranty (375)

price (375)
supply (376)
demand (376)
price competition (377)
non-price competition (377)
product differentiation (377)
markup (379)
breakeven quantity (379)
total revenue (379)
fixed cost (379)
variable cost (379)
total cost (379)
price skimming (382)

penetration pricing (382)
negotiated pricing (383)
secondary-market pricing (383)
periodic discounting (383)
random discounting (383)
odd-number pricing (383)
multiple-unit pricing (383)
reference pricing (383)
bundle pricing (384)
everyday low prices (EDLPs) (384)
customary pricing (384)
captive pricing (384)

premium pricing (385)
price lining (385)
price leaders (385)
special-event pricing (385)
comparison discounting (385)
transfer pricing (386)
discount (386)

REVIEW QUESTIONS

1. What does the purchaser of a product obtain besides the good, service, or idea itself?
2. What are the products of (a) a bank, (b) an insurance company, and (c) a university?
3. What major factor determines whether a product is a consumer or a business product?
4. Describe each of the classifications of business products.
5. What are the four stages of the product life-cycle? How can a firm determine which stage a particular product is in?
6. What is the difference between a product line and a product mix? Give an example of each.
7. Under what conditions does product modification work best?
8. Why do products have to be deleted from a product mix?
9. Why must firms introduce new products?
10. Briefly describe the seven new-product development stages.
11. What is the difference between manufacturer brands and store brands? Between family branding and individual branding?
12. What is the difference between a line extension and a brand extension?

13. How can packaging be used to enhance marketing activities?
14. For what purposes is labeling used?
15. What is the primary function of prices in our economy?
16. Compare and contrast the characteristics of price and non-price competition.
17. How might buyers' perceptions of price influence pricing decisions?
18. List and briefly describe the five major pricing objectives.
19. What are the differences among markup pricing, pricing by breakeven analysis, and competition-based pricing?
20. In what way is demand-based pricing more realistic than markup pricing?
21. Why would a firm use competition-based pricing?
22. What are the five major categories of pricing strategies? Give at least two examples of specific strategies that fall into each category.
23. Identify and describe the main types of discounts that are used in the pricing of business products.

DISCUSSION QUESTIONS

1. Why is it important to understand how products are classified?
2. What factors might determine how long a product remains in each stage of the product life-cycle? What can a firm do to prolong each stage?
3. Some firms do not delete products until they become financially threatening. What problems may result from relying on this practice?
4. Which steps in the evolution of new products are most important? Which are least important? Defend your choices.
5. Do branding, packaging, and labeling really benefit consumers? Explain.
6. To what extent can a firm control its prices in our market economy? What factors limit such control?

7. Under what conditions would a firm be most likely to use non-price competition?
8. Can a firm have more than one pricing objective? Can it use more than one of the pricing methods discussed in this chapter? Explain.
9. What are the major disadvantages of price skimming?
10. What is an "effective" price?
11. Under what conditions would a business most likely decide to employ one of the differential pricing strategies?
12. For what types of products are psychological pricing strategies most likely to be used?

3. Under what set of circumstances would you be willing to change to another competing brand?
4. Discuss how you first began to use this brand.

③ DEVELOPING CRITICAL-THINKING SKILLS

A feature is a characteristic of a product or service that enables it to perform its function. Benefits are the results a person receives from using a product or service. For example, a toothpaste's stain-removing formula is a feature; the benefit to the user is whiter teeth. Although features are valuable and enhance a product, benefits motivate people to buy. The customer is more interested in how the product can help (the benefits) than in the details of the product (the features).

Assignment

1. Choose a product and identify its features and benefits.
2. Divide a sheet of paper into two columns. In one column, list the features of the product. In the other column, list the benefits each feature yields to the buyer.
3. Prepare a statement that would motivate you to buy this product.

④ BUILDING TEAM SKILLS

In his book, *The Post-Industrial Society*, Peter Drucker wrote:

Society, community, and family are all conserving institutions. They try to maintain stability and to prevent, or at least slow down, change. But the organization of the post-capitalist society of organizations is a destabilizer. Because its function is to put knowledge to work—on tools, processes, and products; on work; on knowledge itself—it must be organized for constant change. It must be organized for innovation.

New product development is important in this process of systematically abandoning the past and building a future. Current customers can be sources of ideas for new products and services and ways of improving existing ones.

Assignment

1. Working in teams of five to seven, brainstorm ideas for new products or services for your college.
2. Construct questions to ask currently enrolled students (your customers). Sample questions might include:
   a. Why did you choose this college?
   b. How can this college be improved?
   c. What products or services do you wish were available?
3. Conduct the survey and review the results.
4. Prepare a list of improvements and/or new products or services for your college.

⑤ RESEARCHING DIFFERENT CAREERS

Standard & Poor's Industry Surveys, designed for investors, provides insight into various industries and the companies that compete within those industries. The "Basic Analysis" section gives overviews of industry trends and issues. The other sections define some basic industry terms, report the latest revenues and earnings of more than 1,000 companies, and occasionally list major reference books and trade associations.

Assignment

1. Identify an industry in which you might like to work.
2. Find the industry in *Standard & Poor's*. (*Note: Standard & Poor's* uses broad categories of industry. For example, an apparel or home-furnishings store would be included under "Retail" or "Textiles.")
3. Identify the following:
   a. Trends and issues in the industry
   b. Opportunities and/or problems that might arise in the industry in the next five years
   c. Major competitors within the industry (These companies are your potential employers.)
4. Prepare a report of your findings.

ENDNOTES

1. Based on information in Duane D. Stanford, "PepsiCo Adds Water to Tropicana Products to Juice Margin," *Bloomberg BusinessWeek*, February 16, 2012, www.businessweek.com; E. J. Schultz, "PepsiCo Plans 35% Marketing Boost for Snacks," *Advertising Age*, February 24, 2012, www.adage.com; Karlene Lukovitz, "PepsiCo CFO Talks Pricing, 'Stagflation,'" *MediaPost*, September 8, 2011, www.mediapost.com.
2. Apple, http://apple.com accessed February 13, 2012.
3. "Coming Soon: Barq's Root Beer Redesign," Bev Review, February 22, 2012, www.bevreview.com/2012/02/22/coming-soon-barqs-root-beer-redesign/.
4. AnandK@TWC, "Google to Discontinue 10 Products, Including Google Desktop, Google Pack," The Windows Club, September 3, 2011, www.thewindowsclub.com/google-discontinue-10-products-including-google-desktop-google-pack.
5. Jell-O, www.jello.com, accessed April 2, 2012.
6. Procter & Gamble, http://pg.com/en_US/brands/index.shtml accessed February 13, 2012.
7. General Mills Cereals, www.generalmills.com/en/Brands/Cereals.aspx, accessed March 30, 2012.
8. Nick Bunkley, "GM to Reinforce Battery in its Hybrid Car, the Volt," *The New York Times*, January 20, 2012, www.nytimes.com/2012/01/06/business/gm-to-reinforce-battery-in-hybrid-car.html.
9. Press release, "WD-40 Launches First-Ever Product Line Extension, Introduces New WD-40 Specialist Line of Products," *New York Times*, February 14, 2012, http://markets.on.nytimes.com/research/stocks/news/press_release.asp?docTag=201202141309BIZWIRE_USPRX____BW6491&feedID=600&press_symbol=284382
10. Phil Goldstein, "T-Mobile to Discontinue Sidekick 4G, but May Not Kill Sidekick Brand," Fierce Wireless, March 16, 2012, www.fiercewireless.com/story/t-mobile-discontinue-sidekick-4g-may-not-kill-sidekick-brand/2012-03-16.
11. "A Case for Modernizing Product Planning," (e-paper) Accept Software Corporation, www.accept360.com/resources/modprodplan, accessed April 2, 2012.
12. Google Project Glass, https://plus.google.com/111626127367496192147/posts, accessed April 6, 2012.
13. Emily Glazer and Suzanne Vranica, "Big Firms Mentor Start-Ups on Their Image," *Wall Street Journal*, March 29, 2012, http://online.wsj.com/article/SB10001424052702303816504577309842814468950.html.
14. Joseph Peña, "Aptera Secures Financing, Introduces New 2e Electric Car," *San Diego News Network*, April 14, 2010, sdgln.com/news/2010/04/15/video-aptera-secures-financing-introduces-new-2e-electric-car.

15. Staff writer, "Columbus, Ohio: Test Market of the U.S.A.," CBA News, March 25, 2012, www.cbsnews.com/8301-505125_162-57404087/columbus-ohio-test-market-of-the-u.s.a/.

16. "What Are Store Brands?" PLMA, http://plma.com/storeBrands/factsnew12.html, accessed March 19, 2012; Candace Choi, "Store Brand Groceries Now on Premium Shelves," USA Today, March 25, 2012, www.usatoday.com/money/industries/food/story/2012-03-25/store-brand-groceries/53739828/1.

17. Staff reporter, "Now That's What You Call Brand Loyalty!" *Daily Mail*, March 12, 2012, www.dailymail.co.uk/news/article-2114031/iPad-3-release-date-Pair-sit-head-queue-Apples-new-iPad-5-days-goes-sale.html.

18. Julie Jargon, "Latest Starbucks Concoction: Juice," *Wall Street Journal,* November 11, 2011, http://online.wsj.com/article/SB10001424052970204358004577030112155716538.html, accessed March 19, 2012; Josh Ozersky, "The Big Gulp," *Time,* March 12, 2012, www.time.com/time/magazine/article/0,9171,2108016,00.html.

19. http://amazon.com accessed February 13, 2012.

20. "Pet Insurance," Iams, www.iams.com/pet-health/pet-insurance, accessed April 4, 2012.

21. Matt Haig, *Brand Failures: The Truth about the 100 Biggest Branding Mistakes of All Time,* 2011 (Kogan Page Limited, Philadelphia, PA), p. 58, 77, 88

22. "Cup Summit 3," Starbucks, www.starbucks.com/blog/cup-summit-3/1084, accessed March 21, 2012.

23. "Vitaminwater Accused of Making Misleading Health Claims," Huffington Post, January 3, 2012, www.huffingtonpost.com/2012/01/03/vitaminwater-false-claims_n_1181860.html?ref=food; "Feds Cracking Down on Misleading Labels," National Consumers League, www.nclnet.org/food/85-food-labeling/374-fda-cracking-down-on-misleading-health-claims-on-food-labels, accessed April 1, 2012.

24. Eric Slivka, "Apple Clarifies Warranty Coverage Options for Customers in the European Union," Mac Rumors, March 30, 2012, www.macrumors.com/2012/03/30/apple-clarifies-warranty-coverage-options-for-customers-in-european-union/.

25. Quentin Fottrell, "New Cheap Alternatives to the iPad 3," *Smart Money*, March 7, 2012, http://blogs.smartmoney.com/advice/2012/03/07/new-cheap-alternatives-to-the-ipad-3/?link=SM_hp_ls4e.

26. Vibram Five Fingers, www.vibramfivefingers.com/index.htm, accessed April 4, 2012.

27. Dominic Haber, "Abercrombie & Fitch Plans Further Price Cuts After 1Q Loss," TopNews.com, May 17, 2009, topnews.us/content/25241-abercrombie-fitch-plans-further-price-cuts-after-1q-loss.

28. SF Park, http://sfpark.org/; Leon Neyfahk, "The Case for the $6 Parking Meter," The Boston Globe, January 15, 2012, www.bostonglobe.com/ideas/2012/01/15/the-case-for-parking-meter/H2Ih2QJ8wOEgwiMI7yHdVO/story.html.

29. Arragon Perrone, "Minnesota Twins Expand Dynamic Pricing for Single Games," Ticket News, March 21, 2012, www.ticketnews.com/news/minnesota-twins-expand-dynamic-pricing-for-single-games031221551; Press release, "Demand-Based Pricing for Single Game Tickets at Target Field Starts March 9," March 8, 2012, http://minnesota.twins.mlb.com/news/article.jsp?ymd=20120308&content_id=27106214&vkey=pr_min&c_id=min.

30. Based on information in bludot.com accessed February 21, 2012; "Stuff," bludot.com (accessed February 21, 2012) and originally published in *Minnesota Monthly*; Carl Alviani, "Taking the Middle Ground: Massive Design for the Masses?" Core 77, http://core77.com/reactor/07.05_mIddleground.asp accessed February 13, 2012; interviews with company personnel and the film, "Blu Dot."

31. Jeremiah McWilliams, "PepsiCo Revamps 'Formidable' Gatorade Franchise After Rocky 2009," *The Atlanta Journal-Constitution*, March 23, 2010, http://www.ajc.com/business/pepsico-revamps-formidable-gatorade-397505.html; Martinne Geller, "Pepsi Eyes Emerging Markets, Healthy Fare," *Reuters*, March 22, 2010, http://in.reuters.com/article/2010/03/22/idINIndia-47126620100322; Noreen O'Leary, "Gatorade's G2 Channels Ali to Punch Up Its Messaging," *Adweek*, January 2, 2010, www.adweek.com/news/advertising-branding/gatorades-g2-channels-ali-punch-its-messaging-106901; Emily Bryson and Natalie Zmuda, "What G Isn't Is a Sales Success," *Advertising Age*, August 10, 2009, p. 17; David Sterrett, "New Drinks in Gatorade's Playbook," *Crain's Chicago Business*, November 9, 2009, p. 1; Burt Helm, "Blowing Up Pepsi," *BusinessWeek*, April 23, 2009, http://businessweek.com/magazine/content/09_17/b4128032006687.htm; gatorade.com accessed February 21, 2012.

14 Wholesaling, Retailing, and Physical Distribution

LEARNING OBJECTIVES

Once you complete this chapter, you will be able to:

1. Identify the various channels of distribution that are used for consumer and industrial products.

2. Explain the concept of market coverage.

3. Understand how supply-chain management facilitates partnering among channel members.

4. Describe what a vertical marketing system is and identify the types of vertical marketing systems.

5. Discuss the need for wholesalers and describe the services they provide to retailers and manufacturers.

6. Identify and describe the major types of wholesalers.

7. Distinguish among the major types of retailers.

8. Identify the categories of shopping centers and the factors that determine how shopping centers are classified.

9. Explain the five most important physical distribution activities.

Through Distribution, Chobani Climbs to Number One

How can a brand zoom from startup to market leader in just four years? Greek yogurt maker Chobani had a delicious product, eye-catching packaging, and wallet-friendly pricing. But the real fuel powering its meteoric rise was distribution.

CEO Hamdi Ulukaya got the idea for Chobani when he heard about a yogurt factory for sale near Utica, New York. Instead of the usual yogurt found in grocery stores and supermarkets across America, Ulukaya wanted to market a thick, tangy yogurt not well known to U.S. consumers. Fage, a yogurt imported from Greece, had this product category to itself—for the moment.

Ulukaya bought the factory and hired a yogurt expert. In 2007, after months of development and testing, his Greek yogurt was ready for introduction, complete with a colorful label and a popular price. To get Chobani into the hands of as many consumers as possible, he decided to work with mainstream retailers rather than limit distribution to health-food stores and specialty shops. "We went to the big chains and said we wanted to put it in the regular yogurt section," Ulukaya remembers. Another key decision was to offer in-store samples so customers could taste the new product while shopping and buy that day.

Customers liked the yogurt so much that the first three stores to carry Chobani quickly sold out and reordered. Not long afterward, BJ's Wholesale Club agreed to carry Chobani, followed by Costco, and a growing number of supermarkets across the Northeast. As Chobani added new flavors, retailers made more room on store shelves.

Competition soon crowded in. Fage opened a yogurt plant an hour's drive from Chobani's plant, deep in the heart of New York's dairy belt. Both Dannon and Yoplait introduced Greek yogurt products to take advantage of the booming demand. Only four years after Chobani's debut, it became the top brand in Greek yogurt, with 53 percent of the market, and it was the third-largest overall yogurt brand, thanks in large part to its distribution strategy. How long can Chobani maintain this fast-paced growth?[1]

Did You Know?

Chobani ships 2 million cases of Greek yogurt every week to stores across the United States.

Some companies, like Chobani, use a particular approach to distribution and marketing channels that gives them a sustainable competitive advantage. More than 2 million firms in the United States help to move products from producers to consumers. Store chains such as Dollar General, Starbucks, Sears, and Walmart operate retail outlets where consumers make purchases. Some retailers, such as Avon Products and Amway, send their salespeople to the homes of customers. Still others, such as Amazon, sell exclusively online. Most retailers, however, utilize a mix of distribution channels, which may include retail stores, a Web site with online shopping, and catalogs.

In addition, there are more than half a million wholesalers that sell merchandise to other firms. Most consumers know little about these firms, which work "behind the scenes" and rarely sell directly to consumers. These and other intermediaries are concerned with the transfer of both products and ownership. They thus help to create the time, place, and possession utilities that are critical to marketing. As we will see, they also perform a number of services for their suppliers and their customers.

In this chapter, we initially examine various channels of distribution that products follow as they move from producer to ultimate user. Then we discuss wholesalers and retailers within these channels. Next, we examine the types of shopping centers. Finally, we explore the physical distribution function and the major modes of transportation that are used to move goods.

Identify the various channels of distribution that are used for consumer and industrial products.

CHANNELS OF DISTRIBUTION

A **channel of distribution**, or **marketing channel**, is a sequence of marketing organizations that directs a product from the producer to the ultimate user. Every marketing channel begins with the producer and ends with either the consumer or the business user.

A marketing organization that links a producer and user within a marketing channel is called a **middleman** or **marketing intermediary**. For the most part, middlemen are concerned with the transfer of *ownership* of products. A **merchant middleman** (or, more simply, a *merchant*) is a middleman that actually takes title to products by buying them. A **functional middleman**, on the other hand, helps in the transfer of ownership of products but does not take title to the products.

Channels for Consumer Products

Different channels of distribution generally are used to move consumer and business products. The four most commonly used channels for consumer products are illustrated in Figure 14.1.

Producer to Consumer This channel, often called the *direct channel,* includes no marketing intermediaries. Practically all services and a few consumer goods are distributed through a direct channel. Examples of marketers that sell goods directly to consumers include Dell Computer, Mary Kay Cosmetics, and Avon Products.

Producers sell directly to consumers for several reasons. They can better control the quality and price of their products. They do not have to pay (through discounts) for the services of intermediaries. They can maintain closer ties with customers.

Producer to Retailer to Consumer A **retailer** is a middleman that buys from producers or other middlemen and sells to consumers. Producers sell directly to retailers when retailers (such as Walmart) can buy in large quantities. This channel is used most often for products that are bulky, such as furniture and automobiles, for which additional handling would increase selling costs. It is also the usual channel for perishable products, such as fruits and vegetables, and for high-fashion products that must reach the consumer in the shortest possible time.

Producer to Wholesaler to Retailer to Consumer This channel is known as the *traditional channel* because many consumer goods (especially convenience goods) pass through wholesalers to retailers. A **wholesaler** is a middleman that sells products to other firms. These firms may be retailers, industrial users, or other wholesalers. A producer uses wholesalers when its products are carried by so many retailers that the producer cannot deal with all of them. For example, the maker of Wrigley's gum uses this type of channel.

Producer to Agent to Wholesaler to Retailer to Consumer Producers may use agents to reach wholesalers. Agents are functional middlemen who do not take title to products and are compensated by commissions paid by producers. Often these products are inexpensive, frequently purchased items. For example, to reach a large number of potential customers, a small manufacturer of gas-powered lawn edgers might choose to use agents to market its product to wholesalers, which, in turn, sell the lawn edgers to a large number of retailers. This channel is also used for highly seasonal products (such as Christmas tree ornaments) and by producers that do not have their own sales forces.

Multiple Channels for Consumer Products

Often, a manufacturer uses different distribution channels to reach different market segments. A manufacturer uses multiple channels, for example, when the same product is sold to consumers and

channel of distribution (or marketing channel) a sequence of marketing organizations that directs a product from the producer to the ultimate user

middleman (or marketing intermediary) a marketing organization that links a producer and user within a marketing channel

merchant middleman a middleman that actually takes title to products by buying them

functional middleman a middleman that helps in the transfer of ownership of products but does not take title to the products

retailer a middleman that buys from producers or other middlemen and sells to consumers

wholesaler a middleman that sells products to other firms

Why Dell expanded its distribution channels. Computers are sold through several distribution channels. At one time, Dell sold its computers only through direct distribution. In other words, the company sold them straight to consumers and not to retailers. However, competition forced Dell to add the producer/retailer/consumer channel.

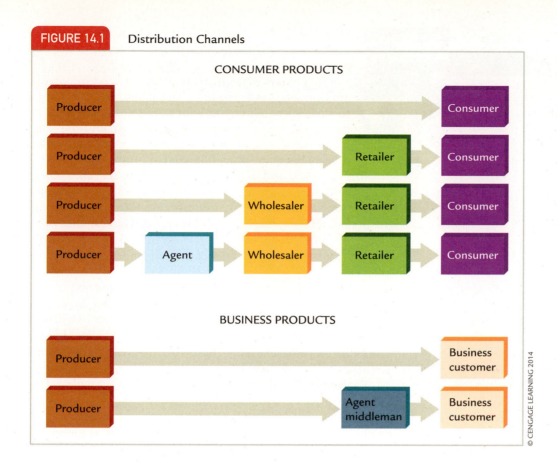

FIGURE 14.1　Distribution Channels

CONSUMER PRODUCTS

BUSINESS PRODUCTS

© CENGAGE LEARNING 2014

business customers. Multiple channels are also used to increase sales or to capture a larger share of the market. With the goal of selling as much merchandise as possible, Firestone markets its tires through its own retail outlets as well as through independent dealers.

Channels for Business Products

Producers of business products generally tend to use short channels. We will outline the two that are used most commonly, which are illustrated in Figure 14.1.

Producer to Business User　In this direct channel, the manufacturer's own sales force sells directly to business users. Heavy machinery, airplanes, and major equipment usually are distributed in this way. The very short channel allows the producer to provide customers with expert and timely services, such as delivery, machinery installation, and repairs.

Producer to Agent Middleman to Business User　Manufacturers use this channel to distribute such items as operating supplies, accessory equipment, small tools, and standardized parts. The agent is an independent intermediary between the producer and the user. Generally, agents represent sellers.

LEVEL OF MARKET COVERAGE

 Explain the concept of market coverage.

The level of market coverage refers to the number of wholesalers and the number of retailers that are used for a specific geographic area. There are three levels of market coverage: intensive distribution, selective distribution, and exclusive distribution.

Personal APPS

Wherever you are—at school, at work, at a ball game, or at a movie—you're likely to see bottled water and snacks for sale. So many people buy these items in so many situations that marketers use intensive distribution to make them available just about everywhere.

Figure 14.2 shows examples of products that are likely to be distributed through each of these levels of market coverage.

Intensive distribution is the use of all available outlets for a product. The producer that wants to give its product the widest possible exposure in the marketplace chooses intensive distribution. The manufacturer saturates the market by selling to any intermediary of good financial standing that is willing to stock and sell the product. For the consumer, intensive distribution means being able to shop at a convenient store and spend a minimum amount of time buying the product. Companies such as Procter & Gamble that produce consumer packaged items rely on intensive distribution for many of their products because consumers want ready availability.

Selective distribution is the use of only a portion of the available outlets for a product in each geographic area. For example, famed high-end clothing designer Missoni switched to selective distribution to make its style more affordable and accessible by designing a low cost ready-to-wear clothing line distributed through Target stores.[2]

Exclusive distribution is the use of only a single retail outlet for a product in a large geographic area. Exclusive distribution usually is limited to very prestigious products. The producer usually places many requirements (such as inventory levels, sales training, service quality, and warranty procedures) on exclusive dealers. For example, Patek Philippe watches, which may sell for $500,000 or more, are available in only a few select locations.

intensive distribution the use of all available outlets for a product

selective distribution the use of only a portion of the available outlets for a product in each geographic area

exclusive distribution the use of only a single retail outlet for a product in a large geographic area

FIGURE 14.2   Levels of Market Coverage

Intensive
Convenience products such as Coke, Pringles, and Duracell batteries
Available in many retail outlets.

Selective
Shopping products such as iPods, televisions, DVD players, and shoes
Available in some outlets.

Exclusive
Specialty products such as haute couture, Mont Blanc pens, BMWs, and Fendi handbags
Available in very few outlets.

Source: William M. Pride and O. C. Ferrell, *Foundations of Marketing* (Mason, OH: South-Western/ Cengage Learning, 2013), 464.

PARTNERING THROUGH SUPPLY-CHAIN MANAGEMENT

3 Understand how supply-chain management facilitates partnering among channel members.

Supply-chain management is a long-term partnership among channel members working together to create a distribution system that reduces inefficiencies, costs, and redundancies while creating a competitive advantage and satisfying customers. Supply-chain management requires cooperation throughout the entire marketing channel, including manufacturing, research, sales, advertising, and shipping. Supply chains focus not only on producers, wholesalers, retailers, and customers but also on component-parts suppliers, shipping companies, communication companies, and other organizations that participate in product distribution. Suppliers are having a greater impact on determining what items retail stores carry. This phenomenon, called *category management,* is becoming common for mass merchandisers, supermarkets, and convenience stores. Through category management, the retailer asks a supplier in a particular category how to stock the shelves. Many retailers and suppliers claim this process delivers maximum efficiency.

Traditionally, buyers and sellers have been adversarial when negotiating purchases. Supply-chain management, however, encourages cooperation in reducing the costs of inventory, transportation, administration, and handling; in speeding order-cycle times; and in increasing profits for all channel members. When buyers, sellers, marketing intermediaries, and facilitating agencies work together, customers' needs regarding delivery, scheduling, packaging, and other requirements are better met. Dunkin' Brands, Inc., the parent company of Dunkin' Donuts and Baskin Robbins, recently signed a long-term supply chain deal with National DCP in order to improve its supply-chain management. NDCP will be the exclusive supply chain provider, handling distribution and procurement, for all Dunkin' outlets in the continental United States. This deal will help Dunkin' streamline its supply chain and provide greater service and product consistency across all of its outlets. This deal will also allow Dunkin' Brands to offer uniform product costs to all of its franchisees in all U.S. markets.[3]

Technology has enhanced the implementation of supply-chain management significantly. Through computerized integrated information sharing, channel members reduce costs and improve customer service. Technology has also allowed for more reciprocal relationships between supply-chain members. The major buyer is no longer necessarily in charge of making all the decisions, which get passed along to the suppliers. Today, all members of a supply chain play important roles in decision making regarding efficiencies and innovation.[4]

supply-chain management long-term partnership among channel members working together to create a distribution system that reduces inefficiencies, costs, and redundancies while creating a competitive advantage and satisfying customers

New automobiles are distributed through selective distribution. Not just anyone can sell new automobiles. Car manufacturers only allow a select number of dealers to sell their brands. The manufacturers generally require their dealers to be located in different geographic areas so they don't directly compete with one another.

VERTICAL MARKETING SYSTEMS

4 Describe what a vertical marketing system is and identify the types of vertical marketing systems.

Vertical channel integration occurs when two or more stages of a distribution channel are combined and managed by one firm. A **vertical marketing system (VMS)** is a centrally managed distribution channel resulting from vertical channel integration. This merging eliminates the need for certain intermediaries. One member of a marketing channel may assume the responsibilities of another member, or it actually may purchase the operations of that member. Apple has utilized a vertical integration model for decades, and other companies such as Oracle, Motorola, and Amazon are following suit. Apple maintains control of much of the operations in its supply chain, including research, design, distribution, marketing, and selling. Apple also, of course, maintains centralized marketing control for the products it produces. While a VMS works well for Apple, many firms find that it is more efficient to remain specialized and to outsource nonessential activities.[5] Total vertical integration occurs when a single management controls all operations from production to final sale. Oil companies that own wells, transportation facilities, refineries, terminals, and service stations exemplify total vertical integration.

vertical channel integration the combining of two or more stages of a distribution channel under a single firm's management

vertical marketing system (VMS) a centrally managed distribution channel resulting from vertical channel integration

There are three types of VMSs: administered, contractual, and corporate. In an *administered VMS*, one of the channel members dominates the other members, perhaps because of its large size. Under its influence, the channel members collaborate on production and distribution. A powerful manufacturer, such as Procter & Gamble, receives a great deal of cooperation from intermediaries that carry its brands. Although the goals of the entire system are considered when decisions are made, control rests with individual channel members, as in conventional marketing channels. Under a *contractual VMS*, cooperative arrangements and the rights and obligations of channel members are defined by contracts or other legal measures. In a *corporate VMS*, actual ownership is the vehicle by which production and distribution are joined. For example, The Limited established a corporate VMS that operates corporate-owned production facilities and retail stores. Most VMSs are organized to improve distribution by combining individual operations.

 Discuss the need for wholesalers and describe the services they provide to retailers and manufacturers.

MARKETING INTERMEDIARIES: WHOLESALERS

Wholesalers may be the most misunderstood of marketing intermediaries. Producers sometimes try to eliminate them from distribution channels by dealing directly with retailers or consumers. Yet wholesalers provide a variety of essential marketing services. Although wholesalers can be eliminated, their functions cannot be eliminated. These functions *must* be performed by other channel members or by consumers. Eliminating a wholesaler may or may not cut distribution costs.

Justifications for Marketing Intermediaries

The press, consumers, public officials, and other marketers often charge wholesalers, at least in principle, with inefficiency and parasitism. Consumers in particular feel strongly that the distribution channel should be made as short as possible. They assume that the fewer the intermediaries in a distribution channel, the lower the price of the product will be.

Those who believe that the elimination of wholesalers will bring about lower prices, however, do not recognize that the services wholesalers perform are still needed. Those services simply are provided by other means, and consumers still bear the costs. Moreover, all manufacturers operating without wholesalers would have to keep extensive records and employ enough personnel to deal with a multitude of retailers individually. Even with direct distribution, products might be considerably more expensive because prices would reflect the costs of producers' inefficiencies. Figure 14.3 shows

FIGURE 14.3   Efficiency Provided by an Intermediary

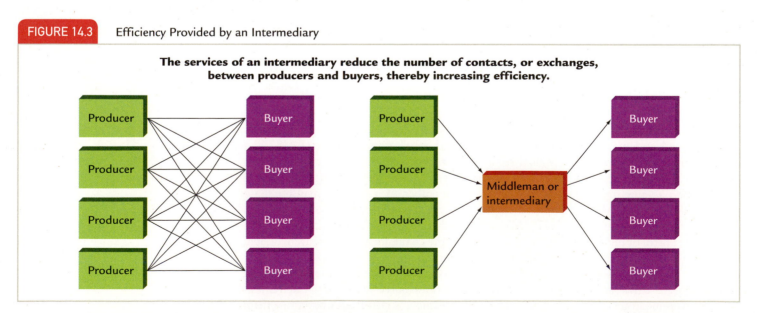

Source: William M. Pride and O. C. Ferrell, *Marketing: Concepts and Strategies*, 17th ed. (Mason, OH: South-Western/Cengage Learning, 2014). Adapted with permission.

that 16 contacts could result from the efforts of four buyers purchasing the products of four producers. With the assistance of an intermediary, only eight contacts would be necessary.

To illustrate further the useful role of wholesalers in the marketing system, assume that all wholesalers in the candy industry were abolished. With thousands of candy retailers to contact, candy manufacturers would be making an extremely large number of sales calls just to maintain the present level of product visibility. Hershey Foods, for example, would have to set up warehouses all over the country, organize a fleet of trucks, purchase and maintain thousands of vending machines, and deliver all of its own candy. Sales and distribution costs for candy would soar. Candy producers would be contacting and shipping products to thousands of small businesses instead of to a limited number of large wholesalers and retailers. The outrageous costs of this inefficiency would be passed on to consumers. Candy bars would be more expensive and likely available through fewer retailers.

Wholesalers' Services to Retailers

Wholesalers help retailers by buying in large quantities and then selling to retailers in smaller quantities and by delivering goods to retailers. They also stock—in one place—the variety of goods that retailers otherwise would have to buy from many producers. Wholesalers provide assistance in three other vital areas: promotion, market information, and financial aid.

Promotion Some wholesalers help to promote the products they sell to retailers. These services are usually either free or performed at cost. Wholesalers, for example, are major sources of display materials designed to stimulate impulse buying. They also may help retailers to build effective window, counter, and shelf displays. Some may even assign their own employees to work on the retail sales floor during special promotions.

Market Information Wholesalers are a constant source of market information. Wholesalers have numerous contacts with local businesses and distant suppliers. In the course of these dealings, they accumulate information about consumer demand, prices, supply conditions, new developments within the trade, and even industry personnel. This information may be relayed to retailers informally though the wholesaler's sales force. Wholesalers often provide information to their customers via Web site, which helps improve transparency and communication between buyers and sellers.

Information regarding industry sales and competitive prices is especially important to all firms. Dealing with a number of suppliers and many retailers, a wholesaler is a natural clearinghouse for such information. Most wholesalers are willing to pass information on to their customers.

Financial Aid Most wholesalers provide a type of financial aid that retailers often take for granted. By making prompt and frequent deliveries, wholesalers enable retailers to keep their own inventory investments small in relation to sales. Such indirect financial aid reduces the amount of operating capital that retailers need.

Wholesalers' Services to Manufacturers

Some of the services that wholesalers perform for producers are similar to those they provide to retailers. Others are quite different.

Providing an Instant Sales Force A wholesaler provides its producers with an instant sales force so that producers' sales representatives need not call on retailers. This can result in enormous savings for producers. For example, Lever Brothers and General Foods would have to spend millions of dollars each year to field a sales force large

PHYSICAL DISTRIBUTION

Physical distribution is all those activities concerned with the efficient movement of products from the producer to the ultimate user. Physical distribution therefore is the movement of the products themselves—both goods and services—through their channels of distribution. It is a combination of several interrelated business functions. The most important of these are inventory management, order processing, warehousing, materials handling, and transportation.

Not too long ago, each of these functions was considered distinct from all the others. In a fairly large firm, one group or department would handle each function. Each of these groups would work to minimize its own costs and to maximize its own effectiveness, but the result was usually high physical distribution costs. Various studies of the problem emphasized both the interrelationships among the physical distribution functions and the relationships between physical distribution and other marketing functions.

Because of such interrelationships, marketers now view physical distribution as an integrated effort that provides important marketing functions: getting the right product to the right place at the right time and at minimal overall cost. Figure 14.4 shows the proportional costs of each of the major physical distribution functions.

Inventory Management

In Chapter 8 we discussed inventory management from the standpoint of operations. We defined **inventory management** as the process of managing inventories in such a way as to minimize inventory costs, including both holding costs and potential stock-out costs. Both the definition and the objective of inventory control apply here as well.

Holding costs are the costs of storing products until they are purchased or shipped to customers. *Stock-out costs* are the costs of sales lost when items are not in inventory. Of course, holding costs can be reduced by minimizing inventories, but then stock-out costs could be financially threatening to the organization. Stock-out costs can be minimized by carrying very large inventories, but then holding costs would be enormous.

FIGURE 14.4   Proportional Cost of Each Physical Distribution Function as a Percentage of Total Distribution Costs.

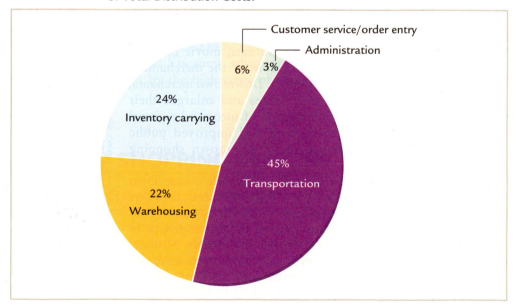

Source: From Pride/Ferrell, *Foundations of Marketing*, 5e. © 2013 Cengage Learning.

physical distribution all the activities concerned with the efficient movement of products from the producer to the ultimate user

inventory management the process of managing inventories in such a way as to minimize inventory costs, including both holding costs and potential stock-out costs

Inventory management, therefore, is a sort of balancing act between stock-out costs and holding costs. The latter include the cost of money invested in inventory, the cost of storage space, insurance costs, and inventory taxes. Often, even a relatively small reduction in inventory investment can provide a relatively large increase in working capital. Sometimes this reduction can best be accomplished through a willingness to incur a reasonable level of stock-out costs.

Companies frequently rely on technology and software to help manage inventory. Efficient inventory management with accurate reorder points is crucial for firms that use a just-in-time (JIT) approach, in which supplies arrive just as they are needed for use in production or for resale. When using JIT, companies maintain low inventory levels and purchase products and materials in small quantities whenever they need them. Usually, there is no safety stock, and suppliers are expected to provide consistently high-quality products. JIT inventory management requires a high level of coordination between producers and suppliers, but it eliminates waste and reduces inventory costs significantly. This approach has been used successfully by many well-known firms, including Chrysler, Harley-Davidson, and Dell Computers, to reduce costs and boost customer satisfaction. When a JIT approach is used in a supply chain, suppliers often move close to their customers.

© DMITRY KALINOVSKY/SHUTTERSTOCK

Wired warehouses and inventory control.
Warehouses and inventory management are becoming increasingly sophisticated. This handheld inventory management device allows employees to get an instant overview of every item—and its price—in a warehouse at any given time. In some warehouses, electronic headsets tell workers exactly where to go to find merchandise—much like GPS devices provide people with directions.

Order Processing

Order processing consists of activities involved in receiving and filling customers' purchase orders. It may include not only the means by which customers order products but also procedures for billing and for granting credit.

Fast, efficient order processing is an important marketing service—one that can provide a dramatic competitive edge. The people who purchase goods for intermediaries are especially concerned with their suppliers' promptness and reliability in order processing. To them, promptness and reliability mean minimal inventory costs as well as the ability to order goods when they are needed rather than weeks in advance. The Internet is providing new opportunities for improving services associated with order processing.

Warehousing

Warehousing is the set of activities involved in receiving and storing goods and preparing them for reshipment. Goods are stored to create time utility; that is, they are held until they are needed for use or sale. Warehousing includes the following activities:

- *Receiving goods*—The warehouse accepts delivered goods and assumes responsibility for them.
- *Identifying goods*—Records are made of the quantity of each item received. Items may be marked, coded, or tagged for identification.
- *Sorting goods*—Delivered goods may have to be sorted before being stored.
- *Dispatching goods to storage*—Items must be moved to specific storage areas, where they can be found later.
- *Holding goods*—The goods are kept in storage under proper protection until needed.
- *Recalling, picking, and assembling goods*—Items that are to leave the warehouse must be selected from storage and assembled efficiently.
- *Dispatching shipments*—Each shipment is packaged suitably and directed to the proper transport vehicle. Shipping and accounting documents are prepared.

order processing activities involved in receiving and filling customers' purchase orders

warehousing the set of activities involved in receiving and storing goods and preparing them for reshipment

Green Logistics

Mega-retailer Walmart has one of the largest private distribution operations in the world, with over 7,000 tractors and 53,000 trailers rolling around the clock and across the country. As part of its green initiative, the company's logistics division has taken a number of important steps to make its fleets more efficient and environmentally friendly, including testing alternative fuels, and using more efficient, aerodynamic trucks along with hybrid vehicles. As a result, Walmart has been able to avoid 40,000 metric tons of carbon dioxide emissions over the past few years—the equivalent of taking 7,600 cars off the road! Read more at:
http://walmartstores.com/Sustainability/9071.aspx.

A firm may use its own warehouses or rent space in public warehouses. A *private warehouse,* owned and operated by a particular firm, can be designed to serve the firm's specific needs. However, the organization must take on the task of financing the facility, determining the best location for it, and ensuring that it is used fully. Generally, only companies that deal in large quantities of goods can justify private warehouses. Some such companies are United Parcel Service (UPS), Walmart, and Sears.

Public warehouses offer their services to all individuals and firms. Most are huge one-story structures on the outskirts of cities, where rail and truck transportation are easily available. They provide storage facilities, areas for sorting and assembling shipments, and office and display spaces for wholesalers and retailers. Public warehouses also will hold—and issue receipts for—goods used as collateral for borrowed funds.

Many organizations locate and design their warehouses not only to be cost-efficient but also to provide excellent customer service.

Materials Handling

Materials handling is the actual physical handling of goods—in warehouses as well as during transportation. Proper materials-handling procedures and techniques can increase the usable capacity of a warehouse or that of any means of transportation. Proper handling can reduce breakage and spoilage as well.

Modern materials handling attempts to reduce the number of times a product is handled. One method is called *unit loading.* Several smaller cartons, barrels, or boxes are combined into a single standard-size load that can be handled efficiently by forklift, conveyer, or truck.

Transportation

As a part of physical distribution, **transportation** is simply the shipment of products to customers. The greater the distance between seller and purchaser, the more important is the choice of the means of transportation and the particular carrier. Transportation is an essential component of the marketing mix that requires careful planning because it can add significant cost. Even in these times of rising fuel costs and concerns over greenhouse gas emissions, some companies are finding ways to maintain or cut costs through improving transportation networks. Large firms like Nike, Walmart, and IKEA have all managed to reduce carbon emissions, cut costs, and improve transportation efficiency through better managing their transportation networks. They have cut emissions through best practices such as transporting products via ships instead of plane or via trains instead of trucks.[18]

A firm that offers transportation services is called a **carrier**. A *common carrier* is a transportation firm whose services are available to all shippers. Railroads, airlines, and most long-distance trucking firms are common carriers. A *contract carrier* is available for hire by one or several shippers. Contract carriers do not serve the general public. Moreover, the number of firms they can handle at any one time is limited by law. A *private carrier* is owned and operated by the shipper.

In addition, a shipper can hire agents called *freight forwarders* to handle its transportation. Freight forwarders pick up shipments from the shipper, ensure that the goods are loaded on selected carriers, and assume responsibility for safe delivery of the

---

materials handling the actual physical handling of goods, in warehouses as well as during transportation

transportation the shipment of products to customers

carrier a firm that offers transportation services

shipments to their destinations. Freight forwarders can often group a number of small shipments into one large load (which is carried at a lower rate). This, of course, saves money for shippers.

The U.S. Postal Service offers *parcel post* delivery, which is used widely by mail-order houses. The Postal Service provides complete geographic coverage at the lowest rates, but it limits the size and weight of the shipments it will accept. UPS, a privately owned firm, also provides small-parcel services for shippers. Other privately owned carriers, such as Federal Express, DHL, and Airborne, offer fast—often overnight—parcel delivery both within and outside the United States. There are also many local parcel carriers, including specialized delivery services for various time-sensitive industries, such as publishing.

The six major criteria used for selecting transportation modes are compared in Table 14.2. Obviously, the *cost* of a transportation mode is important to marketers. At times, marketers choose higher-cost modes of transportation because of the benefits they provide. *Speed* is measured by the total time that a carrier possesses the products, including time required for pickup and delivery, handling, and movement between point of origin and destination. Usually, there is a direct relationship between cost and speed; that is, faster modes of transportation are more expensive. A transportation mode's *dependability* is determined by the consistency of service provided by that mode. *Load flexibility* is the degree to which a transportation mode can provide appropriate equipment and conditions for moving specific kinds of products and can be adapted for moving other kinds of products. For example, certain types of products may need controlled temperatures or humidity levels. *Accessibility* refers to a transportation mode's ability to move goods over a specific route or network. *Frequency* refers to how often a marketer can ship products by a specific transportation mode. Whereas pipelines provide continuous shipments, railroads and waterways follow specific schedules for moving products from one location to another. In Table 14.2, each transportation mode is rated on a relative basis for these six selection criteria. In addition, Table 14.2 shows a breakdown by use of the five different modes of transportation.

Choosing the right transportation modes. More products today are being transported in 40- and 50-foot metal containers like the ones shown on this ship. The containers provide flexibility because they can be transported by ships, railroads, and trucks. Often all three of these transportation modes are used to transport a single container.

TABLE 14.2	Characteristics and Ratings of Transportation Modes by Selection Criteria				
	Railroads	**Trucks**	**Pipelines**	**Waterways**	**Airplanes**
Selection Criteria					
Cost	Moderate	High	Low	Very low	Very high
Speed	Average	Fast	Slow	Very slow	Very fast
Dependability	Average	High	High	Average	High
Load Flexibility	High	Average	Very low	Very high	Low
Accessibility	High	Very high	Very limited	Limited	Average
Frequency	Low	High	Very high	Very low	Average
% Ton-Miles Transported	39.4	28.6	19.6	12.0	0.3
Products Carried	Coal, grain, lumber, heavy equipment, paper and pulp products, chemicals	Clothing, computers, books, groceries, produce, livestock	Oil, processed coal, natural gas	Chemicals, bauxite, grain, motor vehicles, agricultural implements	Flowers, food (highly perishable), technical instruments, emergency parts and equipment, overnight mail

Source: U.S. Bureau of Transportation Statistics, *National Transportation Statistics* (Washington, DC: U.S. Government Printing Office), April 2010, www.bts.gov/publications/national_transportation_statistics/html/table_01_46a.html.

Railroads In terms of total freight carried, railroads are America's most important mode of transportation. They are also the least expensive for many products. Almost all railroads are common carriers, although a few coal-mining companies operate their own lines.

Many commodities carried by railroads cannot be transported easily by any other means. They include a wide range of foodstuffs, raw materials, and manufactured goods. Nearly three-quarters of coal in the United States is transported via rail.[19] Other major commodities carried by railroads include grain, paper and pulp products, liquids in tank-car loads, heavy equipment, and lumber.

Trucks The trucking industry consists of common, contract, and private carriers. It has undergone tremendous expansion since the creation of a national highway system in the 1920s. Trucks can move goods to suburban and rural areas not served by railroads. They can handle freight quickly and economically, and they carry a wide range of shipments. Many shippers favor this mode of transportation because it offers door-to-door service, less stringent packaging requirements than ships and airplanes, and flexible delivery schedules.

Railroad and truck carriers have teamed up to provide a form of transportation called *piggyback*. Truck trailers are carried from city to city on specially equipped railroad flatcars. Within each city, the trailers are then pulled in the usual way by truck tractors. Some companies offer shipping and consolidation services, which may be a good option for smaller companies that do not need to make large shipments because it allows them to take advantage of the reduced costs from economies of scale. Such shipping companies handle the logistics of transporting products via rail and truck to the destination. Piggyback Consolidators is one such carrier. It offers shipping throughout North America using a low-emissions fuel-efficient fleet, as well as tracking and reporting services.[20]

Airplanes Air transport is the fastest but most expensive means of transportation. All certified airlines are common carriers. Supplemental or charter lines are contract carriers.

Because of the high cost, lack of airport facilities in many areas, and reliance on weather conditions, airlines carry less than 1 percent of all intercity freight. Only high-value or perishable items, such as flowers, aircraft parts, and pharmaceuticals or goods that are needed immediately, are usually shipped by air.

Waterways Cargo ships and barges offer the least expensive, but slowest, form of transportation. They are used mainly for bulky nonperishable goods such as chemicals, grain, motor vehicles, and large equipment. Of course, shipment by water is limited to cities located on navigable waterways.

Pipelines Pipelines are a highly specialized mode of transportation. They are used primarily to carry petroleum and natural gas. Plains All American Pipeline, for example, is a fast-growing carrier of crude and refined petroleum and liquefied petroleum gas. The company handles around 3 million barrels of petroleum products a day through a pipeline system that extends all over the United States and Canada.[21]

Pipelines have become more important as the nation's need for petroleum products has increased. Such products as semiliquid coal and wood chips can also be shipped through pipelines continuously, reliably, and with minimal handling.

In the next chapter, we discuss the fourth element of the marketing mix— promotion.

Chobani

To keep up with rising demand for Chobani Greek yogurt, more than four dozen refrigerated tanker trucks filled with milk drive to the company's production facility in upper New York State every day. After the milk is made into yogurt, mixed with fruit for flavored varieties, and poured into plastic cups, convoys of refrigerated trucks take the yogurt to Chobani's coast-to-coast network of retailer partners. In all, Chobani produces 2 million cases of Greek yogurt every week and remains the brand to beat in its category.

When Chobani introduced Champions, its Greek yogurt for children, the product line gained wide distribution in a short time, thanks to strong retail connections. Now the company is testing international distribution, partnering with Loblaw's in Canada and Woolworths in Australia. Watch for retail tests in other markets and new flavors for adults and children as Chobani continues its expansion.

Questions

1. When Chobani decided to pursue distribution in big retail chains, what level of market coverage was it aiming for? Why was this appropriate?
2. When planning physical distribution activities for a perishable food product like Chobani yogurt, what elements do marketers have to pay particular attention to—and why?

SUMMARY

Looking for Success?
Get Flashcards, Quizzes, Games, Crosswords, and more @ www.cengagebrain.com.

 Identify the various channels of distribution that are used for consumer and industrial products.

A marketing channel is a sequence of marketing organizations that directs a product from producer to ultimate user. The marketing channel for a particular product is concerned with the transfer of ownership of that product. Merchant middlemen (merchants) actually take title to products, whereas functional middlemen simply aid in the transfer of title.

The channels used for consumer products include the direct channel from producer to consumer; the channel from producer to retailer to consumer; the channel from producer to wholesaler to retailer to consumer; and the channel from producer to agent to wholesaler to retailer to consumer. There are two major channels of industrial products: (1) producer to user and (2) producer to agent middleman to user.

 Explain the concept of market coverage.

Channels and intermediaries are chosen to implement a given level of market coverage. Intensive distribution is the use of all available outlets for a product, providing the widest market coverage. Selective distribution uses only a portion of the available outlets in an area. Exclusive distribution uses only a single retail outlet for a product in a large geographic area.

 Understand how supply-chain management facilitates partnering among channel members.

Supply-chain management is a long-term partnership among channel members working together to create a distribution system that reduces inefficiencies, costs, and redundancies while creating a competitive advantage and satisfying customers. Cooperation is required among all channel members, including manufacturing, research, sales, advertising, and shipping. When all channel partners work together, delivery, scheduling, packaging, and other customer requirements are better met. Technology, such as bar coding and electronic data exchange (EDI), makes supply-chain management easier to implement.

 Describe what a vertical marketing system is and identify the types of vertical marketing systems.

A VMS is a centrally managed system. It results when two or more channel members from different levels combine under one management. Administered, contractual, and corporate systems represent the three major types of VMSs.

 Discuss the need for wholesalers and describe the services they provide to retailers and manufacturers.

Wholesalers are intermediaries that purchase from producers or other intermediaries and sell to industrial users, retailers, or other wholesalers. Wholesalers perform many functions in a distribution channel. If they are eliminated, other channel members—such as the producer or retailers—must perform these functions. Wholesalers provide retailers with help in promoting products, collecting information, and financing. They provide manufacturers with sales help, reduce their inventory costs, furnish market information, and extend credit to retailers.

 Identify and describe the major types of wholesalers.

Merchant wholesalers buy and then sell products. Commission merchants and brokers are essentially agents and do not take title to the goods they distribute. Sales branches and offices are owned by the manufacturers they represent and resemble merchant wholesalers and agents, respectively.

 Distinguish among the major types of retailers.

Retailers are intermediaries that buy from producers or wholesalers and sell to consumers. In-store retailers include department stores, discount stores, catalog and warehouse showrooms, convenience stores, supermarkets, superstores, warehouse clubs, traditional specialty stores, off-price retailers, and category killers. Nonstore retailers do not sell in conventional store facilities. Instead, they use direct selling, direct marketing, and automatic vending. Types of direct marketing include catalog marketing, direct-response marketing, telemarketing, television home shopping, and online retailing.

 Identify the categories of shopping centers and the factors that determine how shopping centers are classified.

There are three major types of shopping centers: neighborhood, community, and regional. A center fits one of these categories based on its mix of stores and the size of the geographic area it serves.

 Explain the five most important physical distribution activities.

Physical distribution consists of activities designed to move products from producers to ultimate users. Its five major functions are inventory management, order processing, warehousing, materials handling, and transportation. These interrelated functions are integrated into the marketing effort.

KEY TERMS

You should now be able to define and give an example relevant to each of the following terms:

channel of distribution (or marketing channel) (396)
middleman (or marketing intermediary) (396)
merchant middleman (396)
functional middleman (396)
retailer (396)
wholesaler (396)
intensive distribution (398)
selective distribution (398)
exclusive distribution (398)
supply-chain management (399)
vertical channel integration (399)
vertical marketing system (VMS) (399)

merchant wholesaler (402)
full-service wholesaler (402)
general-merchandise wholesaler (402)
limited-line wholesaler (403)
specialty-line wholesaler (403)
limited-service wholesaler (403)
commission merchant (403)
agent (403)
broker (403)
manufacturer's sales branch (403)
manufacturer's sales office (403)
independent retailer (404)
chain retailer (404)

department store (404)
discount store (404)
catalog showroom (404)
warehouse showroom (405)
convenience store (405)
supermarket (406)
superstore (406)
warehouse club (406)
traditional specialty store (406)
off-price retailer (407)
category killer (407)
nonstore retailing (407)
direct selling (407)
direct marketing (408)
catalog marketing (408)
direct-response marketing (408)

telemarketing (409)
television home shopping (409)
online retailing (409)
automatic vending (410)
lifestyle shopping center (411)
neighborhood shopping center (411)
community shopping center (411)
regional shopping center (411)
physical distribution (412)
inventory management (412)
order processing (413)
warehousing (413)
materials handling (414)
transportation (414)
carrier (414)

REVIEW QUESTIONS

1. In what ways is a channel of distribution different from the path taken by a product during physical distribution?
2. What are the most common marketing channels for consumer products? For industrial products?
3. What are the three general approaches to market coverage? What types of products is each approach used for?
4. What is a VMS? Identify examples of the three types of VMSs.
5. List the services performed by wholesalers. For whom is each service performed?

6. What is the basic difference between a merchant wholesaler and an agent?
7. Identify three kinds of full-service wholesalers. What factors are used to classify wholesalers into one of these categories?
8. Distinguish between (a) commission merchants and agents and (b) manufacturers' sales branches and manufacturers' sales offices.
9. What is the basic difference between wholesalers and retailers?

10. What is the difference between a department store and a discount store with regard to selling orientation and philosophy?
11. How do (a) convenience stores, (b) traditional specialty stores, and (c) category killers compete with other retail outlets?
12. What can nonstore retailers offer their customers that in-store retailers cannot?

13. Compare and contrast community shopping centers and regional shopping centers.
14. What is physical distribution? Which major functions does it include?
15. What activities besides storage are included in warehousing?
16. List the primary modes of transportation and cite at least one advantage of each.

DISCUSSION QUESTIONS

1. Which distribution channels would producers of services be most likely to use? Why?
2. Many producers sell to consumers both directly and through middlemen. How can such a producer justify competing with its own middlemen?
3. In what situations might a producer use agents or commission merchants rather than its own sales offices or branches?

4. If a middleman is eliminated from a marketing channel, under what conditions will costs decrease? Under what conditions will costs increase? Will the middleman's functions be eliminated? Explain.
5. Which types of retail outlets are best suited to intensive distribution? To selective distribution? To exclusive distribution? Explain your answer in each case.
6. How are the various physical distribution functions related to each other? To the other elements of the marketing mix?

Video Case 14.1

Taza Cultivates Channel Relationships with Chocolate

Taza Chocolate, a small Massachusetts-based manufacturer of stone-ground organic chocolate made in the classic Mexican tradition, sells most of its products to retailers, wholesalers, and distributors throughout the United States. Individual customers around the world can also buy Taza chocolate bars, baking squares, chocolate-covered nuts, and other specialty items directly from Taza at the company's Web site, and if they live in Somerville (Massachusetts), they might even find a Taza employee riding a "chococycle," selling products and distributing samples at an upscale food truck festival or open market on a weekend.

With a staff of about 20 people, Taza sources all its ingredients directly from certified organic growers with whom the company cultivates a personal relationship. "Because our process here at the factory is so minimal," says the company's director of sales, "it's really important that we get a very high-quality ingredient. . . . The cocoa beans are the most important. . . . When we source those, we pay a premium above even fair-trade prices. We call it direct trade. To make sure that we're getting the absolute cream of the crop, we have a direct face-to-face human relationship between us and the actual farmer that's producing those beans."

The company believes that dealing directly with its suppliers is the best business model for Taza as a small firm, not only because it allows the company to meet its social responsibility goals, but also because it ensures quality, which commands a premium price. "We're a premium brand," says the director of sales, "and because of the way we do what we do, we have to charge more than [the cost of] your average chocolate bar. . .

. There's usually a 40 to 50 percent markup between wholesale sales and the price . . . on the retail store shelf. So, say we sell a chocolate bar for $4.50 . . . then the wholesale price is going to be somewhere around $2.70 for that unit. . . . The distributor price [is] even lower, maybe around $2." Distributors buy in the largest quantities, which for Taza means a pallet load as opposed to a case that a wholesaler would buy. "But wholesale will always be our bread and butter, where we really move the volume and we have good margins. . . . It's been challenging for us to work with distributors. They're always squeezing you on price, or trying to give you charge backs, or run promotions or do sales . . . whereas the average wholesale customer is, in our industry at least, . . . much more used to accepting what we give them in terms of promotions or pricing."

Taza does almost no advertising, relying instead on Facebook, Twitter, a company blog, e-mail, and events that create buzz like chocolate salons, food shows, in-store tastings, and especially frequent sampling in upscale and organic food stores in big metropolitan areas. The company tries to cultivate the same sort of personal relationships with members of its distribution channel as it does with its cocoa farmers. "When we send a shipment of chocolate," says the sales director, "sometimes we'll put in a little extra for the people who work there. That always helps because you're building that kind of human relationship."

A privately owned firm, Taza has just begun shipping its chocolate products internationally to Canada and a handful of European companies. Its marketing channel definitely plays a role in delivering products that are fresh. Shipping perishable products to customers in the summer, for instance, can be a problem. But "having a distributor . . . that has a couple of thousand dollars of inventory in their refrigerated warehouse all the time changes that equation. It means the store can just order from that distributor, pay about the same price that they would pay if they ordered directly from us, [and] get the product probably the next day, with much lower shipping cost."[22]

Questions

1. Which distribution channels does Taza use?
2. In what ways does Taza benefit from selling directly to consumers? What are the potential problems that Taza may experience by selling directly to consumers?
3. If Taza wanted to grow its sales by broadening physical distribution of its products, do you think it should work more closely with its wholesalers or with its distributors? Why?

Case 14.2

Dell Direct and Not-So-Direct

When Michael Dell started his Texas-based computer business in 1984, he chose a distribution strategy that was radically different from that of other computer marketers. Instead of selling through wholesalers and retailers, the company dealt directly with customers. This kept costs low and allowed Dell to cater to customers' needs by building each computer to order. Using a direct channel also minimized inventory costs and reduced the risk that parts and products would become obsolete even before customers placed their orders, a constant concern in high-tech industries.

By 1997, Dell's Web site alone was responsible for $1 million a day in sales. Relying on the strength of its online sales, catalogs, and phone orders, Dell expanded beyond the United States and added new products for four target markets: consumers, large corporations, small businesses, and government agencies. Meanwhile, Apple, Hewlett-Packard, and other competitors were reaching out to many of the same segments with a combination of direct and indirect channels. Apple Stores, for example, proved to be major customer magnets and gave a significant boost to sales of Macintosh computers and other Apple electronics. Hewlett-Packard forged strong ties with value-added resellers (VARs), intermediaries that assemble systems of computers, servers, and other products customized to meet the special needs of business buyers.

Although Dell tested retail distribution on a number of occasions, it never let the experiments go on for too long. In the 1990s, it tried selling PCs through a few big U.S. retail chains, but soon discontinued the arrangement because the profit margins weren't as healthy as in the direct channel. Later, it opened a series of branded retail kiosks in major U.S. markets to display its products and answer customers' questions. Unlike stores, however, the kiosks didn't actually sell anything: Customers could only place orders for future delivery. Dell ultimately closed the kiosks down.

By 2007, with competitors coming on strong, Dell was ready to rethink its worldwide channel strategy. As convenient as online shopping was for many U.S. computer buyers, it was much less popular in many other countries. To gain market share domestically and internationally, Dell would have to follow consumers into stores, malls, and downtown shopping districts. The company began selling a few models through Walmart's U.S. stores, Carphone Warehouse's U.K. stores, Bic Camera's Japanese stores, and Gome's Chinese stores. In addition, it opened Dell stores in Moscow, Budapest, and other world capitals.

By 2010, sales through retailers had gained enough momentum that Dell sought out other retail deals. In another channel change, it began selling through VAR partners that serve small- and medium-sized businesses and lined up wholesalers to distribute its products in Europe, Latin America, and elsewhere. When Dell introduced a new line of smartphones, it needed a new channel arrangement to reach buyers. Therefore, it arranged for mobile phone carriers such as AT&T to sell the new models to their customers.

As successful as Dell has been in revamping its indirect channels, selling directly to customers remains a top priority. Dell invites orders around the clock through Web pages tailored to the needs of each target market. It also maintains an online outlet store to sell discontinued and refurbished products. It mails millions of catalogs and direct-mail pieces every year. And its sales force calls on government officials and big businesses that buy in volume. Dell's Web site notes, with pride, that the ten largest U.S. corporations and five largest U.S. commercial banks "run on Dell."

Moreover, the company is a pioneer in stimulating exchanges with customers through social media. Dell has 139,000 fans on Facebook, for example, and regularly posts offers that drive customers to its various Web sites. It's become a pioneer in selling directly to customers via the microblog site Twitter. In less than three years, it generated $6.5 million in revenue from sales transactions that originated on Twitter. That may be a tiny sliver of Dell's $53 billion in annual revenue, but it demonstrates the company's flexibility in adapting to shifts in customer behavior and environmental forces, such as technological advances.

With market share and profit-margin challenges still facing the company, and global demand just picking up steam after a long, difficult recession, watch for Dell to make more channel adjustments in the coming years.[23]

Questions for Discussion

1. Is Dell using intensive, selective, or exclusive distribution for its market coverage? Why is this appropriate for Dell's products and target markets?
2. What are the major advantages and disadvantages of Dell's use of multiple marketing channels instead of using just the direct marketing channel?
3. In what ways did Dell's physical distribution practices change as it changed to using multiple marketing channels?

Building Skills for Career Success

① SOCIAL MEDIA EXERCISE

Wholesaling, retailing and physical distribution

Gamification is a new trend in social media that essentially uses the ideas and theories behind gaming (rewards, competition, levels and so forth) to engage people online. Fantasy Shopper is a good example of combining the retail experience (in this case fashion retailing) with online games. For example, a luxury handbag by Stella McCartney worth $960 is the prize in a online game to design the best virtual outfit using real items on sale in Matches, a real store. The players of the game choose the winner. Players visit a city (say London, with others to follow) and compete to find bargains and assemble the best outfits using virtual money to spend on goods actually sold in stores. The choices are then published in Facebook newsfeeds and others can vote on these looks. In addition to winning real prizes, players are also rewarded virtually with badges and vouchers to use in real stores. This game is popular with women 20–25 and retailers are excited because it helps them to promote their products and provides instant feedback about what is likely to sell. The real value to retailers is the amount of data generated and passed along by these "social shopping" firms based on the players' behavior. Visit Fantasy Shopper (www.fantasyshopper.com) and take a look about the games available.[24]

1. For what types of retailers are these games most likely to be effective?
2. While the game mentioned above is aimed at women 20–25, what other age and gender segments would be most likely to participate in online games?

② JOURNALING FOR SUCCESS

Discovery statement: In this chapter, you learned that retailers are marketing intermediaries and part of the distribution channel.

Assignment

1. Thinking about brick-and-mortar retail stores, in which store have you had your most enjoyable shopping experience? Describe this retail store.
2. Discuss this shopping experience and why it was such a great shopping experience.
3. At what brick-and-mortar store did you have your worst experience? Describe this store.
4. Discuss this worst shopping experience and be sure to mention the reasons why this shopping experience was the worst one for you.

③ DEVELOPING CRITICAL-THINKING SKILLS

According to the wheel of retailing hypothesis, retail businesses begin as low-margin, low-priced, low-status operations. As they successfully challenge established retailers for market share, they upgrade their facilities and offer more services. This raises their costs and forces them to increase their prices so that eventually they become like the conventional retailers they replaced. As they move up from the low end of the wheel, new firms with lower costs and prices move in to take their place. For example, Kmart started as a low-priced operation that competed with department stores. Over time, it upgraded its facilities and products; big Kmart stores now offer such exclusive merchandise as Martha Stewart's bed-and-bath collection, full-service pharmacies, café areas, and "pantry" areas stocked with frequently bought grocery items, including milk, eggs, and bread. In consequence, Kmart has become a higher-cost, higher-priced operation and, as such, is vulnerable to lower-priced firms entering at the low end of the wheel.

Assignment

1. Investigate the operations of a local retailer.
2. Explain how this retailer is evolving on the wheel of retailing.
3. Prepare a report on your findings.

④ BUILDING TEAM SKILLS

Surveys are a commonly used tool in marketing research. The information they provide can reduce business risk and facilitate decision making. Retail outlets often survey their customers' wants and needs by distributing comment cards or questionnaires.

The following customer survey is an example of a survey that a local photography shop might distribute to its customers.

Assignment

1. Working in teams of three to five, choose a local retailer.
2. Classify the retailer according to the major types of retailers.
3. Design a survey to help the retailer to improve customer service. (You may find it beneficial to work with the retailer and actually administer the survey to the retailer's customers. Prepare a report of the survey results for the retailer.)
4. Present your findings to the class.

⑤ RESEARCHING DIFFERENT CAREERS

When you are looking for a job, the people closest to you can be extremely helpful. Family members and friends may be able to answer your questions directly or put you in touch with someone else who can. This type of "networking" can lead to an "informational interview," in which you can meet with someone who will answer your questions about a career or a company and who can also provide inside information on related fields and other helpful hints.

Assignment

1. Choose a retailer or wholesaler and a position within the company that interests you.
2. Call the company and ask to speak to the person in that particular position. Explain that you are a college student interested in the position, and ask to set up an "informational interview."
3. Prepare a list of questions to ask in the interview. The questions should focus on:
   a. The type of training recommended for the position
   b. How the person entered the position and advanced in it
   c. What he or she likes and dislikes about the work
   d. Present your findings to the class.

By Incorporating Hot Guys and Humor, Old Spice Heats Up on Profits

How can a 1940s brand attract 21st-century audiences? That was the challenge facing Procter & Gamble's marketers when they thought about spicing up the marketing communications of Old Spice, its brand of men's fragrance, body wash, and deodorant products. After decades of popularity, Old Spice was being eclipsed by Unilever's Axe and other new brands with edgier images and flashier advertising. To revitalize Old Spice, P&G teamed up with the ad agency Wieden+Kennedy to launch the multimedia "Old Spice Guy" campaign, aiming to renew interest in the brand, build buzz, and boost sales.

The initial campaign featured former NFL football player Isaiah Mustafa in a series of humorous commercials, online videos, and print ads. Wearing only a towel, as if he had just stepped out of the shower, the muscular Mustafa greeted his audience—"Hello ladies"—and said he was "the man your man could smell like" if they bought Old Spice. This campaign grabbed immediate attention, and Old Spice Guy videos on YouTube quickly drew millions of views. The follow-up was a series of brief online videos featuring Mustafa making clever remarks on camera to influential celebrities and answering questions directed to him on Twitter. The Old Spice Man appeared in so many ads in such a short time that the campaign received widespread publicity for its innovative timing and creative content, adding to the momentum and increasing brand awareness.

A few months later, the agency introduced a new campaign pitting Mustafa against model-turned–romance novelist Fabio in a tongue-in-cheek battle for the title of Old Spice Guy. Through ads, online videos, and social media comments, the two traded wry comments and invited the public to vote for their favorite. In the end, Mustafa won—and so did the brand. The new spice put Old Spice into the spotlight and gave it a bit of attitude to stand out from competing brands. Best of all, "Old Spice leaped into first place in market share and is still growing," says the head of Procter & Gamble's North America division. "We ran out of product and could not keep up with sales."[1]

Marketers employ multiple promotional methods to create very favorable company and product images in the minds of customers. Skillful use of promotion is of great benefit to many brands like Old Spice.

Promotion is communication about an organization and its products that is intended to inform, persuade, or remind target-market members. The promotion with which we are most familiar—advertising—is intended to inform, persuade, or remind us to buy particular products. But there is more to promotion than advertising, and it is used for other purposes as well. Charities use promotion to inform us of their need for donations, to persuade us to give, and to remind us to do so in case we have forgotten. Even the Internal Revenue Service uses promotion (in the form of publicity) to remind us of its April 15 deadline for filing tax returns.

A **promotion mix** (sometimes called a *marketing–communications mix*) is the particular combination of promotional methods a firm uses to reach a target market. The makeup of a mix depends on many factors, including the firm's promotional resources and objectives, the nature of the target market, the product characteristics, and the feasibility of various promotional methods.

In this chapter, we introduce four promotional methods and describe how they are used in an organization's marketing plans. First, we examine the role of advertising in the promotion mix. We discuss different types of advertising, the process of developing an advertising campaign, and social and legal concerns in advertising.

promotion communication about an organization and its products that is intended to inform, persuade, or remind target-market members

promotion mix the particular combination of promotion methods a firm uses to reach a target market

Next, we consider several categories of personal selling, noting the importance of effective sales management. We also look at sales promotion—why firms use it and which sales promotion techniques are most effective. Then we explain how public relations can be used to promote an organization and its products. Also, we illustrate how these four promotional methods are combined in an effective promotion mix. Finally, we discuss the criticisms of promotion.

WHAT IS INTEGRATED MARKETING COMMUNICATIONS?

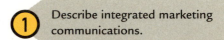
1 Describe integrated marketing communications.

Integrated marketing communications is the coordination of promotion efforts to ensure their maximal informational and persuasive impact on customers. A major goal of integrated marketing communications is to send a consistent message to customers. This approach fosters not only long-term customer relationships but also the efficient use of promotional resources.

The concept of integrated marketing communications has been increasingly accepted for several reasons. Mass-media advertising, a very popular promotional method in the past, is used less today because of its high costs and unpredictable audience sizes. Marketers now can take advantage of more precisely targeted promotional tools, such as cable TV, direct mail, DVDs, the Internet, special-interest magazines, and podcasts. Database marketing is also allowing marketers to be more precise in targeting individual customers. Mass media advertising used to be much more popular than it is today. It is still widely used, but as only one tool in an expanding toolkit of marketing communication options. Marketers today have access to a wide variety of advertising and promotional options. Marketers can now use a mix of high-tech options, such as cable and satellite television, emails, online social media, and podcasts. Thanks to online digital media, marketers today can more precisely identify their target audience with affordable advertising campaigns that directly address their customers' needs and wants. Until recently, specialists handled different aspects of marketing communication campaigns. Advertising agencies created advertising campaigns, sales promotion companies handled sales promotion activities, and public relations firms handled public relations issues. Today, firms can rely on organizations that provide one-stop shopping for all marketing and promotion-related activities. Such firms help to reduce coordination problems and improve integration between different functions. This is beneficial because marketing communications can be very expensive and it is important for firms to ensure that promotional resources are used as efficiently as possible. To appeal to consumers while saving money on their advertising budgets, firms are even relying on customers to help develop effective advertisements and to design promotional activities. Companies like Doritos and Pepsi have utilized consumer advertising and promotion ideas with great success. These campaigns generate a lot of buzz and can be produced much more cheaply than a professional campaign. Viral marketing is another way to achieve broad advertising reach via digital channels for minimal cost. Most marketers now acknowledge the importance and power of utilizing viral marketing.[2]

THE ROLE OF PROMOTION

2 Understand the role of promotion.

Promotion is commonly the object of two misconceptions. Often, people take note of highly visible promotional activities, such as advertising and personal selling, and conclude that these make up the entire field of marketing. People also sometimes consider promotional activities to be unnecessary, expensive, and the cause of higher prices. Neither view is accurate.

The role of promotion is to facilitate exchanges directly or indirectly by informing individuals, groups, or organizations and influencing them to accept a firm's products

integrated marketing communications coordination of promotion efforts to ensure their maximal informational and persuasive impact on customers

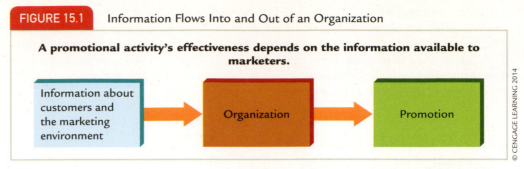

FIGURE 15.1 Information Flows Into and Out of an Organization

A promotional activity's effectiveness depends on the information available to marketers.

Information about customers and the marketing environment → Organization → Promotion

© CENGAGE LEARNING 2014

Source: William M. Pride and O. C. Ferrell, *Marketing: Concepts and Strategies*, 17h ed. (Mason, OH: South-Western/Cengage Learning, 2014). Adapted with permission.

or to have more positive feelings about the firm. To expedite exchanges directly, marketers convey information about a firm's goods, services, and ideas to particular market segments. To bring about exchanges indirectly, marketers address interest groups (such as environmental and consumer groups), regulatory agencies, investors, and the general public concerning a company and its products. The broader role of promotion, therefore, is to maintain positive relationships between a company and various groups in the marketing environment.

Marketers frequently design promotional communications, such as advertisements, for specific groups, although some may be directed at wider audiences. Several different messages may be communicated simultaneously to different market segments. For example, BP must address stakeholders concerned about the aftereffects of the 2010 Deepwater Horizon oil leak and subsequent cleanup efforts; inform customers about its products and services; and update investors about financial performance.

Marketers must plan, implement, and coordinate promotional communications carefully to make the best use of them. The effectiveness of promotional activities depends greatly on the quality and quantity of information available to marketers about the organization's marketing environment (see Figure 15.1). If a marketer wants to influence customers to buy a certain product, for example, the firm must know who these customers are and how they make purchase decisions for that type of product. Marketers must gather and use information about particular audiences to communicate successfully with them. At times, two or more firms partner in joint promotional efforts.

THE PROMOTION MIX: AN OVERVIEW

Marketers can use several promotional methods to communicate with individuals, groups, and organizations. The methods that are combined to promote a particular product make up the promotion mix for that item.

Advertising, personal selling, sales promotion, and public relations are the four major elements in an organization's promotion mix (see Figure 15.2) While it is possible that only one ingredient may be used, it is likely that two, three, or four of these ingredients will be used together in a promotion mix, depending on the type of product and target market involved.

Advertising is a paid nonpersonal message communicated to a select audience through a mass medium. Advertising is flexible enough that it can reach a very large target group or a small, carefully chosen one. **Personal selling** is personal communication aimed at informing customers and persuading them to buy a firm's products. It is more expensive to reach a consumer through personal selling than through advertising, but this method provides immediate feedback and often is more persuasive than advertising. **Sales promotion** is the use of activities or materials as direct inducements to customers or salespersons. It adds extra value to the product or increases the customer's incentive to buy the product. **Public relations** is a broad set of communication activities used to create and maintain favorable relationships between an organization and various public groups, both internal and external.

advertising a paid nonpersonal message communicated to a select audience through a mass medium

personal selling personal communication aimed at informing customers and persuading them to buy a firm's products

sales promotion the use of activities or materials as direct inducements to customers or salespersons

public relations communication activities used to create and maintain favorable relations between an organization and various public groups, both internal and external

FIGURE 15.2 Possible Ingredients of a Promotion Mix

Depending on the type of product and target market involved, one or more of these ingredients are used in a promotion mix.

Advertising

Personal selling

Sales promotion

Public relations

Source: William M. Pride and O. C. Ferrell, *Marketing: Concepts and Strategies*, 17th ed. (Mason, OH: South-Western/ Cengage Learning, 2014). Adapted with permission.

ADVERTISING

③ Explain the purposes of the three types of advertising.

Last year, organizations spent over $144 billion on measured media advertising in the United States.[3] We will discuss how this money is spent by first looking at the type of advertising. Then, we focus on advertising media and the steps involved in developing an advertising campaign.

Types of Advertising by Purpose

Depending on its purpose and message, advertising may be classified into one of three groups: primary demand, selective demand, or institutional.

Primary-Demand Advertising Primary-demand advertising is advertising aimed at increasing the demand for *all* brands of a product within a specific industry The Corn Refiners Association, for example, launched a multimedia campaign designed to educate consumers about high fructose corn syrup in an effort to downplay negative publicity surrounding the refined corn ingredient.[4]

Selective-Demand Advertising Selective-demand (or brand) advertising is advertising that is used to sell a particular brand of product. It is by far the most common type of advertising, and it accounts for the lion's share of advertising expenditures.

Selective advertising that aims at persuading consumers to make purchases within a short time is called *immediate-response advertising*. Most local advertising is of this type. Often local advertisers promote products with immediate appeal. Selective advertising aimed at keeping a firm's name or product before the public is called *reminder advertising*.

Comparative advertising, which has become more popular over the last three decades, compares specific characteristics of two or more identified brands. Of course, the comparison shows the advertiser's brand to be as good as or better than the other identified competing brands. Consumers sometimes become rather guarded concerning claims based on "scientific studies" and various statistical manipulations. Comparative advertising is unacceptable or illegal in a number of countries.

Institutional Advertising Institutional advertising is advertising designed to enhance a firm's image or reputation. A positive public image helps an organization to attract not only customers but also employees and investors. BP's "Still Working, Still

primary-demand advertising advertising aimed at increasing the demand for all brands of a product within a specific industry

selective-demand (or brand) advertising advertising that is used to sell a particular brand of product

institutional advertising advertising designed to enhance a firm's image or reputation

Committed" campaign addresses the company's efforts to clean up and maintain the environment in the Gulf of Mexico after the massive Deepwater Horizon oil leak. This ongoing ad campaign seeks to repair BP's damaged image by demonstrating a commitment to cleaning up pollution in the Gulf, showing a commitment to environmentalism, and restoring consumer faith in the company.[5]

Describe the advantages and disadvantages of the major advertising media.

④

Advertising Media

The **advertising media** are the various forms of communication through which advertising reaches its audience. The major media are newspapers, magazines, direct mail, Yellow Pages, out-of-home displays, television, radio, the Internet, and social media. Figure 15.3 shows the proportion of ad dollars spent on selected media.

Newspapers A very large proportion of newspaper advertising is purchased by local retailers. Retailers use newspaper advertising extensively because it is relatively inexpensive compared with other media. Moreover, since most newspapers provide local coverage, advertising dollars are not wasted in reaching people outside the organization's market area. It is also timely. Ads usually can be placed just a few days before they are to appear.

There are some drawbacks, however, to newspaper advertising. It has a short life span; newspapers generally are read through once and then discarded. Newspaper readership is declining. Color reproduction in newspapers is usually not high quality; thus, most ads are run in black and white. Finally, marketers cannot target specific demographic groups through newspaper ads because newspapers are read by such a broad spectrum of people.

advertising media the various forms of communication through which advertising reaches its audience

 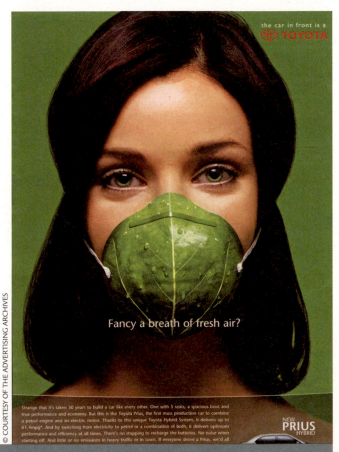

Primary-demand advertising versus selective-demand advertising. The "got milk?" ad is designed to stimulate the demand for *all* milk brands. It is an example of primary-demand advertising. In contrast, the Prius ad is designed to stimulate a *single* car brand. It is an example of selective-demand advertising.

FIGURE 15.3 Proportion of Total Advertising Dollars Spent on Selected Media

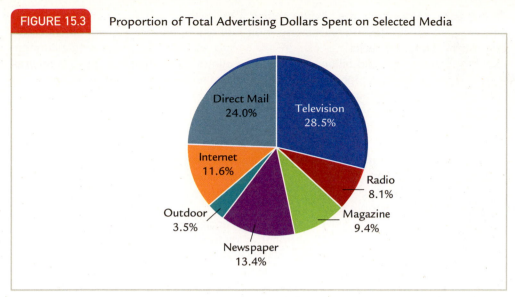

Source: "U.S. Ad Spending Totals," *Advertising Age*, June 20, 2011, p. 18.

Magazines The amount of money companies spend on magazine advertising has been flat over the last few years. However, advertisers can reach very specific market segments through ads in special-interest magazines. A boat manufacturer has a ready-made consumer audience in subscribers to *Yachting* or *Sail*. A number of magazines such as *Time* and *Cosmopolitan* publish regional editions, which provide advertisers with geographic flexibility as well.

Magazine advertising is more prestigious than newspaper advertising, and it allows for high-quality color reproduction. In addition, magazine advertisements have a longer life span than those in other media and the ads they contain may be viewed repeatedly.

The major disadvantages of magazine advertising are high cost and lack of timeliness. Because magazine ads normally must be prepared two to three months in advance, they cannot be adjusted to reflect the latest market conditions. Magazine ads—especially full-color ads—are also expensive. Although the cost of reaching 18 million people may compare favorably with that of other media, the cost of a full-page four-color ad can be very high—$320,000 in *Time*.[6]

Direct Mail Direct-mail advertising is promotional material mailed directly to individuals. Direct mail is the most selective medium; mailing lists are available (or can be compiled) to reach almost any target audience, from airplane enthusiasts to zoologists. The effectiveness of direct-mail advertising can be measured because the advertiser has a record of who received the advertisements and can track who responds to the ads.

Some organizations are using direct e-mail. To avoid customers receiving unwanted e-mail, a firm should ask customers to complete a request form in order to receive promotional e-mail from the company.

The success of direct-mail advertising depends to some extent on maintaining appropriate and current mailing lists. A direct-mail campaign may fail if the mailing list is outdated and the mailing does not reach the right people. In addition, this medium is relatively costly.

Yellow Pages Advertising Yellow Pages advertising appears in telephone directories that are distributed to millions of customers around the United States, as well as online at http://yellowpages.com. Customers use Yellow Pages advertising to save time finding products, to find information quickly, and to learn about products and marketers. Unlike other types of advertising media, Yellow Pages advertisements are purchased for one year and cannot be changed.

direct-mail advertising promotional material mailed directly to individuals

Yellow Pages advertising simple listings or display advertisements presented under specific product categories appearing in print and online telephone directories

Taking advertising to the streets—and other places. Out-of-home advertisements are designed to reach consumers while they are out of their homes. Promotional messages on buses, the backs of street benches, in stadiums, and on backs of the doors of restroom stalls are all examples of out-of-home advertising.

©SHERAB/ALAMY

Out-of-Home Advertising Out-of-home advertising consists of short promotional messages on billboards, posters, signs, and transportation vehicles.

Sign and billboard advertising allows the marketer to focus on a particular geographic area; it is also fairly inexpensive. However, because most outdoor promotion is directed toward a mobile audience, the message must be limited to a few words. The medium is especially suitable for products that lend themselves to pictorial display.

Television Television ranks number one in total advertising expenditures. Approximately 97 percent of American homes have at least one television set and the average American watches 5 hours and 30 minutes of television a day.

Television advertising is the primary medium for larger firms whose objective is to reach national or regional markets. A national advertiser may buy *network time*, which means that its message usually will be broadcast by hundreds of local stations affiliated with the network. However, the opportunity to reach extremely large television audiences has been reduced by the increased availability and popularity of cable channels and home videos. Both national and local firms may buy *local time* on a single station that covers a particular geographic area.

Advertisers may *sponsor* an entire show, participate with other sponsors of a show, or buy *spot time* for a single 10-, 20-, 30-, or 60-second commercial during or between programs. To an extent, they may select their audience by choosing the day of the week and the approximate time of day their ads will be shown. Anheuser-Busch advertises Budweiser beer during televised football games because the majority of viewers are men, who are likely to buy beer.

Marketers also can employ *product placement,* which is paying a fee to have a product appear in a television program, movie, or music video. The product might appear on a table or counter, or one or more of the actors might be using it. Through channel switching and personal digital video recorders (DVRs), television viewers can avoid watching regular television commercials. By placing the product directly into the program, viewers are likely to be exposed to the product. Product placement continues to be a stable advertising method for many marketers. Music videos are increasingly a venue for product placement, particularly if an artist is a representative for a product. Artists like Lady Gaga, Katy Perry, and Rihanna frequently showcase prominently-displayed products and brand names in their music videos. To facilitate the product placement process in music videos, My Product Placement is a new platform that aims to match musical artists and products.[7] Recently researchers reported that 90 percent of all television viewing remains live because more than half of all TV households still do not have access to time-shifting devices (DVRs). Even in households that do have DVRs, only about 20 percent of the viewing time is shifted.

Another option available to television advertisers is the infomercial. An **infomercial** is a program-length televised commercial message resembling an entertainment or consumer affairs program. Infomercials for products such as exercise equipment tell customers why they need the product, what benefits it provides, in what ways it outperforms its competitors, and how much it costs. Although initially aired primarily over cable television, today infomercials are becoming more common on network and local TV as well. Currently, infomercials are responsible for marketing over $1 billion worth of products annually. Even some *Fortune* 500 companies are using them.

Television advertising rates are based on the number of people expected to be watching when the commercial is aired. In 2012, the cost of a 30-second Super Bowl commercial was $3.5 million. Advertisers typically spend over $500,000 for a 30-second television commercial during a top-rated prime-time program.[8]

Radio Like magazine advertising, radio advertising offers selectivity. Radio stations develop programming for—and are tuned in by—specific groups of listeners. There are

out-of-home advertising short promotional messages on billboards, posters, signs, and transportation vehicles

infomercial a program-length televised commercial message resembling an entertainment or consumer affairs program

Going for SUCCESS

IKEA Remodels Perceptions with *Fix This Kitchen*

When viewers watch the reality show *Fix This Kitchen* on the A&E channel, they see renovations starring kitchen cabinets, counters, and cookware from IKEA. The retailer's ad agencies came up with the idea for the series after discovering, through research, that customers viewed IKEA as a store for low-priced accessories, not as a place to design and furnish their dream kitchen. With this in mind, the agencies cooked up *Fix This Kitchen* to achieve two main objectives. The first was to change customers' perceptions of the stores' merchandise by showing a wide range of kitchen makeovers. The second was to draw customers to IKEA's kitchen-design Web site, where they could have fun with a virtual renovation and express their personal style through IKEA's products.

As *Fix This Kitchen* began to air, IKEA also launched a full campaign of advertising, public relations, and special events. When its agencies evaluated the results, they found a 60 percent increase in the number of people who agreed that IKEA offers high-quality materials, plus a 33 percent increase in the number of people using IKEA's kitchen-design tools. Most important, store traffic and sales were on the rise, along with the size of the average sale.

Sources: Based on information in "For Ikea, It's Time to Overhaul Perceptions," *Advertising Age*, December 5, 2011, www.adage.com; Amy-Mae Elliott, "How an Integrated Marketing Campaign Boosted IKEA's Sales over 7%," *Mashable*, December 13, 2011, www.mashable.com; Steve McClellan, "Media Agencies Make Mark as Content Creators," *Advertising Age*, April 25, 2011, www.adage.com.

---

almost half a billion radios in the United States (about six per household), which makes radio the most accessible medium.

Radio advertising can be less expensive than in other media. Actual rates depend on geographic coverage, the number of commercials contracted for, the time period specified, and whether the station broadcasts on AM, FM, or both. Even small retailers are able to afford radio advertising, and a radio advertiser can schedule and change ads on short notice. The disadvantages of using radio are the absence of visual images and (because there are so many stations) the small audience size.

Internet Spending on Internet advertising has increased significantly. Internet advertising can take a variety of forms. The *banner ad* is a rectangular graphic that appears at the top of a Web site. Many Web sites are able to offer free services because they are supported by banner advertisements. Advertisers can use animation and interactive capabilities to draw more attention to their ads. Another type of advertising is *sponsorship* (or *cobranded* ads). These ads integrate a company's brand with editorial content. The goal of this type of ad is to get users to strongly identify the advertiser with the site's mission. For example, a running shoe advertiser such as Nike may choose to place advertisements on a popular lifestyle blog related to running because the site is affiliated with the mission and activities of the firm. The Web site for a cable home-repair network, http://DIYNetwork.com, displays clickable advertisements related to featured articles. Someone browsing articles on windows would find advertisements for different windows on the site. Such online ads also make it easy for consumers to click over to the company's site to make purchases or browse products.[9]

Many Internet advertisers choose to purchase keywords on popular search engines such as Google, Bing, Yahoo!, and MSN. For example, Kellogg's purchased the word *cereal* on Google so that every time someone conducts a search using that word, a link to Kellogg's Web site appears. *Interstitial* ads pop up to display a product. For example, users of www.Hulu.com can watch any of the available TV episodes and movies free of charge by viewing commercials periodically throughout each video.

Harnessing the power of social media—or not? Social media allows a business to reach out to customers in a context that is familiar and comfortable to them. Firms attempt to measure the effectiveness of their social media efforts by gathering statistics on the number of followers and fans they have, traffic to their Web sites, and mentions of their products on social networking sites. Whether or not this type of advertising results in additional sales can be difficult to tell. General Motors pulled its ads off of Facebook after deciding they weren't having much of an impact.

Social MEDIA

The Best Snacks on Earth

Frito-Lay is a key business unit within PepsiCo. The company prides itself on its attention to the health of customers, diversity of suppliers, and the communities in which they operate. The company vision has always included continuously developing products in order to become America's go-to snack food. Frito-Lay's promotional campaign includes all aspects of the promotion mix. One example of TV advertising is illustrated

by the two winning ads that aired during a recent Super Bowl. The company home page www.fritolay.com connects users to all the social media sites. Snack Chatter, the Flavor Kitchen, and Scan the Bag are links found on the Frito-Lay Facebook page (www.facebook.com/FritoLay). Welcome to the Frito-Lay Channel at www.youtube.com/user/OfficialFritoLay#p/c/66ABB6482873A38E. At twitter.com/fritolay, there are over 22,000 followers; and www.snacks.com/ links to the Snack Chat blog.

Social Media In the last few years, the use of social media as an advertising medium has increased dramatically. This is largely due to the perception that marketers can target, interact with, and connect more personally with their customers through the different social-media outlets as opposed to more traditional media. Increasingly, customers expect companies to have an online presence. Most firms have a Web site and many also communicate information and relay promotions via Twitter, Facebook, and LinkedIn. Businesses may also post advertisements on social media sites and blogs. Some companies also have their own branded sites that incorporate aspects and features of social media sites, but focus on their own brands and products. Even the President of the United States leverages social media to promote himself and his message. For example, President Obama released a 17-minute-long documentary narrated by Tom Hanks via YouTube. The documentary functioned like an extended advertisement in a campaign year and the president's staff hoped that it would go viral.[10]

While companies increasingly feel pressure to incorporate digital media, such as social networking sites, into their marketing mixes, research is not clear on the exact benefits of utilizing online social media for advertising. Social media can be a very low-cost advertising medium and it can be an excellent means for reaching a targeted audience, but social media sites are not as good at reaching broad or diverse audiences. To contrast, a television ad broadcast during a major sporting event can reach millions of highly diverse viewers at once. Because of the smaller nature of Internet audiences and the problems of whether online customers actually see the promotions, measuring the return on investment of social media advertising remains a challenge. Firms may measure things like followers and fans, traffic to a site, and social media mentions across other digital platforms, but marketers have a hard time translating this data into an estimate on return on investment. Nevertheless, most marketers feel that online social media are important tools and many firms have full-time social media experts on staff.[11]

Identify the major steps in developing an advertising campaign.

Major Steps in Developing an Advertising Campaign

An advertising campaign is developed in several stages. These stages may vary in number and the order in which they are implemented depending on the company's resources, products, and audiences. The development of a campaign in any organization, however, will include the following steps in some form:

1. Identify and Analyze the Target Audience The target audience is the group of people toward whom a firm's advertisements are directed. To pinpoint the organization's target audience and develop an effective campaign, marketers must analyze such information as the geographic distribution of potential customers; their age, sex, race, income, and education; and their attitudes toward both the advertiser's product and competing products. How marketers use this information will be influenced by the features of the product to be advertised and the nature of the competition. Precise identification of the target audience is crucial to the proper development of subsequent stages and, ultimately, to the success of the campaign itself. Rykä, for example, produces running shoes and accessories aimed at a target audience of female runners. It claims that its products are tailored to fit a woman's foot shape and skeletal structure. As part of its promotional activities, the company partners with exercise programs, such as Jazzercize, that attract more women than men. It also features popular talk show host and avid runner, Kelly Ripa, as its spokeswoman.[12]

2. Define the Advertising Objectives The goals of an advertising campaign should be stated precisely and in measurable terms. The objectives should include the firm's current position, indicate how far and in what direction from that original reference point the company wishes to move, and specify a definite period of time for the achievement of the goals. Advertising objectives that focus on sales will stress increasing sales by a certain percentage or dollar amount or expanding the firm's market share. Communication objectives will emphasize increasing product or brand awareness, improving consumer attitudes, or conveying product information.

3. Create the Advertising Platform An advertising platform includes the important selling points or features that an advertiser wishes to incorporate into the advertising campaign. These features should be important to customers in their selection and use of a product, and, if possible, they should be features that competing products lack. Although research into what consumers view as important issues is expensive, it is the most productive way to determine which issues to include in an advertising platform. For instance, customer research might indicate to the manufacturer of a cold-symptom reliever that customers want a product that relieves your coughing, stops your nose from running, and keeps your eyes from watering.

COURTESY OF THE ADVERTISING ARCHIVES

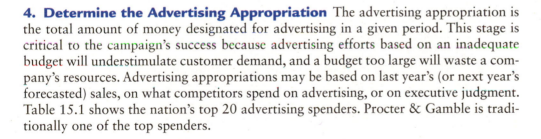

Pinpointing the target audience. Is this ad aimed at everyone? It's unlikely. Most ads are aimed at specific groups of consumers.

4. Determine the Advertising Appropriation The advertising appropriation is the total amount of money designated for advertising in a given period. This stage is critical to the campaign's success because advertising efforts based on an inadequate budget will understimulate customer demand, and a budget too large will waste a company's resources. Advertising appropriations may be based on last year's (or next year's forecasted) sales, on what competitors spend on advertising, or on executive judgment. Table 15.1 shows the nation's top 20 advertising spenders. Procter & Gamble is traditionally one of the top spenders.

5. Develop the Media Plan A media plan specifies exactly which media will be used in the campaign and when advertisements will appear. For example, marketers are not likely to rely on digital media advertising to sell life insurance aimed at retired people because older consumers are not as likely to use the Internet as younger ones. Although cost-effectiveness is not easy to measure, the primary concern of the media planner is to reach the largest number of persons in the target audience for each dollar spent. In addition to cost, media planners must consider the location and demographics of people in the advertising target, the content of the message, and the characteristics of the audiences reached by various media. The media planner begins with general media decisions, selects subclasses within each medium, and, finally, chooses particular media vehicles for the campaign.

6. Create the Advertising Message The content and form of a message are influenced by the product's features, the characteristics of people in the target

Personal APPS

Think about the media plan an advertiser might use to reach you. When do you watch television? Do you ever pass any billboards? Which printed or online newspapers or magazines do you read? These are all questions a media planner would consider when choosing media for a target audience.

audience, the objectives of the campaign, and the choice of media. An advertiser must consider these factors when choosing words and illustrations that will be meaningful and appealing to persons in the advertising target. The copy, or words, of an advertisement will vary depending on the media choice but should attempt to move the audience through attention, interest, desire, and action. Artwork and visuals should complement copy by attracting the audience's attention and communicating an idea quickly. Creating a cohesive advertising message is especially difficult for a company such as eBay that offers such a broad mix of products. eBay developed a "whatever it is" campaign that features a variety of consumers representing all age groups using a variety of products (a car, a television, a dress, and a laptop) all shaped like the letters "it." The tagline, "Whatever *it* is, you can get it on eBay," emphasizes the massive range of products available from the site and effectively showcases the service that the company provides its customers.

7. Execute the Campaign The execution of an advertising campaign requires extensive planning, scheduling, and coordinating because many tasks must be completed on time. Many people and firms, such as production companies, research organizations, media firms, printers, photoengravers,

TABLE 15.1   Who Spends the Most on Advertising?

Rank	Company	Advertising Expenditures (in millions)	Sales (in millions)	Advertising Expenditure as a Percentage of Sales
1	Procter & Gamble Co.	$ 4,615	$ 29,488	15.7
2	AT&T	2,989	123,018	2.4
3	General Motors Co.	2,869	34,514	8.3
4	Verizon Communications	2,451	107,808	2.3
5	American Express Co.	2,223	13,900	16.0
6	Pfizer	2,124	22,504	9.4
7	Walmart Stores	2,055	261,257	0.8
8	Time Warner	2,044	10,960	18.6
9	Johnson & Johnson	2,027	30,330	6.7
10	L'Oreal	1,979	5,742	34.5
11	Walt Disney Co.	1,932	26,389	7.3
12	JPMorgan Chase & Co.	1,917	86,724	2.2
13	Ford Motor Co.	1,915	43,774	4.4
14	Comcast Corp.	1,853	35,996	5.2
15	Sears Holdings Corp.	1,779	36,996	4.8
16	Toyota Motor Corp.	1,736	59,971	2.9
17	Bank of America Corp.	1,553	130,892	1.2
18	Target Corp.	1,508	65,357	2.3
19	Macy's	1,417	23,489	6.0
20	Sprint Nextel Corp.	1,400	32,260	4.3

Source: Reprinted with permission from the June 20, 2011, issue of *Advertising Age*. Copyright Crain Communications Inc., 2011.

Entrepreneurial SUCCESS

Via Ad Agency

With 100 employees and annual revenues of $15 million, Via is a small advertising agency with big ideas. It was founded by John Coleman in 1993 and now operates from a historic 19th-century building that once served as the public library of Portland, Maine. The award-winning agency is known as much for its responsive, results-oriented service as for its creativity in developing distinctive advertising campaigns that help its business clients achieve their promotion objectives.

The chief marketing officer of Samsung Electronics observes that Via's creative experts are good listeners, work collaboratively with clients, and understand the need for measurable results. When Samsung introduced its Galaxy Tab tablet computer, which competes with Apple's iPad, Via was able to crank up a multimedia launch program in only five weeks. Thanks in part to Via's high-performing campaign, Samsung sold more than 1 million Galaxy Tabs in the first three months on the market.

Via's expertise and service have attracted a growing roster of clients from different industries, including Unilever ice creams, Macaroni Grill restaurants, Perdue chicken products, and People's United Bank. No wonder *Advertising Age* recently named Via the best small agency of the year.

Sources: Based on information in Emily Maltby, "New Life for an Old Library," *Wall Street Journal*, February 24, 2012, www.wsj.com; Maureen Morrison, "Via Agency Tapped to Handle Perdue's Marketing," *Advertising Age*, November 29, 2011, www.adage.com; Beth Snyder Bulick, "Small Agency of the Year, Gold: Via," *Advertising Age*, August 8, 2011, www.adage.com; "Via Agency, Baldwin Take Top Honors at Small Agency Awards," *Advertising Age*, July 28, 2011, www.adage.com.

and commercial artists, may contribute to a campaign. Advertising managers constantly must assess the quality of the work and take corrective action when necessary. Situations may also arise that require a change in plans. Designer Marc Jacobs' marketing team had to scramble to release new advertisements after the initial print ad for its Oh, Lola! perfume was banned in the United Kingdom for being inappropriately erotic. Marc Jacobs' marketing team responded by releasing some toned-down advertisements in its place.[13]

8. Evaluate Advertising Effectiveness A campaign's success should be measured in terms of its original objectives before, during, and/or after the campaign. An advertiser should at least be able to estimate whether sales or market share went up because of the campaign or whether any change occurred in customer attitudes or brand awareness. Data from past and current sales and responses to coupon offers and customer surveys administered by research organizations are some of the ways in which advertising effectiveness can be evaluated. While most marketers agree that digital media and online social media are essential marketing tools, it can be difficult to gather measurements on the effectiveness of online advertising, such as return on investment.[14]

Advertising Agencies

Advertisers can plan and produce their own advertising with help from media personnel, or they can hire **advertising agencies**. An advertising agency is an independent firm that plans, produces, and places advertising for its clients. Many large ad agencies offer help with sales promotion and public relations as well. The media usually pay a commission of 15 percent to advertising agencies. Thus, the cost to the agency's client can be quite moderate. The client may be asked to pay for special services that the agency performs. Other methods for compensating agencies are also used.

Firms that do a lot of advertising may use both an in-house advertising department and an independent agency. This approach gives the firm the advantage of being able to call on the agency's expertise in particular areas of advertising. An agency also can bring a fresh viewpoint to a firm's products and advertising plans.

advertising agency an independent firm that plans, produces, and places advertising for its clients

Recognize the various kinds of salespersons, the steps in the personal-selling process, and the major sales management tasks.

PERSONAL SELLING

Personal selling is the most adaptable of all promotional methods because the person who is presenting the message can modify it to suit the individual buyer. However, personal selling is also the most expensive method of promotion.

Most successful salespeople are able to communicate with others on a one-to-one basis and are strongly motivated. They strive to have a thorough knowledge of the products they offer for sale, and they are willing and able to deal with the details involved in handling and processing orders. Sales managers tend to emphasize these qualities when recruiting and hiring.

Many selling situations demand the face-to-face contact and adaptability of personal selling. This is especially true of industrial sales, in which a single purchase may amount to millions of dollars. Obviously, sales of that size must be based on carefully planned sales presentations, personal contact with customers, and thorough negotiations.

The pros and cons of personal selling. Personal selling is more effective than advertising. It's easy to ignore an advertisement. Saying "no" to a salesperson is much harder. The main drawback of personal selling is that it's expensive, which is why it's generally used to sell high-dollar goods and services.

©SUPERSTOCK/ALAMY

Kinds of Salespersons

Because most businesses employ different salespersons to perform different functions, marketing managers must select the kinds of sales personnel that will be most effective in selling the firm's products. Salespersons may be identified as order-getters, order-takers, and support personnel. A single individual can, and often does, perform all three functions.

Order-Getters An **order-getter** is responsible for what is sometimes called **creative selling**—selling a firm's products to new customers and increasing sales to current customers. An order-getter must perceive buyers' needs, supply customers with information about the firm's product, and persuade them to buy the product. Order-getting activities may be separated into two groups. In current-customer sales, salespeople concentrate on obtaining additional sales or leads for prospective sales from customers who have purchased the firm's products at least once. In new-business sales, sales personnel seek out new prospects and convince them to make an initial purchase of the firm's product. The real estate, insurance, appliance, heavy industrial machinery, and automobile industries in particular depend on new-business sales.

Order-Takers An **order-taker** handles repeat sales in ways that maintain positive relationships with customers. An order-taker sees that customers have products when and where they are needed and in the proper amounts. *Inside order-takers* receive incoming mail and telephone orders in some businesses; salespersons in retail stores are also inside order-takers. *Outside* (or *field*) *order-takers* travel to customers. Often, the buyer and the field salesperson develop a mutually beneficial relationship of placing, receiving, and delivering orders. Both inside and outside order-takers are active salespersons and often produce most of their companies' sales.

Support Personnel **Sales support personnel** aid in selling but are more involved in locating *prospects* (likely first-time customers), educating customers, building goodwill for the firm, and providing follow-up service. The most common categories of support personnel are missionary, trade, and technical salespersons.

A **missionary salesperson**, who usually works for a manufacturer, visits retailers to persuade them to buy the manufacturer's products. If the retailers agree, they buy the products from wholesalers, who are the manufacturer's actual customers. Missionary salespersons often are employed by producers of medical supplies and pharmaceuticals to promote these products to retail druggists, physicians, and hospitals.

order-getter a salesperson who is responsible for selling a firm's products to new customers and increasing sales to present customers

creative selling selling products to new customers and increasing sales to present customers

order-taker a salesperson who handles repeat sales in ways that maintain positive relationships with customers

sales support personnel employees who aid in selling but are more involved in locating prospects, educating customers, building goodwill for the firm, and providing follow-up service

missionary salesperson a salesperson—generally employed by a manufacturer—who visits retailers to persuade them to buy the manufacturer's products

A **trade salesperson**, who generally works for a food producer or processor, assists customers in promoting products, especially in retail stores. A trade salesperson may obtain additional shelf space for the products, restock shelves, set up displays, and distribute samples. Because trade salespersons usually are order-takers as well, they are not strictly support personnel.

A **technical salesperson** assists a company's current customers in technical matters. He or she may explain how to use a product, how it is made, how to install it, or how a system is designed. A technical salesperson should be formally educated in science or engineering. Computers, steel, and chemicals are some of the products handled by technical salespeople.

Marketers usually need sales personnel from several of these categories. Factors that affect hiring and other personnel decisions include the number of customers and their characteristics; the product's attributes, complexity, and price; the distribution channels used by the company; and the company's approach to advertising.

The Personal-Selling Process

No two selling situations are exactly alike, and no two salespeople perform their jobs in exactly the same way. Most salespeople, however, follow the six-step procedure illustrated in Figure 15.4.

FIGURE 15.4   The Six Steps of the Personal-Selling Process

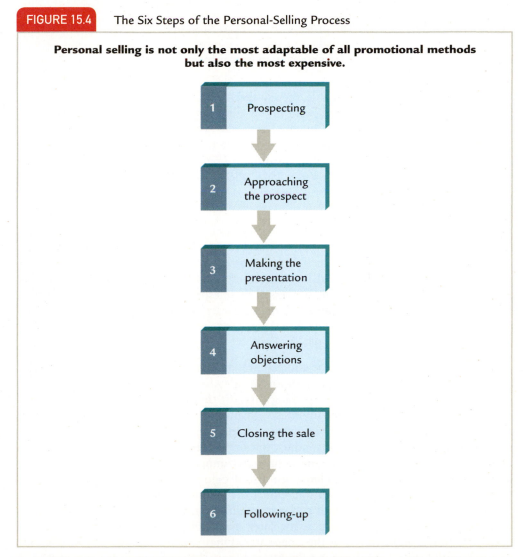

Personal selling is not only the most adaptable of all promotional methods but also the most expensive.

1. Prospecting
2. Approaching the prospect
3. Making the presentation
4. Answering objections
5. Closing the sale
6. Following-up

Source: William M. Pride and O. C. Ferrell, *Marketing: Concepts and Strategies*, 17th ed. (Mason, OH: South-Western/Cengage Learning, 2014). Adapted with permission.

trade salesperson a salesperson—generally employed by a food producer or processor—who assists customers in promoting products, especially in retail stores

technical salesperson a salesperson who assists a company's current customers in technical matters

Prospecting The first step in personal selling is to research potential buyers and choose the most likely customers, or prospects. Sources of prospects include business associates and customers, public records, telephone and trade-association directories, and company files. The salesperson concentrates on those prospects that have the financial resources, willingness, and authority to buy the product.

Approaching the Prospect First impressions are often lasting impressions. Thus, the salesperson's first contact with the prospect is crucial to successful selling. The best approach is one based on knowledge of the product, of the prospect's needs, and of how the product can meet those needs. Salespeople who understand each customer's particular situation are likely to make a good first impression—and to make a sale.

Making the Presentation The next step is actual delivery of the sales presentation. In many cases, this includes demonstrating the product. The salesperson points out the product's features, its benefits, and how it is superior to competitors' merchandise. If the product has been used successfully by other firms, the salesperson may mention this as part of the presentation.

During a demonstration, the salesperson may suggest that the prospect try out the product personally. The demonstration and product trial should underscore specific points made during the presentation.

Answering Objections The prospect is likely to raise objections or ask questions at any time. This gives the salesperson a chance to eliminate objections that might prevent a sale, to point out additional features, or to mention special services the company offers.

Closing the Sale To close the sale, the salesperson asks the prospect to buy the product. This is considered the critical point in the selling process. Many experienced salespeople make use of a *trial closing,* in which they ask questions based on the assumption that the customer is going to buy the product. The questions "When would you want delivery?" and "Do you want the standard model or the one with the special options package?" are typical of trial closings. They allow the reluctant prospect to make a purchase without having to say, "I'll take it."

Following-Up The salesperson must follow up after the sale to ensure that the product is delivered on time, in the right quantity, and in proper operating condition. During follow-up, the salesperson also makes it clear that he or she is available in case problems develop. Follow-up leaves a good impression and eases the way toward future sales. Hence, it is essential to the selling process. The salesperson's job does not end with a sale. It continues as long as the seller and the customer maintain a working relationship.

Managing Personal Selling

A firm's success often hinges on the competent management of its sales force. Although some companies operate efficiently without a sales force, most firms rely on a strong sales force—and the sales revenue it brings in—for their success.

Sales managers have responsibilities in a number of areas. They must set sales objectives in concrete, quantifiable terms and specify a certain period of time and a certain geographic area. They must adjust the size of the sales force to meet changes in the firm's marketing plan and the marketing environment. Sales managers must attract and hire effective salespersons. They must also develop a training program and decide where, when, how, and for whom to conduct the training. They must formulate a fair and adequate compensation plan to keep qualified employees. They must motivate salespersons to boost their productivity. They must define sales territories and determine scheduling and routing of the sales force. Finally, sales managers must evaluate the operation as a whole through sales reports, communications with customers, and invoices.

SALES PROMOTION

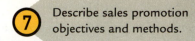

Sales promotion consists of activities or materials that are direct inducements to customers or salespersons. Are you a member of an airline frequent-flyer program? Have you recently received a free sample in the mail or at a supermarket? How about a rebate from a manufacturer? Do you use coupons? All these are examples of sales promotion efforts. Sales promotion techniques often are used to enhance and supplement other promotional methods. They can have a significant impact on sales.

The dramatic increase in spending for sales promotion shows that marketers have recognized the potential of this promotional method. Many firms now include numerous sales promotion efforts as part of their overall promotion mix.

Sales Promotion Objectives

Sales promotion activities may be used singly or in combination, both offensively and defensively, to achieve one goal or a set of goals. Marketers use sales promotion activities and materials for a number of purposes, including

1. To attract new customers
2. To encourage trial of a new product
3. To invigorate the sales of a mature brand
4. To boost sales to current customers
5. To reinforce advertising
6. To increase traffic in retail stores
7. To steady irregular sales patterns
8. To build up reseller inventories
9. To neutralize competitive promotional efforts
10. To improve shelf space and displays

Sales Promotion Methods

Most sales promotion methods can be classified as promotional techniques for either consumer sales or trade sales. A **consumer sales promotion method** attracts consumers to particular retail stores and motivates them to purchase certain new or established products. A **trade sales promotion method** encourages wholesalers and retailers to stock and actively promote a manufacturer's product. Incentives such as money, merchandise, marketing assistance, and gifts are commonly awarded to resellers who buy products or respond positively in other ways. Of the combined dollars spent on sales promotion and advertising, about one-half is spent on trade promotions, about one-fourth is spent on consumer promotions, and about one-fourth is spent on advertising.

A number of factors enter into marketing decisions about which and how many sales promotion methods to use. Of greatest importance are the objectives of the promotional effort. Product characteristics—size, weight, cost, durability, uses, features, and hazards—and target market profiles—age, gender, income, location, density, usage rate, and buying patterns—likewise must be considered. Distribution channels and availability of appropriate resellers also influence the choice of sales promotion methods, as do the competitive and regulatory forces in the environment. Let's now discuss a few important sales promotion methods.

Rebates A **rebate** is a return of part of the product's purchase price. Usually, this refund is offered to consumers who send in a coupon along with a specific proof of purchase. Rebating is a relatively low-cost promotional method. Once used mainly to help launch new product items, it is now applied to a wide variety of products. Some automakers offer rebates on their vehicles because they have found that many car customers are more likely to purchase a car with a rebate than the same car with a lower price and no rebate. One problem with rebates is that many people perceive the redemption process as too complicated. Only about half of individuals who purchase rebated products actually apply for the rebates.

consumer sales promotion method a sales promotion method designed to attract consumers to particular retail stores and to motivate them to purchase certain new or established products

trade sales promotion method a sales promotion method designed to encourage wholesalers and retailers to stock and actively promote a manufacturer's product

rebate a return of part of the product's purchase price

Personal APPS

Samples go far beyond the supermarket or drug store. If you've ever downloaded a trial version of new software or a new digital game, you've taken advantage of a free sample. This is a great way to try before you buy.

coupon an offer that reduces the retail price of a particular item by a stated amount at the time of purchase

sample a free product given to customers to encourage trial and purchase

"Try it! You'll like it!" Companies give away coupons to increase the sales of their products and encourage consumers who are unfamiliar with them to give them a try.

Coupons A **coupon** reduces the retail price of a particular item by a stated amount at the time of purchase. They are made available to customers through newspapers, magazines, direct mail, online, and shelf dispensers in stores. Coupons are precisely targeted at customers. Many firms are utilizing the Internet to target customers with deals and distribute coupons. Constant Contact, for example, offers email and listerv managing capabilities for small businesses. Recently, the company unveiled a Groupon alternative called SaveLocal, which targets customers with specific coupon deals. The service allows businesses to focus on existing customers and provides incentives, chosen by the company, for those customers to notify others about the deals. This method is a low-cost way of promoting a company's products or services among a customer base that will use and appreciate the service. So far, Constant Contact reports that businesses that use the service have found that around 20 percent of coupon users are new to the company, which means the service is effectively attracting new customers.[15]

Although coupon use had been declining steadily for several years, the recent recession caused coupon usage to increase. In 2009, businesses issued 367 billion coupons, the highest level in 30 years. Consumers redeemed 3.3 billion coupons, a 27 percent increase over the previous year, making it the first time in 17 years that consumers used more coupons than they did the year before. In 2010, redemption remained the same, which is interesting according to Bob Carter, President of Inmar's Promotion Services, because "the change in consumer behavior that led to drastic increases in coupon redemption during the economic crisis is holding post-recession."[16] The largest number of coupons distributed are for household cleaners, condiments, frozen foods, medications and health aids, and paper products. Stores in some areas even deduct double or triple the value of manufacturers' coupons from the purchase price as a sales promotion technique of their own. Coupons also may offer free merchandise, either with or without an additional product purchase.

Samples A **sample** is a free product given to customers to encourage trial and purchase. Marketers use free samples to stimulate the trial of a product, increase sales volume in the early stages of a product's life-cycle, and obtain desirable distribution. Samples may be offered via online coupons, direct mail, or in stores. Many customers prefer to receive their samples by mail. Providing samples remains the most expensive sales promotion technique. Although it is used often to promote new products, it can also be used to promote established brands. For example, cosmetics companies may use samples to attract customers. Coca-Cola often gives out free samples of products such as Vitaminwater at business conventions, concerts, and sporting events. In designing a free sample, organizations must consider such factors as seasonal demand for the product, market characteristics, and prior advertising.

Not all samples are free. Some companies have realized that customers will pay a small fee to have regular access to high-end samples. Birchbox is an online company that, for $10 a month, ships customers a monthly box of a variety of high-end beauty product samples. While these samples are not free, customers appreciate the low-cost means of trying out new products and the convenience of having the products shipped directly to their doors. The Sample Society offers a similar service for $15 a month and includes beauty tips from *Allure* magazine editors.[17]

Premiums A **premium** is a gift that a producer offers a customer in return for buying its product. They are used to attract competitors' customers, introduce different sizes of established products, add variety to other promotional efforts, and stimulate consumer loyalty. Creativity is essential when using premiums; to stand out and achieve a significant number of redemptions, the premium must match both the target audience and the brand's image. Examples include a service station giving a free car wash with a fill-up, a free toothbrush available with a tube of toothpaste, and a free plastic storage box given with the purchase of Kraft Cheese Singles. Premiums also must be easily recognizable and desirable. Premiums are placed on or inside packages and also can be distributed through retailers or through the mail.

Frequent-User Incentives A **frequent-user incentive** is a program developed to reward customers who engage in repeat (frequent) purchases. Such programs are used commonly by service businesses such as airlines, hotels, and auto rental agencies. Frequent-user incentives foster customer loyalty to a specific company or group of cooperating companies because the customer is given an additional reason to continue patronizing the business. For example, most major airlines offer frequent-flyer programs that reward customers who have flown a specified number of miles with free tickets for additional travel. There is significant evidence that airline miles are highly valued by customers. Now, more frequent-flyer miles are awarded by non-airline companies than by airline companies. A high proportion of upper-income customers use frequent-user programs, whereas moderate-income customers are not as likely to use these programs.

Point-of-Purchase Displays A **point-of-purchase display** is promotional material placed within a retail store. The display is usually located near the product being promoted. It may actually hold merchandise, or it may simply inform customers about what the product offers and encourage them to buy it. Most point-of-purchase displays are prepared and set up by manufacturers and wholesalers.

Trade Shows A **trade show** is an industry-wide exhibit at which many sellers display their products. Some trade shows are organized exclusively for dealers—to permit manufacturers and wholesalers to show their latest lines to retailers. Others are events designed to stimulate consumer awareness and interest. Among the latter are boat shows, home shows, and flower shows put on each year in large cities. E3, for example, is the world's largest trade show for electronic games and related products. Tens of thousands attend this trade show each year, including all major producers of gaming products, to see the new products being showcased and to network with professionals in the industry.[18]

Buying Allowances A **buying allowance** is a temporary price reduction to resellers for purchasing specified quantities of a product. For example, a laundry detergent manufacturer might give retailers $1 for each case of detergent purchased. A buying allowance may serve as an incentive to resellers to handle new products and may stimulate purchases in large quantities. While the buying allowance is simple, straightforward, and easily administered, competitors can respond quickly by offering a better buying allowance.

Cooperative Advertising Cooperative advertising is an arrangement whereby a manufacturer agrees to pay a certain amount of a retailer's media cost for advertising the manufacturer's products. To be reimbursed, a retailer must show proof that the advertisements actually did appear. A large percentage of all cooperative advertising dollars is spent on newspaper advertisements.

premium a gift that a producer offers a customer in return for buying its product

frequent-user incentive a program developed to reward customers who engage in repeat (frequent) purchases

point-of-purchase display promotional material placed within a retail store

trade show an industry-wide exhibit at which many sellers display their products

buying allowance a temporary price reduction to resellers for purchasing specified quantities of a product

cooperative advertising an arrangement whereby a manufacturer agrees to pay a certain amount of a retailer's media cost for advertising the manufacturer's product

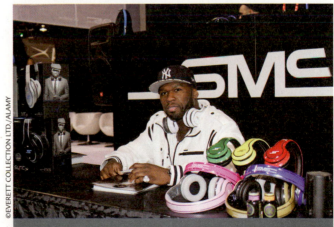

©EVERETT COLLECTION LTD./ALAMY

Using trade shows to generate interest in products. Trade shows help marketers make their products visible to a large number of businesses and consumers. The shows also allow companies to keep an eye on what their competitors are doing and the new products they are launching. In this photo, rapper 50 Cent is promoting a product at the International Consumer Electronics Show held in Las Vegas.

PUBLIC RELATIONS

As noted earlier, public relations is a broad set of communication activities used to create and maintain favorable relationships between an organization and various public groups, both internal and external. These groups can include customers, employees, stockholders, suppliers, educators, the media, government officials, and society in general.

Types of Public-Relations Tools

Organizations use a variety of public-relations tools to convey messages and to create images. Public-relations professionals prepare written materials such as brochures, newsletters, company magazines, annual reports, and news releases. They also create corporate-identity materials such as logos, business cards, signs, and stationery. Speeches are another public-relations tool. Speeches can affect an organization's image and therefore must convey the desired message clearly.

Another public-relations tool is event sponsorship, in which a company pays for all or part of a special event such as a concert, sports competition, festival, or play. Sponsoring special events is an effective way for organizations to increase brand recognition and receive media coverage with comparatively little investment. The Big Apple Barbeque Block Party, for example, is a weekend-long event that occurs every June in New York's Madison Square Park, and features free live music and cooking demonstrations. Barbeque enthusiasts can purchase plates of food from some of the country's top pitmasters, and all proceeds go to the Madison Square Park Conservancy, which maintains the park. Several companies sponsor this event to help promote their brand and the event's charity, including Coca-Cola, Ikea, Dyson, and Southern Living.[19]

Some public-relations tools have been traditionally associated with publicity, which is a part of public relations. **Publicity** is communication in news-story form about an organization, its products, or both. Publicity is transmitted through a mass medium, such as newspapers or radio, at no charge. Organizations use publicity to provide information about products; to announce new product launches, expansions, or research; and to strengthen the company's image. Public-relations personnel sometimes organize events, such as grand openings with prizes and celebrities, to create news stories about a company.

The most widely used type of publicity is the **news release.** It is generally one typed page of about 300 words provided by an organization to the media as a form of publicity. The release includes the firm's name, address, phone number, and contact person. Table 15.2 lists some of the issues news releases can address. There are also several other kinds of publicity-based public-relations tools. A **feature article**, which may run as long as 3,000 words, is usually written for inclusion in a particular publication. For example, a software firm might send an article about its new product to a computer magazine. A **captioned photograph**, a picture accompanied by a brief explanation, is an effective way to illustrate a new or improved product. A **press conference** allows invited media personnel to hear important news announcements and to receive supplementary textual materials and photographs. Finally, letters to the editor, special newspaper or magazine editorials, and videos may be prepared and distributed to appropriate media for possible use.

publicity communication in news-story form about an organization, its products, or both

news release a typed page of about 300 words provided by an organization to the media as a form of publicity

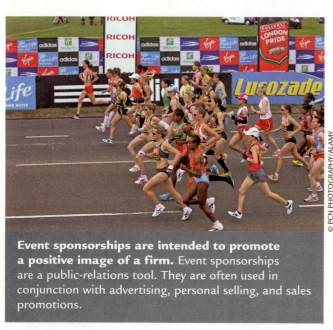

Event sponsorships are intended to promote a positive image of a firm. Event sponsorships are a public-relations tool. They are often used in conjunction with advertising, personal selling, and sales promotions.

© PCN PHOTOGRAPHY/ALAMY

feature article a piece (of up to 3,000 words) prepared by an organization for inclusion in a particular publication

captioned photograph a picture accompanied by a brief explanation

press conference a meeting at which invited media personnel hear important news announcements and receive supplementary textual materials and photographs

The Uses of Public Relations

Public relations can be used to promote people, places, activities, ideas, and even countries. Public relations focuses on enhancing the reputation of the total organization by making people aware of a company's products, brands, or activities and by creating

TABLE 15.2	Possible Issues for News Releases	
Use of new information technology	Packaging changes	
Support of a social cause	New products	
Improved warranties	Creation of new software	
Reports on industry conditions	Research developments	
New uses for established products	Company's history and development	
Product endorsements	Launching of new Web site	
Winning of quality awards	Award of contracts	
Company name changes	Opening of new markets	
Interviews with company officials	Improvements in financial position	
Improved distribution policies	Opening of an exhibit	
Global business initiatives	History of a brand	
Sponsorship of events	Winners of company contests	
Visits by celebrities	Logo changes	
Reports of new discoveries	Speeches of top management	
Innovative marketing activities	Merit awards to the organization	
Economic forecasts	Anniversaries of inventions	

© CENGAGE LEARNING 2014

specific company images such as that of innovativeness or dependability. Social media sites, YouTube, and Twitter can all be great low-cost tools for connecting with consumers and engaging in a dialogue. However, the social media landscape is changing fast. Public relations experts and other marketers must keep track of a growing list of small, niche social media sites. Smaller social media sites that focus on a specific area of interest can be an easy way to target a specific audience. For instance, Tennisopolis is a social media site for tennis enthusiasts and Lookk is a site for fashion enthusiasts and designers. Advertising on sites like these help a brand establish its image and reach its specific target audience. These sites can also be good resources for marketers looking to discover customer needs and wants and new trends.[20]

PROMOTION PLANNING

 9 Identify the factors that influence the selection of promotion-mix ingredients.

A **promotional campaign** is a plan for combining and using the four promotional methods—advertising, personal selling, sales promotion, and public relations—in a particular promotion mix to achieve one or more marketing goals. When selecting promotional methods to include in promotion mixes, it is important to coordinate promotional elements to maximize the total informational and promotional impact on customers. Integrated marketing communication requires a marketer to look at the broad perspective when planning promotional programs and coordinating the total set of communication functions.

In planning a promotional campaign, marketers must answer these two questions:

1. What will be the role of promotion in the overall marketing mix?
2. To what extent will each promotional method be used in the promotion mix?

The answer to the first question depends on the firm's marketing objectives because the role of each element of the marketing mix—product, price, distribution, and promotion—depends on these detailed versions of the firm's marketing goals. The answer to the second question depends on the answer to the first, as well as on the target market.

promotional campaign a plan for combining and using the four promotional methods—advertising, personal selling, sales promotion, and publicity—in a particular promotion mix to achieve one or more marketing goals

Promotion and Marketing Objectives

Promotion is naturally better suited to certain marketing objectives than to others. For example, promotion can do little to further a marketing objective such as "reduce delivery time by one-third." It can, however, be used to inform customers that delivery is faster. Let's consider some objectives that *would* require the use of promotion as a primary ingredient of the marketing mix.

Providing Information This is, of course, the main function of promotion. It may be used to communicate to target markets the availability of new products or product features. It may alert them to special offers or give the locations of retailers that carry a firm's products. In other words, promotion can be used to enhance the effectiveness of each of the other ingredients of the marketing mix.

Increasing Market Share Promotion can be used to convince new customers to try a product while maintaining the product loyalty of established customers. Comparative advertising, for example, is directed mainly at those who might—but presently do not—use a particular product. Advertising that emphasizes the product's features also assures those who *do* use the product that they have made a smart choice. Nature Valley, maker of granola bars, unveiled a new campaign that seeks to increase its already dominant share of the granola bar market. The campaign features a Web site called Nature Valley Trail View, which allows users to virtually hike trails in U.S. national parks. This new promotional campaign is aimed at capturing greater market share by further aligning the Nature Valley brand name with a healthy outdoor lifestyle. Nature Valley gained a 3.9 percent market share and now commands a 41.6 percent share of the market.[21]

Positioning the Product The sales of a product depend, to a great extent, on its competition. The stronger the competition, the more difficult it is to maintain or increase sales. For this reason, many firms go to great lengths to position their products in the marketplace. **Positioning** is the development of a product image in buyers' minds relative to the images they have of competing products.

Promotion is the prime positioning tool. A marketer can use promotion to position a brand away from competitors to avoid competition. Promotion also may be used to position one product directly against another product. For example, in hopes of providing legitimate competition to Apple's iPhone, Motorola is offering the Droid. Looking at its advertising, there is no doubt which phone it is competing against. With statements about its competition like "iDon't have a real keyboard, iDon't allow open development, and iDon't take pictures in the dark," it is very clear that the Droid is positioned head to head with the iPhone.[22]

Stabilizing Sales Special promotional efforts can be used to increase sales during slack periods, such as the "off season" for certain sports equipment. By stabilizing sales in this way, a firm can use its production facilities more effectively and reduce both capital costs and inventory costs. Promotion is also used frequently to increase the sales of products that are in the declining stage of their life-cycles. The objective is to keep them going for a little while longer.

Developing the Promotion Mix

Once the role of promotion is established, the various methods of promotion may be combined in a promotional campaign. As in so many other areas of business, promotion planning begins with a set of specific objectives. The promotion mix then is designed to accomplish these objectives.

Marketers often use several promotion mixes simultaneously if a firm sells multiple products. The selection of promotion-mix ingredients and the degree to which

positioning the development of a product image in buyers' minds relative to the images they have of competing products

they are used depend on the organization's resources and objectives, the nature of the target market, the characteristics of the product, and the feasibility of various promotional methods.

The amount of promotional resources available in an organization influences the number and intensity of promotional methods that marketers can use. A firm with a limited budget for promotion probably will rely on personal selling because the effectiveness of personal selling can be measured more easily than that of advertising. An organization's objectives also have an effect on its promotional activities. A company wishing to make a wide audience familiar with a new convenience item probably will depend heavily on advertising and sales promotion. If a company's objective is to communicate information to consumers—on the features of counter-top appliances, for example—then the company may develop a promotion mix that includes some advertising, some sales promotion to attract consumers to stores, and a lot of personal selling.

The size, geographic distribution, and socioeconomic characteristics of the target market play a part in the composition of a product's promotion mix. If the market is small, personal selling probably will be the most important element in the promotion mix. This is true of organizations that sell to small industrial markets and businesses that use only a few wholesalers to market their products. Companies that need to contact millions of potential customers, however, will emphasize sales promotion and advertising because these methods are relatively inexpensive. The age, income, and education of the target market also will influence the choice of promotion techniques. For example, with less-educated consumers, personal selling may be more effective than ads in newspapers or magazines.

In general, industrial products require a considerable amount of personal selling, whereas consumer goods depend on advertising. This is not true in every case, however. The price of the product also influences the composition of the promotion mix. Because consumers often want the advice of a salesperson on an expensive product, high-priced consumer goods may call for more personal selling. Similarly, advertising and sales promotion may be more crucial to marketers of seasonal items because having a year-round sales force is not always appropriate.

The cost and availability of promotional methods are important factors in the development of a promotion mix. Although national advertising and sales promotion activities are expensive, the cost per customer may be quite small if the campaign succeeds in reaching large numbers of people. In addition, local advertising outlets—newspapers, magazines, radio and television stations, and outdoor displays—may not be that costly for a small local business. In some situations, a firm may find that no available advertising medium reaches the target market effectively.

CRITICISMS OF PROMOTION

 Identify and explain the criticisms of promotion.

Even though promotional activities can help customers to make informed purchasing decisions, social scientists, consumer groups, government agencies, and members of society in general have long criticized promotion. There are two main reasons for such criticism: Promotion does have some flaws, and it is a highly visible business activity that pervades our daily lives. Although people almost universally complain that there is simply too much promotional activity, several more specific issues have been raised. Promotional efforts have been called deceptive. Promotion has been blamed for increasing prices. Other criticisms of promotion are that it manipulates consumers into buying products they do not need, that it leads to a more materialistic society, that customers do not benefit sufficiently from promotion to justify its high costs, and that promotion is used to market potentially harmful products. These issues are discussed in Table 15.3.

motivating sales personnel; creating sales territories; and evaluating sales performance.

 Describe sales promotion objectives and methods.

Sales promotion is the use of activities and materials as direct inducements to customers and salespersons. The primary objective of sales promotion methods is to enhance and supplement other promotional methods. Methods of sales promotion include rebates, coupons, samples, premiums, frequent-user incentives, point-of-purchase displays, trade shows, buying allowances, and cooperative advertising.

 Understand the types and uses of public relations.

Public relations is a broad set of communication activities used to create and maintain favorable relationships between an organization and various public groups, both internal and external. Organizations use a variety of public-relations tools to convey messages and create images. Brochures, newsletters, company magazines, and annual reports are written public-relations tools. Speeches, event sponsorship, and publicity are other public-relations tools. Publicity is communication in news-story form about an organization, its products, or both. Types of publicity include news releases, feature articles, captioned photographs, and press conferences. Public relations can be used to promote people, places, activities, ideas, and even countries. It can be used to enhance the reputation of an organization and also to reduce the unfavorable effects of negative events.

 Identify the factors that influence the selection of promotion-mix ingredients.

A promotional campaign is a plan for combining and using advertising, personal selling, sales promotion, and publicity to achieve one or more marketing goals. Campaign objectives are developed from marketing objectives. Then the promotion mix is developed based on the organization's promotional resources and objectives, the nature of the target market, the product characteristics, and the feasibility of various promotional methods.

 Identify and explain the criticisms of promotion.

Promotion activities can help consumers to make informed purchasing decisions, but they also have evoked many criticisms. Promotion has been accused of deception. Although some deceiving or misleading promotions do exist, laws, government regulation, and industry self-regulation minimize deceptive promotion. Promotion has been blamed for increasing prices, but it usually tends to lower them. When demand is high, production and marketing costs decrease, which can result in lower prices. Promotion also helps to keep prices lower by facilitating price competition. Other criticisms of promotional activity are that it manipulates consumers into buying products they do not need, that it leads to a more materialistic society, and that consumers do not benefit sufficiently from promotional activity to justify its high cost. Finally, some critics of promotion suggest that potentially harmful products, especially those associated with violence, sex, and unhealthy activities, should not be promoted at all.

KEY TERMS

You should now be able to define and give an example relevant to each of the following terms:

promotion (424)
promotion mix (424)
integrated marketing
   communications (425)
advertising (426)
personal selling (426)
sales promotion (426)
public relations (426)
primary-demand
   advertising (427)
selective-demand (or brand)
   advertising (427)

institutional advertising (427)
advertising media (428)
direct-mail advertising (429)
Yellow Pages advertising (429)
out-of-home advertising (430)
infomercial (430)
advertising agency (435)
order-getter (436)
creative selling (436)
order-taker (436)
sales support personnel (436)
missionary salesperson (436)

trade salesperson (437)
technical salesperson (437)
consumer sales promotion
   method (439)
trade sales promotion
   method (439)
rebate (439)
coupon (440)
sample (440)
premium (441)
frequent-user incentive (441)
point-of-purchase display (441)

trade show (441)
buying allowance (441)
cooperative advertising (441)
publicity (442)
news release (442)
feature article (442)
captioned photograph (442)
press conference (442)
promotional campaign (443)
positioning (444)

REVIEW QUESTIONS

1. What is integrated marketing communications, and why is it becoming increasingly accepted?
2. Identify and describe the major ingredients of a promotion mix.
3. What is the major role of promotion?

4. How are selective-demand, institutional, and primary-demand advertising different from one another? Give an example of each.
5. List the four major print media, and give an advantage and a disadvantage of each.

6. Which types of firms use radio, television, and the Internet?
7. Outline the main steps involved in developing an advertising campaign.
8. Why would a firm with its own advertising department use an ad agency?
9. Identify and give examples of the three major types of salespersons.
10. Explain how each step in the personal-selling process leads to the next step.
11. What are the major tasks involved in managing a sales force?

12. What are the major differences between consumer and trade sales promotion methods? Give examples of each.
13. What is cooperative advertising? What sorts of firms use it?
14. What is the difference between publicity and public relations? What is the purpose of each?
15. Why is promotion particularly effective in positioning a product? In stabilizing or increasing sales?
16. What factors determine the specific promotion mix that a firm should use?
17. Is promotion deceptive? What is your evidence that it is or is not deceptive?

DISCUSSION QUESTIONS

1. Discuss the pros and cons of comparative advertising from the viewpoint of (a) the advertiser, (b) the advertiser's competitors, and (c) the target market.
2. Which kinds of advertising—in which media—influence you most? Why?
3. Which kinds of retail outlets or products require mainly order-taking by salespeople?
4. A number of companies have shifted a portion of their promotion dollars from advertising to trade sales promotion methods. Why?

5. Why would a producer offer refunds or cents-off coupons rather than simply lowering the price of its products?
6. How can public-relations efforts aimed at the general public help an organization?
7. Why do firms use event sponsorship?
8. What kind of promotion mix might be used to extend the life of a product that has entered the declining stage of its product life-cycle?

Video Case 15.1

L.L.Bean Employs a Variety of Promotion Methods to Communicate with Customers

Perhaps best known for its beloved mail-order catalog, L.L.Bean was recently placed near the top of Photobrand's list of New England's most powerful brands, beating Ethan Allen and Yankee Candle. L.L.Bean has grown from its founding as a one-product firm in 1912 to a national brand with 14 stores in 10 different states and a thriving online store. Net sales are over $1.5 billion a year.

Marketing communications are more sophisticated now than they were when Leon Leonwood Bean created his first product, a waterproof boot, and publicized it with a homemade brochure. In its early days, the firm thrived on word-of-mouth communication about its reliability and the expert advice of its founder, himself an avid outdoorsman. Determined to build his company and his mailing list, Bean poured all of the company's profits into advertising and talked about the company with one and all. Said one neighbor at the time, "If you drop in just to shake his hand, you get home to find his catalog in your mailbox."

Now the company makes use of marketing database systems to manage and update its mailing lists. The L.L.Bean catalog swelled in size in the 1980s and 1990s, but it has slimmed down as the company's Web site has taken over some of the task of promoting the company's products. The catalog, still a major communication tool for the firm, is also a multiple-industry award-winner. The company uses computer-modeling tools to help it identify what customers want and sends them only the catalogs they desire. Still, says the vice president of stores, "What we find is most customers want some sort of touch point," and the catalog remains very popular.

Online orders recently surpassed mail and phone orders for the first time in the company's history. The relationship between the catalog and the Web site is complicated. As L.L.Bean's vice president for e-commerce explains, customers have begun to shift much of their buying to the Internet, but they still rely on the catalog to browse, plan, and get ideas. Customers take their L.L.Bean catalogs "to soccer games, they read them in the car," she says. "What's changed is what they do next"—often they go online to find more details about an item or to place an order.

L.L.Bean still places print advertising, sometimes small ads that simply offer a free catalog or remind customers that they already have the catalog at home. Since the catalog is expensive to produce, the company tries to support it with other marketing media so it doesn't get lost among all the other messages demanding customers' attention.

A big and growing area for the company's promotion efforts is the Internet, where it uses banner ads on popular sites like Hulu.com allowing customers to click through to the L.L.Bean online store. It also maintains a Facebook page, a Twitter account, and a YouTube channel. The company invests heavily in television advertising as well, particularly around the holidays. Local TV ads are concentrated in the areas around the company's retail stores.

16

Exploring Social Media and e-Business

LEARNING OBJECTIVES

Once you complete this chapter, you will be able to:

1 Examine why it is important for a business to use social media.

2 Discuss how businesses use social media tools.

3 Explain the business objectives for using social media.

4 Describe how businesses develop a social media plan.

5 Explain the meaning of e-business.

6 Understand the fundamental models of e-business.

7 Identify the factors that will affect the future of the Internet, social media, and e-business.

Inside BUSINESS

The Big Business of Angry Birds

A game that didn't exist until 2009 has rocketed its parent company into the big time with $100 million in annual revenue and millions of fans worldwide. Rovio Entertainment, based in Finland, created Angry Birds as a game application in which players use slingshots to send red birds hurtling toward green pigs. The company also started a Facebook page to spread the word and, a few months later, a blog to announce its news and connect with fans.

Within a year, 50 million people had downloaded Angry Birds to smartphones, iPads, and other electronic gadgets, playing either the free version (surrounded by ads) or paying to upgrade to premium versions. For less than the price of a latte, many players were happy to buy access to the game's highest levels. Before the game's third anniversary, the number of players had soared to 500 million, earning Rovio a healthy profit and a global fan base eager for more games and game-related merchandise.

To make the most of the game's popularity, Rovio developed a line of shirts and toys for sale through its e-business online store. Soon it was selling 1 million stuffed pigs and birds plus 1 million branded T-shirts every month through its Web site, along with seasonal items such as Halloween costumes. Then Rovio licensed its brand so that authorized products could be marketed through Amazon.com and other online businesses, as well as in traditional stores. Several times a year, Rovio released new Angry Birds games, some geared to seasonal events (such as the Chinese New Year) and some taking the birds-versus-pigs rivalry to new heights (outer space). Social media helped fuel the frenzy as players compared notes online about their triumphs and frustrations with the latest game variations.

Now, with nearly 1 billion downloads, Angry Birds has transformed the way Rovio makes money, allowing it to move beyond games into other goods and services. "We only care about two things, our fans and our brand," says the chief marketing officer, who views Angry Birds as an entertainment brand for movies, theme parks, and clothing, just like the Disney animated movie characters.[1]

Did You Know?

Rovio Entertainment, the parent company of Angry Birds, rings up more than $100 million every year from global sales of game-related goods and services.

For Rovio Entertainment, the company profiled in the Inside Business feature for this chapter, Angry Birds is big business! With nearly 1 billion downloads and $100 million in annual revenue from global sales of stuffed animals, T-shirts, and other game-related merchandise, Angry Birds and its parent company Rovio Entertainment provide a good example of how fast social media and e-business have developed and the degree to which they are changing the way people live their lives. Take a moment to think about how social media and technology affect your own life. In just a few short years, it has changed the way we communicate with each other, it has changed the way we meet people, and it has changed the way we shop. In this chapter, we explore how these trends affect both individuals and businesses.

We begin this chapter by examining why social media is important for both individuals and business firms. Next, we discuss how companies can use social media to build relationships with customers, the goals for social media usage, and the steps required to build a social media plan and measure the effectiveness of a firm's social media activities. In the last part of this chapter, we take a close look at how firms use technology to conduct business on the Internet and what growth opportunities and challenges affect both social media and e-businesses.

Examine why it is important for a business to use social media.

WHY IS SOCIAL MEDIA IMPORTANT?

If you are a "digital native" (anyone under the age of 32), you know exactly what social media is because you have grown up with technology and are very comfortable sharing information about yourself. If you are anyone else, social media seems like a strange (but exciting) phenomenon where millions of people freely share, create, vote, and connect with other people effortlessly using Internet-based technologies.

What Is Social Media and How Popular Is It?

Today, there are many definitions of social media because it is still developing and continually changing. For our purposes, **social media** represents the online interactions that allow people and businesses to communicate and share ideas, personal information, and information about products and services. Simply put: Social media is about people. It is about a culture of participation, meaning that people can now discuss, vote, create, connect, and advocate much easier than ever before. For

FIGURE 16.1 Timeline of Major Technology Events and Social Media

Like computer technology, developments in social media have been not only rapid, they have also changed the way people connect.

	TECHNOLOGY BREAKTHROUGH
1966	• E-mail
1969	• Advanced Research Projects Agency Network (ARPANET), Compuserve
1979	• USENET
1986	• LISTSERV
1991	• AOL
1995	• Classmates.com; Yahoo
1996	• AOL instant messenger
1998	• MoveOn.org, Google
1999	• Napster, Blogger, Epinions, LiveJournal
2001	• Wikipedia, StumbleUpon
2002	• Friendster, Technorati
2003	• LinkedIn, Wordpress, MySpace, Hi5, Photobucket, Delicious
2004	• Gmail, Flickr, Facebook, Yelp, Digg, Orkut
2005	• YouTube, Mashable, Reddit, Bebo
2006	• Twitter, Ustream
2007	• Tumblr
2008	• Apple's App Store
2009	• Foursquare, Google Wave
2010	• Pinterest,
2011	• Google +
2012	• Facebook sells stock to the public
The Future	• Who knows what the next generation of social media will mean for both individuals and business?

© CENGAGE LEARNING 2014

social media the online interactions that allow people and businesses to communicate and share ideas, personal information, and information about products and services

example, you can post your plans for a weekend trip on Facebook. Then you can share a travel itinerary and chronicle your trip through videos, photos, and ratings on Facebook. People can also use Twitter to raise awareness about bone-marrow donations in order to help a friend find a match. While it's hard to imagine, many popular social media sites like Facebook and Twitter were just created in the past decade (see Figure 16.1).

So how popular is social media? A recent Pew Internet Research study showed that more than two-thirds of online adults use some sort of social media platform like Facebook, LinkedIn, or Twitter. Most of them say staying in touch with family and friends is their primary reason for using social media and roughly half say that reconnecting with old friends is a major reason why they use social media. Other reasons like connecting with people who share interests, making new friends, and reading comments by public figures are less important.[2]

©YURI ARCURS/SHUTTERSTOCK

A new kind of family time. Today, technology has changed the way people communicate and share ideas, personal information, and information about products and services. In this photo, mom, dad, and the kids could be looking at pictures of relatives or reading movie reviews or sending an email to grandma—all social media activities.

Why Businesses Use Social Media

Social media has completely changed the business environment. Early on, companies saw potential in the sheer number of people using social media and that made using social media a top priority for many business firms. By using social media, companies could share information about their products and services and improve customer service. To date (and by the time you read this, the number will be higher), Facebook has not only one of the largest social networks with more than 850 million users, but also one of the "stickiest" Web sites, meaning that a lot of people spend a lot of time on Facebook.[3] As a result, many companies have flocked to build Facebook pages, develop contests, create Facebook ads, and find ways to get as many people as possible to "like" them on Facebook. Coca-Cola, for example, is one of the most effective marketers using Facebook, with more than 41 million likes to date.[4] For more information about why businesses use social media (and the benefits for a business), see Figure 16.2.

The fact that so many people are actively sharing information about themselves and their likes and dislikes online for all to see was a driving force behind many companies' attempts to develop a social media presence. Unlike social media, traditional marketing messages were top down—meaning that companies used television and magazine ads to promote their product to a large audience without any opportunity for feedback. Discussions about products were limited to consumers'

| FIGURE 16.2 | The Five Most Important Benefits for a Business that Uses Social Media |

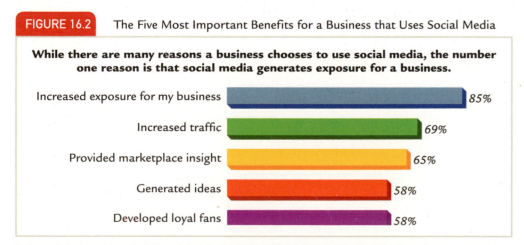

While there are many reasons a business chooses to use social media, the number one reason is that social media generates exposure for a business.

Increased exposure for my business — 85%
Increased traffic — 69%
Provided marketplace insight — 65%
Generated ideas — 58%
Developed loyal fans — 58%

Source: Michael A. Stelzner, "2012 Social Media Marketing Industry Report," The SocialMediaExaminer.com Web site at www.socialmediaexaminer.com, accessed August 14, 2012.

immediate circle of friends and family. With social media, this is no longer the case. If a person has a bad experience with a product or service, they tend to post it on their blog or on Facebook, or tweet about it. A few years ago, Dell, Inc., experienced the wrath of a customer when blogger Jeff Jarvis posted a series of rants called "Dell Hell" after purchasing a Dell laptop. The post caught the attention of others who experienced similar problems; these consumers then proceeded to voice their own Dell Hell stories. As a result, more people knew about the company's mistakes than ever before. Jarvis continued to voice his experience with Dell's customer service department, which at the time was not very effective or responsive. After the story hit the mainstream press and their customer service ratings began to suffer, Dell finally developed a corporate initiative aimed at listening to customers and fixing its customer service problems.[5] Now Dell is considered a leader in monitoring social media and listening to customers. The bottom line: Because of social media, companies no longer have much control over what is said about their products or services, and many are not yet comfortable with the new roles set forth by a consumer-dominated culture.

Discuss how businesses use social media tools. ②

SOCIAL MEDIA TOOLS FOR BUSINESS USE

For a business, part of what makes social media so challenging is the sheer number of ways to interact with other businesses and both existing and potential consumers. Companies are using social media because it allows the company to

- connect with customers;
- listen to its main stakeholders (including but not limited to customers);
- provide another means of customer service;
- develop content that is valuable to customers; and
- engage customers in product development and formulation.

Social content sites allow companies to create and share information about their products and services via blogs, videos, photos, and podcasts. For businesses selling to other businesses, social content sites can also include webinars and online informational promotional materials. For an overview of how businesses can use social media tools, take another look at Figure 16.2.

Business Use of Blogs

For businesses, blogs have become one of the most widely used tools for the effective use of social media. A **blog** is a Web site that allows a company to share information in order to increase customers' knowledge about its products and services, as well as to build trust. Once a story or information is posted, customers can provide feedback through comments, which is one of the most important ways of creating a conversation between business firms and consumers. Some experts believe that every company should have a blog that speaks to current and potential customers, not as customers, but as people.[6]

Blogs are effective at developing better relationships with customers, attracting new customers, telling stories about the company's products or services, and providing an active forum for testing new ideas. For example, Southwest Airlines' *Nuts about Southwest* blog (www.blogsouthwest.com) provides information about the company and allows customers to interact with company employees. By including information

social content sites allow companies to create and share information about their products and services

blog a Web site that allows a company to share information in order to not only increase the customer's knowledge about its products and services, but also to build trust

about webinars and promotional materials, blogs are also effective for businesses that are selling to other businesses.

Photos, Videos, and Podcasts

In addition to blogs, another tool for social content is **media sharing sites**, which allow users to upload multimedia content including photos, videos, and podcasts. Before participating in media sharing, consider the following three factors.

- Who will create the photos, videos, and podcasts that will be used?
- How will the content be distributed to interested businesses and consumers?
- How much will it cost to create and distribute the material?

Podcasts can be not only informative, but also inspirational. As the wife of a retired army sergeant and an army veteran herself, Victoria Parham knows what it is like to experience long separations, job instability, and single parenthood that come with the military lifestyle. Today she shares her experiences and solutions to everyday problems in a free twice-monthly podcast created to inspire, educate, and entertain military spouses.

Today, photo sharing provides a method for companies to tell a compelling story about its products or services through postings on either the company's Web site or a social media site.

Videos have also gained popularity because of their inherent ability to tell stories. Entertainment companies, for example, now traditionally use YouTube as a way to showcase movie trailers. And Home Depot has also posted great do-it-yourself videos on its YouTube channel. Companies know that YouTube, Flickr, and others sites are useful because they are already recognized by other businesses and consumers as a source of both entertainment and information. YouTube is the largest video site and one of the largest general sites in the United States. YouTube is not only large (in terms of visitors), but the characteristics of its users are evenly split among different age groups and sexes.

Podcasts are digital audio or video files that people listen to or watch online on tablets, computers, MP3 players, or smartphones. Think of podcasts as radio shows that are distributed through various means (like iTunes) and not linked to a scheduled time period. The great thing about podcasts is that they are available for download at any time. Both National Public Radio (NPR) and the *New York Times* have used podcasts to share news and information.

Social Media Ratings

Social media enables shoppers to access opinions, recommendations, and referrals from others within and outside of their own social circles. This type of information is available via a social media site and can include reviews and ratings, as well as information on sales promotions programs like Groupon and LivingSocial. Both of these sites provide information about companies that offer deep discounts to customers that redeem an offer.

Sites for ratings and reviews are based on the idea that consumers trust the opinions of others when it comes to purchasing products and services. According to Nielsen Media Research, more than 70 percent of consumers said that they trust online consumer opinions.[7] This statistic was much higher when compared with the same type of research for traditional advertising. Based on the early work of Amazon and eBay, new sites have sprung up allowing consumers to rate local businesses or compare products and services. One of the most popular, Yelp, combines customer ratings with social networking and is now the largest local review directory on the Web.

Social Games

Social games are another area of growth in social media. A **social game** is "a multiplayer, competitive, goal-oriented activity with defined rules of engagement and online connectivity among a community of players."[8] One of the most important aspects of social media is entertainment and games like Angry Birds and FarmVille serve that purpose. Indeed, research shows that the "gamification" of social media is a huge trend because people like the competition, social status, and rewards that they can earn through social gaming.[9] For businesses that create games, it can be very profitable. As mentioned in the Inside Business

media sharing sites allow users to upload multimedia content including photos, videos, and podcasts

podcasts digital audio or video files that people listen to or watch online on tablets, computers, MP3 players, or smartphones

social game a multiplayer, competitive, goal-oriented activity with defined rules of engagement and online connectivity among a community of players

feature for this chapter, Rovio Entertainment, the parent company of Angry Birds, rings up more than $100 million every year from global sales of game-related goods and services. While some businesses elect to create their own games, others choose to place advertising into a game. For example, the search engine Bing placed ads within the Facebook game FarmVille and gained several hundred thousand Facebook fans as a result.[10]

ACHIEVING BUSINESS OBJECTIVES THROUGH SOCIAL MEDIA

Although the popularity of social media is a recent phenomenon, many businesses are already using it to achieve important objectives. Some of these goals are long-term—such as building brand awareness and brand reputation—while others are more short-term—such as increasing Web site traffic or generating sales leads. Regardless of how social media is used, there are a lot of business opportunities. In this section, we explore a few ways that companies have used social media effectively to achieve business objectives.

Social Media Communities

For a business, social media can be used to build a community. **Social media communities** are social networks based on the relationships among people.[11] These electronic communities encourage two-way communication, allow for people to develop profiles, and identify other people to connect with by using technology and the Internet. People in each community can be called friends, fans, followers, or connections. Popular social networking sites include Facebook (the largest), LinkedIn (for professionals), Twitter, Google+, YouTube, Pinterest, and many others. To see how many businesses use the top four social media community sites, see Figure 16.3.

There are social communities for every interest, ethnic group, and lifestyle. Different types of social communities include forums and wikis. Forums were perhaps the earliest form of social community. A **forum** is an interactive version of a community bulletin board that focuses on threaded discussions. These are particularly popular with people who share a common interest such as video games. Another community based on social media is a wiki. A **wiki** is a collaborative online working space that enables members to contribute content that is then sharable with other people. With wikis, members of the community are the editors and gatekeepers ensuring that the content is correct and updated. Wikipedia—the free online encyclopedia—is the best example of a wiki. A community of unpaid experts voluntarily keeps the content on the Wikipedia Web site as updated and accurate as possible.

The whole purpose of social networks is to build communities and develop connections. Today, many companies are using social media to build communities with other businesses and consumers in order to achieve business objectives. Recently, Pepsi used social media to showcase its commitment to real-world communities by shifting the $20 million typically spent on Super Bowl advertising to a Web site that allowed customers to post

social media communities social networks based on the relationships among people

forum an interactive version of a community bulletin board that focuses on threaded discussions

wiki a collaborative online working space that enables members to contribute content that is then sharable with other people

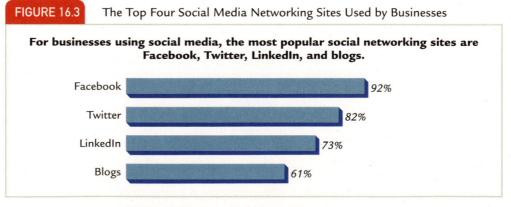

FIGURE 16.3   The Top Four Social Media Networking Sites Used by Businesses

For businesses using social media, the most popular social networking sites are Facebook, Twitter, LinkedIn, and blogs.

Facebook	92%
Twitter	82%
LinkedIn	73%
Blogs	61%

Source: Michael A. Stelzner, "2012 Social Media Marketing Industry Report," The SocialMediaExaminer.com Web site at www.socialmediaexaminer.com, accessed August 14, 2012.

ideas for helping their own communities in areas like education and the environment. The driving force behind its "Refresh Everything" campaign was the belief that the company needed to "walk the walk" and really do something to make an impact. The Pepsi Refresh Project allowed people to upload their ideas or vote for their favorites. Pepsi then funded projects with the most votes. More than 57 million customers voted on different ideas—all designed to improve communities. For Pepsi, this social media project enabled the soft-drink giant to engage its customers who are heavy social media users.[12]

Crisis and Reputation Management

One of the most important reasons for listening to stakeholders is to determine whether there is a crisis brewing. A majority of companies believe that their company is less than a year away from some potential crisis moment and monitor social media for conversations that may predict a crisis.[13] Recently, the organization Susan G. Komen for the Cure decided to withdraw its funding for Planned Parenthood. Immediately, Planned Parenthood sent out an e-mail to its donors in an effort to replace the lost funding. As the news traveled from e-mail to social media, many people expressed their outrage that Komen for the Cure was playing a "political card." According to social media experts, the response from the Komen organization to negative publicity was inadequate. The Komen organization failed to address the issue on Facebook or Twitter even after mainstream media began reporting its controversial decision. It was not until the next day when Nancy Brinker, founder of Susan G. Komen for the Cure, talked about the issue, but by then the organization's public image had already been tarnished.

United Airlines also found out the hard way what happens when customers complain to social networks. Guitarist Dave Carroll accused United Airlines of breaking his guitar during baggage handling in Chicago. After months of moving through the traditional channels and getting nowhere, Dave wrote a song, filmed a video, and posted it on YouTube. He also had friends send out the link to their networks. Soon the video had thousands of views and people started sharing their own negative United Airlines stories. United did try to control the damage on Twitter, but most people saw it as an empty promise to improve customer service. Soon the company was embroiled in bad press (in social media as well as mainstream media), which eventually caused their stock price to fall 10 percent. In the end, it is estimated that neglecting to attend to customer needs cost United Airlines about $180 million.[14]

Listening to Stakeholders

Listening to people, whether they are customers or not, is always an important aspect of a company's social media plan. Indeed, listening is often the first step when developing a social media strategy. Listening to the conversations unfolding on Facebook or Twitter, for example, can be important to understanding just what people think about a company's products and services. By monitoring Facebook, Twitter, and other social media sites, Domino's Pizza found out that people were not very happy with its product quality. Customers described the sauce as "tasting like ketchup" and the crust as "tasting like cardboard." Unfortunately, there were enough comments of a similar nature for the company to use traditional marketing research to verify this information. They found the sentiment to be true and the company then developed a plan to reinvent every aspect of the company—and its pizza products. Did the plan work? Same store sales increased more than 14 percent.[15]

Targeting Customers

Many companies are using social media to increase awareness and build their brand among customers. It is especially valuable in targeting the Millennials. **Millennials** are tech-savvy digital natives born after 1980. When Ford wanted to introduce its

Social media: A new way to handle a crisis.
For years, Walmart—the world's largest retailer—has tried to repair a reputation that's been damaged by decades of criticism and legal problems. Now Walmart has a new public relations tool—social media—to not only monitor what people are saying about the company, but also to tell its side of the story when controversies develop.

Millennials tech-savvy digital natives born after 1980

subcompact car, the Fiesta, to Millennials, it used social media. Ford chose to target Millennials because, as a group, they are also more likely than older consumers to purchase a subcompact car. For this social media promotion, Ford recruited 100 social media users, dubbed "agents," who were given a Ford Fiesta to drive for six months. The only requirement was that each agent talked about the car on social media—using video, posts on Facebook and Twitter, and other social media sites. Initially, Ford set a goal of attracting 144,000 Web site visitors, but by the end of the promotion more than 300,000 people had viewed the Web site. Additional results showed that Ford's social media marketing promotion for the Fiesta worked well and social media could be used to build brand recognition with a specific group of people.[16]

In some cases, awareness is not a problem, but the ability to connect with the customer is. Social media can be used to build that connection. Consider the case of Old Spice. Once thought of as an "old man's" cologne, Old Spice struggled to gain attention for its body wash product in an industry dominated by newcomers like Axe—a brand that had done a very good job of connecting with Millennial men. Old Spice decided to use social media to reposition its body wash with a video launched on YouTube. The video was launched online during the Super Bowl, and then on network television later. The results were so positive that Old Spice followed up with a campaign using online videos based on comments from customers posted on Twitter and Facebook.[17]

Social Media Marketing

According to a survey by eMarketer, 80 percent of U.S. companies with more than 100 employees are using social media tools for marketing. Among small business, the rate of social media use for marketing is closer to 40 percent, and among businesses selling to other businesses, the rate is around 24 percent.[18] **Social media marketing** is the "utilization of social media technologies, channels, and software to create, communicate, deliver and exchange offerings that have value for an organization."[19] As companies become more comfortable with social media, we can expect even more companies to use social media to market products and services to their customers. Already, research indicates that companies are shifting their advertising money from traditional marketing (like television and magazines) to digital marketing (like Internet search engines and social media). Experts now predict that social media will account for 26 percent of all online spending by 2016.[20] The primary reason is simple. People are spending more time online.[21] Often the first step for a business that wants to use social media is to go to LinkedIn, Facebook, or Twitter. As you can tell from the information in Figure 16.4, companies like LinkedIn make using their technology as easy as possible to connect with potential or existing customers.

Today, many companies have been quite successful using social media marketing not only to develop customer awareness, but also to obtain sales leads and increase actual sales. HubSpot, for example, is a software company that helps small and medium-sized companies develop inbound marketing programs. **Inbound marketing** is a marketing term that describes new ways of gaining attention, and ultimately, customers, by creating content on a Web site that pulls customers in. Tools used for inbound marketing programs include search engine optimization, blogging, videos, and social media. In order to market its software products, the software company HubSpot shunned traditional advertising and began to practice what it preached. First, the company developed its own inbound marketing program by creating valuable content and marketing information that was then distributed through social media and search engine Web sites. Companies interested in HubSpot's software were required to enter contact information (name, phone number, and e-mail address) in order to view the information. People provided contact information because they believed the company's software could help them improve their marketing activities. As a result of HubSpot's inbound marketing program, the cost of generating new sales leads was five to seven times less than leads generated by more traditional marketing activities and as a bonus they gained thousands of new customers.[22]

social media marketing the utilization of social media technologies, channels, and software to create, communicate, deliver, and exchange offerings that have value for an organization

inbound marketing a marketing term that describes new ways of gaining attention and ultimately customers by creating content on a Web site that pulls customers in

FIGURE 16.4　LinkedIn's Marketing Solutions for Other Businesses

Like many popular social media communities, LinkedIn's marketing tools make it easy to connect with potential or existing customers.

COURTESY, SUSAN VAN ETTEN

Dell also uses social media to sell its computer and technology products. Unlike other companies experimenting with social media, Dell decided to be more visible and actively use social media to increase sales by using Twitter. The company has sold computers valued at more than $6.5 million by including links in its Twitter account to the DellOutlet Web site. While this represents a tiny percentage of total sales, it does show that products can be sold through social media.[23]

As important as social media is, it is only one aspect of digital marketing. Indeed, digital marketing or online marketing is comprised of several areas, including

- online public relations—developing social media press kits;
- search engine optimization—using keywords in the Web site in order to rank higher in search engine results;
- search engine marketing—buying ads like Google's AdWords to increase traffic to a company's Web site;
- display advertising—buying banner ads;
- e-mail marketing—targeting customers through opt-in email campaigns; and
- content marketing—developing photos, videos, podcasts, blog posts, and other tools to increase the value to the customer.

Generating New Product Ideas

Companies can use social media to conduct much of their consumer-based research. Using insight gained from Facebook or Twitter, for example, allows a company to modify existing products and services and develop new ones. **Crowdsourcing** involves outsourcing tasks to a group of people in order to tap into the ideas of the crowd. In some cases valuable information can be obtained by crowd voting. Frito Lay, for example, has used crowd voting for the last few years when they allowed

crowdsourcing outsourcing tasks to a group of people in order to tap into the ideas of the crowd

© AP PHOTO/ZEF NIKOLIA/DSPD

The face of social media. While many people use Facebook to connect with friends and relatives, the world's largest social media site is so much more! For many businesses, Facebook has created new ways to market their products and services and connect with potential or existing customers. Experts predict that the use of social media sites like Facebook will only increase in the future because people are spending more time online.

Career SUCCESS

Make a Good Impression Using Social Media

When you use social media to promote yourself to potential employers, what you post and how often you post can affect your ability to make a good impression.

- *Do: Show your professional side.* The first thing a visitor will notice is your photo—so be sure you look as professional as you would at an interview. Consider posting a brief "interview" video in which you answer a few questions that employers typically ask, such as what your career goals are or why you're interested in a particular industry. Include a contact link, with an e-mail address that matches the image you want to project.

- *Don't: Post inappropriate material.* One recruiter says he and his colleagues don't judge applicants based on their personal posts, but "we will judge their judgment for putting it on the Internet" if text or photos are offensive or racy. The

head of a marketing research agency warns about using a lot of profanity online. An executive at the Hill Holliday ad agency doesn't like to "see a lot of posts about nothing or points of view that are judgmental or not open-minded. Inappropriate pictures can also [make] a bad impression."

- *Don't: Post too often.* Although many employers welcome active users of social media, they steer clear of applicants who post too often. "Too many Twitter posts from 9 to 5 might make us wonder how you find time for your real job," says the CEO of Zipcar.

Sources: Based on information in Rachel Barsky, "Career Tip Tuesday: How to Leverage Social Media in Your Job Search," *Fox News*, April 3, 2012, www.foxnews.com; Megan Marrs, "The First Step to Building Your Personal Brand," *Forbes*, February 14, 2012, www.forbes.com; Gerrit Hall, "4 Tips for Optimizing Your Resume with Social Media," *Mashable*, November 20, 2011, www.mashable.com; Scott Kirsner, "Social Media Advice for Job-Seekers," *Boston Globe*, September 9, 2011, www.boston.com.

---

people to create and then vote for their favorite television spots for its popular Doritos brand. The winners are then featured during the Super Bowl. Their effort "Crash the Super Bowl" has been wildly successful.[24]

Companies can even build communities for specific brands in order to obtain information and new ideas from consumers. A few years ago, Starbucks built a network called Mystarbucksidea.com that allowed customers to post ideas about how the company could improve. Since the creation of the Web site, thousands of ideas have been posted about Starbucks products, the customer's store experience, and the company's community involvement. The site also enables people to vote on the best ideas, many of which Starbucks has already implemented. For example, getting a free coffee on your birthday if you are a Gold Member or developing a VIP program were both originally customer ideas. In cases such as this one, customers appreciate the ability to share their ideas with a company to whom they are loyal, only to receive reciprocal loyalty when the company implements their ideas.[25]

Recruiting Employees

For years, companies have used current employees to recruit new employees based on the theory that "birds of a feather flock together." The concept is simple: Current employees' friends and family may prove to be good job candidates. Social media takes that concept to a whole new level. LinkedIn, the largest social network for professionals, has been used quite effectively by both large and small companies to recruit employees. Indeed, more than half of *Fortune* 100 companies use LinkedIn to recruit future employees. Using LinkedIn is beneficial for companies because it saves time and lowers recruiting costs. And using a site like LinkedIn also allows employers to see more information about candidates. Companies like Accenture, Home Depot, IBM, and Oracle have all had success with LinkedIn.

How do companies find the right employee?
Answer: More and more companies are using social media sites to recruit employees. Sites like LinkedIn, the largest social network for professionals, are often used by both large and small companies to advertise current job openings and reach out to potential employees located not only in the United States, but also in other parts of the world.

DEVELOPING A SOCIAL MEDIA PLAN

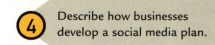
4 Describe how businesses develop a social media plan.

Before developing a plan to use social media, it is important to determine how social media can improve the organization's overall performance and how it "fits" with a company's other operational and promotional activities. For example, if a social media plan attempts to improve customer service, it needs to link to the company's overall organizational efforts to improve customer service.

Steps to Build a Social Media Plan

Once it is determined how social media links to the company's other activities, there are several steps that should be considered.

Step 1: Listen to Determine Opportunities Often social media is used to "listen" to what customers like and don't like about a company's products or services. For example, reading comments on social media sites can yield some insight into how consumers are reacting to a price increase or decrease for an existing product or service. Monitoring social media sites also allows managers and employees to enter the conversation and tell the company's side of the story. In addition, companies can monitor social media sites to gather information about competitors as well as what is being said about the industry.

After the listening phase, it is important to analyze the information to identify the company's strengths and weaknesses. For a company, it is also important to identify opportunities and threats before taking the next step—setting objectives.

Step 2: Establish Social Media Objectives After listening to and analyzing the information obtained from social media sites, it is important to use that information to develop specific objectives. For social media, an objective is a specific statement about what a social media plan should accomplish. Each objective should be specific, measurable, achievable, realistic, and oriented toward the future.

For most companies, the most popular objectives are increasing brand awareness, acquiring new customers, introducing new products, retaining current customers, and gaining customer insight.[26] Other objectives that are often important include improving search engine ranking, showcasing public relations activities, increasing Web site traffic, and generating sales leads.[27] All objectives need to be clear and linked to specific actions that can be used to accomplish each objective.

Step 3: Segment and Target the Social Customer Ideally, a company will have developed a customer profile that describes a typical customer in terms of age, income, gender, ethnicity, etc. When segmenting or targeting customers, it also helps to know how they think, how they spend their time, how much they buy, and how often they buy. In fact, more information about potential customers will help you develop a social media plan to achieve a company's objectives. Lack of information about customers can lead to wasted time and money and the inability to successfully achieve the firm's social media objectives. For example, most companies feel that they must use Facebook and Twitter. But if their core customer does not use these social media sites, then it does not make sense to use them. Additionally it is important to really understand how customers use social media.

- Do they create content like photos, videos, blog posts, etc?
- Do they use social media for ratings and reviews?
- Do they post product reviews and ratings on Facebook accounts?
- Do they spend a lot of time using social media?

According to Forrester Research, there are six types of individuals that use social media. Individuals can be classified as creators, critics, collectors, joiners, spectators, or inactives. In addition to the Forrester classifications of social media users, additional information that can help you target just the "right" social media customer is illustrated in Figure 16.5.

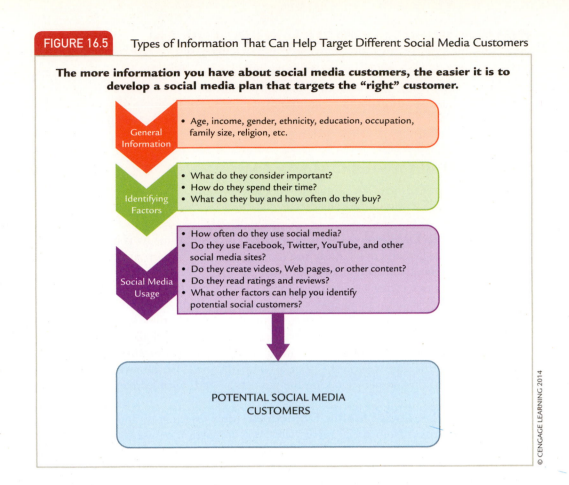

FIGURE 16.5 Types of Information That Can Help Target Different Social Media Customers

The more information you have about social media customers, the easier it is to develop a social media plan that targets the "right" customer.

General Information
- Age, income, gender, ethnicity, education, occupation, family size, religion, etc.

Identifying Factors
- What do they consider important?
- How do they spend their time?
- What do they buy and how often do they buy?

Social Media Usage
- How often do they use social media?
- Do they use Facebook, Twitter, YouTube, and other social media sites?
- Do they create videos, Web pages, or other content?
- Do they read ratings and reviews?
- What other factors can help you identify potential social customers?

POTENTIAL SOCIAL MEDIA CUSTOMERS

© CENGAGE LEARNING 2014

Step 4: Select Social Media Tools The search for the right social media tool(s) usually begins with the company's objectives, outlined in Step 2. It also helps to review the target customer or segment of the market the company is trying to reach (Step 3). With this information, the next step is to choose the right social media tools to reach the right customers. A company can use social communities, blogs, photos, videos, podcasts, or games to reach potential or existing customers. For example, if the goal is to recruit college students for college entry-level jobs, LinkedIn may be a good choice. Remember, it is not necessary (or even advisable) to use all of the above tools. It also helps to remember that social media is not free and can be quite expensive because it costs both time and money.

Step 5: Implement and Integrate the Plan Once social media tools have been identified, a company can implement and integrate the social media plan. Because a social media plan doesn't necessarily have a start and stop date, it is different from traditional advertising campaigns. Some social media activities continue and have a life of their own. For example, Zappos, a very successful and well-respected online retailer, is a company who is always "on" in terms of its social media. Indeed, they do very little traditional advertising and instead rely on social media to promote products, monitor customer service, and enhance the company's reputation. Some companies, on the other hand, feel that it is important to have a mix of short- and long-term social media promotion. In this case, it is important to develop each social media activity to make sure that it is as effective as it can be. For example, if a company is running a Facebook promotion, it is important to consider issues like developing a branded page, updating the page frequently, and providing fresh content to keep customers coming back to the Facebook site. If the same or similar social media activity is used on Twitter, the company must make changes to make sure it works on the Twitter site.

To increase the effectiveness of social media, companies will often integrate online promotions with more traditional or offline promotions. For example, it is not unusual to see the Twitter icon at the end of a television commercial. This signals to consumers that more information about the product or service is provided on Twitter. Indeed, as companies increase the amount of money spent on digital marketing and social media, they will attempt to tie online and offline promotions together in order to get "more bang for the buck."

Measuring and Adapting a Social Media Plan

Because social media is a relatively new method of reaching customers, many companies struggle when attempting to measure social media. Often companies use the same measurements that have been used with long-established media channels like television and radio to determine the effect of social media on the customer's awareness of the company or a specific brand and if sales (and profits) are increasing. Based on this information, the company may try to determine if it is getting a positive return on its investment in social media. Generally, there are two types of social media measurement. While both quantitative and qualitative measurements can be used, most companies tend to use quantitative measurements.

©DAVID J. GREEN-LIFESTYLE 2/ALAMY

Technology that satisfies needs online. Both large and small businesses are using social media to sell products and services to customers 24 hours a day and seven days a week. As an added bonus, today's technology can reach potential and existing customers any place in the world as long as customers have access to the Internet.

Quantitative Social Media Measurement Quantitative social media measurement consists of using numerical measurements, such as counting the number of Web site visitors, number of fans and followers, number of leads generated, and the number of new customers. For example, Coke has 41 million likes on its Facebook page and Dell Computer increases sales revenue by more than $6.5 million by using Twitter. Table 16.1 shows a few popular quantitative ways to measure social media.

Because a company must invest both time and money when it uses social media, it is important to measure the success and make adjustments if needed. In addition to the quantitative measurements already mentioned, a number of companies are using key performance indicators. **Key performance indicators (KPIs)** are measurements that define and measure the progress of an organization toward achieving its objectives. Generally, KPIs are *quantitative* (based on numbers like the number of Twitter followers).

TABLE 16.1	Quantitative Measurements for Selected Social Media Web Sites
Type of Social Media	**Typical Measuremens**
Blogs	• Unique visitors • Number of views • Ratio of visitors to posted comments
Twitter	• Number of followers • Number of tweets and retweets • Click through rate (CTR) of tweeted links • Visits to Web site from tweeted links
Facebook	• Number of fans • Number of likes • Number of comments • Growth of wall response • Visits to Web sites from Facebook links
YouTube	• Number of videos • Number of visitors • Ratio of comments to the number of videos uploaded • Number of embedded links

© CENGAGE LEARNING 2014

quantitative social media measurement using numerical measurements, such as counting the number of Web site visitors, number of fans and followers, number of leads generated, and the number of new customers

key performance indicators (KPIs) measurements that define and measure the progress of an organization toward achieving its objectives

If measuring the success or failure of social media activities with KPIs, the first step is to connect KPIs with objectives. The second step is to set a benchmark—a number that shows what success should look like. For example, Ford said that if 144,000 people visited the Ford Fiesta Web site within a specified time, it would indicate that the company's social media plan to introduce the new subcompact car to Millennials was successful. When measured, more than 300,000 people had visited the Web site. Simply put: The company's social media plan was successful because it surpassed the original benchmark. It is also possible to compare the company's social media KPIs to its benchmarks over time. When trend comparison is used to measure the effectiveness of social media, the trend may be more important than the actual percentage of increase or decrease for just one measurement period.

Qualitative Social Media Measurement Qualitative social media measurement is the process of accessing the opinions and beliefs about a brand. This process primarily uses sentiment analysis to categorize what is being said about a company. Sentiment analysis is a measurement that uses technology to detect the mood, attitudes, or emotions of people who experience a social media activity. Other measurements for determining customer sentiment include:

- *Customer satisfaction score*—defined as the relative satisfaction of customers.
- *Issue resolution rate*—the percentage of customer service inquiries resolved satisfactorily using social media.
- *Resolution time*—defined as the amount of time taken to resolve customer service issues.

When compared to quantitative measurement, it should be noted that many of these qualitative social media measurements are more subjective in nature.

Regardless of the type of measurement used, one of the most powerful aspects of social media—and indeed digital marketing—is the ability to tie the objectives of a social media plan to the results that were achieved. After reviewing results for social media activities against pre-established benchmarks and analyzing trends, changes can be made to increase the effectiveness of social media activities.

Social media is particularly important to businesses that use e-business to sell their products and services online. In the next section, we take a close look at how e-business firms are organized, satisfy needs online, and earn profits.

Explain the meaning of e-business.

DEFINING E-BUSINESS

In Chapter 1, we defined *business* as the organized effort of individuals to produce and sell, for a profit, the products and services that satisfy society's needs. In a simple sense, then, **e-business**, or **electronic business**, can be defined as the organized effort of individuals to produce and sell, for a profit, the products and services that satisfy society's needs *through the facilities available on the Internet*. Sometimes people use the term *e-commerce* instead of *e-business*. In a strict sense, e-business is used when you're talking about all business activities and practices conducted on the Internet by an individual firm or industry. On the other hand, e-commerce is a part of e-business and usually refers only to buying and selling activities conducted online. In this chapter, we generally use the term *e-business* because of its broader definition and scope. As you will see in the remainder of this chapter, e-business is transforming key business activities.

Organizing e-Business Resources

As noted in Chapter 1, to be organized, a business must combine *human, material, informational,* and *financial resources*. This is true of e-business, too (see Figure 16.6), but in this case, the resources may be more specialized than in a typical business. For example, people who can design, create, and maintain Web sites are only a fraction of the specialized human resources required by e-businesses. Material resources must include specialized computers, sophisticated equipment and software, and high-speed

qualitative social media measurement the process of accessing the opinions and beliefs about a brand and primarily uses sentiment analysis to categorize what is being said about a company

sentiment analysis a measurement that uses technology to detect the moods, attitudes, or emotions of people who experience a social media activity

e-business (electronic business) the organized effort of individuals to produce and sell, for a profit, the products and services that satisfy society's needs *through the facilities available on the Internet*

FIGURE 16.6   Combining e-Business Resources

While all businesses use four resources (human, material, informational, and financial), these resources are typically more specialized when used in an e-business.

HUMAN RESOURCES
- Web site designers
- Programmers
- Web masters

INFORMATIONAL RESOURCES
- Customer tracking systems
- Order fulfillment and tracking systems
- Online content-monitoring systems

BUSINESS

MATERIAL RESOURCES
- Computers
- Software
- High-speed Internet connection lines

FINANCIAL RESOURCES
- Investors interested in supporting e-business firms
- Electronic payment from customers

© CENGAGE LEARNING 2014

outsourcing the process of finding outside vendors and suppliers that provide professional help, parts, or materials at a lower cost

Internet connections. Computer programs that track the number of customers who view a firm's Web site are generally among the specialized informational resources required. Financial resources, the money required to start and maintain the firm and allow it to grow, usually reflect greater participation by individual entrepreneurs, venture capitalists, and investors willing to invest in a high-tech firm instead of conventional financial sources such as banks.

In an effort to reduce the cost of specialized resources that are used in e-business, many firms have turned to outsourcing. **Outsourcing** is the process of finding outside vendors and suppliers that provide professional help, parts, or materials at a lower cost. For example, a firm that needs specialized software to complete a project may turn to an outside firm located in another part of the United States, India, or an Eastern European country.

Satisfying Needs Online

Think for a moment about this question: "Why do people use the Internet?" As pointed out in the first part of this chapter, more and more people are using computers, the Internet, and social media as a way to connect with people. The Internet can also be used to purchase products or services. Today, more people use the Internet to satisfy these needs than ever before. Let's start with two basic assumptions.

- The Internet has created some new customer needs that did not exist before the creation of the Internet.
- e-Businesses can satisfy those needs, as well as more traditional ones.

Restoration Hardware (www.restorationhardware.com), for instance, gives customers anywhere in the world access to the same virtual store of hardware and decorative items. And at eBay's global auction site (www.ebay.com), customers can, for a small fee, buy and sell almost anything. In each of these examples, customers can use the Internet to purchase a product or service.

In addition to purchasing products, the Internet can be used by both individuals and business firms to obtain information. For example:

- Internet users can access newspapers, magazines, and radio and television programming at a time and place convenient to them.
- The Internet provides the opportunity for two-way interaction between an Internet firm and the viewer. For example, the CNN news site (www.cnn.com)

©BLOOMBERG VIA GETTY IMAGES

Google—the number 1 search engine. When Google created its now-famous Web site, the developers chose a rather simple opening screen with just the Google name, a search box, and very little else. Users loved the simple format and used the search engine to find information about products and services, investment research, new movies, the current weather, and the latest news stories. Now Google has used its early success to develop new services, including Google Earth, Google+, and mobile apps.

Personal APPS

These days, you can find e-businesses that sell almost anything. Many will help you recognize a new need by offering free trials of apps, games, or other digital products. This is a great way to find out whether the digital product is useful, convenient, and worth buying.

revenue stream a source of revenue flowing into a firm

Using Facebook to reach online customers. Today many retailers like The Container Store are using Facebook and other social network sites to reach consumers. It's just one more way to provide information to consumers that may want to purchase the firm's products or services.

and other news-content sites encourage dialogue among users.

- Customers can respond to information on the Internet by requesting more information or posing specific questions, which may lead to purchasing a product or service.
- Finally, the Internet allows customers to choose the content they are offered. Knowing the interests of a customer allows an Internet firm to direct appropriate, smart advertising to a specific customer. For the advertiser, knowing that its advertisements are being directed to the most likely customers represents a better way to spend advertising dollars.

Creating e-Business Profit

Business firms can increase profits either by increasing sales revenue or by reducing expenses through a variety of e-business activities.

Increasing Sales Revenue Each source of sales revenue flowing into a firm is referred to as a **revenue stream**. One way to increase revenues is to sell merchandise on the Internet. Online merchants can reach a global customer base 24 hours a day, seven days a week, because the opportunity to shop on the Internet is virtually unrestricted. However, shifting revenues earned from customers inside a real store to revenues earned from these same customers online does not create any real new revenue for a firm. The goal is to find *new customers* and generate *new sales* so that *total revenues are increased.*

Intelligent information systems also can help to generate sales revenue for Internet firms such as Amazon.com (www.amazon.com). Such systems store information about each customer's purchases, along with a variety of other information about the buyer's preferences. Using this information, the system can assist the customer the next time he or she visits the Web site. For example, if the customer has bought a Carrie Underwood CD in the past, the system might suggest CDs by similar artists who have either appeared on *American Idol* or won Country Music Awards.

Although some customers may not make a purchase online, the existence of the firm's Web site and the services and information it provides may lead to increased sales in the firm's physical stores. For example, Honda's Web site (www. honda.com) can provide basic comparative information for shoppers so that they are better prepared for their visit to an automobile showroom.

In addition to selling products or services online, e-business revenue streams are created by advertising placed on Web pages and by subscription fees charged for access to online services and content. For example, Hoover's (www.hoovers.com), a comprehensive source for company and industry information, makes some of its online content free for anyone who visits the site, but more detailed information is available only by paid subscription. In addition, Hoover's receives revenue from companies acting as sponsors who advertise their products and services on the site.

Many Internet firms that distribute news, magazine and newspaper articles, and similar content generate revenue from commissions earned from sellers of products linked to the site. Online shopping malls, for example, now provide groups of related vendors of electronic equipment and computer hardware and software with a new method of selling their products and services. In many cases, the vendors share online sales revenues with the site owners.

Reducing Expenses Reducing expenses is the second major way in which e-business can help to increase profitability. Providing online access to information that customers want can reduce the cost of dealing with customers. Sprint Nextel (www.sprint.com), for instance, is just one company that maintains an extensive Web site where potential customers can learn more about products and services, and where current customers can access personal account information, send questions to customer service, and purchase additional products or services. With such extensive online services, Sprint Nextel does not have to maintain as many physical store locations as it would without these online services. We examine more examples of how e-business contributes to profitability throughout this chapter, especially as we focus on some of the business models for activity on the Internet.

FUNDAMENTAL MODELS OF E-BUSINESS

6 Understand the fundamental models of e-business.

One way to get a better sense of how businesses are adapting to the opportunities available on the Internet is to identify e-business models. A **business model** represents a group of common characteristics and methods of doing business to generate sales revenues and reduce expenses. Each of the models discussed in the following text represents a primary e-business model. Regardless of the type of business model, planning often depends on if the e-business is a new firm or an existing firm adding an online presence—see Figure 16.7. It also helps to keep in mind that in order to generate sales revenues and earn profits, a business—especially an e-business—must meet the needs of its customers.

FIGURE 16.7 Planning for a New Internet Business or Building an Online Presence for an Existing Business

The approach taken to creating an e-business plan will depend on whether you are establishing a new Internet business or adding an online component to an existing business.

SUCCESSFUL E-BUSINESS PLANNING

Starting a new Internet business

Building an online presence for an existing business

- Will the new e-business provide a product or service that meets customer needs?
- Who are the new firm's potential customers?
- How do promotion, pricing, and distribution affect the new e-business?
- Will the potential market generate enough sales and profits to justify the risk of starting an e-business?

- Is going online a logical way to increase sales and profits for the existing business?
- Are potential online customers different from the firm's traditional customers?
- Will the new e-business activities complement the firm's traditional activities?
- Does the firm have the time, talent, and financial resources to develop an online presence?

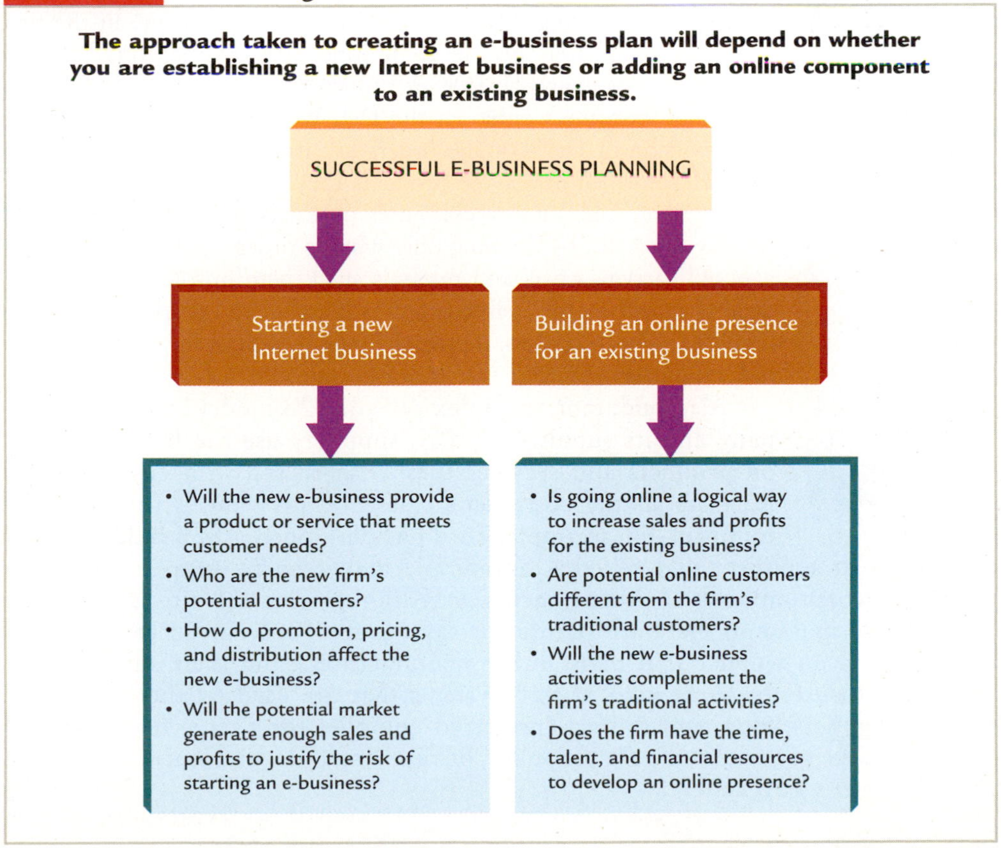

© CENGAGE LEARNING 2014

business model represents a group of common characteristics and methods of doing business to generate sales revenues and reduce expenses

Going for SUCCESS

Macy's and m-Commerce

Through *m-commerce*—mobile commerce, via smartphones and other mobile devices—Macy's is connecting with digital natives who like both fashion and bargains. The retailer operates 800 department stores in 45 states and rings up a total of $26 billion in annual sales. In the past few years, it has stepped up efforts to engage tech-savvy consumers between the ages of 13 and 30.

Macy's created a special version of its popular Web site to fit the size of phone screens, so that customers can browse, look up product details, and buy at any time from any location. It also began inviting customers to subscribe to text messages announcing sales and delivering coupons. Response was so positive that Macy's doubled the size of its text-message subscriber list in just six months. In addition, the retailer includes QR (quick response) codes—boxy, pixilated codes packed with information—in its ads and product displays. Customers use a free QR app to decode the code and access information such as product specifications, demonstration videos, and designer interviews. In one of the store's most popular QR promotions, customers were treated to an exclusive video of beauty expert Bobbi Brown giving a brief makeup lesson. "We're using mobile in every way possible to really complete a customer's experience," explains a Macy's executive.

Sources: Based on information in Sarah Mahoney, "Macy's Revamping Its Bid for Gen Y," *MediaPost*, March 22, 2012, www.mediapost.com; Rimma Kats, "Macy's Mobile Spend Up 70pc: FirstLook Keynote," *Mobile Marketer*, January 20, 2012, www.mobilemarketer.com; Giselle Tsirulnik, "Macy's Is 2011 Mobile Marketer of the Year," *Mobile Marketer*, December 9, 2011, www.mobilemarketer.com.

A new way to reach business customers around the globe. Alibaba.com is a business-to-business (B2B) global trade site that makes it easy for millions of importers and exporters to buy and sell products and services online. Because it meets the needs of its customers, Alibaba.com has become a successful company with offices in more than 70 cities around the globe.

Business-to-Business (B2B) Model

Many e-businesses can be distinguished from others simply by their customer focus. For instance, some firms use the Internet mainly to conduct business with other businesses. These firms are generally referred to as having a **business-to-business (or B2B) model**.

When examining B2B firms, two clear types emerge. In the first type, the focus is simply on facilitating sales transactions between businesses. For example, Dell manufactures computers to specifications that customers enter on the Dell Web site (www.dell.com). A large portion of Dell's online orders are from corporate clients who are well informed about the products they need and are looking for fairly priced, high-quality computer products that will be delivered quickly. Basically, by building only what is ordered, Dell reduces storage and carrying costs and rarely is stuck with unsold inventory. By dealing directly with Dell, customers eliminate costs associated with wholesalers and retailers, thereby helping to reduce the price they pay for equipment.

A second, more complex type of B2B model involves a company and its suppliers. Today, suppliers use the Internet to bid on products and services they wish to sell to a customer and learn about the customer's rules and procedures that must be followed. For example, Ford has developed a B2B model to link thousands of suppliers that sell the automobile maker parts, supplies, and raw materials worth millions of dollars each year. Although the B2B site is expensive to start and maintain, there are significant savings for Ford. Given the potential savings, it is no wonder that many other manufacturers and their suppliers are beginning to use the same kind of B2B systems that are used by the automaker. In fact, suppliers know that to be a "preferred" supplier for a large firm that may purchase large quantities of parts, supplies, or raw materials, they must be tied into the purchaser's B2B system.

business-to-business (or B2B) model a model used by firms that conduct business with other businesses

TABLE 16.2 Other Business Models that Perform Specialized e-Business Activities

Although modified versions of B2B or B2C, these business models perform specialized e-business activities to generate revenues.	
Advertising e-business model	Advertisements that are displayed on a firm's Web site in return for a fee. Examples include pop-up and banner advertisements on search engines and other popular Internet sites.
Brokerage e-business model	Online marketplaces where buyers and sellers are brought together to facilitate an exchange of goods and services. One example is eBay (www.ebay.com), which provides a site for buying and selling virtually anything.
Consumer-to-consumer model	Peer-to-peer software that allows individuals to share information over the Internet. Examples include Bit Torrent (www.bittorrent.com), which allows users to exchange digital media files.
Subscription and pay-per-view e-business models	Content that is available only to users who pay a fee to gain access to a Web site. Examples include investment information provided by Standard & Poor's (www.netadvantage.standardandpoors.com) and business research provided by Forrester Research, Inc. (www.forrester.com).

© CENGAGE LEARNING 2014

Business-to-Consumer (B2C) Model

In contrast with the B2B model, firms such as Barnes and Noble (www.barnesandnoble.com) and online retailer Lands' End (www.landsend.com) clearly are focused on individual consumers. These companies are referred to as having a **business-to-consumer (or B2C) model**. In a B2C situation, understanding how consumers behave online is critical to a firm's success. Typically, a business firm that uses a B2C model must answer the following questions:

- Will consumers use Web sites merely to simplify and speed up comparison shopping?
- Will consumers purchase services and products online or end up buying at a traditional retail store?
- What sorts of products and services are best suited for online consumer shopping?

In addition to providing round-the-clock global access to all kinds of products and services, B2C firms often attempt to build long-term relationships with their customers. Often, firms will make a special effort to make sure that the customer is satisfied and that problems, if any, are solved quickly. Specialized software also can help build good customer relationships. Tracking the decisions and buying preferences as customers navigate a Web site, for instance, helps management to make well-informed decisions about how best to serve online customers. In essence, this is Orbitz's (www.orbitz.com) online selling approach. By tracking and analyzing customer data, the online travel company can provide individualized service to its customers. Although a "little special attention" may increase the cost of doing business for a B2C firm, the customer's repeated purchases will repay the investment many times over.

Today, B2B and B2C models are the most popular business models for e-business. And yet, there are other business models that perform specialized e-business activities to generate revenues. Most of the business models described in Table 16.2 are modified versions of the B2B and B2C models.

THE FUTURE OF THE INTERNET, SOCIAL MEDIA, AND E-BUSINESS

Since the beginning of commercial activity on the Internet, developments in computer technology, social media, and e-business have been rapid and formidable with spectacular successes such as Google, eBay, and Pinterest. However, a larger-than-usual number of technology companies struggled or even failed during the economic crisis. Today, most firms involved in the Internet, social media, and e-business use a more intelligent approach to development. The long-term view held by the vast majority of

7 Identify the factors that will affect the future of the Internet, social media, and e-business.

business-to-consumer (or B2C) model a model used by firms that focus on conducting business with individual consumers

analysts is that the Internet, social media, and e-business will continue to expand to meet the needs of businesses and consumers.

Internet Growth Potential

To date, only a small percentage of the global population uses the Internet. At the beginning of 2012, estimates suggest that about 2.3 billion of the nearly 7 billion people in the world use the Web.[28] Clearly, there is much more growth opportunity. Americans comprise 11 percent of all Internet users.[29] Of the 310 million people making up the American population, 239 million use the Internet. With approximately 77 percent of the American population already using the Internet, potential growth in the United States is limited.[30] On the other hand, the number of Internet users in the world's developing countries is expected to increase dramatically.

Although the number of global Internet users is expected to increase, that's only part of the story. Perhaps the more important question is why people are using the Internet. Primary reasons for using the Internet include the ability to connect with other people, to obtain information, or to purchase a firm's products or services. Of particular interest to business firms is the growth of social media. The number of Facebook users, for example, increased from 664 million to 835 million in the 12-month period from March 2011 to March 2012. And because only 12 percent of the world population currently uses Facebook, the number of Facebook users is expected to continue to increase for years to come.[31] And the number of users for other social media sites like LinkedIn, Twitter, Pinterest, are also expected to increase.

Experts also predict that the number of companies using e-business to increase sales and reduce expenses will continue to increase. Firms that adapt existing business models to an online environment will continue to dominate development. For example, books, CDs, clothing, hotel accommodations, car rentals, and travel reservations are products and services well suited to online buying and selling. These products or services will continue to be sold in the traditional way, as well as in a more cost-effective and efficient fashion over the Internet.

Ethical and Legal Concerns

The social and legal concerns for the Internet, social media, and e-business extend beyond those shared by all businesses. Essentially, the Internet is a new "frontier" without borders and without much control by governments or other organizations.

Ethics and Social Responsibility Socially responsible and ethical behavior by individuals and businesses on the Internet are major concerns. For example, an ethically questionable practice in cyberspace is the unauthorized access and use of information discovered through computerized tracking of users once they are connected to the Internet. Essentially, a user may visit a Web site and unknowingly receive a small piece of software code called a **cookie**. This cookie can track where the user goes on the Internet and measure how long the user stays at any particular Web site. Although this type of software may produce valuable customer information, it also can be viewed as an invasion of privacy, especially since users may not even be aware that their movements are being monitored.

Besides the unauthorized use of cookies to track online behavior, there are several other threats to users' privacy and confidentiality. Monitoring an employee's computer usage may be intended to help employers police unauthorized Internet use on company time. However, the same records can also give a firm the opportunity to observe what otherwise might be considered private and confidential information. Today, legal experts suggest that, at the very least, employers need to disclose the level of surveillance to their employees and consider the corporate motivation for monitoring employees' behavior.

Some firms also practice data mining. **Data mining** refers to the practice of searching through data records looking for useful information. Customer registration forms typically require a variety of information before a user is given access to a site. Based

cookie a small piece of software sent by a Web site that tracks an individual's Internet use

data mining the practice of searching through data records looking for useful information

on an individual's information, data mining analysis can then provide what might be considered private and confidential information about individuals. For instance, assume an individual frequents a Web site that provides information about a life-threatening disease. If this information is sent to an insurance company, the company might refuse to insure this individual, thinking that there is a higher risk associated with someone who wants more information about this disease.

Internet Crime Because the Internet is often regarded as an unregulated frontier, both individuals and business users must be particularly aware of online risks and dangers. For example, a general term that describes software designed to infiltrate a computer system without the user's consent is **malware**. Malware is often based on the creator's criminal or malicious intent and can include computer viruses, spyware, deceptive adware, and other software capable of criminal activities. A more specific term used to describe disruptive software is computer virus. A **computer virus**, which can originate anywhere in the world, is a software code designed to disrupt normal computer activities. The potentially devastating effects of both malware and computer viruses have given rise to a software security industry.

In addition to the risk of computer viruses, identity theft is one of the most common computer crimes that impacts both individuals and business users. A recent study conducted by Javelin Strategy and Research determined that more than 11.6 million Americans were victims of identity theft in just one year.[32] Most consumers are also concerned about fraud. Because the Internet allows easy creation of Web sites, access from anywhere in the world, and anonymity for the creator, it is almost impossible to know with certainty that the Web site, organization, or individuals that you believe you are interacting with are what they seem. As always, caveat emptor ("let the buyer beware") is a good suggestion to follow whether on the Internet or not.

Future Challenges for Computer Technology, Social Media, and e-Business

Today, more information is available than ever before. Although individuals and business users may think we are at the point of information overload, the amount of information will only increase in the future. In order to obtain more information in the future, both individuals and business users must consider the cost of obtaining information and computer technology. For a business, the ability to obtain information or sell products or services with a simple click or touch is expensive. In an effort to reduce expenses and improve accessibility, some companies and individuals are now using cloud computing. **Cloud computing** is a type of computer usage in which services stored on the Internet are provided to users on a temporary basis. When cloud computing is used, a third party makes processing power, software applications, databases, and storage available for on-demand use from anywhere. Instead of running software and storing data on their employer's computer network or their individual computers, employees log onto the third party's system and use (and pay for) only the applications and data storage they actually need. In addition to just cost, there are a number of external and internal factors that a business must consider.

Although the environmental forces at work are complex, it is useful to think of them as either *internal* or *external* forces that affect how a business uses computer

Sustaining the PLANET

Lululemon Develops Lasting Legacies

Lululemon has built an online presence based on demand for their technical athletic apparel for yoga, dancing, and running. Their product line, coupled with the company's social responsibility perspective—which they refer to as Community Legacies—has created a loyal customer base. Viewing efficiency and waste reduction as good business, the company is focused on eliminating waste in their factories, stores, and support centers. Lululemon has an embedded core culture, "Personal responsibility creates global change," that reaches every aspect of the business. For more information, go to www.lululemon.com/community/legacies/focus.

WWW.LULULEMON.COM

malware a general term that describes software designed to infiltrate a computer system without the user's consent

computer virus a software code designed to disrupt normal computer operations

cloud computing a type of computer usage in which services stored on the Internet is provided to users on a temporary basis

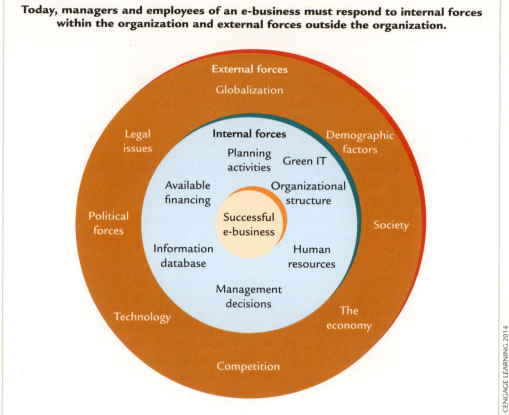

FIGURE 16.8 Internal and External Forces that Affect an e-Business

Today, managers and employees of an e-business must respond to internal forces within the organization and external forces outside the organization.

External forces

Globalization

Internal forces

Legal issues

Demographic factors

Planning activities

Green IT

Available financing

Organizational structure

Successful e-business

Political forces

Society

Information database

Human resources

Management decisions

Technology

The economy

Competition

© CENGAGE LEARNING 2014

technology. Internal environmental forces are those that are closely associated with the actions and decisions taking place within a firm. As shown in Figure 16.8, typical internal forces include a firm's planning activities, organizational structure, human resources, management decisions, information database, and available financing. A shortage of skilled employees needed for a specialized project, for instance, can undermine a firm's ability to sell its services to clients. Unlike the external environmental forces affecting the firm, internal forces such as this one are more likely to be under the direct control of management. In this case, management can either hire the needed staff or choose to pass over a prospective project. In addition to the obvious internal factors that affect how a company operates, a growing number of firms are concerned about how their use of technology affects the environment. The term **green IT** is now used to describe all of a firm's activities to support a healthy environment and sustain the planet. Many offices, for example, are reducing the amount of paper they use by storing data and information on computers.

In contrast, external environmental forces affect a company's use of technology and originate outside the organization. These forces are unlikely to be controllable by a company. Instead, managers and employees of a company generally will react to these forces, attempting to shield the organization from any undue negative effects and finding ways to take advantage of opportunities in an ever-changing technology environment. The primary external environmental forces affecting a company's use of technology include globalization, demographic, societal, economic, competitive, technological, and political and legal forces.

In this chapter, we have explored how both individuals and businesses use social media. We also examined how e-business is changing the way that firms do business. In Chapter 17, we examine a business firm's need for information and why accounting is a major source of information for business.

green IT a term used to describe all of a firm's activities to support a healthy environment and sustain the planet

return to Inside BUSINESS

Angry Birds

Every time Rovio uses Facebook, Twitter, and blogs to announce the release of a new Angry Birds game, it sets the social media world buzzing. Angry Birds Space took social games to new heights when the product introduction featured a NASA astronaut on the International Space Station using an Angry Bird toy and a balloon "pig" to demonstrate the principle of trajectory. Fans downloaded the new space game 10 million times in its first three days, a new record that also helped boost Rovio's e-business revenue for the year.

Now that Angry Birds is an international download phenomenon, Rovio is planning Angry Birds theme parks in Europe, Angry Birds stores in China, and an Angry Birds movie for global release. How long will Rovio's revenues be flying high?

Questions

1. If you were a corporate executive, how could you measure the effectiveness of Rovio's use of social media?
2. Of the environmental forces affecting e-business, which seem to have had the most influence on Rovio's success with Angry Birds?

SUMMARY

 Examine why it is important for a business to use social media.

Millions of people of all ages use social media to interact with people and share ideas, personal information, and information about products and services. Today, more than two-thirds of online adults use some sort of social media platform like Facebook, LinkedIn, or Twitter, according to a recent Pew Internet Research Study. The primary reason for using social media is to stay in touch with family and friends. Other reasons include reconnecting with friends, connecting with people who share interests, making new friends, and reading comments by public figures. Early on, companies saw the potential in the sheer numbers of people using social media. Even though companies have used social media to share information about their products and services and improve customer service, many are still uncomfortable with this new method of communicating with customers because they do not have complete control over what is said about their products or services.

 Discuss how businesses use social media tools.

Companies use social media to connect with customers, listen to stakeholders, provide customer service, provide information to customers, and engage customers in product development and formulation. To share social content (information about products and services), companies can use blogs, photos, videos, and podcasts. In addition, social media also enables shoppers to access opinions, recommendations, and referrals from others within and outside their own social circle. Rating and review sites are based on the idea that people trust the opinions of others when it comes to purchasing products and services. Social games are another area of growth in social media. A social game (like Angry Birds or FarmVille) is a multiplayer, competitive, goal-oriented activity with defined rules of engagement and online connectivity among a community of players. While some businesses elect to create their own game, others choose to place advertising into a game.

 Explain the business objectives for using social media.

Although its popularity is a recent phenomenon, many businesses are already using social media to achieve important goals and objectives. In fact, there are many ways for businesses to use social media to take advantage of business opportunities to build connections with other businesses and consumers. For example, businesses can use social media to build a community. Social media communities are social networks based on the relationships among people. Today, there are social communities for every interest, ethnic group, and lifestyle. Different types of communities include both forums and wikis. Other reasons for using social media include crisis and reputation management, listening to stakeholders, targeting customers, social media marketing, generating new product ideas, and recruiting employees. For a business, social media marketing is especially important because it can not only develop customer awareness, but also obtain sales leads and increase actual sales.

 Describe how businesses develop a social media plan.

Before developing a plan to use social media, it is important to determine how social media can improve the organization's overall performance and how it "fits" with a company's other operational and promotional activities. Once it is determined how social media links to the company's other activities, the first step is to listen to what customers like and don't like about a company's products or services. Typically, the second step is to establish social media objectives that are specific, measurable, achievable, realistic, and time oriented. After listening and establishing objectives, the third step is to identify the customer or market segment a business is trying to reach with a social media promotion. The fourth step is to select the social media tool that will be used to reach customers. While it is not necessary (or even advisable) to use all of the available tools, a company can use social media communities, blogs, photos, videos, podcasts, or games to reach potential or existing customers. Once social media tools have been identified, a company can implement and integrate the social media plan.

Both quantitative and qualitative measurements can be used to determine the effectiveness of a social media plan. Quantitative social media measurement consists of using numerical measurements. Key performance indicators (KPIs), for example, are quantitative measurements. Qualitative measurement is the process of accessing the opinions and beliefs about a brand and primarily uses sentiment analysis to categorize what is being said about a company.

 Explain the meaning of e-business.

e-Business, or electronic business, can be defined as the organized effort of individuals to produce and sell, for a profit, the goods and services that satisfy society's needs *through the facilities available on the Internet*. The human, material, information, and financial resources that any business requires are highly specialized for e-business. In an effort to reduce the cost of e-business resources, many firms have turned to outsourcing.

Using e-business activities, it is possible to satisfy new customer needs created by the Internet as well as traditional ones in unique ways. Meeting customer needs is especially important when an e-business is trying to earn profits by increasing sales and reducing expenses. Each source of revenue flowing into the firm is referred to as a revenue stream.

 Understand the fundamental models of e-business.

e-Business models focus attention on the identity of a firm's customers. Firms that use the Internet mainly to conduct business with other businesses generally are referred to as having a business-to-business, or B2B, model. When examining B2B firms, two clear types emerge. In the first type of B2B, the focus is simply on facilitating sales transactions between businesses. A second, more complex type of the B2B model involves a company and its suppliers. In contrast to the focus of the B2B model, firms such as Amazon or eBay clearly are focused on individual buyers and are thus referred to as having a business-to-consumer, or B2C, model. In a B2C situation, understanding how consumers behave online is critical to the firm's success. Successful B2C firms often make a special effort to build long-term relationships with their customers. While B2B and B2C models are the most popular e-business models, there are other models that perform specialized e-business activities to generate revenues (see Table 16.2).

Identify the factors that will affect the future of the Internet, social media, and e-business.

Since the beginning of commercial activity on the Internet, developments in computer technology, social media, and e-business have been rapid and formidable. Although a number of technology companies struggled or even failed during the recent economic crisis, most firms involved in computer technology, social media, and e-business today use a more intelligent approach to development. The long-term view held by the vast majority of analysts is that use of the Internet will continue to expand along with related technologies. Because approximately 77 percent of Americans now have access to the Internet, potential growth is limited in the United States. On the other hand, only 2.3 billion of the nearly 7 billion people in the world use the Web. Clearly, the number of Internet users in the world's developing countries is expected to increase dramatically.

The future of computer technology and the Internet will be influenced by advances in technology, the increasing popularity of social media, and the increasing use of e-business. Other factors including ethics, social responsibility, and Internet crime will all impact the way that businesses and consumers use computer technology and the Internet. Although the environmental forces at work are complex, it is useful to think of them as either internal or external forces that affect how businesses use computer technology. Internal environmental forces are those that are closely associated with the actions and decisions taking place within a firm. In contrast, external environmental forces are those factors affecting an e-business originating outside an organization.

KEY TERMS

You should now be able to define and give an example relevant to each of the following terms:

social media (458)
social content sites (460)
blog (460)
media sharing sites (461)
podcasts (461)
social game (461)
social media communities (462)
forum (462)
wiki (462)

Millennials (463)
social media marketing (464)
inbound marketing (464)
crowdsourcing (465)
quantitative social media measurement (469)
key performance indicators (KPIs) (469)
qualitative social media measurement (470)

sentiment analysis (470)
e-business (electronic business) (470)
outsourcing (471)
revenue stream (472)
business model (473)
business-to-business (or B2B) model (474)
business-to-consumer (or B2C) model (475)

cookie (476)
data mining (476)
malware (477)
computer virus (477)
cloud computing (477)
green IT (478)

REVIEW QUESTIONS

1. According to material in this chapter, what are the reasons why people use social media?
2. How is using social media to connect with other businesses and consumers different from the top-down traditional advertising approach used with television and magazine ads?
3. What is a blog? How can a business use blogs to develop relationships with customers?
4. What types of content can be used on a media sharing site? What factors should be considered when developing content for a media sharing site?
5. Describe the two ways that businesses can use "gamification" to generate sales revenue.
6. In your own words, describe how social media can help businesses to connect with other businesses and consumers.
7. For a business, why are crisis and reputation management and listening to stakeholders important activities?
8. How can social media be used to segment the market for a firm's products or services and target specific types of customers?

9. Why do you think companies are shifting their advertising monies from traditional advertising (television and newspapers) to social media (Internet search engines and social media)?
10. How can social media help companies generate new product ideas and recruit employees?
11. What are the steps required to develop a social media plan?
12. What is the difference between quantitative and qualitative measurement? Which type of measurement do you think is the most reliable when measuring the effectiveness of a company's social media plan?
13. What are the four major factors contained in the definition of e-business?
14. How do e-businesses generate revenue streams?
15. What are the two fundamental e-business models?
16. Give an example of an unethical use of computer technology by a business.
17. What is the difference between internal and external forces that affect an e-business? How do they change the way an e-business operates?

DISCUSSION QUESTIONS

1. Given the fast pace of everyday life, most people often feel there is not enough time to do everything that needs to be done. Yet, people do find time to post personal information, photos, etc., on Facebook, Twitter, blogs, and other social media sites. Why do you think people are so fascinated with social media?
2. Assume you are the owner of a small company that produces a line of barbeque grills. Describe how you could use social media to connect with customers, improve customer service, increase sales, and reduce expenses.

3. Can advertising provide enough revenue for an e-business to succeed in the long run? What other sources of revenue can an e-business use to generate revenue?
4. Is outsourcing good for an e-business firm? The firm's employees? Explain your answer.
5. What distinguishes a B2B from a B2C e-business model?
6. Experts predict that the Internet, social media, and e-business will continue to expand along with related computer technologies. What effect will this expansion have on how businesses connect with customers in the future?

accounting equation and the three most important financial statements: the balance sheet, the income statement, and the statement of cash flows. Finally, we take a look at how managers evaluate the firm's financial health.

HOW CAN INFORMATION REDUCE RISK WHEN MAKING A DECISION?

Examine how information can reduce risk when making a decision.

As we noted in Chapter 1, information is one of the four major resources (along with material, human, and financial resources) managers must have to operate a business. Although a successful business uses all four resources efficiently, it is information that helps managers reduce risk when making a decision.

Information and Risk

To improve the decision-making process and reduce risk, the information used by individuals and business firms must be relevant or useful to meet a specific need. Using relevant information results in better decisions.

> Relevant information → Better intelligence and knowledge → Better decisions

For businesses, better intelligence and knowledge that lead to better decisions are especially important because they can provide a *competitive edge* over competitors and improve a firm's *profits*.

Theoretically, with accurate and complete information, there is no risk whatsoever. On the other hand, a decision made without any information is a gamble. These two extreme situations are rare in business. For the most part, business decision makers see themselves located someplace between the extremes. As illustrated in Figure 17.1, when the amount of available information is high, there is less risk; when the amount of available information is low, there is more risk.

Suppose that a marketing manager for Procter & Gamble (P&G) responsible for the promotion of a well-known shampoo such as Pantene Pro-V has called a meeting of key people within her department to consider the selection of a new magazine advertisement. The company's advertising agency has submitted two new advertisements in sealed envelopes. Neither the manager nor any of her team has seen them before. Only one selection will be made for the new advertising campaign. Which advertisement should be chosen?

Without any further information, the team might as well make the decision by flipping a coin. If, however, team members were allowed to open the envelopes and examine the advertisements, they would have more information. If, in addition to allowing them to examine the advertisements, the marketing manager circulated a report containing the reactions of a group of target consumers to each of the two advertisements, the team would have even more information with which to work. Thus, information, when understood properly, produces knowledge and empowers managers and employees to make better decisions.

| FIGURE 17.1 | The Relationship Between Information and Risk |

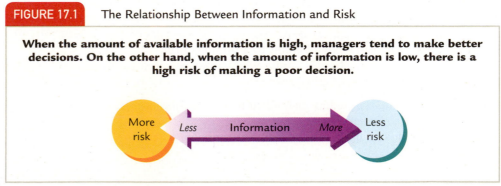

When the amount of available information is high, managers tend to make better decisions. On the other hand, when the amount of information is low, there is a high risk of making a poor decision.

© CENGAGE LEARNING 2014

Information Rules

Marketing research continues to show that discounts influence almost all car buyers. Simply put, if dealers lower their prices, they will sell more cars. This relationship between buyer behavior and price can be thought of as an information rule that usually will guide the marketing manager correctly. An information rule emerges when research confirms the same results each time that it studies the same or a similar set of circumstances.

Because of the volume of information they receive each day and their need to make decisions on a daily basis, businesspeople try to accumulate information rules to shorten the time they spend analyzing choices. Information rules are the "great simplifiers" for all decision makers. Business research is continuously looking for new rules that can be put to good use and looking to discredit old ones that are no longer valid. This ongoing process is necessary because business conditions rarely stay the same for very long.

The Difference Between Data and Information

Many people use the terms *data* and *information* interchangeably, but the two differ in important ways. **Data** are numerical or verbal descriptions that usually result from some sort of measurement. (The word *data* is plural; the singular form is datum.) Your current wage level, the amount of last year's after-tax profit for ExxonMobil Corporation, and the current retail prices of Honda automobiles are all data. Most people think of data as being numerical only, but they can be nonnumerical as well. A description of an individual as a "tall, athletic person with short, dark hair" certainly would qualify as data.

Information is data presented in a form that is useful for a specific purpose. Suppose that a human resources manager wants to compare the wages paid to male and female employees over a period of five years. The manager might begin with a stack of computer printouts listing every person employed by the firm, along with each employee's current and past wages. The manager would be hard pressed to make any sense of all the names and numbers. Such printouts consist of data rather than information.

Now suppose that the manager uses a computer to graph the average wages paid to men and to women in each of the five years. The result is information because the manager can use it for the purpose at hand—to compare wages paid to men with those paid to women over the five-year period. For a manager, information presented in a practical, useful form such as a graph simplifies the decision-making process.

Knowledge Management

The average company maintains a great deal of data that can be transformed into information. Typical data include records pertaining to personnel, inventory, sales, and accounting. Often each type of data is stored in individual departments within an organization. However, the data can be used more effectively when they are organized into a

Personal APPS

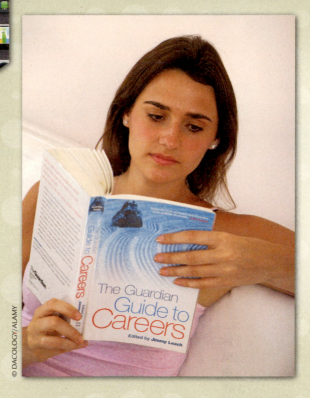

You can reduce the risk in any decision you make—a decision about school, a decision about work, or a decision about buying something expensive—by doing your homework. The more you know about the situation and your alternatives, the better your decision will be.

Technology giant! Cisco Systems is a company known for transforming how people connect, communicate, and collaborate. The technology giant is also a respected innovator that develops state-of-the-art equipment needed by employees, managers, *and* individuals to manage knowledge and information.

database. A **database** is a single collection of data and information stored in one place that can be used by people throughout an organization to make decisions. Although databases are important, the way the data and information are used is even more important—and more valuable to the firm. As a result, management information experts now use the term **knowledge management (KM)** to describe a firm's procedures for generating, using, and sharing the data and information. Typically, data, information, databases, and KM all become important parts of a firm's management information system.

WHAT IS A MANAGEMENT INFORMATION SYSTEM?

Discuss management's information requirements.

A **management information system (MIS)** is a system that provides managers and employees with the information they need to perform their jobs as effectively as possible. The purpose of an MIS (sometimes referred to as an information technology system or simply IT system) is to distribute timely and useful information from both internal and external sources to the managers and employees who need it (see Figure 17.2). Today, most medium-sized to large business firms have an information technology (IT) officer. An **information technology (IT) officer** is a manager at the executive level who is responsible for ensuring that a firm has the equipment necessary to provide the information the firm's employees and managers need to make effective decisions.

Today's typical MIS is built around a computerized system of record-keeping and communications software so that it can provide information based on a wide variety of data. After all, the goal is to provide needed information to all employees and managers.

A Firm's Information Requirements

Employees and managers have to plan for the future, implement their plans in the present, and evaluate results against what has been accomplished in the past. Of course, the specific types of information they need depend on their work area and on their level within the firm.

Today, many firms are organized into five areas of management: *finance, operations, marketing, human resources,* and *administration*. Managers in each of these areas need specific information in order to make decisions.

database a single collection of data and information stored in one place that can be used by people throughout an organization to make decisions

knowledge management (KM) a firm's procedures for generating, using, and sharing the data and information

management information system (MIS) a system that provides managers and employees with the information they need to perform their jobs as effectively as possible

information technology (IT) officer a manager at the executive level who is responsible for ensuring that a firm has the equipment necessary to provide the information the firm's employees and managers need to make effective decisions

FIGURE 17.2 Management Information System (MIS)

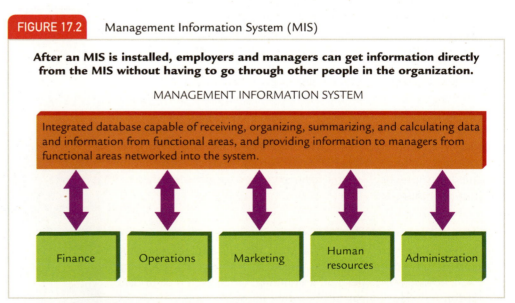

After an MIS is installed, employers and managers can get information directly from the MIS without having to go through other people in the organization.

MANAGEMENT INFORMATION SYSTEM

Integrated database capable of receiving, organizing, summarizing, and calculating data and information from functional areas, and providing information to managers from functional areas networked into the system.

Finance | Operations | Marketing | Human resources | Administration

Source: Adapted from Ricky W. Griffin, *Management* (Mason, OH: Cengage Learning, 2013). Reprinted with permission.

- *Financial managers* are obviously most concerned with a firm's finances. They must ensure that the firm's managers and employees, lenders and suppliers, stockholders and potential investors, and government agencies have the information they need to measure the financial health of the firm. Along with the firm's accountants, financial managers study its debts and receivables, cash flow, future capitalization needs, financial statements, and other accounting information. Of equal importance to financial managers is information about the present state of the economy, interest rates, and predictions of business conditions in the future.

- *Operations managers* are concerned with present and future sales levels, current inventory levels of work in process and finished goods, and the availability and cost of the resources required to produce products and services. They also must keep abreast of any innovative production technology that might be useful to the firm.

- *Marketing managers* need to have detailed information about a firm's products and services and those offered by competitors. Such information includes pricing strategies, new promotional campaigns, and products that competitors are test marketing. Information concerning the firm's customers, current and projected market share, and new and pending product legislation is also important to marketing managers.

- *Human resources managers* must be aware of anything that pertains to a firm's employees. Key examples include current wage levels and benefits packages both within the firm and in firms that compete for valuable employees, current legislation and court decisions that affect employment practices, union activities, and the firm's plans for growth, expansion, or mergers.

- *Administrative managers* are responsible for the overall management of the organization. Thus, they are concerned with the coordination of information—just as they are concerned with the coordination of material, human, and financial resources.

Administrators must ensure that all employees have access to the information they need to do their jobs. Administrative managers must also ensure that the information is used in a consistent manner throughout the firm. Suppose, for example, that General Electric (GE) is designing a new plant that will open in five years. GE's management will want answers to many questions: Is the capacity of the plant consistent with marketing plans based on sales projections? Will human resources managers be able to staff the plant on the basis of employment forecasts? And do sales projections indicate enough income to cover the expected cost of the plant? Next, administrative managers must make sure that all managers and employees are able to use the IT that is available. Certainly, this requires that all employees receive the skills training required to use the firm's MIS. Finally, administrative managers must commit to the costs of updating the firm's MIS and providing additional training when necessary.

Size and Complexity of the System

An MIS must be tailored to the needs of the organization it serves. In some firms, a tendency to save on initial costs may result in a system that is too small or overly simple. Such a system generally ends up serving only one or two management levels or a single department. Managers in other departments "give up" on the system as soon as they find that it cannot process their data.

Almost as bad is an MIS that is too large or too complex for the organization. Unused capacity and complexity do nothing but increase the cost of owning and operating the system. In addition, a system that is difficult to use probably will not be used at all.

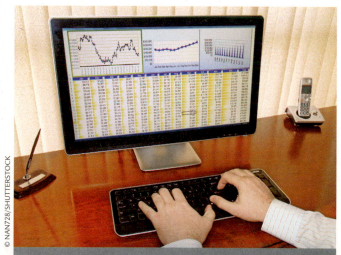

© NAN728/SHUTTERSTOCK

Is all this information really necessary? Today, we live in an information society—that is, a society in which large groups of individuals, employees, and managers generate or depend on information to perform everyday tasks. As a result, all three groups often complain that they have too much information. For many, the problem is not lack of information, but how to determine what information is really needed?

HOW DO EMPLOYEES USE A MANAGEMENT INFORMATION SYSTEM?

To provide information, a management information system (MIS) must perform five specific functions. It must (1) collect data, (2) store the data, (3) update the data, (4) process the data into information, and (5) present the information to users (see Figure 17.3).

Step 1: Collecting Data

A firm's employees, with the help of an MIS system, must gather the data and information needed to establish the firm's *database*. The database should include all past and current data that may be useful in managing the firm. Clearly, the data entered into the system must be *relevant* to the needs of the firm's managers. And perhaps most important, the data must be *accurate*. Irrelevant data are simply useless; inaccurate data can be disastrous. There are two data sources: *internal* and *external*.

Internal Sources of Data Typically, most of the data gathered for an MIS come from internal sources. The most common internal sources of information are managers and employees, company records and reports, and minutes of meetings.

Past and present accounting data can also provide information about the firm's transactions with customers, creditors, and suppliers. Sales reports are a source of data on sales, pricing strategies, and the effectiveness of promotional campaigns. Human resources records are useful as a source of data on wage and benefits levels, hiring patterns, employee turnover, and other personnel variables.

FIGURE 17.3   Five Management Information System Functions

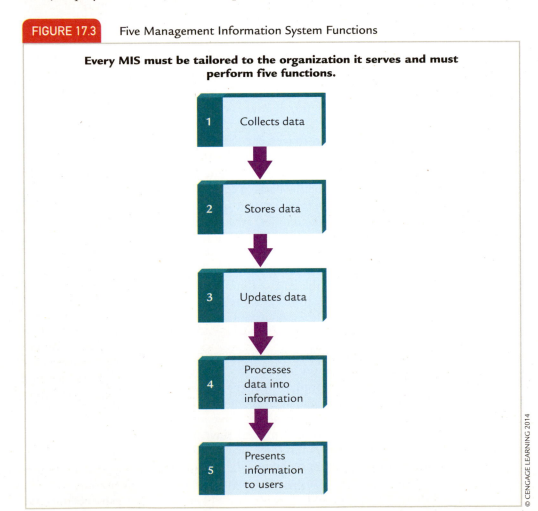

Every MIS must be tailored to the organization it serves and must perform five functions.

1 Collects data

2 Stores data

3 Updates data

4 Processes data into information

5 Presents information to users

© CENGAGE LEARNING 2014

Present and past production forecasts also should be included in the firm's database, along with information indicating how well these forecasts predicted actual events. Specific plans and management decisions—regarding capital expansion and new product development, for example—should also be incorporated into the MIS system.

External Sources of Data External sources of data include customers, suppliers, financial institutions and banks, trade and business publications, industry conferences, online computer services, lawyers, government sources, and firms that specialize in gathering data for organizations. For example, a marketing research company may acquire sales forecasts pertaining to product demand, consumer tastes, and other marketing variables. Suppliers are also an excellent source of information about the future availability and costs of raw materials and component parts. Bankers can often provide valuable economic insights and projections. The information furnished by trade and business publications and industry conferences is usually concerned as much with future projections as with present conditions. Legal issues and court decisions that may affect a firm are discussed occasionally in local newspapers and, more often, in specialized publications such as the *Wall Street Journal, Fortune,* and *BusinessWeek*. Government publications such as the *Monthly Labor Review* and the *Federal Reserve Bulletin* are also quite useful as sources of external data, as are a number of online computer services.

Whether the source of the data is internal or external, always remember the following three cautions:

1. The cost of obtaining data from some external sources, such as marketing research firms, can be quite high.
2. Outdated or incomplete data usually yield inaccurate information.
3. Although computers generally do not make mistakes, the people who use them can make or cause errors. When data (or information) and your judgment disagree, always check the data.

Step 2: Storing Data

An MIS must be capable of storing data until they are needed. Typically, the method chosen to store data depends on the size and needs of the organization. Small businesses may enter data and then store them directly on the hard drive inside an employee's computer. Generally, medium-sized to large businesses store data in a larger computer system and provide access to employees through a computer network. Today, networks take on many configurations and are designed by specialists who work with a firm's IT personnel to decide on what's best for the company.

Step 3: Updating Data

Today, an MIS must be able to update stored data regularly to ensure that the information presented to managers and employees is accurate, complete, and up-to-date. The frequency with which the data are updated depends on how fast they change and how often they are used. When it is vital to have current data, updating may occur as soon as the new data are available. For example, Giant Food Stores, a grocery store chain operating in the eastern part of the United States, has cash registers that automatically transmit data on each item sold to a central computer. The computer adjusts the store's inventory records accordingly. In some systems, the computer may even be programmed to reorder items whose inventories fall below some specified level. Data and information may also be entered into a firm's data bank at certain intervals—every 24 hours, weekly, or monthly.

Step 4: Processing Data

Some data are used in the form in which they are stored, whereas other data require processing to extract, highlight, or summarize the information they contain. **Data processing** is the transformation of data into a form that is useful for a specific purpose.

data processing the transformation of data into a form that is useful for a specific purpose

THE ACCOUNTING EQUATION AND THE BALANCE SHEET

At the beginning of this chapter, *information* was defined as data presented in a form that is useful for a specific purpose. Now, we examine how financial *data* is transformed into financial *information* and reported on three very important financial statements—the balance sheet, income statement, and statement of cash flows. We begin by describing why the fundamental accounting equation is the basis for a firm's balance sheet.

The Accounting Equation

The accounting equation is a simple statement that forms the basis for the accounting process. This equation shows the relationship between a firm's assets, liabilities, and owners' equity.

- **Assets** are the resources a business owns—cash, inventory, equipment, and real estate.
- **Liabilities** are the firm's debts—borrowed money it owes to others that must be repaid.
- **Owners' equity** is the difference between total assets and total liabilities—what would be left for the owners if the firm's assets were sold and the money used to pay off its liabilities.

The relationship between assets, liabilities, and owners' equity is shown by the following **accounting equation**:

$$\text{Assets} = \text{Liabilities} + \text{Owners' equity}$$

The dollar total of all of a firm's assets cannot equal more than the total funds obtained by borrowing money (liabilities) and the investment of the owner(s). Whether a business is a small corner grocery store or a giant corporation such as General Mills, its assets must equal the sum of its liabilities and owners' equity. To use this equation, a firm's accountants must record raw data—that is, the firm's day-to-day financial transactions—using the double-entry system of bookkeeping. The **double-entry bookkeeping system** is a system in which each financial transaction is recorded as two separate accounting entries to maintain the balance shown in the accounting equation. All of the financial transactions can now be summarized in the firm's financial statements. This information is presented in a standardized format to make the statements as accessible as possible to the various people who may be interested in the firm's financial affairs—managers, employees, lenders, suppliers, stockholders, potential investors, and government agencies. In fact the form of the financial statements is pretty much the same for all businesses, from a neighborhood video store or small dry cleaner to giant conglomerates such as Home Depot, Boeing, and Bank of America. A firm's financial statements are prepared at least once a year and included in the firm's annual report. An **annual report** is a report distributed to stockholders and other interested parties that describes a firm's operating activities and its financial condition. Most firms also have financial statements prepared semiannually, quarterly, or monthly.

The Balance Sheet

Question: *Where could you find the total amount of assets, liabilities, and owners' equity for Hershey Foods Corporation?*

Answer: The firm's balance sheet.

A **balance sheet** (sometimes referred to as a **statement of financial position**) is a summary of the dollar amounts of a firm's assets, liabilities, and owners' equity accounts at the end of a specific accounting period. The balance sheet must demonstrate that assets are equal to liabilities plus owners' equity. Most people think of a balance

assets the resources that a business owns

liabilities a firm's debts and obligations

owners' equity the difference between a firm's assets and its liabilities

accounting equation the basis for the accounting process: *assets=liabilities+owners' equity*

double-entry bookkeeping system a system in which each financial transaction is recorded as two separate accounting entries to maintain the balance shown in the accounting equation

annual report a report distributed to stockholders and other interested parties that describes the firm's operating activities and its financial condition

balance sheet (or statement of financial position) a summary of the dollar amounts of a firm's assets, liabilities, and owners' equity accounts at the end of a specific accounting period

FIGURE 17.5   Personal Balance Sheet

Often individuals determine their net worth, or owners' equity, by subtracting the value of their liabilities from the value of their assets.

Marty Campbell
Personal Balance Sheet
December 31, 20XX

ASSETS		LIABILITIES	
Cash	$ 2,500	Automobile loan	$ 9,500
Savings account	5,000	Credit card balance	500
Automobile	15,000	TOTAL LIABILITIES	$10,000
Stereo	1,000		
Television	500		
Furniture	2,500	NET WORTH (Owners' Equity)	16,500
TOTAL ASSETS	$26,500	TOTAL LIABILITIES AND NET WORTH	$26,500

© CENGAGE LEARNING 2014

sheet as a statement that reports the financial condition of a business firm such as the Hershey Foods Corporation, but balance sheets apply to individuals, too. For example, Marty Campbell graduated from college three years ago and obtained a position as a sales representative for an office supply firm. After going to work, he established a checking and savings account and purchased an automobile, stereo, television, and a few pieces of furniture. Marty paid cash for some purchases, but he had to borrow money to pay for the larger ones. Figure 17.5 shows Marty's current personal balance sheet.

Marty Campbell's assets total $26,500, and his liabilities amount to $10,000. Although the difference between total assets and total liabilities is referred to as *owners' equity* or *stockholders' equity* for a business, it is normally called *net worth* for an individual. As reported on Marty's personal balance sheet, net worth is $16,500. The total assets ($26,500) and the total liabilities *plus* net worth ($26,500) are equal. Thus, the accounting equation (Assets = Liabilities + Owners' equity) is still in balance.

Figure 17.6 shows the balance sheet for Northeast Art Supply, a small corporation that sells picture frames, paints, canvases, and other artists' supplies to retailers in New England. Note that assets are reported on the left side of the statement, and liabilities and stockholders' equity are reported on the right side. Let's work through the different accounts in Figure 17.6.

liquidity the ease with which an asset can be converted into cash

current assets assets that can be converted quickly into cash or that will be used in one year or less

Assets

On a balance sheet, assets are listed in order from the *most liquid* to the *least liquid*. The **liquidity** of an asset is the ease with which it can be converted into cash.

Current Assets **Current assets** are assets that can be converted quickly into cash or that will be used in one year or less. Because cash is the most liquid asset, it is listed first. Next are *marketable securities*—stocks, bonds, and other investments—that can be converted into cash in a matter of days.

© NDOELJINDOEL/SHUTTERSTOCK

Checking it once, checking it twice. . . . Before determining the total value of a firm's assets, accountants must determine the value of each type of inventory a firm has on hand to meet customer demand. Accurate accounting procedures for inventory can also determine when it is time to order more inventory.

FIGURE 17.6   Business Balance Sheet

A balance sheet (sometimes referred to as a statement of financial position) summarizes a firm's accounts at the end of an accounting period, showing the various dollar amounts that enter into the accounting equation. Note that assets ($340,000) equal liabilities plus owners' equity ($340,000) and the accounting equation is still in balance.

NORTHEAST ART SUPPLY, INC.

Balance Sheet
December 31, 20XX

ASSETS

Current assets		
Cash		$ 59,000
Marketable securities		10,000
Accounts receivable	$ 40,000	
Less allowance for doubtful accounts	2,000	38,000
Notes receivable		32,000
Merchandise inventory		41,000
Prepaid expenses		2,000
Total current assets		$182,000
Fixed assets		
Delivery equipment	$110,000	
Less accumulated depreciation	20,000	$ 90,000
Furniture and store equipment	$62,000	
Less accumulated depreciation	15,000	47,000
Total fixed assets		137,000
Intangible assets		
Patents		$ 21,000
Total intangible assets		21,000
TOTAL ASSETS		$340,000

LIABILITIES AND STOCKHOLDERS' EQUITY

Current liabilities		
Accounts payable	$ 35,000	
Notes payable	25,675	
Salaries payable	4,000	
Taxes payable	5,325	
Total current liabilities		$ 70,000
Long-term liabilities		
Mortgage payable on store equipment	$ 40,000	
Total long-term liabilities		$ 40,000
TOTAL LIABILITIES		$110,000
Stockholders' equity		
Common stock (25,000×$6)	$ 150,000	
Retained earnings	80,000	
TOTAL OWNERS' EQUITY		230,000
TOTAL LIABILITIES AND OWNERS' EQUITY		$340,000

Next are the firm's receivables. Its *accounts receivable,* which result from allowing customers to make credit purchases, generally are paid within 30 to 60 days. However, the firm expects that some of these debts will not be collected. Thus, it has reduced its accounts receivables by a 5 percent *allowance for doubtful accounts.* The firm's *notes receivable* are receivables for which customers have signed promissory notes. They generally are repaid over a longer period of time than the firm's accounts receivable.

Northeast's *merchandise inventory* represents the value of goods on hand for sale to customers. Since Northeast Art Supply is a wholesale operation, the inventory listed in Figure 17.6 represents finished goods ready for sale to retailers. For a manufacturing firm, merchandise inventory also may represent raw materials that will become part of a finished product or work that has been partially completed but requires further processing.

Northeast Art's last current asset is *prepaid expenses,* which are assets that have been paid for in advance but have not yet been used. An example is insurance premiums. They are usually paid at the beginning of the policy year. The unused portion (say, for the last four months of the time period covered by the policy) is a prepaid expense. For Northeast Art, all current assets total $182,000.

Fixed Assets Fixed assets are assets that will be held or used for a period longer than one year. They generally include land, buildings, and equipment used in the continuing operation of the business. Although Northeast Art owns no land or buildings, it does own delivery equipment that originally cost $110,000. It also owns furniture and store equipment that originally cost $62,000.

fixed assets assets that will be held or used for a period longer than one year

Note that the values of both fixed assets are decreased by their *accumulated depreciation*. **Depreciation** is the process of apportioning the cost of a fixed asset over the period during which it will be used, that is, its useful life. The depreciation amount allotted to each year is an expense for that year, and the value of the asset must be reduced by the amount of depreciation expense. In the case of Northeast's delivery equipment, $20,000 of its value has been depreciated (or used up) since it was purchased. Its value at this time is thus $110,000 less $20,000, or $90,000. In a similar fashion, the original value of furniture and store equipment ($62,000) has been reduced by depreciation totaling $15,000. Furniture and store equipment now has a reported value of $47,000. For Northeast Art, all fixed assets total $137,000.

Intangible Assets **Intangible assets** are assets that do not exist physically but that have a value based on the rights or privileges they confer on a firm. They include patents, copyrights, trademarks, and goodwill. By their nature, intangible assets are long-term assets—they are of value to the firm for a number of years.

Northeast Art Supply lists a *patent* for a special oil paint that the company purchased from the inventor. The firm's accountants estimate that the patent has a current market value of $21,000. The firm's intangible assets total $21,000. Now it is possible to total all three types of assets for Northeast Art. As calculated in Figure 17.6, total assets are $340,000.

Personal APPS

Before you accept a company's job offer or buy its stock, check financials and its business situation. Are profits increasing or decreasing? How is it handling its debt? What are its plans for expansion?

Liabilities and Owners' Equity

The liabilities and the owners' equity accounts complete the balance sheet. The firm's liabilities are separated into two categories—current and long-term liabilities.

Current Liabilities A firm's **current liabilities** are debts that will be repaid in one year or less. Northeast Art Supply purchased merchandise from its suppliers on credit. Thus, its balance sheet includes an entry for accounts payable. *Accounts payable* are short-term obligations that arise as a result of a firm making credit purchases.

Notes payable are obligations that have been secured with promissory notes. They are usually short-term obligations, but they may extend beyond one year. Only those that must be paid within the year are listed under current liabilities.

Northeast Art also lists *salaries payable* and *taxes payable* as current liabilities. These are both expenses that have been incurred during the current accounting period but will be paid in the next accounting period. For Northeast Art, current liabilities total $70,000.

Long-Term Liabilities **Long-term liabilities** are debts that need not be repaid for at least one year. Northeast lists only one long-term liability—a $40,000 *mortgage payable* for store equipment. As you can see in Figure 17.6, Northeast Art's current and long-term liabilities total $110,000.

Owners' or Stockholders' Equity For a sole proprietorship or partnership, the owners' equity is shown as the difference between assets and liabilities. In a partnership, each partner's share of the ownership is reported separately in each owner's name. For a corporation, the owners' equity usually is referred to as *stockholders' equity*. The

depreciation the process of apportioning the cost of a fixed asset over the period during which it will be used

intangible assets assets that do not exist physically but that have a value based on the rights or privileges they confer on a firm

current liabilities debts that will be repaid in one year or less

long-term liabilities debts that need not be repaid for at least one year

dollar amount reported on the balance sheet is the total value of stock plus retained earnings that have accumulated to date. **Retained earnings** are the portion of a business's profits not distributed to stockholders.

The original investment by the owners of Northeast Art Supply was $150,000 and was obtained by selling 25,000 shares at $6 per share. In addition, $80,000 of Northeast Art's earnings has been reinvested in the business since it was founded. Thus, owners' equity totals $230,000.

As the two grand totals in Figure 17.6 show, Northeast Art's assets and the sum of its liabilities and owners' equity are equal—at $340,000. The accounting equation (Assets = Liabilities + Owners' equity) is still in balance.

Read and interpret an income statement. **6**

THE INCOME STATEMENT

Question: *Where can you find the profit or loss amount for Apple, Inc.?*

Answer: The firm's income statement.

An **income statement** is a summary of a firm's revenues and expenses during a specified accounting period—one month, three months, six months, or a year. The income statement is sometimes called the *earnings statement* or *the statement of income and expenses*. Let's begin our discussion by constructing a personal income statement for Marty Campbell. Having worked as a sales representative for an office supply firm for the past three years, Marty now earns $33,600 a year, or $2,800 a month. After deductions, his take-home pay is $1,900 a month. As illustrated in Figure 17.7, Marty's typical monthly expenses include payments for an automobile

FIGURE 17.7   Personal Income Statement

By subtracting expenses from income, anyone can construct a personal income statement and determine if he or she has a surplus or deficit at the end of each month.

Marty Campbell
Personal Income Statement
For the month ended December 31, 20XX

INCOME (Take-home pay)		$1,900
LESS MONTHLY EXPENSES		
Automobile loan	$ 250	
Credit card payment	100	
Apartment rent	500	
Utilities	200	
Food	250	
Clothing	100	
Recreation & entertainment	250	
TOTAL MONTHLY EXPENSES		1,650
CASH SURPLUS (or profit)		$ 250

retained earnings the portion of a business's profits not distributed to stockholders

income statement a summary of a firm's revenues and expenses during a specified accounting period

FIGURE 17.8　Business Income Statement

An income statement summarizes a firm's revenues and expenses during a specified accounting period. For Northeast Art Supply, net income after taxes is $30,175.

NORTHEAST ART SUPPLY, INC.

Income Statement
for the Year Ended
December 31, 20XX

Revenues			
Gross sales		$465,000	
Less sales returns and allowances	$ 9,500		
Less sales discounts	4,500	14,000	
Net sales			$451,000
Cost of goods sold			
Beginning inventory, January 1, 20XX		$ 40,000	
Purchases	$346,000		
Less purchase discounts	11,000		
Net purchases		335,000	
Cost of goods available for sale		$375,000	
Less ending inventory December 31, 20XX		41,000	
Cost of goods sold			334,000
Gross profit			$117,000
Operating expenses			
Selling expenses			
Sales salaries	$ 22,000		
Advertising	4,000		
Sales promotion	2,500		
Depreciation—store equipment	3,000		
Depreciation—delivery equipment	4,000		
Miscellaneous selling expenses	1,500		
Total selling expenses		$ 37,000	
General expenses			
Office salaries	$ 28,500		
Rent	8,500		
Depreciation—furniture	1,500		
Utilities expense	2,500		
Insurance expense	1,000		
Miscellaneous expense	500		
Total general expense		42,500	
Total operating expenses			79,500
Net income from operations			$ 37,500
Less interest expense			2,000
NET INCOME BEFORE TAXES			$ 35,500
Less federal income taxes			5,325
NET INCOME AFTER TAXES			$ 30,175

© CENGAGE LEARNING 2014

loan, credit card purchases, apartment rent, utilities, food, clothing, and recreation and entertainment.

Although the difference between income and expenses is referred to as *profit* or *loss* for a business, it is normally referred to as a *cash surplus* or *cash deficit* for an individual. Fortunately for Marty, he has a surplus of $250 at the end of each month. He can use this surplus for savings, investing, or paying off debts. It is also possible to use the information from a personal income statement to construct a personal budget. A *personal budget* is a specific plan for spending your income—over the next month, for example.

Figure 17.8 shows the income statement for Northeast Art Supply. For a business, revenues *less* cost of goods sold *less* operating expenses equals net income.

Revenues

Revenues are the dollar amounts earned by a firm from selling goods, providing services, or performing business activities. Like most businesses, Northeast Art Supply obtains its revenues solely from the sale of its products or services. The revenues section of its income statement begins with gross sales. **Gross sales** are the total dollar amount

revenues the dollar amounts earned by a firm from selling goods, providing services, or performing business activities

gross sales the total dollar amount of all goods and services sold during the accounting period

of all goods and services sold during the accounting period. Deductions made from this amount are

- *sales returns*—merchandise returned to the firm by its customers;
- *sales allowances*—price reductions offered to customers who accept slightly damaged or soiled merchandise; and
- *sales discounts*—price reductions offered to customers who pay their bills promptly.

The remainder is the firm's net sales. **Net sales** are the actual dollar amounts received by the firm for the goods and services it has sold after adjustment for returns, allowances, and discounts. For Northeast Art, net sales are $451,000.

Cost of Goods Sold

The standard method of determining the **cost of goods sold** by a retailing or a wholesaling firm can be summarized as follows:

> Cost of goods sold = Beginning inventory + Net purchases − Ending inventory

According to Figure 17.8, Northeast Art Supply began its accounting period on January 1 with a merchandise inventory that cost $40,000. During the next 12 months, the firm purchased merchandise valued at $346,000. After deducting *purchase discounts*, however, it paid only $335,000 for this merchandise. Thus, during the year, Northeast had total *goods available for sale* valued at $40,000 plus $335,000, for a total of $375,000.

Twelve months later, at the end of the accounting period on December 31, Northeast had sold all but $41,000 worth of the available goods. The cost of goods sold by Northeast was therefore $375,000 less ending inventory of $41,000, or $334,000. It is now possible to calculate gross profit. A firm's **gross profit** is its net sales *less* the cost of goods sold. For Northeast Art Supply, gross profit was $117,000.

Operating Expenses

A firm's **operating expenses** are all business costs other than the cost of goods sold. Total operating expenses generally are divided into two categories: selling expenses or general expenses.

Selling expenses are costs related to the firm's marketing activities. For Northeast Art Supply, selling expenses total $37,000. *General expenses* are costs incurred in managing a business, in this case, a total of $42,500. Now it is possible to total both selling and general expenses. As Figure 17.8 shows, total operating expenses for the accounting period are $79,500.

Net Income

When revenues exceed expenses, the difference is called **net income**. When expenses exceed revenues, the difference is called **net loss**. As Figure 17.8 shows, Northeast Art's *net income from operations* is computed as gross profit ($117,000) less total operating expenses ($79,500). For Northeast Art, net income from operations is $37,500. From this amount, *interest expense* of $2,000 is deducted to obtain a *net income before taxes* of $35,500. The interest expense is deducted in this section of the income statement because it is not an operating expense. Rather, it is an expense that results from financing the business.

Northeast Art's *federal income taxes* are $5,325. Although these taxes may or may not be payable immediately, they are definitely an expense that must be deducted from income. This leaves Northeast Art with a *net income after taxes* of $30,175. This amount may be used to pay a dividend to stockholders, it may be retained or reinvested in the firm, it may be used to reduce the firm's debts, or all three.

net sales the actual dollar amounts received by a firm for the goods and services it has sold after adjustment for returns, allowances, and discounts

cost of goods sold the dollar amount equal to beginning inventory *plus* net purchases *less* ending inventory

gross profit a firm's net sales *less* the cost of goods sold

operating expenses all business costs other than the cost of goods sold

net income occurs when revenues exceed expenses

net loss occurs when expenses exceed revenues

© TOM MCNEMAR/SHUTTERSTOCK

Would you like to drive one of these to college or work? Although not your typical commuter vehicle, these trucks represent a necessary investment for an electric utility company. Without these "bucket trucks," a utility company would be unable to repair existing electric transmission lines or build new ones. In fact, dollar values for all equipment purchases are reported on a firm's statement of cash flows.

Entrepreneurial SUCCESS

Accounting for First-Time Entrepreneurs

How can a firm be profitable but have no cash? The founder of a small soap-making supply firm was spending money to develop profitable new products more quickly than she was generating cash from sales. She needed to focus on her *statement of cash flows* and on her *cost of goods sold*. She did, and within a few years, she had built the company into a million-dollar business. Entrepreneurs in her situation need to control expenses and have sufficient cash flow to get through occasional unprofitable periods.

What about being so busy selling to new customers that the firm doesn't do much to collect on outstanding invoices? A partner in a commercial tile company was pleased that he had more than $100,000 in accounts receivable—until he learned that some unpaid bills were so old that those customers had gone out of business. Now he pays more attention to his *accounts receivables,* and he doesn't sell to customers until they settle their outstanding balances. Some experts advise entrepreneurs to collect receivables within 30 days of making the sale.

Finally, record *revenues* at the proper time. One entrepreneur booked revenues in December when customers left deposits for custom-made furniture. Because he didn't deliver the items until January, the full sales should have been recorded in that month. Correcting this changed his firm's revenues and profitability for both years.

Sources: Based on information in Deanna Pogorelc, "Accounting 101 for the First-Time Entrepreneur," *Entrepreneurship.org,* March 22, 2012, www.entrepreneurship.org; Darren Dahl, "Basics of Accounting Are Vital to Survival for Entrepreneurs," *New York Times,* August 3, 2011, www.nytimes.com; Don Sadler, "It's All in the Numbers," *Costco Connection,* April 2012, p. 43; "Pay Yourself First," *SCORE,* July 28, 2011, www.score.org.

THE STATEMENT OF CASH FLOWS

 7 Describe business activities that affect a firm's cash flow.

Cash is vital to any business. In 1987, the SEC and the Financial Accounting Standards Board required all publicly traded companies to include a statement of cash flows, along with their balance sheet and income statement, in their annual report. The **statement of cash flows** illustrates how the company's operating, investing, and financing activities affect cash during an accounting period. Whereas a firm's balance sheet reports dollar values for assets, liabilities, and owners' equity and an income statement reports the firm's dollar amount of profit or loss, the statement of cash flows focuses on how much cash is on hand to pay the firm's bills. Executives and managers can also use the information on a firm's statement of cash flows to determine how much cash is available to pay dividends to stockholders. Finally, the information on the statement of cash flows can be used to evaluate decisions related to a firm's future investments and financing needs. Outside stakeholders including investors, lenders, and suppliers are also interested in a firm's statement of cash flows. Investors want to know if a firm can pay dividends in the future. Before extending credit to a firm, lenders and suppliers often use the information on the statement of cash flows to evaluate the firm's ability to repay its debts.

A statement of cash flows for Northeast Art Supply is illustrated in Figure 17.9. It provides information concerning the company's cash receipts and cash payments and is organized around three different activities: operating, investing, and financing.

- *Cash flows from operating activities.* This is the first section of a statement of cash flows. It addresses the firm's primary revenue source—providing goods and services. Typical adjustments include adding the amount of depreciation to a firm's net income. Other adjustments for increase or decrease in amounts for accounts receivable, inventory, accounts payable, and income taxes payable are also required to reflect a true picture of cash flows from operating activities.
- *Cash flows from investing activities.* The second section of the statement is concerned with cash flow from investments. This includes the purchase and sale of land, equipment, and other assets and investments.
- *Cash flows from financing activities.* The third and final section deals with the cash flow from all financing activities. It reports changes in debt obligation and owners'

statement of cash flows a statement that illustrates how the company's operating, investing, and financing activities affect cash during an accounting period

FIGURE 17.9   Statement of Cash Flows

A statement of cash flows summarizes how a firm's operating, investing, and financing activities affect its cash during a specified period—one month, three months, six months, or a year. For Northeast Art Supply, the amount of cash at the end of the year reported on the statement of cash flows is $59,000—the same amount reported for the cash account on the firm's balance sheet.

NORTHEAST ART SUPPLY, INC.

Statement of Cash Flows
for the Year Ended
December 31, 20XX

Cash flows from operating activities		
Net Income		$30,175
Adjustments to reconcile net income to net cash flows		
Depreciation	$ 8,500	
Decrease in accounts receivable	1,000	
Increase in inventory	(5,000)	
Increase in accounts payable	6,000	
Increase in income taxes payable	3,000	13,500
Net cash provided by operating activities		$43,675
Cash flows from investing activities		
Purchase of equipment	$ (2,000)	
Purchase of investments	(10,000)	
Sale of investments	20,000	
Net cash provided by investing activities		8,000
Cash flows from financing activities		
Payments on debt	$(23,000)	
Payment of dividends	(5,000)	
Net cash provided by financing activities		(28,000)
NET INCREASE IN CASH		$23,675
Cash at beginning of year		35,325
CASH AT END OF YEAR		$59,000

equity accounts. This includes loans and repayments, the sale and repurchase of the company's own stock, and cash dividends.

The totals of all three activities are added to the beginning cash balance to determine the ending cash balance. For Northeast Art Supply, the ending cash balance is $59,000. Note that this is the same amount reported for the cash account on the firm's balance sheet. Together, the statement of cash flows, balance sheet, and income statement illustrate the results of past business decisions and reflect the firm's ability to pay debts and dividends and to finance new growth.

Summarize how managers evaluate the financial health of a business.

8

EVALUATING FINANCIAL STATEMENTS

All three financial statements—the balance sheet, the income statement, and the statement of cash flows—can provide answers to a variety of questions about a firm's ability to do business and stay in business, its profitability, and its value as an investment. Often the first step is to compare a firm's financial data with other firms in similar industries and with its own financial results over recent accounting periods.

Comparing Financial Data

Many firms compare their financial results with those of competing firms, with industry averages, and with their own financial results. Comparisons are possible as long as accountants follow GAAPs. Except for minor differences in format and terms, the balance sheet, income statement, and statement of cash flows of Procter & Gamble, for example, will be similar to those of other large corporations, such as Nestle, Clorox, Colgate-Palmolive, and Unilever, in the consumer goods industry. Comparisons among firms give managers a general idea of a firm's relative effectiveness and its standing within the industry. Competitors' financial statements can be obtained from their annual reports—if they are public corporations. Industry averages are published by reporting services such as D&B (formerly Dun & Bradstreet) and Standard & Poor's, as well as by some industry trade associations. Today, most corporations include in their annual reports comparisons of the important elements of their financial statements for recent years. For example, Figure 17.10 shows such comparisons—of revenue, research and development (R&D), operating income, and sales and marketing expenses—for Microsoft Corporation, a world leader in the computer software industry. By examining these data, an operating manager can tell whether R&D expenditures have been increasing or decreasing over the past three years. The vice president of marketing can determine if the total amount of sales and marketing expenses is changing. Stockholders and potential investors, on the other hand, may be more concerned with increases or decreases in Microsoft's revenues and operating income over the same time period. Still another

| FIGURE 17.10 | Comparisons of Present and Past Financial Statements for Microsoft Corporation |

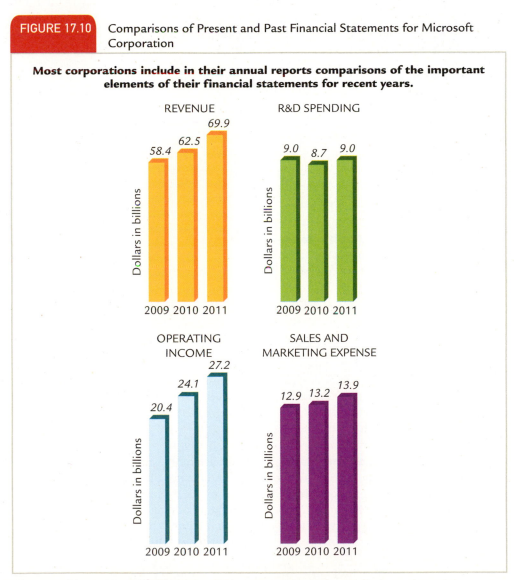

Most corporations include in their annual reports comparisons of the important elements of their financial statements for recent years.

Source: Adapted from the Microsoft Corporation 2011 Annual Report, www.microsoft.com (accessed April 10, 2012).

type of analysis of a firm's financial health involves computation of financial ratios.

Financial Ratios

A **financial ratio** is a number that shows the relationship between two elements of a firm's financial statements. While it is possible to calculate many different financial ratios, we'll only discuss three different ratios that are used to measure a firm's profitability, its ability to pay its debts, and how often it sells its inventory. Like the individual elements in financial statements, these ratios can be compared with those of competitors, with industry averages, and with the firm's past ratios from previous accounting periods. The information required to form these ratios is found in a firm's balance sheet, income statement, and statement of cash flows (in our examples for Northeast Art Supply, Figures 17.6, 17.8, and 17.9).

Measuring a Firm's Ability to Earn Profits A firm's net income after taxes indicates whether the firm is profitable. It does not, however, indicate how effectively the firm's resources are being used. For this latter purpose, a return on sales ratio can be computed. **Return on sales (or profit margin)** is a financial ratio calculated by dividing net income after taxes by net sales. For Northeast Art Supply,

The next step: Going beyond a firm's financial statements. Often accountants must calculate financial ratios to determine the financial "health" of a firm. Among the most useful (and informative) are ratios that measure a firm's profitability, its ability to pay its debts, and how well it manages its inventory and receivables.

© DENIS OPOLJN/SHUTTERSTOCK

$$\text{Return on sales} = \frac{\text{net income after taxes}}{\text{net sales}} = \frac{\$30,175}{\$451,000}$$
$$= 0.067, \text{ or } 6.7 \text{ percent}$$

The return on sales indicates how effectively the firm is transforming sales into profits. A higher return on sales is better than a low one. Today, the average return on sales for all business firms is between 4 and 5 percent. With a return on sales of 6.7 percent, Northeast Art Supply is above average. A low return on sales can be increased by reducing expenses, increasing sales, or both.

Measuring a Firm's Ability to Pay Its Debts A current ratio can be used to evaluate a firm's ability to pay its current liabilities. A firm's **current ratio** is computed by dividing current assets by current liabilities. For Northeast Art Supply,

$$\text{Current ratio} = \frac{\text{current assets}}{\text{current liabilities}} = \frac{\$182,000}{\$70,000} = 2.6$$

This means that Northeast Art Supply has $2.60 of current assets for every $1 of current liabilities. The average current ratio for all industries is 2.0, but it varies greatly from industry to industry. A high current ratio indicates that a firm can pay its current liabilities. A low current ratio can be improved by repaying current liabilities, by reducing dividend payments to stockholders to increase the firm's cash balance, or by obtaining additional cash from investors.

Measuring How Well a Firm Manages Its Inventory A firm's **inventory turnover** is the number of times the firm sells its merchandise inventory in one year. It is approximated by dividing the cost of goods sold in one year by the average value of the inventory.

The average value of the inventory can be found by adding the beginning inventory value and the ending inventory value (given on the income statement) and dividing the sum by 2. For Northeast Art Supply, average inventory is $40,500. Thus

financial ratio a number that shows the relationship between two elements of a firm's financial statements

return on sales (or profit margin) a financial ratio calculated by dividing net income after taxes by net sales

current ratio a financial ratio computed by dividing current assets by current liabilities

inventory turnover a financial ratio calculated by dividing the cost of goods sold in one year by the average value of the inventory

$$\text{Inventory turnover} = \frac{\text{cost of goods sold}}{\text{average inventory}} = \frac{\$334,000}{\$40,500}$$
$$= 8.2 \text{ times per year}$$

Northeast Art Supply sells its merchandise inventory 8.2 times each year, or about once every 45 days. The average inventory turnover for all firms is about 9 times per year, but turnover rates vary widely from industry to industry. For example, supermarkets may have inventory turnover rates of 20 or higher, whereas inventory turnover rates for furniture stores are generally well below the national average. The quickest way to improve inventory turnover is to order merchandise in smaller quantities at more frequent intervals.

Like the three ratios described in this section, the calculations for other financial ratios, including return on owners' ratio, earnings per share, working capital, and debt-to-equity, are based on the information contained in a firm's balance sheet, income statement, and statement of cash flows. For more detailed information on ratio analysis, you may want to read more on the topic in an accounting or finance textbook or use an Internet search engine.

This chapter ends our discussion of management and accounting information. In Chapter 18, we begin our examination of business finances by discussing money, banking, and credit.

return to Inside BUSINESS

PricewaterhouseCoopers

The 21st-century PwC is nothing like the small accounting practice that Samuel Lowell Price set up in London during the mid-19th century. Relying on the knowledge and experience of its global workforce, PwC offers a wide variety of auditing, accounting, and tax services. Its industry specialists also provide expert advice and guidance to banks, law firms, retailers, hospitals, energy firms, travel companies, and many other types of companies, as well as educational institutions, government agencies, and nonprofit groups.

PwC has some very glamorous clients, although its role is behind the scenes rather than on the red carpet. For example, PwC collects and counts the votes for the Academy Awards. Thanks to the firm's extreme measures to ensure secrecy, nobody knows who won until the famous presenters step into the spotlight and make their announcements to the world.

Questions

1. When an accounting firm like PwC has been hired to examine and sign off on a public corporation's annual report, should it limit its consulting work to avoid being influenced by financial ties to the client? Explain your answer.

2. Why would the Academy of Motion Picture Arts and Sciences hire PwC instead of having its own employees count votes for the Academy Awards?

SUMMARY

 Examine how information can reduce risk when making a decision.

The more information a manager has, the less risk there is that a decision will be incorrect. Information produces knowledge and empowers managers and employees to make better decisions. Because of the volume of information they receive each day and their need to make decisions on a daily basis, businesspeople use information rules to shorten the time spent analyzing choices. Information rules emerge when business research confirms the same results each time it studies the same or a similar set of circumstances. Although many people use the terms *data* and *information* interchangeably, there is a difference. Data are numerical or verbal descriptions that usually result from some sort of measurement. Information is data presented in a form that is useful for a specific purpose. A database is a single collection of data and information stored in one place that can be used by people throughout an organization to make decisions. Although databases are important, the way the data and information are used is even more important. As a result, management information experts now use the term *knowledge management* (KM) to describe a firm's procedures for generating, using, and sharing the data and information.

 Discuss management's information requirements.

A management information system (MIS) is a means of providing managers with the information they need to perform their jobs as effectively as possible. The purpose of an MIS (sometimes referred to as an information technology system or simply IT system) is to distribute timely and useful information from both internal and external sources to the decision makers who need it. The specific types of information managers need depend on their area of management and level within the firm. The size and complexity of an MIS must be tailored to the information needs of the organization it serves.

 Outline the five functions of an information system.

The five functions performed by an MIS system are collecting data, storing data, updating data, processing data into information, and presenting information. Data may be collected from such internal sources as company records, reports, and minutes of meetings, as well as from the firm's managers and employees. External sources include customers, suppliers, financial institutions and banks, trade and business publications, industry conferences, online computer services, and information-gathering organizations. An MIS must be able to store data until they are needed and to update them regularly to ensure that the information presented to managers and employees is accurate, complete, and timely. Data processing is the MIS function that transforms stored data into a form useful for a specific purpose. Finally, the processed data (which now can be called information) must be presented for use. Verbal information generally is presented in the form of a report. Numerical information most often is displayed in graphs, charts, or tables. In addition to the five basic functions performed by an MIS, managers and employees can use a decision-support system, an executive information system, and expert system to help improve the decision-making process.

 Explain why accurate accounting information and audited financial statements are important.

Accounting is the process of systematically collecting, analyzing, and reporting financial information. It can be used to answer questions about what has happened in the past; it also can be used to help make decisions about the future. In fact, the firm's accountants and its accounting system often translate goals, objectives, and plans into dollars and cents to help determine if a decision or plan of action makes "financial sense." The purpose of an audit is to make sure that a firm's financial statements have been prepared in accordance with generally accepted accounting principles. To help ensure that

corporate financial information is accurate and in response to the accounting scandals that surfaced in the last few years, the Sarbanes–Oxley Act was signed into law. This law contains a number of provisions designed to restore public confidence in the accounting industry.

 Read and interpret a balance sheet.

A balance sheet (sometimes referred to as a statement of financial position) is a summary of a firm's assets, liabilities, and owners' equity accounts at the end of an accounting period. This statement must demonstrate that the accounting equation is in balance. On the balance sheet, assets are categorized as current, fixed, or intangible. Similarly, liabilities can be divided into current liabilities and long-term liabilities. For a sole proprietorship or partnership, owners' equity is shown as the difference between assets and liabilities. For corporations, the owners' equity section reports the values of stock and retained earnings.

 Read and interpret an income statement.

An income statement is a summary of a firm's financial operations during the specified accounting period. On the income statement, the company's gross profit is computed by subtracting the cost of goods sold from net sales. Operating expenses and interest expense then are deducted to compute net income before taxes. Finally, income taxes are deducted to obtain the firm's net income after taxes.

 Describe business activities that affect a firm's cash flow.

Since 1987, the Securities and Exchange Commission (SEC) and the Financial Accounting Standards Board have required all publicly traded companies to include a statement of cash flows in their annual reports. This statement illustrates how the company's operating, investing, and financing activities affect cash during an accounting period. Together, the cash flow statement, balance sheet, and income statement illustrate the results of past decisions and the business's ability to pay debts and dividends as well as to finance new growth.

 Summarize how managers evaluate the financial health of a business.

The firm's financial statements and its accounting information become more meaningful when compared with information for competitors, for the industry in which the firm operates, and corresponding information for previous years. Such comparisons permit managers, employees, lenders, investors, and other interested people to pick out trends in growth, borrowing, income, and other business variables and to determine whether the firm is on the way to accomplishing its long-term goals. A number of financial ratios can be computed from the information in a firm's financial statements. These ratios provide a picture of a firm's profitability, its ability to pay its debts, and how often it sells its inventory. Like the information on the firm's financial statements, these ratios can and should be compared with information for competitors, for the industry in which the firm operates, and corresponding information for previous years.

KEY TERMS

You should now be able to define and give an example relevant to each of the following terms:

data (488)
information (488)
database (490)
knowledge management (KM) (490)
management information system (MIS) (490)
information technology (IT) officer (490)
data processing (493)
statistic (494)
decision-support system (DSS) (496)
executive information system (EIS) (496)

expert system (496)
accounting (497)
audit (497)
generally accepted accounting principles (GAAPs) (497)
managerial accounting (498)
financial accounting (498)
certified public accountant (CPA) (499)
assets (500)
liabilities (500)
owners' equity (500)
accounting equation (500)
double-entry bookkeeping system (500)

annual report (500)
balance sheet (or statement of financial position) (500)
liquidity (501)
current assets (501)
fixed assets (502)
depreciation (503)
intangible assets (503)
current liabilities (503)
long-term liabilities (503)
retained earnings (504)
income statement (504)
revenues (505)
gross sales (505)
net sales (506)

cost of goods sold (506)
gross profit (506)
operating expenses (506)
net income (506)
net loss (506)
statement of cash flows (507)
financial ratio (510)
return on sales (or profit margin) (510)
current ratio (510)
inventory turnover (510)

REVIEW QUESTIONS

1. In your own words, describe how information reduces risk when you make a personal or work-related decision.
2. What are information rules? How do they simplify the process of making decisions?
3. What is the difference between data and information? Give one example of accounting data and one example of accounting information.
4. List the five functions of an MIS.
5. What are the components of a typical business report?
6. Describe the three types of computer applications that help employees, managers, and executives make smart decisions.
7. What purpose do audits and GAAPs serve in today's business world?
8. How do the major provisions of the Sarbanes–Oxley Act affect a public company's accounting procedures?
9. What is the difference between a private accountant and a public accountant? What are certified public accountants?

10. State the accounting equation, and list two specific examples of each term in the equation.
11. What is the principal difference between a balance sheet and an income statement?
12. How are current assets distinguished from fixed assets? Why are fixed assets depreciated on a balance sheet?
13. Explain how a retailing firm would determine the cost of goods sold during an accounting period.
14. How does a firm determine its net income after taxes?
15. What is the purpose of a statement of cash flows?
16. Explain the calculation procedure for and significance of each of the following:
    a. Return on sales
    b. The current ratio
    c. Inventory turnover

DISCUSSION QUESTIONS

1. Do managers really need all the kinds of information discussed in this chapter? If not, which kinds can they do without?
2. How can confidential data and information (such as the wages of individual employees) be kept confidential and yet still be available to managers who need them?
3. Bankers usually insist that prospective borrowers submit audited financial statements along with a loan application. Why should financial statements be audited by a CPA?
4. What can be said about a firm whose owners' equity is a negative amount? How could such a situation come about?

5. Do the balance sheet, income statement, and statement of cash flows contain all the information you might want as a potential lender or stockholder? What other information would you like to examine?
6. Why is it so important to compare a firm's current financial statements with those of previous years, those of competitors, and the average of all firms in the industry in which the firm operates?

As the "leading supplier of exclusive, high-end audio and video electronics for homes, businesses, educational institutions, and other organizations in greater Chicagoland," The Little Guys has built an enviable reputation since its founding in 1994. The Little Guys sells and installs top-brand home audio and theater equipment and does it well. The company prides itself on its highly knowledgeable salespeople and outstanding customer service, and these have helped it survive strong competition from both "big guys" like the Best Buy electronics chain, which has a store not far away, and economic downturns that have cut consumers' buying power. "We have the best employees," says the company's Web site, and "how we treat our customers makes us great."

David Wexler, the store's co-owner, describes how one of the firm's award-winning salespeople deals with his customers, for instance: "If a guy comes in to buy a $50 DVD player, Ed treats him the same as the guy who's spending $500,000 with us. I think that's what keeps people coming back over and over and over. He fights for them. Frankly, sometimes he fights too much for them. But he's their advocate, and they know it."

In response to recession-slowed sales, the company was recently forced to lay some people off and has reorganized departments from advertising to payroll (the latter is a major and complex expense for The Little Guys because its salespeople earn base pay plus a percentage of their sales). In another cost-cutting move, the company also recently moved to a new location not far from its original store, and it's keeping close track of its cash flows in and out. Salespeople are careful about customers' change orders, too, which often cost the company money. Now, as the economy begins to improve and consumers begin to spend more on electronics, these same cost-cutting measures will help improve the firm's bottom-line profit amount.

With the help of QuickBooks accounting software and a professional accountant who visits regularly, David Wexler and co-owner Evie Wexler have deepened their knowledge of accounting and finance as the business has grown. In the beginning, for instance, they checked sales figures every day, but David quickly realized that this practice created instant information overload.

Now he looks at the numbers about every week or ten days, comparing each set with past results, and the accountant comes in at least once each quarter to help with more complex issues like depreciation of assets and equipment for tax purposes. Taxes are a big concern. As Evie Wexler points out, sometimes the firm has to make a special push to sell off inventory in order to generate extra cash flow when taxes are due, or when it wants to purchase new merchandise that customers are asking for and that will therefore sell faster. Keeping warehoused inventory low saves money, too.

One reason cash flow can be slow is that customers often negotiate prices and repayment terms at The Little Guys, so that an expensive system might not only be sold at a discount, but the customer may also be given extra time to pay. That certainly helps make customers happy, but if it means the company is paying its own suppliers on time while customers lag in their payments, cash can get tight. As David explains, that's partly why The Little Guys limits the number of brands it sells and works with only a few suppliers. Establishing good relationships with these suppliers, largely by ordering regularly and paying on time, allows the company to ask them for special discounts or improved payment terms—even when other retailers aren't getting them—and find yet another way to earn a little more profit on the same volume of sales.[6]

Questions

1. Do you think a fairly small company like The Little Guys still needs a professional accountant after its owners have had so much experience running a successful business? Why or why not?

2. Do you think The Little Guys is doing a good job of using information to manage the business? If so, why, and if not, how can the company improve this function?

3. What are some of the factors that contribute to The Little Guys' cash-flow problems? How might the owners better manage its cash flow?

Will sales and profits meet the expectations of investors and Wall Street analysts? Managers at public corporations must answer this important question quarter after quarter, year after year. In an ideal world—one in which there is never an economic crisis, expenses never go up, and customers never buy competing products—the corporation's price for a share of its stock would soar, and investors would cheer as every financial report showed ever-higher sales revenues, profit margins, and earnings.

In the real world, however, many uncontrollable and unpredictable factors can affect a corporation's performance. Customers may buy fewer units or postpone purchases, competitors may introduce superior products, expenses may rise, interest rates may climb, and buying power may plummet. Faced with the prospect of releasing financial results that fall short of Wall Street's expectations, managers may feel intense pressure to "make the numbers" using a variety of accounting techniques.

For example, some executives at the telecom company WorldCom made earnings look better by booking billions of dollars in ordinary expenses as capital investments. The company was forced into bankruptcy a few weeks after the $11 billion accounting scam was exposed. As another example, top managers at the drug retailer Rite Aid posted transactions improperly to inflate corporate earnings. Later, when Rite Aid had to lower its earnings by $1.6 billion, investors fled and the share price fell.

Under the Sarbanes–Oxley Act, the CEO and CFO now must certify the corporation's financial reports. (For more information about Sarbanes–Oxley, visit www.aicpa.org, the Web site of the American Institute of Certified Public Accountants.) Immediately after this legislation became effective, hundreds of companies restated their earnings, a sign that stricter accounting controls were having the intended effect. "I don't mean to sugarcoat the figure on restatements," says Steve Odland, the former CEO of Office Depot, "but I think it is positive—it shows a healthy system." Yet not all earnings restatements are due to accounting irregularities. "The general impression of the public is that accounting rules are black and white," he adds. "They are often anything but that, and in many instances the changes in earnings came after new interpretations by the chief accountant of the SEC."

Now that stricter regulation has been in force for some time, fewer and fewer corporations are announcing restatements. In fact, the number of corporations restating earnings has declined since it peaked in 2006. The chief reason for the decline is that corporations and their accounting firms have learned to dig deeper and analyze the process used to produce the figures for financial statements, as well as checking the numbers themselves.

Because accounting rules are open to interpretation, managers sometimes find themselves facing ethical dilemmas when a corporation feels pressure to live up to Wall Street's expectations. Consider the hypothetical situation at Commodore Appliances, a fictional company that sells to Home Depot, Lowe's, and other major retail chains. Margaret, the vice president of sales, has told Rob, a district manager, that the company's sales are down 10 percent in the current quarter. She points out that sales in Rob's district are down 20 percent and states that higher-level managers want him to improve this month's

figures using "book and hold," which means recording future sales transactions in the current period.

Rob hesitates, saying that the company is gaining market share and that he needs more time to get sales momentum going. He thinks "book and hold" is not a good business practice, even if it is legal. Margaret hints that Rob will lose his job if his sales figures don't look better and stresses that he will need the book-and-hold approach for one month only. Rob realizes that if he doesn't go along, he won't be working at Commodore for very much longer.

Meeting with Kevin, one of Commodore's auditors, Rob learns that book and hold meets GAAPs. Kevin emphasizes that customers must be willing to take title to the goods before they're delivered or billed. Any book-and-hold sales must be real, backed by documentation such as e-mails to and from buyers, and the transactions must be completed in the near future.

Rob is at a crossroads: His sales figures must be higher if Commodore is to achieve its performance targets, yet he doesn't know exactly when (or if) he actually would complete any book-and-hold sales he might report this month. He doesn't want to mislead anyone, but he also doesn't want to lose his job or put other people's jobs in jeopardy by refusing to do what he is being asked to do. Rob is confident that he can improve his district's sales over the long term. However, Commodore's executives are pressuring Rob to make the sales figures look better right now. What should he do?[7]

Questions

1. What are the ethical and legal implications of using accounting practices such as the book-and-hold technique to inflate corporate earnings?
2. Why would Commodore's auditor insist that Rob document any sales booked under the book-and-hold technique?
3. If you were in Rob's situation, would you agree to use the book-and-hold technique this month? Justify your decision.
4. Imagine that Commodore has taken out a multimillion-dollar loan that must be repaid next year. How might the lender react if it learned that Commodore was using the book-and-hold method to make revenues look higher than they really are?

Building Skills for Career Success

① USING SOCIAL MEDIA

The Security and Exchange Commission (SEC) regulates accounting practices and has pretty specific rules about endorsements and testimonials. Yet, much of the content on social media sites deals with both endorsements and testimonials. For example, Facebook "likes" can be considered a type of endorsement. Recently the SEC weighed in on this. Read a summary of what they had to say at www.accountingtoday.com/news/SEC-Social-Media-Guidelines-61964-1.html.

1. What do you think of these rules? Do you agree or disagree? Why?

2. Can you think of other industries that may have to contend with the transparency of social media?

② JOURNALING FOR SUCCESS

More and more people are using computers and personal finance and accounting software to provide the information they need to manage their finances. To complete this journal entry, use the Internet to research the Quicken software package or a software package offered by a local bank or financial institution. Then answer the following questions.

18 Understanding Money, Banking, and Credit

LEARNING OBJECTIVES

Once you complete this chapter, you will be able to:

1 Identify the functions and characteristics of money.

2 Summarize how the Federal Reserve System regulates the money supply to maintain a healthy economy.

3 Describe the organizations involved in the banking industry.

4 Identify the services provided by financial institutions.

5 Understand how financial institutions are changing to meet the needs of domestic and international customers.

6 Explain how deposit insurance protects customers.

7 Discuss the importance of credit and credit management.

How Umpqua Bank Became "The World's Greatest Bank"

Umpqua Bank, based in Roseburg, Oregon, doesn't operate traditional bank branches. Instead, its 184 "stores" serve as community hubs, "providing banking services plus events and amenities to share with our neighbors," says executive vice-president Lani Hayward. Customers meet with bank employees at concierge desks, relax in easy chairs when opening new accounts, and enjoy a free cup of coffee and free Wi-Fi access whenever they stop in. Some Umpqua stores offer yoga classes, wine tastings, trivia contests, even conference rooms for impromptu business meetings. Customers can also sign up to see the world by joining the bank's travel club. Why all the extras? Because Umpqua wants customers to think of it as "the world's greatest bank," a good neighbor, and a force for positive change in the communities it serves.

Umpqua began with six employees and a single branch in 1953, growing through a combination of new branches, new markets, and bank mergers. Today, the branch system stretches through four states, from the Pacific Northwest through Northern California, serving customers with a mix of full-service branches, commercial bank offices, residential mortgage offices, and ATM-only locations.

In addition to its unique community store concept, Umpqua has a number of unique banking offers. One example is the GreenStreet Lending program, which provides loans to homeowners and businesses for installation of solar panels and other "green" building improvements. As another example, small businesses can borrow $10,000 to $100,000 through the MainStreet Lending program, which supplements the bank's regular business lending services.

Although Umpqua recently celebrated its 60th birthday, it thinks young when it comes to banking technology. Through online banking, mobile banking, and other high-tech systems, the bank can give its customers easy access to their money and information about their money at any hour. And as customers' needs change, Umpqua will be ready with a range of financial services for each new stage of their personal and professional lives.[1]

FYI

Did You Know?

Founded in 1953, Umpqua has grown from one small Oregon branch with six employees to 184 branches with over 2,200 employees in four states.

Most people regard a bank like Umpqua Bank—the financial institution profiled in the Inside Business feature for this chapter—as a place to deposit or borrow money. When you deposit money in a bank like Umpqua, you *receive* interest. When you borrow money from this bank or any financial institution or lender, you must *pay* interest. You may borrow to buy a home, a car, or some other high-cost item. In this case, the resource that will be transformed into money to repay the loan is the salary you receive for your labor.

Businesses also transform resources into money. A business firm (even a new one) may have a valuable asset in the form of an idea for a product or service. If the firm (or its founder) has a good credit history and the idea is a good one, a bank like Umpqua or other lenders may lend it the money to develop, produce, and market the product or service. The loan—with interest—will be repaid out of future sales revenue. In this way, both the firm and the lender will earn a reasonable profit.

In each of these situations, the borrower needs the money now and will have the ability to repay it later. Although the decision to borrow money from a bank or other financial institution should always be made after careful deliberation, the fact is that responsible borrowing enables both individuals and business firms to meet specific needs.

In this chapter, we begin by outlining the functions and characteristics of money that make it an acceptable means of payment for products, services, and resources. Then we consider the role of the Federal Reserve System in maintaining a healthy economy. Next, we describe the banking industry—commercial banks, savings and loan associations, credit unions, and other institutions that offer banking services. Then we turn our attention to how banking practices meet the needs of customers. We also describe the safeguards established by the federal government to protect depositors against losses. In closing, we examine credit transactions and sources of credit information.

Identify the functions and characteristics of money.

WHAT IS MONEY?

The members of some societies still exchange goods and services through barter, without using money. A **barter system** is a system of exchange in which goods or services are traded directly for other goods or services. The trouble with the barter system is that the two parties in an exchange must need each other's products at the same time, and the two products must be roughly equal in value. Thus, even very isolated societies soon develop some sort of money to eliminate the inconvenience of trading by barter.

Money is anything a society uses to purchase products, services, or resources. Historically, different groups of people have used all sorts of objects as money—whales' teeth, stones, beads, copper crosses, clamshells, and gold and silver, for example. Today, the most commonly used objects are metal coins and paper bills, which together are called *currency*.

The Functions of Money

Money aids in the exchange of goods, services, and resources. However, this is a rather general (and somewhat theoretical) way of stating money's function. Let's look instead at three *specific* functions money serves in any society.

Money as a Medium of Exchange A **medium of exchange** is anything accepted as payment for products, services, and resources. This definition looks very much like the definition of money. It is meant to, because the primary function of money is to serve as a medium of exchange. The key word here is *accepted*. As long as the owners of products, services, and resources *accept* money in an exchange, it is performing this function. For example, if you want to purchase a Hewlett-Packard Photosmart printer that is priced at $149 in a Best Buy store, you must give the store the correct amount of money. In return, the store gives you the product.

Money as a Measure of Value A **measure of value** is a single standard or "yardstick" used to assign values to, and compare the values of, products, services, and resources. Money serves as a measure of value because the prices of all products, services, and resources are stated in terms of money. It is thus the "common denominator" we use to compare products and decide which we will buy.

Money as a Store of Value Money received by an individual or firm need not be used immediately. It may be held and spent later. Hence, money serves as a **store of value**, or a means of retaining and accumulating wealth. This function of money comes into play whenever we hold onto money—in a pocket, a cookie jar, a savings account, or whatever.

barter system a system of exchange in which goods or services are traded directly for other goods or services

money anything a society uses to purchase products, services, or resources

medium of exchange anything accepted as payment for products, services, and resources

measure of value a single standard or "yardstick" used to assign values to, and compare the values of, products, services, and resources

store of value a means of retaining and accumulating wealth

© KYRYLO GREKOV/SHUTTERSTOCK

It's all money! Although it's easy for U.S. citizens to think their currency is the only currency in the world, there are many different currencies used throughout the world. Regardless of what their money looks like, people around the world know that their currency must serve as a medium of exchange, a measure of value, and a store of value.

Value that is stored as money is affected by *inflation*. Remember from Chapter 1 that *inflation* is a general rise in the level of prices. Suppose that you can buy a Bose home theater system for $1,000. Your $1,000 has a value equal to the value of that home theater system. However, suppose that you wait and do not buy the home theater system immediately. If the price goes up to $1,025 in the meantime because of inflation, you can no longer buy the same home theater system with your $1,000. Your money has *lost* purchasing power because it is now worth less than the home theater system. To determine the effect of inflation on the purchasing power of a dollar, economists often refer to a consumer price index such as the one illustrated in Figure 18.1. The consumer price index measures the changes in prices of a fixed basket of goods purchased by a typical consumer, including food, transportation, housing, clothing, medical care, recreation, education, communication, and other goods and services. The base amount for the consumer price index is 100 and was established by averaging the cost of the items included in the consumer price index over a 36-month period from 1982 to 1984. In February 2012, it took approximately $228 to purchase the same goods that could have been purchased for $100 in the base period 1982 to 1984.

FIGURE 18.1 The Consumer Price Index and the Purchasing Power of the Consumer Dollar (Base Period 1982–1984 = 100)

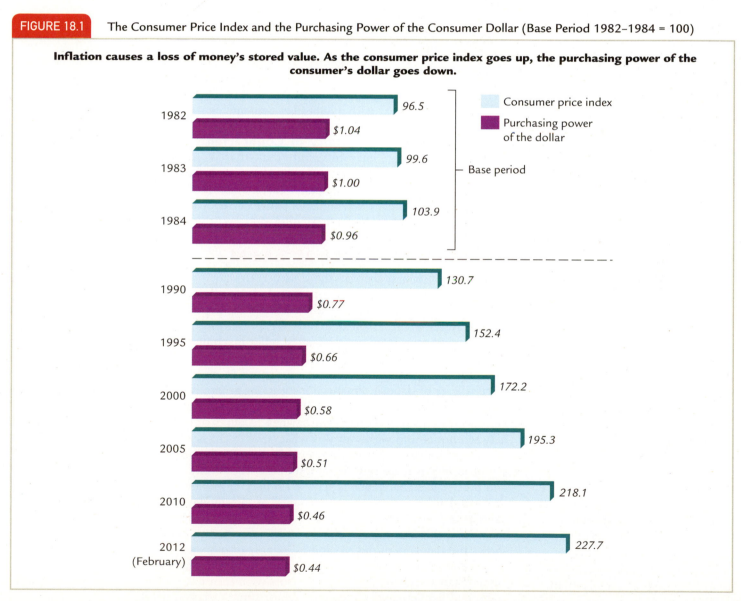

Source: The U.S. Bureau of Labor Statistics Web site, www.bls.gov (accessed March 22, 2012).

Inflation isn't just an economic indicator—it means that you'll pay more for many goods and services. If you're saving to buy a car or a home, the money you put aside won't go as far when prices are on the rise.

Important Characteristics of Money

Money must be easy to use, trusted, and capable of performing the three functions just mentioned. To meet these requirements, money must possess the following five characteristics.

Divisibility The standard unit of money must be divisible into smaller units to accommodate small purchases and large ones. In the United States, our standard is the dollar, and it is divided into pennies, nickels, dimes, quarters, and half-dollars.

Portability Money must be small enough and light enough to be carried easily. For this reason, paper currency is issued in larger denominations—5-, 10-, 20-, 50-, and 100-dollar bills.

Stability Money should retain its value over time. When it does not, people tend to lose faith in their money. When money becomes extremely unstable, people may turn to other means of storing value, such as gold and jewels, works of art, and real estate.

Durability The objects that serve as money should be strong enough to last through reasonable use. To increase the life expectancy of paper currency, most nations use special paper with a high fiber content.

Difficulty of Counterfeiting If a nation's currency were easy to counterfeit—that is, to imitate or fake—its citizens would be uneasy about accepting it as payment. In an attempt to make paper currency more difficult to counterfeit, the U.S. government periodically redesigns its paper currency and uses watermarks and intricate designs to discourage counterfeiting.

The Supply of Money: M_1 and M_2

How much money is there in the United States? Before we can answer this question, we need to define a couple of concepts. A **demand deposit** is an amount on deposit in a checking account. It is called a *demand* deposit because it can be claimed immediately—that is, on-demand—by presenting a properly made out check, withdrawing cash from an automated teller machine (ATM), or transferring money between accounts.

A **time deposit** is an amount on deposit in an interest-bearing savings account or certificate of deposit. Financial institutions generally permit immediate withdrawal of money from savings accounts. However, they can require advance **written notice** before withdrawal of money from savings accounts or certificates of deposit. The time between notice and withdrawal is what leads to the name *time* deposit.

There are two main measures of the supply of money: M_1 and M_2. The M_1 *supply of money* is a narrow definition and consists only of currency, demand deposits and other checkable deposits. The M_2 *supply of money* consists of M_1 (currency and demand deposits) plus savings accounts, certain money-market securities, and certificates of deposit (CDs) of less than $100,000. The M_2 definition of money is based on the assumption that time deposits can be converted to cash for spending. Figure 18.2 shows the elements of the M_1 and M_2 supply of money.

Therefore, the answer to our original question is that the amount of money in the United States depends very much on how we measure it. Generally, economists, politicians, and bankers tend to focus on M_1 or some variation of M_1.

demand deposit an amount on deposit in a checking account

time deposit an amount on deposit in an interest-bearing savings account or certificate of deposit

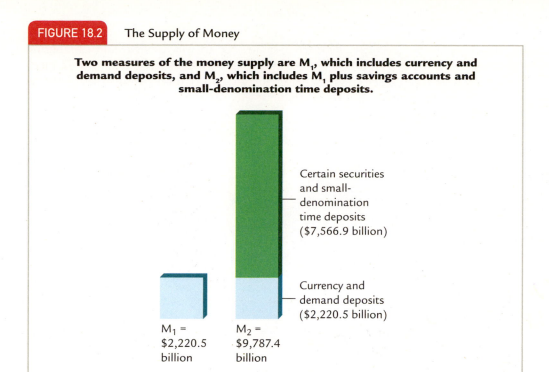

FIGURE 18.2 The Supply of Money

Two measures of the money supply are M_1, which includes currency and demand deposits, and M_2, which includes M_1 plus savings accounts and small-denomination time deposits.

Certain securities and small-denomination time deposits ($7,566.9 billion)

Currency and demand deposits ($2,220.5 billion)

M_1 = $2,220.5 billion

M_2 = $9,787.4 billion

Source: The Federal Reserve Web site, www.federalreserve.gov (accessed March 26, 2012).

THE FEDERAL RESERVE SYSTEM

 2 Summarize how the Federal Reserve System regulates the money supply to maintain a healthy economy.

How do Federal Reserve actions affect me? What is the Federal Reserve System? These are both good questions. First, Federal Reserve Board (often referred to as the Fed) activities have an impact on the interest rates you pay for loans and credit cards. Although many people became aware of the Federal Reserve's actions during the recent economic crisis, the Fed's lending programs have been used since the early 1900s to maintain a healthy economy. Here's how it works. The Fed lowers the interest rates that banks pay to borrow money from the Fed in an effort to shore up a sagging economy. When the Fed lowers rates, banks pay less to borrow money from the Fed. In turn, they often lower the interest rates they charge for business loans, home mortgages, car loans, and even credit cards. Lower rates often provide an incentive for both business firms and individuals to buy goods and services, which, in turn, helps to restore the economic health of the nation. On the other hand, rate increases are designed to sustain economic growth while controlling inflation. When the Fed raises rates, banks must pay more to borrow money from the Fed. And the banks, in turn, charge higher rates for both consumer and business loans.

Now let's answer the second question. The **Federal Reserve System** is the central bank of the United States and is responsible for regulating the banking industry. Created by Congress on December 23, 1913, its mission is to maintain an economically healthy and financially sound business environment in which banks can operate.

The Federal Reserve System is controlled by its seven-member board of governors, who meet in Washington, D.C. Each governor is appointed by the president and confirmed by the Senate for a 14-year term. The president also selects the chairman and vice chairman of the board from among the board members for four-year terms.

The Federal Reserve System consists of 12 district banks located in major cities throughout the United States, as well as 24 branch banks (see Figure 18.3). All national (federally chartered) banks must be members of the Fed. State banks may join if they meet membership requirements. For more information about the Federal Reserve System, visit its Web site at www.federalreserve.gov.

Federal Reserve System the central bank of the United States responsible for regulating the banking industry

FIGURE 18.3 Federal Reserve System

The Federal Reserve System consists of 12 district banks and 24 branch banks.

— Boundaries of Federal Reserve districts
— Boundaries of Federal Reserve branch territories
★ Board of Governors of the Federal Reserve System
■ Federal Reserve Bank cities
● Federal Reserve branch cities

Source: The Federal Reserve Board Web site at www.federalreserve.gov (accessed March 28, 2012).

Economic Crisis and the Fed's Response

Lately, it seems like the Federal Reserve Board has been in the news more than usual. The reason for all the news coverage is quite simple: The Fed was responsible for maintaining the health of the U.S. economy during the recent economic crisis. To maintain a healthy economy, the Federal Reserve Board took a number of specific steps to minimize the effects of the crisis for both business and individuals. Specifically, the Fed[2]

- **Provided liquidity.** The Fed allowed banks in need of cash to borrow money from the Federal Reserve System. If they could not have borrowed money from the Fed, banks would have tightened lending requirements or stopped funding loans to both businesses and individuals.
- **Supported troubled financial markets.** During the first part of the crisis, investors feared that many commercial paper issues would become worthless and they stopped investing in money-market funds that held commercial paper. **Commercial paper** is a short-term promissory note issued by a large corporation. At the same time, many investors were withdrawing money from money-market funds. In order to restore the commercial paper market and lower the cost of this type of short-term financing for businesses, the Federal Reserve provided secured loans to the financial institutions that sell this type of investment; as a result, the commercial paper market is now functioning well.

commercial paper a short-term promissory note issued by a large corporation

- **Supported important financial institutions.** The failure of investment bank Lehman Brothers and the commercial bank Washington Mutual fueled fears that other large financial institutions could fail. The resulting panic threatened to lead to a full-scale "run" on banks and lenders that could have caused the entire financial system to break down. To restore faith in the system, the Fed agreed to provide non-recourse loans to large banks. The ability to borrow money from the Fed and other government agencies helped to calm investors and avoid an even larger financial meltdown.
- **Conducted stress tests of major banks.** In the spring of 2009, the Federal Reserve, along with other federal agencies, conducted an unprecedented review of the financial condition of the 19 largest U.S. banks. This "stress" test measured how well these banks could weather the economic crisis. Banks that failed the test were required to obtain new capital by selling stock or bonds or accept federal government funds. Today, the nation's largest banks still must undergo the Fed's rigorous stress tests to determine if they are able to withstand another economic crisis.

Is Ben Bernanke the nation's most important banker? If you ask that question to bankers, corporate executives, and politicians, the answer would be yes. Simply put: When Mr. Bernanke talks, the financial world listens. Over the last few years, it has been his decisions and the actions taken by the Federal Reserve Board that are responsible for reducing the effects of the recent economic crisis.

The Fed's actions did help to restore confidence in the financial system, to encourage continued lending, to stabilize an unstable economy, and to provide additional time to create a financial rescue plan to restore the nation's economy. At the time of publication, although the health of the banking and financial industry has improved, there are still concerns about the long-term effects of the Federal Reserve's actions, what future actions may be needed to ensure continued economic growth, and the cost of the Fed's actions.

The most important function of the Fed is to use monetary policy to regulate the nation's supply of money in such a way as to maintain a healthy economy. In Chapter 1, *monetary policy* was defined as the Federal Reserve's decisions that determine the size of the supply of money in the nation and the level of interest rates. The goals of monetary policy are continued economic growth, full employment, and stable prices. Three methods—controlling bank reserve requirements, regulating the discount rate, and running open-market operations—are used to implement the Fed's monetary policy.

Regulation of Reserve Requirements

When money is deposited in a bank, the bank must retain a portion of it to satisfy customers who may want to withdraw money from their accounts. The remainder is available to fund loans. By law, the Federal Reserve sets the reserve requirement for financial institutions. The **reserve requirement** is the percentage of its deposits a bank *must* retain, either in its own vault or on deposit with its Federal Reserve district bank. For example, if a bank has *new* deposits of $20 million and the reserve requirement is 10 percent, the bank must retain $2 million. The present reserve requirements range from 0 to 10 percent depending on such factors as the type of account and the total amount individual banks have on deposit.[3]

Once reserve requirements are met, banks can use the remaining funds to create more money and make more loans through a process called *deposit expansion*. In the preceding example, the bank must retain $2 million in a reserve account. It can use the remaining $18 million to fund consumer and business loans. Assume that the bank lends all $18 million to different borrowers and also assume that before using any of the borrowed funds, all borrowers deposit the $18 million in their bank accounts at the lending institution. Now the bank's deposits have increased by an additional $18 million. Because these deposits are subject to the same reserve requirement described earlier, the bank must maintain $1.8 million in a reserve account, and the bank can lend the additional $16.2 million to other bank customers. Of course, the bank's lending

reserve requirement the percentage of its deposits a bank *must* retain, either in its own vault or on deposit with its Federal Reserve district bank

potential becomes steadily smaller and smaller as it makes more loans. Moreover, we should point out that as bankers are usually very conservative by nature; they will not use deposit expansion to maximize their lending activities. Instead, they will take a more middle-of-the-road approach.

The Fed's board of governors sets the reserve requirement. *When it increases the requirement, banks have less money available for lending.* Fewer loans are made, and the economy tends to slow. On the other hand, *by decreasing the reserve requirement, the Fed can make additional money available for lending to stimulate a slow economy.* Although the Fed may change the amount of deposits subject to the reserve requirement from year to year, the Fed seldom changes the reserve requirement because this means of controlling the money supply is so very potent.

Regulation of the Discount Rate

Member banks may borrow money from the Fed to satisfy the reserve requirement. The interest rate the Federal Reserve charges for loans to member banks, called the **discount rate**, is set by the board of directors of each Federal Reserve District bank. For the period from January 2003 to June 2006, the discount rate has been as low as 2 percent and as high as 6.25 percent.[4] In August 2007, in an attempt to stabilize the economy and encourage lending, the Federal Reserve began lowering the discount rate. By February 2010, the discount rate reached its lowest level and remains at 0.75 percent at the time of publication.[5]

When the Fed *lowers* the discount rate, it is easier and cheaper for banks to obtain money. Member banks feel free to make more loans and to charge lower interest rates. This action generally stimulates the nation's economy. When the Fed *raises* the discount rate, banks begin to restrict loans, increase the interest rates they charge for loans, and tighten their own loan requirements. The overall effect is to slow the economy. Although the discount rate has decreased to 0.75 percent, you should remember that the Fed can increase rates in an effort to maintain a healthy economy.

Open-Market Operations

The federal government finances its activities partly by buying and selling government securities issued by the U.S. Treasury. These securities, which pay interest, may be purchased by any individual, firm, or organization—including the Fed. **Open-market operations** are the buying and selling of U.S. government securities by the Federal Reserve System for the purpose of controlling the supply of money.

The Federal Open Market Committee (FOMC) is charged with carrying out the Federal Reserve's open-market operations by buying and selling U.S. Treasury securities through the trading desk of the Federal Reserve Bank of New York. To reduce the nation's money supply, the FOMC simply *sells* government securities. The money it receives from purchasers is taken out of circulation. Thus, less money is available for investment, purchases, or lending. To increase the money supply, the FOMC *buys* government securities. The money the FOMC pays for securities goes back into circulation, making more money available to individuals and firms.

Because the major purchasers of government securities are banking and financial institutions, open-market operations tend to have an immediate effect on lending and investment.

Of the three tools used to influence monetary policy, the use of open-market operations is the most important. When the Federal Reserve buys and sells securities, the goal is to change the federal funds rate. The **federal funds rate** is the interest rate at which a bank lends immediately available funds on deposit at the Fed to another bank overnight to meet the borrowing bank's reserve requirements. Because the Fed funds rate is what banks pay when they borrow, it affects the rates they charge when they lend. Although the FOMC sets a target for the federal funds rate, it does not actually set the rate because it is determined by the open market.[6] (*Note:* There is a difference between the federal funds rate and the discount rate discussed earlier in this section. The *federal funds rate* is the interest rate paid by a bank to borrow funds from other

discount rate the interest rate the Federal Reserve System charges for loans to member banks

open-market operations the buying and selling of U.S. government securities by the Federal Reserve System for the purpose of controlling the supply of money

federal funds rate the interest rate at which a bank lends immediately available funds on deposit at the Fed to another bank overnight to meet the borrowing bank's reserve requirements

TABLE 18.1	Methods Used by the Federal Reserve System to Control the Money Supply and the Economy	
Method Used	Immediate Result	End Result
Regulating Reserve Requirement		
Fed *increases* reserve requirement	Less money for banks to lend to customers—reduction in overall money supply	Economic slowdown
Fed *decreases* reserve requirement	More money for banks to lend to customers—increase in overall money supply	Increased economic activity
Regulating the Discount Rate		
Fed *increases* the discount rate	Less money for banks to lend to customers—reduction in overall money supply	Economic slowdown
Fed *decreases* the discount rate	More money for banks to lend to customers—increase in overall money supply	Increased economic activity
Open-Market Operations		
Fed *sells* government securities	Reduction in overall money supply	Economic slowdown
Fed *buys* government securities	Increase in overall money supply	Increased economic activity

© Cengage Learning 2014

banks. The *discount rate* is the interest rate paid by a bank to borrow funds from the Federal Reserve.) Table 18.1 summarizes the effects of open-market operations and the other tools used by the Fed to regulate the money supply and control the economy.

Other Fed Responsibilities

In addition to its regulation of the money supply, the Fed is also responsible for serving as the government's bank, clearing checks and electronic transfers, inspecting currency, and applying selective credit controls.

Serving as Government Bank The Federal Reserve is the bank for the U.S. government. As the government's bank, it processes a variety of financial transactions involving trillions of dollars each year. For example, the Federal Reserve provides financial services for the U.S. Treasury, including accounts through which incoming tax deposits and outgoing government payments are handled.

Clearing Checks and Electronic Transfers Although not as popular as they once were, many people still use checks to pay their monthly bills and pay for purchases. A check written by a customer of one bank and presented for payment to another bank in the same town may be processed through a local clearinghouse. The procedure becomes more complicated, however, when the banks are not in the same town. Although at one point the Fed was responsible for the prompt and accurate collection of 15 to 17 billion checks each year, today the number of paper checks cleared through the Federal Reserve System is decreasing because of improved automation and electronic equipment.[7] Banks that use the Fed to clear checks are charged a fee for this service. Through the use of automation and electronic equipment, most checks can be cleared within two or three days.

Inspection of Currency As paper currency is handled, it becomes worn or dirty. The typical $1 bill has a life expectancy of less than two years. Most $50 and $100 bills usually last longer because they are handled less. When member banks deposit their surplus cash in a Federal Reserve Bank, the currency is inspected. Bills unfit for further use are separated and destroyed.

Selective Credit Controls The Federal Reserve System (along with the Consumer Financial Protection Bureau that was created in 2010) has the responsibility for enforcing the Truth-in-Lending Act, which Congress passed in 1968. This act requires lenders to state clearly the annual percentage rate and total finance charge for a consumer loan.

The Federal Reserve System is also responsible for setting the margin requirements for securities transactions. The *margin* is the minimum amount (expressed as a percentage) of the purchase price that must be paid in cash or eligible securities. (The investor may borrow the remainder.) The current initial margin requirement is 50 percent. Thus, if an investor purchases $4,000 worth of stock, he or she must pay at least $2,000 in cash or its equivalent in securities. The remaining $2,000 may be borrowed from the brokerage firm. Although the minimum margin requirements are regulated by the Federal Reserve, margin requirements and the interest charged on the loans used to fund margin transactions may vary among brokerage firms and different security exchanges.

Describe the organizations involved in the banking industry.

THE AMERICAN BANKING INDUSTRY

Most bankers will tell you that the last few years have been frustrating for the American banking industry, to say the least. Furthermore, it's not just bankers who felt the impact. Almost everyone has been affected in one way or another by the nation's economic crisis.

Banks, savings and loan associations, credit unions, and other financial institutions were at the center of the nation's economic problems. Aggressive lending practices that led to record numbers of home foreclosures and nonperforming loans caused a financial meltdown. As the economic problems within the banking and financial industry became larger, the ability to borrow money became more difficult for both individuals and business firms—a very serious problem for both borrowers and lenders. In fact, the nation's economic problems (and the world's) became so severe that the government needed to take action. Both the Bush and the Obama administrations developed financial stimulus plans to rescue the economy. In addition, both the Federal Reserve Board and the U.S. Treasury took action. Eventually, the rescue plans did help relieve at least some of the financial problems associated with the economic crisis. Still, there was need for more changes in the way that banks and financial institutions operate.

Banking and Financial Reform: New Regulations

Although there are many critics of increased regulation, it was apparent that something needed to be done to prevent the type of economic problems the nation experienced during the economic crisis. According to President Barack Obama, the goals of new government banking and financial regulations are more than justified in the wake of the crisis and include the following:[8]

- Protect American families from unfair and abusive financial and banking practices.
- Close the gaps in our financial system that allowed large banks and financial firms to avoid strong, comprehensive federal oversight. To accomplish these goals, the Dodd–Frank Wall Street Reform and Consumer Protection Act was passed in 2010. This act addressed many of the issues that led to the economic crisis. Specifically, the act

  - Creates a new Consumer Financial Protection Bureau.
  - Gives the government the power to seize and close down large failing financial firms in an orderly fashion.
  - Increases government regulation of firms in the financial and banking industry.
  - Curbs the high-risk investment strategies that led to the financial problems at some major financial institutions and the nation's economic crisis.
  - Creates a Financial Stability Oversight Council that serves as an early warning system of potential risks and problems in the financial system.

To provide this type of comprehensive reform, it will be necessary to make sure banks and financial institutions are complying with the new regulations. As a result, future regulations will subject banks and financial institutions to more in-depth evaluations to determine their financial health and to spot signs of trouble before they affect individuals, the American economy, and the world economy.

For more information about existing regulations and proposed new regulations, go to the Federal Reserve Board's Web site at www.federalreserve.gov, the U.S. Treasury Web site at www.ustreas.gov, or use a search engine like Google or Yahoo! and enter "banking reform" or "financial reform."

In addition to the nation's economic problems, competition among banks, savings and loan associations, credit unions, and other business firms that want to perform banking activities has never been greater. In fact, many financial institutions are using social media sites like Facebook and Twitter, as well as blogs and their own Web sites, to attract new customers and retain old ones. Let's begin this section with some information about one of the major players in the banking industry—the commercial bank.

When will the sun begin to shine on American banking? Good question. It seems that since the economic crisis began in the fall of 2007, banks have been at the center of the nation's economic problems. For most banks and many financial institutions, aggressive lending practices, record numbers of home foreclosures, and a large number of nonperforming loans caused a financial meltdown and created a situation where it was difficult for both businesses and individuals to borrow money.

Commercial Banks

A **commercial bank** is a profit-making organization that accepts deposits, makes loans, and provides related services to its customers. Like other businesses, the bank's primary goal—its mission—is to meet its customers' needs while earning a profit.

Because they deal with money belonging to individuals and other business firms, banks must meet certain requirements before they receive a charter, or permission to operate, from either federal or state banking authorities. A **national bank** is a commercial bank chartered by the U.S. Comptroller of the Currency. There are approximately 1,400 national banks.[9] These banks must conform to federal banking regulations and are subject to unannounced inspections by federal auditors.

A **state bank** is a commercial bank chartered by the banking authorities in the state in which it operates. State banks outnumber national banks by about four to one, but they tend to be smaller than national banks. They are subject to unannounced inspections by both state and federal auditors. Table 18.2 lists the seven largest banks in the United States. All are classified as national banks.

Other Financial Institutions

In addition to commercial banks, at least eight other types of financial institutions perform either full or limited banking services for their customers.

commercial bank a profit-making organization that accepts deposits, makes loans, and provides related services to its customers

national bank a commercial bank chartered by the U.S. Comptroller of the Currency

state bank a commercial bank chartered by the banking authorities in the state in which it operates

TABLE 18.2	The Seven Largest U.S. Banks, Ranked by 2011 Total Revenues			
Rank	**Company**	**Revenues ($ millions)**	**Profits ($ millions)**	**Employees**
1	Bank of America Corp.	134,194	−2,238	288,122
2	JPMorgan Chase & Co.	115,475	17,370	239,831
3	Citigroup	111,055	10,602	260,000
4	Wells Fargo	93,249	12,362	272,200
5	Goldman Sachs Group	45,967	8,354	38,700
6	Morgan Stanley	39,320	4,703	62,542
7	American Express	30,242	4,057	61,000

Source: From Fortune Magazine, "Fortune 500: Industries: Commercial Banks," May 23, 2011 © 2011 Time Inc. Used under license. Fortune and Time Inc. are not affiliated with, and do not endorse products or services of, Licensee.

Savings and Loan Associations A **savings and loan association (S&L)** is a financial institution that offers checking and savings accounts and CDs and that invests most of its assets in home mortgage loans and other consumer loans. Originally, S&Ls were permitted to offer their depositors *only* savings accounts. However, since Congress passed legislation regarding S&Ls in the 1980s, they have been able to offer other services to attract depositors.

Today, there are approximately 1,050 S&Ls in the United States insured by the Federal Deposit Insurance Corporation.[10] Federal associations are supervised by the U.S. Comptroller of the Currency, a branch of the U.S. Treasury. State-chartered S&Ls are subjected to unannounced audits by state authorities.

Credit Unions The United States currently has an estimated 7,300 credit unions.[11] A **credit union** is a financial institution that accepts deposits from, and lends money to, only those people who are its members. Usually, the membership consists of employees of a particular firm, people in a particular profession, or those who live in a community served by a local credit union. Credit unions may pay higher interest on deposits than commercial banks and S&Ls, and they may provide loans at lower cost. The National Credit Union Administration regulates federally chartered credit unions. State authorities regulate credit unions with state charters.

Organizations that Perform Banking Functions Six other types of financial institutions are involved in banking activities. Although not actually full-service banks, they offer customers some banking services.

- *Mutual savings banks* are financial institutions that are owned by their depositors and offer many of the same services offered by banks, S&Ls, and credit unions, including checking accounts, savings accounts, and CDs. Like other financial institutions, they also fund home mortgages, commercial loans, and consumer loans. Unlike other types of financial institutions, the profits of a mutual savings bank go to the depositors, usually in the form of dividends or slightly higher interest rates on savings. Today, most mutual savings banks are located in the Northeast.
- *Insurance companies* provide long-term financing for office buildings, shopping centers, and other commercial real estate projects throughout the United States. The funds used for this type of financing are obtained from policyholders' insurance premiums.
- *Pension funds* are established by employers to guarantee their employees a regular monthly income on retirement. Contributions to the fund may come from the employer, the employee, or both. Pension funds earn additional income through generally conservative investments in corporate stocks, corporate bonds, and government securities, as well as through financing real estate developments.
- *Brokerage firms* offer combination savings and checking accounts that pay higher-than-usual interest rates. Many people have switched to these accounts because they are convenient and to get slightly higher rates.
- *Finance companies* provide financing to individuals and business firms that may not be able to get financing from banks, S&Ls, or credit unions. Firms such as Ford Motor Credit and GE Capital provide loans to both individuals and business firms. Lenders such as Ace Cash Express, Inc., provide short-term loans to individuals. The interest rates charged by these lenders may be higher than the interest rates charged by other financial institutions.
- *Investment banking firms* are organizations that assist corporations in raising funds, usually by helping sell new issues of stocks, bonds, or other financial securities. Although these firms do not accept deposits or make loans like traditional banking firms, they do help companies raise millions of dollars. More information about investment banking firms and the role they play in American business is provided in Chapter 19.

savings and loan association (S&L) a financial institution that offers checking and savings accounts and CDs and that invests most of its assets in home mortgage loans and other consumer loans

credit union a financial institution that accepts deposits from, and lends money to, only the people who are its members

Careers in the Banking Industry

Take a second look at Table 18.2. The seven largest banks in the United States employ approximately 1,200,000 people. If you add to this amount the people employed by smaller banks not listed in Table 18.2 and those employed by S&Ls, credit unions, and other financial institutions, the number of employees grows dramatically. According to the *Occupational Outlook Handbook*, published by the U.S. Department of Labor, a number of different positions in the banking industry are projected to have average growth between now and the year 2020.[12]

To be successful in the banking industry, employees for a bank, S&L, credit union, or other financial institution must possess the following traits:

1. *You must be honest.* Because you are handling other people's money, many financial institutions go to great lengths to discover dishonest employees.
2. *You must be able to interact with people.* A number of positions in the banking industry require that you possess the interpersonal skills needed to interact not only with other employees but also with customers.
3. *You need a strong background in accounting.* Many of the routine tasks performed by employees in the banking industry are basic accounting functions. For example, a teller must post deposits or withdrawals to a customer's account and then balance out at the end of the day to ensure accuracy.
4. *You need to appreciate the relationship between banking and finance.* Bank officers must interview loan applicants and determine if their request for money is based on sound financial principles. Above all, loan officers must be able to evaluate applicants and their loan requests to determine if the borrower will be able to repay a loan.
5. *You should possess basic computer skills.* Almost all employees in the banking industry use a computer for some aspect of their work on a daily basis.

Depending on qualifications, work experience, and education, starting salaries generally are between $18,000 and $30,000 a year, but it is not uncommon for college graduates to earn $35,000 a year or more.

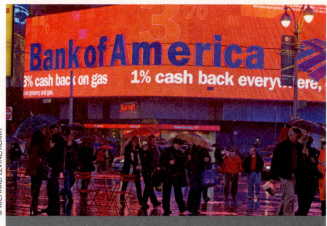

Even "big" banks want more customers. Bank of America, the largest bank in the United States, still wants your business. Like many competitors, the bank offers cash back, competitive rates for savings and loans, online banking, and many other services to attract new customers. Check out the latest promotions at www.bankofamerica.com.

TRADITIONAL SERVICES PROVIDED BY FINANCIAL INSTITUTIONS

> **4** Identify the services provided by financial institutions.

To determine how important banking services are to you, ask yourself just three simple questions:

- How many checks did you write last month?
- Do you have a credit or debit card? If so, how often do you use it?
- How many times did you visit an ATM last month?

If you are like most people and business firms, you would find it hard to live a normal life without the services provided by banks and other financial institutions. Typical services provided by a bank or other financial institution are illustrated in Figure 18.4.

The most important traditional banking services for both individuals and businesses are described in this section. Online banking, electronic transfer of funds, and other significant and future developments are discussed in the next section.

Checking Accounts

Firms and individuals deposit money in checking accounts (demand deposits) so that they can write checks to pay for purchases. A **check** is a written order for a bank or

check a written order for a bank or other financial institution to pay a stated dollar amount to the business or person indicated on the face of the check

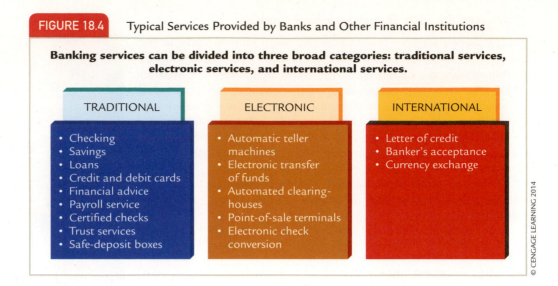

Banking services can be divided into three broad categories: traditional services, electronic services, and international services.

TRADITIONAL	ELECTRONIC	INTERNATIONAL
• Checking	• Automatic teller machines	• Letter of credit
• Savings	• Electronic transfer of funds	• Banker's acceptance
• Loans	• Automated clearing-houses	• Currency exchange
• Credit and debit cards	• Point-of-sale terminals	
• Financial advice	• Electronic check conversion	
• Payroll service		
• Certified checks		
• Trust services		
• Safe-deposit boxes		

© CENGAGE LEARNING 2014

other financial institution to pay a stated dollar amount to the business or person indicated on the face of the check. Today, some financial institutions offer free checking; others charge activity fees (or service charges) for checking accounts. Fees and charges generally range from $5 to $20 per month for individuals. For businesses, monthly charges are based on the average daily balance in the checking account, the number of checks written, or both. Charges for business checking accounts are often higher than those for individual accounts.

Most financial institutions offer interest-paying accounts called NOW (negotiable order of withdrawal) accounts that allow customers to write checks. A **NOW account** is an interest-paying checking account. For these accounts, the usual interest rate is between 0.05 percent and 0.25 percent. Typically, online Internet banks pay slightly higher interest rates. However, individual banks often impose certain restrictions on their NOW accounts.

Although banks and other financial institutions may pay low interest rates on checking accounts, even small earnings are better than no earnings. In addition to interest rates, be sure to compare monthly fees before opening a checking account for your personal use or a business.

Savings Accounts

Savings accounts (time deposits) provide a safe place to store money and a very conservative means of investing. At the time of publication, *passbook savings accounts* earned between 0.05 percent and 0.50 percent in commercial banks and S&Ls and slightly more in credit unions or online Internet banks.

A depositor who is willing to leave money on deposit with a bank for a set period of time can earn a higher rate of interest. To do so, the depositor buys a certificate of deposit. A **certificate of deposit (CD)** is a document stating that the bank will pay the depositor a guaranteed interest rate on money left on deposit for a specified period of time. At the time of publication, interest rates have ranged from 0.50 to 2 percent. The rate always depends on how much is invested and for how long. Generally, the rule is: The longer the period of time until maturity, the higher is the rate. Depositors are penalized for early withdrawal of funds invested in CDs.

Short- and Long-Term Loans

Banks, S&Ls, credit unions, and other financial institutions provide short- and long-term loans to both individuals and businesses. *Short-term business loans* must be repaid within one year or less. Typical uses for the money obtained through short-term loans include solving cash-flow problems, purchasing inventory, monthly expenses, and meeting unexpected emergencies.

NOW account an interest-paying checking account; *NOW* stands for *negotiable order of withdrawal*

certificate of deposit (CD) a document stating that the bank will pay the depositor a guaranteed interest rate on money left on deposit for a specified period of time

Kiva.org Connects Microloan Borrowers and Lenders

Kiva.org is a non-profit organization that connects individual lenders—anyone who can lend at least $25—with borrowers who need a bit of cash to go into business or keep a business running. Microloans are much too small for traditional lenders, but large enough to make a big difference to low-income entrepreneurs who need to buy a fishing net, a box of merchandise for resale, or a bicycle to make deliveries.

Working through local organizations in 61 nations, Kiva posts borrowers' photos and stories on its Web site. Lenders determine which borrowers will receive their money, and Kiva's local partners manage the disbursement and repayment of the loans. As little as $200 can start a borrower in Peru or Kenya on the road to becoming a self-sufficient small business owner. Kiva has arranged loans of up to $10,000, helping entrepreneurs in New Orleans and elsewhere upgrade business equipment or branch out into new services.

Since Kiva was founded in 2005, it has arranged more than $300 million in microloans with money from 740,000 lenders in 218 countries. Nearly 99 percent of all loans are repaid, an extremely high percentage. Once a loan is repaid, the lender can reloan the money to another borrower, starting the cycle over again. "It's a different kind of financing opportunity," says the CEO. "It's personal."

Sources: Based on information in The Kiva Web site (www.kiva.org), accessed April 1, 2012; Joann Pan, "725,000 Loans Granted by Kiva, 2.6 Billion to Go," *Mashable*, March 15, 2012, www.mashable.com; Josh Constine, "Visit Kiva.org to Microlend $1 Million of Reid Hoffman's Money," *TechCrunch*, March 12, 2012, www.techcrunch.com; Matt Silverman, "How Kiva.org's CEO Uses Social Media to Spark a Dialogue of Change," *Mashable*, September 20, 2011, www.mashable.com; Kimberly Quillen, "Kiva CEO Says Entrepreneurial Community Should Include High-Growth and Traditional Firms," *Times-Picayune (New Orleans)*, March 12, 2012, www.nola.com.

To help ensure that short-term money will be available when needed, many firms establish a line of credit. A **line of credit** is a loan that is approved before the money is actually needed. Because all the necessary paperwork is already completed and the loan is pre-approved, the business can obtain the money later without delay, as soon as it is required. Even with a line of credit, a firm may not be able to borrow money if the bank does not have sufficient funds available. For this reason, some firms prefer a **revolving credit agreement**, which is a guaranteed line of credit.

Long-term business loans are repaid over a period of years. The average length of a long-term business loan is generally three to seven years but sometimes as long as 15 years or in a few cases even longer periods of time. Long-term loans are used most often to finance the expansion of buildings and retail facilities, mergers and acquisitions, replacement of equipment, or product development.

Most lenders require some type of collateral for long-term loans. **Collateral** is real estate or property (stocks, bonds, equipment, or any other asset of value) pledged as security for a loan. For example, when an individual obtains a loan to pay for a new Chevrolet Malibu, the automobile is the collateral for the loan. If the borrower fails to repay the loan according to the terms specified in the loan agreement, the lender can repossess the car.

Repayment terms and interest rates for both short- and long-term loans are arranged between the lender and the borrower. For businesses, repayment terms may include monthly, quarterly, semiannual, or annual payments. Repayment terms and interest rates for personal loans vary depending on how the money will be used and what type of collateral, if any, is pledged. However, individuals typically make monthly payments to repay personal loans. Borrowers always should "shop" for a loan, comparing the repayment terms and interest rates offered by competing financial institutions.

line of credit a loan that is approved before the money is actually needed

revolving credit agreement a guaranteed line of credit

collateral real estate or property pledged as security for a loan

How do you pay for your purchases? Today more and more people are using credit and debit cards to pay for their purchases. For consumers, "plastic cards" are convenient and fast. For the merchant, credit and debit card transactions can be converted to cash and improve a firm's cash flow.

Credit Card and Debit Card Transactions

By the end of 2012, 160 million Americans will use credit cards to pay for everything from tickets on American Airlines to Zebco fishing gear.[13] Why have credit cards become so popular?

For a merchant, the answer is obvious. By depositing charge slips in a bank or other financial institution, the merchant can convert credit card sales into cash. In return for processing the merchant's credit card transactions, the financial institution charges a fee that generally ranges between 1.5 and 4 percent. Let's assume that you use a Visa credit card to purchase a microwave oven for $300 from Gold Star Appliance, a retailer in Richardson, Texas. At the end of the day, the retailer deposits your charge slip, along with other charge slips, checks, and currency collected during the day, at its bank. If the bank charges Gold Star Appliance 4 percent to process each credit card transaction, the bank deducts a processing fee of $12 ($300 × 0.04 = $12) for your credit card transaction and immediately deposits the remainder ($288) in Gold Star Appliance's account. Typically, small businesses pay more than larger businesses. The number of credit card transactions, the total dollar amount of credit sales, and how well the merchant can negotiate the fees the bank charges determine actual fees.

Do not confuse debit cards with credit cards. Although they may look alike, there are important differences. A **debit card** electronically subtracts the amount of your purchase from your bank account at the moment the purchase is made. (By contrast, when you use your credit card, the credit card company extends short-term financing, and you do not make payment until you receive your next statement.) Debit cards are used most commonly to obtain cash at ATMs and to purchase products and services from retailers.

 5 Understand how financial institutions are changing to meet the needs of domestic and international customers.

INNOVATIVE BANKING SERVICES

Today, many individuals, financial managers, and business owners are finding it convenient to do their banking electronically. Let's begin by looking at how banking will change in the future.

Changes in the Banking Industry

While the experts may not be able to predict with 100 percent accuracy the changes that will affect banking, they all agree that banking *will* change. The most obvious changes the experts do agree on are as follows:

- More emphasis on evaluating the credit-worthiness of loan applicants as a result of the recent economic crisis
- An increase in government regulation of the banking industry
- A reduction in the number of banks, S&Ls, credit unions, and financial institutions because of consolidation and mergers
- Globalization of the banking industry as the economies of individual nations become more interrelated
- The importance of customer service as a way to keep customers from switching to competitors
- Increased use of credit and debit cards and a decrease in the number of written checks
- Continued growth in online and mobile banking

debit card a card that electronically subtracts the amount of your purchase from your bank account at the moment the purchase is made

Going for SUCCESS

Vying to Run Your Digital Wallet

Cash isn't going away any time soon, but Google, PayPal, Visa, and other big companies are already competing to run the digital wallet that could replace your leather wallet in the future. The idea is to speed up transactions and make them as convenient as the one-click payments many online businesses accept. Instead of handing bills and coins to a cashier or waiting for change, you use your digital wallet (typically, your cell phone) to transfer money electronically to the business you're buying from. Your digital wallet might even alert you to special deals or earn you rewards for certain purchases.

The Google Wallet, for example, uses a wireless technology called near field communication to let your cell phone app "talk" to a cash register and arrange payment (charged to your credit card or another card) with just a tap of the phone. Subway sandwich shops and Macy's were among the first businesses to accept Google Wallet payments. PayPal's system, which works as an app and online, has an interesting feature: After you pay, you have several days to decide where the money will come from—a store credit card or a bank debit card, for example. Billions of dollars in cash transactions are going cashless every year. Is a digital wallet in your future?

Sources: Based on information in Olga Kharif, "Google Said to Rethink Wallet Strategy," *Bloomberg*, March 21, 2012, www.bloomberg.com; Edward C. Baig, "Mobile Wallet Competition Heats Up," *USA Today*, February 28, 2012, www.usatoday.com; Deirdre van Dyk, "The End of Cash," *Time*, January 9, 2012, pp. 48–49.

Online, Mobile, and International Banking

Online banking allows you to access your bank's computer system from home, the office, or even while you are traveling. For the customer, online banking offers a number of advantages, including the following:

- The ability to obtain current account balances
- The capability to deposit checks without leaving your home or office
- The convenience of transferring funds from one account to another
- The ability to pay bills
- The convenience of seeing which checks have cleared
- Simplified loan application procedures

Online banking provides a number of advantages for the financial institution. Probably the most important advantage is the lower cost of processing large numbers of transactions. As you learned in Chapter 17, lower costs often lead to larger profits. In addition to lower costs and increased profits, financial institutions believe that online banking offers increased security because fewer people handle fewer paper documents.

In addition to online banking, many banks now offer mobile banking via text message or apps (software applications) downloaded to cell phones and other electronic devices. The goal is to let customers use technology to check account balances, transfer money, and track deposits at any time, from anywhere. This is especially convenient for busy businesspeople who don't live or work next door to a bank branch and can't always get to a computer to use online banking.

electronic funds transfer (EFT) system a means of performing financial transactions through a computer terminal or telephone hookup

Now you can bank with a click of a computer's mouse. With improved technology, bank customers can now deposit checks without leaving their office or home, obtain current account balances, and pay bills online. In fact, many of the traditional banking services that used to require a trip to the bank can now be completed online. Why not take a look at your bank's Web site to see how online banking can help you manage your finances?

Electronic Funds Transfer (EFT) An **electronic funds transfer (EFT) system** is a means of performing financial transactions through a computer terminal or telephone hookup. The following four EFT applications are changing how banks do business:

1. *Automatic teller machines (ATMs).* An ATM is an electronic bank teller—a machine that provides almost any service a human teller can provide. Once the customer is properly identified, the machine dispenses cash from the customer's checking or savings account or makes a cash advance charged to a credit card. ATMs are located in bank parking lots, supermarkets, drugstores, and even gas stations. Customers have access to them at all times of the day or night. There may be a fee for each transaction.

2. *Automated clearinghouse (ACH).* Designed to reduce the number of paper checks, an automated clearinghouse processes Social Security benefits, tax payments, recurring bill payments, payments for Internet sales, and employee salaries. For example, many large companies use the ACH network to transfer wages and salaries directly into their employees' bank accounts, thus eliminating the need to make out individual paychecks.

3. *Point-of-sale (POS) terminals.* A POS terminal is a computerized cash register located in a retail store and connected to a bank's computer. Assume you want to pay for purchases at a Walmart Supercenter. You begin the process by pulling your credit or debit card through a magnetic card reader. A central processing center notifies a computer at your bank that you want to make a purchase. The bank's computer immediately adds the amount to your account for a credit card transaction. In a similar process, the bank's computer deducts the amount of the purchase from your bank account if you use a debit card. Finally, the amount of your purchase is added to the retailer's account. The Walmart store then is notified that the transaction is complete, and the cash register prints out your receipt.

4. *Electronic check conversion (ECC).* Electronic check conversion is a process used to convert information from a paper check into an electronic payment for merchandise, services, or bills. When you give your completed check to a cashier at a Best Buy store, the check is processed through an electronic system that captures your banking information and the dollar amount of the check. Once the check is processed, you are asked to sign a receipt, and you get a voided (canceled) check back for your records. Finally, the funds to pay for your transaction are transferred into the Best Buy store's account. ECC also can be used for checks you mail to pay for a purchase or to pay on an account.

letter of credit a legal document issued by a bank or other financial institution guaranteeing to pay a seller a stated amount for a specified period of time

Bankers and business owners generally are pleased with online banking and EFT systems. Both online banking and EFT are fast, and they eliminate the costly processing of checks. However, many customers are reluctant to use online banking or EFT systems. Some simply do not like "the technology," whereas others fear that the computer will garble their accounts. Early on, in 1978, Congress responded to such fears by passing the Electronic Funds Transfer Act, which protects the customer in case the bank makes an error or the customer's account information is stolen.

© RICHARD B. LEVINE/ALAMY

Why is a French bank in the United States?
Because it makes perfect business sense in a world where national boundaries blur and multinational firms operate in many different countries. Actually, the number of U.S. banks that operate overseas and the number of foreign banks that operate in the United States are both increasing. For banks, the world is becoming smaller and much more competitive.

International Banking Services For international businesses, banking services are extremely important. Depending on the needs of an international firm, a bank can help by providing a letter of credit or a banker's acceptance.

A **letter of credit** is a legal document issued by a bank or other financial institution guaranteeing to pay a seller a stated amount for a specified period of time—usually 30 to 60 days. With a letter of credit, certain conditions, such as delivery of the merchandise, may be specified before payment is made.

A **banker's acceptance** is a written order for a bank to pay a third party a stated amount of money on a specific date. With a banker's acceptance, no conditions are specified. It is simply an order to pay guaranteed by a bank without any strings attached.

Both a letter of credit and a banker's acceptance are popular methods of paying for import and export transactions. For example, imagine that you are a business owner in the United States who wants to purchase some leather products from a small business in Florence, Italy. You offer to pay for the merchandise with your company's check drawn on an American bank, but the Italian business owner is worried about payment. To solve the problem, your bank can issue either a letter of credit or a banker's acceptance to guarantee that payment will be made. In addition to a letter of credit and a banker's acceptance, banks also can use EFT technology to speed international banking transactions.

One other international banking service should be noted. Banks and other financial institutions provide for currency exchange. If you place an order for merchandise valued at $50,000 from a company in Japan, how do you pay for the order? Do you use U.S. dollars or Japanese yen? To solve this problem, you can use a bank's currency-exchange service. To make payment, you can use either currency. If necessary, the bank will exchange one currency for the other to complete your transaction.

banker's acceptance a written order for a bank to pay a third party a stated amount of money on a specific date

THE FDIC AND NCUA

(6) Explain how deposit insurance protects customers.

During the Great Depression, which began in 1929, a number of banks failed, and their depositors lost all their savings. To make sure that such a disaster did not happen again and to restore public confidence in the banking industry, the U.S. Congress enacted legislation that created the *Federal Deposit Insurance Corporation (FDIC)* in 1933. The primary purpose of the FDIC is to insure deposits against bank failures.

Today, the FDIC provides basic deposit insurance of $250,000 per depositor. Deposits maintained in different categories of legal ownership are insured separately. Thus, you can have increased coverage for different categories of ownership in a single institution. The most common categories of ownership are single (or individual) ownership and joint ownership. A depositor also may obtain additional coverage by opening separate accounts in different financial institutions. To determine if your deposits are insured or if your bank or financial institution is insured, visit the FDIC Web site at www.fdic.gov or call 1-877-ASK-FDIC.

To obtain coverage, banks and S&Ls must pay insurance premiums to the FDIC. In a similar manner, the National Credit Union Administration (NCUA) insures deposits in member credit unions for up to $250,000 per depositor. Like FDIC coverage, increased coverage is provided for accounts with different categories of ownership.

The FDIC and NCUA have improved banking in the United States. When either of these organizations insures a financial institution's deposits, they reserve the right to examine that institution's operations periodically. If a bank, S&L, savings bank, or credit union is found to be poorly managed, it is reported to the proper banking authority.

COURTESY OF FDIC

Ever wonder how safe your money is when you make deposits at a bank? It's easy to find out if your deposits are insured by the FDIC. Just go to the FDIC Web site at www.fdic.gov, and take a look. While you're there, explore the Web site. There are many topics that describe what the FDIC is doing to regulate and improve banking in the United States.

EFFECTIVE CREDIT MANAGEMENT

One of the most important activities of any financial institution or business is making wise decisions regarding to whom it will extend credit. **Credit** is immediate purchasing power that is exchanged for a promise to repay borrowed money, with or without interest, at a later date. For example, suppose that you obtain a bank loan to buy a $150,000 home. You, as the borrower, obtain immediate purchasing power. In return, you agree to certain terms imposed by the lender. Generally, the lender requires that you make a down payment, make monthly payments, pay interest, and purchase insurance to protect your home until the loan is paid in full.

Banks and other financial institutions lend money because they are in business for that purpose. The interest they charge is what provides their profit. Other businesses extend credit to their customers for at least three reasons.

Some customers simply cannot afford to pay the entire amount of their purchase immediately, but they *can* repay credit in a number of smaller payments stretched out over some period of time. Some firms are forced to sell goods or services on credit to compete effectively when other firms offer credit to their customers.

Finally, firms can realize a profit from interest charges that a borrower pays on some credit arrangements.

credit immediate purchasing power that is exchanged for a promise to repay borrowed money, with or without interest, at a later date

Personal APPS

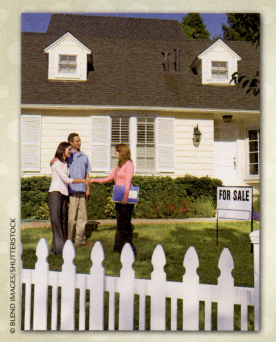

No one likes to pay more than they have to for anything. And yet, many consumers often pay more for loans than necessary. Factors that increase the amount of interest you pay for credit cards, an auto loan, or a home mortgage include how well you have paid your bills in the past, the amount of debt you currently have, and your credit score. It also helps to compare rates for different types of consumer credit. Even a one percent lower interest rate for a home mortgage, for example, can save you thousands of dollars over the life of a home loan.

Getting Money from a Bank or Lender after the Economic Crisis

While lenders need interest from loans to help pay their business expenses and earn a profit, they also want to make sure that the loans they make will be repaid. As a borrower, your job is to convince the lender that you are able and willing to repay the loan.

After the recent economic crisis, bankers, lenders and suppliers, and credit card companies are much more careful when evaluating credit applications.

For individuals, the following suggestions may be helpful when applying for credit:

• Obtain a loan application and complete it at home. At home, you have the information needed to answer *all* the questions on the loan application.
• Be prepared to describe how you will use the money and how the loan will be repaid.
• For most loans, an interview with a loan officer is required. Here again, preparation is the key. Think about how you would respond to questions a loan officer might ask.
• If your loan request is rejected, try to analyze what went wrong. Ask the loan officer why you were rejected. If the rejection is based on incorrect information, supply the correct information and reapply.

Business owners in need of financing may find the following additional tips helpful:

• It is usually best to develop a relationship with your banker before you need financing.
• Help the banker understand what your business is and how you may need future financing for expansion, cash-flow problems, or unexpected emergencies.

- Apply for a pre-approved line of credit or revolving credit agreement even if you do not need the money. View the application as another way to showcase your company and its products or services.
- In addition to the application, supply certified public accountant (CPA)-prepared financial statements and business tax returns for the last three years. If your business is small, you may want to supply your own personal financial statements and tax returns for the same period.
- Update your business plan in case the lender wants to review your plan. Be sure the sales estimates and other projections are realistic.
- Write a cover letter describing how much experience you have, whether you are operating in an expanding market, or any other information that would help convince the banker to provide financing.

The Five C's of Credit Management

When a business extends credit to its customers, it must face the fact that some customers will be unable or unwilling to pay for their credit purchases. To help determine if an individual or business is a good credit risk, lenders often examine a business firm's financial statements. Individuals may be asked to complete a credit application like the one illustrated in Figure 18.5. Most lenders will also consider the five C's of credit, described in Table 18.3.

Checking Credit Information

The five C's of credit are concerned mainly with information supplied by the applicant. But how can a lender determine whether this information is accurate? This depends on whether the potential borrower is a business or an individual consumer.

Credit information concerning businesses can be obtained from the following four sources:

- *Global credit-reporting agencies*. D&B (formerly Dun & Bradstreet) is the world's leading credit-reporting agency. Their reports present detailed credit information about specific companies. For more information on D&B services, visit the company's Web site at www.dnb.com.
- *Local credit-reporting agencies*. These agencies may require a monthly or yearly fee for providing information on a continual basis.
- *Industry associations*. These associations may charge a service fee.
- *Other firms*. This refers to other firms that have given the applicant credit.

TABLE 18.3 The Five C's of Credit

Lenders often use the five C's of credit to determine which credit or loan requests will be approved and which will be rejected.	
Factor to Consider	**Description of Why This Factor Is Important**
Character	The borrower's attitude toward credit obligations
Capacity	The financial ability to meet credit obligations—that is, to make regular loan payments.
Capital	The term *capital* as used here refers to the borrower's assets or the net worth of the individual or business applying for a loan.
Collateral	Real estate or property including stocks, bonds, equipment, or any other asset pledged as security for a loan.
Conditions	General economic conditions that can affect a borrower's ability to repay a loan or other credit obligation.

© Cengage Learning 2014

FIGURE 18.5 Credit Application Form

Lenders use the information on credit application forms to help determine which customers should be granted credit.

Apply today! Just complete this application or call 1-800-438-9222.

Citizens Bank Customer Credit Card Application

Branch # _____

This offer is for existing Citizens Bank Customers applying for a new credit card account

Existing Citizens Bank cardholders should call 1-800-438-9222 for special cardholder rate information.

Citizens Bank VISA® (Code: BVCFNU)

Please tell us about yourself

_____
First Name   Middle Initial   Last Name

_____
Address (street)

_____
(City, state, zip)

_____   ____ — ____ — ____
Date of Birth   Social Security Number

❏ Own   ❏ Rent   ❏ Live with Parents
_____
Years/Months at Present Address

$ _____   (____) _____
Monthly Housing Payment   Home Telephone

_____
Previous Address   Years/Months There
(if less than 2 years at present address)

_____
Mother's Maiden Name

Citizens Bank Account Information

❏ Checking   ❏ Savings   ❏ Loan   ❏ Citizens Circle℠ Checking

account # _____

Please tell us about your employment

_____
Present Employer   Position

_____   (____)
Years/Months Employed There   Business Telephone

_____
Previous Employer   Years/Months There
(if less than 2 years at present employer)

$ _____ $ _____
Gross Monthly Household Income   Other Monthly Income*

*Alimony, child support, or separate maintenance income need not be revealed if you do not wish it to be considered as a basis for repaying this obligation.

24-hour banking convenience

Your card(s) can be encoded with a four-digit personal identification number (PIN) to obtain cash advances at automated teller machines. This four-digit PIN will be known only to you. So that we may properly encode your card(s), please select the four digits of your choice and enter them in the spaces below:

_____   _____   _____   _____

Please send a second card at no cost for

_____
First Name   Middle Initial   Last Name

Please read and sign

_____
Your Signature   Date

All information on this application is true and complete, and Citizens Bank of Rhode Island, the card issuer, is authorized to obtain further credit and employment information from any source. I understand that you will retain this application whether or not it is approved. You may share with others, only for valid business reasons, any information relating to me, this application, and any of my banking relationships with you. I request issuance of a Citizens credit card and agree to be bound by the terms and conditions of the Agreement received with the card(s). I understand that Citizens Bank of Rhode Island will assign a credit line based on information provided and information obtained from any other source; and the issuance of a Gold card is subject to a minimum annual income of $35,000 and qualification for a minimum $5,000 credit line.

Transfer balances and save

Citizens will transfer your high interest rate balances to your new Citizens Bank VISA Card at no extra charge. Use the form below to indicate the amount(s) to be transferred in order of priority. (Citizens Bank will not transfer balances from existing Citizens Bank accounts.) (see reverse side for balance transfer disclosure)

		$ _____
Creditor Name	Account Number	Amount
		$ _____
Creditor Name	Account Number	Amount
		$ _____
Creditor Name	Account Number	Amount

Bank Use Only   Bank Code: ❏ CBMA   ❏ CBRI   ❏ CBCT   Sales ID# _____   Application code: 1122

Source: Courtesy of Citizens Financial Group, Inc., Providence, Rhode Island.

Various credit bureaus provide credit information concerning individuals. The following are the three major consumer credit bureaus:

- Experian—at www.experian.com or toll-free at 888-397-3742
- TransUnion—at www.transunion.com or toll-free at 800-888-4213
- Equifax Credit Information Services—at www.equifax.com or toll-free at 800-685-1111

Protection for Consumers

Consumer credit bureaus are subject to the provisions of the Fair Credit Reporting Act. This act safeguards consumers' rights in two ways. First, you have the right to know what information is contained in your credit bureau file. Second, if you feel that some information in the file is inaccurate, misleading, or vague you have the right to request that the credit bureau verify it. If the disputed information is found to be correct, you can provide a brief explanation, giving your side of the dispute. If the disputed information is found to be inaccurate, it must be deleted or corrected. Furthermore, you may request that any lender or prospective employer that has been supplied an inaccurate credit report in the last six months be sent a corrected credit report.

The Fair and Accurate Credit Transactions Act requires each of the nationwide credit reporting companies—Equifax, Experian, and TransUnion—to provide you with a free copy of your credit report, at your request, once every 12 months. To obtain your free credit report, go to www.annualcreditreport.com. (*Note*: Beware of other sites that may look and sound similar to this site but may charge for information or require that you spend money on credit monitoring.[14])

The Credit Card Act of 2009, which was enacted on February 22, 2010, also provides additional protection for credit card customers. This new federal law is designed to level the playing field between credit card customers and financial institutions that issue credit cards. This act encourages disclosures written in plain language that include more information about due dates, late fees, and the amount of time required to pay off card balances if only minimum monthly payments are made.[15] If you want more information about provisions in the Credit Card Act of 2009, contact the financial institution that issued your credit card, the Federal Reserve Board (www.federalreserve.gov), or conduct a Web search.

In the next chapter, you will see why firms need financing, how they obtain the money they need, and how they ensure that funds are used efficiently, in keeping with their organizational objectives.

return to Inside BUSINESS

Umpqua Bank

How many bank CEOs invite customers to call them with questions, compliments, or complaints? Every Umpqua Bank store (its preferred term for branches) has a direct phone line to the CEO's office, part of the bank's personalized, community-oriented customer service. At a time when so many companies are moving away from face-to-face service, Umpqua Bank is encouraging people to drop in and chat, even when they don't have any transactions to conduct. The bank also connects with customers via Facebook and Twitter, as well as through its own Web site.

Employees go to the World's Greatest Bank University (its in-house training facility) for classes on customer-service techniques and product knowledge. They are also paid for up to 40 hours of volunteer work each year because of the bank's commitment to community involvement. No wonder Umpqua has been named six times to *Fortune*'s list of "100 Best Companies to Work For."

Questions

1. Why would Umpqua go out of its way to make each branch a community hub?
2. Would you like to work for a commercial bank like Umpqua, which serves consumers, small businesses, and corporations? Explain your answer.

Identify the functions and characteristics of money.

Money is anything a society uses to purchase products, services, or resources. Money must serve as a medium of exchange, a measure of value, and a store of value. To perform its functions effectively, money must be divisible into units of convenient size, light and sturdy enough to be carried and used on a daily basis, stable in value, and difficult to counterfeit. The M_1 supply of money is made up of coins and bills (currency) and deposits in checking accounts (demand deposits). The M_2 supply includes M_1 plus savings accounts, certain money-market securities, and certificates of deposits.

 Summarize how the Federal Reserve System regulates the money supply to maintain a healthy economy.

The Federal Reserve System is responsible for regulating the U.S. banking industry and maintaining a sound economic environment. Banks with federal charters (national banks) must be members of the Fed. State banks may join if they can meet the requirements for membership. Twelve district banks and 24 branch banks compose the Federal Reserve System, whose seven-member board of governors is headquartered in Washington, D.C. During the recent economic crisis, it was necessary for the Federal Reserve to take actions in order to reduce the effects of the recent economic crisis. Specifically, the Fed provided liquidity to the banking and financial industry, supported troubled financial markets, supported troubled financial institutions, and conducted stress tests of major banks.

To control the supply of money, the Federal Reserve System regulates the reserve requirement, or the percentage of deposits a bank must keep on hand. It also regulates the discount rate, or the interest rate the Fed charges member banks for loans from the Federal Reserve. It also engages in open-market operations, in which it buys and sells government securities. When the Federal Reserve buys and sells securities, the goal is to increase or decrease the federal funds rate. The federal funds rate is the interest rate at which a bank lends immediately available funds on deposit at the Fed to another bank overnight in order to meet the borrowing bank's reserve requirements. The Fed serves as the government's bank and is also responsible for clearing checks and electronic transfers, inspecting currency, enforcing the Truth-in-Lending Act, and setting margin requirements for securities transactions.

 Describe the organizations involved in the banking industry.

Most everyone has been affected in one way or another by the nation's economic problems. To help resolve the major problems that led to the economic crisis, Congress passed and the president signed the Dodd–Frank Wall Street Reform and Consumer Protection Act that provides new protection for consumers and increased regulation of the financial industry.

A commercial bank is a profit-making organization that accepts deposits, makes loans, and provides related services to customers. Commercial banks are chartered by the federal government or state governments. Savings and loan associations and credit unions offer the same basic services that commercial banks provide. Mutual savings banks, insurance companies, pension funds, brokerage firms, finance companies, and investment banking firms provide some limited banking services. A large number of people work in the banking industry because of the number of banks and other financial institutions.

 Identify the services provided by financial institutions.

Banks and other financial institutions offer today's customers a tempting array of services. Among the most important banking services for both individuals and businesses are checking accounts, savings accounts, short- and long-term loans, and processing credit card and debit card transactions. Other traditional services include financial advice, payroll services, certified checks, trust services, and safe-deposit boxes.

 Understand how financial institutions are changing to meet the needs of domestic and international customers.

Competition among banks, brokerage firms, insurance companies, and other financial institutions has increased. The use of technology will also increase as financial institutions continue to offer online and mobile banking. Increased use of electronic funds transfer systems (automated teller machines, automated clearinghouses, point-of-sale terminals, and electronic check conversion) also will change the way people bank. For firms in the global marketplace, a bank can provide letters of credit and banker's acceptances that will reduce the risk of nonpayment for sellers. Banks and financial institutions also can provide currency exchange to reduce payment problems for import or export transactions.

 Explain how deposit insurance protects customers.

The Federal Deposit Insurance Corporation (FDIC) and the National Credit Union Association (NCUA) insure accounts in member financial institutions for up $250,000. Deposits maintained in different categories of legal ownership are insured separately. The most common ownership categories are single ownership and joint ownership. It is also possible to obtain additional coverage by opening separate accounts in different banks, S&Ls, or credit unions. When either the FDIC or NCUA insures a financial institution's deposits, they reserve the right to examine that institution's operations periodically. If a bank, S&L, or credit union is found to be poorly managed, it is reported to the proper banking authority.

 Discuss the importance of credit and credit management.

Credit is immediate purchasing power that is exchanged for a promise to repay borrowed money, with or without interest, at a later date. Banks lend money because they are in business for that purpose. Businesses sell goods and services on credit because some customers cannot afford to pay cash and because they must keep pace with competitors who offer credit. Businesses also may realize a profit from interest charges.

Decisions on whether to grant credit to businesses and individuals usually are based on the five C's of credit: character, capacity, capital, collateral, and conditions. Credit information can be obtained from various credit-reporting agencies, credit bureaus, industry associations, and other firms. A number of federal regulations even the playing field between consumers and credit card companies and lenders.

KEY TERMS

You should now be able to define and give an example relevant to each of the following terms:

barter system (522)
money (522)
medium of exchange (522)
measure of value (522)
store of value (522)
demand deposit (524)
time deposit (524)
Federal Reserve System (525)
commercial paper (526)

reserve requirement (527)
discount rate (528)
open-market operations (528)
federal funds rate (528)
commercial bank (531)
national bank (531)
state bank (531)
savings and loan association (S&L) (532)

credit union (532)
check (533)
NOW account (534)
certificate of deposit (CD) (534)
line of credit (535)
revolving credit agreement (535)
collateral (535)

debit card (536)
electronic funds transfer (EFT) system (537)
letter of credit (538)
banker's acceptance (539)
credit (540)

REVIEW QUESTIONS

1. How does the use of money solve the problems associated with a barter system of exchange?
2. What are three functions money must perform in a sound monetary system?
3. Explain why money must have each of the following characteristics:
   a. Divisibility
   b. Portability
   c. Stability
   d. Durability
   e. Difficulty of counterfeiting
4. What is included in the definition of the M_1 supply of money? Of the M_2 supply?
5. What is the Federal Reserve System? How is it organized?
6. Describe the actions the Federal Reserve took to maintain a healthy economy during the recent economic crisis. In your opinion, were the actions necessary? Were the Fed's actions effective?
7. Explain how the Federal Reserve System uses each of the following to control the money supply:
   a. Reserve requirements
   b. The discount rate
   c. Open-market operations

8. The Federal Reserve and the Consumer Financial Protection Bureau are responsible for enforcing the Truth-in-Lending Act. How does this act affect you?
9. What is the difference between a national bank and a state bank? What other financial institutions compete with national and state banks?
10. Describe the major banking services provided by financial institutions today.
11. For consumers, what are the major advantages of online banking?
12. How do automated teller machines, automated clearinghouses, point-of-sale terminals, and electronic check conversion affect how you bank?
13. How can a bank or other financial institution help American businesses to compete in the global marketplace?
14. What is the basic function of the FDIC and NCUA? How do they perform this function?
15. How would you check the information provided by an applicant for credit at a department store? By a business applicant at a heavy-equipment manufacturer's sales office?

1. Based on what you know at the time you are answering this question, how would you describe the financial health of the U.S. economy? Of the global economy?
2. It is said that financial institutions use a process called deposit expansion to "create" money when they make loans to firms and individuals. Explain what this means.
3. Why does the Fed use indirect means of controlling the money supply instead of simply printing more money or removing money from circulation when necessary?
4. Why would banks pay higher interest on money left on deposit for longer periods of time (e.g., on CDs)?
5. How could an individual get in financial trouble by using a credit card? If you were in trouble because of credit card debt, what steps could you take to reduce your debts?
6. Assume that you want to borrow $10,000. What can you do to convince the loan officer that you are a good credit risk?

Video Case 18.1   Chase Bank Helps Small Business Owners

JPMorgan Chase & Co. is a global financial holding company formed in 2000 by a merger of the financial institutions that today are its two major brands: Chase (formerly Chase Manhattan Corp.) and J.P. Morgan (formerly J.P. Morgan & Co.). In 2004, the company also acquired Bank One Corp.; later, in 2008, it added both Bear Stearns Companies, Inc., and Washington Mutual, in the process creating the second-largest branch network in the United States and bringing its banking services within the reach of 42 percent of the U.S. population. The bank, which operates in more than 60 countries and employs almost 240,000 people worldwide, holds assets estimated to be worth about $2 trillion and is included in the widely watched stock index, the Dow Jones Industrial Average (DJIA). Despite an economic downturn, the bank still posted profits for the last four years in a row. And now that the nation's economy is improving, the bank is poised for more growth and increased profits.

Most people are probably more familiar with the functions performed on the Chase side of the operation. These operations include conducting everyday banking via branch offices, ATMs, telephone, and online; issuing consumer credit cards; serving small businesses with financing and banking services; offering home mortgages and home equity loans; helping customers with personal retirement and investment planning; and making auto and educational loans.

In its small-business banking operations, Chase exemplifies the words of J.P. Morgan, who told a Senate subcommittee in 1933 that "Another very important use of the banker is to serve as a channel whereby industry may be provided with capital to meet its needs for expansion and development." Providing capital to small businesses is one of the most important functions the bank fulfills for these business clients. Whether small companies need short-term loans to expand their operations or to bridge the time gap between manufacturing a product and collecting money for the sale, a line of credit to ease their cash flow during a tough period, or a commercial mortgage loan to buy a new factory or warehouse, Chase is ready to lend the necessary funds. The bank also offers several kinds of business credit cards, which small-business owners can use for everyday needs when cash is tight. These cards offer different incentives such as no annual fee, cash back for purchases, bonus points, or no interest on balances paid in full each month. Business debit cards are another option, backed by fraud monitoring and account alerts.

Chase is also there to help firms hang on to their money—not only by providing all those branch offices for making deposits but also by handling the safe collection of payments through its lock-box service (through which consumers send bill payments to a post-office box for collection). Chase makes it easier for its small-business customers to deposit checks, too. Now firms can scan paper checks right in their own offices, transforming them into electronic payments so that they can take advantage of online banking's convenience, safety, and speed. Business checking accounts are available as well, with a wide range of specially tailored features and overdraft protection. Business savings accounts and CDs are offered, and business customers can link their accounts to Chase Business Packages to earn additional benefits, such as waived fees and reduced interest rates on borrowing. The bank even offers payroll processing.

Retail firms that accept credit cards like Visa, American Express, MasterCard, and Discover can rely on Chase for payment processing, and they can use the processed funds the very next day. Free technical support is available 24/7, and monthly statements and online reports help firms manage their credit card operations. Business owners can even pay bills, transfer funds, view account balances and transaction history, and send wire transfers by texting the bank from their mobile phones. Additionally, Chase makes it possible for small businesses to conduct transactions globally, whether that means buying goods abroad or accepting orders from international customers.[16]

Questions

1. If you were a small-business owner, would you take advantage of any of Chase's or another bank's small-business banking services? Why or why not?
2. Can you think of any additional financial or banking services that banks could offer to small-business owners?
3. Chase prides itself on its ability to know many of its business customers personally and to keep up-to-date on the industries in which they operate. Why would this familiarity be an advantage for the bank?

Established 62 years before Hawaii became a state, Bank of Hawaii is now one of the top-ranked independent banks in America, known as much for its community involvement as for its financial strength. With 81 branches spread across six Hawaiian islands, American Samoa, Saipan, Guam, and Palau, Bank of Hawaii provides a full range of financial services for corporations, small businesses, and individuals. From traditional checking and savings accounts to loans, mobile banking, online bill payment, and even international trade finance, Bank of Hawaii offers all the services its customers need to achieve their financial goals.

The Honolulu-based bank briefly experimented with an expansion on the mainland before refocusing on its home state, where its heritage and market share are competitive advantages. "The industry recognizes that Hawaii is a challenging place to do business," says CEO Peter Ho. "It's the most ethnically diverse state in the country in many ways." With this diversity in mind, Bank of Hawaii offers customers the choice of communicating in Japanese, Korean, French, Tagalog, Vietnamese, or any of three Chinese dialects. Also, the bank has arranged for the growing number of Chinese tourists who visit Hawaii to use their China UnionPay debit cards at any of Bank of Hawaii's ATMs.

Two-thirds of Hawaiian households use at least one of the bank's services, and it enjoys high customer loyalty within the business community, as well. Bank of Hawaii gave the founder of Yummy's Restaurant Group his first business loan more than 25 years ago. Today, the chain has grown to more than 40 restaurants, and both the company and its founder remain loyal customers. Maui Soda and Ice Works, a family-owned firm that makes ice cream sold throughout the Hawaiian islands, appreciates the bank's professionalism and its expertise in matters such as local economic forecasting. The bank was recently named Small Business Association lender of the year in Hawaii, reflecting its strength in providing financial services for entrepreneurs and growing businesses.

To help customers learn to better manage their money, Bank of Hawaii offers monthly seminars on topics such as buying a home, saving for retirement, developing a business plan, and making investment decisions. More than 2,000 of the bank's employees participate in community projects such as Junior Achievement, the Hawaii Book and Music Festival, and environmental cleanup programs. The annual "employee giving" campaign raises $500,000 every year to benefit local nonprofit groups, and the bank donates tens of thousands of dollars for scholarships and other community needs.

Bank of Hawaii remained profitable even during the recent recession, thanks in large part to its sound lending practices and its ability to adapt to changing economic and technological conditions. As customers began using iPhones and other digital devices, the bank expanded its mobile and online banking services to provide instant, on-the-go access to financial information. Bank representatives tweet and also post on the bank's Facebook page to stay in touch with customers who like to use social media. For added convenience, the bank is opening new branches inside popular stores, allowing customers to bank where they shop. Finally, bank officials have created a "business dashboard" to track performance on key measures of customer service and identify any areas for improvement.[17]

Questions

1. Do you agree with Bank of Hawaii's decision to open branches in stores while it continues to invest in new technology for electronic and mobile banking? Explain your answer.
2. How might Bank of Hawaii adjust its credit policies if the area experiences a sudden or dramatic economic downturn? Suggest at least two adjustments the bank should make when applying the five C's of credit in such a situation.
3. In addition to the many languages spoken throughout the islands, what other challenges do you think banks face in serving the financial needs of individuals and businesses in Hawaii? What are the implications for Bank of Hawaii?

Building Skills for Career Success

① SOCIAL MEDIA EXERCISE

As more and more people have smartphones, it is becoming quite clear that products like Google Wallet will soon become popular electronic money-management tools, especially for Millennials—people born after 1980. Google Wallet is a new way to use your smartphone to pay for things both in store and online. Google says you can "Save time and money by shopping with Google Wallet—a smart, virtual wallet that stores your payment cards, offers, and more on your phone and online." Take a look at Google Wallet to see how it works. www.google.com/wallet.

1. For the consumer, what are the advantages and disadvantages of Google Wallet (and similar services)?
2. For merchants, what are the advantages and disadvantages of Google Wallet (and similar services)?
3. Would you use Google Wallet? Why or why not?

② JOURNALING FOR SUCCESS

You could be one of the 11 million Americans who fall victim to the crime of identity theft every year. Crooks who steal your name, birth date, credit card numbers, bank account numbers, and Social Security number can withdraw money from your bank accounts, charge merchandise in your name, or contract for cell-phone service.

Assignment

1. Use the Internet to obtain information about how to prevent identity theft. Then, according to the professionals, describe the steps someone should take to protect his or her identity.
2. Complete a "security audit" of your personal information and financial records. Based on your audit and the recommendations from professionals, what should you do now to protect your identity?
3. It always helps to have a plan in case your identity is stolen. Based on the information you obtained from your Internet research, what immediate steps should you take if your identity is stolen?

③ DEVELOPING CRITICAL-THINKING SKILLS

Assumption: There are banks, savings and loan associations, credit unions, and other financial institutions that want your business. Therefore, it pays to shop around for the lowest interest rates for loans needed to purchase a home mortgage or an automobile. It's also easy to compare interest rates when investing in certificates of deposit (CDs) or savings accounts. A logical place to start is with the financial institution where you do your banking. You can also compare interest rates at other local banks and financial institutions located close to where you live or work. Finally, you can use the Internet and Web sites like www.bankrate.com or www.interest.com to determine interest rates for loans and CD investments.

Assignment

To answer each of the following questions, contact at least three different financial institutions in your city or town or three different Internet Web sites. *Hint*: If you use the Internet, use a search engine like Google or Yahoo! and enter "interest rates" in the search window.

1. What is the lowest rate you found for a 30-year $150,000 home mortgage?
2. Based on your research, what is the difference between the lowest interest rate and the highest interest rate for a home mortgage? Assuming you pay back the loan in 30 years, how could the difference in interest rates affect the total amount you will pay for your home?
3. What is the highest interest rate you found for a one-year certificate of deposit?
4. Based on your research, what is the difference between the highest rate and the lowest rate for a one-year CD? How could this affect the amount of money you would earn for the 12-month period?

5. In a one- to two-page report, summarize what you have learned from this critical-thinking exercise.

④ BUILDING TEAM SKILLS

Three years ago, Ron and Ginger were happy to learn that, upon graduation, Ron would be teaching history in a large high school, making $35,000 a year, and Ginger would be working in a public accounting firm, starting at $38,000. They married immediately after graduation and bought a new home for $110,000. Since Ron had no personal savings, Ginger used her savings for the down payment. They soon began furnishing their home, charging their purchases to three separate credit cards, and that is when their debt began to mount. When the three credit cards reached their $10,000 limits, Ron and Ginger signed up for one additional credit card with a $10,000 limit. Soon all their monthly payments were more than their combined take-home pay. To make their monthly payments, Ron and Ginger began to obtain cash advances on their credit cards. When they reached the credit ceilings on their four credit cards, they could no longer get the cash advances they needed to cover their monthly bills. Stress began to mount as creditors called and demanded payment. Ron and Ginger began to argue over money and just about everything else. Finally, things got so bad they considered filing for personal bankruptcy; ironically, they could not afford the legal fees. What options are available to this couple?

Assignment

1. Working in teams of three or four, use your local library, the Internet, and personal interviews to investigate the following:
   a. Filing for personal bankruptcy.
      - What is involved in filing for personal bankruptcy?
      - How much does it cost?
      - How does bankruptcy affect individuals?
   b. Review the Money Management International Web site at www.cccsintl.org.
      - What services does this organization provide?
      - How might this organization help Ron and Ginger?
      - What will it cost?
2. Prepare a specific plan for repaying Ron and Ginger's debt.
3. Outline the advantages and disadvantages of credit cards, and make the appropriate recommendations for Ron and Ginger concerning their future use of credit cards.
4. Summarize what you have learned about credit card misuse.

⑤ RESEARCHING DIFFERENT CAREERS

It has long been known that maintaining a good credit record is essential to obtaining loans from financial institutions, but did you know that employers often check credit records before offering an applicant a position? This is especially true of firms that handle financial accounts for others. Information contained in your credit report can tell an employer a lot about how responsible you are with money and how well you manage it. Individuals have the right to know what is in their credit bureau files and to have the credit bureau verify any inaccurate, misleading, or vague information. Before you apply for a job or a loan, you should check with a credit bureau to learn what is in your file.

Assignment

1. Using information in this chapter, use the Internet or call a credit bureau and ask for a copy of your credit report. A small fee may be required depending on the bureau and circumstances.
2. Review the information.
3. Have the bureau verify any information that you feel is inaccurate, misleading, or vague.
4. If the verification shows that the information is correct, prepare a brief statement explaining your side of the dispute, and send it to the bureau.
5. Prepare a statement summarizing what the credit report says about you. Based on your credit report, would a firm hire you as its financial manager?

ENDNOTES

1. Sources: Based on information in Charles Passy, "Banks Branch into Yoga," *Smart Money,* March 13, 2012, www.smartmoney.com; "100 Best Companies to Work For: No. 69, Umpqua Bank," *Fortune,* February 6, 2012, www.fortune.com; Michael Sisk, "Umpqua Keeps Testing New Ideas," *Bank Technology News,* July 1, 2011, p. 18; www.umpquabank.com.
2. "The Economy: Crisis & Response," The Federal Reserve Board of San Francisco Web site at www.frsb.org, accessed April 1, 2012.
3. The Federal Reserve Board Web site at www.federalreserve.gov, accessed March 30, 2012.
4. Ibid.
5. Ibid.
6. The Investopedia.com Web site at www.investopedia.com, accessed March 30, 2012.
7. The Federal Reserve Board at www.federalreserve.gov, accessed March 30, 2012.
8. "Wall Street Reform," the White House Web site at www.whitehouse.gov, accessed June 20, 2010.
9. The Office of the Comptroller of the Currency Web site at www.occ.gov, accessed March 31, 2012.
10. "The Quarterly Banking Profile for December 31, 2011," The Federal Deposit Insurance Corporation Web site at www.fdic.gov, accessed March 31, 2012.
11. U.S. Census Bureau, *Statistical Abstract of the United States, 2012* (Washington, DC: U.S. Government Printing Office), table 1183.
12. "The Occupational Outlook Handbook," the Bureau of Labor Statistics Web site at www.bls.gov, accessed March 31, 2012.
13. U.S. Census Bureau, *Statistical Abstract of the United States, 2012* (Washington, DC: U.S. Government Printing Office), table 1188.
14. The Federal Trade Commission Web site at www.ftc.gov, accessed March 27, 2012.
15. The United States Senate Committee on Banking, Housing, and Urban Affairs Web site at banking.senate.gov, accessed June 15, 2010.
16. Company Web sites www.chase.com and www.jpmorganchase.com, accessed March 31, 2012; "JPMorgan Chase Discloses Results," *American Banking and Market News,* July 15, 2010, www.americanbankingnews.com; Eric Dash, "JPMorgan Chase Easily Exceeds Estimates," *New York Times,* July 15, 2010, www.nytimes.com; and the video, "Chase Bank Helps Small Business Owners."
17. Based on information in Jackie Stewart, "Bank of Hawaii to Shift Some Branches to Grocery Stores," American Banker, February 7, 2012, www.americanbanker.com; Wang Kaihao, "Ready to Say 'Aloha,'" *China Daily,* June 6, 2011, www.chinadaily.com; Kurt Badenhausen, "America's Best and Worst Banks," *Forbes,* December 13, 2011, www.forbes.com; Rachel Witkowski, "Two Hawaiian Banks Find There's No Place Like Home," *American Banker,* May 18, 2011, p. 3; www.boh.com; Bank of Hawaii Annual Report 2011.

19 Mastering Financial Management

LEARNING OBJECTIVES

Once you complete this chapter, you will be able to:

1. Understand why financial management is important in today's uncertain economy.

2. Identify a firm's short- and long-term financial needs.

3. Summarize the process of planning for financial management.

4. Describe the advantages and disadvantages of different methods of short-term debt financing.

5. Evaluate the advantages and disadvantages of equity financing.

6. Evaluate the advantages and disadvantages of long-term debt financing.

How J. M. Smucker Manages Its Money

With a name like Smucker, financial management has to be good. The company is named for its founder, Jerome Monroe Smucker, who began selling apple cider and apple butter in 1897. Today, the Smucker family continues to be involved in running the Orrville, Ohio, firm, which employs 4,500 people and rings up $4.8 billion in food sales every year. Its well-known consumer brands include Smucker's (jams and jellies), Jif (peanut butter), Martha White (baking mixes), and many more that provide tasty food products to customers in both the United States and the global marketplace.

With an eye toward financing faster growth, the J. M. Smucker Co. first sold shares of its common stock to the public in 1959. In recent years, it has made a number of major acquisitions to diversify its product mix and expand its geographical reach. It bought Jif and Crisco from Procter & Gamble in 2002 and then acquired International Multifoods Corporation in 2004. In 2008, Smucker purchased Folgers, the largest U.S. coffee company, from parent Procter & Gamble. In 2011, it purchased Florida-based Rowland Coffee Roasters and folded its $110 million in annual revenues into the corporation's finances. In 2012, the company completed its acquisition of Sara Lee's Douwe Egberts liquid coffee concentrate brand for wholesaling to restaurants and institutions.

Multimillion-dollar acquisitions such as these require excellent financial management. For example, when Smucker bought Douwe Egberts from Sara Lee, it paid $350 million in cash when the deal closed and promised an additional $50 million in payments over the next ten years. The company had funds on hand for this and other acquisitions because it had arranged to borrow money by selling $400 million in bonds during 2010 and another $750 million in bonds during 2011. Although Smucker knew it would have to repay the money to bondholders in the future, it was able to take advantage of promising acquisition opportunities in the short term.

Some of the money is also being spent on investments that will take the company far beyond its Ohio roots. For instance, Smucker paid $35 million to buy a stake in Guilin Seamild Biologic Technology Development Company, a Chinese manufacturer of oatmeal products. "Seamild's portfolio of quality, trusted products aligns with Smucker's strategy of owning and marketing leading food brands," says a Smucker official.[1]

Unfortunately, the J. M. Smucker Co. mentioned in this chapter's opening Inside Business case was the exception when compared to many cash-strapped businesses that struggled to find the funds they needed to operate during the recent economic crisis. In fact, the crisis was a wake-up call for most corporate executives, managers, and business owners because one factor became obvious. The ability to borrow money (debt capital) or obtain money from the owners of a business (equity capital) is necessary for the efficient operation of a business firm *and* our economic system.

In this chapter we examine why financial management is important in an uncertain economy. Then, we discuss how firms find the financing required to meet two needs of all business organizations: the need for money to start a business and keep it going, and the need to manage that money effectively. We also look at how firms develop financial plans and evaluate financial performance. Then we compare various methods of obtaining short-term and long-term financing.

WHY FINANCIAL MANAGEMENT?

Question: How important is financial management for a business firm?

To answer that question, consider the recent financial problems of the "Big Three" U.S. automakers. Both General Motors and Chrysler filed for bankruptcy protection during the recent economic crisis, but Ford had the financial fuel to keep going, despite sagging sales and worldwide economic turmoil. Executives at Ford used aggressive financial planning to anticipate the automaker's need for financing. To avoid the same fate as General Motors and Chrysler—bankruptcy—Ford's financial managers borrowed money in anticipation of a downturn in the company's sales and profits. Ford also sold both stocks and bonds to raise the money it needed to keep the company operating during the crisis and even build for the future. Did that financial plan work? The answer: A definite yes! Today, Ford is selling more cars, developing environmentally friendly engines, creating concept cars for the future, and has returned to profitability. Although there are many factors that account for Ford's success, most experts agree that the firm's financial planning enabled it to weather the economic storm and build for the future.

Although most managers and employees have been affected by the economic crisis, the years since the end of 2007 have been especially difficult for financial managers. After all, they are the ones that must be able to raise the money needed to pay bills and expenses to keep a company's doors open. During the recent economic crisis, many financial managers and business owners found it was increasingly difficult to use many of the traditional sources of short- and long-term financing described later in this chapter. In some cases, banks stopped making loans even to companies that had always been able to borrow money. For example, both GE and AT&T—two premier names in corporate America—could not get the financing they needed.[2] Furthermore, the number of corporations selling stock for the first time to the general public decreased because investors were afraid to invest in new companies. The worst-case scenario: There was an increase in the number of businesses that filed for bankruptcy during the crisis, as illustrated in Figure 19.1. Fortunately, there were many more business firms that were able to weather the economic storm and keep operating because of their ability to manage their finances. And now that the nation's economy is improving, the number of bankruptcies is beginning to decline.

financial management all the activities concerned with obtaining money and using it effectively

How do managers decide how much inventory is needed? One of the most perplexing problems financial managers must deal with is the amount of inventory a retail store needs. If a retailer has too much inventory, then too much money is tied up in merchandise that is not selling. If a retailer has too little inventory, it may not have enough merchandise to meet consumer demand.

The Need for Financial Management

Financial management consists of all the activities concerned with obtaining money and using it effectively. To some extent, financial management can be viewed as a two-sided problem. On one side, the uses of funds often dictate the type or types of financing needed by a business. On the other side, the activities a business can undertake are determined by the types of financing available. Financial managers must ensure that funds are available when needed, that they are obtained at the lowest possible cost, and that they are used as efficiently as possible. In addition, proper financial management must also ensure that:

- Financing priorities are established in line with organizational goals and objectives.
- Spending is planned and controlled.
- Sufficient financing is available when it is needed, both now and in the future.
- A firm's credit customers pay their bills on time, and the number of past due accounts is reduced.
- Bills are paid promptly to protect the firm's credit rating and its ability to borrow money.

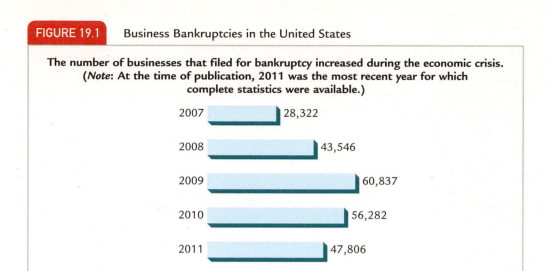

FIGURE 19.1 Business Bankruptcies in the United States

The number of businesses that filed for bankruptcy increased during the economic crisis. (*Note*: At the time of publication, 2011 was the most recent year for which complete statistics were available.)

Year	Bankruptcies
2007	28,322
2008	43,546
2009	60,837
2010	56,282
2011	47,806

Source: Based on The American Bankruptcy Institute Web site at www.abiworld. org (accessed February 24, 2012).

- The funds required for paying the firm's taxes are available when needed to meet tax deadlines.
- Excess cash is invested in certificates of deposit (CDs), government securities, or conservative, marketable securities.

Financial Reform After the Economic Crisis

The job of financial managers became a bit easier as the economy stabilized. Still, it became apparent that something needed to be done to stabilize the financial system and prevent future economic meltdowns. In the wake of the crisis that affected both business firms and individuals, a cry for more regulations and reforms became a high priority. To meet this need, President Obama signed the Dodd–Frank Wall Street Reform and Consumer Protection Act into law on July 21, 2010. Even with the new regulations, some experts say the law did not go far enough while others argue it went too far. Although the U.S. Senate and House of Representatives debate additional regulations, the goals are to hold Wall Street firms accountable for their actions, end taxpayer bailouts, tighten regulations for major financial firms, and increase government oversight. There has also been debate about limiting the amount of executive pay and bonuses, limiting the size of the largest financial firms, and curbing speculative investment techniques that were used by banks before the crisis.

As mentioned in Chapter 18, new regulations will protect American families from unfair, abusive financial and banking practices. For business firms, the impact of new regulations could increase the time and cost of obtaining both short- and long-term financing.

Careers in Finance

After reading the material in the last section, you might be thinking why anyone would want a job in finance. And yet, a career in finance can be rewarding. As an added bonus, the Bureau of Labor Statistics projects there will be an 8 percent increase in the number of jobs in the financial sector of the economy between now and 2018.[3]

Today, there are many different types of positions in finance. At the executive level, most large business firms have a chief financial officer for financial management. A **chief financial officer (CFO)** is a high-level corporate executive who manages a firm's finances and reports directly to the company's chief executive officer or president. Some firms prefer to use the titles vice president of financial management, treasurer, or controller instead of the CFO title for executive-level positions in the finance area.

Although some executives in finance do make $300,000 a year or more, many entry-level and lower-level positions that pay quite a bit less are available. Banks,

chief financial officer (CFO) a high-level corporate executive who manages a firm's finances and reports directly to the company's chief executive officer or president

Did actions by politicians and government officials ease the economic crisis? While people still debate if the government's actions to reduce the effects of the economic crisis were justified, both politicians and government officials did take steps to stabilize the economy. In this photo, Senate majority leader Harry Reid tells reporters—and the nation—about the government's plan to improve the nation's economy.

insurance companies, and investment firms obviously have a need for workers who can manage and analyze financial data. So do businesses involved in manufacturing, services, and marketing. Colleges and universities, not-for-profit organizations, and government entities at all levels also need finance workers.

People in finance must have certain traits and skills. One of the most important priorities for someone interested in a finance career is honesty. Be warned: Investors, lenders, and other corporate executives expect financial managers to be above reproach. Moreover, both federal and state government entities have enacted legislation to ensure that corporate financial statements reflect the "real" status of a firm's financial position. In addition to honesty, managers and employees in the finance area must:

1. Have a strong background in accounting or mathematics.
2. Know how to use a computer to analyze data.
3. Be an expert at both written and oral communication.

Typical job titles in finance include bank officer, consumer credit officer, financial analyst, financial planner, loan officer, insurance analyst, and investment account executive. Depending on qualifications, work experience, and education, starting salaries generally begin at $25,000 to $35,000 a year, but it is not uncommon for college graduates to earn higher salaries. In addition to salary, many employees have attractive benefits and other perks that make a career in financial management attractive.

 Identify a firm's short- and long-term financial needs.

THE NEED FOR FINANCING

Money is needed both to start a business and to keep it going. The original investment of the owners, along with money they may have borrowed, should be enough to open the doors. After that, ideally sales revenues should be used to pay the firm's expenses and provide a profit as well.

This is exactly what happens in a successful firm—over the long run. However, income and expenses may vary from month to month or from year to year. Temporary financing may be needed when expenses are high or sales are low. Then, too, situations such as the opportunity to purchase a new facility or expand an existing plant may require more money than is currently available within a firm.

Short-Term Financing

Short-term financing is money that will be used for one year or less. As illustrated in Table 19.1, there are many short-term financing needs, but three deserve special

short-term financing money that will be used for one year or less

TABLE 19.1	Comparison of Short- and Long-Term Financing
Whether a business seeks short- or long-term financing depends on what the money will be used for.	
Corporate Cash Needs	
Short-Term Financing Needs	**Long-Term Financing Needs**
Cash-flow problems	Business start-up costs
Speculative production	Mergers and acquisitions
Current inventory needs	New product development
Monthly expenses	Long-term marketing activities
Short-term promotional needs	Replacement of equipment
Unexpected emergencies	Expansion of facilities

© Cengage Learning 2014

attention. First, certain business practices may affect a firm's cash flow and create a need for short-term financing. **Cash flow** is the movement of money into and out of an organization. The goal is to have sufficient money coming into the firm in any period to cover the firm's expenses during that period. This goal, however, is not always achieved. For example, California-based Callaway Golf offers credit to retailers and wholesalers that carry the firm's golf clubs, balls, clothing, and golf accessories. Credit purchases made by Callaway's retailers generally are not paid until 30 to 60 days (or more) after the transaction. Callaway therefore may need short-term financing to pay its bills until its customers have paid theirs.

A second major need for short-term financing is speculative production. **Speculative production** refers to the time lag between the actual production of goods and when the goods are sold. Consider what happens when a firm such as Connecticut-based Stanley Black & Decker begins to manufacture electric tools and small appliances for sale during the Christmas season. Manufacturing begins in February, March, and April, and the firm negotiates short-term financing to buy materials and supplies, to pay wages and rent, and to cover inventory costs until its products eventually are sold to wholesalers and retailers later in the year. Take a look at Figure 19.2. Although Stanley Black & Decker manufactures and sells finished products all during the year, expenses peak during the first part of the year. During this same period, sales revenues are low. Once the firm's finished products are shipped to retailers and wholesalers and payment is received (usually within 30 to 60 days), sales revenues are used to repay short-term financing.

Business success often begins with a financial plan. Before the merchandise in this IKEA warehouse can be sold, it must be purchased from manufacturers or suppliers and then stored until it is needed in the retailer's stores. *Successful* businesses often use sound financial planning built on the firm's goals and objectives, different types of budgets, and available sources of funds to make sure financing is available to purchase inventory and other necessities needed to operate a business.

A third need for short-term financing is to increase inventory. Retailers that range in size from Walmart to the neighborhood drugstore need short-term financing to build up their inventories before peak selling periods. For example, Dallas-based Bruce Miller Nurseries must increase the number of shrubs, trees, and flowering plants that it makes available for sale during the spring and summer growing seasons. To obtain this merchandise inventory from growers or wholesalers, it uses short-term financing and repays the loans when the merchandise is sold.

cash flow the movement of money into and out of an organization

speculative production the time lag between the actual production of goods and when the goods are sold

---

FIGURE 19.2   Cash Flow for a Manufacturing Business

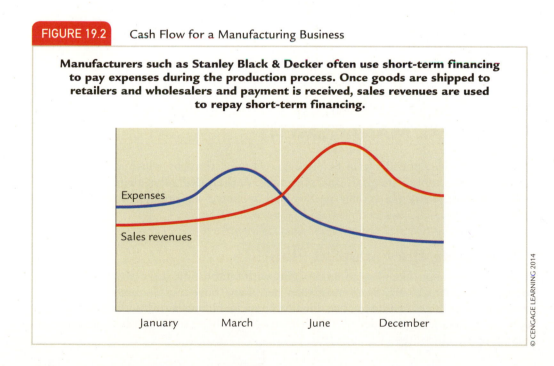

Manufacturers such as Stanley Black & Decker often use short-term financing to pay expenses during the production process. Once goods are shipped to retailers and wholesalers and payment is received, sales revenues are used to repay short-term financing.

Expenses

Sales revenues

January   March   June   December

© CENGAGE LEARNING 2014

Take a moment to write down your short-term and long-term financing needs. Paying for college is a long-term need, for example, as is buying a home. What kinds of short-term financing needs do you have? What can you do to meet your short- and long-term needs in the coming months and years.

long-term financing money that will be used for longer than one year

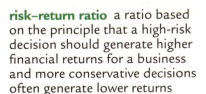

Summarize the process of planning for financial management. ③

risk–return ratio a ratio based on the principle that a high-risk decision should generate higher financial returns for a business and more conservative decisions often generate lower returns

financial plan a plan for obtaining and using the money needed to implement an organization's goals and objectives

Long-Term Financing

Long-term financing is money that will be used for longer than one year. Long-term financing obviously is needed to start a new business. As Table 19.1 shows, it is also needed for business mergers and acquisitions, new product development, long-term marketing activities, replacement of equipment that has become obsolete, and expansion of facilities.

The amounts of long-term financing needed by large firms can seem almost unreal. The 3M Company—a large multinational corporation known for research and development—has invested more than $7 billion over the last five years to develop new products designed to make people's lives easier and safer.[4]

The Risk–Return Ratio

According to financial experts, business firms will find it more difficult to raise both short- and long-term financing in the future for two reasons. First, financial reform and increased regulations will lengthen the process required to obtain financing. Second, both lenders and investors are more cautious about who receives financing. As a result of these two factors, financial managers must develop a strong financial plan that describes how the money will be used and how it will be repaid. When developing a financial plan for a business, a financial manager must also consider the risk–return ratio when making decisions that affect the firm's finances.

The **risk–return ratio** is based on the principle that a high-risk decision should generate higher financial returns for a business. On the other hand, more conservative decisions (with less risk) often generate lesser returns. Although financial managers want higher returns, they often must strive for a balance between risk and return. For example, Ohio-based American Electric Power may consider investing millions of dollars to fund research into new solar technology that could enable the company to use the sun to generate electrical power. Yet, financial managers (along with other managers throughout the organization) must determine the potential return before committing to such a costly research project.

PLANNING—THE BASIS OF SOUND FINANCIAL MANAGEMENT

In Chapter 6, we defined a *plan* as an outline of the actions by which an organization intends to accomplish its goals and objectives. A **financial plan**, then, is a plan for obtaining and using the money needed to implement an organization's goals and objectives.

Developing the Financial Plan

Financial planning (like all planning) begins with establishing a set of valid goals and objectives. Financial managers must then determine how much money is needed to accomplish each goal and objective. Finally, financial managers must identify available sources of financing and decide which to use. The three steps involved in financial planning are illustrated in Figure 19.3.

FIGURE 19.3 The Three Steps of Financial Planning

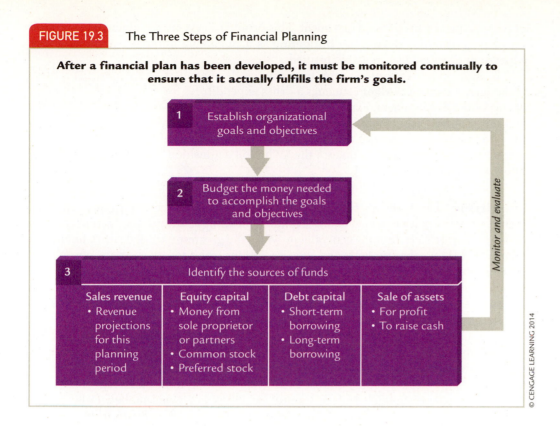

After a financial plan has been developed, it must be monitored continually to ensure that it actually fulfills the firm's goals.

1. Establish organizational goals and objectives

2. Budget the money needed to accomplish the goals and objectives

3. Identify the sources of funds

Sales revenue	Equity capital	Debt capital	Sale of assets
• Revenue projections for this planning period	• Money from sole proprietor or partners • Common stock • Preferred stock	• Short-term borrowing • Long-term borrowing	• For profit • To raise cash

Monitor and evaluate

© CENGAGE LEARNING 2014

Establishing Organizational Goals and Objectives As pointed out in Chapter 6, a *goal* is an end result that an organization expects to achieve over a one- to ten-year period. An *objective* was defined in Chapter 6 as a specific statement detailing what an organization intends to accomplish over a shorter period of time. If goals and objectives are not specific and measurable, they cannot be translated into dollar costs, and financial planning cannot proceed. For large corporations, both goals and objectives can be expensive. For example, have you ever wondered how much McDonald's spends on advertising? Well, to reach the nearly 68 million customers it serves each day, the world's most famous fast-food restaurant chain spends over $685 million each year.[5]

Budgeting for Financial Needs Once planners know what the firm's goals and objectives are for a specific period—say, the next calendar year—they can construct a budget that projects the costs the firm will incur and the sales revenues it will receive. Specifically, a **budget** is a financial statement that projects income, expenditures, or both over a specified future period.

Usually, the budgeting process begins with the construction of departmental budgets for sales and various types of expenses. Financial managers can easily combine each department's budget for sales and expenses into a company-wide cash budget. A **cash budget** estimates cash receipts and cash expenditures over a specified period. Notice in the cash budget for Stars and Stripes Clothing, shown in Figure 19.4, sales receipts and collections are listed at the top for each calendar quarter. Payments for purchases and routine expenses are listed in the middle section. Using this information, it is possible to calculate the anticipated cash gain or loss at the end of each quarter for this retail clothing store.

Most firms today use one of two approaches to budgeting. In the *traditional* approach, each new budget is based on the dollar amounts contained in the budget for the preceding year. These amounts are modified to reflect any revised goals, and managers are required to justify only new expenditures. The problem with this approach is that it leaves room for padding budget items to protect the (sometimes selfish) interests

budget a financial statement that projects income, expenditures, or both over a specified future period

cash budget a financial statement that estimates cash receipts and cash expenditures over a specified period

of the manager or his or her department. This problem is essentially eliminated through zero-base budgeting. **Zero-base budgeting** is a budgeting approach in which every expense in every budget must be justified.

To develop a plan for long-term financing needs, managers often construct a capital budget. A **capital budget** estimates a firm's expenditures for major assets, including new product development, expansion of facilities, replacement of obsolete equipment, and mergers and acquisitions. For example, Berkshire Hathaway, a company known for purchasing well-managed and innovative companies, constructed a capital budget to determine the best way to finance the $9 billion acquisition of the highly successful Lubrizol Corporation in 2011.[6]

Identifying Sources of Funds The four primary sources of funds, listed in Figure 19.3, are sales revenue, equity capital, debt capital, and proceeds from the sale of assets. Future sales revenue generally provides the greatest part of a firm's financing. Figure 19.4 shows that for Stars and Stripes Clothing, sales for the year are expected to cover all expenses and to provide a cash gain of $106,000. However, Stars and Stripes has a problem in the first quarter, when sales are expected to fall short of expenses by $7,000. In fact, one of the primary reasons for financial planning is to provide management with adequate lead time to solve this type of cash-flow problem.

A second type of funding is **equity capital**. For a sole proprietorship or partnership, equity capital is provided by the owner or owners of the business. For a corporation, equity capital is money obtained from the sale of shares of ownership in the business. Equity capital is used almost exclusively for long-term financing.

A third type of funding is **debt capital**, which is borrowed money. Debt capital may be borrowed for either short- or long-term use—and a short-term loan seems made to order for Stars and Stripes Clothing's shortfall problem. The firm probably would borrow the needed $7,000 (or perhaps a bit more) at some point during the first quarter and repay it from second-quarter sales revenue.

Proceeds from the sale of assets are the fourth type of funding. Selling assets is a drastic step. However, it may be a reasonable last resort when sales revenues are declining and equity capital or debt capital cannot be found. Assets also may be sold to increase a firm's cash balance or when they are no longer needed or do not "fit" with the company's core business. In 2011, Pfizer, the world's biggest drug maker, agreed

zero-base budgeting a budgeting approach in which every expense in every budget must be justified

capital budget a financial statement that estimates a firm's expenditures for major assets and its long-term financing needs

equity capital money received from the owners or from the sale of shares of ownership in a business

debt capital borrowed money obtained through loans of various types

---

FIGURE 19.4   Cash Budget for Stars and Stripes Clothing

A company-wide cash budget projects sales, collections, purchases, and expenses over a specified period to anticipate cash surpluses and deficits.

STARS AND STRIPES CLOTHING
Cash Budget   From January 1, 2012 to December 31, 2012

	First Quarter ($)	Second Quarter ($)	Third Quarter ($)	Fourth Quarter ($)	Total ($)
Cash sales and collections	150,000	160,000	150,000	185,000	645,000
Less payments					
Purchases	110,000	80,000	90,000	60,000	340,000
Wages/salaries	25,000	20,000	25,000	30,000	100,000
Rent	10,000	10,000	12,000	12,000	44,000
Other expenses	4,000	4,000	5,000	6,000	19,000
Taxes	8,000	8,000	10,000	10,000	36,000
Total payments	157,000	122,000	142,000	118,000	539,000
Cash gain or (loss)	(7,000)	38,000	8,000	67,000	106,000

to sell its Capsugel manufacturing unit to KKR (Kohlberg Kravis Roberts), a world leading investment company, for $2.4 billion. The cash Pfizer receives from the Capsugel sale will be used to repurchase shares of its own stock.[7]

Monitoring and Evaluating Financial Performance

It is important to ensure that financial plans are implemented properly and to catch potential problems before they become major ones. Despite efforts to raise additional financing, reduce expenses, and increase sales to become profitable, retail and online bookseller Borders filed for bankruptcy protection in 2011. Eventually, the firm was forced to liquidate its inventory and close all its stores because a buyer could not be found for the bankrupt firm.

To prevent such problems, financial managers should establish a means of monitoring financial performance. Interim budgets (weekly, monthly, or quarterly) may be prepared for comparison purposes. These comparisons point up areas that require additional or revised planning—or at least areas calling for a more careful investigation. Budget comparisons can also be used to improve the firm's future budgets.

© OMNITERRA IMAGES

Borders bookstores—no more! After 40 years, Borders closed all of its stores. The firm filed for bankruptcy in early 2011 and was forced to close a large number of stores in order to reorganize. Then in the summer of 2011, the bookseller was forced to liquidate its inventory and remaining stores despite revised financial plans, new financial goals, and its reorganizational efforts. Simply put: A buyer could not be found for the bankrupt firm.

SOURCES OF SHORT-TERM DEBT FINANCING

 4 Describe the advantages and disadvantages of different methods of short-term debt financing.

Typically, short-term debt financing is money that will be repaid in one year or less. During the economic crisis, many business firms found that it was much more difficult to borrow money for short periods of time to purchase inventory, buy supplies, pay salaries, and meet everyday expenses. Today the amount of available short-term financing has increased.

The decision to borrow money does not necessarily mean that a firm is in financial trouble. On the contrary, astute financial management often means regular, responsible borrowing of many different kinds to meet different needs. In this section, we examine the sources of *short-term debt financing* available to businesses. In the next two sections, we look at long-term financing options: equity capital and debt capital.

Sources of Unsecured Short-Term Financing

Short-term debt financing is usually easier to obtain than long-term debt financing for three reasons:

1. For the lender, the shorter repayment period means less risk of non-payment.
2. The dollar amounts of short-term loans are usually smaller than those of long-term loans.
3. A close working relationship normally exists between the short-term borrower and the lender.

Most lenders do not require collateral for short-term financing. If they do, it is usually because they are concerned about the size of a particular loan, the borrowing firm's poor credit rating, or the general prospects of repayment. Remember from Chapter 18 that *collateral* was defined as real estate or property pledged as security for a loan.

Unsecured financing is financing that is not backed by collateral. A company seeking unsecured short-term financing has several options.

unsecured financing financing that is not backed by collateral; unsecured short-term financing offers several options

Entrepreneurs can always use more capital. Even though Body Rest Mattress Company in St. Petersburg, Florida was successful, Carl and Emma Calhoun found that obtaining short-term financing was difficult during the economic crisis. Traditional sources of financing—banks and other financial institutions—tightened the requirements for obtaining unsecured loans or in many cases rejected loan requests.

Trade Credit Manufacturers and wholesalers often provide financial aid to retailers by allowing them 30 to 60 days (or more) in which to pay for merchandise. This delayed payment, known as **trade credit**, is a type of short-term financing extended by a seller who does not require immediate payment after delivery of merchandise. It is the most popular form of short-term financing, because most manufacturers and wholesalers do not charge interest for trade credit. In fact, from 70 to 90 percent of all transactions between businesses involve some trade credit.

Let us assume that Discount Tire Stores receives a shipment of tires from a manufacturer. Along with the merchandise, the manufacturer sends an invoice that states the terms of payment. Discount Tire now has two options for payment. First, the retailer may pay the invoice promptly and take advantage of any cash discount the manufacturer offers. Cash-discount terms are specified on the invoice. For instance, "2/10, net 30" means that the customer—Discount Tire—may take a "2" percent discount if it pays the invoice within ten days of the invoice date. Let us assume that the dollar amount of the invoice is $200,000. In this case, the cash discount is $4,000 ($200,000 × 0.02 = $4,000). If the cash discount is taken, Discount Tire only has to pay the manufacturer $196,000 ($200,000 − $4,000 = $196,000).

A second option is to wait until the end of the credit period before making payment. If payment is made between 11 and 30 days after the date of the invoice, Discount Tire must pay the entire amount. As long as payment is made before the end of the credit period, the retailer maintains the ability to purchase additional merchandise using the trade-credit arrangement.

Promissory Notes Issued to Suppliers A **promissory note** is a written pledge by a borrower to pay a certain sum of money to a creditor at a specified future date. Suppliers uneasy about extending trade credit may be less reluctant to offer credit to customers who sign promissory notes. Unlike trade credit, however, promissory notes usually require the borrower to pay interest. Although repayment periods may extend to one year, most short-term promissory notes are repaid in 60 to 180 days.

A promissory note offers two important advantages to the firm extending the credit.

1. A promissory note is legally binding and an enforceable contract.
2. A promissory note is a negotiable instrument.

Because a promissory note is negotiable, the manufacturer, wholesaler, or company extending credit may be able to discount, or sell, the note to its own bank. If the note is discounted, the dollar amount received by the company extending credit is slightly less than the maturity value because the bank charges a fee for the service. The supplier recoups most of its money immediately, and the bank collects the maturity value when the note matures.

trade credit a type of short-term financing extended by a seller who does not require immediate payment after delivery of merchandise

promissory note a written pledge by a borrower to pay a certain sum of money to a creditor at a specified future date

prime interest rate the lowest rate charged by a bank for a short-term loan

Unsecured Bank Loans Banks and other financial institutions offer unsecured short-term loans to businesses at interest rates that vary with each borrower's credit rating. The **prime interest rate** is the lowest rate charged by a bank for a short-term loan. Figure 19.5 traces the fluctuations in the average prime rate charged by U.S. banks from 1990 to January 2012. This lowest rate generally is reserved for large corporations with excellent credit ratings. Organizations with good to high credit ratings may pay the prime rate plus "2" percent. Firms with questionable credit ratings may have to pay the prime rate plus "4" percent. (The fact that a banker charges a higher interest rate for a higher-risk loan is a practical application of the risk–return ratio

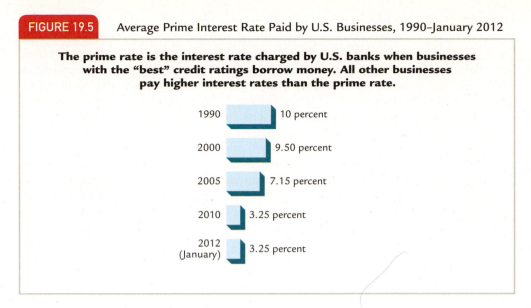

FIGURE 19.5 Average Prime Interest Rate Paid by U.S. Businesses, 1990–January 2012

The prime rate is the interest rate charged by U.S. banks when businesses with the "best" credit ratings borrow money. All other businesses pay higher interest rates than the prime rate.

1990	10 percent
2000	9.50 percent
2005	7.15 percent
2010	3.25 percent
2012 (January)	3.25 percent

Source: Federal Reserve Bank Web site, www.federalreserve.gov (accessed June 6, 2012).

discussed earlier in this chapter.) Of course, if the banker believes that loan repayment may be a problem, the borrower's loan application may well be rejected.

When a business obtains a short-term bank loan, interest rates and repayment terms may be negotiated. As a condition of the loan, a bank may require that a *compensating balance* be kept on deposit at the bank. Compensating balances, if required, are typically 10 to 20 percent of the borrowed funds. The bank may also require that every commercial borrower *clean up* (pay off completely) its short-term loans at least once each year and not use it again for a period of 30 to 60 days.

Commercial Paper Large firms with excellent credit reputations like Microsoft, Procter & Gamble, and Caterpillar can raise large sums of money quickly by issuing commercial paper. As defined in Chapter 18, commercial paper is a short-term promissory note issued by a large corporation. The maturity date for commercial paper is normally 270 days or less.

Commercial paper is secured only by the reputation of the issuing firm; no collateral is involved. The interest rate a corporation pays when it sells commercial paper is tied to its credit rating and its ability to repay the commercial paper. In most cases, corporations selling commercial paper pay interest rates slightly below the interest rates charged by banks for short-term loans. Thus, selling commercial paper is cheaper than getting short-term financing from a bank.

Although it is possible to purchase commercial paper in smaller denominations, larger amounts—$100,000 or more—are quite common. Money obtained by selling commercial paper is most often used to purchase inventory, finance a firm's accounts receivables, pay salaries and other necessary expenses, and solve cash-flow problems.

Sources of Secured Short-Term Financing

If a business cannot obtain enough money through unsecured financing, it must put up collateral to obtain additional short-term financing. Almost any asset can serve as collateral. However, *inventories* and *accounts receivable* are the assets most commonly pledged for short-term financing. Even when it is willing to pledge collateral to back up a loan, a firm that is financially weak may have difficulty obtaining short-term financing.

Loans Secured by Inventory Normally, manufacturers, wholesalers, and retailers have large amounts of money invested in finished goods. In addition, manufacturers carry raw materials and work-in-process inventories. All three types of inventory may be pledged as collateral for short-term loans. However, lenders prefer the much more salable finished merchandise to raw materials or work-in-process inventories.

A lender may insist that inventory used as collateral be stored in a public warehouse. In such a case, the receipt issued by the warehouse is retained by the lender. Without this receipt, the public warehouse will not release the merchandise. The lender releases the warehouse receipt—and the merchandise—to the borrower when the borrowed money is repaid. In addition to paying the interest on the loan, the borrower must pay for storage in the public warehouse. As a result, this type of loan is more expensive than an unsecured short-term loan.

Loans Secured by Receivables As defined in Chapter 17, *accounts receivable* are amounts owed to a firm by its customers. A firm can pledge its accounts receivable as collateral to obtain short-term financing. A lender may advance 70 to 80 percent of the dollar amount of the receivables. First, however, it conducts a thorough investigation to determine the *quality* of the receivables. (The quality of the receivables is the credit standing of the firm's customers, coupled with the customers' ability to repay their credit obligations when they are due.) If a favorable determination is made, the loan is approved. When the borrowing firm collects from a customer whose account has been pledged as collateral, generally it must turn the money over to the lender as partial repayment of the loan. An alternative approach is to notify the borrowing firm's credit customers to make their payments directly to the lender.

Factoring Accounts Receivable

Accounts receivable may be used in one other way to help raise short-term financing: They can be sold to a factoring company (or factor). A **factor** is a firm that specializes in buying other firms' accounts receivable. The factor buys the accounts receivable for less than their face value; however, it collects the full dollar amount when each account is due. The factor's profit thus is the difference between the face value of the accounts receivable and the amount the factor has paid for them. Generally, the amount of profit the factor receives is based on the risk the factor assumes. Risk, in this case, is the probability that the accounts receivable will not be repaid when they mature. In the aftermath of the economic crisis and because of the reluctance of some banks to provide short-term financing, some large financial firms, including CIT Group and GE Capital, are providing additional factoring services to both old and new firms that sell their accounts receivables.[8]

Even though the firm selling its accounts receivable gets less than face value, it does receive needed cash immediately. Moreover, it has shifted both the task of collecting and the risk of non-payment to the factor, which now owns the accounts receivable. Generally, customers whose accounts receivable have been factored are given instructions to make their payments directly to the factor.

Cost Comparisons

Table 19.2 compares the various types of short-term financing. As you can see, trade credit is the least expensive. Factoring of accounts receivable is typically the highest-cost method shown.

For many purposes, short-term financing suits a firm's needs perfectly. At other times, however, long-term financing may be more appropriate. In this case, a business may try to raise equity capital or long-term debt capital.

factor a firm that specializes in buying other firms' accounts receivable

TABLE 19.2 Comparison of Short-Term Financing Methods

Type of Financing	Cost	Repayment Period	Businesses That May Use It	Comments
Trade credit	Low, if any	30–60 days	All businesses with good credit	Usually no finance charge
Promissory note issued to suppliers	Moderate	One year or less	All businesses	Usually unsecured but requires legal document
Unsecured bank loan	Moderate	One year or less	All businesses	Promissory note is required and compensating balance may be required
Commercial paper	Moderate	270 days or less	Large corporations with high credit ratings	Available only to large firms
Secured loan	High	One year or less	Firms with questionable credit ratings	Inventory or accounts receivable often used as collateral
Factoring	High	None	Firms that have large numbers of credit customers	Accounts receivable sold to a factor

© Cengage Learning 2014

SOURCES OF EQUITY FINANCING

Sources of long-term financing vary with the size and type of business. As mentioned earlier, a sole proprietorship or partnership acquires equity capital (sometimes referred to as *owners' equity*) when the owner or partners invest money in the business. For corporations, equity-financing options include the sale of stock and the use of profits not distributed to owners. All three types of businesses can also obtain venture capital and use long-term debt capital (borrowed money) to meet their financial needs.

5 Evaluate the advantages and disadvantages of equity financing.

initial public offering (IPO) occurs when a corporation sells common stock to the general public for the first time

Selling Stock

Some equity capital is used to start every business—sole proprietorship, partnership, or corporation. In the case of corporations, stockholders who buy shares in the company provide equity capital.

Initial Public Offering and the Primary Market An **initial public offering (IPO)** occurs when a corporation sells common stock to the general public for the first time. To raise money, the social networking site Groupon used a 2011 IPO to raise $700 million that it could use to fund expansion and other business activities.[9] In another 2011 IPO, LinkedIn—one of the world's largest social media companies—raised over $350 million.[10] In mid-2012, Facebook used an IPO to raise capital, and it was one of the largest IPOs in recent history. And at the time of the publication of your text, there are more social media and technology IPOs planned for 2012. Corporations in other industries also use IPOs to raise money. In fact, as illustrated in Figure 19.6, the largest IPOs—Visa, General Motors, AT&T Wireless, Kraft Foods, and United Parcel Service—for U.S. companies involve companies from a number of different industries.

© TUPUNGATO/SHUTTERSTOCK

Just a piece of paper—or is it? In fact, a piece of paper can be worth a lot of money when it is a stock certificate. A corporation sells stock to raise needed financing for expansion and to pay for other long-term financial needs. On the other hand, investors purchase stock because they can profit from their investment if the price of the corporation's stock increases and a corporation pays dividends.

Angie's List is now a public company. Angie's List—the company that provides members with information about local professionals for home, health care, and automotive services—sold stock to the public in late 2011 and raised over $100 million. After the initial public offering (IPO), the company's stock was listed on the Nasdaq stock exchange where it can be bought and sold by investors in the secondary market.

Established companies that plan to raise capital by selling subsidiaries to the public can also use IPOs. In 2011, Sunoco sold shares in its metallurgical division and raised over $185 million. The new corporation—SunCoke Energy—will be a separate company and will produce metallurgical coke—a necessary component for manufacturing steel. Monies from the IPO will be used to increase the parent company's cash balance and provide funding for growth opportunities and expansion.[11] In addition to using an IPO to increase the cash balance for the parent company, corporations often sell shares in a subsidiary when shares can be sold at a profit or when the subsidiary no longer fits with its current business plan. Finally, some corporations will sell a subsidiary that is growing more slowly than the rest of the company's operating divisions.

When a corporation uses an IPO to raise capital, the stock is sold in the primary market. The **primary market** is a market in which an investor purchases financial securities (via an investment bank) directly from the issuer of the securities. An **investment banking firm** is an organization that assists corporations in raising funds, usually by helping to sell new issues of stocks, bonds, or other financial securities.

Although a corporation can have only one IPO, it can sell additional stock after the IPO, assuming that there is a market for the company's stock. Even though the cost of selling stock (often referred to as *flotation costs*) is high, the *ongoing* costs associated with this type of equity financing are low for two reasons. First, the corporation does not have to repay money obtained from the sale of stock because the corporation is under no legal obligation to do so. If you purchase corporate stock and later decide to sell your stock, you may sell it to another investor—not the corporation.

A second advantage of selling stock is that a corporation is under no legal obligation to pay dividends to stockholders. As noted in Chapter 4, a *dividend* is a distribution of earnings to the stockholders of a corporation. For any reason (e.g., if a company has a bad year), the board of directors can vote to omit dividend payments. Earnings then are retained for use in funding business operations. Of course, corporate management may hear from unhappy stockholders if expected dividends are omitted too frequently.

primary market a market in which an investor purchases financial securities (via an investment bank) directly from the issuer of those securities

investment banking firm an organization that assists corporations in raising funds, usually by helping to sell new issues of stocks, bonds, or other financial securities

FIGURE 19.6   The All-Time Largest Initial Public Offerings for U.S. Companies

These five corporations raised billions of dollars by selling stock. Visa—the record holder for U.S. companies—raised over $17 billion when it sold stock for the first time in 2008.

Visa	Financial — $17.9 billion
General Motors	Automotive — $15.8 billion
AT&T Wireless	Communications — $10.6 billion
Kraft Foods	Consumer goods — $8.7 billion
United Parcel Service	Transportation — $5.5 billion

Source: Renaissance Capital, Greenwich, CT (www.renaissancecapital.com), accessed February 28, 2012.

Going for
SUCCESS

Investor Relations in the Social Media Era

Tweeting about earnings? Increasingly, public corporations are communicating with their investors via Twitter, Facebook, YouTube, LinkedIn, and other social media. Companies still publish annual reports (in print and online) and hold annual meetings (in person and via webcast). In addition, because stockholders and potential investors want easy access to the latest financial news, companies like Alcoa, Dell, and eBay now use social media to provide official updates. Although the timing and content of these messages must comply with regulatory requirements, the ability to connect quickly and directly with investors is vital at a time when rumors can fly around the world at the click of a mouse.

Alcoa, for example, uses its Facebook page to announce quarterly earnings figures and link to executive webcasts. It also uses its Twitter account to call attention to specific results and invite comments from its followers. For investors who want to dig deeper into quarterly or annual financial reports, the investor relations department shares its electronic presentations on SlideShare.

Thanks to Twitter, YouTube, a dedicated investor relations blog, and other social media, Dell reaches more than five million people when it presents its quarterly financial results. And the online auction site eBay live-tweets earnings results as the CEO announces them. Watch for corporate investor relations departments to become even more social in the years ahead.

Sources: Based on information in Rachel Koning Beals, "Investors Increasingly Tap Social Media for Stock Tips," *U.S. News & World Report,* January 31, 2012, http://money.usnews.com/money; Dominic Jones, "Social Media Investor Relations Reaches Tipping Point," *IR Web Report,* April 14, 2011, http://irwebreport.com; Dave Hogan, "Investor Relations and Social Media: Together at Last," *PR News Online,* May 9, 2011, www.prnewsonline.com; Jennifer Van Grove, "Investor Relations Tool Helps Fortune 500 Companies Get Social," *Mashable,* June 8, 2011, www.mashable.com.

The Secondary Market Although a share of corporate stock is only sold one time in the primary market, the stock can be sold again and again in the secondary market. The **secondary market** is a market for existing financial securities that are traded between investors. Although a corporation does not receive money each time its stock is bought or sold in the secondary market, the ability to obtain cash by selling stock investments is one reason why investors purchase corporate stock. Without the secondary market, investors would not purchase stock in the primary market because there would be no way to sell shares to other investors. Usually, secondary-market transactions are completed through a securities exchange or the over-the-counter (OTC) market.

A **securities exchange** is a marketplace where member brokers meet to buy and sell securities. Generally, securities issued by larger corporations are traded at the New York Stock Exchange (NYSE) (now owned by the NYSE Euronext holding company), or at regional exchanges located in different parts of the country. The securities of very large corporations may be traded at more than one of these exchanges. Securities of firms also may be listed on foreign securities exchanges—in Tokyo or London, for example.

Stocks issued by several thousand companies are traded in the OTC market. The **over-the-counter (OTC) market** is a network of dealers who buy and sell the stocks of corporations that are not listed on a securities exchange. The term *over-the-counter* was coined more than 100 years ago when securities actually were sold "over the counter" in stores and banks. Most OTC securities today are traded through an *electronic exchange* called the Nasdaq (pronounced "nazzdack"). The term Nasdaq stands for National Association of Securities Dealers Automated Quotations. The Nasdaq is now one of the largest securities markets in the world. Today, the Nasdaq is known for its forward-looking, innovative, growth companies, including Intel, Microsoft, Cisco Systems, and Dell Computer.

There are two types of stock: common and preferred. Each type has advantages and drawbacks as a means of long-term financing.

secondary market a market for existing financial securities that are traded between investors

securities exchange a marketplace where member brokers meet to buy and sell securities

over-the-counter (OTC) market a network of dealers who buy and sell the stocks of corporations that are not listed on a securities exchange

Evaluate the advantages and disadvantages of long-term debt financing.

 6

SOURCES OF LONG-TERM DEBT FINANCING

As pointed out earlier in this chapter, businesses borrow money on a short-term basis for many valid reasons other than desperation. There are equally valid reasons for long-term borrowing. In addition to using borrowed money to meet the long-term needs listed in Table 19.1, successful businesses often use the financial leverage it creates to improve their financial performance. **Financial leverage** is the use of borrowed funds to increase the return on owners' equity. The principle of financial leverage works as long as a firm's earnings are larger than the interest charged for the borrowed money.

To understand how financial leverage can increase a firm's return on owners' equity, study the information for Texas-based Cypress Springs Plastics presented in Table 19.3. Pete Johnston, the owner of the firm, is trying to decide how best to finance a $100,000 purchase of new high-tech manufacturing equipment.

- He could borrow the money and pay 7 percent annual interest.
- He could invest an additional $100,000 in the firm.

Assuming that the firm earns $95,000 a year and that annual interest for this loan totals $7,000 ($100,000 × 0.07 = $7,000), the return on owners' equity for Cypress Springs Plastics would be higher if the firm borrowed the additional financing. Return on owners' equity is determined by dividing a firm's net income by the dollar amount of owners' equity. Based on the calculations illustrated in Table 19.3, Cypress Springs Plastics' return on owners' equity equals 17.6 percent if Johnston borrows the additional $100,000. The firm's return on owners' equity would decrease to 15.8 percent if Johnston invests an additional $100,000 in the business.

The most obvious danger when using financial leverage is that the firm's earnings may be lower than expected. If this situation occurs, the fixed interest charge actually works to reduce or eliminate the return on owners' equity. Of course, borrowed money eventually must be repaid.

For a small business, long-term debt financing is generally limited to loans. Large corporations have the additional option of issuing corporate bonds.

Long-Term Loans

financial leverage the use of borrowed funds to increase the return on owners' equity

Many businesses satisfy their long-term financing needs, such as those listed in Table 19.1, with loans from commercial banks, insurance companies, pension funds, and other financial institutions. Manufacturers and suppliers of heavy machinery may also provide long-term debt financing by granting credit to their customers.

TABLE 19.3	Analysis of the Effect of Additional Capital from Debt or Equity for Cypress Springs Plastics, Inc.		
Additional Debt		**Additional Equity**	
Owners' equity	$ 500,000	Owners' equity	$ 500,000
Additional equity	+ 0	Additional equity	+100,000
Total owner's equity	$ 500,000	Total owner's equity	$ 600,000
Loan (@ 7%)	+100,000	No loan	+ 0
Total capital	$ 600,000	Total capital	$ 600,000
Year-End Earnings			
Gross profit	$95,000	Gross profit	$ 95,000
Less loan interest	– 7,000	No interest	– 0
Operating profit	$88,000	Operating profit	$ 95,000
Return on owners' equity	17.6%	Return on owners' equity	15.8%
($88,000 ÷ $500,000 = 17.6%)		($95,000 ÷ $600,000 = 15.8%)	

© Cengage Learning 2014

Term-Loan Agreements A **term-loan agreement** is a promissory note that requires a borrower to repay a loan in monthly, quarterly, semiannual, or annual installments. Although repayment may be as long as 15 to 20 years, long-term business loans normally are repaid in 3 to 7 years.

Assume that Pete Johnston, the owner of Cypress Springs Plastics, decides to borrow $100,000 and take advantage of the principle of financial leverage illustrated in Table 19.3. Although the firm's return on owners' equity does increase, interest must be paid each year and, eventually, the loan must be repaid. To pay off a $100,000 loan over a three-year period with annual payments, Cypress Springs Plastics must pay $33,333 on the loan balance plus $7,000 annual interest, or a total of $40,333 the first year. Although the amount of interest decreases each year because of the previous year's payment on the loan balance, annual payments of this amount are still a large commitment for a small firm such as Cypress Springs Plastics.

The interest rate and repayment terms for term loans often are based on factors such as the reasons for borrowing, the borrowing firm's credit rating, and the value of collateral. Although long-term loans occasionally may be unsecured, the lender usually requires some type of collateral. Acceptable collateral includes real estate, stocks, bonds, equipment, or any asset with value. Lenders may also require that borrowers maintain a minimum amount of working capital.

The Basics of Getting a Loan According to many financial experts, preparation is the key when applying for a long-term business loan. In reality, preparation begins before you ever apply for the loan. To begin the process, you should get to know potential lenders before requesting debt financing. Although there may be many potential lenders that can provide the money you need, the logical place to borrow money is where your business does its banking. This fact underscores the importance of maintaining adequate balances in the firm's bank accounts. Before applying for a loan, you may also want to check your firm's credit rating with a national credit bureau such as D&B (formerly known as Dun & Bradstreet).

Typically, business owners will be asked to fill out a loan application. In addition to the loan application, the lender will also want to see your current business plan. Be sure to explain what your business is, how much funding you require to accomplish your goals, and how the loan will be repaid. Most lenders insist that you submit current financial statements that have been prepared by an independent certified public accountant. Then compile a list of references that includes your suppliers, other lenders, or the professionals with whom you are associated. You may also be asked to discuss the loan request with a loan officer. Hopefully, your loan request will be approved. If not, try to determine why your loan request was rejected. Think back over the loan process and determine what you could do to improve your chances of getting a loan the next time you apply.

Corporate Bonds

In addition to loans, large corporations may choose to issue bonds in denominations of $1,000 to $50,000. Although the usual face value for corporate bonds is $1,000, the total face value of all the bonds in an issue usually amounts to millions of dollars. In fact, one of the reasons why corporations sell bonds is so that they can borrow a lot of money from a lot of different bondholders and raise larger amounts of money than could be borrowed from one lender. A **corporate bond** is a corporation's written

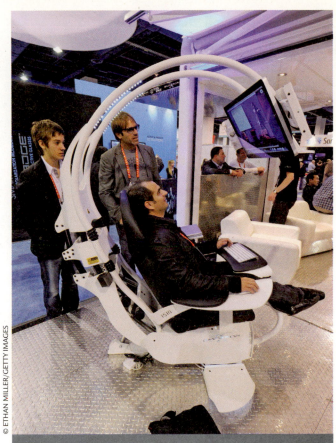

© ETHAN MILLER/GETTY IMAGES

The office of the future. While this product may look like something that should be on the next spaceship to the moon, it is a state-of-the-art office chair designed for people who spend long hours in front of computer monitors. The chair was created by Modern Work Environment (MWE) Lab. Companies that develop innovative products like this one need financing, and they generally have two choices. They can obtain financing from owners and investors or they can borrow money.

term-loan agreement a promissory note that requires a borrower to repay a loan in monthly, quarterly, semiannual, or annual installments

corporate bond a corporation's written pledge that it will repay a specified amount of money with interest

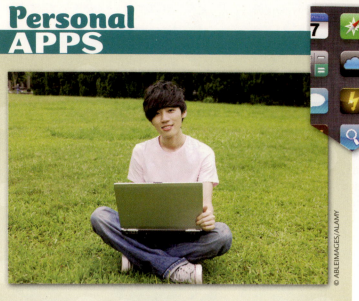

As CFO of your life, you should put your financial house in order before you apply for any loan. Be sure to check your credit report in advance to see how it looks, and think about how you'll repay the loan. Apply only when you know your finances are ready for the spotlight.

maturity date the date on which a corporation is to repay borrowed money

registered bond a bond registered in the owner's name by the issuing company

debenture bond a bond backed only by the reputation of the issuing corporation

mortgage bond a corporate bond secured by various assets of the issuing firm

convertible bond a bond that can be exchanged, at the owner's option, for a specified number of shares of the corporation's common stock

pledge that it will repay a specified amount of money with interest. Interest rates for corporate bonds vary with the financial health of the company issuing the bond. Specific factors that increase or decrease the interest rate that a corporation must pay when it issues bonds include

- The corporation's ability to pay interest each year until maturity.
- The corporation's ability to repay the bond at maturity.

For bond investors, the interest rate on corporate bonds is an example of the risk–return ratio discussed earlier in this chapter. Simply put: Investors expect more interest if there is more risk with more speculative bond issues—see Figure 19.7.

The **maturity date** is the date on which the corporation is to repay the borrowed money. Today, most corporate bonds are registered bonds. A **registered bond** is a bond registered in the owner's name by the issuing company. Many corporations do not issue actual bonds. Instead, the bonds are recorded electronically, and the specific details regarding the bond issue, along with the current owner's name and address, are maintained by computer. Computer entries are safer because they cannot be stolen, misplaced, or destroyed, and make it easier to transfer when a bond is sold.

Until a bond's maturity, a corporation pays interest to the bond owner at the stated rate. For example, owners of American & Foreign Power Company bonds that mature in 2030 receive 5 percent per year for each bond. For each $1,000 bond issued, the corporation must pay bondholders $50 ($1,000 × 0.05 = $50). Because interest for corporate bonds is usually paid semiannually, the owner of an American & Foreign Power bond will receive a $25 payment every six months for each bond they own. On the maturity date, a registered owner will receive cash equaling the face value of the bond.

Types of Bonds Corporate bonds are generally classified as debentures, mortgage bonds, or convertible bonds. Most corporate bonds are debenture bonds. A **debenture bond** is a bond backed only by the reputation of the issuing corporation. To make its bonds more appealing to investors, a corporation may issue mortgage bonds. A **mortgage bond** is a corporate bond secured by various assets of the issuing firm. Typical corporate assets that are used as collateral for a mortgage bond include real estate, machinery, and equipment that is not pledged as collateral for other debt obligations. The corporation can also issue convertible bonds. A **convertible bond** can be

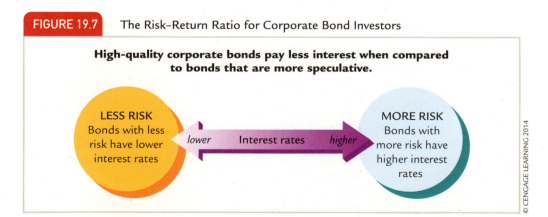

FIGURE 19.7 The Risk–Return Ratio for Corporate Bond Investors

High-quality corporate bonds pay less interest when compared to bonds that are more speculative.

LESS RISK
Bonds with less risk have lower interest rates

lower Interest rates *higher*

MORE RISK
Bonds with more risk have higher interest rates

exchanged, at the owner's option, for a specified number of shares of the corporation's common stock. An Advanced Micro Devices (AMD) bond that matures in 2015 is convertible: Each bond can be converted to 35.6125 shares of AMD common stock.[14] A corporation can gain in three ways by issuing convertible bonds. First, convertibles usually carry a lower interest rate than nonconvertible bonds. Second, the conversion feature attracts investors who are interested in the speculative gain that conversion to common stock may provide. Third, if the bondholder converts to common stock, the corporation no longer has to redeem the bond at maturity.

Repayment Provisions for Corporate Bonds Maturity dates for bonds generally range from 10 to 30 years after the date of issue. Some bonds are callable before the maturity date; that is, a corporation can buy back, or redeem, them. For these bonds, the corporation may pay the bond owner a call premium. The amount of the call premium, if any, is specified, along with other provisions, in the bond indenture. The **bond indenture** is a legal document that details all the conditions relating to a bond issue.

Before deciding if bonds are the best way to obtain corporate financing, managers must determine if the company can afford to pay the interest on the corporate bonds. It should be obvious that the larger the bond issue, the higher the dollar amount of interest that must be paid each year. For example, assume that American Express issues bonds with a face value of $100 million. If the interest rate is 4.875 percent, the interest on this bond issue is $4,875,000 ($100 million × 0.04875 = $4,875,000) each year until the bonds are repaid. In addition, the American Express corporate bonds must all be redeemed for their face value ($100 million) at maturity. If the corporation defaults on (does not pay) either interest payments or repayment of the bond at maturity, owners of bonds can force the firm into bankruptcy and their claims take precedence over the claims of both common and preferred stockholders.

A corporation may use one of three methods to ensure that it has sufficient funds available to redeem a bond issue. First, it can issue the bonds as **serial bonds**, which are bonds of a single issue that mature on different dates. For example, a company may use a 25-year $50 million bond issue to finance its expansion. None of the bonds mature during the first 15 years. Thereafter, 10 percent of the bonds mature each year until all the bonds are retired at the end of the 25th year. Second, the corporation can establish a sinking fund. A **sinking fund** is a sum of money to which deposits are made each year for the purpose of redeeming a bond issue. When Union Pacific Corporation sold a $275 million bond issue, the company agreed to contribute to a sinking fund until the bond's maturity in the year 2025.[15] Third, a corporation can pay off an old bond issue by selling new bonds. Although this may appear to perpetuate the corporation's long-term debt, a number of utility companies and railroads use this repayment method.

A corporation that issues bonds must also appoint a **trustee**, an individual or an independent firm that acts as the bond owner's representative. A trustee's duties are handled most often by a commercial bank or other large financial institution. The corporation must report to the trustee periodically regarding its ability to make interest payments and eventually redeem the bonds. In turn, the trustee transmits this information to the bond owners, along with its own evaluation of the corporation's ability to pay.

Cost Comparisons

Table 19.4 compares some of the methods that can be used to obtain long-term equity *and* debt financing. Although the initial flotation cost of issuing stock is high, selling common stock is generally a popular option for most financial managers. Once the stock is sold and upfront costs are paid, the *ongoing* costs of using stock to finance a business are low. The type of long-term financing that generally has the highest *ongoing* costs is a long-term loan (debt).

To a great extent, firms are financed through the investments of individuals—money that people have deposited in banks or have used to purchase stocks, mutual funds, and bonds. In Chapter 20, we look at how securities markets help people invest their money in business.

bond indenture a legal document that details all the conditions relating to a bond issue

serial bonds bonds of a single issue that mature on different dates

sinking fund a sum of money to which deposits are made each year for the purpose of redeeming a bond issue

trustee an individual or an independent firm that acts as a bond owner's representative

TABLE 19.4 Comparison of Long-Term Financing Methods

Type of Financing	Repayment	Repayment Period	Cost/Dividends Interest	Businesses That May Use It
Equity				
Common stock	No	None	High initial cost; low ongoing costs because dividends not required	All corporations that sell stock to investors
Preferred stock	No	None	Dividends not required but must be paid before common stockholders receive any dividends	Large corporations that have an established investor base of common stockholders
Debt				
Long-term loan	Yes	Usually 3–7 years	Interest rates between 3.25 and 12 percent depending on economic conditions and the financial stability of the company requesting the loan	All firms that can meet the lender's repayment and collateral requirements
Corporate bond	Yes	Usually 10–30 years	Interest rates between 3 and 9 percent depending on the financial stability of the company issuing the bonds and economic conditions	Large corporations that are financially healthy

© CENGAGE LEARNING 2014

return to Inside BUSINESS

The J. M. Smucker Company

More than a century after Jerome Monroe Smucker founded his company, Smucker family members are still making smart financial decisions. Going public in 1959 provided money for growth through investments in product development and other activities. More recently, the firm issued corporate bonds during periods when interest rates were low, keeping long-term borrowing costs low while building Smucker's cash position so that it could make timely acquisitions whenever it spotted good opportunities.

Looking ahead to expansion in China, Smucker has made an equity investment in a leading local oatmeal company. What Smucker learns from this company's knowledge of the market will pave the way for higher sales of its North American products in Asia, as well as the possibility of developing and manufacturing new foods specifically for China.

Questions

1. Why would Smucker prefer to issue more than $1 billion in bonds over 18 months, rather than issuing common or preferred stock?

2. What do you think of Smucker's deal to spread $50 million in payments to Sara Lee over 10 years after paying $350 up front for the liquid coffee concentrate business? Explain your answer.

Understand why financial management is important in today's uncertain economy.

The last few years have been especially difficult for financial managers. Financial managers have had to deal with a downturn in sales and profits. In some cases, banks stopped making loans even to companies that had always been able to borrow money. And the number of companies selling stock for the first time to the general public decreased. The worst-case scenario: There was an increase in the number of businesses that filed for bankruptcy during the crisis. Fortunately, there were many more business firms that were able to weather the economic storm and keep operating because of their ability to manage their finances.

Financial management consists of all activities concerned with obtaining money and using it effectively. Financial management can be viewed as a two-sided problem. On one side, the uses of funds often dictate the type or types of financing needed by a business. On the other side, the activities a business can undertake are determined by the types of financing available. Financial managers must ensure that funds are available when needed, that they are obtained at the lowest possible cost, and that they are used as efficiently as possible. In the wake of the economic crisis, the Dodd–Frank Wall Street Reform and Consumer Protection Act was signed into law. And today, there is an ongoing debate if more regulations are needed. Still, there are a number of rewarding jobs in finance for qualified job applicants.

 Identify a firm's short- and long-term financial needs.

Short-term financing is money that will be used for one year or less. There are many short-term needs, but cash flow, speculative production, and inventory are three for which financing is often required. Long-term financing is money that will be used for more than one year. Such financing may be required for a business start-up, for a merger or an acquisition, for new product development, for long-term marketing activities, for replacement of equipment, or for expansion of facilities. According to financial experts, business firms will find it more difficult to raise both short- and long-term financing in the future because of increased regulations and more cautious lenders. Financial managers must also consider the risk–return ratio when making financial decisions. The risk–return ratio is based on the principle that a high-risk decision should generate higher financial returns for a business. On the other hand, more conservative decisions generate lesser returns.

 Summarize the process of planning for financial management.

A financial plan begins with an organization's goals and objectives. Next, a firm's goals and objectives are "translated" into departmental budgets that detail expected income and expenses. From these budgets, which may be combined into an overall cash budget, the financial manager determines what funding will be needed and where it may be obtained. Whereas departmental and cash budgets emphasize short-term financing needs, a capital budget can be used to estimate a firm's expenditures for major assets and its long-term financing needs. The four principal sources of financing are sales revenues, equity capital, debt capital, and proceeds from the sale of assets. Once the needed funds have been obtained, the financial manager is responsible for monitoring and evaluating the firm's financial activities.

 Describe the advantages and disadvantages of different methods of short-term debt financing.

Most short-term financing is unsecured; that is, no collateral is required. Sources of unsecured short-term financing include trade credit, promissory notes issued to suppliers, unsecured bank loans, and commercial paper. Sources of secured short-term financing include loans secured by inventory and accounts receivable. A firm may also sell its receivables to factors. Trade credit is the least-expensive source of short-term financing. The cost of financing through other sources generally depends on the source and on the credit rating of the firm that requires the financing. Factoring is generally the most expensive approach.

 Evaluate the advantages and disadvantages of equity financing.

A corporation can raise equity capital by selling either common or preferred stock. The first time a corporation sells stock to the general public is referred to as an initial public offering (IPO). With an IPO, the stock is sold in the primary market. Once sold in the primary market, investors buy and sell stock in the secondary market. Usually, secondary market transactions are completed through a securities exchange or the over-the-counter market. Common stock is voting stock; holders of common stock elect the corporation's directors and often must approve changes to the corporate charter. Holders of preferred stock must be paid dividends before holders of common stock are paid any dividends. Another source of equity funding is retained earnings, which is the portion of a business's profits *not* distributed to stockholders. Venture capital—money invested in small (and sometimes struggling) firms that have the potential to become very successful—is yet another source of equity funding. Finally, a private placement can be used to sell stocks and other corporate securities.

6 Evaluate the advantages and disadvantages of long-term debt financing.

For a small business, debt financing is generally limited to loans. Large corporations have the additional option of issuing corporate bonds. Regardless of whether the business is small or large, it can take advantage of financial leverage. Financial leverage is the use of borrowed funds to increase the return on owners' equity. The rate of interest for long-term loans usually depends on the financial status of the borrower, the reason for borrowing, and the kind of collateral pledged to back up the loan. Long-term business loans are normally repaid in 3 to 7 years but can be as long as 15 to 20 years.

Money realized from the sale of corporate bonds must be repaid when the bonds mature. In addition, the corporation must pay interest on that money from the time the bonds are sold until maturity. The interest rate the corporation must pay often depends on the financial health of the firm issuing bonds. Maturity dates for bonds generally range from 10 to 30 years after the date of issue. Three types of bonds—debentures, mortgage bonds, and convertible bonds—are sold to raise debt capital. When comparing the cost of equity and debt long-term financing, the ongoing costs of using stock (equity) to finance a business are low. The most expensive is a long-term loan (debt).

KEY TERMS

You should now be able to define and give an example relevant to each of the following terms:

financial management (552)
chief financial officer (CFO) (553)
short-term financing (554)
cash flow (555)
speculative production (555)
long-term financing (556)
risk–return ratio (556)
financial plan (556)
budget (557)
cash budget (557)

zero-base budgeting (558)
capital budget (558)
equity capital (558)
debt capital (558)
unsecured financing (559)
trade credit (560)
promissory note (560)
prime interest rate (560)
factor (562)
initial public offering (IPO) (563)

primary market (564)
investment banking firm (564)
secondary market (565)
securities exchange (565)
over-the-counter (OTC) market (565)
common stock (566)
preferred stock (566)
retained earnings (566)
private placement (567)
financial leverage (568)

term-loan agreement (569)
corporate bond (569)
maturity date (570)
registered bond (570)
debenture bond (570)
mortgage bond (570)
convertible bond (570)
bond indenture (571)
serial bonds (571)
sinking fund (571)
trustee (571)

REVIEW QUESTIONS

1. For a business firm, what type of activities does financial management involve?
2. How does short-term financing differ from long-term financing? Give two business uses for each type of financing.
3. In your own words, describe the risk–return ratio.
4. What is the function of a cash budget? A capital budget?
5. What is zero-base budgeting? How does it differ from the traditional concept of budgeting?
6. What are four general sources of funds?
7. How does a financial manager monitor and evaluate a firm's financing?
8. How important is trade credit as a source of short-term financing?
9. Why would a supplier require a customer to sign a promissory note?

10. What is the prime rate? Who gets the prime rate?
11. Explain how factoring works. Of what benefit is factoring to a firm that sells its receivables?
12. What are the advantages of financing through the sale of stock?
13. From a corporation's point of view, how does preferred stock differ from common stock?
14. Where do a corporation's retained earnings come from? What are the advantages of this type of financing?
15. For a corporation, what are the advantages of corporate bonds over long-term loans?
16. Describe the three methods used to ensure that funds are available to redeem corporate bonds at maturity.

1. During the recent economic crisis, many financial managers and corporate officers have been criticized for (a) poor decisions, (b) lack of ethical behavior, (c) large salaries, (d) lucrative severance packages worth millions of dollars, and (e) extravagant lifestyles. Is this criticism justified? Justify your opinion.

2. If you were the financial manager of Stars and Stripes Clothing, what would you do with the excess cash that the firm expects in the second and fourth quarters? (See Figure 19.4.)

3. Develop a *personal* cash budget for the next six months. Explain what you would do if there are budget shortfalls or excess cash amounts at the end of any month during the six-month period.

4. Why would a lender offer unsecured short-term loans when it could demand collateral?

5. How can a small-business owner or corporate manager use financial leverage to improve the firm's profits and return on owners' equity?

6. In what circumstances might a large corporation sell stock rather than bonds to obtain long-term financing? In what circumstances would it sell bonds rather than stock?

Video Case 19.1

Financial Planning Equals Profits for Nederlander Concerts

Nederlander Concerts is in the business of booking, promoting, and producing live music shows in the western United States. The company presents artists ranging from James Taylor to Flogging Molly, Bruce Springsteen, Bonnie Raitt, and the Allman Brothers Band. But, says CEO Adam Friedman, "We're not trying to be necessarily a national player or an international player. We seek out opportunities that fit within and leverage our existing portfolio of small- to mid-size venues. . . . It's one of the few remaining family-run entertainment enterprises worldwide. . . . What this means for us on a day-to-day basis is that we can focus on running the business. We're not as guided by Wall Street, we don't have the same constraints, we don't have the same reporting responsibilities, and it allows us to focus on . . . our business strategy for development."

Of course, being a privately owned company and not needing to respond to shareholders (Wall Street) doesn't mean that Nederlander has *no* reporting responsibilities. As the CEO explains, "We assess at the beginning of the year not only concert revenue and expenses but also special event revenue." Nederlander owns some theaters, amphitheaters, and arenas, and it sometimes rents space for concerts and events along the West Coast. "When we rent the facilities to, for example, movie premieres here in Los Angeles, what kind of revenue are we going to see? What kind of expenses are attended to generating that revenue? What's our fixed overhead for the year? Who's on the payroll, whether full-time, or part-time, or seasonal, and how much does it cost us to run the business on a day-to-day basis in order to secure those revenues and pay those expenses? That's wrapped up into an annual budget at the beginning of every year, which is kind of a guideline for me to know how we achieve growth. It also allows me to communicate to our owners what our growth orientation is for that given year. . . . Every event has its own profit and loss statement . . . which is a mini version of that annual plan," says the CEO.

In addition to daily, weekly, and quarterly event reports, Nederlander's financial team generates daily and weekly reports of ticket sales. Monthly reports on company-wide performance feed into quarterly and annual reports. Each annual report is compared to that year's budget. The finance department tallies hundreds of transactions in order to arrive at some of these annual numbers, which are reported to the company's owners to ensure that the company is running as profitably as it can be.

Nederlander's managers say growth in the concert industry must be measured in the long term because the business is cyclical and the cost of real estate is so high that short-term profit is hard to generate. Still, the company is in a strong financial position (it is part of a profitable global theater-ownership company called the Nederlander Organization), so it can afford to fund its own growth and expansion, or it can borrow on favorable terms. "We're very fortunate to have an ownership that is very well capitalized with over 80 years in the business," says the CEO. "Our balance sheet is so strong that we have the ability to tap into debt financing if it makes the most sense. . . . or [use] the corporate treasury. . . . If it makes more sense to borrow the money, we will, and we're typically able to do that on very favorable rates because of very long-term banking relationships."

It can be thrilling to meet some of the artists the company books. "But at the end of the day, it's a business," the CEO points out. "If we're not successful in growing our revenue and managing our expense, ultimately we won't be profitable, and our ownership will not be happy with those results."[16]

Questions

1. Here's what Nederlander's chief operating officer has to say about its business model: "A show has a short lifetime. You go and sell two months out, and the tickets have no value on any day but the day of the show. So it's a very interesting model in that sense." How do you think the short life of the company's products affects its financial planning?

2. The company uses its own arenas and theaters about 90 percent of the time. What are some of the possible advantages and disadvantages of owning its own venues?

3. Why would Nederlander choose to sometimes borrow funds for expansion if it has capital of its own?

Case 19.2

Darden Restaurants Serve Up Long-Term Growth

Growth has been on the menu ever since Bill Darden opened his first Red Lobster restaurant in Florida in 1968. The combination of fresh seafood and casual dining caught on quickly—and quickly caught the eye of General Mills, which bought the fast-growing company in 1970. In 1995, General Mills renamed the company after its founder and spun it off in a public offering. Once it went public, Darden Restaurants used the proceeds to chart a new financial path to long-term growth.

Today, Darden employs 180,000 people and serves more than 400 million meals each year across North America in 1,900 casual, full-service restaurants. The company's seven restaurant brands are: Red Lobster (seafood), Olive Garden (Italian menu), LongHorn Steakhouse (Western-theme steaks and more), The Capital Grille (premium steak house), Bahama Breeze (Caribbean-theme casual dining), Seasons 52 (fresh-grilled foods), and Eddie V's (prime seafood and steaks). In all, Darden's yearly revenue tops $7.5 billion.

Healthy cash flow is definitely on the menu. The average Capital Grille unit rings up $6.5 million in annual sales, the average Olive Garden rings up $4.8 million in annual sales, the average Red Lobster rings up $3.6 million, and the average LongHorn Steakhouse rings up $2.9 million. With the cash generated from restaurant revenue, Darden has been reinvesting in its businesses by opening new units, remodeling existing units, and greening its restaurants with eco-friendly materials and energy-saving touches. Because of its size, it can take advantage of economies of scale in buying foods and beverages from global sources, which in turn helps keep costs under control and supports good profit margins.

Over the years, the company has fueled its continued expansion with a combination of debt and equity. The company can draw on a revolving credit agreement of almost $500 million, which helps smooth out the financial bumps of its seasonal business. Typically, Darden's revenue spikes in the spring and descends to a low point in the fall, although sales are definitely affected by weather conditions, economic circumstances, holidays, and other uncontrollable elements. Having revolving credit in place provides the flexibility to borrow if and when needed.

Darden has also raised money by issuing corporate bonds, some of which mature in 5 years, some in 10 years, some in 20 years, and some with even longer maturities. Twice a year, the company pays interest to its bondholders. On the equity side, Darden's common stock trades on the New York Stock Exchange, and it pays cash dividends to its shareholders. Its cash flow has been so strong, in fact, that Darden increased its dividend not long ago and has focused on paying down debt even as it invests in business.

Looking ahead, Darden expects to continue its growth spurt, despite an unpredictable economy and intense competition from big names in fast food and casual dining. It avoided the heavy, broad-based discounting that some chains used to attract customers during the recent economic crisis. Instead, it used occasional, selective price promotions to heighten its message of affordability. The company's financial stability means that it has money available for making acquisitions, building new restaurants, developing new menu items, training new staff members, and launching new advertising campaigns.

Within the past decade, Darden has used its financial strength to buy and expand the Capital Grill and LongHorn Steakhouse restaurant chains. And Darden acquired the Eddie V's and Wildfish Seafood Grill restaurant chain in 2011. It is also responding to increased consumer interest in healthy dining by opening more of its Seasons 52 restaurants, which feature only steamed, baked, or grilled dishes. As its name implies, Seasons 52 adds new menu items regularly, depending on what's in season. The ever-changing menu brings customers back again and again to try seasonal specialties and enjoy old favorites.

Sometimes Darden closes underperforming units or sells entire chains so that it can put its money and management attention into other growth opportunities. A few years ago, Darden divested its Smokey Bones Barbecue & Grill chain after determining that this restaurant concept did not have the potential for nationwide expansion and profit potential that Darden required. What will Darden do next in its quest for profitable, long-term growth?[17]

Questions

1. Darden is spending heavily to upgrade the interior of many of its Red Lobster and LongHorn Steakhouse restaurants. How would you suggest that the company measure the financial results of this remodeling program?
2. Why would Darden issue corporate bonds with maturities of 5, 10, 20 years or even longer maturities?
3. If Darden needs cash to remodel existing restaurants and open new restaurants, as well as to pay down debt, why would it increase its cash dividend that is paid to its stockholders?

① SOCIAL MEDIA EXERCISE

Turbo Tax is probably one of the best-known tax preparation services in the world. One of the reasons for its popularity is that it provides tax software that people really need. Another reason for its popularity is the company's use of social media through various platforms that include building an online community of users, using Twitter, and developing a YouTube channel. Each video on the TurboTax channel illustrates how a company can use social media to provide valuable information to customers. You can check out Turbo Tax videos at www.youtube.com/user/TurboTax/videos.

1. Visit the YouTube channel for Turbo Tax (www.youtube.com/user/TurboTax/videos). Do you think social media is an effective method of obtaining the tax information you might need to prepare your taxes?
2. Can you think of other companies that could use videos on a YouTube channel to share information that their customers could use?

② JOURNALING FOR SUCCESS

Because many people spend more than they make on a regular basis, they often use credit cards to make routine daily purchases. As a result, the amount they owe on credit cards increases each month and there is no money left to begin a savings or investment program. This exercise will help you to understand (1) how you manage your credit cards and (2) what steps you can take to improve your personal finances.

Assignment

1. How many credit cards do you have?
2. Based on the information on your monthly credit card statements, what types of credit card purchases do you make?
3. Do you pay your balance in full each month or make minimum payments on your credit cards?
4. Most experts recommend that you have one or two credit cards that you use only if you are in an emergency situation. The experts also recommend that you avoid using credit cards to make inexpensive purchases on a daily basis. Finally, the experts recommend that you pay your balance in full each month.
5. Based on the preceding information, what steps can you take to better manage your personal finances?

③ DEVELOPING CRITICAL-THINKING SKILLS

Financial management involves preparing a plan for obtaining and using the money needed to accomplish a firm's goals and objectives. To accomplish your own goals and objectives, you should prepare a *personal* financial plan. You must determine what is important in your life and what you want to accomplish, budget the amount of money required to obtain your goals, and identify sources for acquiring the funds. You should monitor and evaluate the results regularly and make changes when necessary.

Assignment

1. Using the three steps shown in Figure 19.3, prepare a personal financial plan.
2. Prepare a three-column table to display your plan.
   a. In column 1, list at least two goals or objectives under each of the following areas: Financial (savings, investments, retirement), Education (training, degrees, certificates), Career (position, industry, location), and Family (children, home, education, trips, entertainment).
   b. In column 2, list the amount of money it will take to accomplish your goals or objectives.
   c. In column 3, identify the sources of funds for each goal or objective.
3. Describe what you learned from doing this exercise in a comments section at the bottom of the table.

④ BUILDING TEAM SKILLS

Suppose that for the past three years you have been repairing lawn mowers in your garage. Your business has grown steadily, and you recently hired two part-time workers. Your garage is no longer adequate for your business; it is also in violation of the city code, and you have already been fined for noncompliance. You have decided that it is time to find another location for your shop and that it also would be a good time to expand your business. If the business continues to grow in the new location, you plan to hire a full-time employee to repair small appliances. You are concerned, however, about how you will get the money to move your shop and get it established in a new location.

Assignment

1. With all class members participating, use brainstorming to identify the following:
   a. The funds you will need to accomplish your business goals
   b. The sources of short-term financing available to you
   c. Problems that might prevent you from getting a short-term loan
   d. How you will repay the money if you get a loan
2. Have a classmate write the ideas on the board.
3. Discuss how you can overcome any problems that might hamper your current chances of getting a loan and how your business can improve its chances of securing short-term loans in the future.
4. Summarize what you learned from participating in this exercise.

The Vanguard Group Thinks Low-Cost and High-Tech

The Vanguard Group helps investors make the most of their money by offering low-cost investments and high-tech access. From its early days, the company focused not on individual stocks or bonds but on selling shares in mutual funds, pools of money invested in a select group of stocks or bonds. Vanguard was a pioneer in establishing mutual funds tied to a specific group of common stocks or bonds in a particular financial index. Before Vanguard launched its Vanguard 500 Index Fund, individual investors had no way to buy this type of indexed mutual fund directly from an investment company. Today, Vanguard offers hundreds of mutual funds and many other securities for every type of investor and every investment goal, short- and long-term.

Because the Vanguard Group is owned by the different funds it manages, it has a long tradition of operating mutual funds "at cost." As a result, investors pay lower mutual fund fees, and more of their money remains invested to earn returns year after year. Exactly how low is low? By Vanguard's calculations, its average expense ratio is, on average, one-fifth of the industry average. To dramatize this difference, Vanguard recently sent an "At-Cost Café" food truck on tour selling coffee at 28 cents per cup—just one-fifth of the usual price. "The concept of at-cost investing can be difficult to explain," says a Vanguard spokesperson, "so we are trying to help investors 'experience' it through something tangible, such as a routine daily purchase like coffee."

Vanguard also uses the latest technology to let customers check on their accounts and investigate new investment possibilities at any hour, from any place. In addition to its Web site, which offers detailed financial information, online trading, and much more, the company provides downloadable apps for cell phones and tablet computers. Whether investors are just starting out or have a lot of investing experience, they can use the technology of their choice to see their recent transactions, analyze investment performance, buy or sell securities, read Vanguard's research reports, subscribe to its electronic newsletter, and watch its educational videos—all at the touch of a finger or the click of a mouse.[1]

As the saying goes, "I've been rich and I've been poor, but believe me, rich is better." Yet, just dreaming of being rich does not make it happen. Although being rich does not guarantee happiness, managing your personal finances and beginning an investment program are both worthy goals. Firms such as Vanguard Group—the company profiled in the Inside Business feature for this chapter—offer an array of services to help people manage their personal finances, research investments, and buy and sell stocks, bonds, mutual funds, and other securities. Nevertheless, you must be willing to invest the time and effort required to manage your personal finances and become a good investor. Furthermore, do not underestimate how important you are when it comes to managing your money. No one is going to make you manage your money. No one is going to make you save the money you need to fund an investment program. These are your decisions—important decisions that literally can change your life.

Many people ask the question: Why begin an investment program now? To answer that question, you must understand that personal finance experts agree that the best investment program is one that stresses long-term growth over a 20- to 40-year period. As you will see later in this chapter, the dollar value of your investments may decrease over a short time period, but historically the value of quality securities has usually increased over a long time period.

A second compelling reason to start an investment program is that the sooner you start an investment program, the more time your investments have to work for you. So why do people wait to begin investing? In most cases, there are two reasons. First, they do not have the money needed to fund an investment program. However, once you begin managing your personal finances and get your spending under control, you will be able to save the money needed to fund an investment program. The second reason people do not begin investing is because they do not know anything about investing. Again, this chapter provides the basics to get you started.

We begin this chapter by examining everyday money management activities and outlining the reasons for developing a personal investment plan. Next we discuss important factors to consider when choosing investments and describe both traditional and high-risk (or speculative) investments. Then, we explain how to use information to evaluate potential investments. Finally, we examine the methods used to buy and sell investments.

It is time! Take the first step, and begin managing your personal finances.

MANAGING YOUR PERSONAL FINANCES

 1 Explain why you should manage your personal finances and develop a personal investment program.

Although it would be nice if you could accumulate wealth magically, it is not magic. Most people begin by making sure that their "financial house" is in order. In this section, we examine several steps for effective money management that will help you to prepare for an investment program.

Step 1: Tracking Your Income, Expenses, Assets, and Liabilities

Many personal finance experts recommend that you begin the process of managing your money by determining your current financial condition. Often the first step is to construct a personal income statement and balance sheet. (*Note*: Both personal income statements and balance sheets were examined in more detail in Chapter 17.) A *personal income statement* lists your income and your expenses for a specific period of time—usually a month. By subtracting expenses from income, you can determine if you have a surplus or a deficit at the end of the time period. Surplus funds can be used for savings, investing, or for any purpose that you feel is important. On the other hand, if you have a deficit, you must take actions to reduce spending and pay down any debts you may have that will keep you from starting an investment program.

To get another picture of your current financial condition, you should construct a personal balance sheet. A *personal balance sheet* lists your assets and liabilities on a specific date. By subtracting your total liabilities from your total assets, you can determine your net worth. For an individual, **net worth** is the difference between the value of your total assets and your total liabilities. Over time, the goal is to increase the value of your assets (items of value that you own) and decrease liabilities (your debts).

Based on the information contained in these two statements, you can determine your current financial condition and where you spend your money. You can also take the next step: Construct a personal budget.

Step 2: Developing a Budget that Works

A **personal budget** is a specific plan for spending your income. You begin by estimating your income for a specific period—for example, next month. For most people, their major source of income is their salary. The second step is to list expenses for the same time period. Typical expenses include savings and investments, housing, food, transportation, entertainment, and so on. For most people, this is the area where you can make choices and increase or decrease the amount spent on different items listed in your budget. For example, you may decide to reduce the dollar amount spent on entertainment to increase the amount for savings. Above all, it is important to balance

net worth the difference between the value of your total assets and your total liabilities

personal budget a specific plan for spending your income

your budget so that your income is equal to the money you spend, save, or invest each month. For help managing your money and constructing a realistic budget, you may want to visit the Mint.com Web site (www.mint.com), the Motley Fool Web site (www.fool.com), or similar sites on the Internet. Both of these Web sites provide free help and advice that can help you take the necessary steps to improve your personal finances.

After you have constructed your personal budget, you will need to compare the amounts included in your budget with your actual income and expenses. The goal is that the estimated income and expenses are correct and that you have a surplus at the end of the budgeting period. If income is less than anticipated or expenses are more than budgeted, then you will need to take corrective actions to get your budget back on track. Often one change will affect other areas of your budget as well. An increase in your monthly rent payment, for instance, may mean that you have to reduce the amount spent on entertainment to balance your budget. *Caution*: Avoid the temptation to spend more than you make by using credit cards or borrowing money.

Step 3: Managing Credit Card Debt

Unfortunately, many individuals spend more than they make. They purchase items on credit and then make monthly payments and pay finance charges ranging from 10 to 21 percent or more. It makes no sense to start an investment program until payments for credit card and installment purchases, along with the accompanying finance charges, are reduced or eliminated.

Although all cardholders have reasons for using their credit cards, the important point to remember is that it is *very easy* to get in trouble by using your credit cards. Watch for the following five warning signs.

1. Don't fall behind on payments. One of the first warning signs is the inability to pay your entire balance each month.
2. Do not use your credit cards to pay for many small purchases during the month. This can often lead to a "real surprise" when you open your credit card statement at the end of the month.
3. Do not use the cash advance provision that accompanies most credit cards. The reason is simple: The interest rate is usually higher for cash advances.
4. Think about the number of cards you really need. Most experts recommend that an individual have one or two cards and use these cards for emergencies.
5. Get help if you think you are in trouble. Organizations like Consumer Credit Counseling Service (www.cccs.net) or the National Foundation for Credit Counseling (www.nfcc.org) can often help you work out a plan to pay off credit card debt.

By reducing or eliminating credit purchases, eventually the amount of cash remaining after the bills are paid will increase and can be used to start a savings and investment program that will help you obtain your investment goals.

Investment Goals

Personal investment is the use of your personal funds to earn a financial return. Thus, in the most general sense, the goal of investing is to earn money with money. However, such a goal is completely useless for the individual because it is so vague and so easily attained.

In reality, an investment goal must be specific and measurable. It must be tailored to you so that it takes into account your particular financial needs. It must also be oriented toward the future because investing is usually a long-term undertaking. By investing small amounts of money each year over a 20- to 40-year period, you can accumulate money for emergencies and retirement. In addition, if you choose quality investments, the value of your investments will grow over a long period of time. Finally, an investment goal must be realistic in terms of current economic conditions and available investment opportunities.

Some financial planners suggest that investment goals should be stated in terms of money: "By January 1, 2022, I will have total assets of $80,000." Others believe that

personal investment the use of your personal funds to earn a financial return

people are more motivated to work toward goals that are stated in terms of the particular things they desire: "By May 1, 2024, I will have accumulated enough money so that I can take a year off from work to travel around the world." Like the goals themselves, the way they are stated depends on you. The following questions can be helpful in establishing valid investment goals:

1. What financial goals do you want to achieve?
2. How much money will you need, and when?
3. What will you use the money for?
4. Is it reasonable to assume that you can obtain the amount of money you will need to meet your investment goals?
5. Do you expect your personal situation to change in a way that will affect your investment goals?
6. What economic conditions could alter your investment goals?
7. Are you willing to make the necessary sacrifices to ensure that your investment goals are met?

Keep in mind the investment goals you develop may be affected by your career choice. If you choose a career that provides above-average financial rewards, you can develop more challenging investment goals. If you choose a career that provides average or below-average financial rewards, it is still possible to develop an investment program by carefully managing your personal finances. Simply put: You must control spending and manage debt regardless of how much money you make.

Personal APPS

What are your personal, professional, and investment goals? Just like a successful business, you should be looking ahead to what you want to achieve in the next few years and writing down specific goals for yourself. If one goal is to start an investment program, for example, it will help to think about how much you'll need to start investing and how much you will want to accumulate by a specific date.

A Personal Investment Program

Once you have formulated specific goals and have some money to invest, investment planning is similar to planning for a business. It begins with the evaluation of different investment opportunities—including the potential return and risk involved in each. At the very least, this process requires some careful study and maybe some expert advice. Investors should beware of people who call themselves "financial planners" but who are in reality nothing more than salespersons for various financial investments, tax shelters, or insurance plans.

A true **financial planner** has had at least two years of training in investments, insurance, taxation, retirement planning, and estate planning and has passed a rigorous examination. As evidence of training and successful completion of the qualifying examination, the Certified Financial Planner (CFP) Board of Standards (www.cfp.net) in Washington, D.C., allows individuals to use the designation CFP. Similarly, the American College (www.theamericancollege.edu) in Bryn Mawr, Pennsylvania, allows individuals who have completed the necessary requirements to use the designation Chartered Financial Consultant (ChFC). Most CFPs and ChFCs do not sell a particular investment product or receive commissions for their investment recommendations. Instead, they charge consulting fees that range from $100 to $250 an hour.

Many financial planners suggest that you accumulate an "emergency fund"—a certain amount of money that can be obtained quickly in case of immediate need—before beginning an investment program. The amount of money that should be salted away in a savings account varies from person to person. Most financial planners agree that an amount equal to at least three months' living expenses is reasonable. However, you may want to increase your emergency fund in anticipation of a crisis.

financial planner an individual who has had at least two years of training in investments, insurance, taxation, retirement planning, and estate planning and has passed a rigorous examination

Managing your personal finances can improve a relationship! Often money problems can cause relationships to sour and can even lead to divorce for some couples. On the other hand, managing your personal finances can lead to financial stability, peace of mind, and a more stable personal relationship.

TABLE 20.1 Suggestions to Help You Accumulate the Money Needed to Fund an Investment Program

1. *Pay yourself first.* Many financial experts recommend that you (1) pay your monthly bills, (2) save a reasonable amount of money, and (3) use whatever money is left over for personal expenses.

2. *Take advantage of employer-sponsored retirement programs.* Many employers will match part or all of the contributions you make to a 401(k) or 403(b) retirement account.

3. *Participate in an elective savings program.* Elect to have money withheld from your paycheck each payday and automatically deposited in a savings or investment account.

4. *Make a special savings effort one or two months each year.* By cutting back to the basics, you can obtain money for investment purposes.

5. *Take advantage of gifts, inheritances, and windfalls.* During your lifetime, you likely will receive gifts, inheritances, salary increases, year-end bonuses, or federal income tax returns. Instead of spending these windfalls, invest these funds.

Source: Jack R. Kapoor, Les R. Dlabay, and Robert J. Hughes, *Focus on Personal Finance*, 3rd ed. Copyright © 2010 by The McGraw Hill Companies Inc. Reprinted with permission of The McGraw Hill Companies Inc.

After the emergency account is established, you may invest additional funds according to your investment program. Some additional funds may already be available, or money for further investing may be saved out of earnings. For suggestions to help you obtain the money needed to fund your investment program, see Table 20.1.

Monitoring the Value of Your Investment Program

In fall 2007, the stock market, as measured by the Dow Jones Industrial Average, reached an all-time high at 14,000. The **Dow Jones Industrial Average** is an average of 30 leading U.S. corporations that reflect the U.S. stock market as a whole. By March 2009, the same average had declined to 6,600. What happened? The simple answer is that the United States (and most of the world) experienced an economic meltdown. This economic crisis had many causes, including a banking and financial crisis, a downturn in home sales, lower consumer spending, and high unemployment rates. Although the economy shows signs of improving at the time of publication, and the Dow Jones Industrial Average is just over 13,000 at the time of publication, a crisis could happen again.

Although monitoring your investment program and re-evaluating your investment choices are always important, the recent economic crisis underscores the importance of managing your personal finances *and* your investment program. Because of the nation's economic problems, many people were caught off guard. Moreover, some individuals were forced to sell some or all of their investments at depressed prices just to pay for everyday necessities.

To avoid the type of problems just described, you must monitor your investment program and, if necessary, modify it. Always keep in mind your circumstances and economic conditions are both subject to change.

Describe how the factors of safety, risk, income, growth, and liquidity affect your investment program.

IMPORTANT FACTORS IN PERSONAL INVESTMENT

How can you (or a financial planner) tell which investments are "right" for your investment program and which are not? One way to start is to match potential investments with your investment goals in terms of safety, risk, income, growth, and liquidity.

Safety and Risk

Safety and risk are two sides of the same coin. *Safety* in an investment means minimal risk of loss; *risk* in an investment means a measure of uncertainty about the outcome. If you want a steady increase in value over an extended period of time, choose safe investments, such as certificates of deposit (CDs), highly rated government and corporate bonds, and the stocks of highly regarded corporations—sometimes

Dow Jones Industrial Average
an average of 30 leading U.S. corporations that reflect the U.S. stock market as a whole

called blue-chip stocks. A **blue-chip stock** is a safe investment that generally attracts conservative investors. Blue-chip stocks are generally issued by corporations that are industry leaders and have provided their stockholders with stable earnings and dividends over a number of years. Selected mutual funds and real estate may also be very safe investments.

If you want higher dollar returns on investments, you must generally give up some safety. In general, *the potential return should be directly related to the assumed risk.* That is, the greater the risk you assume, the higher the potential monetary reward. As you will see shortly, there are a number of speculative—and potentially profitable—investments.

Often beginning investors are afraid of the risk associated with many investments. However, it helps to remember that without risk, it is impossible to obtain larger returns that really make your investment program grow. In fact, some investors often base their investment decision on projections for rate of return. You can also use the same calculation to determine how much you actually earn on an investment over a specific period of time. To calculate **rate of return**, the total dollar amount of return you receive on an investment over a specific period of time is divided by the amount invested. For example, assume that you invest $5,000 in Home Depot stock, you receive $108 in dividends, and the stock is worth $5,300 at the end of one year. Your rate of return is 8.2 percent, as illustrated here.

Purchasing stocks is one way to invest. Since 1926, stocks have returned just below 10 percent a year—a larger return than most other investment alternatives. So why not just pick a bunch of stocks and begin investing? The truth is that an investment program should begin with a financial checkup to make sure that you are ready to invest and the creation of investment goals before you purchase any investment.

Step 1: *Subtract the investment's initial value from the investment's value at the end of the year.*

$$\$5,300 - \$5,000 = \$300$$

Step 2: *Add the dividend amount to the amount calculated in step 1.*

$$\$108 + \$300 = \$408$$

Step 3: *Divide the total dollar amount of return calculated in step 2 by the original investment.*

$$\$408 \div \$5,000 = 0.082 = 8.2 \text{ percent}$$

Note: If an investment decreases in value, the steps used to calculate the rate of return are the same, but the answer is a negative number. With this information, it is possible to compare the rate of return for different investment alternatives that offer more or less risk.

Investment Income

Investors sometimes purchase certain investments because they want a predictable source of income. For example, CDs, corporate and government bonds, and certain stocks pay interest or dividends each year. Some mutual funds and real estate may also offer steady income potential. Such investments are generally used by conservative investors or retired individuals who need a predictable source of income.

When purchasing investments for income, most investors are concerned about the issuer's ability to continue making periodic interest or dividend payments. Investors in CDs and bonds know exactly how much income they will receive each year. The dividends paid to stockholders can and do vary, even for the largest and most stable corporations. As with dividends from stock, the income from mutual funds and real estate may also vary from one year to the next.

Investment Growth

To investors, *growth* means that their investments will increase in value. For example, growing corporations such as Monster Beverage, Adobe Systems, Questcor Pharmaceuticals, and Silicon Motion Technology usually pay a small cash dividend or no dividend at all. Instead, profits are reinvested in the business (as retained earnings)

blue-chip stock a safe investment that generally attracts conservative investors

rate of return the total dollar amount of return you receive on an investment over a specific period of time divided by the amount invested

to finance additional expansion. In this case, the value of the stock increases as the corporation expands.

Other investments that may offer growth potential include selected mutual funds and real estate. For example, many mutual funds are referred to as growth funds or aggressive growth funds because of the growth potential of the individual securities included in the fund.

Investment Liquidity

Liquidity is the ease with which an investment can be converted into cash. Investments range from cash or cash equivalents (such as investments in government securities or money-market accounts) to the other extreme of frozen investments, which you cannot convert easily into cash.

Although you may be able to sell stock, mutual-fund, and corporate-bond investments quickly, you may not regain the amount of money you originally invested because of market conditions, economic conditions, or many other reasons. It may also be difficult to find buyers for real estate. Furthermore, finding a buyer for investments in certain types of collectibles may also be difficult.

FACTORS THAT CAN IMPROVE YOUR INVESTMENT DECISIONS

 Recognize how you can reduce investment risk and increase investment returns.

We begin this section with an overview of how portfolio management can reduce investment risk and factors that you should consider to choose "just the right" investments. Then in the next two sections, we describe how the investments listed in Table 20.2 can help you to reach your investment goals.

TABLE 20.2 Investment Alternatives
Traditional investments involve less risk than speculative or high-risk investments.
Traditional Investments
Bank accounts
Corporate and government bonds
More Speculative Investments
Common stock
Preferred stock
Mutual funds
Real estate
The Most Speculative Investments
Short transactions
Margin transactions
Stock options
Derivatives
Commodities
Precious metals
Gemstones
Coins
Antiques
Collectibles

© CENGAGE LEARNING 2014

liquidity the ease with which an investment can be converted into cash

Portfolio Management

"How can I choose the right investment?" That's a good question! Unfortunately, there are no easy answers because your investment goals, age, tolerance for risk, and financial resources are different from those of the next person. To help you to decide what investment is right for you, consider the following: Since 1926, as measured by the Standard and Poor's 500 Stock Index, stocks have returned on average just below 10 percent a year. The **Standard & Poor's 500 Stock Index** is an index that contains 500 different stocks that reflect increases or decreases in value for the U.S. stock market as a whole. During the same period, U.S. government bonds have returned about 6 percent.[2] Therefore, why not just invest all your money in stocks or mutual funds that invest in stocks? After all, they offer the largest potential return. In reality, stocks may have a place in every investment portfolio, but there is more to investing than just picking a bunch of stocks or stock mutual funds.

Asset Allocation, the Time Factor, and Your Age

Asset allocation is the process of spreading your money among several different types of investments to lessen risk. Although the term *asset allocation* is a fancy way of saying it, simply put, it really means that you need to diversify and avoid the pitfall of putting all of your eggs in one basket—a common mistake made by investors. Asset allocation is often expressed in percentages. For example, what percentage of my assets do I want to put in stocks and mutual funds? What percentage do I want to put in more conservative investments such as CDs and government bonds? In reality, the answers to these questions are determined by:

- The time your investments have to work for you
- Your age
- Your investment objectives
- Your ability to tolerate risk
- How much you can save and invest each year
- The dollar value of your current investments
- The economic outlook for the economy
- Several other factors

Two factors—the time your investments have to work for you and your age—are so important they deserve special attention.

The Time Factor The amount of time you have before you need your investment money is crucial. If you can leave your investments alone and let them work for five to ten years or more, then you can invest in stocks, mutual funds, and real estate. On the other hand, if you need your investment money in two years, you probably should invest in short-term government bonds, highly rated corporate bonds, or CDs. By taking a more conservative approach for short-term investments, you reduce the possibility of having to sell your investments at a loss because of depressed market value or a staggering economy. For example, during the recent economic crisis, many retirees who were forced to sell stocks and mutual funds to pay for everyday living expenses lost money. On the other hand, many young investors with long-term investment goals could afford to hold their investments until the price of their securities recovered.

Your Age You also should consider your age when developing an investment program. Younger investors tend to invest a large percentage of their nest egg in growth-oriented investments. On the other hand, older investors tend to choose more conservative investments. As a result, a smaller percentage of their nest egg is placed in growth-oriented investments. While no investor regardless of age likes to lose money on an investment, the fact is that younger investors have more time for an investment to recover its original value and even increase in value.

How much of your portfolio should be in growth-oriented investments? Well-known personal financial expert Suze Orman suggests that you subtract your age

Standard & Poor's 500 Stock Index an index that contains 500 different stocks that reflect increases or decreases in value for the U.S. stock market as a whole

asset allocation the process of spreading your money among several different types of investments to lessen risk

from 110, and the difference is the percentage of your assets that should be invested in growth investments. For example, if you are 30 years old, subtract 30 from 110, which gives you 80. Therefore, 80 percent of your assets should be invested in growth-oriented investments, whereas the remaining 20 percent should be kept in safer conservative investments.[3]

Your Role in the Investment Process

Investors want large returns, yet they are often unwilling to invest the time required to become a good investor. They would not buy a car without a test drive or purchase a home without comparing different homes, but for some unknown reason they invest without doing their homework. The suggestions given here will help you choose investments that will increase in value.

- *Evaluate potential investments.* Keep in mind that successful investors evaluate their investments before making investment decisions. Often, it is useful to keep copies of the material you used to evaluate each investment. Then, when it is time to re-evaluate an existing investment, you will know where to begin your search for current information. Much of the information in this chapter in the section "Sources of Financial Information" will help you learn how to evaluate different investment opportunities.
- *Monitor the value of your investments.* Would you believe that some people invest large sums of money and do not know what their investments are worth? They do not know if their investments have increased or decreased in value and if they should sell their investments or continue to hold them. A much better approach is to monitor the value of your investments.
- *Keep accurate and current records.* Accurate record keeping can help you spot opportunities to maximize profits, reduce dollar losses when you sell your investments, and help you decide whether you want to invest additional funds in a specific investment. For tax purposes, you should keep purchase records for each of your investments that include the actual dollar cost of the investment, plus any commissions or fees you paid, along with records of dividends, interest income, or rental income you received.

Explain the reasons people choose conservative investments including bank accounts and bonds.

CONSERVATIVE INVESTMENT ALTERNATIVES

Typically investors who are afraid of the risk associated with stocks, mutual funds, and other investment alternatives, beginning investors, investors that need a predictable source of income, or people worried about a downturn in the economy will often invest their money in bank accounts, government bonds, or corporate bonds.

Bank Accounts

Bank accounts that pay interest—and therefore are investments—include passbook savings accounts, money-market accounts, CDs, and other interest-bearing accounts. These investments were discussed in Chapter 18. The interest paid on bank accounts can be withdrawn to serve as income, or it can be left on deposit and increase the value of the bank account and provide for growth. At the time of this publication, one-year CDs were paying between 0.50 and 1 percent. Although CDs and other bank accounts are risk-free for all practical purposes, many investors often choose other investments because of the potential for larger returns.

Corporate and Government Bonds

In Chapter 19, we discussed why corporations issue bonds to obtain financing. The U.S. government and state and local governments also issue bonds for the same reason. Investors generally choose bonds because they provide a predictable source of income.

Invest in Green Bonds?

Should investors choose green bonds? The World Bank issues green bonds to pay for sustainability projects such as water purification, solar installations, and reforestation. Since 2008, it has issued $3.3 billion worth of green bonds, in 17 currencies, with a range of maturities from 2 to 10 years. For example, Bank of America Merrill Lynch offers World Bank green bonds with 10-year maturities starting with a $1,000 investment. Because repayment is not tied to the performance of the projects they finance, these bonds are rated as low-risk and carry relatively low interest rates.

Nobody questions the need to fund sustainability projects. In fact, some institutional investors see green bonds as a way to support environmental action while diversifying their portfolios. One issue, however, is that the money goes into a World Bank account designated for environmental projects—and investors don't know which project they're supporting. As a result, money from an investor who hopes to preserve the rainforest may actually be used for mass transportation improvements that reduce pollution. Another issue is liquidity. Demand for green bonds is unproven, and they aren't traded as widely or as often as, say, U.S. Treasury bonds. In fact, lack of liquidity may be a real problem for investors who have to sell prior to maturity. So should investors choose green bonds?

Sources: Based on information in Sally Bakewell, "Green Bond Bankers in Japan, Sweden Beat U.S. to $7 Billion," *Bloomberg*, January 24, 2012, www.bloomberg.com; "A Modest, But Important, Addition to Climate Finance," *Economist*, October 29, 2011, www.economist.com; Sonia Kolesnikov-Jessop, "A Change of Heart on Investing in the Climate," *New York Times*, November 27, 2011, www.nytimes.com; Elizabeth O'Brien, "Now Bonds Are Going Green Too," *Smart Money*, October 25, 2011, www.smartmoney.com; www.worldbank.org.

Government Bonds Despite concerns about the increasing dollar amount of national debt for the United States, most investors still consider the nation's government bonds to be risk-free. The other side of the coin is that these bonds pay lower interest than most other investments. Interest paid on U.S. government securities is taxable for federal income tax purposes, but is exempt from state and local taxation. Generally, investors choose from the five different types of U.S. government bonds and securities described in Table 20.3. With the exception of savings bonds, the minimum purchase for each type of U.S. government security is $100 with additional increments of $100 above the minimum. For more information about U.S. government securities, go to www.treasurydirect.gov.

Like the federal government, state and local governments sell bonds to obtain financing. A **municipal bond**, sometimes called a *muni*, is a debt security issued by a state or local government. Municipal bonds are especially attractive to wealthy investors because interest income from municipal bonds may be tax exempt from federal taxes. Whether or not the interest on municipal bonds is tax-exempt often depends on how the funds obtained from their sale are used. *Caution: It is your responsibility, as an investor, to determine whether or not the interest paid by municipal bonds is taxable. It is also your responsibility to evaluate municipal bonds.* Although most municipal bonds are relatively safe, defaults have occurred in recent years.

municipal bond sometimes called a *muni*, a debt security issued by a state or local government

Corporate Bonds Because they are a form of long-term debt financing that must be repaid, investment-grade corporate bonds are generally considered a more conservative investment than either stocks or mutual funds that invest in stocks. One of the principal advantages of corporate bonds is that they are primarily long-term, income-producing investments. Between the time of purchase and the maturity date, the bondholder will receive interest payments—usually semiannually, or every six months. For example, assume that you purchase a $1,000 bond—the usual face value for a corporate bond—issued by the rail-based transportation giant CSX

Can U.S. savings bonds provide an umbrella for a rainy day? Despite concerns about the increasing dollar amount of the national debt for the United States, most investors still consider the nation's savings bonds and securities issued by the U.S. Treasury to be risk-free because they are backed by the full faith and credit of the U.S. government. But be warned: When you invest in these conservative investments, you must accept smaller returns on your investments.

TABLE 20.3 Information about U.S. Government Securities

Type of Security	Maturity	Interest	Notes
Treasury bill (T-bills)	4, 13, 26, or 52 weeks	T-bills are sold at a discount and the actual purchase price is less than $100.	When T-bills mature, you receive the maturity value.
Treasury notes	2, 3, 5, 7, or 10 years	Interest is paid every six months until maturity.	Interest is slightly higher than T-bills because of the longer maturity.
Treasury bonds	30-year	Interest is paid every six months until maturity.	Interest rate is slightly higher than T-bills and Treasury notes because of the longer maturity.
Treasury inflation-protected securities (TIPS)	5, 10, or 30 years. At maturity, you are paid the adjusted principal or original principal, whichever is greater.	Interest is paid every six months until maturity at a fixed rate applied to the adjusted principal.	The principal of TIPS securities increases with inflation and decreases with deflation.
Savings bonds	Pay interest for up to 30 years.	Interest is added to bonds monthly and paid when you redeem savings bonds.	Minimum purchase is $25. Note: If interest is used to pay qualified college expenses, it may be exempt from federal taxation.

© CENGAGE LEARNING 2014

Corporation and that the interest rate for this bond is 6 percent. In this situation, you receive interest of $60 ($1,000 × 0.06 = $60) a year from the corporation. For corporate bonds, interest is usually paid semiannually or every six months. In the case of the CSX bond just described, a bondholder will receive two $30 interest payments each year.

Most beginning investors think that a $1,000 bond is always worth $1,000. In reality, the price of a bond may fluctuate until its maturity date. Changes in the overall interest rates in the economy are the primary cause of most bond price fluctuations. When overall interest rates in the economy increase, the market value of existing bonds with a fixed interest rate typically declines. For example, the value of the CSX bond with a fixed 6 percent interest rate will decline if interest rates in the economy or interest rates for comparable bonds increase. When a bond's price declines, it may be purchased for less than its face value. By holding the bond until maturity, bond owners can redeem the bond for more than they paid for it.

A corporate bond with a fixed interest rate can also increase in value if overall interest rates in the economy decline. In this situation, a bond like the CSX bond with a 6 percent fixed interest rate will increase in value. The difference between the purchase price and the selling price is profit and is in addition to annual interest income.

Before you invest in bonds, remember that the price of a corporate bond can decrease and that interest payments and eventual repayment may be a problem for a corporation that encounters financial difficulty. To compare potential risk and return on corporate bond issues, many investors rely on the bond ratings provided by Moody's Investors Service, Inc., Fitch Ratings, and Standard & Poor's Corporation.

Convertible Corporate Bonds Some corporations prefer to issue convertible bonds because they carry a lower interest rate than nonconvertible bonds—by about 1 to 2 percent. In return for accepting a lower interest rate, owners of convertible bonds have the opportunity for increased investment growth. For example, assume that you purchase an Advanced Micro Devices $1,000 corporate bond that is convertible to 35.6125 shares of the company's common stock. This means that you could convert the bond to common stock whenever the price of the company's stock is $28.08 ($1,000 ÷ 35.6125 = $28.08) or higher.[4] However, owners may opt not to convert their bonds to common stock even if the market value of the common stock does increase to $28.08 or more. The reason for not exercising the conversion feature is quite simple. As the market value of the common stock increases, the price of the convertible bond also increases. By not converting to common stock, bondholders enjoy interest income from the bond in addition to the increased bond value caused by the price movement of the common stock.

MORE SPECULATIVE INVESTMENTS

Identify the advantages and disadvantages of stocks, mutual funds, real estate, and more speculative investments.

Earlier in this chapter, we discussed the concepts of safety and risk. Before you examine more speculative investment alternatives, it may help to review the basic rule: *The potential return should be directly related to the assumed risk*. While all investors want larger returns, you must consider the risk involved with each of the following investments. Above all, keep in mind that dollar returns for the more speculative investments described in this section are not guaranteed.

Common Stock

As mentioned in Chapter 19, corporations issue common stock to finance their business start-up costs and help pay for expansion and their ongoing business activities. Before investing in stock, keep in mind that corporations do not have to repay the money a stockholder pays for stock. Usually, a stockholder may sell her or his stock to another individual.

How do you make money by buying common stock? Basically, there are three ways: through dividend payments, through an increase in the value of the stock, or through stock splits.

stock dividend a dividend in the form of additional stock

capital gain the difference between a security's purchase price and its selling price

market value the price of one share of a stock at a particular time

Dividend Payments One of the reasons why many stockholders invest in common stock is *dividend income*. Generally, dividends are paid on a quarterly basis. At the time of publication, Kraft Foods paid its stockholders an annual dividend of $1.16 per share in quarterly payments of $0.29 every three months. Although corporations are under no legal obligation to pay dividends or can reduce dividends if the company experiences financial difficulties, most corporate board members like to keep stockholders happy (and prosperous). A corporation may pay stock dividends in place of—or in addition to—cash dividends. A **stock dividend** is a dividend in the form of additional stock. It is paid to shareholders just as cash dividends are paid—in proportion to the number of shares owned.

Increase in Dollar Value Another way to make money on stock investments is through a capital gain that occurs when you sell stock. A **capital gain** is the difference between a security's purchase price and its selling price. To earn a capital gain, you must sell when the market value of the stock is higher than the original purchase price you paid for the stock. The **market value** is the price of one share of a stock at a particular time. Let's assume that on March 8,

© RICHARD LEVINE/ALAMY

Should you invest in Cheerios? While most everyone in the United States recognizes the Cheerios brand, did you know that the famous cereal is manufactured and marketed by General Mills? Often you have to dig deeper if you want to invest in a corporation that produces a famous product or service to determine if the "parent" company is a quality investment that will help you obtain your financial goals.

Assumptions: 100 shares of common stock purchased on March 8, 2009, for $37 a share; 100 shares sold on March 8, 2012, for $52 a share; dividends for three years total $4.75 a share.

Cost when Purchased		Return when Sold	
100 shares @ $37	$3,700	100 shares @ $52	$5,200
Plus commission	+25	Minus commission	−25
Total investment	$3,725	Total return	$5,175
Transaction Summary			
Total return	$5,175		
Minus total investment	−3,725		
Profit from stock sale	$1,450		
Plus total dividends (three years)	+475		
Total return for this transaction	$1,925		

Source: Price data and dividend amounts were taken from the Yahoo Finance Web site, http://finance.yahoo.com (accessed March 8, 2012).

2009, you purchased 100 shares of Kellogg common stock at a cost of $37 a share and that you paid $25 in commission charges, for a total investment of $3,725. Let's also assume that you held your 100 shares until March 8, 2012, and then sold the Kellogg stock for $52. Your total return on investment is shown in Table 20.4. You realized a profit of $1,925 because you received dividends totaling $4.75 a share during the three-year period and because the stock's market value increased by $15 a share. Of course, if the stock's market value had decreased, or if the firm's board of directors had voted to reduce or omit dividends, your return would have been less than the total dollar return illustrated in Table 20.4.

Stock Splits   Directors of many corporations feel that there is an optimal price range within which their firm's stock is most attractive to investors. When the market value increases beyond that range, they may declare a *stock split* to bring the price down. A **stock split** is the division of each outstanding share of a corporation's stock into a greater number of shares.

The most common stock splits result in one, two, or three new shares for each original share. For example, in November 2011, the board of directors of Estée Lauder, the company known for skin care, cosmetics, fragrances, and hair-care products, approved a two-for-one stock split. After this split, a stockholder who originally owned 100 shares owned 200 shares. The value of an original share was proportionally reduced. In the case of Estée Lauder, the market value per share was reduced to half the stock's value before the two-for-one stock split. There is no evidence to support that a corporation's long-term performance is improved by a stock split; however, some investors do profit from stock splits on a short-term basis. *Be warned: There are no guarantees that the stock will increase in value after a split.* However, the stock may be more attractive to the investing public because of the potential for a rapid increase in dollar value. This attraction is based on the belief that most corporations split their stock only when their financial future is improving and on the upswing.

Preferred Stock

As we noted in Chapter 19, a firm's preferred stockholders must receive their dividends before common stockholders are paid any dividends. Moreover, the preferred-stock dividend amount is specified on the stock certificate. In addition, the owners of preferred stock have first claim, after bond owners and general creditors, on corporate assets if the firm is dissolved or enters bankruptcy. These features make preferred stock

stock split the division of each outstanding share of a corporation's stock into a greater number of shares

a more conservative investment with an added degree of safety and a more predictable source of income when compared with common stock.

In addition, owners of preferred stock may gain through special features offered with certain preferred-stock issues. Owners of *cumulative* preferred stocks are assured that omitted dividends will be paid to them before common stockholders receive any dividends. Owners of *convertible* preferred stock may profit through growth as well as dividends. When the value of a firm's common stock increases, the market value of its convertible preferred stock also increases. Convertible preferred stock thus combines the lower risk of preferred stock with the possibility of greater speculative gain through conversion to common stock.

Mutual Funds and Exchange-Traded Funds

For many investors, mutual funds are the investment of choice. There are plenty of funds from which to choose. In 1970, there were only about 400 mutual funds. In January 2012, there were over 10,000 funds.[5]

According to the Mutual Fund Education Alliance (www.mfea.com), a **mutual fund** pools the money of many investors—its shareholders—to invest in a variety of different securities.[6] The major advantages of a mutual fund are its *professional management* and its *diversification*, or investment in a wide variety of securities. Most investment companies do everything possible to convince you that they can do a better job of picking securities than you can. In reality, mutual funds are managed by professional fund managers who devote large amounts of time to picking just the "right" securities for their funds' portfolios. *Be warned:* Even the best portfolio managers make mistakes. So you, the investor, must be careful and evaluate different funds before investing. Diversification spells safety because an occasional loss incurred with one security is usually offset by gains from other investments.

Mutual-Fund Basics   There are basically three types of mutual funds: (1) open-end funds, (2) closed-end funds, and (3) exchange-traded funds (ETFs). The investment company sponsoring an *open-end fund* issues and sells new shares to any investor who requests them. It also buys back shares from investors who wish to sell all or part of their holdings. A *closed-end fund* sells shares in the fund to investors only when the fund is originally organized. Once all the shares are sold, an investor must purchase shares from some other investor who is willing to sell them. The investment company is under no obligation to buy back shares from investors.

An **exchange-traded fund (ETF)** is a fund that generally invests in the stocks or securities contained in a specific stock or securities index. Although most investors think of an ETF as investing in the stocks contained in the Standard & Poor's 500 Stock Index, there are many different types of ETFs available that attempt to track all kinds of indexes including different types of stocks, bonds, and even commodities. Exchange-traded funds tend to mirror the performance of a specific index, moving up or down as the individual stocks or securities contained in the index move up or down.

Like a closed-end fund, shares of an exchange-traded fund are traded on a securities exchange or in the over-the-counter market at any time during the business day. Although exchange-traded funds are similar to closed-end funds, there is an important difference. Most closed-end funds are actively managed, with portfolio managers making the selection of stocks and other securities contained in a closed-end fund. Almost

© PONSULAK KUNSUB/SHUTTERSTOCK

Sustaining the PLANET

Green Investing

Interested in earning some green (backs) while you're saving the planet? Maybe green investing is for you! Green investing involves choosing to invest in companies that are involved in operations aimed at improving the environment, such as alternative energy sources, clean air and water projects, or companies that provide environmentally friendly products. Socially Responsible Investing is an organization that provides information about green investing, including green stock investment choices, green mutual funds, and tips for investors. Take a look at http://yesinvesting.com/.

COURTESY OF HTTP://YESINVESTING.COM

mutual fund   pools the money of many investors—its shareholders—to invest in a variety of different securities

exchange-traded fund (ETF)   a fund that generally invests in the stocks or other securities contained in a specific stock or securities index

all exchange-traded funds, on the other hand, normally invest in the stocks, bonds, or securities included in a specific index. Therefore, there is less need for a portfolio manager to make investment decisions. Because of passive management, fees associated with owning shares are generally less when compared to both closed-end and open-end funds. Although increasing in popularity, there are only about 1,100 exchange-traded funds.[7]

The share value for any mutual fund is determined by calculating its net asset value. **Net asset value (NAV)** per share is equal to the current market value of the mutual fund's portfolio minus the mutual fund's liabilities divided by the number of outstanding shares. For most mutual funds, NAV is calculated once a day and is reported in newspapers and financial publications and on the Internet. Because ETFs and closed-end funds trade like stocks, their shares trade at the current market value, which can be more or less than a closed-end fund's or ETF's NAV.

Mutual-Fund Sales Charges and Fees

With regard to costs, there are two types of mutual funds: load and no-load funds. An individual who invests in a *load fund* pays a sales charge every time he or she purchases shares. This charge may be as high as 8.5 percent. Although many exceptions exist, the average load charge for mutual funds is between 3 and 5 percent. Instead of charging investors a fee when they purchase shares in a mutual fund, some funds charge a *contingent deferred sales fee*. Generally, this fee ranges from 1 to 5 percent of the amount withdrawn during the first five to seven years. Typically, the amount of the contingent deferred sales fee declines each year that you own the fund until there is no withdrawal fee.

The purchaser of shares in a *no-load fund* pays no sales charges at all. Although some fund salespeople claim that load funds outperform no-load funds, there is no significant performance difference between funds that charge load charges (commissions) and those that do not.[8] Because no-load funds offer the same type of investment opportunities as load funds, you should investigate them further before deciding which type of mutual fund is best for you.

Mutual funds also collect a yearly management fee of about 0.25 to 1.5 percent of the total dollar amount of assets in the fund. Although fees vary considerably, the average management fee is between 0.50 and 1 percent of the fund's assets. Finally, some mutual funds charge a 12b-1 fee (sometimes referred to as a *distribution fee*) to defray the costs of advertising and marketing the mutual fund. Annual 12b-1 fees are calculated on the value of a fund's assets and cannot exceed 1 percent of the fund's assets. Unlike the one-time sales fees that some mutual funds charge to purchase *or* sell mutual-fund shares, the management fee and the 12b-1 fee are ongoing fees charged each year.

Together, all the different management fees; 12b-1 fees, if any; and additional operating costs for a specific fund are referred to as an **expense ratio**. As a guideline, many financial planners recommend that you choose a mutual fund with an expense ratio of 1 percent or less. To learn more about different mutual fund charges and fees, you should visit the Securities and Exchange Commission Web site at www.sec.gov.

Today, mutual funds can also be classified as A, B, or C shares. With A shares, investors pay commissions when they purchase shares in the mutual fund. With B shares, investors pay commissions when money is withdrawn or shares are sold during the first five to seven years. With C shares, investors often pay no commissions to buy or sell shares but usually must pay higher ongoing management and 12b-1 fees.

Managed Funds Versus Indexed Funds

Most mutual funds are managed funds. In other words, there is a professional fund manager (or team of managers) who chooses the securities that are contained in the fund. The fund manager also decides when to buy and sell securities in the fund.

net asset value (NAV) current market value of a mutual fund's portfolio minus the mutual fund's liabilities divided by the number of outstanding shares

expense ratio all the different management fees; 12b-1 fees, if any; and additional operating costs for a specific fund

© SUSAN VAN ETTEN

How do you choose the right investment and financial company to help you obtain your financial goals? Beginning investors often see the investment world as a jungle because of the different investment alternatives and the large number of companies that want to help you invest. In reality, all investments *and* the companies that want to help you should be evaluated before you make any decisions on how and where to invest.

Instead of investing in a managed fund, some investors choose to invest in an index fund. Why? The answer to this question is simple: Over many years, index funds have outperformed managed funds. The exact statistics vary depending on the year and the specific fund, but a common statistic is that the Standard & Poor's 500 Stock Index outperforms 80 percent of all mutual funds.[9] Simply put: It is hard to beat an index such as the Standard & Poor's 500. If the individual securities included in an index increase in value, the index goes up. Because an index fund contains the same securities as the index, the dollar value of a share in an index fund also increases when the index increases. Unfortunately, the reverse is also true. A second reason why investors choose index funds is the lower fees charged by these passively managed funds. (*Note:* Various indexes are discussed later in this chapter.)

Types of Mutual-Fund Investments Based on the type of securities they invest in, mutual funds generally fall into three broad categories: stocks, bonds, and other. The majority of mutual funds are *stock funds* that invest in stocks issued by small, medium-size, and large corporations that provide investors with income, growth, or a combination of income and growth. *Bond funds* invest in corporate, government, or municipal bonds that provide investors with interest income. The third category includes funds that stress asset allocation and money-market investments or strive for a balance between stocks and bonds. In most cases, the name of the category gives a pretty good clue to the type of investments included in the fund. Typical fund names include:

- Aggressive growth stock funds
- Balanced funds
- Global stock funds
- Growth stock funds
- High-yield (junk) bond funds
- Income stock funds
- Index funds
- Life cycle funds
- Long-term U.S. bond funds
- Regional funds
- Sector stock funds
- Socially responsible funds
- Small-cap stock funds

To help investors obtain their investment objectives, most investment companies now allow shareholders to switch from one fund to another fund within the same family of funds. A **family of funds** exists when one investment company manages a group of mutual funds. For example, shareholders, at their option, can change from the Fidelity International Growth Fund to the Fidelity Small-Cap Discovery Fund. Generally, investors may give instructions to switch from one fund to another fund within the same family either in writing, over the telephone, or via the Internet. Charges for exchanges, if any, are small for each transaction.

Real Estate

Real estate ownership represents one of the best hedges against inflation, but like all investments it has its risks. A piece of property in a poor location, for example, can actually decrease in value. Table 20.5 lists some of the many factors you should consider before investing in real estate.

There are, of course, disadvantages to any investment, and real estate is no exception. If you want to sell your property, you must find an interested buyer with the ability to obtain enough money to complete the transaction. Finding such a buyer can be difficult if loan money is scarce, the real estate market is in a decline, or you overpaid for a piece of property. For example, many real estate investors were forced to hold some properties longer than they wanted because buyers could not obtain financing

family of funds a group of mutual funds managed by one investment company

TABLE 20.5 Real Estate Checklist

Although real estate offers one of the best hedges against inflation, not all property increases in value. Many factors should be considered before investing in real estate.

Evaluation of Property	Inspection of the Surrounding Neighborhood	Other Factors
Is the property priced competitively with similar property?	What are the present zoning requirements?	Why are the present owners selling the property?
What type of financing, if any, is available?	Is the neighborhood's population increasing or decreasing?	How long will you have to hold the property before selling it to someone else?
How much are the taxes?	What is the average income of people in the area?	How much profit can you reasonably expect to obtain?
How much will it cost to repair or remodel a property?	What is the state of repair of surrounding property? Do most of the buildings and homes need repair?	Is there a chance that the property value will decrease?

© CENGAGE LEARNING 2014

during the recent economic crisis. If you are forced to hold your investment longer than you originally planned, taxes, interest, and installment payments can be a heavy burden. As a rule, real estate increases in value and eventually sells at a profit, but there are no guarantees. The degree of your success depends on how well you evaluate different alternatives.

The Most Speculative Investment Techniques

A **high-risk investment** is one made in the uncertain hope of earning a relatively large profit in a short time. (See the most speculative investments category in Table 20.2.) Although all investments have some risk, some investments become high-risk because of the methods used by investors to earn a quick profit. These methods can lead to large losses as well as to impressive gains. They should not be used by anyone who does not fully understand the risks involved. We begin this section with a discussion of selling short. Then we examine margin transactions and other high-risk investments.

Selling Short Normally, you buy stocks expecting that they will increase in value and then can be sold at a profit. This procedure is referred to as **buying long**. However, many securities decrease in value for various reasons. The market value for a share of a corporation's stock, for example, can decrease when sales and profits are lower than expected. When this type of situation occurs, you can use a procedure called selling short to make a profit when the price of an individual stock is falling. **Selling short** is the process of selling stock that an investor does not actually own but has borrowed from a brokerage firm and will repay at a later date. The idea is to sell at today's higher price and then buy later at a lower price. To make a profit from a short transaction, you must proceed as follows:

1. Arrange to borrow a certain number of shares of a particular stock from a brokerage firm.
2. Sell the borrowed stock immediately, assuming that the price of the stock will drop in a reasonably short time.
3. After the price drops, buy the same number of shares that were sold in step 2.
4. Give the newly purchased stock to the brokerage firm in return for the stock borrowed in step 1.

high-risk investment an investment made in the uncertain hope of earning a relatively large profit in a short time

buying long buying a stock with the expectation that it will increase in value and then can be sold at a profit

selling short the process of selling stock that an investor does not actually own but has borrowed from a brokerage firm and will repay at a later date

Your profit is the difference between the amount received when the stock is sold in step 2 and the amount paid for the stock in step 3. For example, assume that you think Barnes & Noble stock is overvalued at $18 a share. You also believe that the stock will decrease in value over the next three to four months. In this example, you can make money with a short transaction—*if the stock's value does decline*. On the other hand, if the market value for a share of Barnes & Noble increases, you lose.

Buying Stock on Margin An investor buys stock *on margin* by borrowing part of the purchase price, usually from a stock brokerage firm. The **margin requirement** is the portion of the price of a stock that cannot be borrowed. This requirement is set by the Federal Reserve Board.

Today, the current margin requirement is 50 percent, which means you can borrow up to 50 percent of the cost of a stock purchase. Some securities exchanges and brokerage firms may impose other restrictions and require that you deposit more cash, which reduces the percentage that can be borrowed. However, why would investors want to buy stock on margin? Simply because they can buy up to twice as much stock that way. Suppose that an investor expects the market price of a share of common stock of American Electric Power Corporation—a U.S. energy company—to increase in the next three to four months. Assume you have enough money to purchase 200 shares of the stock. However, if you buy on margin, you can purchase an additional 200 shares for a total of 400 shares. If the price of American Electric Power's stock increases by $8 per share, your profit will be $1,600 ($8 × 200 = $1,600) if you pay cash. But it will be $3,200 ($8 × 400 = $3,200) if you buy the stock using margin. By buying more shares on margin, you will earn more profit (less the interest you pay on the borrowed money and customary commission charges).

Note that the stock purchased on margin serves as collateral for the borrowed funds. Before you become a margin investor, you should consider two factors. First, if the market price of the purchased stock does not increase as quickly as expected, interest costs mount and eventually drain your profit. Second, if the price of the margined stock falls, your dollar loss will be greater because you own more shares.

If the value of a stock you bought on margin decreases to approximately 60 percent of its original price, you may receive a *margin call* from the brokerage firm. You then must provide additional cash or securities to serve as collateral for the borrowed money. If you cannot provide additional collateral, the stock is sold, and the proceeds are used to pay off the loan and commissions. Any funds remaining after the loan and commissions are paid off are returned to you.

margin requirement the portion of the price of a stock that cannot be borrowed

Other High-Risk Investments We have already discussed two high-risk investments—selling short and margin transactions. Other high-risk investments include the following:

- Stock options
- Derivatives
- Commodities
- Precious metals
- Gemstones
- Coins
- Antiques and collectibles

Without exception, investments of this kind are normally referred to as high-risk investments for one reason or another. For example, the gold market has many unscrupulous dealers who sell worthless gold-plated lead coins to unsuspecting, uninformed investors. It pays to be careful. *Although investments in this category can lead to large dollar gains, they should not be used by anyone who does not fully understand all the potential risks involved.*

© ANAKENM2012/SHUTTERSTOCK

Is gold a conservative or a high-risk investment? Good question. When purchased from reputable dealers, gold can be a conservative investment—especially in troubled economic times. And yet, there are many unscrupulous dealers who sell worthless gold-plated coins to unsuspecting investors who want to make a fast buck. The final answer: Consider the potential risks for a conservative or high-risk investment before investing your money.

SOURCES OF FINANCIAL INFORMATION

A wealth of information is available to investors. Sources include the Internet, professional advisory services, newspapers, brokerage firm reports, business periodicals, corporate reports, and securities averages.

The Internet

By using the Internet, investors can access a wealth of information on most investment and personal finance topics. For example, you can obtain interest rates for CDs; current price information for stocks, bonds, and mutual funds; and experts' recommendations to buy, hold, or sell an investment. You can even trade securities online.

Because the Internet makes so much information available, you need to use it selectively. One of the Web search engines such as Yahoo! (www.yahoo.com) or Google (www.google.com) can help you locate the information you really need. These search engines allow you to do a word search for the personal finance topic or investment alternative you want to explore. Why not take a look? To access a search engine, enter the Web site address and then type in a key term such as *personal finance* or *financial planning* and see the results. In addition to using a search engine to locate information, you can also obtain information from a number of investment sites. For example, the Web sites described in Table 20.6 are often used by successful investors.

Corporations; brokerage firms; investment companies that sponsor mutual funds; real estate brokers and agents; and federal, state, and local governments also have Web sites where you can obtain valuable investment information. You may want to explore the information available on the Internet for two reasons. First, these sites are easily accessible. All you have to do is type in the Web address or use a search engine to locate the site. Second, the information on these sites may be more up-to-date than printed material obtained from published sources. Today, many of the above sources of information also use social media to connect with investors. Charles Schwab, for example, uses Facebook, Twitter, and YouTube to reach existing and potential clients.

In addition, you can access professional advisory services—a topic discussed in the next section—for information on stocks, bonds, mutual funds, and other investment alternatives. Although some of the information provided by these services is free, there is a charge for the more detailed information you may need to evaluate an investment.

TABLE 20.6	Five Popular Web Sites to Help You Establish a Successful Investment Program
Sponsor and Web Address	**Description**
The Motley Fool Web (www.fool.com)	Light-hearted financial advice and step-by-step activities to help you start an investment program
CNN/Money (www.money.cnn.com)	Current financial news and investment information that can help investors sharpen their investment skills
Market Watch (www.marketwatch.com)	Price information about stocks and funds along with information about investing, the economy, and personal financial planning
Yahoo! Finance (http://finance.yahoo.com)	Current price information and general research information for stocks, mutual funds, and bonds
Smart Money (http://smartmoney.com)	Information about how to save, invest, and spend along with easy-to-use financial calculators

© CENGAGE LEARNING 2014

Professional Advisory Services

For a fee, various professional advisory services provide information about investments. Information from these services may also be available at university and public libraries.

As discussed earlier in this chapter, Moody's, Standard & Poor's, and Fitch Ratings provide information that can be used to determine the quality and risk associated with bond issues. Standard & Poor's, Mergent, Inc., and Value Line also rate the companies that issue stock. Each investor service provides detailed financial reports. Take a look at the Mergent's research report for Dollar Tree, Inc., illustrated in Figure 20.1. Notice that there are main sections that provide financial data, summary information about the company's business operations, recent developments, prospects, and other valuable information. Research reports published by Standard & Poor's and Value Line are like the Mergent's report and provide similar information.

A number of professional advisory services provide detailed information on mutual funds. Morningstar, Inc., Standard & Poor's, Lipper Analytical Services, and Value Line are four widely tapped sources for such information. Although some information may be free, a fee is generally charged for more detailed research reports. In addition, various mutual-fund newsletters supply financial information to subscribers for a fee.

Financial Coverage of Securities Transactions

Many local newspapers carry several pages of business news, including reports of securities transactions. The *Wall Street Journal* (published on weekdays) and *Barron's* (published once a week) are devoted almost entirely to financial and economic news. Both include coverage of transactions on major securities exchanges.

Because transactions involving stocks, bonds, and mutual funds are reported differently, we examine each type of report separately.

Common and Preferred Stocks Stock transactions are reported in tables that usually look like the top section of Figure 20.2. Stocks are listed alphabetically. Your first task is to move down the table to find the stock you are interested in. To read the stock quotation, you read across the table. The highlighted line in Figure 20.2 gives detailed information about common stock issued by Aflac—the insurance company with the talking duck.

Bonds Although some newspapers and financial publications provide limited information on certain corporate and government bond issues, it is usually easier to obtain more detailed information on a greater number of bond issues by accessing the Internet. Regardless of the source, bond prices are quoted as a percentage of the face value, which is usually $1,000. Thus, to find the current price, you must multiply the face value ($1,000) by the quotation. For example, a price quoted as 84 translates to a selling price of $840 ($1,000 × 84% = $840). Detailed information obtained from the Yahoo! Finance Web site for a $1,000 AT&T corporate bond, which pays 5.50 percent interest and matures in 2018, is provided in Figure 20.3.

Mutual Funds Purchases and sales of shares of mutual funds are reported in tables like the one shown in Figure 20.4. As in reading stock quotations, your first task is to move down the table to find the mutual fund you are interested in. Then, to find the mutual-fund price quotation, read across the table. The first line in Figure 20.4 gives information for the Vanguard 500 Index mutual fund.

Personal APPS

There is more to successful investing than just luck! In fact, you must "invest" the time needed to research stocks, bonds, mutual funds, and other alternatives before you invest your money. And in order to be a "best" investor, you'll need to continue to evaluate each investment. Continued evaluation can help you decide if you want to hold, sell, or buy more of each investment in your investment portfolio.

FIGURE 20.1   Mergent's Research Report for Dollar Tree, Inc.

A research report from Mergent's is divided into main parts that describe not only the financial condition of a company but also its history and outlook for the future.

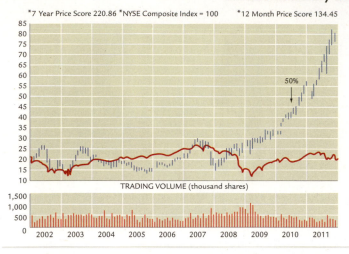

*7 Year Price Score 220.86 *NYSE Composite Index = 100   *12 Month Price Score 134.45

Interim Earnings (Per Share)

Qtr.	Apr	Jul	Oct	Jan
2008–9	0.32	0.28	0.31	0.77
2009–10	0.44	0.42	0.51	1.01
2010–11	0.49	0.61	0.73	1.26
2011-12	0.82	0.77	0.87	

nterim Dividends (Per Share)

No Dividends Paid

Valuation Anaylsis		Institutional Holding	
Forecast EPS	$4.01	No of Institutions	
	(12/10/2011)	545	
Market Cap	$9.7 Billion	Shares	
Book Value	$1.4 Billion	124,758,872	
Price Book	6.70	% Held	
Price/Sales	1.51	N/A	

Business Summary: Retail - General Merchandise/Department Stores (MIC: 2.1.1 SIC: 5331 NAIC: 452990)

Dollar Tree is an operator of discount variety stores providing merchandise at the fixed price of $1.00. Co.'s merchandise mix consists of consumable merchandise, which includes candy and food, health and beauty care, and household consumables; variety merchandise, which includes toys, housewares, gifts, party goods, greeting cards, softlines, and other items; and seasonal goods, which include Easter, Halloween and Christmas merchandise. At Jan 29 2011, Co. operates 4.015 stores in 48 states and the District of Columbia, as well as 86 stores in Canada under the Dollar Tree, Deal$, Dollar Tree Deal$, Dollar Giant and Dollar Bills names.

Recent Developments: For the quarter ended Oct 29 2011, net income increased 12.1% to US$104.5 million from US$93.2 million in the year-earlier quarter. Revenues were US$1.60 billion, up 11.9% from US$1.43 billion the year before. Operating income was US$164.9 million versus US$140.9 million in the prior-year quarter, an increase of 17.0%. Direct operating expenses rose 12.5% to US$1.04 billion from US$920.6 million in the comparable period the year before. Indirect operating expenses increased 8.4% to US$395.7 million from US$365.1 million in the equivalent prior-year period.

Prospects: Our evaluation of Dollar Tree Inc. as of Dec. 11, 2011 is the result of our systematic analysis on three basic characteristics; earnings strength, relative valuation, and recent stock price movement. The company has produced a positive trend in earnings per share over the past 5 quarters and while recent estimates for the company have been raised by analysts, DLTR has posted better than expected results. Based on operating earnings yield, the company is about fairly valued when compared to all of the companies in our coverage universe. Share price changes over the past year indicates that DLTR will perform well over the near term.

Financial Data

(US$ in Thousands)	9 Mos	6 Mos	3 Mos	01/29/2011	01/30/2010	01/31/2009	02/02/2008	02/03/2007
Earning Per Share	3.74	3.60	3.44	3.10	2.37	1.69	1.39	1.23
Cash Flow Per Share	5.53	5.10	5.21	4.09	4.34	2.98	2.56	2.62
Tang Book Value Per Share	10.70	11.55	10.73	10.42	9.87	8.23	6.24	6.83
Income Statement								
Total Revenue	4,684,900	3,088,300	1,545,900	5,882,400	5,231,200	4,644.900	4,242,600	3,969,400
EBITDA	600,100	394,200	201,600	795,200	670,600	526,900	488,800	469,800
Depn & Amortn	119,900	78,800	39,200	159,700	157,800	161,100	158,500	159,600
Income Before Taxes	478,000	313,800	161,500	629,900	507,600	359,100	319,800	302,900
Income Taxes	177,600	117,900	60,500	232,600	187,100	129,600	118,500	110,900
Net Income	300,400	195,900	101,000	397,300	320,500	229,500	201,300	192.000
Average Shares	120,700	123,000	123,500	128,000	135,000	136,200	144,600	155,700
Balance Sheet								
Current Assets	1,332,500	1,408,300	1,325,500	1,333,300	1,305,600	1,073,200	788,800	959,000
Total Assets	2,431,200	2,478,900	2,381,300	2,380,500	2,289,700	2,035,700	1,787,700	1,873,300
Current Liabilities	587,100	495,800	504,700	532,800	475,900	409,900	405,900	383,300
Long-Term Obligations	250,000	250,000	250,000	250,000	250,000	250,000	250,000	250,000
Total Liabilities	984,300	891,200	894,600	921,500	860,500	782,500	799,300	705,600
Stockholders' Equity	1,446,900	1,587,700	1,486,700	1,459,000	1,429,200	1,253,200	988,400	1,167,700
Share Outstanding	119,000	122,300	122,277	123,393	131,284	136,157	134,677	149,495
Statistical Record								
Return on Assets %	19.31	19.07	19.22	17.06	14.86	12.04	11.03	10.29
Return on Equity %	32.38	30.42	31.28	27.59	23.96	20.53	18.72	16.15
EBITDA Margin %	12.81	12.76	13.04	13.52	12.82	11.34	11.52	11.84
Net Margin %	6.41	6.34	6.53	6.75	6.13	4.94	4.74	4.84
Asset Turnover	2.67	2.64	2.69	2.53	2.43	2.44	2.32	2.13
Current Ratio	2.27	2.84	2.63	2.50	2.74	2.62	1.94	2.50
Debt to Equity	0.17	0.16	0.17	0.17	0.17	0.20	0.25	0.21
Price Range	81.74-48.58	70.21-41.04	58.12-39.15	57.36-31.41	34.22-22.45	29.17-19.39	30.38-14.20	21.40-16.30
P/E Ratio	21.86-12.99	19.50-11.40	16.90-11.38	18.50-10.13	14.44-9.47	17.26-9.70	21.86-10.22	17.40-13.25

FIGURE 20.2 **Reading Stock Quotations**

Reproduced at the top of the figure is a portion of the stock quotations listed in the *Wall Street Journal*. At the bottom is an enlargement of the same information. The numbers above each of the enlarged columns correspond to the numbered entries in the list of explanations that appears in the middle of the figure.

STOCK	(SYM)	CLOSE	NET CHG
ABB ADS	ABB	18.33	–0.45
ACE Ltd	ACE	68.41	–0.96
AES Cp	AES	11.72	–0.14
Aflac	AFL	42.89	–0.89

1. Name (often abbreviated) of the corporation: Aflac
2. Ticker symbol or letters that identify a stock for trading: AFL
3. Close is the price paid in the last transaction of the day: $42.89
4. Difference between the price paid for the last share sold today and the price paid for the last share sold on the previous day: –0.89 (in Wall Street terms, Aflac "closed down $0.89" on this day).

1 STOCK	2 (SYM)	3 CLOSE	4 NET CHG
ABB ADS	ABB	18.33	–0.45
ACE Ltd	ACE	68.41	–0.96
AES Cp	AES	11.72	–0.14
Aflac	AFL	42.89	–0.89

Source: The *Wall Street Journal*, December 13, 2011, C8.

FIGURE 20.3 **Reading Bond Quotations**

Reproduced at the top of the figure is bond information obtained from the Yahoo! Finance Web site. The numbers beside each line correspond to numbered entries in the list of explanations that appears at the bottom of the figure.

AT&T INC

OVERVIEW

1. Price	112.28
2. Coupon (%)	5.500
3. Maturity Date	1-Feb-2018
4. Yield to Maturity (%)	3.447
5. Current Yield (%)	4.899
6. Fitch Ratings	A
7. Coupon Payment Frequency	Semi-annual
8. First Coupon Date	1-Aug-2008
9. Type	Corporate
10. Callable	No

1. Price quoted as a percentage of the face value: $1,000 × 112.28% = $1,122.80
2. Coupon (%) is the rate of interest: 5.500 percent
3. Maturity Date is the date when bondholders will receive repayment: February 1, 2018
4. Yield to Maturity (%) takes into account the relationship among a bond's maturity value, the time to maturity, the current price, and the amount of interest: 3.447 percent
5. Current Yield (%) is determined by dividing the dollar amount of annual interest by the current price of the bond: ($55 ÷ $1,122.80 + 0.04899 = 4.899 percent)
6. Fitch Ratings is used to assess risk associated with this bond: A
7. Coupon Payment Frequency tells bondholders how often they will receive interest payments: Semi-annual
8. First Coupon Date: August 1, 2008
9. Type: Corporate
10. Callable: No

Source: The Yahoo! Finance bond Web site at http://bonds.yahoo.com (accessed March 12, 2012).

FIGURE 20.4 Reading Mutual-Fund Quotations

Reproduced at the top of the figure is a portion of the mutual-fund quotations as reported by the *Wall Street Journal*. At the bottom is an enlargement of the same information. The numbers above each of the enlarged columns correspond to numbered entries in the list of explanations that appears in the middle of the figure.

FUND	NAV	NET CHG	YTD %RET
Vanguard 500 Index	126.74	+0.46	9.4
TotBd	11.01	–	0.6
TotIntl	14.60	−0.04	11.8
TotSt	34.44	+0.16	10.1

1. The name of the mutual fund: Vanguard 500 Index
2. The net asset value (NAV) is the value of one share of the Vanguard 500 Index Fund: $126.74
3. The difference between the net asset value today and the net asset value on the previous trading day: +0.46 (in Wall Street terms, the "Vanguard 500 Index fund closed up $0.46" on this day)
4. The YTD% RET gives the total return for the Vanguard 500 Index fund for the year to date: 9.4%

1	2	3	4
FUND	NAV	NET CHG	YTD %RET
Vanguard 500 Index	126.74	+0.46	9.4
TotBD	11.01	–	0.6
TotIntl	14.60	−0.04	11.8
TotSt	34.44	+0.16	10.1

Source: The *Wall Street Journal*, March 10, 2012, B14.

Other Sources of Financial Information

In addition to the Internet, professional advisory services, and financial and newspaper coverage, other sources, which include brokerage firm reports, business periodicals, corporate reports, and securities averages offer information about investment alternatives.

Brokerage Firm Analysts' Reports Brokerage firms employ financial analysts to prepare detailed reports on individual corporations and their securities. Such reports are based on the corporation's sales, profits or losses, management, and planning, plus other information on the company, its industry, demand for its products, its efforts to develop new products, and the current economic environment. The reports, which may include buy or sell recommendations, are usually provided free to the clients of full-service brokerage firms. Brokerage firm reports may also be available from discount brokerage firms, although they may charge a fee.

Business Periodicals Business magazines such as *Bloomberg Businessweek*, *Fortune*, and *Forbes* provide not only general economic news but also detailed financial information about individual corporations. Trade or industry publications such as *Advertising Age* include information about firms in a specific industry. News magazines such as *U.S. News & World Report*, *Time*, and *Newsweek* feature financial news regularly. *Money, Kiplinger's Personal Finance Magazine, Smart Money*, and similar magazines provide information and advice designed to improve your investment skills. These periodicals are available at libraries and are sold at newsstands and by subscription. Many of these same periodicals sponsor an online Web site that may contain all or selected articles that are contained in the print version.

Corporate Reports Publicly held corporations must publish annual reports which include a description of the company's performance, information about the firm's products or services, and detailed financial statements that readers can use to evaluate the firm's actual performance. There should also be a letter from the accounting firm that audited the corporation. As mentioned in Chapter 17, an audit does not guarantee that a company has not "cooked" the books, but it does imply that the company has followed generally accepted accounting principles to report revenues, profits, assets, liabilities, and other financial information.

In addition, a corporation issuing a new security must—by law—prepare a prospectus and ensure that copies are distributed to potential investors. A **prospectus** is a detailed, written description of a new security, the issuing corporation, and the corporation's top management. A corporation's prospectus and its annual reports are available to the general public. You can request both an annual report and a prospectus by mail or telephone. In addition you can obtain an annual report, prospectus, or other financial information online. It's simple: Go to the corporation's Web site and click on "Investor Relations."

Security Averages

Investors often gauge the stock market through the security averages reported in newspapers and on television news programs. A **security average (or security index)** is an average of the current market prices of selected securities. For example, the Dow Jones Industrial Average and the Standard & Poor 500 Stock Index are both used by investors to track the U.S. stock market. Today, there are averages for not only stocks, but also averages for bonds, U.S. Treasury securities, mutual funds, real estate, commodities, natural resources, and many popular investments. Over a period of time, these averages indicate price trends, but they do not predict the performance of individual investments. At best, they can give the investor a "feel" for what is happening to investment prices.

prospectus a detailed, written description of a new security, the issuing corporation, and the corporation's top management

security average (or security index) an average of the current market prices of selected securities

HOW INVESTMENTS ARE BOUGHT AND SOLD

Think back over the material that was covered in this chapter. We began by discussing why it is important to examine your current financial situation and the need to manage your money. Next we talked about the factors that influence your choice of investments,

7 Understand how different investments are bought and sold.

how successful investors are involved in their investment program, and conservative and speculative investment alternatives. Then, in the last section, we discussed how you can evaluate different investment alternatives in order to make an informed decision to buy or sell an investment. Once you understand the information in the previous sections and have researched a potential investment, you can use the options described in this section to buy or sell an investment.

Purchasing Stocks and Bonds

To purchase a Geoffrey Beene sweater, you simply walk into a store that sells these sweaters, choose one, and pay for it. To purchase stocks and bonds, you work through a brokerage firm. In turn, an employee of the brokerage firm buys or sells securities for you.

Brokerage Firms and Account Executives An **account executive**—sometimes called a *stockbroker* or *registered representative*—is an individual who buys and sells securities for clients. Before choosing an account executive, you should have already determined your investment goals. Then you must be careful to communicate these goals to the account executive so that she or he can do a better job of advising you. You must also decide whether you need a *full-service* broker or a *discount* broker. A full-service broker usually charges higher commissions when compared to a discount broker. To help decide if you should use a full-service or a discount brokerage firm, you should consider how much help you need when making an investment decision. Many full-service brokerage firms argue that you need a professional to help you make important investment decisions. Although this may be true for some investors, most account executives employed by full-service brokerage firms are too busy to spend unlimited time with you on a one-on-one basis, especially if you are investing a small amount. On the other side, many discount brokerage firms argue that you alone are responsible for making your investment decisions. Furthermore, they argue that discount brokerage firms have both the personnel and research materials to help you to become a better investor.

The Mechanics of a Transaction Once you decide on a particular stock or bond, you can telephone your account executive or use the Internet to place a market or limit order. A **market order** is a request that a security be purchased or sold at the current market price. Figure 20.5 illustrates one method of executing a market order to sell a stock listed on the New York Stock Exchange (NYSE) at its current market value. It is also possible for a brokerage firm to match a buy order for a security for one of its

account executive an individual, sometimes called a *stockbroker* or *registered representative,* who buys and sells securities for clients

market order a request that a security be purchased or sold at the current market price

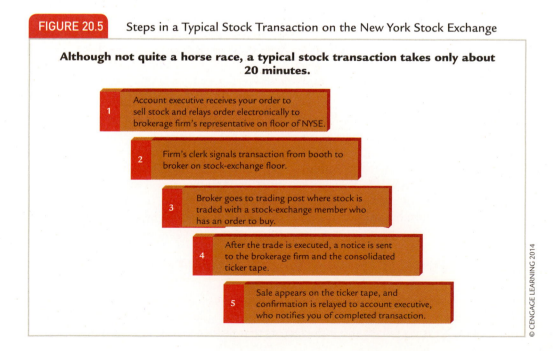

FIGURE 20.5   Steps in a Typical Stock Transaction on the New York Stock Exchange

Although not quite a horse race, a typical stock transaction takes only about 20 minutes.

1. Account executive receives your order to sell stock and relays order electronically to brokerage firm's representative on floor of NYSE.

2. Firm's clerk signals transaction from booth to broker on stock-exchange floor.

3. Broker goes to trading post where stock is traded with a stock-exchange member who has an order to buy.

4. After the trade is executed, a notice is sent to the brokerage firm and the consolidated ticker tape.

5. Sale appears on the ticker tape, and confirmation is relayed to account executive, who notifies you of completed transaction.

© CENGAGE LEARNING 2014

customers with a sell order for the same security from another of its customers. Matched orders are not completed through a security exchange or the over-the-counter market. Regardless of how the security is bought or sold, payment for stocks, bonds, and many other financial securities generally is required within three business days of the transaction.

A **limit order** is a request that a security be bought or sold at a price equal to or better than (lower for buying, higher for selling) some specified price. Suppose that you place a limit order to *sell* Coca-Cola common stock at $70 per share. Your broker's representative sells the stock only if the price is $70 per share or *higher*. If you place a limit order to *buy* Coca Cola at $70, the representative buys it only if the price is $70 per share or *lower*. Usually, a limit order is good for one day, one week, one month, or good until canceled.

Commissions Most brokerage firms have a minimum commission ranging from $7 to $25 for buying and selling stock. Additional commission charges are based on the number of shares and the value of stock bought and sold.

Table 20.7 shows typical commission fees charged by online brokerage firms. Generally, online transactions are less expensive when compared with the costs of trading securities through a full-service brokerage firm. As a rule of thumb, full-service brokerage firms charge as much as 1 to 2 percent of the transaction amount. Commissions for trading bonds, commodities, and options are usually lower than those for trading stocks.

Purchasing Mutual Funds, Real Estate, and Other Investments

The method used to buy or sell mutual funds depends on the type of fund you choose. Open-end funds, for example, can be purchased or sold directly from the investment company that sponsors the fund on any business day. Both closed-end funds and exchange-traded funds can be purchased or sold on any business day through a securities exchange or the over-the-counter market. The amount of sales charge also depends on the type of fund you purchase. The sales charge for load funds can be as high as 8 1/2 percent. For a load fund, the sales charge can be charged when you make a purchase or when you withdraw money from the fund. If you purchase a no-load fund, there is no sales charge. When purchasing shares in a load fund, you usually pay commission to buy *or* sell shares—but not to buy *and* sell shares. Reminder: For fund investments, you will also pay other fees that are usually assessed each year.

Although it is possible to buy or sell real estate without a real estate agent or broker, these professionals are involved in most transactions. Finding an agent or broker that can

© AP PHOTO/DAVID KARP

Case closed—150 years in prison. The common phrase "Don't do the crime if you can't do the time," explains why Bernard "Bernie" Madoff looks so unhappy in this photo. Mr. Madoff was found guilty of securities fraud when the Ponzi scheme he managed collapsed and investors lost almost $65 billion. Perhaps another common phrase, "Crime doesn't pay," is applicable to Bernie Madoff who will spend the rest of his life in prison.

TABLE 20.7	Typical Commission Costs Charged by Online Brokerage Firms		
	Internet ($)	Interactive Voice-Response Telephone System ($)	Broker-Assisted ($)
TD Ameritrade	$9.99	$34.99	$49.99
Charles Schwab	$8.95	13.95	33.95
Fidelity	7.95	12.95	32.95
Scottrade	7.00	17.00	27.00

Source: The Brokerage-Review.com Web site at www.brokerage-review.com (accessed March 13, 2012).

limit order a request that a security be bought or sold at a price that is equal to or better than some specified price

help you to either buy or sell an investment is especially important because she or he can provide professional advice, realistic market values for different properties, and help completing the transaction. You should expect to pay commissions when you sell a property.

A broker (or account executive) is usually involved in the purchase or sell of the most speculative investment alternatives listed in Table 20.2. For example, brokers can help you purchase commodities and precious metals. It is especially important to "know" the person you are dealing with when purchasing many of the speculative investments because of the potential for fraud and misrepresentation. It pays to be careful.

It should be apparent that vast sums of money are involved in securities trading. In an effort to protect investors from unfair treatment, both federal and state governments have acted to regulate securities trading.

Regulation of Securities Trading

Government regulation of securities was begun as a response to abusive and fraudulent practices in the sale of stocks, bonds, and other financial securities. Today, with so many news reports of banks with a portfolio of bad loans and of corporations that are in "hot water" over financial reporting problems that range from simple mistakes to out-and-out fraud, the concerns of both government officials and investors have grown.

Today, a regulatory pyramid consisting of four different levels exists to make sure that investors are protected. The U.S. Congress is at the top of the pyramid. Early on, Congress passed the Securities Act of 1933 (sometimes referred to as the Truth in Securities Act). This act provides for full disclosure. **Full disclosure** means that investors should have access to all important facts about stocks, bonds, and other securities so that they can make informed decisions. This act also requires that corporations issuing new securities file a registration statement and publish a prospectus. Since 1933, Congress has passed additional legislation that includes creating the Securities Investor Protection Corporation to protect investors. Congress also has passed legislation to curb insider-trading abuses. **Insider trading** occurs when insiders—board members, corporate managers, and employees—buy and sell a corporation's stock. Although insiders can buy and sell a corporation's stock, they must disclose their trading activities to the public. More recently, Congress passed the Sarbanes–Oxley Act to improve corporate accountability and financial reporting (see Chapter 17).

On the next level of the regulatory pyramid is the Securities and Exchange Commission (SEC), created in 1934 by the Securities Exchange Act of 1934. The SEC is the agency that enforces federal securities regulations. The SEC also supervises all national exchanges, investment companies, the OTC market, brokerage firms, and just about every other organization involved in trading securities.

On the next level of the regulatory pyramid are individual states. Today, most states require that new security issues be registered with a state agency and that brokerage firms, brokers, and investment advisors operating within the state be licensed. Most state regulations also provide for the prosecution of individuals accused of the fraudulent sale of stocks, bonds, and other securities.

The foundation and most important level of the regulatory pyramid is self-regulation by securities exchanges and brokerage firms. According to the NYSE, self-regulation—the way the securities industry monitors itself to create a fair and orderly trading environment—begins here.[10] To provide guidelines of ethical behavior, the NYSE has published rules, policies, and standards of conduct. These standards are applied to every member in the NYSE's investment community. The NYSE also conducts a thorough examination of each member firm that does business with the public at least once a year.[11] In addition, there are more than 300 brokerage firms that buy and sell securities for their customers. These firms are responsible for ensuring that their employees are highly trained and meet rigorous ethical standards.

Before they can start investing, most people have to decide on a career and obtain a job that will provide the money needed to finance an investment program. To help you find the right job (and the money needed to fund an investment program), read Appendix A where we provide information that can help you to explore different career options (see text Web site @ www.cengagebrain.com).

full disclosure requirement that investors should have access to all important facts about stocks, bonds, and other securities so that they can make informed decisions

insider trading the practice of board members, corporate managers, and employees buying and selling a corporation's stock

The Vanguard Group

Whether investors call the Vanguard Group, visit one of its offices, log onto its Web site, or use its apps, they'll find a wealth of information, tools, and advice to help them manage their investments and achieve their financial goals. Best-known for its low-cost index funds, Vanguard also offers brokerage services, retirement planning services, college investment accounts, and research and educational information for individuals. In addition, it manages pension funds for companies and for nonprofit organizations such as colleges and hospitals.

Because of Vanguard's long-time focus on mutual funds, it didn't begin offering exchange-traded funds (ETFs) until 2001, again keeping costs low as it does with its mutual funds. Now the company has become the third-largest U.S. provider of ETFs, and more than 45 percent of the funds it receives from clients flow into its ETFs—adding up to more than $200 billion in EFT assets.

Questions

1. When investing for a long-term goal such as retirement, how are the costs associated with your investments likely to affect your results? Explain your answer in terms of this chapter's concepts.

2. As an investor, what questions would you like to ask a Vanguard representative? How do these questions relate to your financial goals?

SUMMARY

 Explain why you should manage your personal finances and develop a personal investment program.

Many personal finance experts recommend that you begin the process of managing your money by determining your current financial condition. The first step often is to construct a personal income statement sheet and a personal balance sheet. You can also construct a personal budget. Before you begin investing, you must manage your credit card debts. For most people, the next step is to formulate realistic investment goals. A personal investment program then is designed to implement these goals. Many financial planners also suggest that the investor should establish an emergency fund equivalent to at least three months' living expenses. However, you may want to increase your emergency fund in anticipation of a crisis. Then additional funds may be invested according to the investment program. Finally, all investments should be monitored carefully, and if necessary, the investment program should be modified.

 Describe how the factors of safety, risk, income, growth, and liquidity affect your investment program.

Depending on their particular investment goals, investors seek varying degrees of safety, risk, income, growth, and liquidity from their investments. Safety is, in essence, freedom from the risk of loss. Generally, the greater the risk, the greater should be the potential return on an investment. To determine how much risk you are willing to assume, many investors calculate the rate of return. It is also possible to compare the rate of return for different investments that offer more or less risk. Income is the periodic return from an investment. Growth is an increase in the value of the investment. Liquidity is the ease with which an asset can be converted to cash.

 Recognize how you can reduce investment risk and increase investment returns.

The investments in your investment portfolio should be tailored to your goals, age, tolerance for risk, and financial resources. Asset allocation is the process of spreading your money among several different types of investments to lessen risk. Two other factors—the time your investments have to work for you and your age—should also be considered before deciding where to invest your money. To reduce investment risk and increase the returns on your investments, you should evaluate potential investments before investing your money, monitor the value of your investments on a regular basis, and keep accurate and current records.

 Explain the reasons people choose conservative investments including bank accounts and bonds.

In this section, we examined traditional investments that include bank accounts, government bonds, and corporate bonds. Although bank accounts and bonds can provide investment growth, they are generally purchased by investors who seek a predictable source of income. There are a number of different types of bonds and securities issued by both the U.S. government (see Table 20.3) and local governments. There are also a number of different types of corporate bonds. Both government and corporate bonds are a form of debt financing. As a result, bonds are generally considered a more conservative investment than stocks, mutual funds, or other more speculative investments.

 Identify the advantages and disadvantages of stocks, mutual funds, real estate, and more speculative investments.

With stock investments, investors can make money through dividend payments, an increase in the market value of the stock, or stock splits. The major advantages of mutual-fund investments are professional management and diversification. Today, there are mutual funds to meet just about any conceivable investment objective. The success of real estate investments is often tied to how well each investment alternative is evaluated. High-risk investment techniques can provide greater returns, but they also entail greater risk of loss. You can make money by selling short when the market value of a financial security decreases. An investor can also buy stock on margin by borrowing part of the purchase price, usually from a stock brokerage firm. Because you can purchase up to twice as much stock by using margin, you can increase your return on investment as long as the stock's market value increases. Other high-risk investments include stock options, derivatives, commodities, gemstones, precious metals, antiques, coins, and collectibles.

 Use financial information to evaluate investment alternatives.

Today, there is a wealth of information on stocks, bonds, and other securities and the firms that issue them. There is also a wealth of investment information on other types of investments, including mutual funds, real estate, and high-risk investment alternatives. Two popular sources—the Internet and newspapers—report daily securities transactions.

The Internet can also be used to obtain detailed research information about different investment alternatives. Often, the most detailed research information about securities—and the most expensive—is obtained from professional advisory services. In addition, brokerage firm reports, business periodicals, and corporate reports can also be used to evaluate different investment alternatives. Finally, there are a number of security indexes or averages that indicate price trends but reveal nothing about the performance of individual securities.

 Understand how different investments are bought and sold.

If you invest in stocks and bonds, chances are that you will use the services of an account executive who works for a brokerage firm. It is also possible to use a discount broker or trade securities online with a computer. Both a market order and a limit order can be used to purchase stocks on a securities exchange or in the over-the-counter market. Full-service brokerage firms usually charge higher commissions than discount brokerage firms. With the exception of mutual funds and real estate, you generally pay a commission to buy *and* sell stocks, bonds, commodities, and most other investments.

The method used to buy or sell mutual funds depends on the type of fund you choose. Open-end funds, for example, can be purchased or sold directly from the investment company that sponsors the fund on any business day. Both closed-end funds and exchange-traded funds can be purchased or sold on any business day through a securities exchange or the over-the-counter market. While it is possible to buy or sell real estate without the help of an agent or broker, most investors rely on the professional advice provided by agents and brokers to help complete a real estate transaction.

Today, a regulatory pyramid consisting of four different levels exists to make sure that investors are protected. The U.S. Congress, the Securities and Exchange Commission (SEC), individual states, and securities exchanges and brokerage firms are all involved in regulating the securities industry.

KEY TERMS

You should now be able to define and give an example relevant to each of the following terms:

net worth (581)	Standard & Poor's 500 Stock	exchange-traded fund	prospectus (603)
personal budget (581)	Index (587)	(ETF) (593)	security average (or security
personal investment (582)	asset allocation (587)	net asset value (NAV) (594)	index) (603)
financial planner (583)	municipal bond (589)	expense ratio (594)	account executive (604)
Dow Jones Industrial	stock dividend (591)	family of funds (595)	market order (604)
Average (584)	capital gain (591)	high-risk investment (596)	limit order (605)
blue-chip stock (585)	market value (591)	buying long (596)	full disclosure (606)
rate of return (585)	stock split (592)	selling short (596)	insider trading (606)
liquidity (586)	mutual fund (593)	margin requirement (597)	

1. How could developing a personal budget help you obtain the money needed to fund your investment program?
2. What is an "emergency fund," and why is it recommended?
3. What is the trade-off between safety and risk? How do you calculate rate of return?
4. In general, what kinds of investments provide income? What kinds provide growth?
5. How do you think that asset allocation, the time your investments have to work for you, and your age affect the choice of investments for someone who is 25 years old? For someone who is 59 years old?
6. Characterize the purchase of corporate and government bonds as an investment in terms of safety, risk, income, growth, and liquidity.

7. Describe the three methods by which investors can make money with stock investments.
8. An individual may invest in stocks either directly or through a mutual fund. How are the two investment methods different?
9. What are the risks and rewards of selling short and purchasing stocks on margin?
10. How could the Internet help you to research an investment?
11. In addition to the Internet, what other sources of financial information could help you to obtain your investment goals?
12. Would you use a full-service or a discount brokerage firm? Explain your answer.
13. What is the difference between a market order and a limit order?
14. Describe how the securities industry is regulated.

DISCUSSION QUESTIONS

1. For the time period between 2007 and 2009 people experienced dramatic declines in the market value of stocks, mutual funds, and other investments. Then, the market began to rebound. Based on the current state of the economy and the investment markets at the time you answer this question, do you think that it is a good time to begin an investment program? Justify your answer.
2. What personal circumstances might lead investors to emphasize income rather than growth in their investment planning? What might lead them to emphasize growth rather than income?
3. In this chapter, it was apparent that stocks have outperformed other investment alternatives over a long period of

time. With this fact in mind, why would investors choose to use asset allocation to diversify their investments?
4. What type of individual would invest in government bonds? In growth mutual funds? In real estate?
5. Suppose that you have just inherited 500 shares of IBM common stock. What would you do with it, if anything?
6. What kinds of information would you like to have before you invest in a particular common stock or mutual fund? From what sources can you get that information?
7. Take another look at Figure 20.1 (Mergent's research report for Dollar Tree, Inc.). Based on the research provided by Mergent's, would you buy stock in Dollar Tree? Justify your decision by providing specific examples from Figure 20.1.

Video Case 20.1   Taming the Debt Monster One Budget at a Time

Danny Kofke and his family have purchased some pretty nice things for themselves over the years. They own a lovely home that is about half paid for and have taken nice vacations to places like Europe. He and his wife, Tracy, recently bought a new washer, dryer, refrigerator, and 50-inch flat-screen TV. For the past seven years, Tracy has been able to stay at home to raise their children.

How have the Kofkes, who are only in their thirties, managed to live so well—especially in today's tough economy? Are they members of the 1 percent? Is Danny a highly paid executive or a Wall Street banker, perhaps?

Not hardly. Danny is actually a special-needs teacher who earns just a little over $40,000 a year. That's about $10,000 less than the average family in the United States makes. He and Tracy have figured out how to live well by paying careful attention to their finances. If the Kofkes stick to their financial plan, they are on track to retire with a million dollars or more.

Having a budget has been critical to their success. "The biggest mistake people make when it comes to their money is that they don't keep track of it, and they don't know how they are spending it," Danny explains. Sticking to the budget is also important. The Kofkes carefully prioritize their spending. They don't buy things they don't really want or need just because other people have them. "Don't worry about what your neighbors think," he says. "I know that's hard today when everybody feels like they have to keep up with the Joneses."

Trevor Thomas and his wife, Michelle, are good managers of their money as well. Like the Kofkes, they are diligent budgeters. "A budget can help keep you from overspending during any particular income period or in any particular area," says Trevor. It can help you plan for non-regular expenses, such as car repairs, and help you plan for your financial future." The rising price of gas and food are two areas the Thomases' budget has helped with. "We are a family of six, so these increases have hit us hard," he says. But by examining their budget, he and Michelle were able to figure out how to adjust their spending. As a result, they haven't run up debt on their credit cards like other people without a budget might have done.

In fact, not only do the Thomases have no credit card debt, they don't even have a mortgage on their home. After paying off all of their consumer debt, they regularly saved as much money as they could. They then built an impressive two-story home bit-by-bit over the course of a three-and-a-half-year period. "We built it from the ground up, contracting it and financing it completely by ourselves," Trevor says.

The difference between people who carry credit card debt and those who don't is that the people without it don't feel deprived when they can't have everything they want right away, says Bedda D'Angelo, a certified financial planner. "They're not cheap. They're just not willing to pay for things they don't need and haven't saved for." They also don't lie awake at night wondering how they are going to pay their bills.

The Kofkes admit they have been teased a time or two by people who think they are tightwads. They don't let it get them down, though. In today's debt-addicted world, where so many people, businesses, and even governments are broke, they're happy not to be under a monster-load of debt. "Do what's right for you and your family," Danny advises. "If people who don't do well managing their money—if they are laughing at you and telling you to change—then you must be doing something right."[12]

Questions

1. Is all debt bad? When does going into debt make sense?
2. Why is it so important for people to save and invest when they are young?
3. What steps can you take now to improve your financial outlook?

Case 20.2   Fidelity Helps Investors Prepare for Their Financial Future

Boston-based Fidelity Investments wants its 20 million customers to be able to manage their money and receive responsive assistance from anywhere at any time. Whether customers use an iPad or Android app, tweet for customer service, transfer money electronically, use online chat for service, call a broker, or place orders through the company's Web site, Fidelity is ready to help around the clock.

Founded in 1946, Fidelity now has 39,000 employees worldwide and offers 524 mutual funds that hold a total of $3.6 trillion in assets from individuals and institutional investors. Its mutual funds fall into four main categories: money market, stocks, bonds, and international securities. Fidelity is best known for its managed funds, such as the Contrafund and the Magellan Fund, although it also offers many indexed stock and bond funds. Over the years, it has expanded into a wide range of other financial services, including discount brokerage services, college savings accounts, credit cards, checking accounts, and online bill payment. Fidelity is also the country's largest administrator of 401(k) retirement accounts, handling retirement plans for more than 19,000 corporations, educational institutions, and nonprofit groups.

When the financial markets are open, Fidelity completes 345,000 securities trades per day for its customers. More than 3 million customers click on its user-friendly Web site every day to read analysts' reports, learn about investment and account options, view market update webinars, monitor their portfolios, or place a trade. For in-person service and advice, customers can visit one of the 168 Fidelity Investor Centers around the United States or attend a local seminar featuring Fidelity's investment experts.

Technology has always been one of Fidelity's strengths, so it's not surprising that the company has a Facebook page with 55,000 "likes" and a Twitter account with 48,000 followers. "Our expectation is that over time, we'll be interacting with not tens of thousands, but millions of people on these channels," says Fidelity's head of digital distribution. On the company's Web site, customers are invited to rate brokerage products and services for convenience, value, and features on a scale of one to five stars. In addition, they can write detailed reviews of what they like and don't like. This allows investors to see what other investors think, as well as giving Fidelity vital feedback and fresh ideas for new products.

Given Fidelity's diverse menu of offerings, "The time has arrived when a lot of people can do very well with a firm like Fidelity for all of their cash management [needs]," says a senior executive. For example, customers can deposit checks to non-retirement accounts using a smart phone app, and withdraw money from any local bank's ATM—Fidelity pays the ATM fee. In fact, customers now click to make 7 million transfers of money to or from Fidelity accounts every year, a number that is growing as customers shift more of their personal finances to Fidelity.

Are young people going to have the money they need to enjoy retirement decades in the future? Fidelity's research shows that, thanks to new U.S. laws, more employees are being automatically enrolled in their employers' retirement plans. The earlier people begin to build their savings, the more money they will have when they reach retirement age. Among the plans that Fidelity administers, more than half of company employees now participate in the plan—triple the number of employees who participated in 2006. When these people need help with other financial matters, Fidelity will be ready.[13]

Questions

1. Why would Fidelity offer 524 mutual funds? What are the advantages to the company and to investors?
2. What are the pros and cons of having a checking account with Fidelity rather than with a local bank or credit union?
3. If you were trying to evaluate a specific mutual fund, where would you obtain the research information needed to choose the right fund? Assuming that you have found the right fund, would you prefer to invest online or talk with a Fidelity broker to complete the transaction?

① SOCIAL MEDIA EXERCISE

A growing number of personal finance- and investment-related ventures are starting to take advantage of the power of social media by connecting people beyond the boundaries of Facebook and Twitter. Peer-to-peer collaboration is now part of a new reality in the personal finance and investment fields. Online investor communities like Investorvillage (http://investorvillage.com), Covestor (http://covestor.com), and SocialPicks (http://social-picks.com) allow people to compare their investment ideas and their investment portfolio's performance to those of peers, professional analysts, and financial bloggers. According to SocialPicks, the site is "a trusted online investing community where investors and traders invest smarter together."

1. Do you think peer-to-peer investment and personal finance Web sites like these are valuable? Why or why not?
2. Do you trust peer-to-peer collaboration when it comes to investing and personal finance? Why or why not?

② JOURNALING FOR SUCCESS

According to many financial experts, the logical place to begin the search for a quality investment is to examine the products and services you use on a regular basis—products and services that provide a high level of consumer satisfaction.

The preceding statement is based on the assumption that if you like the product or service and you feel that you got excellent value for your money, other consumers will too. And while it may be obvious, a satisfied, growing customer base can mean increased sales, profits, and ultimately higher stock values for the company that manufactured the product or provided the service.

Assignment

1. To begin this journal exercise, think about purchases you made over the last month. Describe one product or service that you feel "was worth the money."
2. For the product or service you chose, describe the attributes or features that impressed you.
3. Determine if the company that made the product or provided the service is a public company that has issued stock.* Then use the Internet or go to the library to research the investment potential for this company. Finally, describe why you feel this would be a good or bad investment at this time.

   *If the company that manufactured the product or service you chose is not a public company, choose another product or service.

③ DEVELOPING CRITICAL-THINKING SKILLS

One way to achieve financial security is to invest a stated amount of money on a systematic basis. This investment strategy is called *dollar-cost averaging*. When the cost is lower, your investment buys more shares. When the cost is higher, your investment buys fewer shares. A good way to begin investing is to select a mutual fund that meets your financial objectives and to invest the same amount each month or each year.

Assignment

1. Select several mutual funds from the financial pages of the *Wall Street Journal* or a personal finance periodical such as *Money, Kiplinger's Personal Finance,* or *SmartMoney* that provides information about mutual funds. Call the toll-free number for each fund and ask about its objectives. Furthermore, request that the company send you a prospectus and an annual report.
2. Select one fund that meets your financial objectives.
3. Prepare a table that includes the following data:
   a. An initial investment of $2,000 in the mutual fund you have selected
   b. The net asset value (NAV)
   c. The number of shares purchased
4. Record the investment information on a weekly basis. Look in the *Wall Street Journal* or on the Internet to find the NAV for each week.
5. Determine the value of your investment until the end of the semester.
6. Write a report describing the results. Include a summary of what you learned about investments. Be sure to indicate if you think that dollar-cost averaging (investing another $2,000 next year) would be a good idea.

④ BUILDING TEAM SKILLS

Investing in stocks can be a way to beat inflation and accumulate money. Traditionally, stocks have earned just below 10 percent per year since 1926. Bonds and certificates of deposit, on the other hand, often earn little more than the inflation rate, making it very difficult to accumulate enough money for retirement.

Assignment

1. Form teams of three people. The teams will compete against each other, striving for the largest gain in investments.
2. Assume that you are buying stock in three companies; some should be listed on the NYSE, and some should be traded in the Nasdaq over-the-counter market.
   a. Research different investments, and narrow your choices to three different stocks.
   b. Divide your total investment of $25,000 into three amounts.
   c. Determine the number of shares of stock you can purchase in each company by dividing the budgeted amount by the price of the stock. Allow enough money to pay for the commission. To find the cost of the stock, multiply the number of shares you are going to purchase by the closing price of the stock.

d. Assume that the commission is 1 percent. Calculate it by multiplying the cost of the stock by 0.01. Add the dollar amount of commission to the cost of the stock to determine the total purchase price.

3. Set up a table to reflect the following information:
   a. Name of the company
   b. Closing price per share
   c. Number of shares purchased
   d. Amount of the commission
   e. Cost of the stock

4. Record the closing price of the stock on a weekly basis. Prepare a chart to use for this step.

5. Before the end of the semester, assume that you sell the stock.
   a. Take the closing price on the day you sell your stocks and multiply it by the number of shares; then calculate the commission at 1 percent.
   b. Deduct the amount of commission from the selling price of the stock. This is the total return on your investment.

6. Calculate your profit or loss. Subtract the total purchase price of the stock from the total return. If the total return is less than the total purchase price, you have a loss.

7. Prepare a report summarizing the results of the project. Include the table and individual stock charts, as well as a statement describing what you learned about investing in stocks.

⑤ RESEARCHING DIFFERENT CAREERS

Today many people choose a personal financial advisor to help develop an investment program that will help them achieve their financial goals. Not only is this career choice an opportunity to help others, it is also one of the fastest growing career fields in the United States. According to the *Occupational Outlook Handbook*, the job opportunities for personal financial advisors are expected to increase by 32 percent between now and the year 2020. For help completing this exercise, use the *Occupational Outlook Handbook* in your college's library or career center or go to www .bls.gov/ooh.

Assignment

1. Answer the following questions based on information obtained in the *Occupational Outlook Handbook*.
   a. What is the nature of the work performed by personal financial advisors?
   b. What type of training or qualifications is required for a career in financial planning?
   c. Where are the job opportunities for personal financial advisors?
   d. What are typical annual wages for a personal financial advisor?

2. Summarize your findings in a report. Be sure to include if you would choose this career and why.

Running a Business   PART 7   Graeter's

Plans for Financing Growth

Almost as soon as Richard, Chip, and Robert Graeter became fourth-generation owners of the business their family had built, they started talking about expansion. They worked with Kroger, now their largest distribution partner, to put pints of Graeter's ice cream on store shelves many miles from the company's Cincinnati headquarters. Year by year, they increased their distribution reach with new retail partners—which meant they would need sufficient production capacity to fill all their orders, especially during months of peak demand.

Graeter's Reading Road factory, opened in 1934, was a printing plant before its conversion to ice-cream production. But it was bursting at the seams, and despite dramatic improvements in production efficiency, the Graeters recognized the increasingly urgent need to construct a new facility to support ongoing expansion.

FROM ONE FACTORY TO TWO

The economic situation was less than ideal for obtaining financing for a new factory, because the country—and the world—was in the grip of a severe and prolonged financial crisis. After scouting possible locations and exploring various options, Graeter's signed a 20-year deal with the city of Cincinnati. It paid the city a token amount for land in the Bond Hill neighborhood and borrowed $10 million from the city to pay for construction of a new 28,000-square-foot factory. The loan carried low interest rates and would be repaid over 20 years. In turn, Cincinnati issued $10 million in bonds to provide Graeter's with this funding.

Graeter's received a total package of financial incentives worth $3.3 million toward its new Bond Hill factory. In exchange, Graeter's committed to "stay and grow" in Cincinnati for at least 20 years, creating new jobs when the facility opened and even more as Graeter's growth continued.

Following months of construction, the new facility officially opened in 2010, during Graeter's landmark 140th anniversary year. "As a Cincinnati-based, family-run company, we are proud of our association with this wonderful city and look forward to new generations of success," said Richard Graeter II, Graeter's CEO. "We are incredibly grateful [for the City's assistance], because not only will their support help us expand nationally, but it is also helping us create jobs locally."

FROM TWO FACTORIES TO THREE

Even as the Bond Hill facility was nearing opening day, Graeter's was presented with an unexpected opportunity. Its largest franchisee wanted to sell the franchise operation, complete with stores and an ice-cream factory, and Graeter's had the right to buy the franchise back. The timing was almost perfect for its growth strategy, giving Graeter's not one, not two, but three production facilities to fuel expansion. On the other hand, how would the company pay for this unanticipated acquisition?

"That was not planned, not part of our strategic vision," explains Richard Graeter, "but the opportunity came up, and we had to look at it." If the Graeters decided to move ahead with the acquisition, "we had to come up with several millions of dollars in additional financing over and above what we had borrowed to build our new plant. So that means working with the bankers and lawyers and accountants to model how the business would look after the acquisition to determine if it makes financial sense, and then going out and raising the investment that you need to make the acquisition."

In the end, after looking at what the business had done in the past and where it was going in the future, the three great-grandsons of Graeter's founders decided that this unexpected acquisition would be a good move. They put together the financing needed to buy the stores and factory from the franchisee. Now Graeter's has the added strength of a sizable retail chain as well as three factories equipped to make the company's signature French-pot ice cream, one small batch after another—the right combination of ingredients for expanding from coast to coast and beyond.[14]

Questions

1. What kinds of questions do you think Cincinnati officials asked Graeter's owners before agreeing to loan the company $10 million? Why would Graeter's go with this financing arrangement rather than borrowing from a bank to pay for the Bond Hill factory?
2. One of the financing strategies Graeter's has not used is to sell common stock to the general public. Why would Graeter's hesitate to go public? Do you agree with its decision to use debt rather than equity financing?
3. As an investor, would you be willing to buy shares in Graeter's if it decided to go public through an IPO? Explain why the company's stock would or would not be a good investment for you.

Building a Business Plan   PART 7

In this last section, provide some information about your exit strategy, and discuss any potential trends, problems, or risks that you may encounter. These risks and assumptions could relate to your industry, markets, company, or personnel. Make sure to incorporate important information not included in other parts of the business plan in an appendix. Now is also the time to go back and prepare the executive summary, which should be placed at the beginning of the business plan.

THE EXIT STRATEGY COMPONENT

Your exit strategy component should at least include answers to the following questions:

7.1 How do you intend to get yourself (and your money) out of the business?

7.2 Will your children take over the business, or do you intend to sell it later?

7.3 Do you intend to grow the business to the point of an IPO?

7.4 How will investors get their money back?

THE CRITICAL RISKS AND ASSUMPTIONS COMPONENT

Your critical risks and assumptions component should answer at least the following questions:

7.5 What will you do if your market does not develop as quickly as you predicted? What if your market develops too quickly?

7.6 What will you do if your competitors underprice or make your product obsolete?

7.7 What will you do if there is an unfavorable industry-wide trend?

7.8 What will happen if trained workers are not available as predicted?

7.9 What will you do if there is an erratic supply of products or raw materials?

THE APPENDIX COMPONENT

Supplemental information and documents are often included in an appendix. Here are a few examples of some documents that can be included:

- Résumés of owners and principal managers
- Advertising samples and brochures
- An organization chart
- Floor plans of a retail facility or factory

REVIEW OF BUSINESS PLAN ACTIVITIES

As you have discovered, writing a business plan involves a long series of interrelated steps. As with any project involving a number of complex steps and calculations, your business plan should be reviewed carefully and revised before you present it to potential investors or lenders.

Remember, there is one more component you need to prepare after your business plan is completed: The executive summary should be written last, but because of its importance, it appears after the introduction.

THE EXECUTIVE SUMMARY COMPONENT

In the executive summary, give a one- to two-page overview of your entire business plan. This is the most important part of the business plan and is of special interest to busy bankers, investors, and other interested parties. Remember, this section is a summary; more detailed information is provided in the remainder of your business plan.

Make sure that the executive summary captures the reader's attention instantly in the first sentence by using a key selling point or benefit of the business.

Your executive summary should include answers to at least the following:

7.10 *Company information*. What product or service do you provide? What is your competitive advantage? When will the company be formed? What are your company objectives? What is the background of you and your management team?

7.11 *Market opportunity*. What is the expected size and growth rate of your market, your expected market share, and any relevant market trends?

Once again, review your answers to all the questions in the preceding parts to make sure that they are all consistent throughout the entire business plan.

Although many would-be entrepreneurs are excited about the prospects of opening their own business, remember that it takes a lot of hard work, time, and in most cases a substantial amount of money. Though the business plan provides an enormous amount of information about your business, it is only the first step. Once it is completed, it is now your responsibility to implement the plan. Good luck in your business venture.

ENDNOTES

1. Sources: Based on information in Chris Flood, "Vanguard ETF Assets Surge to Top $200 bn," *Financial Times,* March 25, 2012, www.ft.com; Jackie Noblett, "Vanguard Drives Home Low-Cost Mantra, in a Mobile Café," *Financial Times,* March 21, 2012, www.ft.com; Jason Kephart, "Vanguard Steps Up Efforts to Woo Advisers," *Investment News,* March 12, 2012, p. 2; Robert Steyer, "Providers Going Big with Technology," *Pensions & Investments,* October 31, 2011, p. 2; www.vanguard.com.

2. "Money 101 Lesson 4: Basics of Investing," the CNN/Money Web site at www.money.cnn.com, accessed March 8, 2012.

3. Suze Orman, *The Road to Wealth* (New York: Riverbend Books, 2001), 371.

4. The 2010 Advanced Micro Devices Annual Report, the Advanced Micro Devices Web site at www.amd.com, accessed March 8, 2012.

5. The Investment Company Institute Web site at www.ici.org, accessed August 21, 2012.

6. The Mutual Fund Education Alliance Web site at www.mfea.com, accessed March 8, 2012.

7. The Investment Company Institute Web site at www.ici.org, accessed August 21, 2012.

8. Bill Barker, "Loads," the Motley Fool Web site at www.fool.com, accessed March 8, 2012.

9. "The Low Down on Index Funds," the Investopedia Web site at www.investopedia.com, accessed October 23, 2009.

10. "The Regulatory Pyramid," the New York Stock Exchange Web site, accessed March 10, 2012.

11. Ibid.

12. Based on information in Julia Gabriel, "Little Money? Live Rich on Simple Financial Wisdom," *CBN News,* October 30, 2011, www.cbn.com; Trevor Thomas, "Living Debt Free," *American Thinker*, July 24, 2011, www.americanthinker.com; Shelly K. Schwartz, "You Can Live Debt Free," *CNBC*, August 12, 2008, www.cnbc.com.

13. Based on information in John McCrank, "E-Brokerages Tap Social Media for Faster Service," *Reuters*, April 5, 2012, www.reuters.com; Stephen Miller, "Pension Protection Act Changes Plan Design, Motivates Saving," *HR Magazine*, February 2012, p. 14; Dan McCrum, "Original US Fidelity Business Thrives," *Financial Times*, April 11, 2012, www.ft.com; Ari I. Weinberg, "Coming to Your 401(k): Fidelity ETFs?" *Wall Street Journal*, January 3, 2012, www.wsj.com; William Baldwin, "Who Needs Bank Branches?" *Forbes*, August 3, 2011, www.forbes.com; www.fidelity.com.

14. Sources: Based on information from Kimberly L. Jackson, "Graeter's Premium Chocolate Chip Ice Cream Lands at Stop & Shop," *Newark Star-Ledger (NJ)*, April 4, 2012, www.nj.com; "Graeter's Ice Cream Debuts in Bay Area," *Tampa Bay Times (St. Petersburg, FL)*, January 10, 2012, p. 4B; Jim Carper, "Graeter's Runs a Hands-on Ice Cream Plant," *Dairy Foods*, August 2011, pp. 36+; Jim Carper, "The Greater Good," *Dairy Foods*, August 2011, pp. 95+; "Graeter's Unveils New 'Mystery Flavor,'" *Dayton Daily News*, March 29, 2012, www.daytondailynews.com; Bob Driehaus, "A Cincinnati Ice Cream Maker Aims Big," *New York Times*, September 11, 2010, www.nytimes.com; Lucy May, "Graeter's Northern Kentucky Franchisee Puts Stores on the Block," *Business Courier*, August 6, 2010, http://cincinnati.bizjournals.com; "Cincinnati Officials Help Dedicate New Graeter's Plant," *Cincinnati Economic Development*, September 2010, www.choosecincy.com; www.graeters.com; interviews with company staff and Cengage videos about Graeter's.

GLOSSARY

A

absolute advantage the ability to produce a specific product more efficiently than any other nation (71)

accessory equipment standardized equipment used in a firm's production or office activities (360)

accountability the obligation of a worker to accomplish an assigned job or task (195)

account executive an individual, sometimes called a *stockbroker* or *registered representative,* who buys and sells securities for clients (604)

accounting the process of systematically collecting, analyzing, and reporting financial information (497)

accounting equation the basis for the accounting process: *assets = liabilities + owners' equity* (500)

ad hoc committee a committee created for a specific short-term purpose (204)

administrative manager a manager who is not associated with any specific functional area but who provides overall administrative guidance and leadership (175)

advertising a paid nonpersonal message communicated to a select audience through a mass medium (426)

advertising agency an independent firm that plans, produces, and places advertising for its clients (435)

advertising media the various forms of communication through which advertising reaches its audience (428)

affirmative action program a plan designed to increase the number of minority employees at all levels within an organization (55)

agency shop a workplace in which employees can choose not to join the union but must pay dues to the union anyway (317)

agent a middleman that expedites exchanges, represents a buyer or a seller, and often is hired permanently on a commission basis (403)

alien corporation a corporation chartered by a foreign government and conducting business in the United States (116)

analytical process a process in operations management in which raw materials are broken into different component parts (215)

analytic skills the ability to identify problems correctly, generate reasonable alternatives, and select the "best" alternatives to solve problems (176)

annual report a report distributed to stockholders and other interested parties that describes the firm's operating activities and its financial condition (500)

arbitration the step in a grievance procedure in which a neutral third party hears the two sides of a dispute and renders a binding decision (318)

asset allocation the process of spreading your money among several different types of investments to lessen risk (587)

assets the resources that a business owns (500)

audit an examination of a company's financial statements and the accounting practices that produced them (497)

authority the power, within an organization, to accomplish an assigned job or task (195)

autocratic leadership task-oriented leadership style in which workers are told what to do and how to accomplish it; workers have no say in the decision-making process (177)

automatic vending the use of machines to dispense products (410)

automation the total or near-total use of machines to do work (233)

B

balance of payments the total flow of money into a country minus the total flow of money out of that country over some period of time (74)

balance of trade the total value of a nation's exports minus the total value of its imports over some period of time (73)

balance sheet (or statement of financial position) a summary of the dollar amounts of a firm's assets, liabilities, and owners' equity accounts at the end of a specific accounting period (500)

banker's acceptance a written order for a bank to pay a third party a stated amount of money on a specific date (539)

bargaining unit the specific group of employees represented by a union (312)

barter an exchange in which goods or services are traded directly for other goods or services without using money (25)

barter system a system of exchange in which goods or services are traded directly for other goods or services (522)

behavior modification a systematic program of reinforcement to encourage desirable behavior (288)

benchmarking a process used to evaluate the products, processes, or management practices of another organization that is superior in some way in order to improve quality (181)

bill of lading document issued by a transport carrier to an exporter to prove that merchandise has been shipped (86)

blog a Web site that allows a company to share information in order to not only increase the customer's knowledge about its products and services, but also to build trust (460)

blue-chip stock a safe investment that generally attracts conservative investors (585)

board of directors the top governing body of a corporation, the members of which are elected by the stockholders (117)

bond indenture a legal document that details all the conditions relating to a bond issue (571)

boycott a refusal to do business with a particular firm (320)

brand a name, term, symbol, design, or any combination of these that identifies a seller's products as distinct from those of other sellers (369)

brand equity marketing and financial value associated with a brand's strength in a market (371)

brand extension using an existing brand to brand a new product in a different product category (373)

brand loyalty extent to which a customer is favorable toward buying a specific brand (371)

brand mark the part of a brand that is a symbol or distinctive design (369)

brand name the part of a brand that can be spoken (369)

breakeven quantity the number of units that must be sold for the total revenue (from all units sold) to equal the total cost (of all units sold) (379)

broker a middleman that specializes in a particular commodity, represents either a buyer or a seller, and is likely to be hired on a temporary basis (403)

budget a financial statement that projects income, expenditures, or both over a specified future period (557)

bundle pricing packaging together two or more complementary products and selling them for a single price (384)

business the organized effort of individuals to produce and sell, for a profit, the goods and services that satisfy a society's needs (10)

business buying behavior the purchasing of products by producers, resellers, governmental units, and institutions (348)

business cycle the recurrence of periods of growth and recession in a nation's economic activity (20)

business ethics the application of moral standards to business situations (37)

business model represents a group of common characteristics and methods of doing business to generate sales revenues and reduce expenses (473)

business plan a carefully constructed guide for the person starting a business (144)

business product a product bought for resale, for making other products, or for use in a firm's operations (359)

business service an intangible product that an organization uses in its operations (360)

business-to-business (or B2B) model a model used by firms that conduct business with other businesses (474)

business-to-consumer (or B2C) model a model used by firms that focus on conducting business with individual consumers (475)

buying allowance a temporary price reduction to resellers for purchasing specified quantities of a product (441)

buying behavior the decisions and actions of people involved in buying and using products (348)

buying long buying stock with the expectation that it will increase in value and then can be sold at a profit (596)

C

capacity the amount of products or services that an organization can produce in a given time (221)

capital budget a financial statement that estimates a firm's expenditures for major assets and its long-term financing needs (558)

capital gain the difference between a security's purchase price and its selling price (591)

capital-intensive technology a process in which machines and equipment do most of the work (222)

capitalism an economic system in which individuals own and operate the majority of businesses that provide goods and services (14)

captioned photograph a picture accompanied by a brief explanation (442)

captive pricing pricing the basic product in a product line low, but pricing related items at a higher level (384)

carrier a firm that offers transportation services (414)

cash budget a financial statement that estimates cash receipts and cash expenditures over a specified period (557)

cash flow the movement of money into and out of an organization (555)

catalog marketing a type of marketing in which an organization provides a catalog from which customers make selections and place orders by mail, telephone, or the Internet (408)

catalog showroom a retail outlet that displays well-known brands and sells them at discount prices through catalogs within the store (404)

category killer a very large specialty store that concentrates on a single product line and competes on the basis of low prices and product availability (407)

caveat emptor a Latin phrase meaning "let the buyer beware" (48)

centralized organization an organization that systematically works to concentrate authority at the upper levels of the organization (196)

certificate of deposit (CD) a document stating that the bank will pay the depositor a guaranteed interest rate on money left on deposit for a specified period of time (534)

certified public accountant (CPA) an individual who has met state requirements for accounting education and experience and has passed a rigorous accounting examination (499)

chain of command the line of authority that extends from the highest to the lowest levels of an organization (191)

chain retailer a company that operates more than one retail outlet (404)

channel of distribution (or marketing channel) a sequence of marketing organizations that directs a product from the producer to the ultimate user (396)

check a written order for a bank or other financial institution to pay a stated dollar amount to the business or person indicated on the face of the check (533)

chief financial officer (CFO) a high-level corporate executive who manages a firm's finances and reports directly to the company's chief executive officer or president (553)

closed corporation a corporation whose stock is owned by relatively few people and is not sold to the general public (115)

closed shop a workplace in which workers must join the union before they are hired; outlawed by the Taft–Hartley Act (317)

cloud computing a type of computer usage in which services stored on the Internet are provided to users on a temporary basis (477)

code of ethics a guide to acceptable and ethical behavior as defined by the organization (41)

collateral real estate or property pledged as security for a loan (535)

collective bargaining the process of negotiating a labor contract with management (313)

command economy an economic system in which the government decides what goods and services will be produced, how they will be produced, for whom available goods and services will be produced, and who owns and controls the major factors of production (16)

commercial bank a profit-making organization that accepts deposits, makes loans, and provides related services to its customers (531)

commercial paper a short-term promissory note issued by a large corporation (526)

commission a payment that is a percentage of sales revenue (258)

commission merchant a middleman that carries merchandise and negotiates sales for manufacturers (403)

common stock stock owned by individuals or firms who may vote on corporate matters but whose claims on profits and assets are subordinate to the claims of others (116, 566)

communication skills the ability to speak, listen, and write effectively (176)

community shopping center a planned shopping center that includes one or two department stores and some specialty stores, along with convenience stores (411)

comparable worth a concept that seeks equal compensation for jobs requiring about the same level of education, training, and skills (257)

comparative advantage the ability to produce a specific product more efficiently than any other product (71)

comparison discounting setting a price at a specific level and comparing it with a higher price (385)

compensation the payment employees receive in return for their labor (256)

compensation system the policies and strategies that determine employee compensation (256)

competition rivalry among businesses for sales to potential customers (21)

component part an item that becomes part of a physical product and is either a finished item ready for assembly or a product that needs little processing before assembly (360)

computer-aided design (CAD) the use of computers to aid in the development of products (233)

computer-aided manufacturing (CAM) the use of computers to plan and control manufacturing processes (233)

computer-integrated manufacturing (CIM) a computer system that not only helps to design products but also controls the machinery needed to produce the finished product (234)

computer virus a software code designed to disrupt normal computer operations (477)

conceptual skills the ability to think in abstract terms (175)

consumer buying behavior the purchasing of products for personal or household use, not for business purposes (348)

consumer price index (CPI) a monthly index that measures the changes in prices of a fixed basket of goods purchased by a typical consumer in an urban area (19)

consumer product a product purchased to satisfy personal and family needs (359)

consumerism all activities undertaken to protect the rights of consumers (51)

consumer sales promotion method a sales promotion method designed to attract consumers to particular retail stores and to motivate them to purchase certain new or established products (439)

convenience product a relatively inexpensive, frequently purchased item for which buyers want to exert only minimal effort (359)

convenience store a small food store that sells a limited variety of products but remains open well beyond normal business hours (405)

convertible bond a bond that can be exchanged, at the owner's option, for a specified number of shares of the corporation's common stock (570)

contingency plan a plan that outlines alternative courses of action that may be taken if an organization's other plans are disrupted or become ineffective (171)

continuous process a manufacturing process in which a firm produces the same product(s) over a long period of time (234)

controlling the process of evaluating and regulating ongoing activities to ensure that goals are achieved (172)

cookie a small piece of software sent by a Web site that tracks an individual's Internet use (476)

cooperative an association of individuals or firms whose purpose is to perform some business function for its members (123)

cooperative advertising an arrangement whereby a manufacturer agrees to pay a certain amount of a retailer's media cost for advertising the manufacturer's product (441)

core competencies approaches and processes that a company performs well that may give it an advantage over its competitors (168)

corporate bond a corporation's written pledge that it will repay a specified amount of money with interest (569)

corporate culture the inner rites, rituals, heroes, and values of a firm (201)

corporate officers the chairman of the board, president, executive vice presidents, corporate secretary, treasurer, and any other top executive appointed by the board of directors (118)

corporation an artificial person created by law with most of the legal rights of a real person, including the rights to start and operate a business, to buy or sell property, to borrow money, to sue or be sued, and to enter into binding contracts (115)

cost of goods sold the dollar amount equal to beginning inventory *plus* net purchases *less* ending inventory (506)

countertrade an international barter transaction (89)

coupon an offer that reduces the retail price of a particular item by a stated amount at the time of purchase (440)

craft union an organization of skilled workers in a single craft or trade (304)

creative selling selling products to new customers and increasing sales to present customers (436)

credit immediate purchasing power that is exchanged for a promise to repay borrowed money, with or without interest, at a later date (540)

credit union a financial institution that accepts deposits from, and lends money to, only the people who are its members (532)

cross-functional team a team of individuals with varying specialties, expertise, and skills that are brought together to achieve a common task (200, 293)

crowdsourcing outsourcing tasks to a group of people in order to tap into the ideas of the crowd (465)

cultural (or workplace) diversity differences among people in a workforce owing to race, ethnicity, and gender (6, 249)

currency devaluation the reduction of the value of a nation's currency relative to the currencies of other countries (76)

current assets assets that can be converted quickly into cash or that will be used in one year or less (501)

current liabilities debts that will be repaid in one year or less (503)

current ratio a financial ratio computed by dividing current assets by current liabilities (510)

customary pricing pricing on the basis of tradition (384)

customer lifetime value a measure of a customer's worth (sales minus costs) to a business over one's lifetime (333)

customer relationship management (CRM) using information about customers to create marketing strategies that develop and sustain desirable customer relationships (333)

D

data numerical or verbal descriptions that usually result from some sort of measurement (488)

database a single collection of data and information stored in one place that can be used by people throughout an organization to make decisions (490)

data mining the practice of searching through data records looking for useful information (476)

data processing the transformation of data into a form that is useful for a specific purpose (493)

debenture bond a bond backed only by the reputation of the issuing corporation (570)

debit card a card that electronically subtracts the amount of your purchase from your bank account at the moment the purchase is made (536)

debt capital borrowed money obtained through loans of various types (558)

decentralized organization an organization in which management consciously attempts to spread authority widely in the lower levels of the organization (195)

decision making the act of choosing one alternative from a set of alternatives (179)

decision-support system (DSS) a type of computer program that provides relevant data and information to help a firm's employees make decisions (496)

delegation assigning part of a manager's work and power to other workers (194)

deflation a general decrease in the level of prices (18)

demand the quantity of a product that buyers are willing to purchase at each of various prices (22, 376)

demand deposit an amount on deposit in a checking account (524)

departmentalization the process of grouping jobs into manageable units (193)

departmentalization by customer grouping activities according to the needs of various customer populations (193)

departmentalization by function grouping jobs that relate to the same organizational activity (193)

departmentalization by location grouping activities according to the defined geographic area in which they are performed (193)

departmentalization by product grouping activities related to a particular product or service (193)

department store a retail store that (1) employs 25 or more persons and (2) sells at least home furnishings, appliances, family apparel, and household linens and dry goods, each in a different part of the store (404)

depreciation the process of apportioning the cost of a fixed asset over the period during which it will be used (503)

depression a severe recession that lasts longer than a typical recession and has a larger decline in business activity when compared to a recession (21)

design planning the development of a plan for converting an idea into an actual product or service (220)

directing the combined processes of leading and motivating (171)

direct-mail advertising promotional material mailed directly to individuals (429)

direct marketing the use of the telephone, Internet, and nonpersonal media to introduce products to customers, who can then purchase them via mail, telephone, or the Internet (408)

direct-response marketing a type of marketing in which a seller advertises a product and makes it available, usually for a short time period, through mail, telephone, or online orders (409)

direct selling the marketing of products to customers through face-to-face sales presentations at home or in the workplace (407)

discount a deduction from the price of an item (386)

discount rate the interest rate the Federal Reserve System charges for loans to member banks (528)

discount store a self-service general-merchandise outlet that sells products at lower-than-usual prices (404)

discretionary income disposable income *less* savings and expenditures on food, clothing, and housing (349)

disposable income personal income *less* all additional personal taxes (349)

dividend a distribution of earnings to the stockholders of a corporation (117)

domestic corporation a corporation in the state in which it is incorporated (116)

domestic system a method of manufacturing in which an entrepreneur distributes raw materials to various homes, where families process them into finished goods to be offered for sale by the merchant entrepreneur (25)

double-entry bookkeeping system a system in which each financial transaction is recorded as two separate accounting entries to maintain the balance shown in the accounting equation (500)

Dow Jones Industrial Average an average of 30 leading U.S. corporations that reflect the U.S. stock market as a whole (584)

draft issued by the exporter's bank, ordering the importer's bank to pay for the merchandise, thus guaranteeing payment once accepted by the importer's bank (86)

dumping exportation of large quantities of a product at a price lower than that of the same product in the home market (75)

E

e-business (electronic business) the organized effort of individuals to produce and sell *through the Internet,* for a profit, the products and services that satisfy society's needs (26, 470)

economic community an organization of nations formed to promote the free movement of resources and products among its members and to create common economic policies (83)

economic model of social responsibility the view that society will benefit most when business is left alone to produce and market profitable products that society needs (49)

economics the study of how wealth is created and distributed (13)

economy the way in which people deal with the creation and distribution of wealth (13)

electronic funds transfer (EFT) system a means of performing financial transactions through a computer terminal or telephone hookup (537)

embargo a complete halt to trading with a particular nation or of a particular product (75)

employee benefit a reward in addition to regular compensation that is provided indirectly to employees (259)

employee ownership a situation in which employees own the company they work for by virtue of being stockholders (291)

employee training the process of teaching operations and technical employees how to do their present jobs more effectively and efficiently (260)

empowerment making employees more involved in their jobs by increasing their participation in decision making (291)

entrepreneur a person who risks time, effort, and money to start and operate a business (14)

entrepreneurial leadership personality-based leadership style in which the manager seeks to inspire workers with a vision of what can be accomplished to benefit all stakeholders (178)

Equal Employment Opportunity Commission (EEOC) a government agency with the power to investigate complaints of employment discrimination and the power to sue firms that practice it (56)

equity capital money received from the owners or from the sale of shares of ownership in a business (558)

equity theory a theory of motivation based on the premise that people are motivated to obtain and preserve equitable treatment for themselves (282)

esteem needs our need for respect, recognition, and a sense of our own accomplishment and worth (278)

ethics the study of right and wrong and of the morality of the choices individuals make (37)

everyday low prices (EDLPs) setting a low price for products on a consistent basis (384)

exchange-traded fund (ETF) a fund that generally invests in the stocks or other securities contained in a specific stock or securities index (593)

exclusive distribution the use of only a single retail outlet for a product in a large geographic area (398)

executive information system (EIS) a computer-based system that facilitates and supports the decision-making needs of top managers and senior executives by providing easy access to both internal and external information (496)

expectancy theory a model of motivation based on the assumption that motivation depends on how much we want something and on how likely we think we are to get it (283)

expense ratio all the different management fees; 12b-1 fees, if any; and additional operating costs for a specific fund (594)

expert system a type of computer program that uses artificial intelligence to imitate a human's ability to think (496)

Export-Import Bank of the United States an independent agency of the U.S. government whose function is to assist in financing the exports of American firms (91)

exporting selling and shipping raw materials or products to other nations (72)

express warranty a written explanation of the producer's responsibilities in the event that a product is found to be defective or otherwise unsatisfactory (375)

external recruiting the attempt to attract job applicants from outside an organization (252)

F

factor a firm that specializes in buying other firms' accounts receivable (562)

factors of production resources used to produce goods and services (13)

factory system a system of manufacturing in which all the materials, machinery, and workers required to manufacture a product are assembled in one place (25)

family branding the strategy in which a firm uses the same brand for all or most of its products (373)

family of funds a group of mutual funds managed by one investment company (595)

feature article a piece (of up to 3,000 words) prepared by an organization for inclusion in a particular publication (442)

federal deficit a shortfall created when the federal government spends more in a fiscal year than it receives (21)

federal funds rate the interest rate at which a bank lends immediately available funds on deposit at the Fed to another bank overnight to meet the borrowing bank's reserve requirements (528)

Federal Reserve System the central bank of the United States responsible for regulating the banking industry (525)

financial accounting generates financial statements and reports for interested people outside an organization (498)

financial leverage the use of borrowed funds to increase the return on owners' equity (568)

financial management all the activities concerned with obtaining money and using it effectively (552)

financial manager a manager who is primarily responsible for an organization's financial resources (173)

financial plan a plan for obtaining and using the money needed to implement an organization's goals and objectives (556)

financial planner an individual who has had at least two years of training in investments, insurance, taxation, retirement planning, and estate planning and has passed a rigorous examination (583)

financial ratio a number that shows the relationship between two elements of a firm's financial statements (510)

first-line manager a manager who coordinates and supervises the activities of operating employees (173)

fiscal policy government influence on the amount of savings and expenditures; accomplished by altering the tax structure and by changing the levels of government spending (21)

fixed assets assets that will be held or used for a period longer than one year (502)

fixed cost a cost incurred no matter how many units of a product are produced or sold (379)

flexible benefit plan compensation plan whereby an employee receives a predetermined amount of benefit dollars to spend on a package of benefits he or she has selected to meet individual needs (260)

flexible manufacturing system (FMS) a single production system that combines electronic machines and computer-integrated manufacturing (234)

flextime a system in which employees set their own work hours within employer-determined limits (288)

foreign corporation a corporation in any state in which it does business except the one in which it is incorporated (116)

foreign-exchange control a restriction on the amount of a particular foreign currency that can be purchased or sold (76)

form utility utility created by converting production inputs into finished products (215, 333)

forum an interactive version of a community bulletin board and focuses on threaded discussions (462)

franchise a license to operate an individually owned business as though it were part of a chain of outlets or stores (151)

franchisee a person or organization purchasing a franchise (151)

franchising the actual granting of a franchise (151)

franchisor an individual or organization granting a franchise (151)

free enterprise the system of business in which individuals are free to decide what to produce, how to produce it, and at what price to sell it (4)

frequent-user incentive a program developed to reward customers who engage in repeat (frequent) purchases (441)

full disclosure requirement that investors should have access to all important facts about stocks, bonds, and other securities so that they can make informed decisions (606)

full-service wholesaler a middleman that performs the entire range of wholesaler functions (402)

functional middleman a middleman that helps in the transfer of ownership of products but does not take title to the products (396)

G

Gantt chart a graphic scheduling device that displays the tasks to be performed on the vertical axis and the time required for each task on the horizontal axis (228)

General Agreement on Tariffs and Trade (GATT) an international organization of 153 nations dedicated to reducing or eliminating tariffs and other barriers to world trade (81)

generally accepted accounting principles (GAAPs) an accepted set of guidelines and practices for companies reporting financial information and for the accounting profession (497)

general-merchandise wholesaler a middleman that deals in a wide variety of products (402)

general partner a person who assumes full or shared responsibility for operating a business (110)

generic product (or brand) a product with no brand at all (370)

goal an end result that an organization is expected to achieve over a one- to ten-year period (168)

goal-setting theory a theory of motivation suggesting that employees are motivated to achieve goals that they and their managers establish together (284)

grapevine the informal communications network within an organization (204)

green IT a term used to describe all of a firm's activities to support a healthy environment and sustain the planet (478)

grievance procedure a formally established course of action for resolving employee complaints against management (317)

gross domestic product (GDP) the total dollar value of all goods and services produced by all people within the boundaries of a country during a one-year period (18)

gross profit a firm's net sales *less* the cost of goods sold (506)

gross sales the total dollar amount of all goods and services sold during the accounting period (505)

H

hard-core unemployed workers with little education or vocational training and a long history of unemployment (56)

high-risk investment an investment made in the uncertain hope of earning a relatively large profit in a short time (596)

hostile takeover a situation in which the management and board of directors of a firm targeted for acquisition disapprove of the merger (124)

hourly wage a specific amount of money paid for each hour of work (258)

human resources management (HRM) all the activities involved in acquiring, maintaining, and developing an organization's human resources (246)

human resources manager a person charged with managing an organization's human resources programs (174)

human resources planning the development of strategies to meet a firm's future human resources needs (247)

hygiene factors job factors that reduce dissatisfaction when present to an acceptable degree but that do not necessarily result in high levels of motivation (279)

I

import duty (tariff) a tax levied on a particular foreign product entering a country (75)

import quota a limit on the amount of a particular good that may be imported into a country during a given period of time (75)

importing purchasing raw materials or products in other nations and bringing them into one's own country (72)

inbound marketing a marketing term that describes new ways of gaining attention and ultimately customers by creating content on a Web site that pulls customers in (464)

incentive payment a payment in addition to wages, salary, or commissions (258)

income statement a summary of a firm's revenues and expenses during a specified accounting period (504)

independent retailer a firm that operates only one retail outlet (404)

individual branding the strategy in which a firm uses a different brand for each of its products (373)

industrial union an organization of both skilled and unskilled workers in a single industry (305)

inflation a general rise in the level of prices (18)

infomercial a program-length televised commercial message resembling an entertainment or consumer affairs program (430)

informal group a group created by the members themselves to accomplish goals that may or may not be relevant to an organization (204)

informal organization the pattern of behavior and interaction that stems from personal rather than official relationships (204)

information data presented in a form that is useful for a specific purpose (488)

information technology (IT) officer a manager at the executive level who is responsible for ensuring that a firm has the equipment necessary to provide the information the firm's employees and managers need to make effective decisions (490)

initial public offering (IPO) occurs when a corporation sells common stock to the general public for the first time (563)

injunction a court order requiring a person or group either to perform some act or to refrain from performing some act (310)

insider trading the practice of board members, corporate managers, and employees buying and selling a corporation's stock (606)

inspection the examination of the quality of work-in-process (230)

institutional advertising advertising designed to enhance a firm's image or reputation (427)

intangible assets assets that do not exist physically but that have a value based on the rights or privileges they confer on a firm (503)

integrated marketing communications coordination of promotion efforts to ensure their maximal informational and persuasive impact on customers (425)

intensive distribution the use of all available outlets for a product (398)

intermittent process a manufacturing process in which a firm's manufacturing machines and equipment are changed to produce different products (234)

internal recruiting considering present employees as applicants for available positions (253)

international business all business activities that involve exchanges across national boundaries (71)

International Monetary Fund (IMF) an international bank with 188 member nations that makes short-term loans to developing countries experiencing balance-of-payment deficits (93)

International Organization for Standardization (ISO) a network of national standards institutes and similar organizations from over 160 different countries that is charged with developing standards for quality products and services that are traded throughout the globe (231)

interpersonal skills the ability to deal effectively with other people (176)

inventory control the process of managing inventories in such a way as to minimize inventory costs, including both holding costs and potential stock-out costs (226)

inventory management the process of managing inventories in such a way as to minimize inventory costs, including both holding costs and potential stock-out costs (412)

inventory turnover a financial ratio calculated by dividing the cost of goods sold in one year by the average value of the inventory (510)

investment banking firm an organization that assists corporations in raising funds, usually by helping to sell new issues of stocks, bonds, or other financial securities (564)

invisible hand a term created by Adam Smith to describe how an individual's personal gain benefits others and a nation's economy (14)

J

job analysis a systematic procedure for studying jobs to determine their various elements and requirements (251)

job description a list of the elements that make up a particular job (251)

job enlargement expanding a worker's assignments to include additional but similar tasks (287)

job enrichment a motivation technique that provides employees with more variety and responsibility in their jobs (287)

job evaluation the process of determining the relative worth of the various jobs within a firm (257)

job redesign a type of job enrichment in which work is restructured to cultivate the worker–job match (288)

job rotation the systematic shifting of employees from one job to another (192)

job security protection against the loss of employment (316)

job sharing an arrangement whereby two people share one full-time position (289)

job specialization the separation of all organizational activities into distinct tasks and the assignment of different tasks to different people (192)

job specification a list of the qualifications required to perform a particular job (251)

joint venture an agreement between two or more groups to form a business entity in order to achieve a specific goal or to operate for a specific period of time (123)

jurisdiction the right of a particular union to organize particular groups of workers (313)

just-in-time inventory system a system designed to ensure that materials or supplies arrive at a facility just when they are needed so that storage and holding costs are minimized (227)

K

key performance indicators (KPIs) measurements that define and measure the progress of an organization toward achieving its objectives (469)

knowledge management (KM) a firm's procedures for generating, using, and sharing the data and information (490)

L

labeling the presentation of information on a product or its package (375)

labor-intensive technology a process in which people must do most of the work (222)

labor union an organization of workers acting together to negotiate their wages and working conditions with employers (303)

leadership the ability to influence others (177)

leading the process of influencing people to work toward a common goal (171)

lean manufacturing a concept built on the idea of eliminating waste from all of the activities required to produce a product or service (232)

letter of credit a legal document issued by a bank or other financial institution guaranteeing to pay a seller a stated amount for a specified period of time (86, 538)

liabilities a firm's debts and obligations (500)

licensing a contractual agreement in which one firm permits another to produce and market its product and use its brand name in return for a royalty or other compensation (85)

lifestyle shopping center an open-air-environment shopping center with upscale chain specialty stores (411)

limited liability a feature of corporate ownership that limits each owner's financial liability to the amount of money that he or she has paid for the corporation's stock (119)

limited-liability company (LLC) a form of business ownership that combines the benefits of a corporation and a partnership while avoiding some of the restrictions and disadvantages of those forms of ownership (121)

limited-line wholesaler a middleman that stocks only a few product lines but carries numerous product items within each line (403)

limited partner a person who contributes capital to a business but has no management responsibility or liability for losses beyond the amount he or she invested in the partnership (110)

limited-service wholesaler a middleman that assumes responsibility for a few wholesale services only (403)

limit order a request that a security be bought or sold at a price that is equal to or better than some specified price (605)

line-and-staff structure an organizational structure that utilizes the chain of command from a line structure in combination with the assistance of staff managers (198)

line extension development of a new product that is closely related to one or more products in the existing product line but designed specifically to meet somewhat different customer needs (364)

line manager a position in which a person makes decisions and gives orders to subordinates to achieve the organization's goals (198)

line of credit a loan that is approved before the money is actually needed (535)

line structure an organizational structure in which the chain of command goes directly from person to person throughout the organization (198)

liquidity the ease with which an asset can be converted into cash (501, 586)

lockout a firm's refusal to allow employees to enter the workplace (320)

long-term financing money that will be used for longer than one year (556)

long-term liabilities debts that need not be repaid for at least one year (503)

lump-sum salary increase an entire pay raise taken in one lump sum (258)

M

macroeconomics the study of the national economy and the global economy (13)

maintenance shop a workplace in which an employee who joins the union must remain a union member as long as he or she is employed by the firm (317)

major equipment large tools and machines used for production purposes (359)

Malcolm Baldrige National Quality Award an award given by the President of the United States to organizations judged to be outstanding in specific managerial tasks that lead to improved quality for both products and services (229)

malware a general term that describes software designed to infiltrate a computer system without the user's consent (477)

management the process of coordinating people and other resources to achieve the goals of an organization (165)

management by objectives (MBO) a motivation technique in which managers and employees collaborate in setting goals (285)

management development the process of preparing managers and other professionals to assume increased responsibility in both present and future positions (260)

management information system (MIS) a system that provides managers and employees with the information they need to perform their jobs as effectively as possible (490)

managerial accounting provides managers and employees with the information needed to make decisions about a firm's financing, investing, marketing, and operating activities (498)

manufacturer (or producer) brand a brand that is owned by a manufacturer (370)

manufacturer's sales branch essentially a merchant wholesaler that is owned by a manufacturer (403)

manufacturer's sales office essentially a sales agent owned by a manufacturer (403)

margin requirement the portion of the price of a stock that cannot be borrowed (597)

market a group of individuals or organizations, or both, that need products in a given category and that have the ability, willingness, and authority to purchase such products (336)

market economy an economic system in which businesses and individuals decide what to produce and buy, and the market determines quantities sold and prices (15)

marketing the activity, set of institutions, and processes for creating, communicating, delivering, and exchanging offerings that have value for customers, clients, partners, and society at large (334)

marketing concept a business philosophy that a firm should provide goods and services that satisfy customers' needs through a coordinated set of activities that allow the firm to achieve its objectives (334)

marketing information system a system for managing marketing information that is gathered continually from internal and external sources (344)

marketing manager a manager who is responsible for facilitating the exchange of products between an organization and its customers or clients (174)

marketing mix a combination of product, price, distribution, and promotion developed to satisfy a particular target market (337)

marketing plan a written document that specifies an organization's resources, objectives, strategy, and implementation and control efforts to be used in marketing a specific product or product group (342)

marketing research the process of systematically gathering, recording, and analyzing data concerning a particular marketing problem (344)

marketing strategy a plan that will enable an organization to make the best use of its resources and advantages to meet its objectives (337)

market order a request that a security be purchased or sold at the current market price (604)

market price the price at which the quantity demanded is exactly equal to the quantity supplied (23)

market segment a group of individuals or organizations within a market that share one or more common characteristics (339)

market segmentation the process of dividing a market into segments and directing a marketing mix at a particular segment or segments rather than at the total market (339)

market value the price of one share of a stock at a particular time (591)

markup the amount a seller adds to the cost of a product to determine its basic selling price (379)

Maslow's hierarchy of needs a sequence of human needs in the order of their importance (277)

mass production a manufacturing process that lowers the cost required to produce a large number of identical or similar products over a long period of time (215)

master limited partnership (MLP) a limited partnership that has units of ownership that can be traded on security exchanges much like shares of ownership in a corporation (111)

materials handling the actual physical handling of goods, in warehouses as well as during transportation (414)

materials requirements planning (MRP) a computerized system that integrates production planning and inventory control (227)

matrix structure an organizational structure that combines vertical and horizontal lines of authority, usually by superimposing product departmentalization on a functionally departmentalized organization (199)

maturity date the date on which a corporation is to repay borrowed money (570)

measure of value a single standard or "yardstick" used to assign values to, and compare the values of, products, services, and resources (522)

media sharing sites allow users to upload multimedia content including photos, videos, and podcasts (461)

mediation the use of a neutral third party to assist management and the union during their negotiations (320)

medium of exchange anything accepted as payment for products, services, and resources (522)

merchant middleman a middleman that actually takes title to products by buying them (396)

merchant wholesaler a middleman that purchases goods in large quantities and then sells them to other wholesalers or retailers and to institutional, farm, government, professional, or industrial users (402)

merger the purchase of one corporation by another (124)

microeconomics the study of the decisions made by individuals and businesses (13)

middleman (or marketing intermediary) a marketing organization that links a producer and user within a marketing channel (396)

middle manager a manager who implements the strategy and major policies developed by top management (173)

Millennials tech-savvy digital natives born after 1980 (463)

minority a racial, religious, political, national, or other group regarded as different from the larger group of which it is a part and that is often singled out for unfavorable treatment (55)

mission a statement of the basic purpose that makes an organization different from others (167)

missionary salesperson a salesperson—generally employed by a manufacturer—who visits retailers to persuade them to buy the manufacturer's products (436)

mixed economy an economy that exhibits elements of both capitalism and socialism (15)

monetary policies Federal Reserve decisions that determine the size of the supply of money in the nation and the level of interest rates (21)

money anything a society uses to purchase products, services, or resources (522)

monopolistic competition a market situation in which there are many buyers along with a relatively large number of sellers who differentiate their products from the products of competitors (23)

monopoly a market (or industry) with only one seller, and there are barriers to keep other firms from entering the industry (24)

morale an employee's feelings about his or her job and superiors and about the firm itself (275)

mortgage bond a corporate bond secured by various assets of the issuing firm (570)

motivating the process of providing reasons for people to work in the best interests of an organization (171)

motivation the individual internal process that energizes, directs, and sustains behavior; the personal "force" that causes you or me to behave in a particular way (275)

motivation factors job factors that increase motivation, although their absence does not necessarily result in dissatisfaction (279)

motivation–hygiene theory the idea that satisfaction and dissatisfaction are separate and distinct dimensions (279)

multilateral development bank (MDB) an internationally supported bank that provides loans to developing countries to help them grow (93)

multinational enterprise a firm that operates on a worldwide scale without ties to any specific nation or region (89)

multiple-unit pricing the strategy of setting a single price for two or more units (383)

municipal bond sometimes called a *muni,* a debt security issued by a state or local government (589)

mutual fund pools the money of many investors—its shareholders—to invest in a variety of different securities (593)

N

National Alliance of Business (NAB) a joint business–government program to train the hard-core unemployed (57)

national bank a commercial bank chartered by the U.S. Comptroller of the Currency (531)

national debt the total of all federal deficits (21)

National Labor Relations Board (NLRB) the federal agency that enforces the provisions of the Wagner Act (309)

natural monopoly an industry requiring huge investments in capital and within which any duplication of facilities would be wasteful and thus not in the public interest (24)

need a personal requirement (277)

negotiated pricing establishing a final price through bargaining (383)

neighborhood shopping center a planned shopping center consisting of several small convenience and specialty stores (411)

net asset value (NAV) current market value of a mutual fund's portfolio minus the mutual fund's liabilities divided by the number of outstanding shares (594)

net income occurs when revenues exceed expenses (506)

net loss occurs when expenses exceed revenues (506)

net sales the actual dollar amounts received by a firm for the goods and services it has sold after adjustment for returns, allowances, and discounts (506)

network structure an organizational structure in which administration is the primary function, and most other functions are contracted out to other firms (201)

net worth the difference between the value of your total assets and your total liabilities (581)

news release a typed page of about 300 words provided by an organization to the media as a form of publicity (442)

non-price competition competition based on factors other than price (377)

nonstore retailing a type of retailing whereby consumers purchase products without visiting a store (407)

nontariff barrier a nontax measure imposed by a government to favor domestic over foreign suppliers (75)

not-for-profit corporation a corporation organized to provide a social, educational, religious, or other service rather than to earn a profit (122)

NOW account an interest-paying checking account; *NOW* stands for *negotiable order of withdrawal* (534)

O

objective a specific statement detailing what an organization intends to accomplish over a shorter period of time (168)

odd-number pricing the strategy of setting prices using odd numbers that are slightly below whole-dollar amounts (383)

off-price retailer a store that buys manufacturers' seconds, overruns, returns, and off-season merchandise for resale to consumers at deep discounts (407)

oligopoly a market (or industry) in which there are few sellers (24)

online retailing retailing that makes products available to buyers through computer connections (409)

open corporation a corporation whose stock can be bought and sold by any individual (115)

open-market operations the buying and selling of U.S. government securities by the Federal Reserve System for the purpose of controlling the supply of money (528)

operating expenses all business costs other than the cost of goods sold (506)

operational plan a type of plan designed to implement tactical plans (171)

operations management all the activities required to produce goods and services (213)

operations manager a manager who manages the systems that convert resources into goods and services (174)

order-getter a salesperson who is responsible for selling a firm's products to new customers and increasing sales to present customers (436)

order processing activities involved in receiving and filling customers' purchase orders (413)

order-taker a salesperson who handles repeat sales in ways that maintain positive relationships with customers (436)

organization a group of two or more people working together to achieve a common set of goals (190)

organization chart a diagram that represents the positions and relationships within an organization (190)

organizational height the number of layers, or levels, of management in a firm (197)

organizing the grouping of resources and activities to accomplish some end result in an efficient and effective manner (171)

orientation the process of acquainting new employees with an organization (256)

out-of-home advertising short promotional messages on billboards, posters, signs, and transportation vehicles (430)

outsourcing the process of finding outside vendors and suppliers that provide professional help, parts, or materials at a lower cost (471)

over-the-counter (OTC) market a network of dealers who buy and sell the stocks of corporations that are not listed on a securities exchange (565)

overtime time worked in excess of 40 hours in one week (under some union contracts, time worked in excess of eight hours in a single day) (316)

owners' equity the difference between a firm's assets and its liabilities (500)

P

packaging all the activities involved in developing and providing a container with graphics for a product (373)

participative leadership leadership style in which all members of a team are involved in identifying essential goals and developing strategies to reach those goals (177)

partnership a voluntary association of two or more persons to act as co-owners of a business for profit (110)

part-time work permanent employment in which individuals work less than a standard work week (289)

penetration pricing the strategy of setting a low price for a new product (382)

perfect (or pure) competition the market situation in which there are many buyers and sellers of a product, and no single buyer or seller is powerful enough to affect the price of that product (22)

performance appraisal the evaluation of employees' current and potential levels of performance to allow managers to make objective human resources decisions (262)

periodic discounting temporary reduction of prices on a patterned or systematic basis (383)

personal budget a specific plan for spending your income (581)

personal income the income an individual receives from all sources *less* the Social Security taxes the individual must pay (349)

personal investment the use of your personal funds to earn a financial return (582)

personal selling personal communication aimed at informing customers and persuading them to buy a firm's products (426)

PERT (Program Evaluation and Review Technique) a scheduling technique that identifies the major activities necessary to complete a project and sequences them based on the time required to perform each one (228)

physical distribution all the activities concerned with the efficient movement of products from the producer to the ultimate user (412)

physiological needs the things we require for survival (277)

picketing marching back and forth in front of a place of employment with signs informing the public that a strike is in progress (320)

piece-rate system a compensation system under which employees are paid a certain amount for each unit of output they produce (276)

place utility utility created by making a product available at a location where customers wish to purchase it (333)

plan an outline of the actions by which an organization intends to accomplish its goals and objectives (170)

planning establishing organizational goals and deciding how to accomplish them (167)

planning horizon the period during which an operational plan will be in effect (223)

plant layout the arrangement of machinery, equipment, and personnel within a production facility (223)

podcasts digital audio or video files that people listen to or watch online on tablets, computers, MP3 players, or smartphones (461)

point-of-purchase display promotional material placed within a retail store (441)

pollution the contamination of water, air, or land through the actions of people in an industrialized society (57)

positioning the development of a product image in buyers' minds relative to the images they have of competing products (444)

possession utility utility created by transferring title (or ownership) of a product to a buyer (334)

preferred stock stock whose owners usually do not have voting rights but whose claims on dividends and assets are paid before those of common-stock owners (116, 566)

premium a gift that a producer offers a customer in return for buying its product (441)

premium pricing pricing the highest-quality or most-versatile products higher than other models in the product line (385)

press conference a meeting at which invited media personnel hear important news announcements and receive supplementary textual materials and photographs (442)

price the amount of money a seller is willing to accept in exchange for a product at a given time and under given circumstances (375)

price competition an emphasis on setting a price equal to or lower than competitors' prices to gain sales or market share (377)

price leaders products priced below the usual markup, near cost, or below cost (385)

price lining the strategy of selling goods only at certain predetermined prices that reflect definite price breaks (385)

price skimming the strategy of charging the highest possible price for a product during the introduction stage of its life-cycle (382)

primary-demand advertising advertising aimed at increasing the demand for all brands of a product within a specific industry (427)

primary market a market in which an investor purchases financial securities (via an investment bank) directly from the issuer of those securities (564)

prime interest rate the lowest rate charged by a bank for a short-term loan (560)

private placement occurs when stock and other corporate securities are sold directly to insurance companies, pension funds, or large institutional investors (567)

problem the discrepancy between an actual condition and a desired condition (179)

problem-solving team a team of knowledgeable employees brought together to tackle a specific problem (292)

process material a material that is used directly in the production of another product but is not readily identifiable in the finished product (360)

producer price index (PPI) an index that measures prices that producers receive for their finished goods (19)

product everything one receives in an exchange, including all tangible and intangible attributes and expected benefits; it may be a good, a service, or an idea (358)

product deletion the elimination of one or more products from a product line (365)

product design the process of creating a set of specifications from which a product can be produced (221)

product differentiation the process of developing and promoting differences between one's products and all competitive products (23, 377)

product life-cycle a series of stages in which a product's sales revenue and profit increase, reach a peak, and then decline (360)

product line a group of similar products that differ only in relatively minor characteristics (220, 363)

product mix all the products a firm offers for sale (363)

product modification the process of changing one or more of a product's characteristics (364)

productivity the average level of output per worker per hour (18)

profit what remains after all business expenses have been deducted from sales revenue (11)

profit-sharing the distribution of a percentage of a firm's profit among its employees (258)

promissory note a written pledge by a borrower to pay a certain sum of money to a creditor at a specified future date (560)

promotion communication about an organization and its products that is intended to inform, persuade, or remind target-market members (424)

promotional campaign a plan for combining and using the four promotional methods—advertising, personal selling, sales promotion, and publicity—in a particular promotion mix to achieve one or more marketing goals (443)

promotion mix the particular combination of promotion methods a firm uses to reach a target market (424)

prospectus a detailed, written description of a new security, the issuing corporation, and the corporation's top management (603)

proxy a legal form listing issues to be decided at a stockholders' meeting and enabling stockholders to transfer their voting rights to some other individual or individuals (117)

proxy fight a technique used to gather enough stockholder votes to control a targeted company (124)

publicity communication in news-story form about an organization, its products, or both (442)

public relations communication activities used to create and maintain favorable relations between an organization and various public groups, both internal and external (426)

purchasing all the activities involved in obtaining required materials, supplies, components, and parts from other firms (225)

Q

qualitative social media measurement the process of accessing the opinions and beliefs about a brand and primarily uses sentiment analysis to categorize what is being said about a company (470)

quality circle a team of employees who meet on company time to solve problems of product quality (230)

quality control the process of ensuring that goods and services are produced in accordance with design specifications (230)

quantitative social media measurement using numerical measurements, such as counting the number of Web site visitors, number of fans and followers, number of leads generated, and the number of new customers (469)

R

random discounting temporary reduction of prices on an unsystematic basis (383)

rate of return the total dollar amount of return you receive on an investment over a specific period of time divided by the amount invested (585)

ratification approval of a labor contract by a vote of the union membership (314)

raw material a basic material that actually becomes part of a physical product; usually comes from mines, forests, oceans, or recycled solid wastes (359)

rebate a return of part of the product's purchase price (359, 439)

recession two or more consecutive three-month periods of decline in a country's GDP (20)

recruiting the process of attracting qualified job applicants (252)

reference pricing pricing a product at a moderate level and positioning it next to a more expensive model or brand (383)

regional shopping center a planned shopping center containing large department stores, numerous specialty stores, restaurants, movie theaters, and sometimes even hotels (411)

registered bond a bond registered in the owner's name by the issuing company (570)

reinforcement theory a theory of motivation based on the premise that rewarded behavior is likely to be repeated, whereas punished behavior is less likely to recur (281)

relationship marketing establishing long-term, mutually satisfying buyer–seller relationships (333)

replacement chart a list of key personnel and their possible replacements within a firm (248)

research and development (R&D) a set of activities intended to identify new ideas that have the potential to result in new goods and services (219)

reserve requirement the percentage of its deposits a bank must retain, either in its own vault or on deposit with its Federal Reserve district bank (527)

reshoring a situation in which U.S. manufacturers bring manufacturing jobs back to the United States (214)

responsibility the duty to do a job or perform a task (195)

retailer a middleman that buys from producers or other middlemen and sells to consumers (396)

retained earnings the portion of a business's profits not distributed to stockholders (504, 566)

return on sales (or profit margin) a financial ratio calculated by dividing net income after taxes by net sales (510)

revenues the dollar amounts earned by a firm from selling goods, providing services, or performing business activities (505)

revenue stream a source of revenue flowing into a firm (472)

revolving credit agreement a guaranteed line of credit (535)

risk–return ratio a ratio based on the principle that a high-risk decision should generate higher financial returns for a business and more conservative decisions often generate lower returns (556)

robotics the use of programmable machines to perform a variety of tasks by manipulating materials and tools (233)

S

safety needs the things we require for physical and emotional security (277)

salary a specific amount of money paid for an employee's work during a set calendar period, regardless of the actual number of hours worked (258)

sales forecast an estimate of the amount of a product that an organization expects to sell during a certain period of time based on a specified level of marketing effort (343)

sales promotion the use of activities or materials as direct inducements to customers or salespersons (426)

sales support personnel employees who aid in selling but are more involved in locating prospects, educating customers, building goodwill for the firm, and providing follow-up service (436)

sample a free product given to customers to encourage trial and purchase (440)

Sarbanes–Oxley Act of 2002 provides sweeping new legal protection for employees who report corporate misconduct (41)

savings and loan association (S&L) a financial institution that offers checking and savings accounts and CDs and that invests most of its assets in home mortgage loans and other consumer loans (532)

S-corporation a corporation that is taxed as though it were a partnership (121)

scheduling the process of ensuring that materials and other resources are at the right place at the right time (227)

scientific management the application of scientific principles to management of work and workers (275)

secondary market a market for existing financial securities that are traded between investors (565)

secondary-market pricing setting one price for the primary target market and a different price for another market (383)

securities exchange a marketplace where member brokers meet to buy and sell securities (565)

security average (or security index) an average of the current market prices of selected securities (603)

selection the process of gathering information about applicants for a position and then using that information to choose the most appropriate applicant (253)

selective-demand (or brand) advertising advertising that is used to sell a particular brand of product (427)

selective distribution the use of only a portion of the available outlets for a product in each geographic area (398)

self-actualization needs the need to grow and develop and to become all that we are capable of being (278)

self-managed teams groups of employees with the authority and skills to manage themselves (292)

selling short the process of selling stock that an investor does not actually own but has borrowed from a brokerage firm and will repay at a later date (596)

seniority the length of time an employee has worked for an organization (316)

sentiment analysis a measurement that uses technology to detect the moods, attitudes, or emotions of people who experience a social media activity (470)

serial bonds bonds of a single issue that mature on different dates (571)

Service Corps of Retired Executives (SCORE) a group of businesspeople who volunteer their services to small businesses through the SBA (148)

service economy an economy in which more effort is devoted to the production of services than to the production of goods (26, 217)

shopping product an item for which buyers are willing to expend considerable effort on planning and making the purchase (359)

shop steward an employee elected by union members to serve as their representative (317)

short-term financing money that will be used for one year or less (554)

sinking fund a sum of money to which deposits are made each year for the purpose of redeeming a bond issue (571)

Six Sigma a disciplined approach that relies on statistical data and improved methods to eliminate defects for a firm's products and services (231)

skills inventory a computerized data bank containing information on the skills and experience of all present employees (248)

slowdown a technique whereby workers report to their jobs but work at a slower pace than normal (320)

small business one that is independently owned and operated for profit and is not dominant in its field (135)

Small Business Administration (SBA) a governmental agency that assists, counsels, and protects the interests of small businesses in the United States (147)

small-business development centers (SBDCs) university-based groups that provide individual counseling and practical training to owners of small businesses (149)

small-business institutes (SBIs) groups of senior and graduate students in business administration who provide management counseling to small businesses (149)

small-business investment companies (SBICs) privately owned firms that provide venture capital to small enterprises that meet their investment standards (150)

social audit a comprehensive report of what an organization has done and is doing with regard to social issues that affect it (62)

social content sites allow companies to create and share information about their products and services (460)

social game a multiplayer, competitive, goal-oriented activity with defined rules of engagement and online connectivity among a community of players (461)

social media the online interactions that allow people and businesses to communicate and share ideas, personal information, and information about products and services (27, 458)

social media communities social networks based on the relationships among people (462)

social media marketing the utilization of social media technologies, channels, and software to create, communicate, deliver, and exchange offerings that have value for an organization (464)

social needs the human requirements for love and affection and a sense of belonging (278)

social responsibility the recognition that business activities have an impact on society and the consideration of that impact in business decision making (44)

socioeconomic model of social responsibility the concept that business should emphasize not only profits but also the impact of its decisions on society (49)

sole proprietorship a business that is owned (and usually operated) by one person (106)

span of management (or span of control) the number of workers who report directly to one manager (196)

special-event pricing advertised sales or price cutting linked to a holiday, season, or event (385)

specialization the separation of a manufacturing process into distinct tasks and the assignment of the different tasks to different individuals (25)

specialty-line wholesaler a middleman that carries a select group of products within a single line (403)

specialty product an item that possesses one or more unique characteristics for which a significant group of buyers is willing to expend considerable purchasing effort (359)

speculative production the time lag between the actual production of goods and when the goods are sold (555)

staff manager a position created to provide support, advice, and expertise within an organization (198)

stakeholders all the different people or groups of people who are affected by the policies and decisions made by an organization (12)

Standard & Poor's 500 Stock Index an index that contains 500 different stocks that reflect increases or decreases in value for the U.S. stock market as a whole (587)

standard of living a loose, subjective measure of how well off an individual or a society is, mainly in terms of want satisfaction through goods and services (24)

standing committee a relatively permanent committee charged with performing some recurring task (204)

state bank a commercial bank chartered by the banking authorities in the state in which it operates (531)

statement of cash flows a statement that illustrates how the company's operating, investing, and financing activities affect cash during an accounting period (507)

statistic a measure that summarizes a particular characteristic of an entire group of numbers (494)

stock the shares of ownership of a corporation (115)

stock dividend a dividend in the form of additional stock (591)

stockholder a person who owns a corporation's stock (115)

stock split the division of each outstanding share of a corporation's stock into a greater number of shares (592)

store (or private) brand a brand that is owned by an individual wholesaler or retailer (370)

store of value a means of retaining and accumulating wealth (522)

strategic alliance a partnership formed to create competitive advantage on a worldwide basis (88)

strategic plan an organization's broadest plan, developed as a guide for major policy setting and decision making (170)

strategic planning process the establishment of an organization's major goals and objectives and the allocation of resources to achieve them (167)

strike a temporary work stoppage by employees, calculated to add force to their demands (304)

strikebreaker a non-union employee who performs the job of a striking union member (320)

supermarket a large self-service store that sells primarily food and household products (406)

superstore a large retail store that carries not only food and nonfood products ordinarily found in supermarkets but also additional product lines (406)

supply the quantity of a product that producers are willing to sell at each of various prices (22, 376)

supply an item that facilitates production and operations but does not become part of a finished product (360)

supply-chain management long-term partnership among channel members working together to create a distribution system that reduces inefficiencies, costs, and redundancies while creating a competitive advantage and satisfying customers (399)

sustainability meeting the needs of the present without compromising the ability of future generations to meet their own needs (27)

SWOT analysis the identification and evaluation of a firm's strengths, weaknesses, opportunities, and threats (168)

syndicate a temporary association of individuals or firms organized to perform a specific task that requires a large amount of capital (123)

synthetic process a process in operations management in which raw materials or components are combined to create a finished product (215)

T

tactical plan a smaller scale plan developed to implement a strategy (170)

target market a group of individuals or organizations, or both, for which a firm develops and maintains a marketing mix suitable for the specific needs and preferences of that group (337)

task force a committee established to investigate a major problem or pending decision (204)

team two or more workers operating as a coordinated unit to accomplish a specific task or goal (292)

technical salesperson a salesperson who assists a company's current customers in technical matters (437)

technical skills specific skills needed to accomplish a specialized activity (176)

telecommuting working at home all the time or for a portion of the work week (290)

telemarketing the performance of marketing-related activities by telephone (409)

television home shopping a form of selling in which products are presented to television viewers, who can buy them by calling a toll-free number and paying with a credit card (409)

tender offer an offer to purchase the stock of a firm targeted for acquisition at a price just high enough to tempt stockholders to sell their shares (124)

term-loan agreement a promissory note that requires a borrower to repay a loan in monthly, quarterly, semiannual, or annual installments (569)

Theory X a concept of employee motivation generally consistent with Taylor's scientific management; assumes that employees dislike work and will function only in a highly controlled work environment (281)

Theory Y a concept of employee motivation generally consistent with the ideas of the human relations movement; assumes responsibility and work toward organizational goals, and by doing so they also achieve personal rewards (280)

Theory Z the belief that some middle ground between type A and type J practices is best for American business (281)

time deposit an amount on deposit in an interest-bearing savings account or certificate of deposit (524)

time utility utility created by making a product available when customers wish to purchase it (334)

top manager an upper-level executive who guides and controls the overall fortunes of an organization (172)

total cost the sum of the fixed costs and the variable costs attributed to a product (379)

total quality management (TQM) the coordination of efforts directed at improving customer satisfaction, increasing employee participation, strengthening supplier partnerships, and facilitating an organizational atmosphere of continuous quality improvement (181)

total revenue the total amount received from sales of a product (379)

trade credit a type of short-term financing extended by a seller who does not require immediate payment after delivery of merchandise (560)

trade deficit a negative balance of trade (73)

trademark a brand name or brand mark that is registered with the U.S. Patent and Trademark Office and thus is legally protected from use by anyone except its owner (369)

trade name the complete and legal name of an organization (370)

trade sales promotion method a sales promotion method designed to encourage wholesalers and retailers to stock and actively promote a manufacturer's product (439)

trade salesperson a salesperson—generally employed by a food producer or processor—who assists customers in promoting products, especially in retail stores (437)

trade show an industry-wide exhibit at which many sellers display their products (441)

trading company provides a link between buyers and sellers in different countries (89)

traditional specialty store a store that carries a narrow product mix with deep product lines (406)

transfer pricing prices charged in sales between an organization's units (386)

transportation the shipment of products to customers (414)

trustee an individual or an independent firm that acts as a bond owner's representative (571)

U

undifferentiated approach directing a single marketing mix at the entire market for a particular product (337)

unemployment rate the percentage of a nation's labor force unemployed at any time (19)

union–management (labor) relations the dealings between labor unions and business management both in the bargaining process and beyond it (303)

union security protection of the union's position as the employees' bargaining agent (317)

union shop a workplace in which new employees must join the union after a specified probationary period (317)

unlimited liability a legal concept that holds a business owner personally responsible for all the debts of the business (108)

unsecured financing financing that is not backed by collateral; unsecured short-term financing offers several options (559)

utility the ability of a good or service to satisfy a human need (215)

V

variable cost a cost that depends on the number of units produced (379)

venture capital money that is invested in small (and sometimes struggling) firms that have the potential to become very successful (150)

vertical channel integration the combining of two or more stages of a distribution channel under a single firm's management (399)

vertical marketing system (VMS) a centrally managed distribution channel resulting from vertical channel integration (399)

virtual team a team consisting of members who are geographically dispersed but communicate electronically (293)

W

wage survey a collection of data on prevailing wage rates within an industry or a geographic area (257)

warehouse club a large-scale members-only establishment that combines features of cash-and-carry wholesaling with discount retailing (406)

warehouse showroom a retail facility in a large, low-cost building with a large on-premises inventory and minimal service (405)

warehousing the set of activities involved in receiving and storing goods and preparing them for reshipment (413)

whistle-blowing informing the press or government officials about unethical practices within one's organization (42)

wholesaler a middleman that sells products to other firms (396)

wiki a collaborative online working space that enables members to contribute content that is then sharable with other people (462)

wildcat strike a strike not approved by the strikers' union (320)

World Trade Organization (WTO) powerful successor to GATT that incorporates trade in goods, services, and ideas (82)

Y

Yellow Pages advertising simple listings or display advertisements presented under specific product categories appearing in print and online telephone directories (429)

Z

zero-base budgeting a budgeting approach in which every expense in every budget must be justified (558)

NAME INDEX

Horatio Alger Award, 5
Horizon Ventures, 13
Houston Community College system, 167
Houston Wire & Cable Company, 402
Howard Johnson Company, 152
HRTMS, 251
HubSpot, 464
Hufbauer, Gary, 77
Hulu, 431, 449
Human Proteome Folding Project, 45
The Human Side of Enterprise (McGregor), 279
Hurt, Alan, 61
Hyatt Corporation, 176
Hyundai USA, 177

I

Iams, 373
IBM, 45, 148, 165, 182, 190, 230, 283, 344, 371, 373, 466
IKEA, 170, 414, 431, 442, 555
Illumina, Inc., 233
Immelt, Jeffrey R., 171
IncrEibles Breakaway Foods, 369
Industrial Workers of the World (IWW), 305
Information Resources, Inc., 346
Ingersoll Rand, 250
Inmar's Promotion Services, 440
Innovision Technologies, 137
InstyMeds vending machines, 410
Intel Corporation, 10, 150, 214, 269–270, 371, 565
Inter-American Development Bank (IDB), 91, 92
Intergovernmental Panel on Climate Change, 59
Internal Revenue Service, 424
International Accounting Standards Board, 497
International Financial Reporting Standards (IFRS), 497
International Franchise Association, 155
International Monetary Fund (IMF), 78, 93
International Multifoods Corporation, 551
International Organization for Standardization (ISO), 231
International Trade Administration, 91
Intuit, 109
Invensys, 245
iPads, 496
iPhone, 496
Isenberg, Daniel, 139
IVY Planning Group, 110

J

Jackson Kayak, 496
Jacobs, Marc, 435
Jaguar, 44
Japan Post Holdings, 89
Jarvis, Jeff, 460
Jason Wu, 337
Javelin Strategy and Research, 477
Jazzercize, 433
JCPenney, 106, 134, 404, 408
Jeni's Ice Cream, 368
Jeter, Derek, 391
Jewelry Television, 409
Jif, 551
J.M. Smucker Company, 551, 572
Jobs, Steve, 174, 177, 178
Johns Manville building products, 130

Johnson, Lyndon, 57
Johnson & Johnson, 27, 434
Johnston, Pete, 568, 569
Jordan Furniture, 130
J.P. Morgan (formerly J.P. Morgan & Co.), 546
JPMorgan Chase & Co., 124, 434, 531, 546
Jubilant Foodworks, 88
Junior's Restaurant, 107

K

Kaufelt, Rob, 158
Kazemi, Masoud Mir, 86
Kelley, Harry, 145
Kellogg's, 191, 215, 345, 363, 431
Kennedy, John F., 51, 81
KFC (Kentucky Fried Chicken), 152
Khunu, 366
Kimpton, Bill, 105
Kimpton Hotel & Restaurant Group, 105, 127
Kinder Morgan Energy Partners, 111
King Soopers grocery chain, 452
Kiplinger's Personal Finance Magazine, 602
Kirby Company, 407, 408
Kiva.org, 535
KKR (Kohlberg Kravis Roberts), 559
Kmart, 116, 196, 337, 404
Knights of Labor, 304–305
Kodak, 180
Koehn, Nancy F., 139
Kofke, Danny, 609
Kofke, Tracy, 609
Kohler, 333
Kolesnik, Kris, 42
Kotter, John, 292
Kotter International, 292
Kozlowski, Leo Dennis, 38
KPMG, 499
Kraft Foods, Inc., 10, 189, 205, 345, 353, 363, 387, 441, 563, 564, 591
Kroger, 9, 158, 405, 406, 452, 612
Kroopf, Jackson, 145
Krummer, Robert, Jr., 145

L

LAB Series, 337
Lady Gaga, 430
LaFalce, John, 41
Lagerfeld, Karl, 337
Lamy, Pascal, 82, 93, 94
Lands' End, 289, 475
Lauper, Cyndi, 31
Lavrov, Sergey, 75
Lay's, 410
Learning Express, 134
Lehman Brothers, 527
Lenovo, 208
LensCrafters, 159
Leondakis, Niki, 105
Lever Brothers, 401–402
Levi Strauss, 225, 370
LEXIS-NEXIS, 346
The Limited, 400
Lincoln Electric, 233
Lindquist, Lee, 65
LinkedIn, 6, 180, 245, 252, 261, 267, 270, 432, 459, 462, 464, 465, 466, 468, 476, 499, 563, 565

Lipper Analytical Services, 599
Litow, Stanley S., 45
The Little Guys, 514
Live Nation, 31
LiveOps, 283
LivingSocial, 461
Liz Claiborne, 234
L.L.Bean, Inc., 140–141, 184, 298, 449–450
Loblaw's, 417
Locker Lookz, 134, 156
Lockheed Martin, 44, 230
LongHorn Steakhouse, 576
Lookk, 443
Loopt, 137
L'Oreal, 434
Lowe's, 292, 405
Lufthansa AG, 88
Luke's Lobster, 482
Lululemon, 477
Lupron cancer drug, 37

M

Macaroni Grill, 435
MacArthur Foundation, 6
Macy's, 72, 404, 434, 474, 537
Madecasse Chocolate, 226
Madison Square Park Conservancy, 442
Madoff, Bernard "Bernie," 38, 605
Magellan Fund, 610
Maggiano's Little Italy Restaurant, 218
Magic Bullet, 408
Mailchimp (software), 333
Major League Baseball players' union, 319
Malcolm Baldrige National Quality Award, 229
Mantega, Guido, 96
Marathon Oil Corporation, 215
Marilyn's Gift Gallery and Sound World Music, 148
Market Watch, 598
Marks, Richard, 38
Maroon 5, 31
Marriott, 153
Marriott Hotels, 373
Marriott International, 5
Mars, 115
Marshall, John, 114–115
Marshalls, 407
Marx, Karl, 17
Mary Kay, 396, 407, 408
Maslow, Abraham, 277–278
Massachusetts Export Center, 156
Massachusetts Nurses Association, 324
Master Lock, 214
MasterCard, 546
Mattel, Inc., 21
Maui Soda and Ice Works, 547
Maxim Integrated Products, Inc., 223
Mayo, Elton, 276
Mayo Clinic, 166
Mayrhuber, Wolfgang, 88
Maytag, 52
McCafés, 97
McCarron, Suzanne, 46
McCormick, Chris, 184
McDonald's Corporation, 96, 97, 140, 151, 152, 153, 154, 155, 180, 196, 199, 224, 343, 371, 372, 557
McFaul, Gerald, 38

McFollum, Tim, 226
McGregor, Douglas, 279–280
McGuinness, Joe, 153
McMillion, Denver, 149
Meany, George, 306
MediaBistro, 252
Mercedes-Benz, 230, 333
Merck & Co., Inc., 47
Mergent,Inc., 599
Merkle, 344
Merrill Lynch, 124
Michael and Susan Dell Foundation, 45
Michelin tires, 371
Mickelson ExxonMobil Teachers Academy, 46
Microsoft Corporation, 115, 371, 483, 509, 561, 565
Midvale Steel Company, 275
Mills, Karen, 141, 150, 151
Minnesota Twins, 380
Minority Business Development Agency, 148
Mint.com, 109
Minute Maid, 358
Missoni, 398
Modern Work Environment (MWE) Lab, 569
Money, 602
Monopoly game, 361
Monster Beverage, 585
Monster.com, 6, 175, 252
Mont Blanc pens, 339
Montgomery Ward, 408
Monthly Labor Review, 493
Moody's Investors Service, Inc., 590, 599
Morgan, J.P., 546
Morgan Stanley, 124, 531
Morningstar, Inc., 599
Motley Fool Web site, 582, 598
Motorola, 229, 230, 231, 399, 444
Mozilla, 293
MSN, 431
Murray's Cheese, 158–159
Mustafa, Isaiah, 424, 446
Mutual Fund Education Alliance, 593
MySpace, 207, 483

N

Nabisco, 365
Nader, Ralph, 52
Nanigian, Daniel J., 156
Nanmac Corporation, 156
NASDAQ (National Association of Securities Dealers Automated Quotations), 565
National Alliance of Business (NAB), 57
National Basketball Association (NBA), 303, 321
National Black McDonald's Operators Association, 153
National Center for Employee Ownership, 291
National Consumers' League, 52
National Credit Union Administration (NCUA), 532, 539
National DCP (NDCP), 399
National Football League, 32
National Foundation for Credit Counseling, 582
National Highway Safety Administration, 364
National Labor Relations Board (NLRB), 309
National Nurses United, 324
National Public Radio (NPR), 461
National Whistle Blower Center, 42
Nature Valley, 444

Nature Valley Trail View Web site, 444
Nautica, 370
NCR, 214
Nebraska Furniture Mart, 130, 131
Nederlander Concerts, 31, 575
Nederlander Organization, 575
Nespresso, 331, 350
Nestlé, 96, 99, 212, 222, 331, 509
Nestlé Purina, 229
Netapp, 275
Netflix, 185, 341, 409
NetJets, 130–131
New Scientist magazine, 346
New United Motor Manufacturing, Inc. (NUMMI), 88
New York Stock Exchange (NYSE), 565, 604, 606
New York Times, 461
Newport News, 408
Newsweek, 602
New-Wave Fashions, Inc., 194
Nielsen marketing research, 347
Nielsen Media Research, 461
Nike, 189, 199, 333, 369, 370, 414, 431
Nisource (Columbia Gas), 149
Nissan, 24, 337
Nixon, Richard, 38
NLRB, 312, 313
Nortel Networks Corporation, 39
North American Free Trade Agreement (NAFTA), 84
Northeast Art Supply, 501, 502, 503, 504, 505–506, 507–508, 510–511
Northrop Grumman Corporation, 230
Noxema, 369
Numi Organic Tea, 207–208
NYSE Euronext holding company, 565

O

Obama, Barack, 85, 90, 92, 150–151, 432, 530, 553
Occupational Safety and Health Administration (OSHA), 266
Ocean Spray Cranberries, Inc., 123
Odland, Steve, 515
Office Depot, 407, 408, 515
OfficeMax, 339–340
Office of the U.S. Trade Representative, 84
Old Spice, 424, 446, 464
Oliberte, 226
Olive Garden, 218, 576
Olyai, Nikki, 137
Omnicon Group, 332
Online Women's Business Center, 149
Oovoo, 254
OPEC (Organization of Petroleum Exporting Countries), 85
Open Pantry, 406
Oracle Corporation, 124, 399, 466
Orbitz, 475
Organization of Petroleum Exporting Countries (OPEC), 85
Orman, Suze, 587–588
Ouchi, William, 280–281
Outback Steakhouse, 150
Oxley, Michael J., 41

P

PA Live Bait Vending, 410
Packard, Dave, 208

Page, Brandt, 145
Page, Larry, 177
Palm, 208
Pampered Chef, 130, 408
Panasonic, 221
Panera Bread, 36
Panera Cares, 36, 63
Papa John's Pizza, 118
Parham, Victoria, 461
Parker Brothers, 361
Patek Philippe watches, 398
Pateer, Aaron, 109
Patient Assistance Program, 47
Pattillo, Aaron, 366
PayPal, 537
Pencil Makers Association, 75
Pennsylvania Association of Staff Nurses and Allied Professionals, 324
People's United Bank, 435
Pepsi, 378, 425, 462–463
PepsiCo, 106, 152, 155, 194, 353–354, 358, 387, 390, 432
Perdue chicken products, 435
Perry, Herman, 153
Perry, Katy, 430
PERT (Program Evaluation and Review Technique), 228–229
Petcare, 229
Pfizer, 434, 558–559
Philip Morris, 51, 89
Phillips Petroleum, 44
Pier 1 Imports, 70
Piggyback Consolidators, 416
Pincus, Mark, 3, 28
Pinterest, 462, 475, 476, 482, 567
Pixar, 32
Pizza Hut, 220, 370
Plains All American Pipeline, 416
Planned Parenthood, 463
Plumbing Warehouse, 405
Polaroid, 141
Polman, Paul, 66
Polo, 370
Pomerantz, Carrie Schwab, 46
Porcino Paul, 517
Prevot, Corinne, 145
Price, Samuel Lowell, 511
PricewaterhouseCoopers (PwC), 38, 250, 487, 499, 511
Prius, 428
Private Label Manufacturer's Association, 370
Procter, William, 114
Procter & Gamble (P&G), 27, 39, 106, 114, 115, 140, 148, 191, 203, 208, 212, 214, 292, 363, 367, 369, 373, 384, 398, 400, 424, 433, 434, 446, 488, 509, 551, 561
Providence Sacred Heart Medical Center, 324
Puck, Wolfgang, 105
Pulte Homes, 496
Putin, Vladimir, 125

Q

Qantas Airways, 315
Quaker Oats, 260, 390
Qualified Resources, Inc., 149
Questcor Pharmaceuticals, 585
Questor Corporation, 86

SUBJECT INDEX

goal, defined, 168
goal-setting theory, 284
going price, accepting, 22
"Going the Extra Mile" award, at REI, 296
gold, investing in, 597
goods, 358
government
    role in a mixed economy, 16
    role in capitalism, 15
    role in encouraging ethics, 41
government accounting, 499
government bank, Federal Reserve serving as, 529
government bonds, 588–591
government export assistance programs, U.S., 91
government involvement, increasing, 48
government regulation, of corporations, 120
governmental markets, 336
grapevine, 204–205
graph, example, 495
Great Depression, 25, 48
green, saving natural resources, 13
"green" audits, 487
green bonds, investing in, 589
green IT, 478
green marketing, signs of, 65
Greensburg, Kansas, 65
GreenStreet Lending program, at Umpqua, 521
gRide program, 290
grievance procedure, 317–318
gross domestic product (GDP), 18, 79–80
gross profit, 506
gross sales, 505–506
growth
    from within, 124
    of business, 124–126
    of investments, 585
    plans for financing, 612–613
    through mergers and acquisitions, 124–126
    using structure to support, 208
growth stage, of the product life-cycle, 361–362
"Guppy Love" program, 105

H

hard-core unemployed, training programs for, 56–57
Hawthorne Studies, 276–277
Haymarket riot of 1886, 304
health of citizens, protecting with trade restrictions, 77
health-care benefits, working full- or part-time, 274
higher prices, from imposition of tariffs, 77
Himalayan herders, 366–367
holding costs, 226, 412–413
honesty, in business, 38
Horatio Alger Award, 5
horizontal merger, 125
hostile takeover, 124
hourly wage, 258
households, in a mixed economy, 16
HRM. See human resources management (HRM)
human factors, responsible for experiment results, 277
Human Proteome Folding Project, 45
human relations movement, in management, 277
human resource managers, 491
human resources, 10, 166, 222–223, 470
    cultural diversity in, 249
    importance of an organization's, 171
    maintaining, 246
human resources demand, forecasting, 247

human resources management (HRM)
    legal environment of, 264–267
    phases of, 246
    responsibility for, 246–247
human resources managers, 174–175
human resources planning, 246, 247–248
human resources supply, forecasting, 248
The Human Side of Enterprise (McGregor), 279
Hurricanes Katrina and Rita, small businesses affected by, 150
hygiene factors, 279

I

idea generation, 366–367
identity theft, 477, 536
imitations, 366
immediate-response advertising, 427
import and export transactions, paying for, 539
import duty, 75
import quota, 75
importing, 72
inbound marketing, 464
incentive payments, 258
income, types of, 349
income and wealth, inequality of, 20
income levels, for whites, blacks, Hispanics, and Asians, 55
income statement, 504–506, 507
incorporation process, beginning by consulting a lawyer, 115, 116
independence, in a small business, 143
independent retailer, 404
index funds, 595
India, 78, 88
individual branding, 373
individual factors, affecting ethics, 40
individual knowledge, affecting ethics, 40
individual wages, 257
industrial markets, 336
industrial products, 359, 445
industrial union, 305
industries
    attracting small businesses, 136–137
    protecting new or weak with trade restrictions, 77
inflation, 18, 523
inflation rate, 20
infomercial, 430
informal groups, 204
informal leadership, 177
informal organization, 204
information, 10, 166
    defined, 489, 500
    described, 487–488
    presenting, 494–495
    providing in a promotion, 444
    risk and, 488
    rules, 489
information technology system (IT system), 490
informational resources, 471
infringement, on an existing brand, 372
initial public offering (IPO), 563–564
injunction, 310
innovations, 12, 141, 214, 366
inputs, contributed to the organization, 282
input-to-outcome ratio, 282
inside order-takers, 436
insider trading, 606

insourcing, 214
inspection, of work-in-process, 230
institutional advertising, 427–428
institutional markets, 336
in-store retailers, classes of, 404–407
insurance companies, 532
insurance packages, 259
intangible assets, 503
integrated marketing communications, 425
intensive distribution, 398
Intergovernmental Panel on Climate Change, 59
intermediaries, 374, 395
intermittent process, 234
internal environmental forces, in an e-business, 478
internal recruiting, 253
internal sources
    of data, 492–493
    marketing data from, 344
International Accounting Standards Board, 497
international banking services, 538–539
international business
    basis for, 71–74
    extent of, 78–80
    financing, 91–94
    methods of entering, 85–90
    restrictions to, 74–77
international economic organizations, working to foster trade, 83–85
International Financial Reporting Standards (IFRS), 497
International Franchise Association, 155
international markets
    exporting to, 86–87
    steps in entering, 90
international resources, misallocation of, 77
international trade, 70, 73
international trade agreements, 81–85
International Trade Loan program, SBA's, 156
Internet
    advertising on, 431
    affecting ethics, 40
    conducting job searches on, 252
    creating new customer needs, 471
    crime, 477
    ethics on, 476–477
    financial information on, 598
    growth potential, 476
    as a major force in economy, 25
    making marketing information easily accessible, 347
    marketing on, 372
    relationship marketing and, 332
    selling merchandise on, 472
    social responsibility on, 476–477
Internet business, starting a new, 473
internships, unpaid, 203
interpersonal skills, of managers, 7, 176
Interstate Commerce Act (1887), 48
interstitial ads, 431
interview questions, difficult to answer, 255
interviews, 254–256
intranets, 347
introduction component, of a business plan, 100, 102
introduction stage, of the product life-cycle, 361
inventories, 226, 561, 562
inventory control, 226–227
inventory costs, wholesalers reducing, 402
inventory management, 412–413
inventory turnover, 510–511